ADVANCES IN THE INVESTIGATION OF PSYCHOLOGICAL STRESS

ADVANCES IN THE INVESTIGATION OF PSYCHOLOGICAL STRESS

Edited by
RICHARD W. J. NEUFELD

WILEY

A Wiley-Interscience Publication

JOHN WILEY & SONS

New York / Chichester / Brisbane / Toronto / Singapore

Library of Congress Cataloging in Publication Data:

Advances in the investigation of psychological stress.

    (Wiley series on health psychology/behavioral
medicine)
    Includes bibliographies.
    1. Stress (Psychology) 2. Medicine and psychology.
I. Neufeld, Richard W. J. [DNLM: 1. Stress,
Psychological. WM 172 A244]
RC455.4.S87A38   616'.0019   88-20458
ISBN 0-471-81598-5

Contributors

Yitzchak Binik, Ph.D., Associate Professor, Department of Psychology, McGill University, Montreal, Quebec, Canada

Sheldon Cohen, Ph.D., Professor, Department of Psychology, Carnegie Mellon University, Pittsburgh, Pennsylvania

Gerald M. Devins, Ph.D., Associate Professor, Department of Psychology, University of Calgary, Calgary, Alberta, Canada

Jeffrey R. Edwards, Ph.D., Academic Assistant Professor, School of Business, University of Virginia, Charlottesville, Virginia

Michael W. Eysenck, Ph.D., Professor and Head Department of Psychology, Royal Holloway and Bedford New College, University of London, London, England

Myles Genest, Ph.D., Associate Professor, Department of Psychology, University of Saskatchewan, Saskatoon, Saskatchewan, Canada

James A. Hanley, Ph.D., Professor, Department of Epidemiology and Biostatistics, McGill University, Montreal, Quebec, Canada

David S. Holmes, Ph.D., Professor, Department of Psychology, The University of Kansas, Lawrence, Kansas

Nicholas A. Kuiper, Ph.D., Professor, Department of Psychology, University of Western Ontario, London, Ontario, Canada

Normand Martin, M.A., Department of Psychology, University of Montreal, Montreal, Quebec, Canada

Rod A. Martin, Ph.D., Assistant Professor, Department of Psychology, University of Western Ontario, London, Ontario, Canada

Kevin D. McCaul, Ph.D., Associate Professor and Chairman, Department of Psychology, North Dakota State University of Agriculture and Applied Science, Fargo, North Dakota

Richard W. J. Neufeld, Ph.D., Professor, Department of Psychology, University of Western Ontario, London, Ontario, Canada

Ian R. Nicholson, M.A., Graduate Student, Department of Psychology, University of Western Ontario, London, Ontario, Canada

L. Joan Olinger, Ph.D., Department of Psychology, London Psychiatric Hospital, London, Ontario, Canada

Carolee M. Orme, Ph.D., Department of Psychology, Glenside Hospital, Bristol, England.

Robert Oseasohn, M.D., Professor and Associate Dean, School of Public Health, University of Texas Health Science Center, San Antonio, Texas

Randolph J. Paterson, M.A., Graduate Student, Department of Psychology, University of Western Ontario, London, Ontario, Canada

Ethel Roskies, Ph.D., Professor, Department of Psychology, University of Montreal, Montreal, Quebec, Canada

Peter Seraganian, Ph.D., Associate Professor, Department of Psychology, Concordia University, Montreal, Quebec, Canada

Christine Smilga, M.A., Department of Psychology, University of Montreal, Montreal, Quebec, Canada

Series Preface

This series is addressed to clinicians and scientists who are interested in human behavior relevant to the promotion and maintenance of health and the prevention and treatment of illness. *Health psychology* and *Behavioral medicine* are terms that refer to both the scientific investigation and interdisciplinary integration of behavioral and biomedical knowledge and technology to prevention, diagnosis, treatment, and rehabilitation.

The major and purposely somewhat general areas of both health psychology and behavioral medicine which will receive greatest emphasis in this series are: theoretical issues of bio-psycho-social function, diagnosis, treatment, and maintenance; issues of organizational impact on human performance and an individual's impact on organizational functioning; development and implementation of technology for understanding, enhancing, or remediating human behavior and its impact on health and function; and clinical considerations with children and adults, alone, in groups, or in families that contribute to the scientific and practical/clinical knowledge of those charged with the care of patients.

The series encompasses considerations as intellectually broad as psychology and as numerous as the multitude of areas of evaluation, treatment, prevention, and maintenance that make up the field of medicine. It is the aim of the series to provide a vehicle which will focus attention on both the breadth and the interrelated nature of the sciences and practices making up health psychology and behavioral medicine.

THOMAS J. BOLL

The University of Alabama in Birmingham
Birmingham, Alabama

Contents

Introduction

The study of psychological stress and its effects on psychological and physical functioning has mushroomed over the last decade. Efforts to develop and evaluate techniques for preventing or managing stress and its effects have accelerated as well. The chapters in this book represent a cross section of some of the more prominent lines of investigation.

One theme running through the treatments of the various topics is the importance of discerning genuine advances in knowledge and research procedures. The literature is critically evaluated. An effort has been made to extract those advances that are valid. New proposals are offered with appropriate caveats regarding limitations in empirical support. Therapeutic investigations that are primarily guided by theory at this point are identified as such. Finally, weaknesses in commonly used methods of investigation are noted and improvements suggested.

In Part I, conceptual principles in theory and research on psychological stress are reviewed. Subjects covered include situational cues giving rise to stress response, the nature of the stress response, and ways of controlling the response. Material has been selected in part to provide a survey of concepts, distinctions, and classes of events that to date have had important roles in theory, and have been used extensively to organize research findings. This material should provide readers not entirely familiar with the study of psychological stress with some important background for the subsequent chapters.

Part II reviews laboratory research on stress. The first chapter in this section, Chapter 3, extensively treats methodological aspects of laboratory research. A good deal of this subject matter will be of greater interest to laboratory investigators than to consumers of research findings. Nevertheless, a reading of the chapter by the latter audience should lead to a better understanding of how laboratory research on stress is conducted, and an appreciation of its role in the overall context of investigation. This chapter sets the stage for the two chapters to follow.

It has long been known that stress arousal can disrupt thinking and problem solving. Michael Eysenck discusses in Chapter 4 the workings whereby stress arousal may impair cognitive processes. He integrates his observations with findings on cognitive task performance among individuals who typically are more reactive to stressors than others (high-trait-anxious individuals). The result is a compelling set of observations on the nature of susceptibility to stress-induced disruption of cognitive processes among such individuals.

One of the topics most frequently studied in the stress laboratory is defense mechanisms. In particular, individuals thought to be disposed toward repression, denial, or projection as a means of coping with stress have been exposed to laboratory conditions intended to activate these mechanisms. David Holmes and Kevin McCaul provide a penetrating and comprehensive evaluation of claims that have been made for the operation of these defense mechanisms, in the first instance, and effects of these mechanisms on stress arousal, in the second. This review presents a convincing challenge to the traditional view on the operation of defense mechanisms and their potential stress-reducing effects.

Part III, field and clinical investigations, begins with Rod Martin's chapter on research methods and data analysis. He describes and comments on assessment of stressing events and their consequences, as well as on variables considered to temper the consequences of stressing events. Discussed also are alternate methods of data analysis and their respective advantages and limitations. This chapter, Chapter 6, highly informative in its own right, can provide a useful orientation to the remaining chapters of this section.

Sheldon Cohen and Jeffrey Edwards examine claims that certain personality characteristics can moderate the relationship between stress and physical or psychological disorder. They lay out clearly the methodological requirements and data-analytic hurdles that must be met before results from a study can be interpreted as supporting the existence of relationship-moderating effects. Literature on this topic is scrutinized in the light of these requirements and, to a large degree, is found wanting. These authors argue persuasively that future research efforts should be more theory-driven than past efforts, attending to processes and mechanisms whereby moderating effects may come about.

In Chapter 8, we turn to risk of coronary heart disease associated with the well-known type A behavior pattern. Ethel Roskies, Peter Seraganian,

Robert Oceasohn, Christine Smilga, Normand Martin, and James Hanley describe treatment programs designed to reduce the risk of coronary heart disease among currently healthy type A males. A major strength of the approach taken by these investigators is the adherence to established theoretical frameworks concerning stress and coping in designing their preventative programs. These authors discuss the strengths and limitations of the specific programs they describe.

Chapter 9 by Yitzchak Binik and Gerald Devins takes us into the medical setting where we examine coping under the stress of a life-threatening disorder—that of irreversible kidney failure. This disorder essentially had been fatal until the advent of the hemodialysis machine and kidney transplantation. As these methods of treatment became increasingly successful, survival depended more and more on coping with the lifestyle that the treatment regimens imposed. The authors review research findings on patients with kidney failure from three areas of investigation: depression, marital adjustment, and adherence to treatment programs. They discuss several methodological issues involved in carrying out research in this setting. The importance of employing relevant theory on stress and coping in designing studies and interpreting findings once again is underscored.

Stress and rheumatoid arthritis is the subject dealt with by Myles Genest in Chapter 10. He discusses the possible influences of personality-related stress proneness, and of the presence of stressful life events on the disease process. In turn, the stressing properties of the disease are examined in detail. Genest notes that interventions designed to modify the stress impact of the disease should be beneficial not only from an immediate therapeutic perspective, but also from the perspective of improved basic understanding of the disorder and its relation to stress.

Chapter 11 by Nicholas Kuiper and Joan Olinger examines some of the most common symptoms of psychological disturbance associated with stress—those of depression. The authors present theory and research on the sequence of events leading to depression as stress increases. Their focus is on individuals who may be especially vulnerable to stress-related depression because of their styles of evaluating self-worth. This chapter represents an intriguing account of the interface between cognitive dispositions and experienced stress in producing depression.

Relations between stress and one of the most debilitating forms of psychological disorder—schizophrenia—are considered in the final chapter by Ian Nicholson and Richard Neufeld. Attention is given to hypotheses about the role of stress in precipitating the occurrence of this syndrome and in affecting its course. The disorder itself is seen to be a major source of stress and to erode coping ability; schizophrenic behavior has a disrupting effect on the patient's environment, and the efficiency of several psychological processes decline with the disorder. With regard to the latter difficulties, specific forms of reduced efficiency that may compromise the patient's ability to negotiate stress are discussed with special reference to paranoid schizophrenia.

This book cuts across a fairly broad band of subject matter. Material ranges from laboratory investigations and studies of basic processes, to clinical investigations and studies of psychopathology. At the same time, an effort has been made to stay within the domain of *psychological* studies of stress and coping, although the boundaries of such a domain admittedly are somewhat arbitrary. Emphasis, for example, has been placed on personality factors as opposed to forms of social support as possible moderators of the effects of stress; the expression of stress in psychopathology as opposed to, say, disruption of small-group functioning, has been included, and so on.

There are a number of instances where material covered in one chapter complements that of another; a point discussed briefly in one chapter may be elaborated upon in another. An effort has been made to draw attention to such instances within the chapters themselves.

All in all, it is hoped that the variety of topics presented and the tenor of their exposition will make for an informative book and will give readers an appreciation of many of the genuine advances that had been made in the investigation of psychological stress.

PART **I**

CONCEPTUAL PRINCIPLES IN THEORY AND RESEARCH ON PSYCHOLOGICAL STRESS

1

The Stress Response and Parameters of Stressful Situations

RANDOLPH J. PATERSON
RICHARD W. J. NEUFELD

INTRODUCTION

The stress response appears to be a critical fieldpiece in the arsenal of behavioral mechanisms nurturing our ancestors' struggle for survival. In most primitive environments, survival involved striving to attain food and avoid predators. Organisms that accomplished these tasks survived to reproduce. Traits contributing to survival were passed on to become more common in the population. In most stages of mammalian development, the stress response conferred considerable advantage to the organism equipped with it. Increased heart rate, respiration, and alertness, the diversion of blood from the digestive system toward the skeletal musculature, and other components of the threat reaction observed among modern humans benefited both predation and avoiding the predation of others. Greater strength

7

and endurance enabled more effective combat and escape (hence the so-called "fight-or-flight response"). By releasing endorphins and increasing the blood's clotting ability, this response enhanced the body's defenses against wounds obtained in battle and prevented the individual from being disabled by pain should such wounds occur. The stress response represents an ideal adaptation to "life in the wild."

Another benefit of humanity's genetic heritage is the capacity to use tools and reason to structure their surroundings to the best advantage: In addition to adapting to the environment, humans have forced the environment to adapt to *them*. The speed of the resulting cultural and technological evolution has far outstripped the capacity of biological evolution to keep pace (Barash, 1986). As a consequence, human beings find themselves equipped with bodies that are in some respects suited more to the wild than to modern life. In the environment in which most humans find themselves today, the stress response is more often a liability than an asset. The vigorous physical activity which the stress response prepares them for is rarely an appropriate response to the stressors encountered. Instead, in many modern situations the stress response impairs adaptive coping. Further, in the wild the stress response commonly was activated by transitory stressors and declined soon thereafter. There was little selection pressure to develop mechanisms to handle longer-lasting forms of stress. Today, many stressors are long-term rather than immediate, resulting in more extended elevations of arousal levels. This can impair the functioning of various organ systems, including the immune system, leaving the body more open to disease.

Thus humanity is, in a sense, a victim of its own ingenuity. The ability to manipulate the environment has led to the development of a society to which our bodies are not suited. One response to this is to agree that on the whole our present environment is better than the one our ancestors had (after all, we appear to live longer), and accept its disadvantages as inevitable penance. Another is to alter the environment to more closely suit our supposed nature, as the "back-to-the-land" movement of the 1960s attempted to do. While there are undoubtedly ways of humanizing the modern urban environment that should be investigated, the environment that our bodies are best adapted for is the wild—an option rejected in favor of civilization by our forebears.

The response of science has been to embark upon a detailed scientific investigation of the nature of stress, both its internal biological manifestations and its properties in the context of the surrounding culture. Such study can provide compromises and interventions between the demands of the environment and the nature of the species. During the past 30 years, there has been a mushrooming interest in the topic of stress. Some of this research has examined the properties of stimuli that elicit stress responses. Some has examined the relationship between the resources that can be brought to bear on a situation and the amount of stress that results. Some researchers have used stress as a means to understanding individual differences, both in the normal range of behavior and in the development of psychopathology. In recent years, a number of researchers have begun to examine the relationship between stress and illness, with stress playing the multiple roles of etiologic factor, exacerbating influence, and consequence of illness.

In this chapter, some of the conceptual underpinnings of the research literature on stress are examined. First, the terminology in the field is examined both historically and from a theoretical viewpoint. Additionally examined are the various components of the stress response and the issue of whether stress can be a positive influence. Next, a model of the stress process based on past work is proposed. The model places strong emphasis on the process of appraisal, whereby the individual interprets environmental cues and formulates responses. The literature on the properties of stimuli which set the process of appraisal, arousal, and coping into motion is then reviewed.

Chapter 2 examines the literature on control and coping, and expands on the part of the model covering the selection of coping options and the determinants of the level of stress produced in controllable situations. Chapter 2 also reviews the effects of stress upon the capacity to process information in appraisal and response selection.

Throughout Chapters 1 and 2, an attempt is made to move beyond a stimulus-response view and assess the internal processes that may mediate the relationship between environmental events and emotional, behavioral, and physiological reactions. Observations regarding likely sites for the operation and influence of individual differences are made where appropriate.

THE CONCEPT OF STRESS

Theory and research on stress are plagued with a lack of agreement regarding basic terminology—particularly regarding the definition of stress itself. Breznitz and Goldberger (1982) argue that this is to be expected from a rapidly expanding area of inquiry, indicative of little more than the dynamism of the field. They caution against prematurely defining the boundaries of the domain of stress by using strict definitions. The lack of a precise definition has not deterred psychologists from investigating stress, nor has it prevented the public from becoming conversant with the concept. Mandler (1962) notes that most people have difficulty defining many words that they use quite regularly, such as emotion, morality, or consciousness, despite an intuitive sense that they understand the concepts. Stress seems to be another example of this. Most complex ideas have somewhat vague boundaries, and attempting to define them gives one a sense of arbitrariness. We propose—at least for the time being—to allow the term stress to retain this somewhat amorphous character. Within the field denoted by the term, however, there are specific concepts that must be more precisely defined. These are discussed within a framework for conceptualizing the stress process.

While the scientific study of stress from a psychological perspective is a relatively recent development, the concept itself has a long history. The word stress has its origins in the Latin words *strictus*, meaning tight or narrow, and *stringere*, the verb meaning to tighten. These root words reflect the internal feelings of tightness and constriction of the muscles and breathing reported by many under stress. However, in early usage the term was used more frequently to refer to difficult environmental situations (Cox, 1978). The term began to be used in engineering in the 1800s. In this context, load refers to a force acting upon an object, stress is the load divided by the area over which it acts (expressed, for example, in pounds per square inch), and strain refers to the effects of the force on the object, including weakening and changes in shape. Stress occasionally was used in a similar manner in medicine by the late nineteenth century, denoting the entire range of pressures and challenges to health undergone by the body.

In the 1930s, Hans Selye began his landmark studies of stress that provided much of the impetus for current psychological investigation. Selye noticed that many medical conditions had common elements. That is, while each disorder had unique, distinctive symptoms, there was also a pool of symptoms held in common with most other disorders. Whereas the primary thrust of the science of diagnosis had been to identify the unique symptoms, Selye turned in the opposite direction and began studying the commonalities in illness. He defined stress as "the nonspecific (that is, common) result of any demand upon the body, be the effect mental or somatic" (1982, p. 7). This response-based definition was a natural outgrowth of his perspective. It was only reasonable to give the name stress to the unified response rather than to the multifarious etiologies.

Others disagreed, seeing in the response an enormously complicated syndrome and in the stimulus the common feature of an extreme demand upon the individual. This is paralleled by everyday usage, in which a person is often described as being *under* stress, that is, feeling weighed down or pressured by external events. Some research has indicated that the stress response is not nearly as general and nonspecific as Selye's work at first indicated. Different stressors may produce somewhat different patterns of stress reaction, and different individuals may have different characteristic modes of response (Lacey, 1967; Lacey, Bateman, & Van Lehn, 1953).

Spielberger (1976) suggests that stress should refer to the objective characteristics of a situation, and that threat should denote the perception of danger by the individual. Still others emphasize that stress is neither an external situation nor an internal state, but rather proceeds entirely from a complex interaction between environmental demands, perceptions of these demands, and the perceived ability to meet or alter them. Here stress is used to describe either (a) the midpoint of the interaction at the interface between demands and resources or (b) the total transaction from the demand to the resolution. Lazarus (1966; Lazarus & Folkman, 1984), one of the most influential investigators of stress, takes the latter position. He argues that stress cannot be adequately understood without reference to external conditions, internal evaluative processes, personal resources, and, of course, the psychological and physical outcome.

Which of these views is the most relevant, given the current status of the field? The aggregate view, that stress should refer to the entire range of concerns, has the disadvantage of being extremely general. It refers to all things and, in so doing, describes nothing very well. Yet it is axiomatic that the more precise the definition, the less comprehensive it becomes. If we were to develop a strictly delimited description of one part of the process to be referred to as stress, we would be eliminating from consideration parts of the process that are intimately related. Further, stress would be both the name for a field of study, a connotation which the word can hardly be expected to lose, and a specific process or focus within that field. Confusion seems inevitable with such a duality.

It appears better at this stage of the field's development for stress to be retired as a theoretical term and be retained as the name of the field of study—a position it already holds. In Mandler's (1962) words, stress is best regarded as a "chapter-heading" term, one that gathers "under one rubric what are believed to be related phenomena, experiments, and observations" (p. 276). Lazarus (1966) agrees, reviewing the different elements of the field and concluding "Stress is not any one of these things; nor is it stimulus, response, or intervening variable, but rather a collective term for an area of study" (p. 27).

If stress is to be left as a general term, then other terms must be used for the elements and phases of which it is composed. Here there is more agreement among researchers. The stimuli, or environmental situations, that set the whole process in motion are typically referred to as *stressors*. The consequences of these stressors within the individual are collectively called the *stress response*.

Three periods of interaction between the stressor and the individual may be identified. The first is the period before the stressful event actually occurs. For example, an individual walking across a street may suddenly notice an oncoming car. Here the stressor is a *threat*. Threat alone has the capacity to elicit a stress response. If nothing is done to avert the stressor's occurrence, *impact* may ensue. Following this is the *post-impact period* during which the individual may still suffer from some of the residual effects of the event. It may take time for the parasympathetic nervous system to return the body to the resting state. Other post-impact effects may also occur: After a disease the individual may take some time to return to the premorbid level of functioning, and after a severe psychological stressor the individual may suffer from some form of post-traumatic stress disorder or phobia.

Many stressors, perhaps most, do not impinge directly on the body. Instead, they must be perceived and evaluated before they can elicit a stress response in a process called *appraisal*. Some stressors, including disease, fatigue, and injury, do have direct effects. While most of these are also subject to appraisal, they may activate a stress response quite apart from their appraisal-mediated effects. An individual who is injured and rendered unconscious in the process may still show some of the effects Selye described, despite being unable to appraise the stressor. Indeed, the stressors that initially concerned Selye were physiological stressors such as these. It is unknown, however, exactly how closely such a stress response resembles those produced via appraisal. Most psychological investigators prefer to consider mainly those problems that are clearly subject to appraisal. This narrowed field is usually what is meant by the label of *psychological stress*.

The stress response itself, whether produced by physiological or psychological stressors, has a number of different components: physiological, cognitive, emotional, and behavioral. All may have transient and cumulative effects, although this distinction is presently clearest among the physiological effects. Transient physiological effects include the symptoms of sympathetic nervous system arousal, among them elevated heart rate, blood pressure, respiration, adrenaline release, peripheral muscle tension, perspiration, and reduced digestive activity. These are best brought under the rubric of *arousal*. Cumulative, or more long-term effects, include ulcers, heart disease, colitis, and other illnesses. Occasionally, these effects may appear soon after impact, as when an executive has a heart attack upon being fired, but generally such a situation is preceded by years of damage making the "cumulative" label appropriate. Certain other effects, such as sleep and appetite disturbances, seem best grouped with the physiological effects, but it may be unclear whether these are transient or cumulative. They are clearly not as transient as surges in heart rate, but do not fit well into the cumulative category either.

Normally accompanying the physiological manifestations of stress are certain emotional reactions, such as *anxiety*. Indeed, Endler and Edwards (1982) noted that the words "stress" and "anxiety" are used almost interchangeably in much of the literature. Lewis (1970) described anxiety as an unpleasant emotion closely related to fear and involving transient physiological responses. As such, anxiety appears to be the subjective experience of physiological arousal combined with a negative tone. An alternative is to view anxiety as a somewhat generic emotional concomitant of arousal that may be combined with various feeling tones. When a stressor represents a danger of harm or loss and seems likely to occur, anxiety may take the form of fear. In situations where the stressor is caused by the arbitrary action of another individual, the anxiety may be expressed as anger. When the stressor is a situation of achievement or some voluntarily precipitated event (such as climbing a mountain peak or riding a roller coaster), the subjective experience may be one of excitement or exhilaration. Anxiety accompanied by pessimistic predictive judgments concerning the utility of coping may be associated with depression (witness the seemingly intractable linking of depression with anxiety; Neufeld, 1982).

In the area of cognition, stress may affect both content and capacity. With regard to content, the individual may ruminate about the stressor (*worry*), assessing the likelihood of damage or seeking a way out of the situation. These are the functions of appraisal. Capacity may also be affected, although this area is poorly understood. One suggested effect is that, as arousal increases, the breadth of attention narrows (Easterbrook, 1959). This is offered as a potential explanation of the Yerkes-Dodson law of performance under stress, which states that as arousal increases, performance improves and then, with further increases, decays. There may be other changes in cognitive processing, such as reductions in the capacity to process information in parallel, but these remain largely uninvestigated. Such changes are further explored in Chapter 3.

Stress may also have a number of behavioral effects. Most obvious are the tremors and increased general activity level (pacing, fidgeting) commonly associated with anxiety. In addition, where a stressor is potentially controllable, the individual is quite likely to engage in coping behavior, the form of which may be largely determined by the context. Another form of behavioral effect is choice. If several avenues are open to an individual and one of these is associated with an aversive stressor, it may be expected that this option will be selected less often than the others. The exercise of choice is a primary measure of stress in many studies of both animals and humans. With animals, the exercise of choice may be the only way to assess the internal evaluation of an event; if the animal avoids one route, behavior, or stimulus, it is often inferred that that option is stressful in some way. Similarly, in humans the choice of one option over the other may be regarded as more indicative of internal evaluations than self-report ratings that have no impact on future events. A common paradigm is to expose subjects to two stressful procedures and have them select one of these for a subsequent set of trials, which may or may not actually be delivered (e.g., Katz & Wykes, 1985). Of course, caution must be used in such designs, as stressfulness is not the sole determinant of decision making. Esthetics and personal likes and dislikes also influence choices. But where options are carefully designed to differ only along a stress-relevant dimension, preferences may more confidently be attributed to their aversiveness.

This aspect of choice raises the issue of an ongoing debate in the stress literature: the stressfulness of apparently welcome events. Stress is frequently discussed in negative terms as a damaging influence that is always avoided. But many situations, such as rock climbing, amusement park rides, and viewing frightening films, indisputably elicit stress reactions and are willingly engaged in. The active selection of these activities appears to violate the choice criterion of stressfulness just described. Many other arousal-inducing events, such as promotions and surprise parties, are not subject to choice but are often greeted with apparent pleasure and leave the impression that if a choice had been possible, these events would have been actively sought.

The inclusion of positive stressful events is the subject of some controversy in the life events literature, which attempts to relate the occurrence of major stressors to subsequent changes in health and functioning. The scales used to assess environmental stress typically include events such as marriage, vacations, and the birth of children. One justification for this practice is simply that positive events lead to stress, whatever their emotional concomitants, and so are appropriately included. An alternative view is that most events have positive and negative components. The positive components fulfill needs and desires and so are tension-reducing. The negative components are responsible for arousal. Thus, while a mountain climber gains in perceived competence and self-esteem from success, it is the negative components of danger and effort that produce the stress response. If the anticipated gains outweigh the perceived dangers, then the aversion to risk will be overcome. Similarly, the birth of a child may involve love, pride, and satisfaction, but it is the negative aspects of changing diapers, sleep loss, and continual demands on one's time that may cause stress reactions.

Regardless of the view taken, the argument becomes somewhat academic in the face of some evidence (as yet insufficient to close the issue) suggesting that positively regarded stressful events may have less damaging long-term effects than aversive stressors. In a number of studies in which subjects rated various aspects of the life events they have experienced, it was found that event undesirability is a more effective predictor of later dysfunction than change per se (e.g., Suls & Mullen, 1981; Vinokur & Selzer, 1975). In an approach similar to the life events literature but concentrating on more minor everyday events, Kanner, Coyne, Schaefer, and Lazarus (1981) developed two scales, one for positive and one for negative events. While the latter, the Hassles Scale, was found to predict psychological symptoms (and with greater strength than a major life events scale), no such relation was found for the former, the Uplifts Scale. (See Chapter 6 for a more thorough discussion of the life events literature.)

Finally, recent research (largely beyond the scope of this chapter) finds differing physiological reactions to stressors differing in controllability. For example, it appears that uncontrollable stress leads to more suppression of the immune system than does controllable stress (Laudenslager, Ryan, Drugan, Hyson, & Maier, 1983; Sklar & Anisman, 1979). Perhaps events that are viewed positively and hence are willingly engaged in are inherently more controllable than others—indeed, perhaps their controllability is what causes them to be viewed in a positive light. In consequence, perhaps these positive events, while stressful, do not increase the organism's vulnerability to disease.

Several attempts have been made to explain the attraction of certain stressful events. Selye (1976) stated that stress should be regarded as a neutral term. He uses the word *distress* to describe the reaction to unwelcome stressors, and *eustress* to refer to reactions to positively regarded events—those actively sought out or greeted with pleasure. Selye regards the task of much of life as that of minimizing distress and maximizing eustress. The implication is that the negative effects of stress are primarily a consequence of distress. Eustress is regarded as an innocuous or even a health-promoting influence. Little indication is given of the biological differences between the two forms of stress, and no theoretical device is formulated to predict when a stimulus would produce eustress as opposed to distress. This would be a desirable feature since the distinction cannot be made strictly on the basis of the nature of the stimulus—many sources of stress that are sought after by some people are avoided and feared by others.

Another view suggests that there is a homeostatic balance in the amount of stress that humans prefer. The traditional stress literature examines the situation when environmental demands are too great. But it can be argued that too little environmental stimulation and demand are likewise aversive. Thus, the literature on industrial psychology lists both work *overload* and *underload* as potential causes of job stress (French, Caplan, & Van Harrison, 1982). This view suggests that when one's everyday life contains too little stimulation, one might be more attracted to stressful leisure activities. Whether underload, the absence of stressors, can be listed as a stressor in itself is open to some question, however. It seems more appropriate to suggest that two separate homeostatic mechanisms deal with deviations from an optimal level of stimulation. The stress response may serve to motivate the individual to overcome external stressors when demand is too high. When demand is too low, perhaps boredom (rather than stress) serves as the motivator for the individual to seek out more stimulation.

Another criticism of this approach is that, unlike Selye's distinction between eustress and distress, it offers no distinctions between alternative forms of stress. It seems unlikely, for example, that an understimulated individual would welcome a stressor causing personal harm or loss in order to return to an optimal level of stimulation. To this criticism it may be argued that there is a correlation between the form of stress (harm/loss vs. challenge) and level of stimulation, such that most harm/loss stressors cause the individual to overshoot the homeostatic balance level in the opposite direction, resulting in overstimulation. This may be a valid point, but there is little evidence addressing the issue of such a correlation. Thus, the homeostatic view is valuable in that it suggests why an individual might want to seek out stress deliberately, but it does not provide guidelines for understanding which stressors will be sought. For this aspect another view is required.

Lazarus (1966) suggests that there are four primary outcomes of the appraisal of a situation. The first is a neutral outcome: Upon analysis it appears that the situation has no relevance for the individual. There has not been nor will there be any impact on the appraiser or on persons or objects in which the appraiser has any emotional investment, and, therefore, no arousal is produced. Second, appraisal can reveal the presence of a threat—an impending impact of some kind—which is capable of eliciting arousal. In this context, threat refers to an event which is perceived to be unlikely to yield to attempts to control or avert it. Lazarus suggests that the likely emotional response is fear. The third outcome is an appraisal of harm or loss, in which an impact has already occurred with consequences for the appraiser. Finally, appraisals of challenge reveal that the situation offers the potential for either harm or mastery. These situations may arise unavoidably, as do the others. But, unlike the others, they may also be deliberately sought out. Sporting activities and viewing frightening films are two examples of situations frequently appraised as challenges and voluntarily engaged in. The attraction of these forms of stress appears to be the opportunity for the enhancement of one's self-image through demonstrated expertise or endurance. The individual may come away from challenges successfully met with the respect of others and/or feeling more capable of meeting challenges in the future.

Unlike the homeostatic view, this approach does not postulate a specific optimal level of stimulation. Instead, the amount of stimulation sought will be a product of the interaction between environmental opportunities and the individual's style of appraisal. A history of failure with a certain form of stressor may cause the individual to appraise a situation involving that stressor as a threat rather than as a challenge, resulting in avoidance. A history of unbroken success in dealing with the stressor may produce a neutral appraisal, resulting in indifference. But a history of variable success may produce an appraisal of challenge, resulting in voluntary participation. The ratio of successes to failures which results in an appraisal of challenge is likely to be idiosyncratic—a product of temperament, generalized confidence, past success experience in other areas, or personal investment in the specific form of situation.

A MODEL OF STRESS

In earlier years, the stress literature was typified by purely stimulus- and response-based examinations of stress. In these models, events in the environment directly produce the biological changes associated with the stress response. In his 1966 book, however, Lazarus emphasized that most stressors cannot provoke a response unless the individual becomes aware of them and assesses them in some way. In place of the stimulus-response model, Lazarus proposed a stimulus-appraisal-response model. Appraisal was thought to have two functions. In *primary appraisal*, the individual perceives that stress cues are present in the environment and evaluates the nature and amount of danger present. In *secondary appraisal*, the resources that can be brought to bear on the problem are assessed.

An expanded model incorporating primary and secondary appraisal is illustrated in Figure 1.1. The process begins with the emergence of cues in the environment that have some personal relevance. In certain cases, usually involving bodily injury or illness, appraisal may not be necessary for

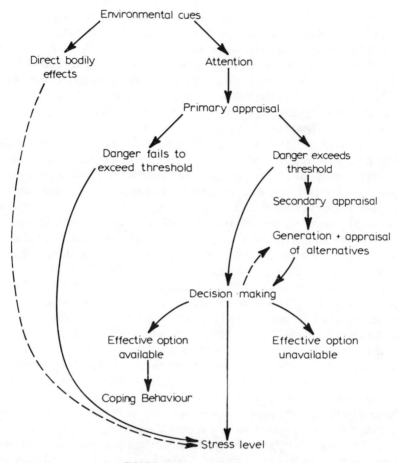

FIGURE 1.1. A model of stress.

the body to launch a physiological stress reaction as described by Selye (1976). Consequently, a dotted line (representing the relative infrequency of this route) leads directly to the stress response, bypassing the entire appraisal process.

Most stressors, however, do not impact directly on the body. Even when they do, the individual will usually engage in some interpretive activity to assign psychological meaning to the injury or illness. The individual is assumed to be scanning the environment in the course of day-to-day activities. In order for environmental cues to trigger appraisal, they must attract the attention. (For a dissenting view, see Tyrer, Lewis, & Lee, 1978, who report anxiety in response to subliminal presentations of stress-related stimuli.) Once this is accomplished, primary and secondary appraisals occur. In primary appraisal, the individual assesses the stressfulness of the situation in the event that the present course of action is maintained. In most situations, this means the amount of stress associated with not mounting any retaliatory coping behavior. Little research has been conducted to examine the internal course of this process directly. It may occur in multiple passes, each having greater depth than the last. In the first pass, a cursory glance at the cues would provide a global impression of whether threat is present or not. If it is, then a second, more detailed examination could follow.

Fisher (1986) suggests how stressor cues may be identified. She argues that the individual carries an implicit internal model of the desired or ideal state of the environment. When processing external cues, the state of reality is compared with this ideal state. Although Fisher does not emphasize the point, presumably the ideal represents not an individual's most extravagant desires and fantasies, but a reasonable level of expectation based on past experience (there is oxygen to breathe, one's marriage is not endangered, promotional opportunities are available at work, and so on). Deviations from the ideal state represent targets for coping behavior. According to Fisher, stress may arise at this point if the present state does not seem amenable to change through coping. Her model resembles points made by Selye (1982), who saw drive as a product of deviation from a steady state or set point. When deviations from these internally held set points, or expectations, are perceived, motivation to reduce the deviation arises. Stressors may act in several ways. They may actively remove the individual from the desired state (for example, by introducing aversive stimuli such as loud noise or criticism by superiors), or they may threaten to do so in the future. In the case of appetitive drives that require regular attention (such as hunger and thirst), stressors may prevent or threaten to prevent the behavior necessary for maintaining homeostasis (such as eating and drinking) by restricting supplies or somehow restraining the individual.

If, after at least a first glance at the stimulus, danger appears to be present, then secondary appraisal is activated. Danger in some form and degree is likely to be perpetually present in most people's lives; it is not a discrete present-or-absent variable. Consequently there is likely to be some kind of threshold below which secondary appraisal—the search for coping options—does not occur and above which it does. Individuals may vary in the height of this threshold. Stoics and repressors, those individuals tending to deny or ignore stress, may have a very high threshold, simply accepting many stressors as they occur without attempting to cope. Sensitizers—the opposites of repressors in that they react more than usual to given levels of stimulation—may have a very low threshold, more readily launching searches for alternatives. The height of the threshold may also vary according to the nature of the stressor. Some individuals may be very brave in most respects but have a particular sensitivity to heights. If the level of danger or injury does not exceed the threshold, then the appraisal process ceases and the level of stress is determined by the primary appraisal outcome.

If the danger or injury exceeds the threshold, then secondary appraisal occurs. Secondary appraisal addresses the availability of coping options.

Pearlin and his associates described three types of coping behavior (Pearlin, Menaghan, Lieberman, & Mullan, 1981; Pearlin & Schooler, 1978). *Stimulus-directed coping* is directed toward the stressor cues themselves, aimed at eliminating or moderating the original trigger. Examples of this type of coping include lifting a fallen tree off one's leg, dousing a fire in the kitchen, and complaining to the shop foreman about the lack of hearing guards for machine operators. *Response-directed coping* is aimed at reducing the magnitude of the stress response (the term is preferable to Pearlin et al.—"emotion-focused coping"—since it may be aimed at any or all facets of the stress response). Exercise, meditation, and cue-controlled relaxation are a few examples. Finally, *appraisal-directed coping* involves various cognitive coping techniques. Among these are defenses such as denial and repression. Given that arousal is produced not by stressor cues but by the perception of stressor cues, the individual may attempt to cope by altering the perception or appraisal of the threat. A person may avoid reading a layoff notice, downplay the significance of current marital problems, or inflate the imagined effectiveness of another form of coping technique (for example, by optimistically planning to catch up on an entire term's material by studying the evening before the exam). This form of coping, involving psychological defenses, has traditionally been the turf of psychodynamic clinicians. Only recently has it been subjected to extensive empirical investigation (see Chapter 5).

It may be possible to create a hierarchy of the desirability of these options. Stimulus-directed coping appears to be the most effective form. Stress, like pain, is fundamentally an alarm system that provides a useful service. Whereas pain provides a cue that there is something wrong with the body, stress provides a cue that something is unusual in the environment: The surroundings are demanding something of the individual. In the case of pain, it is undesirable to proceed directly to the application of analgesics without first investigating the causal agent. Often the pain will signal a problem that needs to be corrected, and if corrected, the pain will abate. Similarly it appears that the first and only response to stress should not be a relaxation technique designed to shut off the alarm. Nor should the individual distort the perception of the environment to prevent the alarm from ringing. Instead, in most situations, it would seem appropriate to examine the source of the stress response and attempt to resolve it. If this is successfully accomplished, the arousal may fade of its own accord.

Many situations, however, are not controllable in this way. Many jobs, for example, are inherently stressful and cannot be altered by the individual occupying the position. While it may be useful for consultants, corporate officers, and others to attempt to redesign such jobs (and, along the same lines, for planners, social workers, and community psychologists to focus on the environment to reduce ambient sources of stress), the individual is often forced to accept the stressful nature of many situations. Rather than suffer a permanently elevated arousal level, it may be preferable to reduce it using other forms of coping. Further, even when stimulus-directed coping is available it frequently requires a cool, relaxed demeanor to carry out successfully. Whereas evolution has supplied humanity with an aggressive, active biological response that would have been beneficial in many primitive coping situations, stimulus-directed coping in the modern world frequently requires us to rein in this tendency. Thus, other forms of coping may be useful as adjuncts to stimulus-directed coping.

In the same way that stimulus-directed coping, when available, seems preferable to other forms, response-directed coping may similarly be a more valuable response than many forms of appraisal-directed coping. Human beings are part of an interactive system between organism and environment. In order to ensure optimal functioning, it is necessary that the senses and intellect have a generally accurate picture of the surroundings. Even when the environment signals the unavailability of stimulus-directed control, these signals may change, or other dangers requiring assessment may arise. Consequently, it may be undesirable for the individual to distort perceptions and appraisals through appraisal-directed coping. It seems better in most circumstances to continue accepting messages from the environment and control the stress response directly.

Despite these arguments, there remain certain situations in which appraisal-directed coping can be valuable. First, many individuals have poor control over their arousal responses and thus are unable to engage in effective response-directed coping. Victims of anxiety disorders seem to fit into this category. Rather than accepting their anxiety or taking steps to reduce it, they may engage in internal distortions of the appraisal process. Obsessive-compulsives appear to be victimized by the implicit belief that some ritualistic and plainly ineffective series of thoughts or behaviors are essential to remove the source of their anxiety. Others engage in irrational denials or projections in an effort to create a view of an external reality that is less threatening. Psychodynamic theorists feel that these strategies are precarious because reality itself is not changed or controlled and constantly threatens to provide incontrovertible evidence of the falsehood of the distortions. A major part of the treatment of these individuals in clinical work is to improve their relaxation skills, presumably because response-directed coping can provide a better management technique. Likewise, assertiveness training may enable more effective stimulus-directed coping.

There are also some extreme situations in which control is unavailable and the incoming stimuli are too overwhelming for relaxation efforts to succeed. Many combat veterans report such situations, as do some survivors and rescue workers involved in hostage situations and serious disasters (Dunning & Silva, 1980; Raphael, Singh, Bradbury, & Lambert, 1983; Siegel, 1984). Workers at the site of a fatal air crash may avoid thinking about the lives and concerns of the people now strewn about on the ground. Instead, they may try to make the job easier by thinking of the bodies as those of animals, by imagining that the bodies are actually store-window dummies, or by pretending they are in a movie about an air crash (see, e.g., Taylor & Frazer, 1982). Similarly, most chronic pain patients are unable to remove the source of their discomfort since it is internal (often the result of enduring tissue damage), and many find that relaxation provides relief only while the relaxation procedure is being carried out (Melzack & Wall, 1982). Many find that the most effective coping tool they have is simply to ignore, deny, or distort the pain (e.g., by redefining it as tingling and not pain at all). This allows them to continue with their daily activities. Thus in the absence of effective relaxation skills or in the presence of overwhelming stimuli, appraisal-directed coping may be the most effective strategy available.

The use of different forms of control seems likely to influence the future choice of coping options. For example, if stimulus-directed coping is successful, then the individual's perceived competence, at least with regard to the type of coping required, is likely to increase. Greater experience may enhance the ability to generate coping options in similar situations in the future, and may cause these options to be appraised as more likely to succeed. Consequently success would tend to increase the probability of engaging in stimulus-directed coping in the future. As discussed earlier, success in surviving voluntary stressors (skydiving, whitewater rafting) raises one's perceived ability to control the environment, hence one's self-esteem. Conversely failure may cause the person to believe that estimates of the likelihood of success of the coping are overly optimistic. Future estimates then may be more cautious. In extreme cases, the individual may develop a belief that outcomes are completely noncontingent on coping attempts. If attributed to the stimulus, this engenders a belief that control is simply unavailable. If attributed to the quality of the coping response, beliefs regarding personal competence are affected. In either case, a state approximating learned helplessness (Seligman, Maier, & Solomon, 1971) may ensue.

Similar learning can affect the future performance of response- and appraisal-directed coping. Successful response-directed coping may tend to increase the future use of the technique. In the short term, this may increase both perceived competence in exercising this form of coping and the acceptance of unavoidable situations. In extreme cases, it may produce a bias in favor of this form of coping over stimulus-directed coping, resulting in a somewhat passive response style. Failure may encourage more attempts at stimulus-directed coping, even in the face of events better dealt with through relaxation. A driven, obsessive style may be evidenced. Alternatively, appraisal-directed coping may become more likely. The reinforcement of appraisal-directed coping through success may cause the individual to engage in defensive, denying responses in the face of future stresses. Failure may encourage more adaptive forms of coping, provided the individual has the ability to carry them out.

To return to the model, in secondary appraisal the individual compares the existing situation with the available resources that may be used in attempts to cope. Specific alternative plans of action are generated. The degree of threat associated with actually carrying out each option is appraised, perhaps in a manner similar to the appraisal of the original situation. These appraisals are then compared with the primary appraisal (hence the link between primary appraisals which exceed the danger threshold and decision making in the diagram) in order to select a strategy. If every alternative involves more threat than the original situation, then nothing is done. If, however, an option can be found that is associated with less threat and does not involve so much effort that its advantages are outweighed, it is selected and carried out.

Two ways of making the decision present themselves. The individual may adopt a *maximizing* strategy (Janis & Mann, 1977) in which all possible options are generated, each is thoroughly appraised and compared with the existing situation, and the single best option (that associated with the least threat or impact) is selected for action. Alternatively, the individual may adopt a *satisficing* strategy, represented in Figure 1.1 by the recursive line from decision making back to the generation of alternatives. Here the individual selects a specific level of threat as a criterion for accepting an option. This may be based on the level of danger from the primary appraisal, the amount of time available in which to decide, and so forth. Options are generated one at a time, appraised, and compared with the criterion. If the level of threat associated with an option is lower than the criterion, the option is carried out. If not, another option is generated. While faster than a maximizing strategy, satisficing has the disadvantage of not necessarily yielding the best option available.

The decision-making strategy used may be universal, but more likely depends on the personality of the individual (e.g., perhaps obsessive-compulsives adopt maximizing strategies more often), the amount of time available for option generation, and the difficulty of generating options. The two strategies are not necessarily as distinct as they appear. One individual may generate and attempt to pick the best of only a few of the possible options; another may make the criterion so stringent that a satisficing strategy becomes, in effect, a maximizing one; and still another may start out with a maximizing strategy and gradually adopt a satisficing strategy as time runs out.

Whichever strategy is used, eventually a course of action is selected and carried out (even if that course of action is simply to let the stressor occur as threatened). For the sake of simplicity, the different types of coping behavior are represented separately in Figure 1.2. Stimulus-directed coping attempts to influence the environmental cues. If successful, ongoing monitoring will detect a reduction in threat and this will, in turn, reduce the level of arousal. Appraisal-directed coping influences the primary appraisal and, in some cases, the appraisal of other coping options. The aim is to reduce the perceived threat or bolster confidence in alternative coping strategies. With reduced perceived threat or heightened perceived efficacy

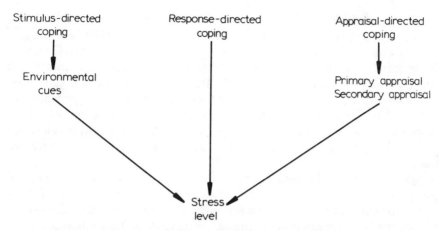

FIGURE 1.2.   Effects of different coping strategies.

of coping, arousal levels may abate. Response-directed coping, of course, attempts to intervene with the stress response directly.

The intensity of the stress response may be influenced by a number of variables. Becoming aware of the stressor cues in the attention stage may cause an arousing startle response. The magnitude of danger from the primary appraisal may induce a stress reaction, as may the availability or unavailability of coping options. But perhaps the best candidate for the most potent determinant of arousal is the degree of threat associated with the least stressful alternative.

During appraisal, particularly the appraisal of threat, the individual is attempting to predict the future. If, as a result of primary appraisal, the future seems bleak, then secondary appraisal is engaged. Here the individual assesses the availability and relative stressfulness of alternative futures that can be created by engaging in different coping behaviors. It is presumed that generally the least threatening future is selected from among these. If anticipatory stress arises from anticipating the future occurrence of a stressor, then its strength should be determined by the future that has been selected. Hence the strongest predictor of the stress response in this model is the future course that has been decided upon. In addition, the actual performance of the coping behavior may result in a new situation that is better or worse than expected, and this too may affect the intensity of the response later on. The stressfulness of different choice situations is dealt with further in Chapter 3.

The model in Figure 1.1 is proposed primarily as a descriptive, rather than predictive, representation of the stress process. While it examines the process in somewhat more depth than many other approaches, it remains somewhat atheoretical. The existence, effectiveness, or operation of the specific elements of the model are left unstated. These may be determined by predictive theories and empirical investigation. The model provides an organizing framework. For example, on occasion, or for certain individuals, it may be that any amount of perceived danger automatically leads to secondary appraisal and attempts to cope. This does not make the threshold for proceeding to secondary appraisal incorrect; it simply determines that the level of the threshold is zero in these instances. Similarly, it does not state the aspects of the stimulus that are considered in primary appraisal. Nor does it give specific guidelines regarding whether stimulus-, response-, or appraisal-directed coping will be selected in any given situation (although some suggestions regarding this selection procedure are made).

Many aspects of the model are substantially untested. However, several portions have been subject to considerable empirical scrutiny. One of these is the influence of various characteristics of a threatening stimulus on the perception and production of the stress response. This corresponds to the subject matter of primary appraisal and is the concern of the remainder of the chapter. Another area that has been investigated in some detail is the effect of the availability of stimulus-directed control on the stress response. This is the focus of much of Chapter 3.

STIMULUS FACTORS AND STRESS

Two primary areas of research have focused on stressful stimuli. The first, which may be called a *macroscopic* approach, is the literature on stressful life events. The area details the long-term, cumulative effects of stress on health. (As previously mentioned, a review of this approach can be found in Chapter 6; also, in Chapter 7 the literature on suspected moderators of these effects is reviewed.) The second approach, which is more *microscopic,* is the large literature in which aspects of stressful situations are manipulated in the laboratory and the stress response is measured. This approach differs from the life events literature in that the stressors are usually anxiety-provoking but relatively mild in the overall context of the subject's life. It also focuses on the transient, rather than cumulative, effects of stress. As such it may be more open than the life events literature to criticisms relating to external validity. But in their tightly controlled designs, these studies often have the advantage of strong internal validity and are more specific in their findings than are the life events studies (for further comment, see Chapter 3 on laboratory methods).

Most of these studies attempt to control for the effects of appraisal. The meaning of the cues is given explicitly rather than being subject to individual differences in appraisal ability. The interpretation of the event by the person is partially controlled by using very basic, isolated stressors within a testing environment that is kept constant across subjects. Still, some subjects will have a better memory for sample stimuli than will others. As well, individual differences in response to even the most basic stressors are inevitable, and subjects bring different sets of preconceptions, fears, and motivations to the laboratory. Some subjects may appraise the administration of loud noise as a threat to be endured, while others will see it as a challenge to see how much volume they can withstand.

Consequently, while appraisal may not be the explicit subject of study, variability attributable to differences in appraisals invariably creep into the results of these experiments, generally as unaccounted-for variance. This imposes an upper bound on the amount of understanding that can be gained from a strict stimulus-based approach. Lazarus, DeLongis, Folkman, and Gruen (1985) point out that findings of wide individual differences in response to identical stressors constitute compelling evidence that appraisal is an important determinant of responses to stressful stimuli. Significant findings obtained by manipulating environmental cues, however, indicate that this earlier stage also constitutes an important source of variability. Further, the approach has the advantage of a degree of objectivity that is difficult to achieve with assessments of internal cognitive processes.

Similarly, in most of these studies, an attempt is made to eliminate any effects attributable to situation controllability. In order to ensure that the individual reacts to the threat of the stimulus and not a lesser degree of threat associated with a coping option, most stimulus-directed coping options are eliminated. Subjects are explicitly told that the stimulus *will* be presented and that there is no way to prevent it short of withdrawing from the study (a necessary proviso which imposes some limits on the nature of stressors that can be examined). It is difficult, however, to eliminate the possibility of response- or appraisal-directed coping. A few studies include tasks designed to prevent the most obvious internal strategies of relaxation or attention diversion, but more often nothing is done to prevent these forms of coping. In the absence of controls for these strategies, some subjects may use them while others do not. As with appraisal, variability attributable to these aspects of coping usually remains unaccounted for in most designs, thus operating against finding effects attributable to stimulus factors alone. That such effects are obtained despite this handicap is further testimony to the importance of some aspects of the stimulus array.

Responses to manipulations of stimulus characteristics may be examined in any of the three stressor periods: threat, impact, or post-impact. But in laboratory research the post-impact effects tend not to last for long (due to the mild nature of most laboratory stressors), and some effects at impact and post-impact may be specific to the type of stressor used (e.g., noise versus shock). Further, a number of the stimulus variables that have been examined are most relevant to the anticipatory period. Among these are the length of anticipation, the probability of actual occurrence, and ambiguity about the timing and form of the stimulus. Obviously once impact has begun, the subject knows the probability of occurrence and most forms of ambiguity are resolved. Consequently, most of the research in this area examines responses occurring in the anticipatory period.

A number of stressful stimuli have been used in these studies including loud noise, electric shock, cold pressor pain, situations demanding achievement, warnings about the consequences of ongoing behavior (such as cigarette smoking), aversive visual stimuli (such as films on industrial accidents), and, for patient populations, impending surgical or medical procedures.

The research can be divided into four main areas according to the aspect of stressor presentation that is manipulated. The first concerns the nature of the stressor itself, its form and intensity. Next is the timing of the presentation of the stressor, including the effects of imminence and the length of time spent anticipating the event. The third is the stated probability of impact actually occurring. (These three factors have been examined in greater detail in Paterson & Neufeld, 1987.) Finally, any of these parameters may be left unstated or uncertain, making the stressor ambiguous along one or more dimensions.

Severity of Stressor Occurrence

One of the most fundamental considerations in the appraisal of a threat is the severity of stressor impact should it occur. As discussed earlier, Fisher (1986) and Selye (1982) suggest that severity can be viewed in terms of deviations from internally held models of the expected or desired state. The goal of the individual is to attain or maintain this state. Striving is dormant until cues arise that deviations from the goal state exist or will soon exist. In the case of certain appetitive drives, these cues may arise internally (for example, an individual who has not eaten in some hours will begin to receive internal cues that may trigger eating). These and other drives are also subject to external cues signaling actual or potential deviations from the ideal, as, for example, when a diver suddenly realizes that the oxygen tank is almost empty, or when the climber of Everest sees that an avalanche has blocked the way ahead. Stress occurs, according to Selye (1982), when cues signal a significant deviation from the expected state that strain or exceed the capacity of the individual to overcome.

Within this perspective, stressor severity can be viewed as the product of three influences: the number of goals (or aspects of the expected or desired state) that are threatened, the importance of each, and the degree to which they are threatened. In an earlier article (Paterson & Neufeld, 1987), we combined these quantitatively as follows:

$$\text{Severity} = \sum_{i=1}^{N} (\text{Goal importance}_i \times \text{Intensity of deprivation}_i)$$

where N is the number of goals threatened.

This model provides a basis for subsequent discussion rather than a formal statement of fact; most humans likely deviate from it. For example, in most stressful situations, it is hard to imagine an individual exhaustively taking stock of all possible goals, appraising the likely effects of the impending event on each one, and summing the result to form an estimation of how much trouble is coming. Limited information processing capacity and diminishing relevance as successively less-related goals are assessed make such an effort overwhelming and in most situations unnecessary. Instead, it seems likely that only threats to the most obviously related goals are assessed. Further, cognitive biases may distort the appraisal process. For example, primacy and/or recency effects may cause greater weight to be placed on some goals purely as a function of their order of consideration. Finally, humans generally prefer rule-based reasoning over the use of such mathematical estimations (Slovic, Fischoff, & Lichtenstein, 1977). It may be possible to test precisely how most people deviate from the model, but no one has attempted this to date.

The three basic components of the model can be subjected to empirical scrutiny more easily. The influence of goal importance on the degree of threat perceived can be assessed either by comparing the effects of similar threats to two separate goals that differ in importance or by comparing the effects of threatening a single goal on subjects who vary in the degree to which they value the goal. To our knowledge, no studies have been conducted using the former approach. Several have used the latter. Hodges and Spielberger (1966) found that subjects highly fearful of shock demonstrated significantly greater increases in heart rate in response to the threat of shock than did subjects low in fear of shock. Vogel, Raymond, and Lazarus (1959) classified high school boys as high or low in achievement and affiliation motivations and selected two groups in which members were high in one motivation and low in the other. When given somewhat threatening tasks presented as tests of either achievement ability or friendliness, subjects in both groups demonstrated more arousal in response to the test of the more valued goal than to the less valued one.

From a different perspective, Endler (1975) proposes that anxiety-provoking situations differ by type (e.g., physical danger, ego/interpersonal threat) and that different individuals vary in their vulnerability to anxiety in each type of situation. A number of studies provide evidence that vulnerability to a given type predicts the level of anxiety produced when individuals are actually confronted with that type and does not predict anxiety in response to other types (e.g., Endler, King, Edwards, Kuczynski, & Diveky, 1983). Other studies fail to support this finding with certain situation types (e.g., Ackerman & Endler, 1985; Mothersill, Dobson, & Neufeld, 1986).

That the number of different goals threatened influences the strength of the anticipatory stress response is an implicit part of several models, including those of Janis and Mann (1977) and Lazarus and Folkman (1984). No studies have been conducted to examine this proposition, however. It may be possible to assess the effect by comparing reactivity when one goal is threatened versus reactivity when a second goal is threatened in addition to the first. For example, one could have subjects attempt to estimate the intensity of a shock to be administered. In one group, the shock alone would serve as the threat, whereas subjects in the other group could be told that accuracy in the task was strongly correlated with emotional health. A design of this type was used by Barton and Buckhout (1969), but that study was mainly concerned with the effects of different response styles, and anticipatory arousal levels were not assessed. While this aspect of severity seems plausible, it also seems likely that with subsequent additions of goals one would obtain smaller and smaller increments in arousal. It is unlikely that the influence of multiple goals is strictly additive, both because of ceiling effects and less than comprehensive appraisal strategies.

Finally, it seems likely that the stressfulness of impact is influenced by the intensity of the deprivation caused. Greater intensity can be achieved by increasing either the magnitude of impact or its duration; longer or stronger administrations of stressors should produce greater distress than brief or weak administrations of the same type of stimulus. As with the number of goals disrupted, however, it seems unlikely that intensity will produce strictly additive effects. A volume of noise twice as loud as another is unlikely to produce twice the increment of arousal over baseline as that of the weaker volume. Further, stressor duration may have different effects depending on the nature of the goal state that is disrupted. Increasing duration may cause habituation to the stimulus, as occurs in the case of shock (Katz & Wykes, 1985), resulting in minimal increases in arousal with greater stressor duration. In the case of appetitive goals, however, increasing duration may cause marked increases in distress (consider the effect of doubling a period of oxygen deprivation from 90 to 180 seconds).

Deane (1969) found that subjects who were told they would receive a strong shock demonstrated more heart rate acceleration than those told to expect a weak shock, at least on the first trial. On later trials, subjects appeared to base their apprehension on the actual level of the shock received, which was the same across conditions, and the differences disappeared. Franzini (1970) found that subjects' ratings of the aversiveness of anticipatory periods covaried with the strength of shock expected. Elliott (1966), however, found no relationship between anticipatory heart acceleration or rated tension and expected shock intensity. Averill and Rosenn (1972) report that subjects adopted a more vigilant strategy during the anticipatory period when threatened with stronger shocks.

To summarize, it appears that the most obvious influence on anticipatory stress levels is the aversiveness of stressor impact. This very obviousness, however, seems to have discouraged investigators from extensive study of the principle. Few studies have examined the effects of stimulus intensity on arousal, fewer still have assessed the effects of goal importance, and none has looked directly at the effects of threatening multiple goals. While the components of the model given above seem intuitively plausible (although unlikely to follow neat mathematical rules), extensive empirical evidence is lacking. The evidence available, however, seems to confirm the importance of these aspects of stressful stimuli.

Temporal Factors

Two aspects of the timing of the anticipatory period appear to influence the amount of arousal produced. The first is the imminence of the event. Generally, the more distant in time is an aversive event, the less is its capacity to produce arousal (Breznitz, 1967; Monat, 1976). The second temporal factor relating to perceived stressfulness is the length of time that the individual has to anticipate the event. Franzini (1970) found that subject ratings of the aversiveness of anticipation intervals are linear increasing functions of their length. Nomikos, Opton, Averill, and Lazarus (1968) edited a stressor film to provide shorter or longer periods of anticipation and found that significantly greater rises in skin conductance occurred among subjects viewing the film with longer buildups.

Upon first receiving a threat of an event to occur at some point in the future, there is generally an increase in the level of arousal (Breznitz, 1967). If the stressor does not follow immediately, this initial burst of arousal subsides. Over time, the arousal level rises again as the event becomes more imminent. It appears that the height of the final rise is determined at least in part by the length of the anticipation period. Breznitz (1971) refers to the latter phenomenon as the incubation of threat, and ascribes it to the subject's spending the anticipation time worrying about stressor impact. The act of worry may make the stressor more aversive.

A number of studies have demonstrated that when given a choice, subjects tend to select stressors with shorter anticipation times, despite the greater stressor imminence in these conditions (Badia, McBane, Suter, & Lewis, 1966; Badia, Suter, & Lewis, 1967; Breznitz, 1967; D'Amato & Gumenik, 1960). This may be evidence of awareness that the ultimate aversiveness of the event will be greater if they choose the less imminent alternative. Unfortunately, some of these studies confound the influences of worry and predictability. In these studies and in many everyday life situations, the timing of an imminent event is clear and unambiguous, while much less certainty exists regarding the moment of impact of a more distant event (Seligman, Maier, & Solomon, 1971). In one such study (Maltzman & Wolff, 1970), the short-delay interval was fixed, whereas the long delay varied from 15 to 25 seconds. Even if the long delay is fixed, however, subjects may find it difficult to count down the seconds accurately enough to predict precisely when impact will occur. A signal just before impact in both conditions would remove this confound with predictability. To date it remains somewhat unclear whether preferences for immediate stressors are attributable to awareness of the incubation phenomenon or to an aversion to ambiguity regarding the time of onset (a factor to be examined shortly).

Regardless, the timing of the anticipation interval seems to influence the magnitude of the stress response in two ways. The first is the length of time that passes between the initial warning and the time of measurement, with longer times yielding higher arousal (aside from the initial burst of arousal at the time of the warning). The second is the length of time yet to come before the stated time of impact, shorter periods being associated with higher arousal.

Event Probability

So far the discussion implicitly presumes that the threat is valid and that the stressor actually occurs. Many threatened events are not inevitable, however. Coping behavior may avert or avoid many stressors. Even if no coping behavior is carried out, many threats are possibilities, not certainties. The river may not overflow, job layoffs may not come, and an onrushing car may soon return to its own lane. Generally, people seem to worry more about events that are somewhat probable (such as drowning while swimming at a beach known for undertows) than about unlikely events (such as drowning in the bathtub). This seems reasonable if one views anticipatory arousal as the product of the anticipated future event. As the probability of stressor occurrence falls below 1.0, there emerges a progressively greater chance that the impact will be nil. We can represent threat as being the product of event probability and the severity of impact:

$$\text{Threat} = [p(\text{Occurrence}) \times \text{Severity of impact}] + [p(\text{Nonoccurrence}) \times 0]$$

$$= p(\text{Occurrence}) \times \text{Severity of impact}$$

That is, perceived threat is determined by the anticipated severity of impact associated with the potential outcomes. These severities are weighted according to their likelihood. Where there are two possible outcomes (occurrence/nonoccurrence) the degree of threat is determined by the impact of each (zero in the case of nonoccurrence) multiplied by its probability. This equation suggests that when the threatened severity of impact remains constant (e.g., a noise burst of 100 db), a linear relationship between the probability of event occurrence and the degree of threat perceived (hence the strength of the stress response) is obtained. The slope of a graph of probability against perceived threat is determined by the anticipated severity of impact.

Unfortunately, this simple relationship has not been obtained in the few studies examining the effect of probability on arousal (Deane, 1969; Epstein & Roupenian, 1970; Gaines, Smith, & Skolnick, 1977; Monat, Averill, & Lazarus, 1972). The results of these studies are conflicting but in no case provide the positive linear relationship suggested by the equation. In most cases, the highest probability failed to elicit the most arousal.

Part of the difficulty appears to be that two factors are confounded. In addition to the greater threat associated with greater event probability, uncertainty appears to play a role. Uncertainty regarding whether impact will occur is nil at the extreme probabilities of 0 and 1.0, and is greater at intermediate values. Uncertainty within the context of a stressful situation seems to bring with it an element of stressfulness. Lovibond (1968) represented the contributions of both objective threat and uncertainty as shown in Figure 1.3. The objective level of threat increases linearly with the probability of event occurrence, in accord with the equation. The degree of uncertainty varies with the probability of occurrence. The greatest uncertainty is present when the probability of occurrence is 50%, and uncertainty is absent when stressor occurrence is either certain (100%) or impossible (0%). The third curve represents the levels of uncertainty and objective threat added together.

The contributions of uncertainty and objective threat may vary, resulting in different relative heights of the objective threat and uncertainty curves and, consequently, differing probabilities of maximum situation aversiveness overall. In some situations, uncertainty may not be particularly aversive, resulting in a lower uncertainty curve and a point of maximum aversiveness at or near a probability of 100%. In other situations, the stimulus itself may not be particularly aversive relative to the uncertainty, resulting in a smaller slope of the objective threat line and a point of greatest aversiveness closer to 50%.

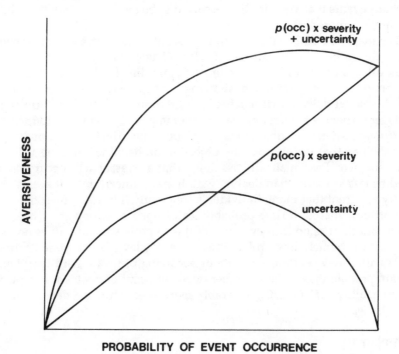

FIGURE 1.3. Levels of stress or aversiveness as determined by objective threat and by uncertainty (adapted from Lovibond, 1968).

Lovibond (1968) obtained a pattern of self-reported aversiveness ratings in response to various shock probabilities that approximated the combined threat and uncertainty curve. However, there was a tendency for probability conditions above 50% to fall short of the curve and for the one condition below 50% to exceed the expected height (indicating perhaps that uncertainty has a more dramatic effect at lower probability levels). Other studies have found evidence of greatest arousal at probabilities of 50% or lower (e.g., Deane, 1969). Epstein and Roupenian (1970) found the greatest reactivity occurring as low as 5%. In an attempt to explain their results, Epstein and Roupenian assumed that uncertainty is considerably more aversive than the objective threat. They suggested that subjects tend to prepare themselves for impact even when it is unlikely that it will occur in order to avoid being caught unprepared. For most probabilities, this involves inflating the subjective estimate of the likelihood of impact to 100%. But, they argue, at very low probabilities this is more difficult; the individual cannot escape the very real possibility that impact will not occur. These probabilities are inflated only to moderate probability levels, which actually cause greater arousal (due to uncertainty) than they would if left uninflated. Presumably at extremely low probabilities this inflation does not occur, or we would all be subject to overwhelming fears of drowning in the bathtub. Perhaps events that are initially perceived to be below a certain probability are simply ignored.

The literature on event probability is scanty and contradictory. It seems likely that both objective threat levels and uncertainty contribute to the stressfulness of situations where impact is not inevitable. Lovibond (1968) has provided an elegant model showing how these effects might combine. But the model does not fit much of the literature which frequently shows stronger responses to lesser probabilities of impact. Epstein and Roupenian's (1970) suggestion that subjects may be responding to inflated internally held probabilities that differ from the objective probabilities may be valid for some subjects. Pessimistically assuming that a stressor will occur may indeed be less stressful than dealing with hopeful uncertainty. It seems intuitively apparent that many individuals frequently "blow a danger out of all proportion," that is, inflate probabilities of impact beyond their objective levels. But there is no firm evidence of this hypothesis, and it does not deal well with extremely low probabilities. In everyday life everyone routinely deals with low-level dangers without becoming prostrate with fear; below certain probabilities inflation either does not occur or, instead, is replaced by probability *deflation*. Considerably more research is needed to resolve these issues.

Ambiguity

Ambiguity refers to situations in which some information regarding the situation parameters just described is unknown. As such, ambiguity is present in a majority of everyday situations and represents a departure from many laboratory situations in which all of the parameters are precise and explicit. Any of the three dimensions may be ambiguous in some way: It may be unclear how great an impact an event will have, how likely it is to happen, or when it will happen.

Ambiguity differs from the three previous stimulus dimensions in at least one important respect. A threat must have some degree of severity and some probability of occurring at some point in the future. Severity, probability, and imminence are all essential and together are sufficient to elicit a stress response. In contrast, ambiguity is neither essential—an utterly unambiguous threat may still produce a stress response—nor, in most cases, is it sufficient. Certain situations lacking in obvious threat cues may produce apprehension due to past conditioning (as in the case of phobias), but here the situation itself may be regarded as a cue. Also, a lack of information may impair striving toward an otherwise unimpeded goal, but the resulting stress may be viewed as a product of the threat to the goal, not the ambiguity itself. It seems likely that ambiguity is normally stressful only in the context of other cues signalling the presence of threat.

For the sake of precision, it is useful to consider ambiguity regarding each of the three primary stimulus dimensions separately. Ambiguity regarding probability implies a situation in which the odds of receiving a stressor are unknown. Little work has been conducted on this particular aspect, but several studies have examined the effects of ambiguity regarding occurrence; that is, whether or not a stressor will be administered. This is the dimension of uncertainty included in Lovibond's model of responding across different probabilities. Badia, Suter, and Lewis (1967) found that when shock was certain to occur, subjects showed no significant preference for a warning signal just prior to administration. When shock was uncertain, however, such a preference emerged. In a similar study, Pervin (1963) compared conditions in which warning lamps either did or did not distinguish between shock occurrence and nonoccurrence trials and found that the unambiguous condition was preferred and produced less anxiety than the other. A similar preference has been observed by Lanzetta and Driscoll (1966).

Ambiguity regarding stimulus severity has likewise been found to potentiate situation stressfulness. Subjects have been found to react with greater anticipatory increases in heart rate to threatened shock of unknown than known intensity (Deane, 1961; Elliott, 1966). It may be that when severity is unknown, subjects adopt a strategy of preparing for the worst (just as they may do when the probability of occurrence is less than 1.0), resulting in high levels of anticipatory arousal. This strategy would prevent the individual from being surprised by a stressor of greater magnitude than anticipated. Averill (1979) suggests, however, that sometimes the provision of information regarding stimulus intensity can actually increase arousal levels, perhaps by preventing appraisal-directed coping strategies aimed at minimizing the threat.

Other studies have found that accurate expectations influence reactivity at the point of impact. Staub and Kellett (1972) varied the presentation of information about both the safety of the shock apparatus and the sensations to be expected from the shocks. They found that subjects receiving both types of information had significantly higher thresholds for labeling the shock as painful and were willing to tolerate more intense shock than groups receiving only one type of information or none at all. Other studies in which subjects were given information regarding the sensations to be expected from aversive medical procedures or immersion of a hand in ice water indicate that such information effectively reduces the stressfulness of these procedures at the time of impact (Friedman, Thompson, & Rosen, 1985; Johnson, 1973; Johnson & Leventhal, 1974; Johnson, Morrissey, & Leventhal, 1973). This form of information may reduce fears that something has gone wrong and permanent damage is occurring. Thus, while leaving the physical sensations unchanged (Friedman, Thompson, & Rosen, 1985), information may remove the emotional alarm component from the experience. Again, in the face of uncertainty there may be a tendency to fear the worst.

The greatest amount of research has been conducted on ambiguity regarding the timing of the stressful event. Most of these studies compare conditions in which impact is or is not preceded by a warning signal. Badia, Harsh, and Abbott (1979) published a review of the animal literature on this issue, concluding that signalled shock is generally preferred by a number of species across a number of different paradigms. Many studies with humans have likewise found less behavioral or physiological evidence of stress with predictable stressor onset. Lovibond (1968) observed greater habituation to predictable than to unpredictable shocks. Katz and Wykes (1985) found that relative to unpredictable shock trials, predictable trials are met with less self-reported anticipatory distress, fewer fluctuations in skin resistance, and lower ratings of shock aversiveness. When, at the end of the experiment, subjects were asked to choose one condition for an additional block of trials, 64% chose predictable shock. Glass, Singer, and Friedman (1969) found that unpredictable noise resulted in lower tolerance for frustration and lower efficiency on subsequent tasks than did predictable noise.

Some studies, however, have not favored predictable stressor conditions. Elliott (1966) found no differences between predictable and unpredictable conditions on measures of heart rate acceleration or self-reported tension. Averill, O'Brien, and DeWitt (1977) found that when no effective control option was available most subjects preferred to listen to music rather than listen for a warning signal preceding shock. It may be that in some situations, particularly when stimulus-directed control is unavailable, having to monitor warning signals interferes with response- or appraisal-directed coping strategies more than the advantages of having the warning warrants.

A number of theories have been proposed to attempt to account for the apparent stressfulness of ambiguity found in most studies. The preparatory response hypothesis, proposed by Perkins (1968), argues that predictability allows subjects to prepare for the moment of impact. While no stimulus-directed coping option may be available, the subject may be able to engage in some strategy (such as tensing the muscles or redirecting the attention) that can reduce the subjective experience of impact, but only if onset is anticipated precisely. This theory clearly addresses the issue of ambiguity regarding onset most directly, but may be extended to the effects of ambiguity regarding probability and severity: Perhaps precise expectations along all dimensions facilitate the selection of internal coping strategies suited to the stimulus.

The preparatory response hypothesis suggests that predictability allows the stressfulness of impact to be reduced. An alternative is offered by the safety signal hypothesis, advanced by Seligman, Maier, and Solomon (1971), which states that predictability primarily affects the stressfulness of the anticipatory period. The value of the signal, according to this view, is not that it predicts danger by its presence but that it predicts safety by its absence. In unsignaled conditions the stressor may occur at any moment, and the subject is in a state of chronic fear. When impact is signaled, periods of relative safety appear and the individual becomes aroused only when the signal comes on. Less stress is experienced overall. While intuitively appealing, the safety signal hypothesis has some difficulty accounting for findings of reduced reactivity at the time of impact. The theory seems limited to an explanation of the effects of ambiguity regarding onset.

Miller (1979) proposed the minimax hypothesis primarily as an explanation of the stress-reducing effects of situation controllability, although it may also be applied to predictability. According to the minimax hypothesis, individuals in uncontrollable situations fear that stressors will be so severe as to be overwhelming and that stimulus-directed control allays this fear by allowing them to avoid or escape any stimulus they feel they cannot endure. Information may not afford any opportunity to moderate or avoid the stimulus, but in most laboratory situations it is likely to reassure the subject that the stimulus is not beyond the bearable range. The minimax hypothesis is most applicable to ambiguity regarding stimulus severity. The hypothesis is vulnerable to the criticism that in most laboratory studies subjects are already aware of the upper limit of stimulation, having been given samples before consenting to participate. It seems unlikely that consent would be obtained if subjects felt they could not endure the stimuli. While questionable as an explanation of laboratory findings, the minimax hypothesis may be valuable as an explanation of preferences for predictability in patients undergoing medical procedures and in other real-life situations, in which there may be no guarantee that the stimulation will not be overwhelming.

An observation rarely made is that surprise within the context of a stressful situation may be aversive in itself. The highly aroused individual is particularly vulnerable to startle reactions to unanticipated stimuli. These startle responses are subjectively extremely unpleasant, even when the triggering stimuli are relatively innocuous (as anyone who has been touched on the shoulder while watching a horror film can attest). Greater anticipatory distress and greater reactivity at impact under conditions of ambiguity may occur simply because, in addition to the stressfulness of the stimulus, ambiguity introduces the element of unpleasant surprise. This applies in varying degrees to all forms of ambiguity, though it most clearly relates to ambiguity regarding the timing of onset. It might also explain the apparent tendency of subjects to expect the worst (e.g., by engaging in probability inflation). Perhaps stimulus occurrence and unexpectedly high intensities are more startling than stimulus nonoccurrence and unexpectedly mild intensities. If so, a useful strategy is to develop an expectation that the stimulus will occur and be of maximum magnitude.

While potentially valuable, this hypothesis substantially fails to address the question of why surprise is aversive. According to Berlyne's (1960) information-seeking theory, uncertainty causes unpleasant conflict in the individual, which provides a motivation to seek information and reduce the uncertainty. The conflict causes the elevated arousal levels associated with ambiguity. There may be several reasons for this. One is that exercising stimulus-directed control typically requires an understanding of the nature of the stimulus. Past associations between control and stress-reduction may create a general preference for situations of control and a general aversion to situations of no control (this possibility will be discussed in more detail in Chapter 2). By extension, the individual may develop an aversion to ambiguous situations and hence a general motivation to overcome ambiguity. Where this cannot be done, the individual may simply bear the discomfort associated with the ambiguity. This appears in laboratory studies as an increment in arousal levels when ambiguity is present.

A similar view from a more ethological perspective is advanced by Milburn and Watman (1981). They observe that, in threatening surroundings, animals survive by exerting control over the environment. They find or build safe shelters, avoid or battle predators, and gather food. Each of these activities is more effective when the relevant information is available (i.e., which building materials are sturdier, where the best hunting is, and what the weaknesses of a predator are). Organisms having and using this information are more successful than others. Consequently, there is a selection pressure favoring those who gather knowledge and overcome uncertainty. There may therefore be an inborn drive to reduce ambiguity in threatening situations, or a set of predispositions that ensure such a drive is developed. As just described, Berlyne (1960) proposed that the predisposing factor is a natural aversion to conflict, resulting in the reinforcement of efforts to overcome it. A simple alternative is that conditioning experience over time tends to produce a preference for certainty and control through associations of ambiguity and lack of control with negative outcomes. Another influence encouraging the development of a tendency to seek information may be the apparently universal aversiveness of the startle response.

Averill (1979) offers a number of factors that may moderate the relationship between information and stress. First, there are individual differences in preferred coping styles and hence in the degree to which ambiguity is aversive. For example, repressors may prefer ambiguity in many situations because it facilitates avoidant forms of coping. In contrast, sensitizers may strongly prefer information in the hope that it will enable some form of stimulus-directed coping. Second, the source of the information is likely to influence how it is used and how much faith is put in it. For example, assurances from a low-credibility source regarding the aversiveness of a stimulus may not reduce arousal levels. Third, the time between the receipt of the information and impact may influence how the information is used. The provision of information about all possible coping options may result in the adoption of a maximizing strategy if sufficient time is available to process it all; if time is short, a satisficing strategy might be used instead. Fourth, the magnitude of threat is likely to influence the motivation to seek out and process information. Finally, the type of information provided influences how it is used and its effects on the stress response. Averill distinguishes between information regarding the objective characteristics of the stressor (relevant to the discussion of ambiguity), the sensations to be expected at impact (which relates to the research on information-giving in medical procedures), the nature of the stress response itself, recommended stimulus-directed coping strategies, and recommended internal forms of coping (including both response- and appraisal-directed coping).

CONCLUSION

A number of factors are relevant in the primary appraisal of threat. Greater stimulus severity appears to result in appraisals of greater threat. Greater imminence also seems to be associated with greater threat, as may be the amount of time spent worrying about the stressor. The probability of stressor occurrence influences appraisal in poorly understood ways; greater likelihood may contribute to greater perceptions of threat, but other factors, such as the degree of uncertainty and the expectation strategy adopted, appear to have influences that obscure this relation. Finally, ambiguity seems to be generally aversive except where it facilitates response- or appraisal-directed coping strategies (although it remains unclear how to predict which effect it will have). Unambiguous stressors may be preferred because they: (1) enable the individual to prepare internally for impact, (2) provide safe periods during which it is known that impact will not occur, (3) allay fears that they will overwhelm all defenses, (4) lessen the startle response upon impact, and/or (5) satisfy drives to eliminate ambiguity that developed either through past associations between ambiguity and negative outcomes or through natural selection. In all likelihood, more than one, if not all, of these explanations contribute to the preference for complete information about threatening events.

The product of primary appraisal is an assessment of the degree of danger posed by cues in the environment. The model presented in Figure 1.1 suggests that if this degree passes an internally held threshold, the individual is motivated to engage in some form of coping. This is the subject of secondary appraisal, which assesses both the stressor for potential avenues for exerting control, and the self for resources that may be brought to bear. A considerable amount of theory and research is concerned with control, decisionmaking, and stress. The following chapter is concerned with such factors.

References

Ackerman, C. A., & Endler, N. S. (1985). The interaction of anxiety and central treatment. *Journal of Research in Personality, 19,* 78–88.

Averill, J. R. (1979). A selective review of cognitive and behavioral factors involved in the regulation of stress. In R. A. Depue (Ed.), *The psychobiology of the depressive disorders: Implications for the effects of stress* (pp. 365–387). New York: Academic.

Averill, J. R., O'Brien, L., & Dewitt, G. W. (1977). The influence of response effectiveness on the preference for warning and on psychophysiological stress reactions. *Journal of Personality, 45,* 395–418.

Averill, J. R., & Rosenn, M. (1972). Vigilant and nonvigilant coping strategies and psychophysiological stress reactions during the anticipation of electric shock. *Journal of Personality and Social Psychology, 23,* 128–141.

Badia, P., Harsh, J., & Abbott, B. (1979). Choosing between predictable and unpredictable shock conditions: Data and theory. *Psychological Bulletin, 86,* 1107–1131.

Badia, P., McBane, B., Suter, S., & Lewis, P. (1966). Preference behavior in an immediate versus variably delayed shock situation with and without a warning signal. *Journal of Experimental Psychology, 72,* 847–852.

Badia, P., Suter, S., & Lewis, P. (1967). Preference for warned shock: Information and/or preparation. *Psychological Reports, 20,* 271–274.

Barash, D. P. (1986). *The hare and the tortoise: Culture, biology, and human nature.* New York: Penguin.

Barton, M., & Buckhout, R. (1969). Effects of objective threat and ego threat on repressors and sensitizers in the estimation of shock intensity. *Journal of Experimental Research in Personality, 3,* 197–205.

Berlyne, D. E. (1960). *Conflict, arousal and curiosity.* New York: McGraw-Hill.

Breznitz, S. (1967). Incubation of threat: Duration of anticipation and false alarm as determinants of the fear reaction to an unavoidable frightening event. *Journal of Experimental Research in Personality, 2,* 173–179.

Breznitz, S. (1971). A study of worrying. *British Journal of Social and Clinical Psychology, 10,* 271–279.

Breznitz, S., & Goldberger, L. (1982). Stress research at a crossroads. In L. Goldberger & S. Breznitz (Eds.), *Handbook of stress: Theoretical and clinical aspects* (pp. 3–6). New York: Free Press.

Cox, T. (1978). *Stress.* New York: Macmillan.

D'Amato, M. R., & Gumenik, W. E. (1960). Some effects of immediate versus randomly delayed shock on an instrumental response and cognitive processes. *Journal of Abnormal and Social Psychology, 60,* 64–67.

Deane, G. E. (1961). Human heart rate responses during experimentally induced anxiety. *Journal of Experimental Psychology, 61,* 489–493.

Deane, G. E. (1969). Cardiac activity during experimentally induced anxiety. *Psychophysiology, 6,* 17–30.

Dunning, C., & Silva, M. (1980). Disaster-induced trauma in rescue workers. *Victimology: An International Journal, 5,* 287–297.

Easterbrook, J. A. (1959). The effect of emotion on cue utilization and the organization of behaviour. *Psychological Review, 66,* 183–201.

Elliott, R. (1966). Effects of uncertainty about the nature and advent of a noxious stimulus (shock) upon heart rate. *Journal of Personality and Social Psychology, 3,* 353–356.

Endler, N. S. (1975). A person-situation interaction model for anxiety. In D. C. Spielberger & I. G. Sarason (Eds.), *Stress and anxiety* (Vol. 1, pp. 145–164). Washington, DC: Hemisphere.

Endler, N. S., & Edwards, J. (1982). Stress and personality. In L. Goldberger & S. Breznitz (Eds.), *Handbook of stress: Theoretical and clinical aspects* (pp. 36–48). New York: Free Press.

Endler, N. S., King, P. R., Edwards, J. M., Kuczynski, M., & Diveky, S. (1983). Generality of the interaction model of anxiety with respect to two social evaluation field studies. *Canadian Journal of Behavioral Science, 15,* 60–69.

Epstein, S., & Roupenian, A. (1970). Heart rate and skin conductance during experimentally induced anxiety: The effect of uncertainty about receiving a noxious stimulus. *Journal of Personality and Social Psychology, 16,* 20–28.

Fisher, S. (1986). *Stress and strategy.* London: Erlbaum.

Franzini, L. R. (1970). Magnitude estimations of the averseness of the interval preceding shock. *Journal of Experimental Psychology, 84,* 526–528.

French, J. R. P., Jr., Caplan, R. D., & Van Harrison, R. (1982). *The mechanisms of job stress and strain.* New York: Wiley.

Friedman, H., Thompson, R. B., & Rosen, E. F. (1985). Perceived threat as a major factor in tolerance for experimentally induced cold-water pain. *Journal of Abnormal Psychology, 94,* 624–629.

Gaines, L. L., Smith, B. D., & Skolnick, B. E. (1977). Psychological differentiation, event uncertainty, and heart rate. *Journal of Human Stress, 3,* 11–25.

Glass, D. C., Singer, J. E., & Friedman, L. N. (1969). Psychic cost of adaptation to an environmental stressor. *Journal of Personality and Social Psychology, 12,* 200–210.

Hodges, W. F., & Spielberger, C. D. (1966). The effects of shock on heart rate for subjects who differ in manifest anxiety and fear of shock. *Psychophysiology, 2,* 287–294.

Janis, I. L., & Mann, L. (1977). *Decision making: A psychological analysis of conflict, choice, and commitment.* New York: Free Press.

Johnson, J. E. (1973). Effects of accurate expectations about sensations on the sensory and distress components of pain. *Journal of Personality and Social Psychology, 27,* 261–275.

Johnson, J. E., & Leventhal, H. (1974). Effects of accurate expectations and behavioral instructions on reactions during a noxious medical examination. *Journal of Personality and Social Psychology, 29,* 710–718.

Johnson, J. E., Morrissey, I. F., & Leventhal, H. (1973). Psychological preparation for an endoscopic examination. *Gastrointestinal endoscopy, 19,* 180–182.

Kanner, A. D., Coyne, J. C., Schaefer, C., & Lazarus, R. S. (1981). Comparisons of two modes of stress measurement: Daily hassles and uplifts versus major life events. *Journal of Behavioral Medicine, 4,* 1–39.

Katz, R., & Wykes, T. (1985). The psychological difference between temporally predictable and unpredictable stressful events: Evidence for information control theories. *Journal of Personality and Social Psychology, 48,* 781–790.

Lacey, J. I. (1967). Somatic response patterning and stress: Some revisions of activation theory. In M. H. Appley & R. Trumbull (Eds.), *Psychological stress: Issues in research* (pp. 14–42). New York: Appleton-Century-Crofts.

Lacey, J. I., Bateman, D. E., & Van Lehn, R. (1953). Autonomic response specificity: An experimental study. *Psychosomatic Medicine, 15,* 71–82.

Lanzetta, J. T., & Driscoll, J. M. (1966). Preference for information about an uncertain but unavoidable outcome. *Journal of Personality and Social Psychology, 3,* 96–102.

Laudenslager, M. L., Ryan, S. M., Drugan, R. C., Hyson, R. L., & Maier, S. F. (1983). Coping and immunosuppression: Inescapable but not escapable shock suppresses lymphocyte proliferation. *Science, 221,* 568–570.

Lazarus, R. S. (1966). *Psychological stress and the coping process.* New York: McGraw-Hill.

Lazarus, R. S., DeLongis, A., Folkman, S., & Gruen, R. (1985). Stress and adaptational outcomes: The problem of confounded measures. *American Psychologist, 40,* 770–779.

Lazarus, R. S., & Folkman, S. (1984). *Stress, appraisal, and coping.* New York: Springer.

Lewis, A. (1970). The ambiguous word "anxiety." *International Journal of Psychiatry, 9,* 62–79.

Lovibond, S. H. (1968). The aversiveness of uncertainty: An analysis in terms of activation and information theory. *Australian Journal of Psychology, 20,* 85–91.

Maltzman, P. O., & Wolff, C. (1970). Preference for immediate versus delayed noxious stimulation and the concomitant GSR. *Journal of Experimental Psychology, 83,* 76–79.

Mandler, G. (1962). Emotion. In R. Brown, E. Galanter, E. H. Hess, & G. Mandler (Eds.), *New directions in psychology* (pp. 268–343). New York: Holt, Rinehart & Winston.

Melzack, R., & Wall, P. (1982). *The challenge of pain* (rev. ed.). Harmondsworth, Eng.: Penguin.

Milburn, T. W., & Watman, K. H. (1981). *On the nature of threat: A social psychological analysis.* New York: Praeger.

Miller, S. M. (1979). Controllability and human stress: Method, evidence and theory. *Behavior Research and Therapy, 17,* 287–304.

Monat, A. (1976). Temporal uncertainty, anticipation time, and cognitive coping under threat. *Journal of Human Stress, 2*(2), 32–43.

Monat, A., Averill, J. R., & Lazarus, R. S. (1972). Anticipatory stress and coping reactions under various conditions of uncertainty. *Journal of Personality and Social Psychology, 24,* 237–253.

Mothersill, K. J., Dobson, K. S., & Neufeld, R. W. J. (1986). The interactional model of anxiety: An evaluation of the differential hypothesis. *Journal of Personality and Social Psychology, 51,* 640–648.

Neufeld, R. W. J. (1982). On decisional processes instigated by threat: Some possible implications for stress-related deviance. In R. W. J. Neufeld (Ed.), *Psychological stress and psychopathology* (pp. 240–270). New York: McGraw-Hill.

Nomikos, M. S., Opton, E. M., Jr., Averill, J. R., & Lazarus, R. S. (1968). Surprise versus suspense in the production of stress reaction. *Journal of Personality and Social Psychology, 8,* 204–208.

Paterson, R. J., & Neufeld, R. W. J. (1987). Clear danger: Situational determinants of the appraisal of threat. *Psychological Bulletin, 101,* 404–416.

Pearlin, L. I., Menaghan, E. G., Lieberman, M. A., & Mullan, J. T. (1981). The stress process. *Journal of Health and Social Behavior, 22,* 337–356.

Pearlin, L. I., & Schooler, C. (1978). The structure of coping. *Journal of Health and Social Behavior, 19,* 2–21.

Perkins, C. C., Jr. (1968). An analysis of the concept of reinforcement. *Psychological Review, 75,* 155–172.

Pervin, L. A. (1963). The need to predict and control under conditions of threat. *Journal of Personality, 31,* 570–587.

Raphael, B., Singh, B., Bradbury, L., & Lambert, F. (1983). Who helps the helpers? The effects of a disaster on the rescue workers. *Omega, 14,* 9–20.

Seligman, M. E. P., Maier, S. F., & Solomon, R. L. (1971). Unpredictable and uncontrollable aversive events. In F. R. Brush (Ed.), *Aversive conditioning and learning* (pp. 347–400). New York: Academic.

Selye, H. (1976). *The stress of life* (rev. ed.). New York: McGraw-Hill.

Selye, H. (1982). History and present status of the stress concept. In L. Goldberger & S. Breznitz (Eds.), *Handbook of stress: Theoretical and clinical aspects* (pp. 7–17). New York: Free Press.

Siegel, R. K. (1984). Hostage hallucinations: Visual imagery induced by isolation and life-threatening stress. *Journal of Nervous and Mental Disease, 172,* 264–272.

Sklar, L. S., & Anisman, H. (1979). Stress and coping factors influence tumor growth. *Science, 205,* 513–515.

Slovic, P., Fischoff, B., & Lichtenstein, S. (1977). Behavioral decision theory. *Annual Review of Psychology, 28,* 1–39.

Spielberger, C. D. (1976). The nature and measurement of anxiety. In C. D. Spielberger & R. Diaz-Guerrero (Eds.), *Cross-cultural anxiety* (pp. 3–12). Washington, DC: Hemisphere.

Staub, E., & Kellett, D. S. (1972). Increasing pain tolerance by information about aversive stimuli. *Journal of Personality and Social Psychology, 21,* 198–203.

Suls, J., & Mullen, B. (1981). Life events, perceived control and illness: The role of uncertainty. *Journal of Human Stress, 7*(2), 30–34.

Taylor, A. J. W. & Frazer, A. G. (1982). The stress of post-disaster body handling and victim identification work. *Journal of Human Stress, 8*(4), 4–12.

Tyrer, P., Lewis, P., & Lee, I. (1978). Effects of subliminal and supraliminal stress on symptoms of anxiety. *Journal of Nervous and Mental Disease, 166,* 88–95.

Vinokur, A., & Selzer, M. L. (1975). Desirable versus undesirable life events: Their relationship to stress and mental distress. *Journal of Personality and Social Psychology, 32,* 329–337.

Vogel, W., Raymond, S., & Lazarus, R. S. (1959). Intrinsic motivation and psychological stress. *Journal of Abnormal and Social Psychology, 58,* 225–233.

2

Issues Concerning Control and Its Implementation

RICHARD W. J. NEUFELD
RANDOLPH J. PATERSON

In Chapter 1, we discussed how the stress response appears to have evolved and how it frequently ill-suits modern humans and their problems. A model of the appraisal process, in which environmental cues are assessed for their relevance to the individual, was presented. Finally, the empirical literature on the nature of the cues that elicit an initial perception of threat was reviewed. These are all important issues in the understanding of stress. As important as the forces that set the stress process in motion, however, is the functional significance of the stress response. The increase in arousal and apparent focusing of attention was originally brought about by the increased survival rate they conferred in stressful situations. The stress response is apparently designed to enhance the organism's capacity for active coping in response to an environmental demand. While the specific form of the stress response may not suit the requirements of the situation today, the response is still activated when some form of threat, challenge, or harm is perceived. The subsequent actions of the individual determine the future course of the stimuli and the stress response itself.

As discussed in Chapter 1, the individual under stress may attempt to cope by intervening with the stressor cues, with the outcome of the appraisal process, or with the stress response itself. The latter two mainly represent adaptations to situations when external control is inappropriate or unavailable. This chapter is primarily concerned with the active response to the initial perception of threat. The first section outlines a model of the coping process, including decision making and the amount of stress to be expected in different situations of control. An examination of the theoretical and empirical literature on control follows. Then, existing accounts are extended and some new perspectives are discussed. Finally, the effects of the stress response itself on the cognitive faculties are considered. The appraisal of stressor cues, identification of potential avenues for control, and the formulation and execution of coping plans all require information processing to some degree. Yet, the very stress response they are designed to overcome may itself affect the ability to do so.

A MODEL OF CHOICE AND CONTROL

Neufeld (1982) developed a diagram to represent the choices made under different contingencies and the magnitude of the stress response to be expected. This is presented in somewhat modified form as Figure 2.1. The figure describes a case in which a single coping option is available to deal with a threatened event. At the heart of the representation is a ratio of the perceived threat should the coping behavior be performed (plus a weighted value of the amount of effort that the coping response would require) to the perceived threat if nothing is done.

The horizontal axis represents the value of the ratio. The lower the value, the more effective is the coping response in reducing the perceived threat with a minimum of effort. Values higher than 1.0 describe situations in which either (1) performing the coping option actually increases the threat (perhaps by reducing the original threat but creating a greater one, in an "out of the frying pan, into the fire" situation), or (2) the advantages of performing the option are outweighed by the effort required. The vertical axis represents the likelihood of using the coping response. Generally, the more effective the response, the more likely one is to use it. The closer the ratio is to 1, the more difficult is the decision whether or not to use it. The depth axis represents the magnitude of the stress response produced by the situation. As can be seen, decisional uncertainty is a postulated source of stress. But the major determinant of the degree of stress is the threat associated with the option selected. When the option requires little effort to perform, this will be the least threatening of the available alternatives.

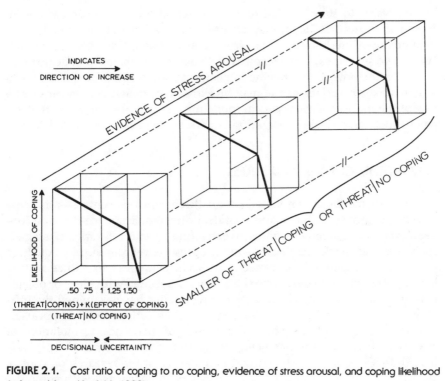

FIGURE 2.1. Cost ratio of coping to no coping, evidence of stress arousal, and coping likelihood (adapted from Neufeld, 1982).

The assumptions within the figure are largely untested, but suggest a number of questions for empirical study. For example, as drawn the figure suggests that the probability of making use of a coping option is a linear function of its efficiency relative to doing nothing. Instead, it may be that when adequate information is available the probability of active coping will be high when the ratio is below 1.0, quickly declining to become quite low above 1.0. Further, perhaps the steepness of the curve as it passes 1.0 depends upon the ease of making the decision. When all of the information is readily available, then perhaps below 1.0 the probability of active coping is 100% and above 1.0 it is 0%, with the only occasion of uncertainty coming at exactly 1.0. When the information is incomplete, or difficult to obtain or process, uncertainty may spread across more values of the ratio. When absolute ambiguity is present, and there is no information on which to base the decision, the curve may be flat.

It may also be that the hypothesized decisional stress near ratio values of 1.0 is greater the more stress there is. At low levels of threat, the decision may make little difference; at extremely high levels, the decision may be considerably more difficult and involve, in itself, much more stress. (One is reminded of the novel *Sophie's Choice*, in which the protagonist is required by the Nazis to select which of her two children will be sent to die in Birkenau, Styron, 1976.) It may also be that the level of decisional stress depends upon the aspect of the threat manipulated. Having to decide between two severities, such as noises of 95 db and 96 db, may not be difficult at all. On the other hand, having to decide between two probabilities, as in a high-stakes blackjack game, may be extremely stressful. These are just a few of the more esoteric issues in modeling the appraisal of stress that are amenable to empirical investigation but which have yet to be tested.

CONTROL, COPING, AND STRESS

Research has been conducted on all three types of control—stimulus-directed, response-directed, and appraisal-directed. Response-directed coping has been examined in studies investigating various relaxation strategies, such as biofeedback, meditation, and progressive relaxation. Most of these studies have examined the capacity of such techniques to reduce resting levels of arousal, or to overcome the anxiety associated with ideas or objects that are irrationally feared. Relatively few studies have examined the efficacy of these techniques in the context of objective threat. Appraisal-directed coping has largely been the domain of theoretical formulations of anxiety and therapy and has been the subject of less study in the past, although this seems to be changing. The majority of the research on control and coping within the stress literature has been concerned with stimulus-directed control, which refers to the perception that an option is available that is potentially capable of altering some aspect of the threatened event. It is this literature that forms the basis of the present section.

Although the perception of control is typically viewed as a part of secondary appraisal, in which one's personal resources are assessed, it equally depends upon the characteristics of the stimulus situation. The situation must not be implacable, beyond the capacity of any human being to influence. There must be aspects of the situation that afford the opportunity for some action on the part of the threatened individual. Like stress, stimulus-directed control is not a discrete bipolar variable. The individual may be neither totally helpless nor absolutely in charge of the situation.

A number of different forms of control are possible. The greatest of these is control over stressor occurrence. With this form of control, the individual can avert or avoid the stressor altogether. Less absolute is control over impact probability, in which the individual can reduce the likelihood that the event will occur. Control over severity, another form, may not allow the threat to be eliminated, but allows the impact of the event to be affected by the effort of the individual. Any of the different aspects of stressor severity discussed in Chapter 1 might afford attempts at intervention. The individual may be able to reduce the number of goals threatened, perhaps by developing alternative means of goal attainment. The importance of certain goals may be reduced by cognitive restructuring as a part of appraisal-directed coping. More common in the research literature is for the absolute magnitude of the stressor to be controllable, allowing the individual to select lesser intensities of stimulation. A related aspect, also commonly used in research, is control over duration, in which the individual is given an option that can be exercised to terminate the stressor once impact has already begun. Imminence may also be controllable, allowing the individual to select when onset will occur while having no influence over the objective characteristics of the event. The most common forms of control examined in the research literature are control over onset, offset, occurrence, and magnitude.

Like the literature examining the elements of primary appraisal, the literature on control typically attempts to minimize variability attributable to other sources. The form of control available is usually made very explicit, in order to eliminate individual differences in the ability to detect control options. The option itself is usually made very easy to perform, in order to eliminate differences in ability. The focus of study is on the effects of the presence of readily available options on the stress response.

This makes the situations somewhat artificial. In everyday situations, one typically has to engage in some amount of effort in order to determine what forms of controllability are available, if any. No experimenter comes along to supply this information in a predigested form. One then has to assess one's own resources to determine whether the type of coping required is within one's range of ability. The effort involved in actually performing the response is considered; if the effort is too great then this form of coping may be discarded for some other form, or one may simply endure stressor impact. In contrast, laboratory options generally involve minimal effort (such as pressing a button), so the expense of coping is virtually nil. Finally, in everyday situations one must assess the likelihood that an initiated response will be successfully completed and have the desired effect. Often an option will seem feasible but not certain to be met with success, and frequently one has less than absolute faith that one's behavior will have the desired consequences. In most laboratory studies, the option is certain to be completed adequately and the effect that successful completion will have is assured by the experimenter. Thus, many of these studies do not consider a wide range of factors associated with coping. This is not to say that the laboratory method cannot be adapted to examine these factors, only that so far few have done so. Instead, they focus on a quite narrow issue: Whether coping that is free from uncertainty and effort can reduce stress levels.

The issue of stimulus-directed control might initially seem obvious, certainly in the case of control over severity and occurrence. If stress is a response to environmental stimulation, then if one removes the stressor there should be no response. Similarly, if the level of such stimulation can be reduced, then the degree of arousal should likewise be reduced, all other factors remaining equal. That this should be the case for reactivity at impact and post-impact seems self-evident. In the case of the anticipatory period, the degree of arousal should be roughly proportional to the degree of threat associated with the future that will be selected; if one can select a less threatening future, then less arousal should result. The matter becomes substantially less self-apparent in the face of evidence that the perception that one is in control of a situation reduces stress even if impact is not affected. A number of experimental paradigms have been developed to examine the effects of control independent of impact reduction.

One of these paradigms is self-administration. In these studies, subjects are typically threatened with an aversive stimulus such as shock. In one condition, the experimenter administers the stressor, often by pressing a button. In the other condition, subjects press the button themselves. Usually there is some type of signal given to the subjects that tells them when to administer the stimulus. The objective characteristics of the stimulus do not vary by condition, and occurrence is certain in either case. Thus, the subject has control over administration but little else. Studies conducted using this paradigm have demonstrated preferences for self-administration (Ball & Vogler, 1971; Pervin, 1963) and some evidence for reduced reactivity during the anticipatory and impact periods (Haggard, 1943), although other studies have found no differences in reactivity at impact (Pervin, 1963; Staub, Tursky, & Schwartz, 1971).

A major difficulty for this and some other paradigms is that the perception of control can be easily confounded with predictability. Self-administration allows the subject to select a time to initiate the stimulus, thus giving a certain amount of control over onset. Usually this control is limited, because the subject is expected to initiate the stimulus within a period of a few seconds after being given the signal to do so. But the use of control gives absolute predictability regarding the time of onset. When the experimenter administers the stimulus, there is no such predictability. In the Haggard study, there was not even a signal indicating approximately when the experimenter would be initiating the stressor. The problem is less severe if, as in the Pervin (1963) study, the signal lamp lights regardless of whether the subject has control or not. But even in this case, knowledge about stimulus onset is more certain in the control condition than in the no-control condition. The finding that self-administration is preferred is useful knowledge from a practical perspective, since it may have implications for patients undergoing aversive procedures, but it is problematic when attempting to attribute the effects obtained to predictability or control.

A second paradigm, that can be called actual control equated for impact, gives actual control over the stressor to subjects in the experimental condition. Subjects in the condition without control receive exactly the same stimulation, usually through the use of a yoking procedure. The control available may influence stressor severity, probability, occurrence, or duration. Results in this paradigm usually favor the control condition (e.g., Geer & Maisel,

1972; Hokanson, DeGood, Forrest, & Brittain, 1971; Szpiler & Epstein, 1976). While suggestive that control may be valuable, this paradigm, too, tends to confound control with predictability. When subjects have control over some aspect of a stressor, that aspect becomes predictable. With control over offset, for example, there is no ambiguity about the duration of the stimulus, whereas subjects without control typically do not know what the duration will be. While predictability may well be one of the advantages of controllability in most everyday situations, it is best regarded as a by-product of control and not a form of control itself. In order for control to be regarded as an independent source of stress-reducing effects, the comparison conditions must be equated for predictability.[1]

This is accomplished in studies where control is absent but perceived by subjects to be present. Subjects in the experimental condition are told that some aspect of the stressor (often occurrence) is contingent on their responding to a criterion level. Usually the level at which control is said to occur is left somewhat ambiguous so that the actual noncontingency of stress on performance does not become immediately transparent. Often subjects in the no-control condition are asked to perform the same response, but are told that it has no effect on the stimulus. Geer, Davison, and Gatchel (1970) found that subjects with perceived control reacted with fewer anticipatory nonspecific skin conductance responses (SCRs) and lower skin conductance at shock impact than no-control subjects, although pain ratings were not affected. Glass et al. (1973) found no differences in SCR, but controlling subjects gave lower pain ratings and performed better on a post-impact task than subjects without perceived control. Although the specific effects of this form of perceived control vary, results generally favor perceived control conditions.

A final paradigm along these lines, "potential control," is one in which the experimental group is given a "panic button" that will affect impact usually by terminating a stressor, thus giving subjects control over offset and consequently stressor duration. Generally subjects are told that the

---

[1] An additional, penetrating criticism of yoking procedures has been pointed out by Costello (1978), observed originally by Church (1964). In both the control-present and the (yoked) control-absent conditions, some subjects may be acutely sensitive to aversive stimulation. These subjects should expend substantial effort to minimize stimulation when given the option. When instead yoked to someone in the control-present condition, the sensitive subject is the recipient of whatever controlling efficiency is provided by the controlling member of the pair. It usually is a toss-up as to whether the controlling member will be as sensitive and display a corresponding level of effort to capitalize on control, or will prove thick-skinned and decline to expend effort to avoid the stressor at all. Consequently, the subjective impact of aversive stimulation experienced by the control-absent group is probably greater on the average than is that of the control-present group. Corresponding differences in measured evidence of stress arousal should be observed.

button is to be used only if the stimulation becomes intolerable, and in most studies it is rarely or never used. Thus, subjects in the experimental and no-control conditions receive the same stimulation; the only difference is that experimental subjects believe they can escape the stressor should they want to. It should be noted that in all experiments using humans, subjects in all conditions have, in effect, such an escape response; they may simply withdraw. The provision of an actual escape button simply makes the response more salient and easier to perform. Despite this limitation, results typically favor subjects with the escape button. Miller (1980) found that a majority of subjects selected the potential control condition when given a choice, particularly those most anxious about receiving shock. Glass, Reim, and Singer (1971) found reduced anticipatory arousal with potential control, and Bowers (1968) found that subjects who believed they were going to have control exhibited much higher tolerance for shock than subjects who believed they would not have control. There is little evidence, however, that potential control reduces arousal upon impact or improves performance on a behavioral task during impact (Glass, Singer, & Friedman, 1969; Glass et al., 1971; Sherrod & Downs, 1974).

To summarize, it appears that the perception that one has control over a stressful stimulus reduces some aspects of the stress response. While some findings are confounded to a degree with predictability, others demonstrate that control has effects independent of predictability. Nor are these results solely attributable to the effects of control on the stressor, since many studies have demonstrated that groups receiving the same stimulation and differing only in controllability still exhibit differing stress responses. The research is not extensive enough at this date to determine whether all types of control reduce arousal, which stress indices are affected and which are not, or the relative efficacy of different forms of control in reducing arousal. It seems clear, however, that various degrees of control have differential effects. In virtually every study, subjects have ultimate control over stressor occurrence by virtue of being volunteers. The reduction of stress by the provision of further control indicates that control, like threat, is not a unitary phenomenon but rather a matter of degree.

There are a number of theories to account for this capacity of control to reduce stress. Several of these also apply to the effects of ambiguity and are described in that section of Chapter 1; these will be covered more briefly here. When comparing these it is important to keep in mind that the failure of any theory to account for all of the available evidence does not constitute evidence against the theory. To argue otherwise (as does Miller, 1980) is to assume that there is a single explanation for the effect. There is no evidence to support such an assumption. Multiple theories may vary not in whether or not they are correct, but in the amount of the effect that they account for.

One theory, illustrated in Figure 2.1, states that arousal is equivalent to the level of threat associated with the least threatening of the available futures. Where control offers an alternative future that is less threatening than the original threat, this future may determine the intensity of the stress response. This should hold provided that the alternative is perceived, that the individual has the capacity to perform the coping response, and that the costs associated with performing the coping response (attaining the offered future) do not exceed the benefits in stress reduction. This theory is frequently regarded as a confound in the control literature and not an explanation at all, but in most circumstances it is likely to be the single most powerful reason for control to be stress-reducing. The theory is supported by research indicating that subjects taking a less stressful alternative exhibit less arousal. However, it does not account for findings of stress reduction with other paradigms in which control or perceived control has no real effect on the stimulus relative to a group without control.

The internality hypothesis, described by Miller (1980) and based on an argument by Church (1964), suggests that control is preferred because it enables individuals to regulate the stressor according to fluctuations in internal resistance. The theory relates most clearly to control over onset, as in the self-administration paradigm. It assumes that internal resistance to stressors varies over time. When subjects are given the opportunity to self-administer stressors, they do so when internal resistance is at a high point, thus reducing the subjective impact of the stressor. The theory bears a strong resemblance to the preparatory response hypothesis, described in the preceding chapter, which attempts to explain ambiguity effects. Both argue that subjects attempt to match the moment of stressor occurrence to periods of high resistance. According to the preparatory response hypothesis, subjects develop an internal state of readiness when they know a stressor is about to occur, whereas according to the internality hypothesis, subjects vary the timing of the stressor to suit spontaneous fluctuations in readiness. Regardless, the subject manages to vary the subjective impact of the stressor without affecting its objective impact. Both adequately explain the effects of self-administration. Miller (1980) argues that the internality hypothesis also explains the effects of potential control, since subjects in these conditions anticipate being able to terminate stressors that are too subjectively intense.

Miller (1979, 1980) also proposes the minimax hypothesis as an explanation of the effects of control. This theory states that control is preferred and reduces arousal because it allows the subject to determine the maximum stimulation they will be forced to bear. Should stimulation exceed internal tolerance, subjects in control conditions anticipate being able to eliminate it. The minimax hypothesis, involving a perception of personal efficacy rather than actual effects on the stimulus, can be used as an explanation of the effects of actual control, actual control equated for impact, and potential control—at least when the actual or promised form of control exerts influence over stressor occurrence or severity (or, to a lesser extent, over duration).

It is more difficult to see how the hypothesis could account for reductions in arousal when the control influences only the probability of stressor occurrence or the timing of onset. Miller (1980) claims that it adequately explains the effects of self-administration, but it is difficult to see how this could be the case. In self-administration paradigms, only the time of onset is typically affected; the individual rarely has any influence over the maximum severity of the event (at least in any way that differs from experimenter-administration groups).

In an attempt to resolve this difficulty, Miller (1979) suggests that when the experimenter administers a stimulus, subjects may anticipate greater than threatened stimuli due to experimenter incompetence or some surprise feature of the study, whereas greater trust is held in the self (". . . if you are scheduled to give yourself five shocks, you will not give yourself six shocks. Nor will you hold the plunger down too long . . . A subject who must rely on the experimenter, however, cannot know if the experimenter will fall asleep, or forget in the future, or become sadistic, no matter how efficient he has been to date," p. 295). This seems a bit of a stretch that is unnecessary for the theory's explanations of other forms of control. If the goal is the avoidance of overwhelming stress, one could as easily imagine subjects preferring experimenter administration. The experimenter is more knowledgeable and experienced with the equipment, and is more likely to know what to do should difficulties occur than is an anxious subject confronted with a novel situation and poorly understood apparatus.

Miller (1979) compares her theory with several others and concludes that the minimax hypothesis more closely fits the data, which seems to demonstrate preferences for control and less anticipatory arousal in all major paradigms. This is accomplished by assuming that the mere potential for minimizing maximum stimulation in the future would yield advantages for control conditions. This is not an unreasonable assumption. The same assumption is not made for the other theories, however. The anticipation of less surprising stimuli (the information-seeking model) or of safety periods (the safety signal hypothesis—described in Chapter 1) in the future is not assumed to reduce arousal levels. This seems to be an inequitable comparison.

The final model to be discussed is the conditioning/evolutionary model described in Chapter 1 under ambiguity. According to this model, situations of control are preferred and are less arousing because in the past they have been associated with less aversive outcomes than have uncontrollable situations. Predictability is likewise preferred because it enables available control to be utilized to the greatest effect. The bias in favor of control may be acquired through conditioning experiences over the course of each individual's life. Alternatively, because the effective search for and use of stimulus-directed control is likely associated with greater adaptive fitness, a bias in favor of control and information may have evolved and hence be inborn. This hypothesis, that there is a learned or inherited drive for control over threatening situations, could be used to explain the preference for control in all of the research paradigms described. If frustration of this drive is aversive, then it could also explain the differences in arousal obtained in these conditions.

Variations of this hypothesis have been proposed with some frequency. Hendrick (1942) stated that the desire to exert mastery over the environment is a major instinct, and the exercise of mastery is a primary reinforcer. From a related point of view, Fernichel (1945) argued that mastery is negatively reinforcing: Failing to exert mastery is anxiety-provoking. White (1959) suggested that competence in dealing with the environment is its own reward. De Charms (1968) and Maslow (1968) both stated that self-esteem and a sense of competence are actual needs, which may be fed by mastering the environment. Presumably mastering situations which strain one's ability are particularly rewarding, expanding one's sense of competence beyond past limits more than trivial or oft-repeated acts. Lazarus (1966) stated that the emotional tone of an appraisal depends upon the likelihood of mastery of the situation. If mastery seems possible, then an appraisal of challenge results. Situations so appraised may be accompanied by positive affect such as excitement or exhilaration, and may be engaged in willingly.

Each of the models proposed likely contributes to the research findings to some extent. All have intuitive appeal. As suggested by Figure 2.1, arousal levels do seem to be commensurate with the least stressful alternative. A pedestrian standing on the street and noticing an oncoming car is unlikely to feel much anxiety if a sidewalk can readily be reached before the time of impact. On a highway with high guard rails and no shoulders, the level of arousal is likely to be higher, simply because a low-threat alternative cannot be performed.

The internality and preparatory response hypotheses also seem plausible, stating that the subjective intensity of impact is determined in part by the internal state of readiness. When faced with an aversive stimulus such as an injection, many individuals attempt to prepare themselves by looking away, thinking about other things, or tensing the muscles.

The minimax hypothesis simply states that in threatening situations individuals like to be able to set the upper bound in the amount of aversive stimulation they will have to endure. Testing this poses some problems in laboratory settings, where it is unlikely that stimulation will ever be unbearable and subjects always have the option of withdrawing from the study. But in real life, there are often no ethical concerns limiting pain or suffering and it is quite likely that individuals would prefer to be able to set the upper limit of emotional or physical pain that they are required to experience.

Finally, the idea that there is a drive to achieve mastery appeals to many. All of the other theories discuss control as a method of minimizing the damage or aversiveness of stressful events. None account for situations in which stressful and potentially dangerous situations are willingly engaged in. Yet dangerous sports such as downhill skiing, hang-gliding, mountain climbing, and skydiving are regularly tried by many thousands of people. Of these, many try only once or only until they reach some personal criterion of success, later explaining "I just wanted to see if I could do it." The conclusion that success in mastering or simply surviving dangerous activities boosts the sense of self-esteem is almost inescapable. Seligman's linkage of the perceived lack of mastery, learned helplessness, with the development of depression (Abramson, Seligman, & Teasdale, 1978) is salient here.

One could argue that there are other gains from hazardous activities, such as companionship, which simply outweigh the aversiveness of many situations. But in our laboratory, we have conducted numerous experiments in which students are subjected to loud bursts of white noise and have found that some subjects spontaneously select louder volumes in choice conditions. When asked about this later, many describe a desire to boost their ability to withstand stress, to see how much they can take. That this should occur with a stressor such as white noise, an uncommon sound they are unlikely to be asked to endure at high volumes again, seems particularly surprising. They gain something from this activity, and it appears that what they gain is an enhanced sense of competence under pressure, or toughness. The desire to establish mastery seems to be a strong one if it can overcome the threat of so many situations. The drive theory suggests that it is precisely the degree of threat, in conjunction with the possibility of overcoming or enduring it, that motivates the willing selection of stressful activities.

TYPES OF CONTROL: RELATIONS AMONG EXISTING ACCOUNTS AND SOME NEW PERSPECTIVES

We begin this section by consolidating existing formulations into an informal taxonomy of stress-directed control. Subsequently, relations among the types of control making up the taxonomy will be considered. The composition of certain of these types, and the benefits they potentially bestow, are examined in detail. Finally, some factors entering into decisions concerning the exercising of control are discussed.

As presented in the preceding chapter and reiterated above, Pearlin and his coworkers (Pearlin, Menaghan, Lieberman, & Mullan, 1981; Pearlin & Schooler, 1978) have differentiated stimulus-directed, response-directed, and appraisal-directed coping. Stimulus-directed coping is said to be aimed at some aspect of impending or ongoing stressful events. Efforts may be made to reduce the probability that an impending event will actually occur, or to terminate the event's duration or severity, if it is already happening. Response-directed coping seeks to interfere with stress arousal through incompatible behaviors such as relaxing or meditating. Appraisal-directed coping is designed to lessen stress arousal indirectly, through altering the perception or appraisal of the event.

The division between internally- and externally-directed coping appears in other accounts of control as well. Leventhal (1970) has referred to control directed toward external sources of stress arousal as "danger control"; while controlling behavior designed to inhibit the stress arousal itself has been labeled "fear control." Similarly, Lazarus and Folkman (1984) have pointed to "problem-focused and emotion-focused coping."

Other accounts resemble the above. On the stimulus-directed side, Thompson (1981) has referred to "behavioral control," which is similar to Averill's (1973) "instrumental control." Here, some action is performed in order to favorably affect one or more of the stressor parameters—its probability of occurrence, intensity in the event of occurrence, time of onset, duration, or the degree to which its effects are widespread in the individual's immediate environs. Instrumental or behavioral control, then, closely resembles Pearlin et al.'s stimulus-directed coping.

Another form of control put forth by Averill (1973) is "decisional control." This refers to the availability of choice between options for reducing existing threat. Implicit in decisional control is increased accessibility to a less threatening future should an effective decision be made. In its simplest form, for example, choice may be available at a construction job site from among some number of tasks, say eight. In another instance, two task options may be chosen from. The maximum number of discernible task options, were there no curtailment of choice, might be 10. Availability of eight choices, rather than two, carries less risk of being barred from the option carrying the least amount of threat (assuming no bias in availability). Decisional control, then, does not necessarily affect the stressful event directly. Rather, it affects the individual's relation to the event by allowing the selection of an alternative outcome.

Appraisal-directed control, as put forth by Pearlin et al., is paralleled in Averill's (1973) and Thompson's (1981) typologies by "cognitive control." Altering appraisal or perception of the stressing agent can take several forms. The individual may engage in a "comforting redefinition" of the circumstances at hand into more favorable terms. Covert verbalization and imagery which contradict stressor potency and the inevitability of acute responding may be employed (Meichenbaum & Cameron, 1983). Cognizance may be taken of one's abilities for dealing with impending events. Thoughts about the stressful event may be replaced by other thoughts, or some distracting activity may be used (Gal & Lazarus, 1975). Existing beliefs and attitudes might be modified to reinterpret initially stressing cues as more welcome occurrences (Sarbin, 1969).

Another type of control that is directed toward stress arousal but does not impinge directly on the stressor is "somatic control." This type of control is related somewhat to Pearlin et al.'s response-directed control. Its immediate targets are muscle tension and autonomic nervous-system activation. Specific forms may include muscle-relaxation procedures, autogenic relaxation (repetition of soothing phrases), and meditation. These forms of somatic control represent "behavioral antagonists" of automatic arousal and skeletal muscle tension. Somatic control can also include the ingestion of chemical compounds that dampen psychophysiological responding.

Functional Relations among Types of Control

The alternate types of control described above might play different roles at different times over the course of events in a stressing situation. At the outset, the individual may scan alternate facets of the presenting situation so as to ascertain whether some are less threatening than others. For example, tasks at the construction job site might be evaluated for the relative levels of danger they contain. Or, at a social function, a diffident individual may survey fellow guests for signs of prospective interchanges that may prove to be abrasive. Assuming that some tasks, or individuals, are more palatable than others, the person may set about identifying which potential alternatives within the setting are realistically available; of these, the least threatening presumably is selected. The activities described thus far pertain to decisional control, a form of stimulus-directed control. In Figure 2.2, the alternate facets (tasks or fellow guests) making up the situation are represented by the array of alley ways. An open gate indicates entry is available, meaning that the alley represents an available option. Threat is reduced (minimized) through decisional control by avoiding all but the least threatening of these options.

At this point, instrumental control putatively comes into play. The person may take steps, for example, to reduce the encountered threat even further. Special precautions may be taken on the job site to, for example, minimize the risk of injury from a power tool or swinging girders.

Still, threat cannot be eliminated. The probability of an untoward event may remain within a certain "danger zone." To deal with the residual threat, the individual may engage in "comforting cognitions" so as to assuage continuing stress arousal via appraisal-directed control. Perhaps some form of somatic control, such as rhythmical deep breathing, or, in the social setting, moderate alcohol ingestion, might also be undertaken.

Clearly the schema portrayed in Figure 2.2 is among the simplest of those eligible. First, it is assumed that each form of control is possible. In fact, the individual may have at his disposal decisional control alone. Perhaps only a single course of action is available, and stimulus-directed stress reduction rests entirely on instrumental control. If this form of control is unavailable, and the parameters of the stressing event are unalterable, then control is possible only through appraisal-directed or somatic coping.

Second, the figure depicts an ordered sequence of transactions. Control may not be successive, or serial, as portrayed, but "parallel," as follows. While engaging in decisional control, the individual may be preparing defensive strategies appropriate to cognitive or somatic control. For example,

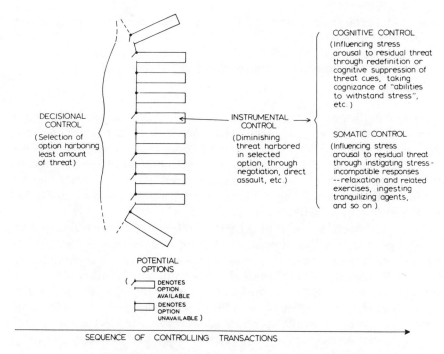

FIGURE 2.2.   Progression of alternate types of control.

he or she may be anticipating those reinterpretations that might prove to be effective in quelling the stress response. Simultaneous with the exercise of instrumental control, the individual may be rehearsing forms of somatic control that have been found useful in the past.

Furthermore, the alternate forms of control may be interdependent. The option selected in the decisional control phase may be determined by the projected feasibility of effective instrumental control within that option. (The task selected on the job site may be based on the ease of responding quickly when called upon to maneuver foreign objects or malfunctioning equipment out of harm's way.) Accessing available opportunities for effective instrumental control may require effective implementation of decisional control. Effective instrumental control may pave the way for cognitive or somatic control. If the residual threat referred to in the right-most portion of the figure is beyond a certain threshold, cognitive or somatic control may be impotent at influencing stress arousal downward (Lazarus & Averill, 1972).

Other conditions, such as the nonrecursiveness of the forms of control, may contribute to artificial simplicity. The simplifying assumptions need not be stated exhaustively to make the point that the functional relations among alternate forms of control very often will not behave as neatly as portrayed in this schema. As with most formulations of this nature, the schema is best looked upon as a building block whose elements are combined, permuted and downplayed in different ways at different times in different circumstances of stress.

Decisional Considerations concerning the Exercising of Control Options

Implicit in the preceding layout was that individuals automatically would exercise control if it were available. Note, however, that engaging in available control is volitional. As with any discretionary behavior, the relative costs of participation, over and against benefits, enter the picture. In the case of instrumental control, costs may entail the physical effort of modifying the stressor agent, stressful interpersonal negotiation, prolonged activity involving escape, and the like.

Decisional control as well may carry a toll—that of effortful cognitive activity, or cognitive load. Implementing decisional control means selecting the available option that minimizes threat relative to the remaining options. To identify the option of absolute minimal threat, however, the available options must be considered exhaustively. The likelihood and severity of stressor occurrence must be predicted for each option, in comparison to all other available options. Moreover, as decisional control increases, so does the number of predictive appraisals that must be generated and compared.

It has been known for some time that covert information processing can be stressful, as evidenced on commonly used laboratory indexes of stress (Lacey & Lacey, 1970; Obrist, 1976, 1981; Solomon, Holmes, & McCaul, 1980; Wright, 1984; commonly used indexes are described in the next chapter). Such findings have been shown to generalize to the specific type of predictive judgments that mediate the threat-reduction benefits of decisional control (Kukde, 1985; Morrison, Neufeld, & Lefebvre, in press). A mathematical and empirical analysis of decisional control has been presented elsewhere (Morrison, Neufeld, & Lefebvre, in press).

These kinds of considerations—outlay of resources over and against anticipated benefits of control—also may apply to cognitive and somatic forms of control. On balance, then, the likelihood of engaging in controlling activity, and possibly the degree of involvement and effort allocated to the activity after it is instigated, would be expected to reflect the decisional factors raised here.

A representation of the decisions open to an individual facing a stressor is presented in Figure 2.3. As it stands, the figure is oversimplified in several ways, but it suffices for a description of several factors entering into the decisional process. The column titles in Figure 2.3 represent the likely outcomes of the situation should the person decline to exercise control and instead allow events to run their course. The rows represent the outcomes of the decision whether to exercise control or not. The decision maker is assumed to be ignorant of the likely outcome held in store by the natural course

OUTCOME, GIVEN ABSTINENCE FROM AVAILABLE CONTROL

		RELATIVE SAFETY	ABSENCE OF RELATIVE SAFETY
COURSE OF ACTION	EXERCISE AVAILABLE CONTROL	Utility of relative safety, but the cost of implementing control	Utility of relative safety, but the cost of implementing control
	ABSTAIN FROM CONTROL	Utility of relative safety, and no cost of implementing control	Absence of relative safety, but no cost of implementing control

FIGURE 2.3.   Utility considerations surrounding the exercise of available control.

of events. In each cell the net utility (or net negative cost) of the corresponding row/column combination is given.

In the upper left cell, the individual exercises control and experiences the utility of relative safety, but at the cost of outlaying the resources necessary to exert control. In the upper right cell the same net utility is obtained. But in this instance the stressor would never have occurred anyway and so the exercise of control turns out to have been a waste of effort. Note that the amount of relative safety obtained in these two cells is assumed to be equal. Moving to the lower left cell, the individual decides not to exercise control and gains the benefits of safety without the outlay of effort. In the lower right cell effort is again avoided, but safety is lost.

When it comes to making the decision as to whether or not to adopt the controlling option, any of several strategies may be employed (Blackwell & Girshick, 1979; Rappaport, 1983). First, when using a *maximax* strategy the individual targets the outcome with the greatest net utility in the matrix. This appears in the lower left cell of the figure, in which the individual gains the benefit of safety without the cost of effort. In this instance, the decision would be not to exercise control. The maximax strategy is a strategy of optimism, in which the individual targets the best possible outcome and ignores the risks associated with it.

An alternative is the *maximin* strategy. Using this more pessimistic strategy the individual acts as though assuming the worst possible outcome of any decision will occur. Thus, the worst possible outcome of each course of action is assessed and compared. The decision made is that which avoids the most objectionable cell in the matrix. If the benefits of relative safety outweigh the costs of exerting control, then the individual faced with the matrix in Figure 2.3 would choose to exert control, because this avoids the objectionable outcome in the lower right cell. Note that if the effort involved in exerting control outweighed the benefit of safety, then the individual would elect not to exert control, since this would avoid the objectionable costs in the upper pair of cells.

A *minimax regret* strategy may also favor exerting control. Here the individual attempts to avoid the distressing consequences of contrasting the outcome of a decision with what could have been obtained if only the other choice had been made. Each possible outcome of one decision is compared with each outcome of the other, and the individual selects the option associated with least regret. To begin, the relative utilities given an eventual outcome of safety might be compared. If effort is expended to exert control, then this is done needlessly, as both options result in the benefit of safety. Thus, the regret in this case accompanies a decision to exert control. The same process is carried out for a situation in which relative absence of safety would occur in the absence of coping. Here the decision to exert control again incurs the cost of effort, but it avoids the regret of deciding not to exert control and suffering the absence of safety. Finally the various outcomes are combined. If the regret of failing to achieve safety exceeds the regret of exerting control needlessly, then the individual will opt to exert control.

The plot thickens, needless to say, as the constraints imposed for simplicity of presentation are removed. There may be more than two options, the relative safety achieved with each may not be equal, and the cost of effort may not be clear at the outset. Further, the individual may reconsider the adopted course as matters unfold and the situation appears to be working out badly.

In addition, the model ignores the differential probabilities of the respective net utilities. As depicted in the top row of Figure 2.3, engaging in control assures the net utility of relative safety, minus the cost of whatever demands need to be met to implement control. But implementing available instrumental or decisional control may not guarantee the absence of threat; instead it simply may reduce its likelihood. In this case, the probability of completely avoiding the threatened event is less than 1.0, but the probability of reducing the *threat* of the event is 1.0. If control is not exerted, the probability of safety may be dwarfed by the probability of its absence.

The entry of such differential probabilities implicates immediately the construct of *expected utility*. Expected utility for a given course of action is equal to the sum of the respective net utilities associated with the action, each cross-multiplied by its probability of occurrence. With reference to Figure 2.3, the individual net utilities in each row are multiplied by their respective probabilities of occurrence, and then summed. The course of action corresponding to the row with the maximum sum of cross products is the one selected. The expected utility of exercising available control would be the following: the probability of relative safety, given the exercise of available control, multiplied by the net utility of relative safety under this course of action, plus the probability of absence of relative safety, given the exercise of available control, multiplied by the net utility of absence of relative safety, under this course of action. In this example, the first probability is 1.0, and the second is 0, since safety is invariably present, whether the exercise of available control was responsible (right-hand cell) or not (left-hand cell). We may write more concisely:

$$EU_{control} = 1.0 \, [(\text{Utility of relative safety}) - (\text{Cost of implementing control})]$$
$$+ \, 0 \, [(0) - (\text{Cost of implementing control})]$$
$$= 1.0 \, [(\text{Utility of relative safety}) - (\text{Cost of implementing control})].$$

The expected utility of abstaining from control is the probability of relative safety, given the absence of controlling activity, multiplied by the net utility of relative safety under this course of action, plus the probability of absence of relative safety, given abstinence from available control, multiplied by the corresponding net utility. Here, we may write:

$$EU_{Abstinence} = Pr \, (\text{Relative safety} \,|\, \text{Abstinence from control})$$
$$(\text{Utility of relative safety})$$
$$+ \, Pr \, (\text{Absence of relative safety} \,|\, \text{Abstinence from}$$
$$\text{control}) \, (\text{Utility of absence of relative safety}).$$

Since (Utility of absence of relative safety) = 0,

$$EU_{Abstinence} = Pr \, (\text{Relative safety} \,|\, \text{Abstinence from control})$$
$$(\text{Utility of relative safety}).$$

The course of action to be taken is the one having the higher expected utility. The structures of the preceding equations demonstrate clearly that the indicated course of action will be dictated by the cost of implementing control over and against the contingent probability of relative safety, given abstinence from control. We may expect the value placed on avoiding the lower probability of relative safety, given abstinence from control, to vary across individuals. Similarly, the value placed on avoiding the cost of implementing control may vary from person to person.

Because they have technical tone to them, the developments presented above may need to be worked through quite methodically by the less initiated reader. The payoff, however, is perhaps a deeper insight into how such developments can systematically make salient some of the issues that confront individuals faced with the prospect of control in a situation of potential stress. Decision and choice behavior under such conditions can be understood in terms of the construction and comparison of subjective expected utilities of this nature. As mentioned in the preceding chapter, however, the actual construction of such values probably does not follow the orthodox statistical prescription laid out in the above equations. Nevertheless, such formulations underscore the factors that bear on the choice at hand. Indeed, they point out the types of comparisons that should occur, according to statistically orthodox criteria. In this sense, while recognizing human frailties in conforming to such requirements, conceptualization of factors entering into choosing whether or not to implement available control options can be guided by the variables that these requirements specify.

STRESS AROUSAL AND INFORMATION PROCESSING

We now turn our attention to possible associations between stress arousal and information processing. If stress affects the processing of information, then when stress arousal is increased, the efficiency of any number of information-dependent tasks may rise or fall. Selection and execution of controlling activity directed toward stress embraces a subset of such tasks. Therefore, stress may impinge upon the very operations directed toward its control.

Stress arousal has been shown to affect a variety of perceptual and cognitive operations. Hence, information from one's environment may be processed less or more quickly and/or accurately. In addition, at least some elementary preliminary processing is necessary to efficiently separate those stimuli or stimulus features that are relevant to a given processing goal from those that are irrelevant. This ability to attend to the portion of environmental stimulation containing information most relevant to the task at hand (selective attention) may suffer or improve with changes in the arousal level.

In other words, tasks depending on the processing of information either lodged in the environment or contained in memory may be performed differently as stress arousal increases. Performance may improve or become worse, depending on task demands and the level of stress response that occurs. On this note, we might observe that the Yerkes-Dobson inverted-U relation between performance and "activation" has been etched into the minds of most behavioral scientists. The primary emphasis here, however, is on adverse rather than facilitative effects of stress on performance.

A fairly large amount of work has been carried out on the effects of stress arousal on information processing (e.g., Glass & Singer, 1972; Hamilton & Warburton, 1979; Hockey, 1983). An especially noteworthy contribution to this literature is the recent volume by Fisher (1986).

For example, considerable research has been undertaken on the effects of the stress response on efficiency in detecting environmental stimuli and/or their task-relevant stimulus features. Stress arousal has been found to reduce the efficiency of such operations (Broadbent, 1971), in part because of a tendency to restrict the breadth of stimuli attended to (Hockey, 1973; Teichner, 1968). This tendency to respond to a narrower range of stimuli is strengthened by a bias to check or recheck peripheral stimulus arrays less when the individual is experiencing stress arousal induced by increased task complexity (Broadbent, 1971; Hockey, 1973). If a task requires the involvement of stimulus information which occupies a peripheral location in the individual's attentional field (according to the individual's predisposition to the array at large), then performance should deteriorate; conversely, if stimuli in the periphery are irrelevant to the task, then performance is unlikely to deteriorate and may improve due to a reduced level of distraction (Hockey & MacLean, 1981).

Turning to memory, two of the more prominent sets of findings have involved the input and retrieval of presented items. One set of findings concerns the clustering or mnemonic organization of materials derived from latent semantic structures. To illustrate, words signifying pleasant emotions and/or excitedness (e.g., delighted, elated, content) may be grouped together; those representing large household furnishings (e.g., couch, table, etc.) may tend to form clusters, and so on. For such mnemonic processes to be effective, individuals must be sensitive to the categories which divide some stimuli from others. The stressor of moderate noise levels, for example, has been found to impair such processes (Broadbent, 1971). At the retrieval stage, the likelihood of centering memory search processes on stored information that is most salient or accessible is greater when stress arousal is activated to a certain degree (Eysenck, 1976).

Many perceptual and memory functions such as these may constitute the selection and execution of stress-controlling operations. Space does not permit a comprehensive summary of such functions and the susceptibility of each in turn to levels of the stress response. The sources cited above may be consulted for detailed accounts.

At a more general level, Mandler (1984) has interpreted the effects of stress on cognitive operations as being both direct-automatic and indirect, as follows. The former type of effect includes the increased selectivity of stimuli that are responded to, as described above. The more indirect effects involve the absorption of one's limited information-processing capacity (Kahneman, 1973; see also Hasher & Zacks, 1979). To the extent that the individual must deal with existing tasks, the residual capacity for other tasks is supposedly reduced. Among the "tasks" introduced by stress arousal that leave less processing capacity for other perceptual/cognitive operations may be the increased confrontations one faces with intrusive and irrelevant thoughts (Horowitz, 1975; Sarason, 1975).

All things considered, then, while the stress response may have an alerting function regarding potential harm (as described toward the beginning of this chapter), at the same time it may interfere with the efficient development, appraisal, and performance of controlling options. This apparent paradox may be understood in part in light of possible differences between modern and early survival demands, as referred to in Chapter 1. Survival response to threat during earlier times may have depended more on immediate attack or escape, requiring a minimum of thought. Reduced cognitive activity, perhaps even facilitating such earlier forms of survival behavior, now may translate into inefficiency in carrying out forms of control that depend on cognitive operations.

CONCLUSION

A substantial body of literature has been concerned with the interaction of stress and control. At one level, control over a threatening situation can provide the individual with the opportunity to select a less threatening future than might otherwise come about. Given that the magnitude of the stress response appears related to the intensity of threatened events, it seems likely that the response to a controllable situation is proportional to the degree of threat present in the most attractive of the available options.

This does not account for all of the existing data, however. Control can come in other forms, including control over the appraisal of environmental events and control over the stress response itself. And direct control over the stimulus need not necessarily reduce impact or threatened impact in order to have stress-reducing effects. A large literature exists in which one group of individuals are given a perception of control over a stressor, but in fact receive identical stimulation to another group without control. This is accomplished by providing control over event timing rather than severity, by yoking the stimulation levels given to the controlling and noncontrolling groups, by obscuring the ineffectiveness of a putative coping behavior, and by offering an escape route with accompanying social influence so that it is never actually used. Results in all of these paradigms suggest that a simple perception that one is in control of a situation is sufficient to reduce stress levels. Theories advanced to account for these findings suggest variously that control is used to match stressor occurrence to moments of internal readiness, that humans feel less anxious when they can determine the maximum impact they will have to experience, and that evolution or past conditioning have provided the species with a general preference for situations of control.

In addition to their stress-reducing effects, different forms of control are of interest in the way that they influence behavior in stressful situations. When multiple forms of control are available, individuals may select certain courses of action not only for their direct effects on their respective targets (stimuli, the stress response, or stress appraisals), but also for the way in which they inhibit or potentiate the use of other forms of control. This perspective is supportive of a more inclusive form of investigation which considers resources in all spheres of control. A number of strategies that may be used in the selection of coping options have been identified. While yet at an early stage of development, these models of the decision-making process hold promise for a more precise delineation of the appraisal and coping process than has so far been possible using more basic descriptive methods. An essential part of this more analytic view of the coping process will be a thorough examination of the changes in cognitive function and capacity attendant upon increases in the level of arousal. For example, a narrowing of the range of cues attended to may aid in processing relatively simple information, but impair the ability to consider more complex or peripheral stimuli.

References

Abramson, L. Y., Seligman, M. E. P., & Teasdale, J. D. (1978). Learned helplessness in humans: Critique and reformulation. *Journal of Abnormal Psychology, 87,* 49–74.

Averill, J. R. (1973). Personal control over aversive stimuli and its relationship to stress. *Psychological Bulletin, 80,* 286–303.

Ball, T. S., & Vogler, R. E. (1971). Uncertain pain and the pain of uncertainty. *Perceptual and Motor Skills, 33,* 1195–1203.

Blackwell, D., & Girshick, M. A. (1979). *Theory of games and statistical decisions.* New York: Dover.

Bowers, K. (1968). Pain, anxiety, and perceived control. *Journal of Consulting and Clinical Psychology, 32,* 596–602.

Broadbent, D. E. (1971). *Decision and stress.* New York: Academic.

Church, R. M. (1964). Systematic effect of random error in the yoked-control design. *Psychological Bulletin, 62,* 1221–1231.

Costello, C. G. (1978). A critical review of Seligman's laboratory experiments on learned helplessness in depression in humans. *Journal of Abnormal Psychology, 87,* 21–31.

De Charms, R. (1968). *Personal causation.* New York: Academic.

Eysenck, M. W. (1976). Arousal, learning, and memory. *Psychological Bulletin, 83,* 389–404.

Fernichel, O. (1945). *The psychoanalytic theory of neurosis.* New York: Norton.

Fisher, S. (1986). *Stress and strategy.* London: Erlbaum.

Gal, R. G., & Lazarus, R. S. (1975). The role of activity in anticipating and confronting stressful situations. *Journal of Human Stress, 4,* 4–20.

Geer, J. H., Davison, R., & Gatchel, J. (1970). Reduction of stress in humans through non-veridical perceived control of aversive stimulation. *Journal of Personality and Social Psychology, 16,* 731–738.

Geer, J. H., & Maisel, E. (1972). Evaluating the effects of the prediction-control confound. *Journal of Personality and Social Psychology, 23,* 314–319.

Glass, D. C., Reim, B., & Singer, J. E. (1971). Behavioral consequences of adaptation to controllable and uncontrollable noise. *Journal of Experimental Social Psychology, 7,* 244–256.

Glass, D. C., & Singer, J. E. (1972). *Urban stress.* New York: Academic.

Glass, D. C., Singer, J. E., & Friedman, L. N. (1969). Psychic cost of adaptation to an environmental stressor. *Journal of Personality and Social Psychology, 12,* 200–210.

Glass, D. C., Singer, J. D., Leonard, H. S., Krantz, D., Cohen, S., & Cummings, H. (1973). Perceived control of aversive stimulation and the reduction of stress responses. *Journal of Personality, 41,* 577–595.

Haggard, E. S. (1943). Experimental studies in affective processes: I. Some effects of cognitive structure and active participation on certain autonomic reactions during experimentally induced stress. *Journal of Experimental Psychology, 33,* 257–284.

Hamilton, V., & Warburton, D. M. (1979). *Human stress and cognition: An information-processing approach.* New York: Wiley.

Hasher, L., & Zacks, R. T. (1979). Automatic and effortful processes in memory. *Journal of Experimental Psychology: General, 108,* 356–388.

Hendrick, L. (1942). Instinct and the ego during infancy. *Psychoanalytic Quarterly, 11,* 33–58.

Hockey, R. (1973). Changes in information selection patterns in multisource monitoring as a function of induced arousal shifts. *Journal of Experimental Psychology, 101,* 35–42.

Hockey, R. (Ed.). (1983). *Stress and fatigue in human performance.* Chichester: Wiley.

Hockey, R., & MacLean, A. (1981). State changes and the temporal patterning of component resources. In A. Baddeley & J. Long (Eds.), *Attention and Performance IX* (pp. 106–142). Hillsdale, NJ: Erlbaum.

Hokanson, J. E., DeGood, D. E., Forrest, M. S., & Brittain, T. M. (1971). Availability of avoidance behaviors in modulating vascular-stress responses. *Journal of Personality and Social Psychology, 19,* 60–68.

Horowitz, M. J. (1975). Intrusive and repetitive thoughts after experimental stress: A summary. *Archives of General Psychiatry, 32,* 1457–1463.

Kahneman, D. (1973). *Attention and effort.* Englewood Cliffs, NJ: Prentice Hall.

Kukde, M. P. (1985). *The electrophysiology of control-mediating predictive stress appraisals.* Unpublished master's thesis, Department of Psychology, University of Western Ontario, London, Ontario, Canada.

Lacey, J. I., & Lacey, B. C. (1970). Some autonomic-central nervous system interrelationships. In P. Black (Ed.), *Physiological correlates of emotion.* New York: Academic.

Lazarus, R. S. (1966). *Psychological stress and the coping process.* New York: McGraw-Hill.

Lazarus, R. S., & Averill, J. R. (1972). Emotion and cognition. With special reference to anxiety. In C. D. Spielberger (Ed.), *Anxiety: Current trends in theory and research* (pp. 241–283). New York: Academic.

Lazarus, R. S., & Folkman, S. (1984). *Stress, appraisal, and coping.* New York: Springer.

Leventhal, H. (1970). Findings and theory in the study of fear communications. In L. Berkowitz (Ed.), *Advances in educational social psychology* (Vol. 5). New York: Academic.

Mandler, G. (1984). *Mind and body: Psychology of emotion and stress.* New York: Norton.

Maslow, A. H. (1968). *Toward a psychology of being.* Princeton, NJ: Van Nostrand.

Meichenbaum, D., & Cameron, R. (1983). Stress inoculation training: Toward a general paradigm for training coping skills. In D. Meichenbaum & M. E. Jaremko (Eds.), *Stress reduction and prevention* (pp. 115–154). New York: Plenum.

Miller, S. M. (1979). Controllability and human stress: Method, evidence, and theory. *Behavior Research and Therapy, 17,* 287–304.

Miller, S. M. (1980). When is a little information a dangerous thing? Coping with stressful events by monitoring versus blunting. In S. Levine & H. Ursin (Eds.), *Coping and health* (pp. 145–169). New York: Plenum.

Morrison, M. S., Neufeld, R. W. J., & Lefebvre, L. A. The economy of probabilistic stress: Interplay of controlling activity and threat reduction. *British Journal of Mathematical and Statistical Psychology*, in press.

Neufeld, R. W. J. (1982). On decisional processes instigated by threat: Some possible implications for stress-related deviance. In R. W. J. Neufeld (Ed.), *Psychological stress and psychopathology* (pp. 240–270). New York: McGraw-Hill.

Obrist, P. A. (1976). The cardiovascular-behavioral interaction as it appears today. *Psychophysiology, 13,* 95–107.

Obrist, P. A. (1981). *Cardiovascular psychophysiology: A perspective.* New York: Plenum.

Pearlin, L., Menaghan, E. G., Lieberman, M. A., & Mullan, J. T. (1981). The stress process. *Journal of Health and Social Behavior, 22,* 337–356.

Pearlin, L., & Schooler, C. (1978). The structure of coping. *Journal of Health and Social Behavior, 19,* 2–21.

Pervin, L. A. (1963). The need to predict and control under conditions of threat. *Journal of Personality, 31,* 570–587.

Rappaport, A. (1983). *Mathematical models in the social and behavioral sciences.* New York: Wiley.

Sarason, I. G. (1975). Anxiety and self-preoccupation. In I. G. Sarason & C. D. Spielberger (Eds.), *Stress and anxiety* (Vol. 2). New York: Wiley.

Sarbin, T. R. (1969). Schizophrenic thinking: A role-theoretical analysis. *Journal of Personality, 37,* 190–206.

Sherrod, D. R., & Downs, R. (1974). Environmental determinants of altruism: the effects of stimulus overload and perceived control on helping. *Journal of Experimental Social Psychology, 10,* 468–479.

Solomon, S., Holmes, D., & McCaul, K. (1980). Behavioral control over aversive events: Does control that requires effort reduce anxiety and physiological arousal? *Journal of Personality and Social Psychology, 39,* 729–736.

Staub, E., Tursky, B., & Schwartz, G. E. (1971). Self-control and predictability: Their effects on reactions to aversive stimulation. *Journal of Personality and Social Psychology, 18,* 157–162.

Styron, W. (1976). *Sophie's choice.* New York: Random House.

Szpiler, F. A., & Epstein, S. (1976). Availability of an avoidance response as related to autonomic arousal. *Journal of Abnormal Psychology, 85,* 73–82.

Teichner, W. H. (1968). Interaction of behavioral and physiological stress reactions. *Psychological Review, 75,* 271–291.

Thompson, S. C. (1981). Will it hurt if I can control it? A complex answer to a simple question. *Psychological Bulletin, 90,* 89–101.

White, R. W. (1959). Motivation re-considered: The concept of competence. *Psychological Review, 66,* 297–333.

Wright, R. A. (1984). Motivation, anxiety, and the difficulty of avoidance control. *Journal of Personality and Social Psychology, 46,* 1376–1388.

PART **II**

LABORATORY
INVESTIGATIONS

3

Methodological Aspects of Laboratory Studies of Stress

RICHARD W. J. NEUFELD

The field of "stressology" has a substantial heritage of laboratory investigation. Some of the most engaging problems within this arena of study have involved research methodology. The present chapter is oriented toward methodological issues in a way that hopefully complements, rather than repeats other treatments.

CONTEXT OF EMPIRICAL INVESTIGATION

Before embarking on specific methodological considerations, laboratory studies are considered in the overall context of empirical investigation (see Figure 3.1). Contributions available from laboratory data should become apparent as advantages and disadvantages are considered for each of the respective sources, in turn.

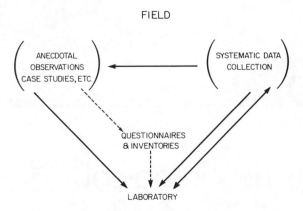

FIGURE 3.1.   Overall context of empirical investigation.

We begin with informal observations of events occurring in the field, or natural setting (e.g., descriptive surveys, single-case studies, ad hoc information from personal experiences). To take a simple example, the investigator may examine clinical case reports of individuals complaining of stress when dealing with other people. The investigator may notice that the reported stress appears to occur primarily in novel situations where decisive action is called for. Moreover, because of their novelty, it is not readily apparent in these situations that assertive behavior will be appropriate and effective in favorably influencing the progression of events. Accordingly, the investigator may surmise that individuals do not decide to use particular counter-stress strategies if cues signifying their effectiveness are ambiguous. This hunch may be checked against case material dealing with other types of stress (e.g., that involving basic physical needs); it may also be checked for compatibility with pertinent findings from investigations reported in the literature.

Informal field studies may be valuable for the generation and revision of tentative ideas about the subject matter, for insights involving novel applications of "existing knowledge," and so on. This is the least scientifically rigorous stage of study. However, some investigators have extolled this stage as the "honeymoon period" of research activity; it is lauded for allowing creative energies to operate in a relatively unconstrained fashion. Fresh ideas can germinate unencumbered by immediate concerns with systematic controls, nuances of statistical analysis, and formal rules of inference. Whether the researcher has an affinity for the "free thinking" afforded by this stage of inquiry or has antipathy toward its lack of structure, informal field observation is often an essential initial step in a new area of investigation.

Another source of data is the laboratory study, the main subject of this chapter. This source is often employed following initial field observation. For instance, tentative predictions may be examined in a preliminary fashion in order to formulate questions emanating from the field more clearly; in turn, a more elaborate laboratory study may be undertaken. The most obvious advantage of laboratory investigation is that it lends itself to experimental manipulation of target variables. Consider the earlier hunch regarding ambiguity of cues and decisions to activate counter-stress strategies. With some refinement, the hunch may be consolidated into a hypothesis that the propensity to engage in counter-stress behavior (instrumental stimulus-directed control; see Chapter 2) is some specified function of ambiguity of cues signifying the behavior's effectiveness. The targeted independent variable may be the level of ambiguity that is manipulated.

The laboratory setting also lends itself to control of nontarget variables (e.g., sex of experimenter, format of instructions, individual differences in reactivity). Control of the latter variables can be achieved by holding them constant, by matching or counterbalancing across groups, or by leaving them free to vary randomly with respect to the target independent variable(s).

A well-known risk attending data collection from the laboratory is that results may not generalize to the natural setting. That is, the pattern of findings may not be representative of events outside the laboratory; the configuration of dependent-variable values associated with the target independent variable, may systematically change. Obtained effects may disappear, become more pronounced, or assume different directions.

One contributor to change in results may be the extraneous variables that have been held constant. Patterns of findings may change as the "constant experimenter" is replaced in the field by the absence of any experimenter; or as the absence of distraction in the laboratory gives way to many distracting events outside the laboratory. Changes in patterns of the dependent variable(s) representing effects of the target independent variable can be viewed in terms of interactions between the target independent variable and the respective extraneous variables (Neufeld, 1970). Similar considerations apply to the independent variable and constant but incidental features of the laboratory (e.g., room temperature, wall color, floor space).

Another hazard to generalization pertains to the laboratory version of the independent variable(s). The degradation in cues signifying counter-stress behavior effectiveness, for example, may bear a tenuous correspondence to the ambiguity of such cues in extra-laboratory settings. Other factors contributing to the artificiality of manipulations include subjects' awareness that ethical constraints protect them from substantial harm or serious discomfort. In this sense, the severity and duration of experiences contrast with those of the natural setting. This peril to generalization may bear more heavily on "traumatic stressors" (see, e.g., Dohrenwend & Dohrenwend, 1974) than on microstressors or hasslelike experiences (e.g., Lazarus & Folkman, 1984; McLean, 1976); the latter are presumably more readily contrived in the laboratory.

We turn now to consider barriers to generalization deriving from sample characteristics. Results are supposedly generalizable on statistical grounds to the population from whom the sample has been selected. Practical constraints make this mode of generalization hardly feasible and it is seldom taken seriously by investigators. Generalization usually rests on an apparent absence of demographic differences between the sample characteristics and those of the population to which generalization is desired. If such differences exist, they are judged informally with respect to the likelihood of their interacting with the target independent variables (Edgington, 1966; Neufeld, 1977).

An empirical approach to assessing generalizability can take the following form. Variables representing potential barriers to generalization can be incorporated directly into the laboratory setting. For example, a "constant human experimenter" versus an automated delivery of laboratory procedures might form a two-level factor in the research design of the study. Similarly, specific laboratory settings might comprise a between-subjects factor in a split-plot factorial design (Hicks, 1973). The target independent variable might take on alternate formats as well. Ambiguity of counter-stress related cues, for example, may be manipulated using different methods for inducing uncertainty/salience. Finally, subsets of subjects who systematically differ demographically (e.g., with respect to age, socioeconomic status, etc.) can be worked into the analysis. (Spohn & Fitzpatrick, 1980, have elaborated on the latter procedure in the context of psychopathology research.) In each of these instances, the effects of principal interest are the interactions between the variables potentially threatening generalization and the target independent variable(s).[1]

Unfortunately, such empirical estimates of changes in results as a function of factors specific to the laboratory tend to be economically unrealistic. They certainly speak to replicability of findings within the laboratory; and they are suggestive regarding applicability of findings outside the laboratory. But such procedures usually cannot experimentally implement stressful situations as they appear in the natural setting. Little or no interaction with the target independent variable may be observed when variations of nontarget variables are limited to formats that are feasible within the laboratory. The more extreme variation from laboratory to nonlaboratory settings, on the other hand, may introduce important effects. To illustrate, there may be little influence of the presence of a human experimenter versus the automated

---

[1] In the case of continuous demographic variables such as age and education level, and dichotomous variables such as sex, samples need not be subdivided. Each demographic variable can simply be examined for significant heterogeneity in coefficients of regression involving itself and the dependent variable(s) across levels of the target independent variable. Such tests for heterogeneity can be found in most commonly used computer program packages for Analysis of Covariance. Significant heterogeneity of regression coefficients is indicative of an interaction between the demographic and target independent variables.

delivery of experimental procedures on the effects of the target independent variable. A discernable influence may occur, however, if an additional level of such a factor could be introduced—specifically, the essentially unstructured atmosphere hosting the target independent variable in the field setting.

In a similar vein, alternate modes of varying ambiguity may make little or no difference to ambiguity's effects on counter-stress behavior as observed in the laboratory. Suppose each of several subsets of subjects receives a different manipulation of this target independent variable (e.g., visual vs. auditory presentation of cue information). Suppose, further, that there is no ambiguity by type-of-manipulation interaction. In all likelihood, ambiguity will be a "within-subjects factor"; that is, each subject receives each designated level of ambiguity. Due to practical constraints, furthermore, the respective levels are presented in fairly rapid succession over the laboratory session. The resulting effects may not match those that occur when levels of the ambiguity factor occur more or less in temporal isolation, as in some natural settings. For these reasons, there seems to be little alternative to at least complementing laboratory data collection with that from systematic field investigation.

Systematic field observations might incorporate cross-sectional surveys, longitudinal data in the form of repeated interviews or questionnaires, or a combination of these procedures (involving observations of two or more strata of individuals over time). Furthermore, direct observations may be carried out longitudinally and/or cross sectionally. The reader is referred to the evaluative review of field methodology by R. Martin, in Chapter 6 in this volume. The present discussion focuses on the role of field investigations in the current context of the data-collection enterprise.

In the field setting, laboratory-constrained versions of the independent variables of principal interest presumably give way to the "natural formats" of these variables. The network of extraneous and incidental variables that hosts the independent variables is thought to take on a nonartificial status as well. A factor potentially undermining this authenticity involves intrusive observations, such as measurements that might sensitize subjects to the purpose of the study and thereby distort their behavior. A chief disadvantage is the difficulty in attributing with confidence the observed variation in the designated dependent variable(s) to that of the independent variable.

Controlled manipulations of the independent variable may be difficult, but not impossible in the field (see, e.g., Dooley, 1985). Such manipulations may permit stronger inferences regarding sources of variation in dependent variables. But, unfortunately, substantial impediments to clear inferences of this type are ever present. First, strength of the manipulation, despite its more natural format, may be weakened. For example, increased ambiguity of the experimentally manipulated cues relating to counter-stress effectiveness may be offset by other sources of information regarding its potential effectiveness.[2] On the other hand, effects may be overestimated because of factors augmenting the target independent variable. As ambiguity of cues signifying effectiveness of counter-stress activity diminishes, the actual effectiveness of the activity may increase. The provision of cues clearly indicating that a social context is amenable to assertive behavior may also be instructive regarding strategic timing and format of the behavior. Such knowledge may carry incentive to generate counter-stress behavior over and above that provided by cue-salience per se.

A frequent approach to the preceding type of problem is that of statistical adjustment through part and partial correlation and related procedures such as hierarchical multiple regression. These approaches, however, require exhaustive identification of confounding variables. This is necessary if statistical adjustments are to "purify" the variance of the designated variables into unconfounded residual variance for subsequent correlations. Even if such a chimerical task were accomplished, a number of barriers to clear interpretation remain. Similar and often identical problems attend statistical adjustment of laboratory data. These are elaborated upon in a later section on analysis.

On the more positive side, convergence and discrepancy of field findings with those of the laboratory can sometimes be assessed reciprocally as follows. Questionnaires can be completed and diaries kept by subjects participating in the laboratory experiment. For instance, the diary/questionnaire may address frequencies of counter-stress assertiveness during social encounters along with relevant characteristics of those encounters, on a daily basis. Results may be checked against laboratory findings. Subsets of subjects for whom generality of laboratory findings appear to differ might be identified; in turn, demographic and other characteristics (e.g., organismic) of the subsamples might be noted. An excellent example of this technique, as used in a different context, has been presented by Baddeley, Sutherland, and Harris (1982). In studying memory deficits among head-injured patients, they demonstrated significant generalization of laboratory findings

---

[2] It may be argued that identifying an active agent of variation in a dependent variable(s) inside the laboratory is of little value if an effect-nullifying correlate is intrinsic to the agent in its "natural format." On the contrary, estimates of whether null findings in the field result from inherent impotence of the suspected agent, or counter-action of a correlated antagonist can be important, as follows. The opposing variable may be weak or absent under other field-setting circumstances. Depending on whether earlier effects were cancelled, or were zero *ab initio*, variation in the dependent variable(s) now will or will not be predicted.

A parallel is available from the field of quantum mechanics, where the phase sequences of complex functions (Schrodinger wave functions) cancel out. In principle, knowing the specific functions underlying this "null" epiphenomenon may affect predictions about epiphenomena under other conditions, where possibly a subset of the phase-sequence values are operative.

when time and format of diary measures were adapted to subjects' specific handicaps.

Similar refinements of laboratory procedures and interpretation of findings are likely to stem from diary/questionnaire findings. This give-and-take transaction between laboratory and field is represented by the double arrow in Figure 3.1.

Another source of data is made up of questionnaires and inventories. For such questionnaires and inventories, stress-relevant scenarios are constructed as items (e.g., "You falter in a seminar given before a class whose mandate is to be highly critical"). Subjects, in turn, are asked to make various judgments about the items. For example, the items may be judged with respect to their "global similarity" to one another; or judgments may be made along specified dimensions (e.g., controllability of events within the described scenarios). The judgments are commonly submitted to multivariate analyses in order to estimate the types of stressing properties couched in the situations, and/or interrelations among these properties (e.g., Magnusson & Ekehammar, 1975).

An advantage of using this type of questionnaire and inventory is the opportunity to incorporate extra-laboratory situations and events into items. Results speak to how subjects cognitively map this extra-laboratory subject matter. In addition, findings also may implicate direct effects of field encounters to some degree; correspondence to these encounters can be facilitated if items describe specific situations in relatively concrete terms (Semin & Greenslade, 1985).

This type of data collection can augment informal field observations when initially generating ideas about the subject matter. As well, it might provide a preliminary test of ideas that have sprung from field observations. Unfortunately, certain factors may perturb the veracity of results. The judgmental data is based on imagined experiences that may be qualitatively different from direct experiences (e.g., Craig, 1968). Also, judgmental errors and biases are well-documented (see, e.g., Estes, 1976; Pitz & Sachs, 1984) and appear to extend to stress-relevant judgments (e.g., Neufeld, 1982). A related influence stems from judges' preconceived ideas about stressing situations and their effects (Shweder, 1975). On balance, the use of questionnaires and inventories in the manner indicated can augment laboratory and field studies. Results are tentative, however, as indicated in Figure 3.1 by the dashed arrow.

Returning to the overall context depicted in Figure 3.1, note that the enterprise of empirical study is considered to be iterative. Systematic field observations may be superimposed upon other less-structured field observations; the latter observations may instantiate our current network of information, and/or suggest extensions and refinements. The cycle of investigation is thus reinitiated. All things considered, the data-acquisition route depicted by the solid arrows should ultimately instill the greatest confidence in our statements about psychological stress. The segment incorporating laboratory studies and systematic field observations should be emphasized. There is reasonable support for a belief that a given independent variable affects a given dependent variable in the natural setting if (a) the laboratory version of the independent variable affects the laboratory version of the dependent variable, and (b) the field format of the independent variable correlates with the field format of the dependent variable(s).

In Defense of the Laboratory

Certain prominent investigators of psychological stress and coping (Lazarus, Coyne, & Folkman, 1982; Lazarus & Folkman, 1984) have extolled the value of findings obtained from the field (natural-setting and everyday-life) over those obtained in the laboratory. They have argued that the meaningfulness of future research rests on a redirection of efforts away from the laboratory and toward the field (e.g., Lazarus & Folkman, 1984, pp. 301–302). Arguments for their position primarily revolve around the issues of generalizability of laboratory findings, discussed in this chapter.

Such a position may be premature. The laboratory arena of data collection should not be stripped of its importance; it should not even be given second priority. A survey of current journal articles and volumes on psychological stress clearly indicates that we have, in some respects, barely tapped the wealth of information available from the laboratory. For example, constructs such as appraisal and coping (see Chapters 1 and 2), used extensively in field research, have in no way been fine-tuned sufficiently to afford the abandonment of laboratory investigation. Among other approaches, models and corresponding paradigms from experimental cognitive psychology have yet to be exploited. Included among such models are those addressing memory processes (e.g., Estes, 1976; Hunt & Lansman, 1986). How might these processes be involved in the development and implementation of appraisals concerning the imminence, probability, and intensity of threatening events—or the duration and consequences of ongoing experiences? What decision/ choice operations (Luce & Weber, 1986; Pitz & Sachs, 1984) determine the selection of coping alternatives?

If laboratory findings have been disappointing to some, rather than blaming the artificiality of the setting, we might look to shortcomings in tapping the setting's strengths. Among these shortcomings are a frequent lack of innovation and rigor in designing manipulations and methods of measurement; a failure to implement and extend relevant paradigms from other research domains and frequently superficial evaluations of results (see also Holmes & McCaul, this volume).

In any event, inherent interest in "natural-setting" or "everyday" versions of stress may tempt many researchers to relegate laboratory work to back-burner status. A valid case can be made, however, that laboratory efforts should take precedence over field investigations. In the laboratory, the sources of variation in dependent variables can be more precisely identified.

In turn, these influences *may* operate similarly outside the laboratory. The belief that a feature influences a dependent variable in the laboratory and the field is greater if the agent is found at least to influence measures of the dependent variable within the laboratory. Such knowledge stemming from laboratory findings has substantial endorsement from the history of empirical science. To encourage or discourage existing views is a chief function of data acquisition (Garber, 1983). Because of the elusiveness of control over potential confounding variables in the field and consequent vulnerability of causal inferences, data from field studies can rarely modify these beliefs with much empirical force.

We now attend to two of the more prominent potential roadblocks to life-likeness of laboratory studies. These have been labeled "controllability" and "open-endedness" (Lazarus & Folkman, 1984). The first refers to the ethical constraints on laboratory investigators to allow a subject to leave the setting altogether if the experience becomes too distasteful. Open-endedness, on the other hand, refers to the durations of laboratory stressors, which are usually short intervals relative to ongoing stressors in everyday life. Do these and related qualities of field experiences *de facto* invalidate laboratory findings? The answer requires a consideration of interactions between the independent variable(s) of interest and the above qualities of field versus laboratory stress. (Such interactions were described earlier, with reference to target independent variables, "extraneous variables" that are deliberately held constant, and incidental features of the laboratory setting.) While we may suspect that such interactions take place, categorical statements to this effect at this juncture can be somewhat gratuitous. The current state of this research domain urges investigators to continue using all means at their disposal to ferret out and elucidate focal parameters of stress phenomena. Doing so should continuously upgrade our estimates of where obtained findings do and do not apply.

The fruits of such persistence are illustrated by the recent history of investigation into a particular form of stress—pain. In 1957, a leading pain researcher, H. K. Beecher, strongly indicated laboratory studies of pain; his rationale closely resembled that underlying the current championing of field research.

Laboratory pain had been induced by agents such as radiant heat to the forearm, pressure-cuff muscle ischemia, hand-immersion into ice water, etc. Such pain differed from field (clinical) forms of pain in terms of duration (chronicity), locus (peripheral vs. e.g., visceral), and significance of danger (clinical pain might signal severe illness or death). Nonetheless, laboratory investigators persevered. Their efforts subsequently led to promising, noninvasive control strategies for some forms of clinical pain (Tan, 1982) and substantially improved measurement techniques (Clark, 1987). Interestingly, Beecher softened his skepticism as possible sources of reduced generalization from laboratory to clinical pain became apparent with continued study. Hebben (1985) has sketched these developments, as follows:

Wolff (1978) has reported how Beecher's disapproval of experimentally induced pain studies slowed pain research, and, more importantly, devalued the studies of Hardy, Wolff, and Goodell. Beecher later reversed his position and allowed that experimental pain techniques which involved suprathreshold sensations might be useful in the measurement of clinical pain. Following this, it was once more acceptable to study pain in humans with experimental techniques; consequently, the scientific study of pain has flourished over the last two decades (pp. 451–452).

It would be unfortunate if researchers unwittingly repeated the above cycle with nonpainful stress.

Finally, without the laboratory setting, it would be impossible to pursue a number of deserving lines of investigation. Among these is the impact of stress on "molecular psychological processes," described in Chapter 2.

METHODS OF FORMULATING RESEARCH QUESTIONS

The purpose of this section is to describe options for formulating questions addressed in laboratory stress research. Emphasis is placed on the format of posing the questions, over and above their specific content. The options are examined primarily with respect to their "formal" versus "informal" status as "scientific subsystems" (Braithwaite, 1968; Earman, 1983). Formal subsystems generally involve mathematical deduction; informal subsystems depend mainly on "verbal reasoning."

Laboratory stress research is dominated by the posing of research questions informally, as depicted in the top segment of Figure 3.2. To illustrate, we return to our previous example. The research question concerning relations between ambiguity of cues signifying effectiveness of counter-stress activity and propensity to engage in such activity might develop as follows:

Propensity to engage in counter-stress activity is inversely related to apparent effectiveness of such activity. (This statement might be supported according to the clinical observations, etc., described in the preceding section.) Therefore, propensity to engage in the activity should decrease to the extent that cues signifying its effectiveness become ambiguous. Consequently, evidence of counter-stress activity should be more apparent where cues signifying its effectiveness are least ambiguous, less apparent where they are moderately ambiguous, and least apparent where the cues are most ambiguous.

The question spoken to by the laboratory study is, "Does this order of stress magnitude occur empirically?"

Operationalizing the independent variable may involve the generating of cues signifying the intended effectiveness of counter-stress activity. For example, the researcher may employ a probability-learning paradigm that associates initially neutral stimuli with a specific history of success of the

FORMAL SUBSYSTEM(S)   INFORMAL SUBSYSTEM(S)

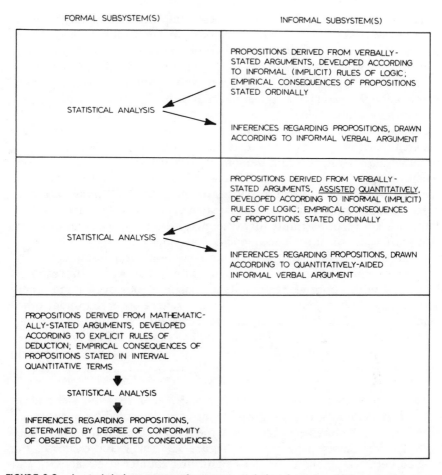

STATISTICAL ANALYSIS

PROPOSITIONS DERIVED FROM VERBALLY-
STATED ARGUMENTS, DEVELOPED ACCORDING
TO INFORMAL (IMPLICIT) RULES OF LOGIC;
EMPIRICAL CONSEQUENCES OF PROPOSITIONS
STATED ORDINALLY

INFERENCES REGARDING PROPOSITIONS, DRAWN
ACCORDING TO INFORMAL VERBAL ARGUMENT

STATISTICAL ANALYSIS

PROPOSITIONS DERIVED FROM VERBALLY-
STATED ARGUMENTS, ASSISTED QUANTITATIVELY,
DEVELOPED ACCORDING TO INFORMAL (IMPLICIT)
RULES OF LOGIC; EMPIRICAL CONSEQUENCES
OF PROPOSITIONS STATED ORDINALLY

INFERENCES REGARDING PROPOSITIONS, DRAWN
ACCORDING TO QUANTITATIVELY-AIDED
INFORMAL VERBAL ARGUMENT

PROPOSITIONS DERIVED FROM MATHEMATIC-
ALLY-STATED ARGUMENTS, DEVELOPED
ACCORDING TO EXPLICIT RULES OF
DEDUCTION; EMPIRICAL CONSEQUENCES OF
PROPOSITIONS STATED IN INTERVAL
QUANTITATIVE TERMS

STATISTICAL ANALYSIS

INFERENCES REGARDING PROPOSITIONS,
DETERMINED BY DEGREE OF CONFORMITY
OF OBSERVED TO PREDICTED CONSEQUENCES

FIGURE 3.2. Logical deductive scientific systems, including formal and informal subsystems.

activity (e.g., Estes, 1976). The previously neutral stimuli, now imbued with the intended cue properties, may be presented under alternate conditions of ambiguity. For instance, the stimuli may be embedded in varying amounts of ambient, distracting stimulation.

Turning to the dependent variable, propensity to engage in counter-stress activity may be measured in terms of reported behavioral intent, perhaps augmented with direct behavioral observations (e.g., immediacy, intensity, and duration of the designated behavior). Measurement values are then submitted to statistical analysis. Note that, in contrast to the posing of the research question, the analysis is considered to comprise a formal scientific subsystem; computations are determined by mathematical theorems and propositions with closed proof (e.g., Scheffe, 1959).

Results of statistical analysis are then used to pass judgment on the tenability of the stated proposition(s). Did the ordinal consequences of variation in the independent variable occur empirically? Emphasis is most often placed on arithmetic means, conjoint with probability values of their observed separation, under a null hypothesis of "no true differences." With this information in hand, the investigator estimates whether or not the empirical findings have approximated the proposition-consequences closely enough to convince colleagues that ordinal support for the proposition has been obtained.

Examples of this system of scientific inquiry abound in laboratory stress research. For example, in many instances, reference is made to responses by individuals with differing personality dispositions (e.g., "Repression-Sensitization," "Internal-External Perceived Locus of Control"); propositional consequences concern responses by the individuals under alternate stressing conditions thought to bear on such dispositions (e.g., inevitability of the stressor vs. opportunity for avoidance, predominance of task success vs. failure, and so on). Consequences may now pertain to interactions between the dispositional and stressing-condition variables; but the consequences remain ordinal in nature, as follows. Differences in response associated with opposite personality dispositions observed under some stressing conditions should exceed the differences observed under other conditions; or, direction of such differences should change (e.g., Endler, King, Edwards, Kuzcynski, & Divecky, 1983; Pagano, 1973; also, see especially Chapter 5 by Holmes & McCaul, this volume). Measures of dependent variables are then analyzed statistically, with attention focused on the stated interaction.

The second system presented in Figure 3.3 represents an elaboration of the first system. Verbal propositions are supplemented by quantitative statements; such statements often take the form of graphical presentation. Consider, for example, the graph in Figure 3.3. This graph expresses the relation between ambiguity of cues signifying counter-stress activity and propensity toward engaging in the activity. In this quantitative portrayal, however, the initial argument has been embellished.

First, two contingent probabilities have been introduced; the probability of a stressing occurrence, given that the individual engages in counter-stress activity; and the probability of a stressing occurrence, given the absence of the counter-stress activity. These contingent probabilities are denoted in Figure 3.3 as Pr(stressing occurrence | counter-stress activity), and Pr(stressing occurrence | $\overline{\text{counter-stress activity}}$), respectively. Propensity to engage in counter-stress activity is considered to vary with the amount by which the second probability exceeds the first. This difference is eroded as the cues signifying that the first probability is less than the second become increasingly ambiguous; that is, the "effective" (conveyed) difference is reduced as cue-ambiguity increases.

The potential or "true" effectiveness of counter-stress activity is the highest value of Pr(stressing occurrence | $\overline{\text{counter-stress activity}}$) $- Pr$(stressing

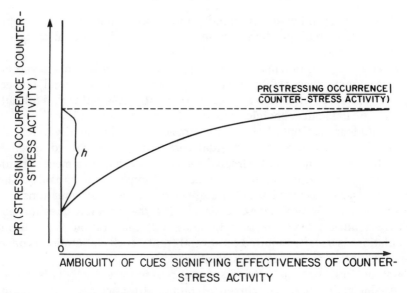

FIGURE 3.3. Conveyed effectiveness of counter-stress activity as a function of ambiguity of cues (see text).

occurrence | counter-stress activity), as presented in Figure 3.3. This value, denoted h, is apparent to the subject under 0 ambiguity. One other noteworthy feature of Figure 3.3 is that increasing ambiguity has diminishing effects to the extent that its existing effects are already high. Thus, ambiguity of the relevant cues takes its major toll on activity-propensity by dislodging the relative "certainty" of counter-stress effectiveness associated with the difference, h; "diminishing returns" on increases in ambiguity are observed thereafter.

Empirical assessment, in this instance may proceed much as before. However, attention is directed to certain additional operations. Of particular interest is the "baseline condition" of 0 ambiguity. Also, the conveyed contingent probabilities over the various levels of ambiguity may be monitored, in addition to evidence of propensity to engage in counter-stress activity. Furthermore, perhaps several values along the ambiguity continuum might be implemented; corresponding ordinal increases in evidence of propensity to engage in counter-stress activity would be expected.

Statistically significant increases at lower levels of ambiguity, along with nonsignificant differences at higher levels might be interpreted as supportive of the "leveling off" of effects, as indicated in Figure 3.3. More convincingly, reduced effects of ambiguity incrementation at higher levels of existing ambiguity, might be registered as a significant "incrementation-by-existing-levels" interaction. Perhaps even more convincing would be the demonstration of significant linear and quadratic trends.[3] In the preceding ways, the integration of results with propositional consequences is aided by the earlier quantitative statements.

The above description indicates how quantitative supplements to verbally stated arguments can elaborate such arguments, and in several respects provide greater specificity. Examples of quantitatively aided verbal formulations are available in economic accounts of stress (Caplan, 1983; Cox, 1978; French, Rodgers, & Cobb, 1974). Here, stress is viewed primarily in terms of the imbalance between environmental demands (e.g., keyboard speed required by an employer) and personal resources available to meet such demands (e.g., words-per-minute of which the employee is capable). Such imbalance is expressed in a set of straight-forward algebraic equations.

Consideration is now given to developing the research question as a formal scientific subsystem (part 3, Figure 3.2). Elaboration of pre-formal formulations is usually required on several fronts; such elaboration is developed next with reference to the current example.

First, potential or "true" effectiveness of counter-stress activity is defined as the value of Pr(stressing occurrence | $\overline{\text{counter-stress activity}}$) − Pr(stressing occurrence | counter-stress activity) at 0 ambiguity. This value corresponds to h, the contingent probability difference in the preceding formulation. We label this difference the "signal," that is embedded in the cues signifying effectiveness of counter-stress activity. Ambiguity now is identified as the obscurity or lack of clarity of the signal (as opposed, say, to equivocalness of the "message" comprising the signal). In turn, ambiguity is dissected into the following two sources.

The first source is the "unobtrusiveness" of the medium or cues carrying the signal. An analogy in the field of visual information processing might be the dimness of a target shape in a visual search task; a comparable analogy in the auditory modality would be the attenuation of those stimuli of a dichotic listening task that are to be shadowed. In the present example, reference would be made to stimuli previously associated with effectiveness of counter-stress activity. Such stimuli may be social in nature, as in apparent relief displayed by others having successfully dealt with threat. Unobtrusiveness of cues in the current context may increase as such responding becomes progressively subdued. In the deliberations that follow, the degree of unobtrusiveness of the relevant cues is denoted m.

The second source of ambiguity, superimposed onto m, consists of stimulation competing with the signal-carrying cues, or environmental noise. Included is ambient stimulation, such as distracting events, and extraneous

---

[3] Obtaining significant (positive) linear and quadratic trends might be viewed as elevating propositional consequences, and supporting empirical results, beyond ordinal status. However, these significant trends together simply indicate a decelerative increase; quantitative-interval status would require, for example, specification, of amount of deceleration involved.

information. This source is denoted n. Last, the focal response is pin-pointed. In particular, interest lies in the relative incidence of counter-stress activity under the effective, or conveyed values of Pr(stressing occurrence | counter-stress activity) – Pr(stressing occurrence | counter-stress activity).

In the following treatment, we assume that the Pr(stressing occurrence | counter-stress activity) remains constant over the various levels of noise in the stressing situation under consideration. Therefore, emphasis is placed on variation in Pr(stressing occurrence | counter-stress activity), since it is now the sole determinant of the relative differences in the contingent probabilities.

The proposed function defining the path of Pr(stressing occurrence | counter-stress activity) over n, $y(n)$ is

$$y(n) = (y(0) - \overline{P})e^{-mn} + \overline{P}$$

where n = environmental noise, $y(0)$ = the value of $y(n)$ when $n = 0$, $\overline{P} = Pr$(stressing occurrence | counter-stress activity), and e = the base of the natural logarithm, or 2.72. (The reader may wish to consult the Appendix to this chapter for the derivation of this function and the incidence of counter-stress activity function that follows.)

Note that the unobtrusiveness implied by m in particular refers to the susceptibility of the signal-carrying cues to obscurity by environmental noise. Hence, where $n = 0$, the signal is equally accessible under alternate values of m, since supposedly there are no undermining effects of noise stimulation present. The signal fades more quickly, however, for values of $n > 0$ as m increases (compare the path of $y(n)$ involving m to that involving m' in Figure 3.4). Accordingly, the amount of counter-stress activity over

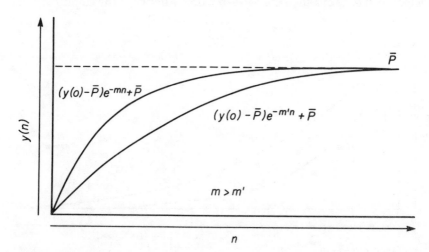

FIGURE 3.4.   Conveyed effectiveness of counter-stress activity as a function of environmental noise (n) and unobtrusiveness of cues (m).

the range of $n \geq 0$ should decrease, and its relative incidence should be shifted toward lower values of n. As m decreases, on the other hand, the amount should be increased and occurrences distributed more evenly over n (compare the distributions involving m and m' in Figure 3.5).

The relative incidence of counter-stress activity over n is now considered in more detail. We first set $\overline{P} = 1$ and $y(0) = 0$; these values correspond to maximum potential effectiveness of counter-stress activity. They also facilitate calculation of the relative behavioral incidence of current interest. The latter is proportional to the function illustrated in Figure 3.5. The specific function is as follows (readers who wish to bypass this notation can do so without losing the main points of the passage):

$$1 - F(n) = e^{-mn}; \int_0^\infty e^{-mn}dn = 1/m$$

For instance, the relative amount of counter-stress activity associated with an interval of n between n'' and n' is proportional to

$$\{[1 - F(n)] | n'' < n \leq n')\} = \int_{n''}^{n'} 1 - F(n) \, dn = -1/m \; e^{-mn}]_{n''}^{n'}$$

The functions illustrated in Figures 3.4 and 3.5 embody propositions whose empirical consequences follow rather immediately; variation in values of relevant *observed* behaviors should vary with those defined by the stated functions. Laboratory operations follow immediately as well. The cues signifying $(\overline{P} - y(0) = 1)$ are presented under levels of competing noise stimulation; proportion of total presentations of each value of n leading to counter-stress response is tabulated; estimates of $\overline{P}$ and $y(n)$ may be obtained so as to monitor conveyed effectiveness of counter-stress activity, $[\overline{P} - y(n)]$.

Regarding statistical analysis, "tests for goodness of fit" may be conducted; such tests evaluate the correspondence between the empirical values

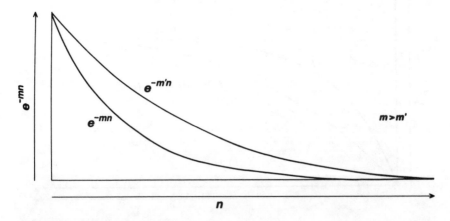

FIGURE 3.5. Relative incidence of counter-stress activity as a function of environmental noise (n) and unobtrusiveness of cues (m).

and those predicted by the functions just stated.[4] Preferably, the analysis may compare the adequacy of these functions in accounting for the empirical data to that of some competing function(s) (see, e.g., Townsend, 1984).

Observe that in formally posing our research question, we have been forced to become somewhat more explicit about the variables of interest. Implementing the question mathematically has compelled greater attention to detail, as illustrated in the elaboration of variables such as ambiguity, discussed earlier. The functions relating these variables have had to be spelled out and the response parameter of principal interest specified. Such increased precision exemplifies that required of formalized research questions generally (see also Restle & Greeno, 1970; Staddon, 1984).

In practice, variations on this type of development are often employed. For example, mathematical deductions can be augmented by computer simulations to derive predictions for specific experimental conditions (see, e.g., Hunt & Lansman, 1986). In some cases, propositions are derived against a backdrop of a computer algorithm, whose sequential arguments in turn are expressed mathematically (e.g., Hintzman, 1986).

In still other instances, wholesale systems of proven propositions and theorems may be applied to a specific content domain. For example, a series of intervariable relations may be stated mathematically; in turn, the expressed relations may be viewed as having application to a class of phenomena transcending highly diverse content domains. Such an approach is part of *general systems* theorizing. A prominent recent example is *Catastrophe Theory* (e.g., Golubitsky, 1979). *Catastrophe Theory* quantifies sudden changes occurring in a given variable as a function of continuous changes occurring in other variables. The system of equations of *Catastrophe Theory* may be brought to bear, for instance, on structural collapse as a function of continuously escalating physical stresses; the system may also be brought to bear on a "breakdown in coping behavior" as a function of continuously escalating psychological stresses.

An increasingly popular form of theory development that can take on formal status is the construction of "structural equations"; such equations depict the relative importance of selected variables in determining the values of some other variable(s) of principal interest. The relative importance of the first variables are represented by their corresponding weights in the structural equation or "weighted combination of variables." For instance, semi-independent variables of speed and accuracy representing

---

[4] Parameters of a stated function (e.g., m) must be estimated from empirical observations. We assume that n can be "objectively quantified" through, for instance, Thurstonian scaling methods.

Note that empirical observations have been used both to estimate parameters of the function, and to test the function's goodness of fit to the data. However, as a rule of thumb, to the extent that the number of independent observations exceeds the number of parameters estimated, a valid test of the function's fit is available.

performance on a choice-reaction-time task might be related to semi-independent psychometric scores of subjects' sensitivity to the threat of error versus delay in responding. An expected link between sensitivity to error-threat and performance accuracy would be represented by corresponding relatively substantial weights for these two variables.

A currently favorite method of constructing structural equations is to use one of the computational algorithms known as Linear Structural Relationships (LISREL; e.g., Joreskog & Sorbom, 1981). Such algorithms can be used to arrive at a structural equation best representing the pattern of empirical data at hand (employing "goodness-of-fit" criteria). The weights in the equation are determined so as to make the empirical configuration maximally likely, given the equation's specific grouping of variables ("maximum-likelihood estimation"). Some of the constituent variables in the structural equation are "inferred" or "latent" variables. They represent sources of variation that underlie overlapping behavior among subsets of directly measured variables, similar to factor scores in traditional factor analysis. Upon cross validation, the obtained structural equation represents a model for the network of relations among the selected set of measured and latent variables (for elaboration see Bynner & Romney, 1985). The term "formal model" appears applicable inasmuch as development has proceeded according to specified computational constraints; and the set of relations among the variables is described according to quantitative-interval values.

The LISREL algorithms can also be used to empirically assess a structural model formulated independently of the algorithm. The role played by the algorithm then becomes essentially one of statistical analysis (see Figure 3.2). Furthermore the tested structural model is seldom developed "formally," as judged by the criteria described earlier. With respect to Figure 3.2, the second rather than the third system descriptor is more applicable. Finally, note that LISREL emerges from a lineage of methods for developing theoretical models in the format of linear combinations of variables (Estes, 1976; Rodwan & Hake, 1964; Tukey, 1954). A brief but penetrating description of LISREL as applied to psychological-stress research has been provided by Dooley (1985).

Examples of formal theorizing in the research area of psychological stress are rare, but certainly not absent. Osuna (1985) has presented a theory of the psychological stress resulting from waiting for an anticipated event, as commonly occurs in queues. His mathematically stated propositions, sustained by closed proofs, bear several interesting empirical ramifications. For example, the author quantifies precisely the accumulation and momentary increases of stress arousal over the waiting interval. Also, strategic periods are specified when information about time left to wait will most effectively ameliorate stress. Osuna has offered some concrete suggestions for experimentally testing his predictions.

Staddon (1984) has formally addressed the process of "stressor-stressee" interaction over time. The stressor in this instance involves the "hassle" of a child's unruly behavior and the stressee is a guardian responsible for punishment. Such roles are easily reversed in Staddon's example (and probably would be, from the child's perspective); they can also be held by each player in the transaction concomitantly. The author has shown how a series of relatively simple differential equations can generate unexpected but plausible predictions regarding the progressive interaction. The model demonstrates the sequence of events leading eventually to an equilibrium state of mutual accommodation.

An account of abrupt shifts in coping effectiveness resulting from varying levels of stress has been presented by Booth (1985). The stress, in this instance, comprises autonomic arousal and apprehension about performance instigated by test taking; "coping" simply takes the form of test performance. Booth has implemented *Catastrophe Theory* in setting forth his model. In the model, sudden changes in coping range from a collapse in performance to abandoning the test; these changes are described as a function of graded increases in autonomic arousal and performance apprehension.

Critics of formal development of research questions have often leveled the following type of accusation: Such developments appear sophisticated and rigorous, but the price paid for these qualities is an oversimplification of the subject matter of interest. The richness of the phenomenon is sacrificed for the sake of theoretical neatness.

These apparent difficulties stem largely from the "simplifying assumptions" often necessary to launch formal theorizing. Consider again the account of stress incurred through prolonged waiting, as proposed by Osuna (1985). One simplifying assumption is that a subject's initial set of beliefs about possible waiting times brought to the queuing situation remains constant. As time progresses, the individual may revise his/her subjective probabilities about time still remaining by using the information couched in the initial set of beliefs; but the beliefs themselves remain the same. By putting in place a condition that expedites formal modeling, the theorist may be relinquishing a *sine qua non* of "true stress processes": change in the store of properties associated with an encountered stressing situation in long-term memory.

Such accusations have been countered by Staddon (1984) as follows (see also Blalock, 1969, 1982; Kingma, 1987; Lakatos, 1978; Meehl, 1978). Staddon's defense of formalization takes place in the context of his observations on Bandura's theoretical approach to social-learning and self-regulation phenomena. However, his defense applies to the more general issue raised here. He notes that the above type of accusation tacitly harbors a claim that informal theories (unaided verbal reasoning) are less restricted than formal theories in the type of subject matter they can deal with. However, informal theories appear to be more versatile because they readily make reference to the complexities of a phenomenon and state the difficulties in dealing with them; unfortunately, they make little or no headway in resolving the complexities. Resolution compels the investigator to develop an expanded formal theory—one that accommodates a broader set of conditions, as opposed to dealing with the latter through simplifying assumptions. For example, Osuna (1985) presents an additional formulation on the "stress of waiting" which relaxes the assumption of constancy of initial beliefs about the stressing situation.

The following statement has been made by Staddon in response to Bandura's (1978, p. 356) claim that computational models of human functioning neglect important factors such as "reflective self-awareness":

> Maybe so; my argument shows that this neglect stems not from the inability of formal models to handle these subtle concepts but from the requirement to be precise in specifying relations between inferred and measured variables that they impose. Bandura's models incorporate internal factors with ease, not because they go beyond information processing theories but because they are not (formal) theories at all.[5] (p. 504)

It would be naive to suggest that stress researchers will embrace these arguments and make formalization the order of the day. Doing so is more than a matter of argument or taste. Adopting formal procedures imposes the added encumbrance of facility with the mathematical-deductive apparatus that carries the theoretical arguments. Nevertheless, because of the cogency of apologetics like Staddon's, a case can be made that this class of theorizing should be given priority as an ultimate goal, however distant. Meanwhile psychological stress researchers should be more receptive to contributions assuming this format than is often the case.

MEASURES OF DEPENDENT VARIABLES IN LABORATORY STUDIES OF STRESS

Having formulated the question(s) to be addressed, and designed the relevant experimental manipulations, the laboratory researcher is faced with the task of measuring the effects of those manipulations. The literature on laboratory stress studies reveals a substantial array of available measures. Moreover, new measures continue to emerge at a fairly steady rate, often appearing first in connection with studies addressed to specific substantive problems. Relatively rare are studies devoted expressly to relevant psychometric properties of alternate measures. More work directed toward the "underlying structure" of the various measures appears in order. For example, documentation of comparative sensitivities of the various measures to competing sources of variance (e.g., differential stressor intensity, "organismic traits," or "individual-difference" variables, intensity/organismic-variable interaction) may be especially useful. Such documentation may facilitate the

---

[5] The interested reader can consult Bandura's (1984) reply.

selection of an efficient measurement battery for a given study—a battery that comprehensively taps the response dimensions of interest as unobtrusively as possible.

In keeping with the orientation of this chapter, an exhaustive catalog of available measures is not the main concern. Rather, the general "measurement domain" is described. Reference is made to some of the more prominent developments regarding measures and measurement procedures. Also, alluded to are some broad considerations surrounding measurement strategy.

Evidence of Stress Arousal

In 1970, McGrath enumerated categories of stress measures as follows:

One is the *physiological* level, having to do with body functions and conditions. The second is the *psychological* level, having to do with cognitive, emotional, and motivational functions and conditions. The third can be termed *behavioral;* it has to do with (overt) responses, including both interpersonal and task behaviors. (p. 65)

McGrath noted a further distinction between behavioral measures involving, first decrement of performance on tasks such as mirror-tracing or word association, not directed toward an environmental stressor, and second, measures of task performance directly relevant to the stressor, such as "learning a discrimination to turn off shock," or "repairing a damaged radio in a military training situation." Although both types of measures involve overt behavior, the former type, unlike the latter, is aimed at the subject's responding in the "psychological" rather than the behavioral domain. These observations on measurement categories by and large were representative of prevalent viewpoints of the day (e.g., Kahn, 1970; Leventhal, 1970; Weick, 1970). In several ways, however, they summarize the current state of laboratory stress measures.

Consequently, the taxonomy employed here is not dissimilar to that discussed previously. Current categories of measures are arranged along a continuum reflecting "directness, and observability of measurement." To illustrate, at one pole are "molar behaviors" that eliminate or neutralize encountered stressors; included may be direct physical assault on the stressor, negotiation, or some other instrumental act aimed at a source of stress in the environment. At the other extreme might be certain psychophysiological responses that can be detected only electronically.

Consider first behaviors that may eliminate or neutralize encountered stressors. A potential difficulty with such behaviors of course involves their actual effects on the stressor: Eliminating or neutralizing the stressor will nullify the remainder of the laboratory session, assuming that continuing stressor presence is required. Consequently, the stressor (e.g., shock threat, aversive loud noise, time/task-load pressure and/or task-failure threat) typically remains under experimental control. A subject may simply be informed that some parameter of the stressor—its probability of occurrence, intensity, or duration—will be lessened relative to what it would have been without the behavior. The subject is presumably unaware of what the value of the parameter otherwise would have been, allowing the information to impute an apparent effect to the designated response (e.g., Burger & Arkin, 1980; Wright, 1984). Various features of responding might be examined, including frequency, latency, duration, intensity, efficiency, and so on (see, e.g., Douglas & Anisman, 1975; Miller & Seligman, 1982; Nielson & Neufeld, 1986). It goes without saying that microprocessor technology and increased availability of multivariate quantitative methods have increased dramatically the comprehensiveness with which overt-behavioral stress response can be tapped.

Such behaviors entail "confronting the stressor" in a way that reduces its likelihood and/or impact. Rather than confronting the stressor, the individual may escape its presence. These behaviors again present the laboratory investigator with practical problems surrounding post-escape stressor elimination. Certain investigators have monitored other formats of "escape." These formats involve attending to versus escaping information about the time of stressor occurrence as opposed to escaping the stressor itself (Miller, 1979). Overt activity generated for purposes of distraction may serve a similar "information-escaping function" (Gal & Lazarus, 1975).

Another category of measures concern individuals' self-reports of their subjective states. These measures too, are relatively direct and observable in the following sense. Subjects are required to participate in the measurement process by answering specific questions.

For example, standardized inventories may be used. Representatives include the "state version" of the State-Trait Anxiety Inventory (STAI, Spielberger, Gorsuch, & Lushene, 1970). Eighteen statements, such as "I feel calm," are answered on a four-point scale ranging from "Not at all" through "Very much so," according to the individual's current feelings.

The Multiple Affect Adjective Checklist (MAACL, Zuckerman & Lubin, 1965) Anxiety Scale also is a frequently used inventory. Like the STAI, the MAACL can be administered under instructions designed to elicit subjects' current status, as opposed to instructions targeted toward their more general dispositions. This distinction will be returned to in a later subsection. The MAACL comprises 132 mood adjectives. Subjects are required to indicate those adjectives from among the entire list which characterize their present mood. A subset of 21 adjectives form the Anxiety Scale; other adjectives are assigned to Hostility and Depression Scales.

Note that item factor analyses of the entire MAACL have suggested one or two factors may describe responding (e.g., Gotlib & Meyer, 1986; Howarth & Schokman-Gates, 1981). In other words, three factors corresponding to the Anxiety, Hostility, and Depression Scales were not apparent. Gotlib and

Meyer's findings, for example, suggest two factors—one reflecting "negative affect" [e.g., "afraid," "alone," and "angry" having high (rotated) factor loadings] and the other reflecting positive affect (e.g., "active," "agreeable," "alive" having high loadings). The proportion of extracted variance accounted for by the two factors was 30%. The first factor following *Varimax rotation* contributed 16.2% and the second contributed 13.8%.[6] Because of the potentially similar influence of negative- and positive-affect items on the MAACL *in toto,* users may wish to score only the subset of items associated with the first rotated factor (regardless of the items' nominal scale membership). Observe that "psychological stress" has been recurrently associated primarily with negative affect.

The Anxiety Differential (Alexander & Husek, 1962) is a scale whose items have been selected according to their empirically determined sensitivity to laboratory manipulations. Specifically, various instructional sets and emotion-provoking films (e.g., of highway-accidents) have been employed to assess item and scale validity. The format resembles that of the well-known Semantic Differential (Osgood, Suci, & Tannenbaum, 1957). In the current instance, 28 items are rated on corresponding seven-point scales anchored by opposite adjectives (e.g., Fingers: loose-tight; Anxiety: clear-hazy). The Anxiety Differential has not been as prominent in the laboratory stress literature as certain other scales (e.g., the STAI). This is surprising, since criteria for item selection were based upon sensitivity specifically to laboratory stimuli, as opposed to, for instance, intersubject differences in "anxiety proneness" across settings. Furthermore, the Anxiety Differential appears to have a more construct-valid item factor structure than more popular scales (e.g., the MAACL Anxiety Scale).

On several occasions, ad hoc single-item scales have apparently been satisfactorily sensitive to experimental manipulations (e.g., Dobson & Neufeld, 1981; Monat, Averill, & Lazarus, 1972). These scales simply require ratings on a continuum, such as "disturbed-relaxed," or "tense-calm." Subjects need not be restricted to rating categories; for more refined gradations, they can place a slash along a line representing an analogue to the continuum (e.g., Mothersill & Neufeld, 1985).

A measure developed in a military field setting, but one which appears very useful in laboratory settings, is the Subjective Stress Scale (SSS; Berkun, Bialek, Kern, & Yagi, 1962). The SSS is a one-item scale reflecting the designated "continuum of subjective stress." Fourteen adjectives (e.g., indifferent, worried) are located at various points along the continuum. Their locations are assigned numerically according to mean ratings of association with stress obtained from a military sample. If undergraduate students, or similar research samples are employed, a different set of values are more appropriate. These values are derived from Thurstonian successive-interval

---

[6] Thanks are extended to Ian Gotlib and John Meyer for the full rotated factor matrix necessary for these computations.

scaling analyses of ratings from undergraduate judges (Neufeld & Davidson, 1972). The adjectives have been shown to vary along a unidimensional continuum of subjective stress, and to be highly consistent in this regard across subjects (Neufeld, 1973).[7]

The SSS might be extolled for its ease of administration and its apparent sensitivity to variation in experienced stress. It has exceeded the sensitivity of members of a battery of competing measures to effects of socially and physically aversive stimuli (Davidson & Neufeld, 1974; Neufeld & Davidson, 1974). The SSS also has been used successfully to monitor therapeutic changes in obsessional ruminations (Kazarian & Evans, 1977). Versatility of this scale is indicated by the range of settings in which it has been used, such as those involving military maneuvers (Berkun et al., 1962) and concert performances (Kendrick, Craig, Lawson, & Davidson, 1982).

We now move along the continuum of directness and observability of measures to the index of stress—facial expression. Facial expression is perhaps more subtle than overt instrumental activity or subjective judgments about experienced stress; however, it does not require "electronic sensors" such as polygraphs for detection. Indeed, Prkachin, Currie, and Craig (1983) have shown that untrained observers are quite sensitive to variation in aversive experiences of others. There has been a long history of interest in the relation between facial muscle activity and emotion [Izard, 1971; see especially Zajonc's (1985) description of Waynbaum's hypotheses regarding the possible role of facial expression in regulating emotion, dating back to 1906]. Now a method is available for systematically scoring these expressions (Ekman & Friesen, 1978). Craig, Prkachin, and their colleagues have used effectively this method to study social influences on experienced pain (e.g., Patrick, Craig, & Prkachin, 1986).

The association of facial expression with other stress indexes, specifically measures of autonomic-nervous-system activity (see next), has been the subject of study, and some debate. Interestingly, lowered facial expressiveness has been associated with reduced autonomic activity (Notarius & Levenson, 1979; Notarius, Wemple, Ingraham, Burns, & Kollar, 1982). On the other hand, the production of facial expressions has been found to instigate autonomic changes associated with emotionality (Ekman, Levenson, & Friesen, 1983).

Consideration is now given to indexes of stress based on behavioral disruption. Stress and anxiety have long been considered to adversely affect the performance of complex tasks (e.g., Maher, 1966). Such tasks are not directed toward somehow eliminating or neutralizing the stressor, or escaping

---

[7] The unidimensionality of this continuum does not contraindicate multidimensionality of *sources* of stress arousal (e.g., threat of physical injury, social embarrassment, and so on; Ekehammar et al., 1975). It merely indicates that the *subjective experience* instigated by such various sources is unidimensional, as reflected in the current set of adjectives.

from it; nor are they aimed at reducing one's level of stress arousal. Task completion is considered to be more or less an end in itself (e.g., the mirror-tracing task referred to by McGrath, 1970). A variety of such tasks have been available for laboratory research for several decades. Such measures include pursuit-rotor tracking, the digit-span-backwards subtest of the Weschler Adult Intelligence Scale, perceptual discrimination tasks, and so on. Other such tasks include errors in copyediting prose (Glass & Singer, 1972), inaccuracies in performing computer-presented analogies (Keinan, 1987), and speech disruption.

Disruption of motor performance would be expected from "stress-induced" muscle tremor and/or difficulty in suppressing strong but irrelevant responses in complex tasks (Maher, 1966). Concerning cognitive efficiency, stress may instigate "intrusive thoughts" (Horowitz, 1975; Sarason, 1984) and/or consume attention (Hasher & Zacks, 1979).

There are psychophysiological reasons why stress might express itself in vocal performance. Siegman (1982) has written:

> The increase in muscle tone under stress and the deepening of respiration and dilation of the bronchi under stress (Gray, 1971) would lead one to expect higher intensity and higher fundamental frequency in the speech signal, caused by increased subglottal pressure and higher medial compression and tension of the vocal folds, as well as a shift of the energy concentration in the spectrum to higher frequencies (p. 315).

Spence (1982) has provided an evaluative review of quantifiable speech attributes such as rate, amount, and faults. He points out that the significance of these attributes depends on consideration of contextual factors:

> Better knowledge of background conditions would alert us to the more promising stress markers in each situation. In a similar fashion, general knowledge of certain kinds of speech faults, such as filled and unfilled pauses, would make us better able to separate signal from noise; to tell when a long pause, for example, is used for emphasis as opposed to delay or evasion (p. 304).

At this point, consideration is given to a category of measures typically involving electronic instrumentation. Such measures most often fall under the rubric of "psychophysiological recordings"; in the domain of stress, these measures are directed usually toward activity of the autonomic nervous system (ANS). Responses such as respiration and pulse rates occasionally have been recorded directly; but generally responses including these are monitored with polygraphic equipment, increasingly used in tandem with personal computers.

An exhaustive treatment of psychophysiological measures of stress is not feasible here. Instead, a full volume such as that edited by Martin and Venables (1980) presents authoritative accounts of accurate recording and interpretation of a variety of somatic responses. These responses range from relatively easily obtained galvanic skin responses and body-temperature changes, to high-frequency electrocortical activity. Contributors to this volume present clear descriptions of methods and issues surrounding response quantification, as well. These methods vary from statistical adjustment for individual differences in "tonic heart rate" preceding any experimental manipulation (see also, Obrist, 1981), to rapid Fourier transformations of electrocortical activity.

Modifications in personal-computer software, and in solid-state technology lead to new developments almost daily. Keeping abreast of these developments requires continued examination of catalogues and circulars. Nearly gone are the days of laborious hand-scoring of polygraph charts; table-top recording units for on-line digital quantification of responses are increasingly available.

As just mentioned, by and large stress researchers have been interested in psychophysiological measures of ANS activity. This interest of course has stemmed from the longstanding clinical association of autonomic reactions with "stress and anxiety" (see, e.g., Maher, 1970). Focus, therefore, has been on measures such as heart rate, electrodermal responses, and respiration rate. Muscle tension, specifically that of the frontalis region (recorded midway between the hairline and eyebrows), has proven to be a worthwhile adjunct to the preceding set of measures. This measure often detects experimental effects that may go undetected by the other indexes, especially for female subjects (see, e.g., discussion by Dobson & Neufeld, 1981). More recently, cardiovascular responding as reflected in "pulse transit time," and pulse volume (elaborated upon below) have joined the roster of psychophysiological stress measures.

Interpretation of these measures has depended primarily on the usual psychometric considerations of construct validity. That is, the validity of any one of these indexes of "stress arousal" is derived largely from its responsiveness to the presence of "stressing events," such as threatened or experienced physical discomfort, and/or its increased responsiveness for individuals considered to be particularly susceptible to such events. Measures such as skin conductance, however, tend to be affected by a variety of stressing and nonstressing stimulus events, including those that are said to elicit "attention." Similarly, increased heart rate may occur to sexual arousal, physical movement, and covert problem solving. Therefore, interpretation of a given index as reflecting "magnitude of stress arousal" must be supported according to the nature and salience of contextual events (Averill & Opton, 1968; Cacioppo, Petty, & Marshall-Goodell, 1984).

As already mentioned, initial interest among stress researchers in psychophysiological measures had stemmed in good part from the association of the ANS with "stress and anxiety." While the validity of psychophysiological indexes has not been determined by neurological considerations, the latter have contributed to the construct validity of these indexes. The significance ascribed to elevation in certain measures such as frequency of galvanic skin responses, and phasic (event-related) elevations in heart rate have been viewed as according more or less with the apparent functions of selected neurological systems (e.g., limbic and ascending reticular activating systems; e.g., Eysenck, 1970; Kilpatrick, 1972; Lefave & Neufeld, 1980).

Recent additions to the battery of psychophysiological stress indexes have been motivated to a large extent by the upsurge of interest in cardiovascular correlates of stress (e.g., Glass, 1977). Interpretation of these measures has depended in good part on the nature of events affecting them and on the relevance to stress of the cardiovascular functions which they reflect. For example, finger-pulse volume has been shown to increase during periods of relaxation (Obrist, 1981). Hence, increased volume, with certain qualifications, may be indicative of lessened stress-related activation (e.g., Solomon, Holmes, & McCaul, 1980).

Interest in "cardiovascular arousal" under stressing conditions increasingly has led to the monitoring of systolic and diastolic blood pressure. Obtaining these measures unfortunately can be somewhat cumbersome and intrusive. The measures can be read directly by a technician using a mercury sphygmomanometer and stethoscope. An alternative is to automate recording with the aid of a microcomputer or commercially available physiological-recording hardware (e.g., Nielson & Neufeld, 1986; Pittner, Houston, & Spiridigliozzi, 1983). In this case, the subject still experiences periodic cuff inflation and deflation in the nondominant arm, to allow a microphone attached to the arm to register the systolic and diastolic values.

A measure frequently augmenting systolic and diastolic blood pressure in the measurement of cardiovascular arousal is pulse transit time. Pulse transit time consists of the period between the EKG R-wave, and pulse registration at a peripheral site, often the radial artery (consequently, the more accurate but less popular term, "R-wave pulse interval"—RPI—has been endorsed by Obrist, 1981). Precise recording of RPI to all intents and purposes necessitates the use of a microcomputer, or commercially available specialized hardware.

Obrist has suggested that the reciprocal of RPI may be one of the more promising measures of "beta-adrenergic cardiac activity"; this activity, in turn, has been linked to efforts to "gain control over sources of threat." Consequently, RPI has been used, for example, in studies of individuals whose response to threat is characterized by such efforts, and who have been thought to be at risk for cardiovascular disorders (e.g., Nielson & Neufeld, 1986). These individuals have been described as having a "cardiac-prone behavior pattern" (also known as "Type A behavior," e.g., Matthews, 1982; Roskies et al., Chapter 8, this volume). This measure, however, has been used in other contexts, as well. For instance, Gottman and Levenson (1985) employed RPI as an index of stress arousal during high- and low-conflict marital interactions.

If the foregoing measures related to cardiovascular responding are involved, the following is more so. Moreover, it is somewhat invasive. This measure taps neuroendocrine stress responses that may mediate pathogenic processes leading to heart problems. Focus centers on hormones such as cortisol, adrenocorticotropic hormone, and catecholamines, epinephrine and norepinephrine. A catheter, indwelling in the subject's "antecubital vein" of the nondominant arm, is required for periodic monitoring of these substances over the course of experimental events. Blood samples are extracted and centrifuged for separation of plasma. The latter is then frozen for later submission to radioimmunoassay and related analyses (see, e.g., Weicker, Feraudi, Hagele, & Pluto, 1984).

Needless to say, measures such as these are not common even in studies expressly addressed to cardiovascular implications of stress. Nevertheless, they are included here because it is expected that they may increase in prominence as this area of research continues to progress.

More common at this point are measures of cortisol levels and catecholamine metabolites in the urine. Post-experimental readings, referred to pre-experimental readings, can be used as summary estimates of response to the experimental session (e.g., Frankenhaeuser, Lundberg, & Forsman, 1980). In contrast, employing the indwelling-catheter technique permits sampling at regular intervals, say every 10 minutes, over the course of the session.

The relation between stress and health has been the source of another measure prominent of late. This measure is addressed to immunological response to infectious disease. Levels of secretory immunoglobulin A (S-Ig A) are estimated from saliva samples employing radial immunodiffusion assays (see Martin's Chapter 6, this volume; also, Stone, Cox, Valdimarsdottir, & Neale, 1987). This index has been used most often in field studies of stress and health; however, it is mentioned here since S-Ig A is potentially a valuable measure in laboratory studies where interest lies in the effects of stress specifically on protection against infectious diseases (e.g., McClelland, cited in Stone et al., 1987).

It was stated earlier that polygraphically obtained psychophysiological measures frequently serving in laboratory stress studies derive their construct validity in good part from their empirical correlates. The latter include the nature of ongoing events to which the measures appear responsive. Certain derivatives of these measures owe their very development and, in part, their construct validity, to theoretical formulations concerning stress and coping. For example, two stress-relevant measures of ANS activation have been based on a description of "components of autonomic responding" presented by Pribram and McGuinness (1975). These are the visceroautonomic arousal system, and the somatomotor "activation system." The former is said to reflect in part "responsiveness to sensory input" while the latter reflects one's "readiness to respond defensively to aversive stimulation." The term "defense," in this instance, refers to autonomic activation which supposedly functions to reduce subjective effects of aversive stimulation. These two components have pointed to two parameters of the distribution of autonomic-response magnitudes generated by aversive stimuli of varying intensities. The distributional parameters are estimated according to computations prescribed by the theory of signal detectability (d' and C_x, Lefave & Neufeld, 1980; Clark & Marmor, 1969). In one study (Lefave & Neufeld, 1980), these parameters were computed for distributions of heart-rate and skin-conductance responses to aversive noise. Only readiness to respond defensively (C_x) was affected by apprehensiveness about the noise induced through preliminary information. The index of responsivity to sensory input, or autonomic sensitivity to aversive stimulation (d'), however, was unaffected. Contrasting results were obtained for comparisons between subject groups formed on the basis of psychometrically measured differences in levels of typical stress arousal. In this instance, d' was elevated among higher-scoring subjects, but C_x was not. This pattern was considered to favor accounts of responsiveness to stressing events based on increased sensitivity to such events of "neurological punishment/reward centers" (Gray, 1970, 1971) and excitability of limbic and ascending reticular activating systems (Eysenck, 1967, 1970). These measures derived from the theory of signal detectability, then, may be differentially affected by alternate "sources of stress elevation," and, in some instances, may speak to the composition of these sources.

The final index of stress arousal discussed here is relatively "indirect and molecular." This index consists of information-processing capacity (e.g., Kahneman, 1973; Navon & Gopher, 1980; Wickens, 1984). Information-processing capacity is considered to be adversely affected by stress (Hasher & Zacks, 1979; Mandler, 1984; elaborated upon in Neufeld & Paterson, Chapter 2, this volume). Identification of effects on such capacity does not require the electronic monitoring of imperceptible somatic events involved in psychophysiological stress measures; in the present instance, however, precise measurement does require the consideration of formal (mathematical) models of memory/perceptual processes, and corresponding experimental paradigms. Within these models and paradigms, rigorous definitions of capacity are available in terms of *rates of processing quantified informational loads*. Also, computational procedures for estimating capacity in this format are available (Townsend, 1984; Townsend & Ashby, 1983).

For example, subjects may be required to perform a relatively simple "visual scanning task." They may be presented with a three-stimulus array and be asked to indicate whether the pattern in the center of the array matches that to its left or its right. The task may be performed under several conditions comprising high/low illumination of the array, and high/low compatibility between the matching-stimulus location and response registration requirements. Low compatibility may be induced, for instance, by requiring a left-hand response button to be pressed whenever the matching stimulus is on the right, and the opposite (e.g., Biederman & Kaplan, 1970). In turn, performance may be carried out with and without the presence of an external stressor (e.g., aversive loud noise). Response speed may be monitored under all conditions (error rates are assumed to be relatively stable and low).

Employing formal models and computations referred to above, rates of carrying out the scanning and response operations involved in this task can be estimated (see, e.g., Townsend, 1984). Moreover, separate estimates are available for the alternate conditions under which the task is performed. Consequently, comparisons can be made between rates for these operations when they occur under the presence of an external stressor, and when they do not. As yet, such measures largely have been untapped, although less formal approximations to these procedures have been attempted (Millar, 1980).

Coping

A number of laboratory measures have been directed toward individuals' coping activity in response to stressing events. Reference has already been made toward the beginning of this section to such activity as indicating the strength of stressing events. In particular, mention was made of behaviors directed toward parameters of stressor severity, such as probability of occurrence, and magnitude of impact (e.g., Burger & Arkin, 1980; Nielson & Neufeld, 1986); behaviors designed to reduce or eliminate stress-associated cues were referred to as well (Miller, 1979).

Investment in the aforementioned forms of coping, then, has been considered to reflect at least in part the severity of experienced or anticipated stress (consider the contingent expectancy of threat given absence of coping activity in the contingent-expectancy formulations presented in Chapter 2 of this volume). Degree of engagement in coping activity is of course meaningful in its own right; it is affected by factors other than severity of experienced or anticipated stress. Such factors relate, for instance, to appraised potency of available coping activity (consider, for instance, the contingent expectancy of threat, given coping activity in the contingent expectancy formulations, as referred to in Chapter 2).

These observations come into play with respect to forms of coping other than "instrumental or behavioral control." Several measures have been designed to monitor efforts in the way of "cognitive control." Examples of this form of control include covertly distracting oneself from stress-related stimulation through competing thoughts, reinterpreting one's experiences into more favorable terms (e.g., "Although uncomfortable, this is an important experience that will make me stronger"), and so on (see Neufeld & Paterson, Chapter 2, this volume).

A relatively straightforward method of assessing covert distraction from stress-related stimulation has been presented by Monat et al., (1972). Subjects are presented with three or so statements descriptive of thoughts that avoid stress-related stimulation [e.g., "I thought about things not related to the noise (shock, or other stressor), such as movies, songs, etc."]; contrasting these are three statements descriptive of thoughts focusing on stress-related stimulation [e.g., "I tried to attend to the task at hand, noting my reactions to the noise (shock, etc.)"]. The subject indicates on a rating scale the degree to which each statement characterizes her/his thoughts during the earlier period of stress (e.g., 1 = not at all to 5 = very frequently).

Certain forms of coping entail active covert information processing. Consider, for example, "decisional control." This form of control refers to "the number of options or choices available to the individual in a stressing situation" (Averill, 1973; discussed further in Neufeld & Paterson, Chapter 2, this volume). Exercising decisional control involves, first, generating predictive judgments concerning the severities of stress associated with the respective options; and, second, comparing the predictions so as to select the most advantageous option.

A psychophysiological measure of covert information processing, including that which might be involved in decisional control, concerns facial muscle activity near the lips and chin (electromyography of obicularis oris and digistracus muscle regions; Cacioppo & Petty, 1981). This measure has closely reflected quantified availability of decisional control (Kukde, 1985). It has been positively related to more indirect measures of covert processing, such as elevation in heart rate and skin conductance (Kukde, 1985; Morrison, Neufeld, & Lefebvre, in press). Further, lip and chin electromyographic activity has covaried directly with the amount of reduction in stressor probability effected by decisional control (Kukde, 1985; Morrison et al., in press).

Lip and chin-muscle electromyography, then, would appear to be a useful means of monitoring coping activity involving covert information processing. Cacioppo, Petty, and Marshall-Goodell (1984) have concluded:

> Results support the efficacy of myographic studies of covert affective processing given that subjects are generally quiescent, unobtrusively observed, unaware that somatic activity is being recorded, and involved in the task. (p. 85)

The final "measure" of coping discussed here comprises the *configuration* of self-report and psychophysiological stress measures. As the relative level of a subject's psychophysiological responding exceeds self-reported levels of stress, denial of aversive stimulus properties—a form of "intrapsychic coping," according to Lazarus and Averill (1972)—is thought to be evident. Relative level of psychophysiological responding is obtained by standardizing the subject's score against the distribution of scores of the other experimental subjects; self-report expression of stress is obtained in a similar fashion. An intriguing use of this measure has been reported by Shean, Faia, and Schmaltz (1974), who studied responses of paranoid and nonparanoid schizophrenics. Among other findings, these investigators observed that paranoid subtypes had larger standardized-score differences when faced with affective visual stimuli (slides of mutilated bodies).

Comment

It is clear that the laboratory researcher has available a reasonable arsenal of measures to tap evidence of stress arousal; a smaller selection of measures is available to estimate coping activity. On the basis of the fore-going observations (and past experience in our own laboratory), certain recommendations can be made regarding a "minimal battery" for indicating evidence of stress arousal. The battery includes the Subjective Stress Scale (Berkun et al., 1962; rescaled according to Neufeld & Davidson, 1972, if an undergraduate or similar sample are serving as subjects); the Anxiety Differential, in addition to the Subjective Stress Scale, if experimentally feasible; frontalis muscle tension; and heart rate. This set of measures should be sufficiently comprehensive to register treatment effects in many laboratory studies. Furthermore, it is considered to be relatively nonredundant; it spans subjective and psychophysiological sub-domains of response, and makes some provision for possible sex differences in response.

General Considerations in Measure Selection: Tautology

A risk often encountered in laboratory studies of stress is that of tautology. Tautology occurs when the dependent-variable measure is informationally redundant to the operational independent variable; variation in the dependent measure is essentially a restatement of that in the independent variable.

The risk of tautology most often occurs when differing measuring instruments tap the same source of variance. The following is a rudimentary illustration from the field setting. Let us suppose that persistent disruption of routine daily activities is suspected of promoting signs of psychological disturbance. Separate psychometric measures are targeted to these two variables, and found to correlate positively. Upon detailed examination of the two measures, it is found that items composing the second measure to all intents and purposes are a subset of those composing the first measure. The items, for example, revolve around a decline in the frequency of completing routine tasks (an experience not uncommon with "psychological disturbance"). Depending on the relative size of the subset of items, then, the second measure is merely a restatement of the first measure.[8] This type of difficulty appears to be more pronounced whenever the operational

---

[8] Such problems are far from new in the study of relations between signs of disturbance and normal personality (Cattell & Bolton, 1969) and between prodromal symptoms and stress (Spring & Coons, 1982).

independent variable and the dependent-variable measure(s) are obtained from the same source (e.g., subjects' self report). Martin refers to such problems under "measurement contamination" in his chapter on field-study procedures (Chapter 6, this volume).[9]

A similar form of tautology occurs where the independent variable can be viewed essentially as an algebraic function of dependent-measure values. Such tautology may take place with varying degrees of subtlety. A rather blatant version is presented first, for purposes of illustration.

Consider a study where a group of 30 subjects have been exposed to three stressing events of equally spaced, graded severities. Suppose further that stress arousal has been measured for each event. The investigator then proceeds to compute the mean value over all stressing events for each subject. Using a tertile split of mean responses, the total sample may be divided into high, medium and low responders, and labeled, "High, Medium and Low Stress-Prone subsamples." The pattern of results for such a scenario may appear as in Figure 3.6. (Note that replacing the subsamples with three individual subjects would suffice to make the present points.)

The investigator now reports the finding that stress arousal escalates more rapidly, the more stress-prone is the subsample of individuals (consider the three slopes portrayed in Figure 3.6). The "algebraic function" tautology in this instance is straightforward. The difference between any two subsamples in mean stress arousal, calculated over k equally-spaced levels of stressing-event severity, is equal to $1/2(k + 1) \times$ [(slope for subsample 1) − (slope for subsample 2)] + [(intercept for subsample 1) − (intercept for subsample 2)]. Apart from compensating differences in intercepts, then, differences in mean values—the operational "independent variable"—are an algebraic consequence of differences in slope—a designated property of dependent-measure data.

---

[9] Tautologous findings can be considered in the light of the contribution of new evidence to the tenability of a theoretical relation, as stated in Bayesian terms:

$$P(T \mid E) = [P(T)P(E \mid T)] / [P(T)P(E \mid T) + P(\overline{T})P(E \mid \overline{T})],$$

where $P(T \mid E)$ = the probability of the theoretical relation being true, given the evidence from the study at hand (*posterior probability*); $P(T)$ = the probability of the theoretical relation being true, prior to the evidence (*prior probability*); $P(E \mid T)$ = the probability of the obtained evidence, given that the theoretical relation is true; $P(\overline{T})$ = the probability that the theoretical relation is not true, prior to the evidence; and, $P(E \mid \overline{T})$ = the probability of the obtained evidence, given that the theoretical relation is not true.

Note that a tautologous finding is one that occurs whether or not the theoretical relation is true. That is, $P(E \mid T) = P(E \mid \overline{T}) = 1$. This equality represents an instance where the evidence is of no diagnostic value concerning the theoretical relation. Thus, from the initial equation, $P(T \mid E) = P(T)$; that is, the prior probability of the relation is unaffected by the evidence.

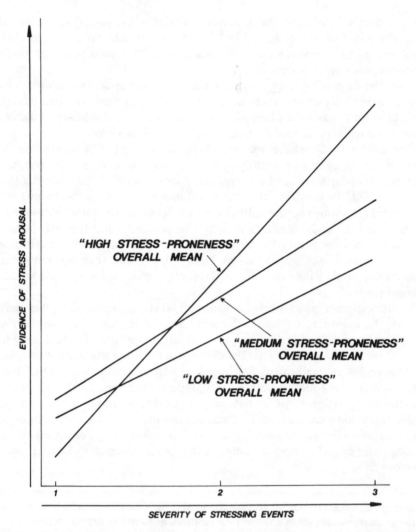

FIGURE 3.6. Evidence of stress arousal, severity of stressing events, and levels of stress proneness.

In practice, intervariable redundancy is much more indirect. Subsamples of subjects are not flagrantly formed according to the very data to be submitted to statistical analysis. However, "surrogate data" may be used as follows. Subjects may be instructed to indicate on a questionnaire their levels of stress arousal "in general" (see, e.g., Allen & Potkay, 1981). These responses may then be used to categorize subjects with respect to levels of "stress proneness."

Presumably judgments to such questionnaires are affected by prior experiences as they are represented in "episodic" long-term memory (e.g., Tulving,

1985). Furthermore, such representations would be expected to correlate positively with mean responding to the k stressing events under current consideration. Hence, data of a given study, such as those depicted in Figure 6, are not necessarily employed directly to classify subjects and then to show significant differences among the classes on certain properties of the same data. However, such a scenario is approximated to the extent that subjects have simply summarized on a questionnaire responses that are in the offing according to past experience (see, e.g., Dobson & Neufeld, 1981).

Furthermore, to data patterns like those of Figure 3.6, an appreciable interaction between the k (in this case, 3) events and designated proneness levels is apparent. As such interaction or nonadditivity increases, the correlation across "proneness levels" between the overall mean responses and those recorded at each of the k events separately will on the average be lessened.

Moreover, two measures addressing similar evidence of stress arousal should display similar patterns of values over events and proneness levels. Inasmuch as they share a similar psychometric structure, the two measures should correlate appreciably across proneness levels within any one of the k events. Indeed, the latter correlation may easily exceed a correlation computed between a measure's values within a given event, and the measure's average values. (The inequality would be expected to increase if an approximation of the averages was used in the form of questionnaire-obtained estimates of such averages, as referred to previously.) In general, the intermeasure correlation computed across proneness levels within events, should exceed the within-event—overall-average correlation, computed across proneness levels within measures, (a) as the two measures increase in their structural similarity; and (b) as nonadditive effects on stress arousal of proneness levels and events exceeds variance associated with average proneness differences. Surprisingly, such inequalities in correlation have been used as a defense against earlier suggestions of tautology not unlike the concerns raised here (cf. Allen & Potkay, 1981; Fridhandler, 1986; Zuckerman, 1983). The inequalities have been construed, for example, as indicating orthogonal information concerning the nature of individual response differences. The usual inference drawn from nonadditivity, however, is that differences in overall averages ("main effects") may have no representation among the sets of differences composing them, and in that sense, are merely uninformative (a point elaborated upon in most standard statistical manuals).

It should be emphasized that the foregoing cautions are not intended to devalue questionnaire measures of individual differences in "typical stress response." They are intended to underscore risks inherent in certain dependent measures—dependent measures that can render operational independent variables as essentially (indirect) linear combinations of dependent-measure values.

On the contrary, such questionnaire measures can be of considerable value for convenient preliminary screening of individuals in terms of their probable levels of responding. Resulting subsamples can then immediately be examined for differences in nontautologous dependent measures such as those relating to neuropsychological substrates, capacity to process information (described earlier in this section), and so on.

Reliability

A question commonly raised about a dependent measure to be used in a given study is, "How reliable is the measure?" It is generally assumed that the more reliable a measure is, the more sensitive it will be to the effects of experimental treatments. An appropriate qualifying question is, "Given that the measure is acceptably reliable, what is the reliability's structure? Does it consist primarily of substantial true-score variance, or low-measurement error variance?" The significance of this qualification should become clear from the discussion that follows.

Measurement variance known as true-score variance is that associated with relatively enduring and systematic sources of variation. In contrast, measurement-error variance is that associated with unsystematic or random influences on the measure. Therefore, as true-score variance increases, so supposedly does the comparative impact of treatment effects on the measure (see, e.g., Chapman & Chapman, 1973).

In traditional psychometric treatments, however, sources of reliability have been identified with "individual differences," meaning relatively permanent subject-to-subject variation in personality traits, mental abilities, and so on. Effects of experimental manipulations, on the other hand, take place typically with respect to *groups* of subjects ("between-subjects effects") or the same *group* of subjects under different conditions ("within-subjects effects"). This discussion focuses on measure reliability and between-subjects experimental effects; the arguments are similar for reliability and within-subjects effects, and these will be described briefly later in this subsection.

Consider for illustrative purposes a simple experiment where subjects have been assigned randomly to one of k experimental treatments (e.g., k preliminary descriptions of a stressing conventional pursuit rotor task). A measure of stress arousal in terms of psychomotor disturbance may consist of the proportion of time the stylus misses the pursuit rotor target over a given interval. The (Fisherian) linear model for analysis of variance of this data is

$$y_{ij} = \mu + \beta_j + e_{ij(o)}$$

where y_{ij} = the observed score for subject i ($i = 1, 2, \ldots, n$) in treatment j ($j = 1, 2, \ldots, k$); μ is the grand mean of treatment populations; β_j = the effect of treatment j, considered to be constant for all subjects within treatment population j; and $e_{ij(o)}$ = an effect on y_{ij} unique to subject ij, and independent of all other $e_{ij(o)}$

In turn, $e_{ij(o)}$ can be broken down into true-score and measurement-error effects:

$$e_{ij(o)} = e_{ij(T)} + e_{ij(m)}$$

The "between-treatment expected mean square" is

$$\sigma_T^2 + \sigma_m^2 + 1/(k-1)\, (n\sum_1^k \beta^2_j);$$

where $\sigma_T^2 =$ true-score variance; $\sigma_m^2 =$ measurement-error variance; and, $1/(k-1)\sum_1^k \beta^2_j =$ treatment-effect variance.

The "error-term expected mean square" is

$$\sigma_T^2 + \sigma_m^2$$

Allowing the usual independence among the above variance components, as well as communality of σ_T^2 and σ_m^2 among treatment groups, traditional psychometric reliability of the current measure is equal to

$$\sigma_T^2/(\sigma_T^2 + \sigma_m^2).$$

Note that decreasing σ_m^2 will increase reliability; it also will decrease the error-term expected mean square relative to the between-treatment expected mean square. Thus, increasing reliability through reducing σ_m^2 should increase the power of the F ratio. Reduction in σ_m^2 can be achieved by various methods. For example, performance may be averaged over several trials, the averages rather than individual scores being submitted to statistical analysis; a more exact timing device may be used, and so on.

Another route to increasing reliability comprises increasing σ_T^2. This might be accomplished, for example, by increasing or decreasing the speed of the pursuit rotor. By adjusting difficulty level, the measure may more accurately reflect individual differences in skills subserving task performance, thus increasing σ_T^2. An increased influence on the measure of the differential effects of experimental treatments, however, is not necessarily forthcoming. Therefore, elevation in σ_T^2 may result in a greater increase in the error-term expected mean square relative to the between-treatment expected mean square. Accordingly, the probability of correctly rejecting the null hypothesis (power of the F ratio) will be diminished.

The following example illustrates just such an instance. It employs data presented in a prominent publication on this issue by Chapman and Chapman (1973). These investigators examined measure reliability and the detection of "experimental effects" in the context of "psychopathology and cognitive deficit." The measure involved performance on a multiple-choice analogies test, and the "between-subjects treatment factor" was diagnostic category—schizophrenia ($n = 49$) versus normal ($n = 206$). Results, however, are similarly instructive regardless of content area.

Two forms of the test were administered; these forms differed in (coefficient alpha) reliability, the first coefficient being .47, the second being .80.

The power for each measure was calculated using sample values as estimates of β_j and σ_o^2, based on maximum-likelihood rationale (Winkler & Hays, 1975).[10]

The following values were obtained for the less reliable version of the measure:

$$\beta_1 = \beta_2 = 1.15$$
$$\sigma_{(o)}^2 = 2.76$$
$$\sigma_{(T)}^2 = 1.3$$
$$\sigma_{(m)}^2 = 1.46$$

If n per treatment group were 10, the power of the F ratio for detecting treatment effects at $\alpha = .05$ would be .835, and at $\alpha = .01$ is .58.

Increasing reliability by selecting different test items so as to elevate $\sigma_{(T)}^2$ resulted in these values:

$$\beta_1 = \beta_2 = 1.65$$
$$\sigma_{(o)}^2 = 7.84$$
$$\sigma_{(T)}^2 = 6.27$$
$$\sigma_{(m)}^2 = 1.57$$

Power of the F ratio with $\alpha = .05$ decreased from .835 to .69, and that with $\alpha = .01$ decreased from .58 to $< .30$. Clearly, the more reliable version of the measure was less likely to detect treatment effects.

The association between measure reliability and statistical power has been the subject of considerable debate and research (e.g., Chapman & Chapman, 1983; Cleary, Linn, & Walster, 1970; Neufeld, 1984; Neufeld & Broga, 1977; Nicewander & Price, 1983; Overall & Woodward, 1976; Sutcliffe, 1980). The lesson to be drawn from these efforts is that, in general, if reliability is increased through reduction in $\sigma_{(m)}^2$, power will increase. On the other hand, elevating $\sigma_{(T)}^2$ will increase power only if there is a commensurate or disproportionate increase in sensitivity to experimental treatment effects. Otherwise, increasing reliability through methods that elevate σ_T^2 can reduce power. Conversely, reducing reliability by reducing σ_T^2 can increase power, if there is comparatively lower toll on sensitivity to treatment effects, as illustrated in the above numerical example.

Turning briefly to within-subject treatment manipulations, similar arguments apply. Consider for instance, a study where k treatments have been administered in random order to the same group of subjects. Now, σ_T^2 does not enter into the between-treatment or error term expected mean squares for within-subject effects. Thus enhancing reliability through methods that elevate σ_T^2 should improve power only if they commensu-

---

[10] Estimates of variance components based on expected mean squares, adopting a least-squares approach to unequal n's, gives similar results.

rately or disproportionately enhance sensitivity to the within-subject treatment effects. Once again, reducing σ_m^2 through combining observations, increasing precision of measurement, and so forth should elevate both reliability and statistical power.

ANALYSIS

This section deals with a selection of issues that accompany some typical approaches to the analysis of laboratory-stress data. These approaches include chiefly standard univariate and multivariate analyses of variance and covariance. Accordingly, the primary concern in this section is with the first and second systems of scientific inquiry presented earlier in Figure 3.2. The analyses of principal interest are those applied to data that bear on informally posed research questions—analyses assumed to be most familiar to investigators.

One troubling theme shared by discussions of analysis in almost any research area is the following. Difficulties in meeting the assumptions for valid application of a method often stand in the way of obtaining very desirable information from one's data that the method could otherwise provide. It is not uncommon to encounter analyses compelling in the information they potentially harbor, while carrying *sui generis* forbidding assumptions. A prominent example involves the application of cross-lagged panel correlation (Kenny, 1979). This method holds great appeal with respect to certain research questions. Specifically, it addresses whether an association between two variables separated in time is a spurious effect of some third variable. For example, the first variable may be efficiency in performing a stress-prophylactic exercise, and the second may be psychomotor disruption after a stressing period. The third variable conceivably could be physical health, that both enhances efficiency in performing the exercise, and improves psychomotor performance. The assumptions underlying valid inferences from cross-lagged panel correlation, however, have been considered by Rogosa (1980) to be prohibitive to the point of negating the method as an option.

Often, the trade-off to adopting some analytical alternative technically less troublesome than one's initial choice, is a less than ideal yield of information. In general, though, it appears advisable to employ a technically less demanding procedure, than one whose informational appeal risks being undermined by invalid inferences. One instance of appealing but technically troublesome methodology involves the attempted control of extraneous variables through statistical adjustments.

Statistical Control of Extraneous Variables.

Efforts to control sources of variance extraneous to those of principal interest often take the form of statistical adjustment. The most common procedure is to use analysis of covariance (ANCOVA). The covariate, whose influence computationally is to be extricated from the dependent measure, may be some extraneous organismic variable (e.g., age, education, or IQ). Perhaps even individual differences in stress response represent an unwanted source of variance, and self-report measures of typical reactions, as described in the preceding section, may form the covariate (e.g., Neufeld, 1976).

A variable commonly allocated to nuisance or wastebasket status in laboratory stress research is that of pre-treatment level of stress arousal. Pre-treatment, or initial value on an index, is considered to be an important determinant of post-treatment value on the index. A post-treatment value obviously is the sum of the initial value, and some change from the initial value. The initial value correlates not only perfectly with itself, but it correlates also with the change portion of the final score. This latter relation reflects what is commonly known as Wilder's law of initial values. Given a broad range of initial values, the latter will tend to be negatively correlated with increases in an index. The net association between the final and initial values of the index can be identified and "removed"; effects are then examined with respect to the variance in the dependent variable over and above that associated with the covariate. Either ANCOVA or one of its variants can be used to these ends (e.g., Solomon et al., 1980; Turpin, Lobstein, & Siddle, 1980).

In effect, covariance adjustment of data for initial values implies that a given amount of increase in an index requires more of an elevation in "activation," or "underlying stress arousal," if the baseline value is higher than if it is lower. The increased elevation presumably is necessary to overcome the reduced latitude for change when the baseline value is already high. In essence, the covariance adjustment credits scores with the degree of elevation in stress arousal necessary for observed changes, given the scores' baseline values. In a certain sense, then, the rationale for statistical adjustment of this nature rests largely on the *tacit assumption* of differential expression, with varying baselines, of elevation in underlying stress arousal.

The use of covariance adjustments in general may be carried out to remove effects of the extraneous variables that are confounded with those of focal independent variables. Furthermore, they may be carried out to increase power for detecting treatment effects by reducing the F-ratio error-term mean square, according to the "within-treatment" association between the covariate and dependent variable.

In the first instance, the extraneous variable systematically varies over levels of the focal independent variable (e.g., at the .10 level of significance). The focal independent variable, for example, may comprise the division of subjects into two or more groups experiencing differing levels of subclinical psychological disturbance. The investigator, interested in a possible decline in cognitive/perceptual performance, may decide to examine reaction time on a "stressing vigilance task." Here the subject must indicate as rapidly as possible when a target stimulus appears on a screen.

A factor complicating interpretation of results is, say, the positive association of subclinical disturbance with age. Age, in turn, can be correlated with reaction time. Consequently, slowed vigilance performance may be a reflection of the disturbed group's age. It seems reasonable, therefore, to employ ANCOVA, treating age as a covariate. Unfortunately, genuine effects of disturbance on performance speed can be inadvertently removed to the degree that such effects are not statistically distinguishable from those of age differences (Cochran, 1957). For example, the effects of "subclinical disturbance" and of "age" on performance may be redundant to one another, rather than being additive. To illustrate, disturbance and age might independently reduce speed of responding by similar amounts. Average reduction in speed of responding for disturbed subjects may correspond to that ascribable to age, according to the within-group regression coefficient employed in analysis of covariance. The reduction also may take subjects to their respective "floors of response speed," curtailing the full expression of *both* age and disturbance effects. As the effects are not "additive," the observed average reduction is mistakenly "attributed" exclusively to group differences in age. The analysis, in other words, leaves no residual significant differences among group means following their adjustment for estimated "effects of the covariate."[11]

The researcher may be relieved to observe that the pattern of significant differences among treatment means remains the same, whether or not the data are covariance adjusted. In other words, the effects of the independent variable are sufficiently incremental to those of the covariate to be detected in the analysis. At this point, however, a different problem may be encountered. The problem is one of incomplete removal of its effects if the covariate is not quantified without measurement error. That is to say, the true-score values of the covariate are required if the resulting test for effects of the independent variable is not to be positively biased (e.g., Humphreys, 1976; 1978). This assumption can be particularly hazardous where the covariate is a single initial score on some index of stress arousal (see, e.g., Turpin et al., 1980).

Note that in the current example the covariate varies systematically over levels of the independent variable possibly because of its effects on the latter

---

[11] It might be contended that the relation between the covariate and dependent variable may be underestimated for groups with more extreme scores on the former (e.g., Evans & Anastasio, 1968); thus ANCOVA would be contraindicated at the outset because of violation of the assumption of homogeneity of within-group regression coefficients. In practice, however, such problems in many instances do not occur. In the present example, it is quite conceivable that response speed could be reduced among the respective older subjects below some common critical value, beyond which incremental, and therefore isolable, effects of disturbance are overridden. The specific speeds beyond this critical value nevertheless may parallel age no less than they do in the younger and less disturbed group. Hence, the regression coefficients of the two groups may remain homogeneous.

(i.e., aging may increase susceptibility so subclinical psychological stress). In most instances, the direction of influence is likely to be in the opposite direction. To illustrate from the present example, the investigator may be inclined to divide the vigilance task into "visual scanning" and "response processes." The former processes may be of special interest. Hence, time for response processes may be estimated according to latencies of response to a simple two-choice reaction-time task, obtained beforehand. The mean latencies then, may constitute a covariate. Clearly, the independent variable of disturbance may affect this (fallible) measure of response processes.

All in all, overestimation or underestimation of independent-variable effects are risked when the covariate varies systematically over levels of the independent variable. Such systematic variation happens when the independent and dependent variables co-occur naturally by similar amounts and/or when they influence one another.

If the covariate is distributed randomly over levels of the independent variable, ANCOVA may be employed primarily to increase power by reducing the F-ratio error-term mean square according to the dependent variable's association with the covariate. It must be remembered, however, that inferences concerning effects of the independent variable are restricted to the adjusted version of the dependent variable (Winne, 1983). The structure of the residualized dependent variable is not interchangeable with that of the intact dependent variable. Reliability of the residualized variable is diminished (Nicewander & Price, 1983)[12], and consequently, the structure of its reliable variance (see, e.g., Harman, 1976) will likely be altered. In the earlier example involving vigilance performance, inferences are restricted to a vigilance response-time dependent measure independent of age (at least as age is represented in the given sample). Similarly, where response time estimates serve as the covariate, inferences are restricted to a dependent measure that is "free" of this source of variation. The residualized dependent measures, then, are reconceptualized according to the nature of the covariance adjustments. The final status of one's measure may be quite acceptable, given the research questions at hand. The point to be made is that the structure of the dependent measure is shifted from its original version according to the residualization procedure. In some instances, the shift may render a measure that has little or no counterpart in the natural environment. Examples may include dependent measures of stress-related dysphoria or depression, dissociated statistically with measured anxiety; or, general levels of stress-related symptoms of disturbance dissociated from the dimension of "social desirability." To the extent that external validity of measures is part and parcel of desired interpretations, the latter may be undermined—the adjusted measure may be a statistical creation unique to the research setting.

---

[12] As noted by these authors, this represents another instance of increased statistical power being associated with *reduced* reliability.

Given the several difficulties associated with ANCOVA on measures of stress arousal, it may be tempting simply to analyze the variance of unadjusted scores. Indeed, analysis of unadjusted scores has much to recommend it. First it avoids problems of unwarranted specificity of inferences—specificity that goes beyond that safely permitted by the data. The benefits of potentially isolating a treatment effect from the influence of some covariate (baseline value, or otherwise), may not be worth the risk of distorted findings.

Second, one of the apparent liabilities of analyzing unadjusted scores may turn out actually to be an asset, as follows. It was mentioned above that statistical power for detecting treatment effects may be increased with ANCOVA. That is, the analysis of adjusted scores may substantially increase the probability of uncovering genuine treatment effects. On the other hand, it may be argued that parametric effects tending not to produce statistically significant results with unadjusted scores are of questionable importance. For instance, those effects which largely are not detectable when they happen in a context of naturally occurring baseline differences may be of little theoretical or practical interest. On balance, results from analysis of unadjusted scores should at the very least accompany those of adjusted scores. The merits and demerits of each should be kept firmly in mind, and perhaps stated explicitly.

Before leaving this topic, mention should be made of a method of adjustment that is sometimes used as an alternative to ANCOVA. Difference scores, or "gain scores," may be calculated; initial values are straightforwardly subtracted from final scores, followed by analysis of variance on the residuals. The problems already listed are simply increased with this procedure. To start, as has long been known, potential increase in power is eroded as the regression of the final score onto the initial score departs from 1.0 (e.g., Kirk, 1968). Second, the interpretation of apparent treatment effects on difference scores is highly problematic. Consider even the simplest of research designs—one involving a single two-level independent variable. Results from analysis of variance on difference scores are a function of the following constituents: the correlation between the initial and final scores; the ratio of final-to-initial score standard deviations; the (point biserial) correlation between the independent variable and the initial scores; and the correlation between the independent variable and the final scores (Gardner & Neufeld, 1987).

To conclude, an informed interpretation of results will depend in good part on the comprehensiveness of presentation. Analysis of unadjusted scores has certain advantages and can be sufficiently informative in its own right. To restate the earlier recommendation, if ANCOVA is undertaken, it ideally should be accompanied by the analysis of unadjusted scores, with full cognizance of assets and liabilities of each type of analysis. Any apparent discrepancies in findings between the two sets of results should be considered in connection with the assumptions associated with covariance adjustments.

Aggregating Data Prior to Analysis

As indicated in the earlier subsection on reliability, power for detecting effects of a laboratory treatment on some dependent measure is increased as measurement-error variance declines. Operationally, one method of suppressing measurement error was to employ as the data submitted to analysis sums or averages of several observations. For instance, scores on an index of stress arousal or coping might be combined from a number of trials or periods within a given treatment condition. Measurement-error variance is reduced because random effects on the measure tend to offset one another over successive observations. Combining data prior to analysis, then, may aid in establishing the existence of a non-zero effect.

The tenability of a non-zero effect having been established, the time will come to find out more about the nature of the effect. Of particular interest is the effect's strength, or magnitude.[13] Strength or magnitude translates into mainly two properties. The first property is the consistency of significant effects attributable to the treatment over repeated studies. The second of these is the strength of association within studies of the independent variable with dependent measure(s). Strength of association may be indexed by the proportion of total variance in the dependent-measure accounted for by the independent variable, ω^2, and so on.

Consider first consistency of findings. Statistical power speaks directly to consistency of significant effects. The probability of a significant finding for a given study is tantamount to the expected percentage of successive studies that replicate positive results. Therefore, results from studies employing aggregated data stand more to be consistently positive than would be the case for unaggregated data.[14]

Similarly, strength of association between an independent variable and aggregate-score dependent measure is apt to be elevated relative to that available from single scores. Less measurement error variance means less competition for treatment-effect variance; the latter thus is thrown into greater relief, implying higher ω^2, etc. It may be tempting, then, to opt as often as possible for pre-analysis data aggregation in laboratory stress research. In other areas of experimental personality research, this method has been heralded as a knight errant, restoring to their rightful throne of theoretical import intervariable relations that had been deposed as notably

---

[13] Strength or magnitude of an effect is not to be confused with *importance* of the effect. A small effect of some treatment manipulation can have substantial theoretical importance, though perhaps less direct practical importance (Neufeld & Gardner, 1987).

[14] The net impact of score aggregation depends on several factors, such as intercorrelations among the constituent scores. A statistical discussion of the implications of aggregation is available elsewhere (Neufeld & Gardner, 1987).

weak or inconsistent imposters (see, e.g., Epstein & O'Brien, 1985; Rushton, Brainerd, & Pressley, 1983).

Pre-analysis data aggregation, however, carries a not easily dismissed price tag. The price tag comprises inferential boundaries resembling those described for statistically adjusted scores in the preceding subsection. Deductions concerning treatment effects technically are restricted to the aggregate format of measurement.

Suppose, for example, an investigator is interested in the effectiveness of a procedure designed to ameliorate psychomotor disruption resulting from physical discomfort. The procedure is taught and the subject is told to exercise it prior to each of several uncomfortable events. The events might include experiencing loud white noise, a mild direct electrical current to the fingers, immersion of the nondominant hand into ice water, the squeezing of a hand dynamometer for a protracted period, and radiant heat to the forearm. Following each of the randomly-ordered stressors, psychomotor disruption is measured according to task performance involving some fine stylus manipulation. The performance of subjects undergoing this protocol is to be compared to that of subjects administered control procedures. Each subject's datum comprises the sum of the performance scores taken after the respective stressors. The target procedure may be found to significantly improve performance; as well, the independent variable involving the target and control procedures may account for nearly one half the total variance in the analyzed data. Furthermore, repeated studies perhaps indicate appreciable reliability of these findings.

It cannot be overemphasized that this apparently desirable state of affairs is specific to the aggregate structure of the dependent measure. It is conceivable that the investigator might be content to restrict inferences to a statistical entity—the sum of constituent performance scores. In the meantime, moving with similar inferences to the level of observable, individual performance measures, would be fallacious (Kenny, 1979; Robinson, 1950; Thorndike, 1939). Unfortunately, gratuitous crossing from one level of data integration to another with inferences all but intact is somewhat rampant in the literature advocating essentially routine pre-analysis data aggregation. Errors usually, but not always, are in the direction of overestimation of associational strength and consistency of significant results. The degree and direction of error is readily demonstrable in quantitative terms (Neufeld & Gardner, 1987).

In general, pre-analysis data aggregation is contraindicated when treatment-effect potency and consistency (over and against treatment-effect "existence") are at issue. Multiple measures nevertheless may be invoked to span more fully the addressed measurement domain (e.g., estimates of psychomotor disruption to each of several stressors). Analyses of choice under these circumstances are multivariate methods which summarize the behaviors of multiple measures collectively, in ways that provide for inferences to the level of individual measurement (e.g., multivariate analysis of variance). Similarly, appropriate multivariate estimates of associational strength are recommended (Neufeld & Gardner, 1987).

Analyses Involving Dissimilar Groups of Subjects

Laboratory stress research is replete with studies of individual-difference factors thought to affect stress and coping. Often these take the form of personality variables, such as "Repression-Sensitization," "Coronary-Prone-Behavior Pattern," "Dysphoric—Obsessive-Compulsive Coping Style," and so forth. A measure purported to tap the variable of interest is administered, and subjects then are divided into groups according to their scores. The sample may be divided at the median of the distribution, the top and bottom thirds of the distribution may be studied, or some division similar to these may be employed. Usually, a treatment manipulation to which the contrasting groups are expected to respond differently is applied. Such manipulations may include variation in opportunities for distraction, presentation of a threatening event in alternate informational contexts, and so on.

One reason for the popularity of this paradigm is that results are cast into the familiar Fisherian model of main effects and interactions of categorical independent variables. The paradigm, furthermore, is not complicated procedurally, and it sports a fairly healthy history as a prominent and seemingly productive avenue for studying individual differences in stress and coping.

Some of the main objections to the approach are as follows. It "sacrifices information" regarding gradations of the independent variable within groups. Arbitrary group divisions are not veridical with respect to the assumed continuous nature of the variable. Subjects are assigned to the same level of the independent variable even though they differ from others within the same designated range. Indeed, with a median split procedure, subjects near the median differ more from the more extreme members of their group, than they do from those who are adjacent to them but fall just on the opposite side of the median.

One consequence of employing this type of design is the misappropriation of variance to the category of "error," or "residual." The total dependent-variable variance within groups contributes to the F ratio error term; a goodly portion of this variance, however, actually may represent covariance with the continuous individual-difference variable. Net effects on statistical power will depend in good part on the degree to which extremes of the distribution make up the groups.

Another objection concerns the shape of the distribution of dependent-measure scores. The individual-differences variable presumably follows a normal distribution. The current procedure fragments the distribution by splitting it, or by extracting portions from opposite ends. Shape of the dependent measure within groups may be affected accordingly to the extent that the measure correlates with the individual-difference variable. The up-shot of this design is the probable violation of assumptions of normality.

An obvious antidote to such difficulties is to treat the individual-differences variable as continuous in the analysis. The reader is referred to Martin's chapter in this volume, Chapter 6, for a discussion of regression approaches to analysis of variance, involving a mixture of continuous and categorical variables. In some instances, ANCOVA may serve a similar purpose. To illustrate, subjects may be assigned randomly to levels of the treatment manipulation. The individual-differences variable of interest assumes for purposes of analysis, the role of covariate. The significance test for heterogeneity of within-level regression coefficients can be used to evaluate the interaction between the treatment-manipulation variable and the individual-difference variable; the test on the pooled within-level regression coefficient is tantamount to the test on the main effects of the individual-differences variable. Procedures for dissecting significant interactions within this framework have been presented by Rogosa (1980) and by Karpman (1983). An introductory overview is given by Dance and Neufeld (1988).

Some additional observations concerning the theme of continuity-discontinuity are in order. Whether or not they have been analyzed as such, certain personality and other stress-relevant organismic variables generally have been assumed to be continuous. Continuity, however, may not be as prevalent as is typically imagined (Gangestad & Snyder, 1985). Instead, discontinuity, or categoricalness may characterize the distribution of certain individual differences. The distinct possibility of "types," however, is no license to impose arbitrary divisions among subjects, as discussed above. Rather, in each instance, such discontinuity first needs to be established empirically (Meehl & Golden, 1982). Secondly, the optimal cutoff on the fallible index of the discontinuous trait (minimizing misclassifications) needs to be ascertained. Furthermore, these procedures are carried out in a context of "consistency tests" (Meehl, 1983)—alternate methods of measurement and analysis converge on both the viability of discontinuity, and validity of the selected indicator(s). Taken together, such procedures are too elaborate for routine use. In some cases, however, they may already have been carried out. One such case is that of "self-monitoring," a typology that appears to reflect, in part, differential susceptibility to threat of social embarrassment (Gangestad & Snyder, 1985).

Alternate Forms of Analyses

There are several areas of behavioral science where new methods of analysis have been developed to deal with specific research problems. Such methods have been determined by the theoretical framework within which the research questions have been posed (see, e.g., Adam, 1978; Meehl & Golden, 1982; Schaie, 1965; Townsend, 1984).

The area of psychological stress to this author's knowledge has not originated analytical options uniquely tailored to its own set of problems. Some existing procedures, though, have been very effectively adapted to certain research issues; such methods include regression procedures as employed in epidemiological field stress research (see chapters 6 and 7, by Cohen & Edwards and by Martin, in this volume). In the laboratory, too, a number of nonstandard analyses seem custom-made for dealing with certain research questions.

One such method is "Stochastic process analysis," or "Markov-chain analysis." Briefly, this method of analysis can be used to quantify patterns of successive categorical events. Its basic datum is the probability of one event (a "consequent," in the parlance of Markovian analysis) following another ("antecedent"). The events can refer to the states of subjects undergoing stressing events over time; they also can refer to the nature of stressing events themselves.

Within this analysis, a shift from one state of the organism or stressor to another is referred to as a "transition." The number of transitions required to reach a particular state can be ascertained. Altogether, then, the method can be employed to describe patterns of change in states of stress arousal, coping, or the stressor itself. For technicalities of Markovian analysis, including assumptions, the reader is referred to the volume by Kemeny and Snell (1960). More elementary presentations include those of Hertel (1972), and Neufeld (1977). Recent developments incorporate mathematical models of decision and choice in describing transitions in organismic states. In addition, they provide for the evaluation of treatment interventions on the stochastic chain of events (Holtgrave, 1983).

Of particular interest to stress researchers are analyses that can implement probabilistic interactions between "stressor" and "stressee." A given state of the stressor may lead to a given state of the stressee, and the opposite. Such analyses are apt to be especially appealing to investigators interested in the transactional approach to stress. This approach has been espoused most notably by Lazarus and Folkman (1984). Here, the stressor itself may be influenced by the individual's overt reaction to its effects. In turn, the organism's state as it relates to these effects may undergo a series of changes. Analysis of stochastic interactions have been described by Benjamin (1979) and by Gottman (1979), and Gottman and Bakeman (1979; see also Dumas, 1986).

Another method of analysis that can be valuable in stress research is multidimensional scaling. Multidimensional scaling may be used to uncover the composition of stressing events, in the following sense. Stressing events may comprise several dimensions, such as likelihood of occurrence, imminence, and severity; "content dimensions" may include risk of social embarrassment, risk of physical discomfort, and unavoidable prolonged physical or mental exertion. Multidimensional scaling requires only that subjects indicate the overall proximities among the judged objects. Judgments typically take the form of ratings of similarity between stimuli, presented in successive pairs. Multidimensional scaling then proceeds to identify the dimensions implicitly having contributed to the perceived relative similarities among the stimuli. Individual differences in the salience of these dimensions can be estimated also.

Multidimensional scaling has been used to elucidate the "dimensionality" of described stressing events (e.g., Neufeld, 1978), as have methods closely aligned with multidimensional scaling (e.g., Ekehammar, Schalling, & Magnusson, 1975). The method has been used also to examine the dimensional structure of directly-experienced common laboratory stressors (Neufeld & Davidson, 1974). A very versatile multidimensional scaling computer program currently is available in the Statistical Package for the Social Sciences – X (1986).

Finally, survival analysis might be considered as being especially appropriate for certain research problems. Survival analysis as a rule deals with the duration—survival—of a given state of individuals; rates of relinquishing the state as time progresses is the focus. In medical research, for example, remaining alive following the onset of illness may be the state of interest. The laboratory stress researcher may care to study the duration of "normal psychomotor functioning" or the maintenance of positive mood after the inception of experimental stress. Rates of relinquishing the state at hand are referred to as "rates of failure." These rates determine the form of the distribution of failures, which, in turn, affects four noteworthy mathematical functions.

One function is the "probability density function," which refers roughly to the proportion of the total sample failing during a given time interval. A second function is the conditional-rate-of-failure function, or hazard function. This function indicates the proportion of those individuals who not yet having failed, do so during the interval. The third function is the probability distribution function, which identifies the cumulative proportion of the total sample failing by the end of the interval. And the fourth function is the survival function, which simply indicates the proportion of the total sample surviving after the interval.

Probability-density, distribution, and survival functions were referred to earlier in this chapter (section on formulation of research questions, and the Appendix). Survival functions of the exponential distribution with differing parameter values are plotted in Figure 3.5. Recall that these particular functions did not express the distribution of a given state as time progressed. Rather, they expressed the distribution of a state—"persistence of counter-stress activity"—with incremental detracting stimulation. The survival functions in Figure 3.5 portray the "survival of counter-stress activity" with incremental detracting stimulation (labeled "noise").

Survival analysis has been treated in depth by Cox (e.g., Cox, 1962). The computer program, "Survival," is available in the Statistical Package for the Social Sciences – X (1986). Comparisons of distributions across samples are provided; both omnibus and pair-wise comparison tests are included in the program. These tests, for instance, would allow treatments designed to forestall selected forms of failure under stress to be evaluated.

Taken together, the above examples merely illustrate the availability of lesser known analytical options—analytical options that nonetheless may have special relevance to research questions addressed in the psychological stress laboratory. We can look for a substantial increase in the creative application of such methods as we continue to progress in this domain of investigation.

CONCLUDING REMARKS

In this chapter, the research enterprise has been segmented into the formulation of research questions, the measurement of dependent variables, and statistical analyses. In practice, of course, such segmentation is artificial; each of these aspects of the research enterprise interfaces with the others. Research questions must be formulated with measurement and analysis options kept firmly in mind, and so forth. Throughout, an effort has been made to emphasize guiding concepts, distinctions, and more or less broad alternate approaches and associated issues, in transacting each segment of the research enterprise. It is hoped that the treatment has been sensitive to problems of special relevance to the psychological stress laboratory.

An area of research activity that in its own right has not been addressed here is that of operationalizing independent variables—that is, putting into effect stress-inducing and/or coping variables, and administering different treatment manipulations. Considerations of experimental procedures by and large tend to be experiment-specific; as such, they are given comparatively little space in a chapter devoted to topics that are general across studies. However, related material has been dealt with from time to time. Mention has been made of ethical constraints of laboratory procedures; of different "sources of stress" that might be studied, according to past multivariate experimental findings; and of forms of coping as put forth in theoretical accounts.

As a general observation, methodological neatness perhaps should never take precedence over theoretical relevance when deciding strategies of investigation. It might be said that the mission of the investigator when it comes to matters methodological is twofold: to provide for the minimization of unknowns when it comes time to interpret results, and to remain faithful to the content of the research question(s) that motivated the study in the first place. Practical constraints in laboratory stress research should of course never be used to excuse less than the maximum possible rigor. It goes without saying that the knowledge value of results from a given study is limited by the methodology employed in generating the results. At the same time, it is retrogressive in scientific inquiry to await the resolution of all methodological impediments to clear cut interpretations. The continued acquisition of imperfect knowledge progressively elevates the fidelity of interpretations: effects that otherwise might be suspect as artifacts at some point stand to be exonerated on theoretical grounds. In a "boot-strapping" sense, reduction of ambiguity, in turn, enhances the harvest of theory-enhancing information; and so it goes.

A side of laboratory stress research not separately dealt with in this chapter is that of applied research. As the term implies, findings from applied research generally are intended to have rather immediate practical implications—implications for stress reduction, for improved effectiveness of coping, or for prevention of adverse effects of stress on psychological or physical functioning. The evaluation of treatment interventions designed to have beneficial effects such as these carries its own additional set of considerations. An informed assessment of the importance of effects requires the evaluation of their relative magnitude. Highly statistically significant effects can be trivial from a practical standpoint if they account for little variance in the outcome variable. Whether or not a practically meaningful impact on the outcome actually has occurred weighs heavily on whether the treatment will survive a cost-effectiveness assessment (Drummond, Stoddart, & Torrance, 1987; Neufeld, 1977).

APPENDIX

In this appendix, we quantify: (a) the effects of ambiguity of cues signifying effectiveness of counter-stress activity on conveyed effectiveness of such activity; and (b) the conveyed effectiveness of counter-stress activity on the latter's relative frequency of occurrence.

Conveyed effectiveness of counter-stress activity is defined as Pr(stressing occurrence | counter-stress activity) $-$ [conveyed Pr(stressing occurrence | counter-stress activity)]. In the following development, the first probability is denoted $\overline{P}$, which remains constant; the second probability varies over levels of environmental noise, n, and is denoted $y(n)$; m is an appropriately-scaled index of susceptibility to noise of cues signifying effectiveness of counter-stress activity, or the "initial unobtrusiveness" of such cues.

Let the incremental effects on $y(n)$ of raising environmental noise constantly be reduced as its existing effects on $y(n)$ increase. Furthermore, let the rate of reduction be proportional to m, the initial unobtrusiveness of the relevant cues. Then the change in $y(n)$, $dy(n)$, is a positive linear function of the degree to which $\overline{P}$ exceeds $y(n)$. In derivative format,

$$\frac{dy(n)}{dn} = m(\overline{P} - y(n)),$$

and

$$\frac{dy(n)}{dn} + my(n) = mP.$$

Applying the general solution to a first-order linear differential equation,

$$y(n) = e^{-\int m\,dn}(A + \int m\overline{P}e^{\int m\,dn}\,dn)$$
$$= e^{-\int m\,dn}(A + \int m\overline{P}e^{mn}\,dn)$$
$$= e^{-mn}(A + 1/m\,(m\overline{P}e^{mn}))$$
$$= Ae^{-mn} + \overline{P}$$

At $n = 0$, $y(0) = A + \overline{P}$, and $A = y(0) - \overline{P}$. Substituting the right-hand value for A yields

$$y(n) = (y(0) - \overline{P})\,e^{-mn} + \overline{P}.$$

We now turn our attention to the relative incidence of counter-stress activity. Observe that elevation in $y(n)$ is considered to reduce this incidence. Thus, we seek a function whose values vary continuously with $y(n)$, but in the opposite direction. The function identified below fulfills these conditions.

First, let $\overline{P} = 1$, and $y(0) = 0$, as stated in the text. Then $y(n) = 1 - e^{-mn}$. But this is the distribution function, $F(n)$, of an exponential distribution, with parameter, m (see, e.g., McGill, 1963). The corresponding survival function, $1 - F(n)$, is equal to

$$1 - y(n) = e^{-mn}.$$

This function will vary continuously with $y(n)$, since they both involve exponential functions with the same parameters; second, the directionality requirement is met (see Figure 5 of text). Based on these properties, then, e^{-mn} can serve as a hypothetical function describing variation in counter-stress activity over values of n.

Another function of the exponential distribution, meeting such minimal requirements, is the probability density function,

$$f(n) = \frac{d(1 - e^{-mn})}{d(n)} = me^{-mn}.$$

However, $\int_0^\infty f(n)\,dn = 1$, regardless of m; on the other hand, $\int_0^\infty e^{-mn}dn = 1/m$, conveying reduced cumulative counter-stress activity over n ($n \geqq 0$) as m increases.

References

Adam, J. (1978). Sequential strategies and the separation of age, cohort, and time-of-measurement contributions to developmental data. *Psychological Bulletin, 85,* 1309–1316.

Alexander, S., & Husek, T. R. (1962). The anxiety differential: Initial steps in the development of a measure of situational anxiety. *Educational and Psychological Measurement, 22,* 325–348.

Allen, B. P., & Potkay, C. R. (1981). On the arbitrary decision between states and traits. *Journal of Personality and Social Psychology, 41,* 916–928.

Averill, J. R. (1973). Personal control over aversive stimuli and its relationship to stress. *Psychological Bulletin, 80,* 287–303.

Averill, J. R., & Opton, E. M. (1968). Psychophysiological assessment: Rationale and problems. In P. McReynolds (Ed.), *Advances in psychological assessment,* (Vol. 1). Palo Alto, CA: Science and Behavior Books.

Baddeley, A., Sutherland, A., & Harris, J. (1982). How well do laboratory-based psychological tests predict patients' performance outside the laboratory. In S. Corkin (Ed.), *Alzheimer's disease: A report of progress, Vol. 19: Aging* (pp. 141–148). New York: Raven.

Bandura, A. (1978). The self-system in reciprocal determinism. *American Psychologist, 33,* 344–358.

Bandura, A. (1984). Representing personal determinants in causal structures. *Psychological Review, 91,* 508–511.

Benjamin, L. S. (1979). Use of structural analysis of social behaviors (SASB) and Markov chains to study dyadic interactions. *Journal of Abnormal Psychology, 88,* 303–319.

Berkun, M. M., Bialek, H. M., Kern, R. P., & Hagi, K. (1962). Experimental studies of psychological stress in man. *Psychological Monographs, 76,* (15, Whole No. 534).

Biederman, I., & Kaplan, R. (1970). Stimulus discriminability and S-R compatibility: Evidence for independent effects in choice reaction time. *Journal of Experimental Psychology, 86,* 434–439.

Blalock, H. M. (1969). *Theory construction: From verbal to mathematical formulations.* Englewood Cliffs, NJ: Prentice Hall.

Blalock, H. M. (1982). *Conceptualization and measurement in the social sciences.* Beverly Hills, CA: Sage.

Booth, P. I. (1985). A geometric interpretation of the effects of anxiety on test performance. *The Mathematical Intelligencer, 7,* 56–63.

Braithwaite, R. B. (1968). *Scientific explanation.* London: Cambridge University Press.

Burger, J. M., & Arkin, R. M. (1980). Prediction, control, and learned helplessness. *Journal of Personality and Social Psychology, 38,* 482–491.

Bynner, J. M., & Romney, D. M. (1985). LISREL for beginners. *Canadian Psychology, 26,* 43–49.

Cacioppo, J. T., & Petty, R. E. (1981). Electromyographic specificity during covert information processing. *Psychophysiology, 18,* 518–523.

Cacioppo, J. T., Petty, R. E., & Marshall-Goodell, B. S. (1984). Electromyographic specificity during simple physical and attitudinal tasks: Location and topographical features of integrated EMG responses. *Biological Psychology, 18,* 85–121.

Caplan, R. D. (1983). Person-environment fit: Past, present, and future. In C. L. Cooper (Ed.), *Stress research.* New York: Wiley.

Cattell, R. B., & Bolton, L. S. (1969). What pathological dimensions lie beyond the normal dimensions of the 16PF. *Journal of Consulting and Clinical Psychology, 33,* 18–29.

Chapman, L. J., & Chapman, J. P. (1973). Problems in the measurement of cognitive deficit. *Psychological Bulletin, 79,* 380–385.

Chapman, L. J., & Chapman, J. P. (1983). Reliability and the discrimination of normal and pathological groups. *Journal of Nervous and Mental Disease, 171,* 658–661. ⌡

Clark, W. C. (1987). Quantitative models for the assessment of clinical pain: Individual differences scaling and sensory decision theory. In Burrows, Elton, & Stanley (Eds.), *Handbook of chronic pain management.* Amsterdam: Elsevier.

Clark, W. C., & Marmor, E. (1969). *Comparison of sensory sensitivities (d') determined from verbal and autonomic responses to electrical stimulation.* Paper presented at the meetings of the Eastern Psychological Association.

Clearly, T. A., Linn, R. L., & Walster, G. W. (1970). Effects of reliability and validity on power of statistical tests. In E. F. Borgatta & G. W. Bohrnstedt (Eds.), *Sociological methodology.* San Francisco: Jossey-Bass.

Cochran, W. G. (1957). Analysis of covariance: Its nature and uses. *Biometrics, 13,* 261–281.

Cox, D. R. (1962). *Renewal theory.* London: Methuen.

Cox, T. (1978). *Stress.* Baltimore: University Park Press.

Craig, K. D. (1968). Physiological arousal as a function of imagined, vicarious and direct stress experiences. *Journal of Abnormal Psychology, 73,* 513–520.

Dance, K., & Neufeld, R. W. J. (1988). Aptitude-treatment interaction in the clinical setting: An attempt to dispel the patient-uniformity myth. *Psychological Bulletin,* in press.

Davidson, P. O., & Neufeld, R. W. J. (1974). Response to pain and stress: A multivariate analysis. *Journal of Psychosomatic Research, 18,* 25–32.

Dobson, K., & Neufeld, R. W. J. (1981). Sources of differential stress response associated with psychometrically-designated anxiety proneness. *Journal of Personality and Social Psychology, 40,* 951–961.

Dohrenwend, B. P., & Dohrenwend, B. S. (1974). Social and cultural influences on psychopathology. In M. R. Rosenzweig & L. W. Porter (Eds.), *Annual Review of Psychology.* Palo Alto, CA: Annual Reviews.

Dooley, D. (1985). Causal inference in the study of social support. In S. Cohen & S. L. Syme (Eds.), *Social support and health* (pp. 109–125). New York: Academic.

Douglas, D., & Anisman, H. (1975). Helplessness or expectation in congruency: Effects of aversive stimulation on subsequent performance. *Journal of Experimental Psychology: Human Perception and Performance, 1,* 411–417.

Drummond, M. F., Stoddart, G. L., & Torrance, G. W. (1987). *Methods for the economic evaluation of health care programmes.* Oxford: Oxford University Press.

Dumas, J. E. (1986). Controlling for autocorrelation in social interaction analysis. *Psychological Bulletin, 100,* 125–127.

Earman, J. (Ed.). (1983). *Minnesota Studies in the Philosophy of Science, Volume X: Testing scientific theories.* Minneapolis: University of Minnesota Press.

Edgington, E. S. (1966). Statistical inference and nonrandom samples. *Psychological Bulletin, 66,* 485–487.

Ekehammar, B., Schalling, D., & Magnusson, D. (1975). Dimensions of stressful situations: A comparison between response analysis and stimulus analytical approach. *Multivariate Behavioral Research, 10,* 155–164.

Ekman, P., & Friesen, W. V. (1978). *Manual for the Facial Action Coding System.* Palo Alto, CA: Consulting Psychologists Press.

Ekman, P., Levenson, R. W., & Friesen, W. V. (1983). Autonomic activity distinguishes among emotions. *Science, 221,* 1208–1210.

Endler, N. S., King, P. R., Edwards, J. M., Kuczynski, M., & Divecky, S. (1983). Generality of the interaction model of anxiety with respect to two social evaluation field studies. *Canadian Journal of Behavioral Science, 15,* 60–69.

Epstein, S., & O'Brien, E. J. (1985). The person-situation debate in historical and current perspective. *Psychological Bulletin, 98,* 513–517.

Estes, W. K. (1976). The cognitive side of probability learning. *Psychological Review, 83,* 37–64.

Evans, S. H., & Anastasio, E. (1968). Misuse of analysis of covariance when treatment effect and covariate are confounded. *Psychological Bulletin, 69,* 225–234.

Eysenck, H. J. (1967). *The biological basis of personality.* Springfield, IL: Thomas.

Eysenck, H. J. (1970). A dimensional system of psychodiagnostics. In A. R. Maher (Ed.), *New approaches to personality classification.* New York: Columbia University Press.

Frankenhaeuser, M., Lundberg, U., & Forsman, L. (1980). Dissociation between sympathetic-adrenal and pituitary-adrenal responses to an achievement situation characterized by high controllability: Comparison between type A and type B males and females. *Biological Psychology, 10,* 79–91.

French, J. R., Rodgers, W., & Cobb, S. (1974). Adjustment as person-environment fit. In G. B. Coelho, D. A. Hamburg, & J. E. Adams (Eds.), *Coping and adaptation.* New York: Basic Books.

Fridhandler, B. M. (1986). Conceptual note on state, trait, and the state-trait distinction. *Journal of Personality and Social Psychology, 50,* 169–174.

Gal, R. G., & Lazarus, R. S. (1975). The role of activity in anticipating and confronting stressful situations. *Journal of Human Stress, 4,* 4–20.

Gangestad, S., & Snyder, M. (1985). "To carve nature at its joints": On the existence of discrete classes in personality. *Psychological Review, 92,* 317–349.

Garber, D. (1983). Old evidence and logical omniscience in Bayesian confirmation theory. In J. Earman (Ed.), *Minnesota studies in the philosophy of science, Vol. X: Testing scientific theories.* Minneapolis: University of Minnesota Press.

Gardner, R. C., & Neufeld, R. W. J. (1987). The simple difference score in correlational analyses. *Educational and Psychological Measurement, 47,* 849–864.

Glass, D. C. (1977). *Behavior patterns, stress, and coronary disease.* New York: Wiley.

Glass, D. C., & Singer, J. E. (1972). *Urban stress.* New York: Academic.

Golubtisky, M. (1979). An introduction to catastrophe theory and its applications. *General Systems, 24,* 65–100.

Gotlib, I. H., & Meyer, J. P. (1986). Factor analysis of the multiple affect adjective check list: A separation of positive and negative affect. *Journal of Personality and Social Psychology, 50,* 1161–1165.

Gottman, J. M. (1979). *Marital interaction: Experimental investigations.* New York: Academic.

Gottman, J. M., & Bakeman, R. (1979). The sequential analysis of observational data. In M. E. Lamb, S. J. Suomi, & G. R. Stephenson (Eds.), *Social interaction analysis: Methodological issues* (pp. 185–206). Madison: University of Wisconsin Press.

Gottman, J. M., & Levenson, R. W. (1985). A valid procedure for obtaining self-report of affect in marital interaction. *Journal of Consulting and Clinical Psychology, 53,* 151–160.

Gray, J. (1970). Strength of the nervous system, introversion-extraversion, condition-ability, and arousal. In H. J. Eysenck (Ed.), *Readings in extraversion-introversion: Theoretical and methodological issues.* London: Staples.

Gray, J. (1971). *The psychology of fear and stress.* New York: McGraw-Hill.

Harman, H. (1976). *Modern factor analysis* (3rd Ed.). Chicago: University of Chicago Press.

Hasher, L., & Zacks, R. T. (1979). Automatic and effortful processes in memory. *Journal of Experimental Psychology: General, 108,* 356–388.

Hebben, N. (1985). Toward the assessment of clinical pain. In G. M. Aranoff (Ed.), *Evaluation and treatment of chronic pain.* Baltimore: Urban & Schwarzenberg.

Hertel, R. K. (1972). Application of stochastic process analyses to the study of psychotherapeutic processes. *Psychological Bulletin, 77,* 421–430.

Hicks, C. R. (1973). *Fundamental concepts in the design of experiments* (2nd Ed.). New York: Holt, Rinehart & Winston.

Hintzman, D. L. (1986). "Schema abstraction" in a multiple-trace memory model. *Psychological Review, 93,* 411–428.

Holmes, D. S. and McCaul, K. D. (1989). Laboratory research on defense mechanisms. In R. W. J. Neufeld (Ed.), *Advances in the investigation of psychological stress* (pp. 161–192). New York: Wiley.

Holtgrave, D. R. (1983). *Psychological measurement and models of individual streams of behavior.* Unpublished doctoral dissertation, Department of Psychology, University of Illinois at Urbana-Champaign.

Horowitz, M. J. (1975). Intrusive and repetitive thoughts after experimental stress: A summary. *Archives of General Psychiatry, 32,* 1457–1463.

Howarth, E., & Schokman-Gates, K. (1981). Self-report multiple mood instruments. *British Journal of Clinical Psychology, 25,* 46–53.

Humphreys, L. G. (1976). Analysis of data from pre- and post-test designs: A comment. *Psychological Reports, 38,* 639–642.

Humphreys, L. G. (1978). Differences between correlations in a single sample: A correction and amplification. *Psychological Reports, 43,* 657–658.

Hunt, E., & Lansman, M. (1986). Unified model of attention and problem solving. *Psychological Review, 93,* 446–461.

Izard, C. E. (1977). *Human emotions.* New York: Plenum.

Joreskog, G., & Sorbom, D. G. (1981). *LISREL V user's guide.* Chicago: International Educational Enterprises.

Kahn, R. L. (1970). Some propositions toward a researchable conceptualization of stress. In J. E. McGrath (Ed.), *Social and psychological factors in stress.* New York: Holt, Rinehart & Winston.

Kahneman, D. (1973). *Attention and effort.* Englewood Cliffs, NJ: Prentice Hall.

Karpman, M. B. (1983). The Johnson-Neyman technique using SPSS or BMDP. *Educational and Psychological Measurement, 43,* 137–147.

Kazarian, S. S., & Evans, D. R. (1977). Modification of obsessional ruminations: A comparative study. *Canadian Journal of Behavioral Science, 9,* 91–100.

Keinan, G. (1987). Decision making under stress: Scanning of alternatives under controllable and uncontrollable threats. *Journal of Personality and Social Psychology, 52,* 639–644.

Kemeny, J. G., & Snell, J. L. (1960). *Finite Markov chains.* New York: Van Nostrand.

Kendrick, M. J., Craig, K. D., Lawson, D. M., & Davidson, P. O. (1982). Cognitive and behavioral therapy for musical-performance anxiety. *Journal of Consulting and Clinical Psychology, 50,* 353–362.

Kenny, D. A. (1979). *Correlation and causality.* New York: Wiley.

Kilpatrick, D. (1972). Differential responsiveness of two electrodermal indices to psychological stress and performance of a complex cognitive task. *Psychophysiology, 9,* 218–226.

Kingma, J. (1987). The new two-state model of learning: A tool for analyzing the loci of memory differences in intellectually impaired children. In J. Bisanz, C. J. Brainerd, & R. V. Kail (Eds.), *Formal methods of cognitive development.* New York: Springer-Verlag.

Kirk, R. E. (1968). *Research design: Procedures for the behavioral sciences.* Belmont, California: Brooks/Cole.

Kukde, M. P. (1985). *The electrophysiology of control-mediating predictive stress appraisals.* Unpublished master's thesis, University of Western Ontario, Department of Psychology, London, Ontario, Canada.

Lakatos, I. (1978). Falsification and the methodology of scientific research programs. In J. Worrell & G. Currie (Eds.), *The methodology of scientific research: Imre Lakatos Philosophical Papers* (Vol. 1, pp. 139–167). Cambridge: Cambridge University Press.

Lazarus, R. S., & Averill, J. R. (1972). Emotion and cognition. With special reference to anxiety. In C. D. Spielberger (Ed.), *Anxiety: Current trends in theory and research.* New York: Academic.

Lazarus, R. S., Coyne, J. C., & Folkman, S. (1982). Cognition, emotion and motivation: The doctoring of Humpty Dumpty. In R. W. J. Neufeld (Ed.), *Psychological stress and psychopathology.* New York: McGraw-Hill.

Lazarus, R. S., & Folkman, S. (1984). *Stress, appraisal, and coping.* New York: Springer.

Lefave, M. K., & Neufeld, R. W. J. (1980). Anticipatory threat and physical-danger trait anxiety: A signal-detection analysis of effects on autonomic responding. *Journal of Research in Personality, 14,* 283–306.

Leventhal, H. (1970). Findings and theory in the study of fear communication. In L. Berkowitz (Ed.), *Advances in experimental social psychology* (Vol. 5). New York: Academic.

Luce, R. D., & Weber, E. U. (1986). An axiomatic theory of conjoint, expected risk. *Journal of Mathematical Psychology, 30,* 188–205.

Magnusson, D., & Ekehammar, B. (1975). Perceptions of and reactions to stressful situations. *Journal of Personality and Social Psychology, 31,* 1147–1154.

Maher, B. (1966). *Principles of psychopathology: An experimental approach.* New York: McGraw-Hill.

Maher, B. (1970). *Introduction to research in psychopathology.* New York: McGraw-Hill.

Mandler, G. (1984). *Mind and body: Psychology of emotion and stress.* New York: Norton.

Martin, I., & Venables, P. H. (1980). *Techniques of psychophysiology.* Toronto: Wiley.

Martin, R. (1989). In R. W. J. Neufeld (Ed.), *Advances in the investigation of psychological stress* (pp. 135–194). New York: Wiley.

Matthews, K. A. (1982). Psychological perspectives on the type A behavior pattern. *Psychological Bulletin, 91,* 293–323.

McGill, W. J. (1963). Stochastic latency mechanisms. In R. D. Luce, R. R. Bush, & El Galanter (Eds.), *Handbook of mathematical psychology* (Vol. 1, pp. 33–60). New York: Wiley.

McGrath, J. E. (1970). Settings, measures, and themes: An integrative review of some research on social-psychological factors in stress. In J. E. McGrath (Ed.), *Social and psychological factors in stress.* New York: Holt, Rinehart & Winston.

McLean, P. D. (1976). Depression as a specific response to stress. In I. G. Sarason & C. D. Spielberger (Eds.), *Stress and anxiety* (Vol. 3). Washington: Hemisphere.

Meehl, P. E. (1978). Theoretical risks and tabular asterisks: Sir Karl, Sir Ronald, and the slow progress of soft psychology. *Journal of Consulting and Clinical Psychology, 46,* 806–834.

Meehl, P. E. (1983). Consistency tests in estimating the completeness of the fossil record: A neo-Popperian approach to statistical paleontology. In J. Earman (Ed.), *Minnesota studies in the philosophy of science, Vol. X: Testing scientific theories.* Minneapolis: University of Minnesota Press.

Meehl, P. E., & Golden, R. R. (1982). Taxometric methods. In P. C. Kendall & J. N. Butcher (Eds.), *Handbook of research methods in clinical psychology.* New York: Wiley.

Millar, K. (1980). *Loud noise and retrieval of information.* Unpublished doctoral dissertation, University of Dundee.

Miller, S. M. (1979). Controllability and human stress: Method, evidence, and theory. *Behavioral Research and Therapy, 17,* 287–304.

Miller, S., & Seligman, M. E. P. (1982). The reformulated model of helplessness and depression: Evidence and theory. In R. W. J. Neufeld (Ed.), *Psychological stress and psychopathology* (pp. 149–178). New York: McGraw-Hill.

Monat, A., Averill, J. R., & Lazarus, R. S. (1972). Anticipating stress and coping reactions under various conditions of uncertainty. *Journal of Personality and Social Psychology, 24,* 237–253.

Morrison, M. S., Neufeld, R. W. J., & Lefebvre, L. A. in press. The economy of probabilistic stress: Interplay of controlling activity and threat reduction. *British Journal of Mathematical and Statistical Psychology.*

Mothersill, K., & Neufeld, R. W. J. (1985). Probability learning and coping in dysphoria and obsessive-compulsive tendencies. *Journal of Research in Personality, 19,* 152–165.

Navon, D., & Gopher, D. (1980). Task difficulty, resources, and dual-task performance. In R. S. Nickerson (Ed.), *Attention and performance, VIII* (pp. 297–315). Hillsdale, NJ: Erlbaum.

Neufeld, R. W. J. (1970). Generalization of results beyond the experimental setting: Statistical vs. logical considerations. *Perceptual and Motor Skills, 31,* 443–446.

Neufeld, R. W. J. (1973). Semantic dimensionality of the subjective stress scale. *Psychological Reports, 33,* 885–886.

Neufeld, R. W. J. (1976). Evidence of stress as a function of experimentally-altered appraisal of stimulus aversiveness and coping adequacy. *Journal of Personality and Social Psychology, 33,* 632–646.

Neufeld, R. W. J. (1977). *Clinical quantitative methods.* New York: Grune & Stratton.

Neufeld, R. W. J. (1978). Veridicality of cognitive mapping of stressor effects: Sex differences. *Journal of Personality, 3,* 85–121.

Neufeld, R. W. J. (1982). On decisional processes instigated by threat: Some possible implications for stress-related deviance. In R. W. J. Neufeld (Ed.), *Psychological stress and psychopathology.* New York: McGraw-Hill.

Neufeld, R. W. J. (1984). Elaboration of incorrect application of traditional test discriminating-power formulations to diagnostic group studies. *Journal of Nervous and Mental Disease, 172,* 373–374.

Neufeld, R. W. J., & Broga, M. I. (1977). *Fallacy of the reliability-discriminability principle in research on differential cognitive deficit.* Department of Psychology Research Bulletin #360, University of Western Ontario, London, Ontario, Canada.

Neufeld, R. W. J., & Davidson, P. O. (1972). Scaling of the subjective stress scale with a sample of university undergraduates. *Psychological Reports, 31,* 821–822.

Neufeld, R. W. J., & Davidson, P. O. (1974). Sex differences in stress responses: A multivariate analysis. *Journal of Abnormal Psychology, 83,* 178–185.

Neufeld, R. W. J., & Gardner, R. C. (1987). *Data aggregation as an analytical option: Multivariate and logical-deductive considerations.* University of Western Ontario, Department of Psychology Research Bulletin #652, London, Ontario, Canada.

Nicewander, W. A., & Price, J. M. (1983). Reliability of measurement and the power of statistical tests: Some new results. *Psychological Bulletin, 94,* 524–533.

Nielson, W., & Neufeld, R. W. J. (1986). Type A behavior and cardiovascular response to uncontrollable stress: A multidimensional approach. *Canadian Journal of Behavioral Science, 18,* 224–237.

Notarius, C. I., & Levenson, R. W. (1979). Expressive tendencies and physiological response to stress. *Journal of Personality and Social Psychology, 37,* 1204–1210.

Notarius, C. I., Wemple, C., Ingraham, L. J., Burns, T. J., & Kollar, E. (1982). Multichannel responses to an interpersonal stressor: Interrelationships among facial display, heart rate, self-report of emotion, and threat appraisal. *Journal of Personality and Social Psychology, 43,* 400–408.

Obrist, P. A. (1981). *Cardiovascular psychophysiology: A perspective.* New York: Plenum.

Osgood, C. E., Suci, G., & Tannenbaum, P. (1957). *The measurement of meaning.* Urbana: University of Illinois Press.

Osuna, E. E. (1985). The psychological cost of waiting. *Journal of Mathematical Psychology, 29,* 82–105.

Overall, J. E., & Woodward, J. A. (1976). Reassertion of the paradoxical power of tests of significance based on unreliable difference scores. *Psychological Bulletin, 83,* 776–777.

Pagano, D. (1973). Effects of task familiarity on stress responses of repressors and sensitizers. *Journal of Consulting and Clinical Psychology, 40*, 22–26.

Patrick, C. J., Craig, K. D., & Prkachin, K. M. (1986). Observer judgments of acute pain: Facial action determinants. *Journal of Personality and Social Psychology, 50*, 1291–1298.

Pittner, M. S., Houston, B. K., & Spiridigliozzi, G. (1983). Control over stress. Type A behavior pattern and response to stress. *Journal of Personality and Social Psychology, 44*, 627–637.

Pitz, G. F., & Sachs, N. J. (1984). Judgment and decision. In M. R. Rosenzweig & L. W. Porter (Eds.), *Annual Review of Psychology, 28*, 1–39.

Pribram, K. H., & McGuinness, D. (1975). Arousal, activation, and effort in the control of attention. *Psychological Review, 82*, 116–149.

Prkachin, K. J., Currie, N. A., & Craig, K. D. (1983). Judging on nonverbal expressions of pain. *Canadian Journal of Behavioral Science, 15*, 409–421.

Restle, F., & Greeno, J. G. (1970). *Introduction to mathematical psychology.* Reading, MA: Addison-Wesley.

Rodwan, A., & Hake, H. (1964). The discriminant function as a model for perception. *American Journal of Psychology*, 380–397.

Robinson, W. S. (1950). Ecological correlations and the behavior of individuals. *American Sociological Review, 15*, 351–357.

Rogosa, D. (1980). A critique of cross-lagged correlation. *Psychological Bulletin, 88*, 245–258.

Rushton, J. P., Brainerd, C. J., & Pressley, M. (1983). Behavioral development and construct validity: The principle of aggregation. *Psychological Bulletin, 94*, 18–36.

Sarason, I. (1984). Stress, anxiety, and cognitive interference: Reactions to tests. *Journal of Personality and Social Psychology, 46*, 929–938.

Schaie, K. W. (1965). A general model for the study of developmental problems. *Psychological Bulletin, 64*, 92–107.

Scheffe, H. (1959). *The analysis of variance.* New York: Wiley.

Semin, G. R., & Greenslade, L. (1985). Differential contributions of linguistic factors to memory-based ratings: Systematizing the systematic distortion hypothesis. *Journal of Personality and Social Psychology, 49*, 1713–1723.

Shean, G., Faia, C., & Schmaltz, E. (1974). Cognitive appraisal of stress and schizophrenic subtype. *Journal of Abnormal Psychology, 83*, 523–528.

Shweder, R. A. (1975). How relevant is an individual difference theory of personality? *Journal of Personality, 43*, 455–484.

Siegman, A. W. (1982). Nonverbal correlates of anxiety and stress. In L. Goldberger & S. Breznitz (Eds.), *Handbook of stress: Theoretical and clinical aspects* (pp. 306–319). New York: Free Press.

Solomon, S., Holmes, D., & McCaul, K. (1980). Behavioral control over aversive events: Does control that requires effort reduce anxiety and physiological arousal? *Journal of Personality and Social Psychology, 39*, 729–736.

Spence, D. P. (1982). Verbal indicators of stress. In L. Goldberger & S. Breznitz (Eds.), *Handbook of stress: Theoretical and clinical aspects* (pp. 295–305). New York: Free Press.

Spielberger, C. D., Gorsuch, R. L., & Lushene, R. E. (1970). *Manual for the state-trait anxiety inventory (self-evaluation questionnaire)*. Palo Alto, CA: Consulting Psychologists Press.

Spohn, H. E., & Fitzpatrick, T. (1980). Informed consent and bias in samples of schizophrenic subjects at risk for drug withdrawal. *Journal of Abnormal Psychology, 89,* 79–92.

Spring, B., & Coons, H. (1982). Stress as a precursor of schizophrenic episodes. In R. W. J. Neufeld (Ed.), *Psychological stress and psychopathology.* New York: McGraw-Hill.

SPSS, Inc. (1986). *Statistical package for the social sciences – X.* New York: McGraw-Hill.

Staddon, J. E. R. (1984). Social learning theory and the dynamics of interaction. *Psychological Review,* 502–507.

Stone, A. A., Cox, D. S., Valdimarsdottir, H., & Neale, J. M. (1987). Secretory IgA as a measure of immunocompetence. *Journal of Human Stress, 13,* 136–140.

Sutcliffe, J. P. (1980). On the relationship of reliability to statistical power. *Psychological Bulletin, 88,* 509–515.

Tan, S. Y. (1982). Cognitive and cognitive-behavioral methods for pain control: A selective review. *Pain, 12* 201–228.

Thorndike, E. L. (1939). On the fallacy of imputing the correlations found for groups to the individuals or smaller groups composing them. *American Journal of Psychology, 52,* 122–124.

Townsend, J. T. (1984). Uncovering mental processes with factorial experiments. *Journal of Mathematical Psychology, 28,* 363–400.

Townsend, J. T., & Ashby, F. G. (1983). *Stochastic modeling of elementary psychological processes.* London: Cambridge University Press.

Tukey, J. W. (1954). Causation, regression, and path analysis. In O. K. Kempthorne, T. A. Bancroft, J. W. Gowen, & J. L. Lush (Eds.), *Statistics and mathematics in biology* (pp. 35–66). Ames: Iowa State University Press.

Tulving, E. (1985). How many memory systems are there? *American Psychologist, 40,* 385–398.

Turpin, G., Lobstein, T., & Siddle, D. A. (1980). Phase activity: The influence of prestimulus variability. In I. Martin & P. H. Venables (Eds.), *Techniques in psychophysiology* (pp. 210–217). New York: Wiley.

Weick, K. E. (1970). The "ess" in stress: Some conceptual and methodological problems. In J. E. McGrath (Ed.), *Social and psychological factors in stress.* New York: Holt, Rinehart & Winston.

Weicker, H., Feraudi, M., Hagele, H., & Pluto, R. (1984). Clinical detection of catecholiamines in urine and plasma after separation with HPLC. *Clinica Chimica Acta (Amsterdam), 141,* 17–25.

Wickens, C. D. (1984). Attentional resources. In R. Parasuraman & D. R. Davies (Eds.), *Varieties of attention.* New York: Academic.

Winkler, R. L., & Hays, W. L. (1975). *Statistics: Probability, inference, & decision (2nd ed.).* New York: Holt, Rinehart & Winston.

Winne, P. H. (1983). Distortions of construct validity in multiple regression analysis. *Canadian Journal of Behavioural Science, 15,* 187–202.

Wolff, B. B. (1978). Behavioral measurement of human pain. In R. A. Sternbach (Ed.), *The psychology of pain.* New York: Raven.

Wright, R. A. (1984). Motivation, anxiety, and the difficulty of avoidant control. *Journal of Personality and Social Psychology, 46,* 1376–1388.

Zajonc, R. B. (1985). Emotional and facial efference: A theory reclaimed. *Science, 228(4695),* 15–21.

Zuckerman, M. (1983). The distinction between trait and state scales is *not* arbitrary: Comment on Allen and Potkay's "On the arbitrary distinction between traits and states." *Journal of Personality and Social Psychology, 44,* 1083–1086.

Zuckerman, M., & Lubin, B. (1965). *The multiple affect adjective checklist.* San Diego, CA: Educational and Industrial Testing Service.

4

Personality, Stress Arousal, and Cognitive Processes in Stress Transactions

MICHAEL W. EYSENCK

INTRODUCTION

There is almost universal agreement that the systematic investigation of psychological stress is of considerable practical and theoretical importance. As a result, there has been a large-scale investment of resources and research effort into the causes of, and cures for, psychological stress. Despite this, the answers that have emerged have been disappointingly incomplete and inconclusive. In part, the difficulty lies in the great variety of ways in which stress can be viewed. It is indisputable that at one level stress is a physiological state of the individual, but it is also partly a function of individual personality, of cognitive interpretations of the environment, and of various social and interpersonal problems.

It would be tempting in the face of such considerations to adopt an eclectic approach in which approximately equal weight is assigned to each of the factors that may cause psychological stress. However, a rather different and more challenging theoretical position is proposed here. This position is based on two key assumptions that have not as yet met with general approval. The first such assumption is that there are pronounced individual differences in susceptibility to stress and that, in consequence, any serious attempt to understand why it is that some individuals develop stress symptoms whereas others do not must take account of human personality. A theory along these lines was proposed by Slater (1943). In essence, he argued that neuroses occur as a result of the interactive influences of personality characteristics and the severity and number of stressful life events experienced. Thus, for example, people who are normally high in trait anxiety will on average require fewer stressful life events than those low in trait anxiety for an anxiety neurosis to occur. Recent evidence supporting this theoretical position was reported by McKeon, Roa, and Mann (1984) in a study of patients with obsessive-compulsive neurosis. They discovered that those patients with a highly anxious premorbid personality had experienced approximately half as many life events as patients with a nonanxious premorbid personality during the year preceding the onset of illness.

The second major assumption is that cognitive factors help to determine the extent to which environmental events are perceived as stressful. As Lazarus (1981) and others have pointed out, stress does not depend solely on environmental demands; rather, it is determined interactively by environmental demands and by the extent to which the individual appraises his or her coping skills as adequate to deal successfully with those demands. Thus, an apparently extremely demanding situation may be perceived as challenging if the individual in that situation feels that he or she has a reasonable chance of mastering it, whereas what is objectively the same situation will be perceived as stressful and threatening if the necessary resources and skills for mastery are thought to be lacking.

While the theoretical approach adopted by Lazarus (1981) is a plausible one in many ways, there is inadequate empirical evidence pinpointing the precise mechanisms involved in appraisal and coping. However, it is at least clear that cognitive appraisal is important, since altering appraisal has predictable effects on physiological and self-reported stress (Lazarus & Alfert, 1964).

There are great difficulties involved in attempting to amalgamate the personality and cognitive approaches to psychological stress. Personality theorists have often identified very general traits that allegedly are determined in large measure by heredity and are relatively invariant over time. In contrast, most cognitive theorists have focused on relatively specific aspects of cognition and behavior, and their interest has centered on the role played by learning and experience in modifying cognition. The basic dimensions of personality will be considered first, followed by an attempt to suggest ways in which the theoretical approaches favored by trait and cognitive researchers may be reconciled.

THE TRAIT APPROACH

The Basic Factors

The first task of personality theorists attempting to delineate the structure of human personality is to identify the major personality dimensions or traits. Factor theorists have been prominent here, but it is often argued that their efforts have proved unsuccessful. It is certainly true that different theorists have emphasized different factors, and the number of factors identified also varies substantially from theorist to theorist. At one extreme, Eysenck and Eysenck (1985) claimed that there are only three major dimensions of personality (extraversion, neuroticism, and psychoticism), whereas at the other extreme Cattell (e.g., Cattell, Eber, & Tatsouka, 1970) has concluded that there are at least 16 important personality factors. When one considers that several other factor theorists have each produced their own idiosyncratic sets of factors, it appears at a superficial level that matters are decidedly chaotic and unclear.

In fact, as Eysenck and Eysenck (1985) demonstrated in their review of the literature, a reasonable amount of clarification is possible. The first important requirement is to draw a distinction between first-order or primary factors, that are relatively specific, correlated factors, and second-order factors, that are both general and orthogonal to each other. In terms of this distinction, Cattell has focused largely on first-order factors, whereas Eysenck has concentrated on second-order factors. When Cattell's 16 Personality Factor (16 P.F.) questionnaire is analyzed so as to extract second-order factors, two of the largest, resultant factors clearly resemble Eysenck's factors of extraversion and neuroticism (cf. Hundleby & Connor, 1968). In other words, the evidence is quite strong that many (if not most) of the disagreements among factor theorists occur simply as a result of looking at the same reality from different perspectives.

Is it more useful to explore personality in terms of first-order or second-order factors? Analysis at the first-order level appears to offer the prospect of a more detailed and comprehensive picture of the richness of human personality than can be accomplished at the second-order level. As Cattell et al. (1970) argued, "The primary factors give one most information, and we would advocate higher strata contributors only as supplementary concepts . . . It is a mistake, generally, to work at the secondary level only, for one certainly loses a lot of valuable information present initially at the primary level." However, while that argument may seem convincing, the advantages that first-order or primary factors possess in principle have never been realized in practice. First-order factors are generally very difficult to replicate, and even now there is nothing even approaching consensus concerning the nature of these factors. In contrast, numerous studies have reported second-order factors identical (or highly similar) to Eysenck's factors of extraversion, neuroticism, and psychoticism. More-over, first-order factors typically add surprisingly little to the information contained in second-order factors. For example, Saville and Blinkhorn (1981) administered the Cattell scales and the Eysenck Personality Inventory (EPI) to large groups of people. When all of the variance attributable to extraversion and neuroticism was removed from the 16 P.F. data, little in the way of useful information about personality remained.

A question that has not been addressed very often is nevertheless of crucial significance in this area: Why exactly is it that the orthogonal factors of extraversion and neuroticism (plus possibly psychoticism) occur in all cultures? Is it merely a biological quirk, or is there some persuasive theoretical reason for this? A very interesting answer has recently been provided by Tellegen (1985). His starting position was that there are very close inter-relationships between mood and personality. Detailed analysis of self-report mood scales revealed the existence of two major orthogonal dimensions of mood: positive affect (e.g., elated, active, enthusiastic) and negative affect (e.g., distressed, fearful, hostile) (Zevon & Tellegen, 1982). Re-analysis of the data from previous studies, that had identified several relatively specific mood factors also revealed the existence of the two broad factors of positive affect and negative affect. If mood and personality are closely related, then it should follow that two particularly important personality dimensions involve susceptibility to positive affect and susceptibility to negative affect, respectively.

Which personality dimensions most successfully predict individual differences in positive affect and negative affect? The evidence so far indicates that extraversion (and especially its sociability component) is related to positive affect, with extraverts experiencing much more positive affect than introverts (Costa & McCrae, 1980; Tellegen, 1985). Not surprisingly, neuroticism or the related personality dimension of anxiety is most predictive of negative affect, with those high in neuroticism or anxiety being considerably more susceptible to negative affect than individuals low in those dimensions. The fact that positive affect and negative affect are quite separate rather than simply being the opposite of each other is shown by the further findings that the level of extraversion does not predict the amount of negative affect experienced, and positive affect is not affected by the level of neuroticism or anxiety.

Clearly Tellegen (1985) has provided powerful theoretical arguments to account for the universal prominence of extraversion and neuroticism. This theoretical conceptualization also sheds light on the old controversy concerning the distinction between the two stress-induced mood disorders of anxiety and depression. While most clinicians and psychologists continue to argue that there is a valid distinction between anxiety and depression, this argument is weakened by the substantial correlations that are typically obtained between questionnaire measures of anxiety and depression (Watson & Clark, 1984). Tellegen (1985) has proposed a simple and elegant theoretical analysis of the distinction, arguing in essence that anxious mood involves primarily very high negative affect, whereas depressed mood depends in large measure on very low positive affect. Among psychiatric patients, it was found that a reported lack of pleasurable experiences was often associated with a diagnosis of depression, whereas the experience of distressing life events was related more specifically to anxiety (Hall, 1977). In a questionnaire study, Tellegen (1985) discovered that a measure of anxiety was correlated more highly with negative affect than was a measure of depression, whereas the opposite was the case for correlations with low positive affect. This pattern was fairly clear-cut, despite the fact that the anxiety and depression scales correlated +.83 with each other.

The distinction between anxiety and depression is more complex than suggested by Tellegen (1985). Moreover, high negative affect and low positive affect are often found together, especially in clinical populations. Nevertheless, the view of anxiety as a stressful engagement in life, whereas depression involves disengagement from pleasurable experiences, appears to capture an important truth.

In sum, any attempt to relate individual differences in susceptibility to stress to personality should be based on the "big two" personality dimensions of extraversion and neuroticism or anxiety. These two dimensions have special status not only because of their prominence in most factor analytic studies but also because they are strongly predictive of levels of positive and negative affect, respectively. Not surprisingly, most research in this area has focused on the anxiety or neuroticism dimension, because it seems more directly associated with stress susceptibility. However, it is probable that the effects of stressful experiences on those high in neuroticism or anxiety will depend to some extent on the level of extraversion. Neurotic extraverts, with their greater susceptibility to positive affect, may be better able than neurotic introverts to cope with the stresses of everyday life.

What Is Trait Anxiety?

The position argued for so far has implied that the personality dimension of neuroticism or anxiety (i.e., trait anxiety) is primarily a measure of susceptibility to negative affect. In other words, it is a mood-dispositional dimension. This general position has been adopted by a number of theorists (e.g., Spielberger, Gorsuch, & Lushene, 1970; Watson & Clark, 1984). Spielberger et al. (1970) specifically defined trait anxiety as "relatively stable individual differences in anxiety proneness." However, other theorists have offered somewhat different interpretations of the essential nature of trait anxiety or neuroticism. Eysenck (1967) has favored a physiological theory in which individual differences in neuroticism depend upon the functioning of the "visceral brain," that is, the hippocampus, amygdala, cingulum, septum, and hypothalamus. More specifically, individuals who are high in neuroticism usually produce more activity in the visceral brain than those low in neuroticism. Gray (1981) has proposed a related view. He distinguished between neuroticism and anxiety, arguing that anxiety is an amalgam of neuroticism and introversion. Trait anxiety, in his opinion, is determined by a Behavioral Inhibition System consisting of the septo-hippocampal system, its neocortical projection in the frontal lobe and its monoaminergic afferents from the brain stem. The Behavioral Inhibition System is responsive to signals of punishment and frustrative nonreward; hence, anxious individuals are particularly affected by punishment.

A radically different view of trait anxiety was offered by Hamilton (1983):

> *Anxiety* should be regarded as a particular set or network of connotative data that, on the basis of past experience and autonomous elaboration of their cognitive structures, provides a store of long-term memories. These are available for retrieval when stimulated, just like other long-term memory data . . . The greater the predisposition to generate aversive expectancies or behavior outcomes, the greater the appropriate memory store, the lower the retrieval threshold for this type of information, and the greater the response bias toward primary processes of identifying and avoiding real or potential aversiveness (p. 114).

Which of these various explanations of the basis of trait anxiety is to be preferred? All of these explanations are over-simplified, and some kind of synthesis is required. In order to sustantiate that view, let us consider the predictions made by the various theories, together with the relevant evidence. Theorists such as Eysenck (1967), Gray (1981), and Spielberger et al. (1970) all regard neuroticism or trait anxiety as determined substantially by heredity, whereas Hamilton (1983) apparently does not. The evidence (which is reviewed in considerable detail by Eysenck and Eysenck, 1985) indicates strongly that heredity plays an important role in determining the level of neuroticism or trait anxiety. Shields (1962), for example, used an early version of the Maudsley Personality Inventory with various different types of twins. He discovered that dizygotic twins brought up together had an intraclass correlation coefficient of +.11 for neuroticism, whereas monozygotic twins brought up together had one of +.38, and monozygotic twins brought up apart had one of +.53. The findings that monozygotic twins were much more similar in neuroticism than dizygotic twins and that monozygotic twins brought up apart were much more alike in neuroticism than dizygotic twins brought up together (despite the much greater environmental similarity in the latter group) are in line with the genetic determination of neuroticism.

More recently, an especially thorough study was reported by Floderus-Myrhed, Pedersen, and Rasmusson (1980). They administered a short form of the Eysenck Personality Inventory to a total of 12,898 twin pairs in

Sweden. The estimated heritability for neuroticism for males was .50, and for females it was .58. Since there are several other studies reporting findings basically in line with those of Shields (1962) and Floderus-Myrhed et al. (1980), Eysenck and Eysenck (1985) drew the following conclusion: "No serious worker in this field denies that genetic factors account for at least something like half of the variance, and equally none would deny the importance of environmental variables" (p. 96).

As would be expected from the hereditarian position, trait anxiety demonstrates reasonable longitudinal consistency. Longitudinal evidence from a range of measures of anxiety or neuroticism (including the hypochondriasis scale of the Minnesota Multiphasic Personality Inventory, Bell's scale of Emotional Maladjustment, the neuroticism scale of the Eysenck Personality Inventory, and the 0 scale of the 16 P.F.) was reviewed by Conley (1984). When allowance is made for the rather poor internal consistency or period-free reliability of some of these measures, then the annual stability of anxiety or neuroticism is approximately .98. Thus, while levels of trait anxiety do vary over time, the changes tend to be relatively modest unless long time intervals are involved.

So far, the traditional conceptualization of trait anxiety has fared better than the more modern cognitive interpretation proposed by Hamilton (1983). However, the traditional approach is severely limited in some ways. First, the notion of trait anxiety as a predisposition to experience anxiety that is largely determined by heredity is a remarkably static view. A complete understanding of trait anxiety must take account of the substantial impact of the environment and of the fact that the longitudinal consistency of trait anxiety is far from perfect. In other words, there seems to be a need for a dynamic model that accounts for the ways in which trait anxiety fluctuates throughout an individual's life.

Second, the view that an individual's level of neuroticism or trait anxiety depends on the functioning of a single physiological system such as the visceral brain or the Behavioral Inhibition System implies that trait anxiety is a unidimensional construct. If it is simply the case that some individuals have more responsive physiological systems than others, then the natural expectation is that those with very responsive systems should be highly anxious across all stressful situations, whereas those with very unresponsive physiological systems should be relatively immune from anxiety. This prediction of across-the-board anxiety or lack of anxiety can be contrasted with an interactionist perspective, according to which some people will be anxious in one particular stressful situation but not in another, whereas other people will manifest the opposite pattern. This kind of theory was advocated by Endler and Edwards (1982), who claimed that the existence of consistent interactions between individuals and situations in determining the level of anxiety experienced meant that trait anxiety should be regarded as multidimensional rather than unidimensional. Unfortunately there is much disagreement concerning both the number and the nature of dimensions of anxiety. However, the two dimensions that have received the most empirical support so far are those of ego threat or social evaluation and physical danger. Traditional measures of trait anxiety that are based on the unidimensional view typically assess the ego-threat dimension rather than the physical-danger dimension (Endler, Magnusson, Eke- hammar, & Okada, 1976; Hodges, 1968).

A relatively direct test of the multidimensional view of trait anxiety is to obtain separate measures of two dimensions of trait anxiety (e.g., social evaluation and physical danger), and then to expose the subjects to situations that are stressful because they involve either social evaluation or physical danger. In one such study (Donat, 1983), social evaluation and physical danger anxiety were assessed by means of the Stimulus-Response Inventory of General Trait Anxiety. The subjects were then placed in situations designed to create either social evaluation anxiety (ego-involving instructions on a task) or physical danger anxiety (threat of electric shock). The findings were consistent with an interactionist theory. All measures (i.e., self-report, heart rate, task performance) indicated higher levels of anxiety when the nature of the subject's anxiety was congruent with the type of anxiety induced in the experimental situation than when there was a lack of congruence. Some other studies (e.g., Kendall, 1978) have produced similar results.

If trait anxiety is best regarded as a multidimensional construct, then it is likely that the differentiation of anxiety occurs as a result of life experiences. Heredity may influence whether or not an individual's moods are generally anxious, but it is less likely that heredity is of importance in determining the kinds of environmental situations that will be responded to with more or less anxiety. This differential responsiveness can most readily be accommodated by more cognitive approaches such as the one proposed by Hamilton (1983). If one has a series of stressful experiences relating to, say, physical danger, then this will influence the information that is stored in long-term memory. This stored information, in turn, will influence subsequent cognitive inter- pretations of similar environmental events.

A third limitation of the traditional view (and one that has attracted little attention) involves an intriguing paradox. Theorists associated with the trait approach to personality typically maintain the Behaviorist tradition of denigrating introspective evidence and cognitive processes in general, and yet the major method of assessing trait anxiety or neuroticism is based firmly on introspective evidence! Hamilton's (1983) emphasis on the role of long-term memory in anxiety makes much sense when one considers that questionnaire assessment of anxiety involves a series of items requiring the retrieval of relevant information from long-term memory.

In spite of cogent arguments that trait anxiety should be regarded from a cognitive perspective, there is more to consider. As Lang (1971) pointed out, there are three somewhat separate systems involved in anxiety: the behav- ioral, the physiological, and the verbal. While most theorists have assumed implicitly that these three systems respond concordantly, this assumption must be rejected. For example, Craske and Craig (1984) investigated anxiety in 40 competent pianists who played alone and in front of an audience. The different systems involved in anxiety were assessed by taking several measures, including state anxiety on the State-Trait Anxiety Inventory, heart rate, skin conductance, respiration, and quality of piano playing. A number of within-systems correlations (e.g., correlating one physiological measure with another) were statistically significant, but the more crucial between-systems correlations were mostly weak and insignificant.

Why is it that behavioral, physiological, and verbal components of anxiety so often fail to co-vary? One important reason is that none of the components is affected solely by the prevailing level of anxiety; rather, there are numerous factors in addition to anxiety that may affect each of the measures; for example, the situational and social constraints typically present in everyday life tend to prevent the "natural" behavioral response of passive avoidance.

The cases in which there are genuine and systematic discordances among the various components of anxiety are of rather greater theoretical interest than the cases we have considered so far. For example, there is reasonable evidence that at least some individuals who appear low in anxiety as assessed verbally are rather high in anxiety as assessed physiologically and behaviorally (e.g., Weinberger, Schwartz, & Davidson, 1979). While it might be argued that such individuals are simply "faking" their questionnaire answers, it appears rather that they are people who exercise considerable cognitive self-control and who have a preoccupation with mastering negative emotional states such as anxiety.

In sum, approaches to trait anxiety that are based exclusively on biology, physiology, or cognition all seem to be doomed to failure. The notion that an individual's level of trait anxiety is determined by heredity is partially supported by twin studies and evidence of longitudinal consistency, but this biological model does not provide an adequate account of the dynamic changes in anxiety over time. In contrast, cognitive models can potentially account for change, but do not explain why heredity plays an important role. An amalgam of these two approaches might offer a more complete explanation, and a few preliminary thoughts along those lines are discussed next.

Towards a Theoretical Framework

The discussion in earlier sections has indicated that it is necessary to assume that the cognitive system and the physiological system both play significant roles in anxiety. It is also apparent that the trait approach needs to become more dynamic in the sense that changes over time in trait anxiety and the development of multiple dimensions of trait anxiety require explanation. In essence, it is proposed here that genetically determined individual differences in physiological functioning produce some stability in trait anxiety as construed unidimensionally, whereas the cognitive system is instrumental in producing changes in trait anxiety over time, including the gradual differentiation of multiple dimensions of anxiety. In other words, the consistency and generality or unidimensionality are attributable largely to the physiological system, whereas the specificity or multidimensionality of trait anxiety stems from the cognitive system. Of course, the physiological and cognitive systems usually operate interdependently, so that the differences between the two systems may well over-state a complex reality.

How does the functioning of the cognitive system vary between high-anxiety and low-anxiety individuals? The best way of conceptualizing the relationship between trait anxiety and long-term memory is not obvious. However, it may be useful to postulate a hierarchical structure of information storage, with rather general schemata (i.e., broad memory structures) at the top of the hierarchy and more specific units of information (e.g., worries) towards the bottom. Butler and Mathews (1983) have argued that anxious patients, but not normal controls, possess "danger schemata." This claim was based on the finding that anxious patients regarded themselves as significantly more "at risk" than other people from potential environmental dangers. At a more specific level, those high in trait anxiety worry significantly more than those low in trait anxiety, even when the initial level of state anxiety of the two groups is equated (Eysenck, 1984b). This difference in the incidence of worrying may well reflect the larger number of worries that high-anxiety individuals have stored in long-term memory, as well as the more organized nature of those worries. In other words, individuals high and low in trait anxiety probably differ in both the number and nature of anxiety-related schemata, and in the number and organization of specific worries. These differences in long-term memory may play an important role in affecting the perceptual, attentional, and interpretative processes that are applied to environmental stimuli, as will be discussed in the next section.

One of the great advantages of a schema-based theory is that it provides a theoretical framework to account for the multidimensionality of trait anxiety and for changes in trait anxiety over time. There are multiple dimensions of trait anxiety because there are a number of different underlying schemata. Changes in anxiety level can easily be accommodated, because schemata are constantly being modified and refined as a result of interactions with the environment. However, schemata tend to change slowly rather than radically over time. Thus, schemata may prove important in accounting for the gradual alterations in trait anxiety over time that appear in nearly all of the longitudinal studies (Conley, 1984).

The physiological component of trait anxiety probably closely resembles the Behavioral Inhibition System postulated by Gray (1981). The precise bidirectional influences of the cognitive and physiological systems upon each other remain obscure. However, the perceptual, attentional, and interpretative processes of the cognitive system will determine, at least in part, the degree of subsequent activation of the Behavioral Inhibition System. In the other direction, the influence of the physiological system on mood states will produce effects on the content of the information stored in long-term memory.

At the very least, these sketchy theoretical notions may provide a useful orientation to research. It is clear that much more needs to be discovered about the inter-relationships between the cognitive and physiological systems. In addition, the structure and content of long-term memory in individuals high and low in trait anxiety are almost completely unexplored, and the impact of schemata and other memory structures on psychological processes such as attention and stimulus interpretation is unclear. Rather more is known about the physiological processes involved in anxiety than about the cognitive processes. The rest of this chapter is devoted to an examination of current knowledge concerning anxiety and cognition.

COGNITIVE PROCESSES

There are various different strands of research that have examined the effects of anxiety on cognitive processes and cognitive-task performance. The approach that is of most immediate relevance to an understanding of how trait anxiety might predispose to anxiety neurosis is based on the assumption that individuals high and low in trait anxiety differ in their immediate reactions to *threatening* stimuli, but not to *neutral* stimuli. This line of research stems from Byrne's (1964) distinction between repressors and sensitizers, and has produced reasonably clear-cut effects of trait anxiety on a variety of cognitive processes.

An alternative approach has been more concerned with possible effects of trait anxiety on the processing capacity that is available for cognitive-task performance. High levels of trait anxiety are usually associated with relatively poor levels of task performance, at least on complex tasks. As a consequence, the main theoretical issue has been to identify the processes and mechanisms responsible for this adverse effect of anxiety. This line of research is dealt with in a later section.

The links between the research evidence and the theoretical speculations discussed in the previous section are not as close as one would like. This is inevitable, however, because the research was designed to test theoretical formulations antedating the one put forward above.

Repression-Sensitization

At a relatively crude level of analysis, it is possible to identify two major strategies that could be applied when someone is initially confronted by threatening or threat-related environmental stimuli:

1. An approach strategy, in which the threatening stimuli are thoroughly attended to and processed
2. An avoidance strategy, in which there is minimal attention to, and processing of, the threatening stimuli

The most prominent theorist who has argued for such a classification of strategies is Byrne (1964). He referred to the approach strategy as "sensitization," a label under which he subsumed Freudian defense mechanisms such as intellectualization, obsessive behavior, and ruminative worrying. He called the opposite or avoidance strategy "repression," a term intended to include denial and rationalization as well as ordinary repression.

Perhaps Byrne's greatest contribution was to argue that there are characteristic individual differences in preferred strategy, and to support that argument by devising the Repression-Sensitization Scale, a test which is based largely on items selected from the Minnesota Multiphasic Personality Inventory. The basic assumption lying behind the construction of this test was that individuals can meaningfully be ordered along a continuum, with an extreme tendency to avoid threatening stimuli defining one end of this continuum and an extreme tendency to approach threatening stimuli defining the other end.

Byrne (1964) claimed that his Repression-Sensitization Scale should not be regarded purely and simply as a measure of trait anxiety, but the evidence indicates that he is mistaken. As Watson and Clark (1984) have shown in their review of the evidence, scores on the Repression-Sensitization Scale correlate on average +.80 or higher with standard measures of trait anxiety (e.g., Taylor's Manifest Anxiety Scale). Since these correlation coefficients are only a little lower than the test-retest reliabilities of the tests concerned, it must be concluded that the Repression-Sensitization Scale and standard tests of trait anxiety are measuring the same construct. As a consequence, it will be assumed that the Repression-Sensitization Scale is, in essence, a measure of trait anxiety. Thus, repressors are low-anxiety individuals and sensitizers are high-anxiety individuals.

The first issue that needs to be examined is whether it is indeed the case that sensitizers tend to approach threatening stimulation whereas repressors avoid such stimulation. If the evidence supports that hypothesis, then it would be important to establish the boundary conditions for the existence of these differential processing strategies. Finally, the specific cognitive processing mechanisms underlying these approach and avoidance strategies would need to be identified.

Watson and Clark (1984) were very definite in their assessment of the evidence relating to the first issue, that is, the hypothesis of consistent approach-avoidance tendencies to threat associated with repression-sensitization or trait anxiety. First they identified the dimension measured by scales of repression-sensitization and trait anxiety as one of negative affectivity. They briefly reviewed the findings from studies in which the association between the Repression-Sensitization Scale or some equivalent measure and approach-avoidance tendencies to sexually provocative stimuli, to taboo words, or to painful or gruesome stimuli was examined. They came to the following conclusion:

> These studies have used a wide variety of designs and measures and, although a few inconsistencies do appear, the results have been overwhelmingly negative. Taken together, they indicate that NA (i.e., negative affectivity) is unrelated to the approach/avoidance of these types of threatening stimuli. (p. 481)

It will be argued very strongly here that this conclusion is unwarrantedly pessimistic, and that clear-cut differences in the processing of threat-related stimuli can be demonstrated under some circumstances. However, it will be useful to consider first some of the negative findings that led Watson and Clark (1984) to their conclusion. Many of the negative results have emerged from studies of perceptual defense, which is perhaps the most researched task in the investigation of repression-sensitization. In this task, stimuli are presented tachistoscopically for progressively longer periods of time until they can be recognized. Perceptual defense is said to occur when taboo or emotionally disturbing stimuli have higher recognition thresholds than neutral stimuli (Dixon, 1981). If perceptual defense depends upon partial avoidance of, and reduced processing of, threat-related stimuli, then it is reasonable to assume that greater perceptual defense should be shown by repressors than by sensitizers.

In fact, the experimental evidence provides rather little support for this hypothesis, although early research produced some positive findings (e.g., Greenbaum, 1956; Tempone, 1962). In the study by Greenbaum (1956), for example, the recognition thresholds for hostile and friendly faces were assessed. Those high in trait anxiety (i.e., sensitizers) had on average lower recognition thresholds for the hostile faces than for the friendly ones, whereas those low in trait anxiety (i.e., repressors) exhibited the opposite tendency.

In spite of these positive findings, other early researchers failed to discover any difference in perceptual defense between repressors and sensitizers (e.g., Bitterman & Kniffin, 1953). Moreover, all of these early studies share the same limitation, in that the recognition-threshold data do not indicate whether the perceptual defense effects obtained are genuine perceptual effects or whether they are due to response bias. One way of permitting an unequivocal interpretation of the data is to use the measures provided by signal-detection theory—a measure of perceptual sensitivity and a measure of response cautiousness. Precisely this approach was adopted by Van Egeren (1968). He discovered that neutral and affective words did not differ in perceptual sensitivity, but the response threshold was higher or more stringent for the affective words. There was no difference between repressors and sensitizers with respect to either perceptual sensitivity or response cautiousness.

Further negative findings were obtained in an interesting study by Wagstaff (1974), who made use of a different way of observing the effects of threat-related stimuli on perceptual sensitivity uncontaminated by possible response bias. The subject's task was to estimate the relative brightness of pairs of light signals that were actually of identical brightness. The light signals were superimposed on subliminally presented words. In general, the threat-related words appeared subjectively to be less bright than the neutral stimuli, which is consistent with the typical perceptual defense effect. However, repressors and sensitizers did not differ as predicted in their performance on this task.

All in all, the perceptual defense studies provide minimal support for the hypothesis of consistent differences between high-anxiety and low-anxiety subjects in the processing of threat-related stimuli. It is noteworthy that the studies employing the best methodology (i.e., Van Egeren, 1968; Wagstaff, 1974) failed to support the hypothesis, while the studies providing evidential support for the hypothesis made use of methodologically inadequate designs. These negative findings might lead one to conclude, as Watson and Clark (1984) did, that there are no consistent differences between low-anxiety and high-anxiety individuals in their immediate processing of threat-related stimuli. However, it could also be argued that the perceptual defense paradigm possesses certain features that render it inappropriate as a complete test of the hypothesis. Two features deserve particular emphasis. The first is that a perceptual recognition task may require only relatively low-level perceptual processes, whereas the approach and avoidance strategies may operate at a somewhat higher level of cognitive functioning. The second feature is that nearly all of the studies of perceptual defense have used paradigms involving perceptual recogniton of one word at a time. This would be a serious limitation if individuals high and low in trait anxiety differ primarily in terms of how they allocate processing resources to two or more concurrent stimuli. Such selective allocation of resources clearly could not be detected within the confines of the typical perceptual defense experiment.

There is already available in the literature some evidence suggesting that the failure of high- and low-anxiety individuals to differ in the size of the perceptual defense effect may not be because the perceptual defense paradigm involves early and low-level perceptual processes. There have been a number of experimental studies (e.g., Carroll, 1972; Lewinsohn, Berquist, & Brelje, 1972) in which threat-related and neutral stimuli were presented visually for relatively long periods of time that permitted the use of high-level perceptual processes. Despite this, the typical finding is that repressors and sensitizers have the same duration of visual attention to threat-related pictures of mutilated bodies and corpses.

More promising findings were obtained by Neufeld (1975). He compared subjective stress in repressors and sensitizers to slides of homicide victims and skin-diseased patients. Two separate signal-detection measures were calculated: subjective sensitivity to the stimuli and the criterion for reporting stress. In general, repressors exhibited lower stress sensitivity than sensitizers, but the two groups did not differ in their criteria. These findings differ from those of Van Egeren (1968), who also used signal-detection theory measures, but the tasks used were rather different. In addition, as Neufeld pointed out, his stimuli may have been more stressful than those used by Van Egeren.

The remaining alternative is that high-anxiety and low-anxiety individuals differ in their approach/avoidance tendencies towards threatening stimuli only when at least one threatening and one neutral stimulus are presented concurrently. The first of a series of studies was carried out by Christos Halkiopoulos, in unpublished research. In essence, he used a dichotic listening task in which pairs of words were presented concurrently, one to each ear. The subjects were required to attend to and repeat back aloud all of the words presented to one ear. A mixture of threatening (e.g., grave, fail) and nonthreatening (e.g., chairs, sale) words were presented on the attended channel, but only neutral or nonthreatening words were presented on the nonshadowed or unattended ear. Occasionally a tone occurred on either the attended or unattended ear shortly after a pair of words had been presented, and the subject's task was to respond as quickly as possible whenever a tone was detected. The rationale was that the speed of response to each tone would provide an indication of the allocation of processing resources or attention at that time. The Facilitation-Inhibition Scale (Ullmann, 1962), which correlates very highly with Byrne's Repression-Sensitization Scale, was administered to all of the subjects.

The differences between facilitators (i.e., high-anxiety individuals) and inhibitors (i.e., low-anxiety individuals) in terms of the response latencies to tones following threatening and nonthreatening words were quite striking and were reflected in a highly significant interaction involving facilitation-inhibition, attended word type (threatening vs. nonthreatening), and tone channel (attended vs. unattended). Facilitators responded very rapidly to the tone when it followed a threatening word in the same ear, but they responded very slowly when it followed a threatening word in the other ear. In other words, they allocated processing resources preferentially to the ear on which a threatening word had been presented. In contrast, inhibitors showed exactly the opposite pattern, as if they actively avoided attending to the ear on which a threatening word had just been presented.

These findings are potentially of great interest, because at last we have convincing evidence of threat avoidance by low-anxiety individuals and threat approach by high-anxiety individuals as originally proposed by Byrne (1964). Of course, it would be desirable to replicate such an important finding, and this has been done by MacLeod, Mathews, and Tata (1986). They used a visual analog of the paradigm employed by Halkiopoulos, in which pairs of words were presented together on a screen, with the subject being instructed to read the top word out loud and attend to that area of the screen.

One of the words was sometimes replaced by a dot that required a rapid response. Their subjects consisted of a group of patients with a primary diagnosis of generalized anxiety and a group of normal controls. The former group had a much higher mean trait anxiety score than the latter group. The basic pattern of results obtained by MacLeod et al. (1986) closely resembled that of Halkiopoulos. Anxious patients responded faster to the probe when it replaced a threatening word than when it replaced a neutral one, thus manifesting a sensitizing tendency. On the other hand, the control subjects responded faster to the probe when it replaced a neutral word; this reflects a defensive strategy.

The basic similarity between the findings of Halkiopoulos (unpublished) and of MacLeod et al. (1986) indicates the robustness of these approach and avoidance tendencies. Additional research by Broadbent (personal communication) and by myself (research in progress) provides even more conclusive support for the predicted differences in processing resource allocation between high-anxiety and low-anxiety individuals on this visual task.

There are various theoretical implications of these findings, but before discussing them it is necessary to discuss some limitations of the data. First, it remains unclear whether trait anxiety is directly responsible for the observed effects, or whether the effects of trait anxiety are mediated by anxious mood state during the experiment. If trait anxiety turns out to be directly responsible, it would then be necessary to decide whether the schemata stored in long-term memory influence approach and avoidance tendencies to threat-related stimuli. Second, it seems highly probable that there are substantial individual differences in allocation of processing resources among concurrent threatening and neutral stimuli only when mildly threatening stimuli are presented. It would seem to be virtually a biological imperative that major sources of threat should pre-empt everyone's processing resources. Third, the level of processing at which the selective allocation biases operate has not been definitely established. However, MacLeod et al. (1986) reported that the selective biases on their visual task were equally apparent whether the dot appeared in the "attended" or the "unattended" part of the screen. Since there was a general lack of awareness of the meanings of those words presented in the unattended or bottom area of the screen, this is suggestive evidence that the selective biases may be preattentive in nature. Additional evidence pointing to the same conclusion was obtained by Mathews and MacLeod (1986). They discovered that selective biases with threat words were operating in a dichotic listening task, despite the fact that there was no conscious awareness of any of these words.

At a theoretical level, it is now clear that Watson and Clark (1984) were unwarranted in their rejection of Byrne's (1964) theory, because quite powerful perceptual and attentional differences between high-anxiety and low-anxiety individuals in their reactions to threatening stimuli have been demonstrated. However, these differences manifestly do not appear under all circumstances, as was claimed by Byrne (1964). Instead, what we need theoretically is an account of what distinguishes those situations in which processing biases towards threatening stimuli are and are not found. As a first approximation, it is reasonable to assume that high-anxiety individuals have a preattentive bias in favor of threatening stimuli, and low-anxiety individuals have a preattentive bias against threatening stimuli. Since these are *selective* biases, they will normally influence performance only when the stimulus situation permits selective allocation of resources (i.e., when at least one threatening and one neutral stimulus are presented concurrently).

These selective biases may play an important role in everyday life, since we are often confronted with mildly threatening stimuli of one kind or another. If anxious individuals typically attend selectively to such stimuli and then engage in excessive processing of them, this could account for the fact that anxious patients feel themselves to be more "at risk" than normal controls (Butler & Mathews, 1983). The strong tendency for those high in trait anxiety to be more anxious than those low in trait anxiety even in apparently relaxing conditions (Watson & Clark, 1984) may also be due in part to selective processing of threatening stimuli.

Preattentive selective biases may be of relevance to an understanding of some of the adverse effects of trait anxiety on task performance that are discussed in the next section. It has often been assumed (e.g., Eysenck, 1979) that anxiety influences the allocation of processing resources away from the experimental task and to task-irrelevant, threat-related information. However, empirical support for the notion that anxiety affects the allocation of processing resources in this way has often been extremely indirect, sometimes being based entirely on postexperimental questioning (e.g., Deffenbacher, 1978). In contrast, the studies of Halkiopoulos (unpublished) and MacLeod et al. (1986) have provided unequivocal evidence of processing allocation biases, and it is plausible to assume that many of the detrimental effects of trait anxiety on the performance of cognitive tasks are caused by these biases.

So far the emphasis has been on possible differences between high-anxiety and low-anxiety individuals in their allocation of processing resources to environmental stimuli. It is possible, however, that individual differences in approach and avoidance tendencies towards threatening stimuli extend to other aspects of cognitive functioning. In particular, a paradigm that seems related to the one used by Halkiopoulos (unpublished) and MacLeod et al. (1986) is one in which subjects interpret an ambiguous stimulus that has a threatening and a nonthreatening interpretation. While there are some inconsistencies in the literature, most of the evidence indicates that all of the possible interpretations of ambiguous stimuli are activated automatically, an assumption that is explicitly incorporated into the exhaustive access model (Simpson, 1984). If preattentive selective biases partially determine which interpretation reaches conscious awareness, then high-anxiety individuals may show a bias towards threatening interpretations of ambiguous stimuli, whereas the opposite bias should characterize low-anxiety individuals.

Historically the attempt to obtain consistent individual differences in the interpretation of ambiguous stimuli within personality research has not proved particularly successful. There is a long tradition of using projective tests such as the Rorschach ink-blot test and the Thematic Apperception Test to assess personality, but typically the tests have poor reliability and validity. In one study discussed by Eysenck and Eysenck (1981), 50 anxious patients and 50 normal controls were administered the Rorschach test. Subsequent analysis by experts of the interpretations of the ink blots provided by the subjects revealed essentially no ability to discriminate between the responses of the two groups.

The disappointing results obtained from projective tests are somewhat surprising, because the underlying rationale for their use seems to be sound. Interpretation of a stimulus situation depends interactively on the information contained within the situation and on interpretative processes and structures within the individual perceiver. If the situation is totally unambiguous (e.g., a plane's engines stall and it plummets towards the ground), then individual differences in interpretative processes and structures become largely irrelevant, because the stimulus information permits only one interpretation. In contrast, ambiguous situations afford maximal scope for individual differences in interpretation.

Why is there this mismatch between theory and practice? A major problem is that most projective tests are simply too unconstrained, and allow too many different interpretations. As a consequence, a given individual often provides quite different interpretations of the same stimulus on two separate occasions. A further difficulty is that the stimuli used in some projective tests are rather remote from most people's experience, and thus may not properly engage their major cognitive schemata or structures. This is perhaps especially true of the ink blots of the Rorschach test.

This analysis of projective tests suggests that high- and low-anxiety individuals will differ in their interpretation of ambiguous stimuli only under certain conditions. More specifically, the stimuli should permit a strictly limited number of alternative interpretations, and the stimuli should be of relevance to the subjects' previous experience and to their cognitive schemata. A few studies conforming to these guidelines have been reported, and the results to date are reasonably encouraging. For example, Blaylock (1963) presented homographs having both aggressive and neutral meanings to a group of subjects and discovered that sensitizers were more likely than repressors to perceive the homographs as aggressive in content. However, repression-sensitization failed to correlate with homograph interpretation in a second study.

A related study was carried out by Haney (1973). Ambiguous sentences (e.g., The index finger was placed on the tray) were followed by two resolutions of the ambiguity (e.g., Finger: Pointing, Amputation), one of which was threatening and the other of which was neutral. The subjects were asked to select the interpretation that more closely approximated their own natural interpretation. Sensitizers selected significantly more threatening or negative interpretations than repressors. It is also of interest that Haney (1973) found with negative sentences that both repressors and sensitizers chose predominantly negative interpretations. These various findings led Haney to the following conclusion:

> While the presentation of blatantly negative stimuli has been a characteristic method of producing ego-threat and concomitant approach-avoidance behaviors in repressors and sensitizers, it appears that the utilization of ambiguous stimuli may, under some circumstances, be even more effectively discriminative. (p. 98)

Eysenck, MacLeod, and Mathews (1987) made use of homophones having a threatening or negative interpretation and a neutral interpretation (e.g., mourn, morn). The homophones (together with some nonhomophones) were presented auditorily, and subjects simply wrote down the first spelling of each word that occurred to them. The basic finding was that high-anxiety subjects were much more likely than low-anxiety subjects to select the threatening interpretations. The threatening interpretation for half of the homophones was related to physical health (e.g., die, dye), whereas for the remaining homophones it was related to social problems (e.g., guilt, gilt). It was anticipated that those who reported worrying relatively more about social than about physical health problems might select more social threat interpretations than physical health interpretations, whereas those who reported worrying relatively more about physical health than social problems might show the opposite tendency. In fact, the major type of worry reported did not predict the type of homophone that produced the greater number of threatening interpretations.

These findings can be interpreted by assuming that the initial automatic activation of both meanings of the homophones rapidly provides information concerning the threat value, and that a preattentive selective bias making use of this information explains the tendency of high-anxiety subjects to become aware of the threatening interpretations of ambiguous stimuli. However, there are other alternative explanations. In general, it has been clearly established that people tend to select the more familiar or frequently occurring interpretation of homophones. If, as seems likely, high-anxiety subjects have greater familiarity than low-anxiety subjects with the threatening interpretations of the homophones, then this differential familiarity could account for the findings. Another possibility that would be more consistent with the theoretical framework outlined earlier is that homophone interpretation was determined by the nature and strength of the relevant schemata and other cognitive structures in long-term memory.

Whatever the appropriate interpretation, there are important implications of the finding that high trait anxiety is associated with an enhanced probability of interpreting ambiguous stimuli in a threat-related fashion. This is, of course, consistent with the well-established finding that anxious people regard the environment as more threatening than nonanxious ones (Butler & Mathews, 1983). In addition, it appears that the cognitive system plays a major role in accounting for differences between high-anxiety and low-anxiety individuals. Presumably what happens is that the cognitive system determines how a stimulus is interpreted, and this then affects the subsequent involvement of other systems related to anxiety (e.g., the physiological; the behavioral).

There is an important theoretical assumption made by Byrne (1964) that deserves consideration at this point. According to Byrne (1964), extreme repressors and sensitizers are fundamentally alike in that they are very affected by threatening stimulation, differing primarily in the preferred strategy for responding to it. Those who are intermediate between repressors and sensitizers are allegedly less affected by threat, and can thus in some sense be regarded as healthier than repressors or sensitizers. Byrne (1964) discussed this issue with respect to a continuum ranging from strong avoidance reactions to threat at one end to powerful approach reactions to threat at the other end: "A curvilinear relationship should be found between an individual's position on this continuum and various indices of his maladjustment" (p. 212).

Byrne's (1964) theoretical position can be contrasted with the more conventional view (e.g., Eysenck, 1967) that there is a monotonic function relating susceptibility to anxiety neurosis and level of trait anxiety. There is scattered evidence of an underlying similarity between repressors and sensitizers. When repressors and sensitizers were shown a film called *It Didn't Have to Happen*, in which progressively more serious woodworking shop accidents are depicted, eye-movement data showed that repressors and sensitizers both engaged in more perceptual scanning than those intermediate on the repression-sensitization continuum. It may be that threat is more relevant and important to repressors and sensitizers than to those not clearly belonging to either group.

So far as maladjustment is concerned, the crucial group theoretically consists of repressors or low-anxiety individuals. Byrne (1964) argued that this group should be high in maladjustment, whereas Eysenck (1967) and others make the opposite prediction. An impressive attempt to clarify matters was made by Weinberger, Schwartz, and Davidson (1979). They proposed a compromise view, in which some individuals low in trait anxiety are genuinely free of anxiety, whereas others are susceptible to threat but try to handle it by adopting a repressive or avoidance strategy. In order to test this hypothesis, Weinberger et al. (1979) divided subjects low in trait anxiety into low anxious and repressors on the basis of their scores on the Marlowe-Crowne Social Desirability Scale. This scale appears to measure affect inhibition, defensiveness, and protection of self-esteem, and thus high scorers were assigned to the repressor category. On a moderately stressful task, there were large differences between repressors and low-anxious subjects. Although the repressors actually scored lower than the low anxious on trait anxiety, three separate physiological measures taken during the task (i.e., heart rate, spontaneous skin resistance responses, and forehead muscle tension) and three task-performance measures all indicated that the repressors were significantly more stressed than the low-anxious subjects.

In sum, there are a number of theoretically significant differences between individuals high and low in trait anxiety in terms of immediate reactions to threatening stimulation. These differences include a preattentive selective bias that directs processing resources towards or away from threat-related stimuli presented concurrently with neutral stimuli, and semantic interpretations of ambiguous stimuli having threatening and neutral interpretations. The preattentive selective bias operates only when two or more stimuli are presented concurrently, when there is a mixture of threatening and neutral stimuli, and when there is time for information concerning threat value to affect the subsequent allocation of processing resources. Such conditions are probably widespread in everyday life, but are not always found under laboratory conditions (e.g., perceptual defense studies).

In more general terms, the fact that high- and low-anxiety individuals differ systematically in their use of preattentive, attentional, and interpretative mechanisms demonstrates beyond peradventure that individual differences in trait anxiety cannot be understood unless the functioning of the cognitive system is examined. Many of these processing differences may depend to a greater or lesser extent on differences in underlying schemata, but this remains an article of faith rather than an established fact.

Cognitive-Task Performance

There has been considerable research interest over the years in the effects of trait anxiety and psychological stress (often in the form of failure feedback) on the performance of cognitively demanding tasks. While there are some exceptions, and the effects are sometimes surprisingly small, it is usually found that the combination of high trait anxiety and high psychological stress is associated with poorer performance than any other combination of high and low trait anxiety and high and low stress (see Eysenck, 1982, 1984a, for literature reviews).

When the effects of anxiety on two or more tasks are compared, it is usually found that anxiety interacts with task difficulty (defined in various ways). More specifically, the typical finding is that anxiety has a greater adverse effect on complex tasks than on easy ones (cf. Eysenck, 1982). For example, Mayer (1977) investigated the effects of trait anxiety on a number of relatively difficult or complex cognitive tasks (e.g., anagrams; water-jar problems) and of easy tasks (e.g., simple mathematical operations; visual search). High trait anxiety reduced the percentage of complex cognitive tasks solved correctly from 80 percent to a little over 40 percent. On the other hand, anxiety failed to have any effect on performance of the easy tasks.

From the perspective of contemporary cognitive psychology, differential effects of anxiety across a range of tasks can provide useful insights into the cognitive mechanisms most affected by anxiety. Eysenck (1979, 1982) argued that some understanding of the interaction between anxiety and task diffi- culty could be obtained with reference to the working memory model origi- nally formulated by Baddeley and Hitch (1974). Since the working memory system is crucially involved in the processing and transient storage of infor- mation, more difficult tasks make greater use than easy tasks of its resources. The most important component of working memory is the central executive, which is a modality-free system of limited capacity that resembles attention. The evidence (summarized by Eysenck, 1982) suggests that anxiety reduces the capacity of the central executive that is available for task performance, perhaps because task-irrelevant cognitive activities such as worry make use of some of its capacity in high-anxiety subjects. This reduced capacity in high anxiety would be expected to impair performance mainly when the task be- ing performed was demanding or difficult, which thus accounts for the inter- action between anxiety and task difficulty. However, it must be admitted that relatively little is known of the functioning of the central executive. There have been no successful attempts to measure its allegedly limited capacity, and its modality-free status cannot be said to have been established.

There are various limitations associated with most of the empirical re- search in which the effects of trait anxiety on tasks varying in difficulty level have been compared. In many studies, the easy and difficult tasks have differed in a number of ways from each other, so that it is virtually impossible to acount for any differences in the effects of trait anxiety on them. There are still likely to be interpretative problems even when the tasks are carefully selected to be as comparable as possible. Eysenck (1985) illustrated the problems by taking as an example an 'easy' task that requires processes a, b, and c, and a 'difficult' task that makes use of processes a, b, c, and d. If there are any differential effects of anxiety on these tasks, then there would be a natural tendency to attribute this differential effect en- tirely to the effects of anxiety on process d. However, such a conclusion is warranted only if it is assumed that processes a, b, and c are all unaffected by the introduction of the additional process d, and that assumption will frequently be erroneous. A related limitation is that data are usually avail- able only for overall task performance, despite the fact that any difficult or complex task is likely to comprise a number of different components or processes. As a consequence, it is impossible to identify unequivocally the process or processes affected by anxiety.

What is required in order to increase our understanding of the effects of trait anxiety on task performance? Hockey, MacLean, and Hamilton (1981) pointed out in a different context the importance of using tasks where the microstructure is clear, and where it is possible to measure each component of task performance separately. They used a letter-transformation task to illustrate their point. This task involves transforming between one and four letters by moving a specified distance through the alphabet, and then producing the results of the transformation as the response when all of the letters have been transformed. Thus, for example, the answer to the four-letter problem 'FDRE + 4' is 'JHVI'. After practice the error rates are relatively low, so that the main emphasis is on speed of performance.

According to Hockey et al. (1981), the microstructure of the letter-transformation task is as follows. There are three sequential processing stages involved in the processing of each letter: (1) access to long-term memory to locate the appropriate starting place in the alphabet; (2) letter transformation; and (3) rehearsal and storage of the accumulating answer. Thus, for four-letter problems there are 12 processing stages in all, and Hockey et al. (1981) provided methods for assessing the duration of each stage.

Eysenck (1985) applied these ideas to trait anxiety in two experiments. In the first experiment, there was a highly significant interaction between trait anxiety and the number of letters in the problem; this was consistent with other anxiety × task difficulty interactions, in that anxiety impaired (i.e., slowed down) performance only when three or four letters required transformation. In the second experiment, an attempt was made to clarify the effects of anxiety on four-letter problems by performing a componential analysis. This analysis revealed that the detrimental effects of anxiety on speed of performance of four-letter problems were limited to only three of the 12 processing stages involved: these were the rehearsal and storage stage for the second, third, and fourth letters. Obviously, this fine-grain analysis provides much more information about the effects of anxiety on the letter-transformation task than is available simply from knowledge of overall solution times.

It is possible to make some theoretical sense of these findings by reference to Eysenck's (1979) theory of anxiety, according to which anxiety disrupts the functioning of working memory, and especially the central executive component. The demands on working memory in terms of concurrent processing and transient storage increase systematically from letter to letter, and thus adverse effects of anxiety should be most pronounced towards the end of the problem. However, this does not explain why it is rehearsal and storage rather than access to long-term memory or transformation that is affected by anxiety. Eysenck (1985) speculated that accessing long-term memory may be unaffected because it is a relatively 'automatic' process, and the transformation process may be unaffected because it primarily requires use of the articulatory loop or rehearsal component of working memory. In contrast, rehearsal and storage make greater demands on the attentional resources of the central executive, and it is for this reason that this stage is affected by anxiety.

Eysenck (1979, 1982) argued that measures of cognitive-task performance often fail to reflect accurately the effects of anxiety on the cognitive system. He distinguished between efficiency and effectiveness. However, the meanings he gave to those terms were the opposite of the conventional ones, and here we will use them in their customary sense. Performance effectiveness thus refers to the quality of performance, and is what is usually measured in studies of task performance (e.g., percentage correct, time taken). Processing efficiency refers to the relationship between the effectiveness of task performance and the effort or processing resources invested to produce that level of performance. In essence, Eysenck (1979, 1982) argued that anxiety is more likely to affect processing efficiency than performance effectiveness. The reason for this is that adverse effects of anxiety on processing efficiency are often camouflaged by compensatory activities on the part of the anxious individual to prevent task performance from suffering.

How can this hypothesis be tested? The most direct method is to consider those situations in which anxiety does not affect performance effectiveness. While the usual conclusion is that anxiety has had no effect at all, Eysenck's hypothesis suggests that there might often be adverse effects of anxiety on processing efficiency. The evidence is reviewed in detail by Eysenck and Eysenck (1985), and will be mentioned only briefly here. Broadly speaking, there is considerable support for the hypothesis. Even when anxiety has no effect on task performance, high-anxiety individuals report significantly greater self-reported perceived effort than low-anxiety individuals (Dornic, 1977, 1980). If high-anxiety subjects invest more processing resources than low-anxiety subjects in main task performance, then they will have less spare processing capacity. When spare processing capacity has been assessed by using a subsidiary task, this prediction has been confirmed (Calvo, 1982; Eysenck, unpublished; Hamilton, 1978). A third line of research combines behavioral and physiological evidence. Weinberg and Hunt (1976) and Weinberg (1978) discovered that high-anxiety and low-anxiety subjects did not differ in their performance on a throwing task, but there were substantial differences in electromyography as a function of anxiety. As Weinberg and Hunt (1976) concluded, "High-anxious subjects were using more energy than necessary, and expending it over longer periods of time, than were low-anxious subjects" (p. 223).

An interesting alternative method of testing the hypothesis in issue was adopted by Calvo (1985). If subjects high in trait anxiety are typically investing more of their resources in task performance than subjects low in trait anxiety, then they would be less able to respond to incentive by increased effort. This is precisely what Calvo (1985) found. There was an interaction between trait anxiety and incentive conditions on an inductive non-verbal reasoning test, in which only those low in anxiety benefitted from the introduction of monetary incentive.

In sum, the emphasis in this section has been on attempts to specify as precisely as possible the cognitive processes and mechanisms affected by anxiety. While some progress has been made in this direction, the fact that performance effectiveness often camouflages the adverse effects of anxiety on processing efficiency means that both effectiveness and efficiency must be assessed.

The difficulties encountered by high-anxiety individuals can be seen clearly in the context of Schönpflug's (1983) claim that the amount of stress experienced depends on the relationship between the demands imposed by problems or tasks and an individual's capacities or abilities. Maximal stress is experienced when demands marginally exceed capacities; that is to say, stress occurs as a consequence of an individual being unable to cope with the demands placed upon him or her. As we have seen, the high-anxiety individual may experience greater demands than the low-anxiety individual, because of the need to process task-irrelevant as well as task-relevant information. At the same time, the capacity for cognitive functioning appears to be reduced, whether due to lowered central executive capacity or to some other limitation. Thus, high-anxiety individuals are more likely than low-anxiety individuals to be unable to cope and so to experience stress, especially when relatively demanding tasks need to be performed.

In real-world situations, there may be a tendency for a vicious circle to develop. The nature of this vicious circle is that an anxious person who initially fails to cope with a task experiences stress as a result, and the increase in stress level reduces the chances of coping with the task subsequently.

SUMMARY

The main thrust of the argument presented in this chapter is that theories of trait anxiety should consider both the physiological and cognitive systems involved. In this connection, an attempt was made to assess the contributions made by each system towards an understanding of anxiety. Particular attention was paid to the cognitive system, and to the identification of salient differences in cognitive functioning between those high and low in trait anxiety. Several such differences have now been identified. The ultimate hope is that progress towards a more complete account of these cognitive differences should have implications for the treatment of anxiety neurosis by means of cognitive therapy.

References

Baddeley, A. D., & Hitch, G. (1974). Working memory. In G. H. Bower (Ed.), *The psychology of learning and motivation* (Vol. 8). London: Academic.

Bitterman, M. E., & Kniffin, C. W. (1953). Manifest anxiety and "perceptual defense." *Journal of Abnormal and Social Psychology, 48*, 248–252.

Blaylock, B. A. H. (1963). *Repression-sensitization, word association responses, and incidental recall.* Unpublished Master's Thesis, University of Texas, Austin.

Butler, G., & Mathews, A. (1983). Cognitive processes in anxiety. *Advances in Behavior Research & Therapy, 5,* 51–62.

Byrne, D. (1964). Repression-sensitization as a dimension of personality. In B. A. Maher (Ed.), *Progress in experimental personality research.* New York: Academic.

Calvo, M. G. (1982). *Analisis cognitivo de la ansiedad y el redimiento en situaciones evaluativas.* Unpublished doctoral dissertation, University of Salamanca, Spain.

Calvo, M. G. (1985). Effort, aversive representations and performance in test anxiety. *Personality and Individual Differences, 6,* 563–571.

Carroll, D. (1972). Repression-sensitization and duration of visual attention. *Perceptual and Motor Skills, 34,* 949–950.

Cattell, R. B., Eber, H. W., & Tatsouka, M. M. (1970). *Handbook for the sixteen personality factor questionnaire (16 P.F.).* Champaign, IL: Institute for Personality and Ability Testing.

Conley, J. J. (1984). The hierarchy of consistency: A review and model of longitudinal findings on adult individual differences in intelligence, personality and self-opinion. *Personality and Individual Differences, 5,* 11–25.

Costa, P. T., & McCrae, R. R. (1980). Influence of extraversion and neuroticism on subjective well-being: Happy and unhappy people. *Journal of Personality and Social Psychology, 38,* 668–678.

Craske, M. G., & Craig, K. D. (1984). Musical performance anxiety: The three-systems model and self-efficacy theory. *Behaviour Research and Therapy, 22,* 267–280.

Deffenbacher, J. L. (1978). Worry, emotionality, and task-generated interference in test anxiety: An empirical test of attentional theory. *Journal of Educational Psychology, 70,* 248–254.

Dixon, N. F. (1981). *Preconscious processing.* Chichester: Wiley.

Donat, D. C. (1983). Predicting state anxiety: A comparison of multidimensional and unidimensional trait approaches. *Journal of Research in Personality, 17,* 256–262.

Dornic, S. (1977). Mental load, effort, and individual differences. *Reports of the Department of Psychology, University of Stockholm,* No. 509.

Dornic, S. (1980). Efficiency vs. effectiveness in mental work: The differential effect of stress. *Reports of the Department of Psychology, University of Stockholm,* No. 568.

Endler, N. S., & Edwards, J. (1982). Stress and personality. In L. Goldberger and S. Breznitz (Eds.), *Handbook of stress: theoretical and clinical aspects.* London: Free Press.

Endler, N. S., Magnusson, D., Ekehammar, B., & Okada, M. (1976). The multidimensionality of state and trait anxiety. *Scandinavian Journal of Psychology, 17,* 81–96.

Eysenck, H. J. (1967). *The biological basis of personality.* Springfield, IL: Thomas.

Eysenck, H. J., & Eysenck, M. W. (1981). *Mindwatching.* London: Joseph.

Eysenck, H. J., & Eysenck, M. W. (1985). *Personality and individual differences.* New York: Plenum.

Eysenck, M. W. (1979). Anxiety, learning, and memory: A reconceptualization. *Journal of Research in Personality, 13,* 363–385.

Eysenck, M. W. (1982). *Attention and arousal: cognition and performance.* Berlin: Springer.

Eysenck, M. W. (1984a). *A handbook of cognitive psychology.* London: Erlbaum.

Eysenck, M. W. (1984b). Anxiety and the worry process. *Bulletin of the Psychonomic Society, 22,* 545–548.

Eysenck, M. W. (1985). Anxiety and cognitive-task performance. *Personality and Individual Differences, 6,* 579–586.

Eysenck, M. W., MacLeod, C., & Mathews, A. (1987). Cognitive functioning and anxiety. *Psychological Research, 49,* 189–195.

Floderus-Myrhed, B., Pedersen, N., & Rasmusson, I. (1980). Assessment of heritability for personality based on a short form of the Eysenck Personality Inventory. *Behavior Genetics, 10,* 153–162.

Gray, J. A. (1981). A critique of Eysenck's theory of personality. In H. J. Eysenck (Ed.), *A model for personality.* Berlin: Springer.

Greenbaum, M. (1956). Manifest anxiety and tachistoscopic recognition of facial photographs. *Perceptual and Motor Skills, 6,* 245–248.

Hall, C. A. (1977). *Differential relationships of pleasure and distress with depression and anxiety over a past, present and future time framework.* Unpublished doctoral dissertation, University of Minnesota.

Hamilton, V. (1978). *The cognitive analysis of personality related to information-processing deficits with stress and anxiety.* Paper presented at the British Psychological Society meeting, London.

Hamilton, V. (1983). *The cognitive structures and processes of human motivation and personality.* Chichester: Wiley.

Haney, J. N. (1973). Approach-avoidance reactions by repressors and sensitizers to ambiguity in a structured free-association task. *Psychological Reports, 33,* 97–98.

Hockey, R., MacLean, A., & Hamilton, P. (1981). State changes and the temporal patterning of component resources. In J. Long and A. Baddeley (Eds.), *Attention and Performance* (Vol. 9). Hillsdale, NJ: Erlbaum.

Hodges, W. F. (1968). Effects of ego threat and threat of pain on state anxiety. *Journal of Personality and Social Psychology, 8,* 364–372.

Hundleby, J. D., & Connor, W. H. (1968). Interrelationships between personality inventories: The 16 P.F., the MMPI, and the MPI. *Journal of Consulting and Clinical Psychology, 32.*

Kendall, P. C. (1978). Anxiety: States, traits—situations? *Journal of Consulting and Clinical Psychology, 46,* 280–287.

Lang, P. (1971). The application of psychophysiological methods to the study of psychotherapy and behavior modification. In A. Bergin & S. Garfield (Eds.), *Handbook of psychotherapy and behavior change.* New York: Wiley.

Lazarus, R. S. (1981). The stress and coping paradigm. In C. Eisdorfer, D. Cohen, A. Kleinman, & P. Maxim (Eds.), *Theoretical Bases for Psychopathology.* New York: Spectrum.

Lazarus, R. S., & Alfert, E. (1964). The short-circuiting of threat by experimentally altering cognitive appraisal. *Journal of Abnormal and Social Psychology, 69,* 194–205.

Lewinsohn, P. M., Berquist, W. H., & Brelje, T. (1972). The repression-sensitization dimension and emotional response to stimuli. *Psychological Reports, 31,* 707–716.

MacLeod, C., Mathews, A., & Tata, P. (1986). Attentional bias in emotional disorders. *Journal of Abnormal Psychology, 95,* 15–20.

Mathews, A., & MacLeod, C. (1986). Discrimination of threat cues without awareness in anxiety state. *Journal of Abnormal Psychology, 95,* 1–8.

Mayer, R. E. (1977). Problem-solving performance with task overload: Effects of self-pacing and trait anxiety. *Bulletin of the Psychonomic Society, 9,* 282–286.

McKeon, J., Roa, B., & Mann, A. (1984). Life events and personality traits in obsessive-compulsive neurosis. *British Journal of Psychiatry, 144,* 185–189.

Neufeld, R. W. J. (1975). Effect of cognitive appraisal on d' and response bias to experimental stress. *Journal of Personality and Social Psychology, 31,* 735–743.

Saville, P., & Blinkhorn, S. (1981). Reliability, homogeneity and the construct validity of Cattell's 16 P.F. *Personality and Individual Differences, 2,* 325–333.

Schönpflug, W. (1983). Coping efficiency and situational demands. In R. Hockey (Ed.), *Stress and fatigue in human performance.* Chichester: Wiley.

Shields, J. (1962). *Monozygotic twins.* Oxford: Oxford University Press.

Simpson, G. B. (1984). Lexical ambiguity and its role in models of word recognition. *Psychological Bulletin, 96,* 316–340.

Slater, E. (1943). The neurotic constitution. *Journal of Neurology, Neurosurgery, and Psychiatry, 6,* 1.

Spielberger, C. D., Gorsuch, R., & Lushene, R. (1970). *The state-trait anxiety inventory (STAI) test manual form X.*

Tellegen, A. (1985). Structures of mood and personality and their relevance to assessing anxiety, with an emphasis on self-report. In A. H. Tuma and J. Maser (Eds.), *Anxiety and the anxiety disorders.* London: Erlbaum.

Tempone, V. J. (1962). Extension of the repression-sensitization hypothesis to success and failure experience. *Psychological Reports, 15,* 39–45.

Ullmann, L. P. (1962). An empirically derived MMPI scale which measures facilitation-inhibition of recognition of threatening stimuli. *Journal of Clinical Psychology, 18,* 127–132.

Van Egeren, L. (1968). Repression and sensitization: Sensitivity and recognition criteria. *Journal of Experimental Research in Personality, 3,* 1–8.

Wagstaff, G. F. (1974). The effects of repression-sensitization on a brightness scaling measure of perceptual defense. *British Jorunal of Psychology, 65,* 395–401.

Watson, D., & Clark, L. A. (1984). Negative affectivity: The disposition to experience aversive emotional states. *Psychological Bulletin, 96,* 465–490.

Weinberg, R. S. (1978). The effects of success and failure on the patterning of neuromuscular energy. *Journal of Motor Behavior, 10,* 53–61.

Weinberg, R. S., & Hunt, V. (1976). The interrelationships between anxiety, motor performance, and electromyography. *Journal of Motor Behavior, 8,* 219–224.

Weinberger, D. A., Schwartz, G. E., & Davidson, R. J. (1979). Low-anxious, high-anxious, and repressive coping styles: Psychometric patterns and behavioral and physiological responses to stress. *Journal of Abnormal Psychology, 88,* 369–380.

Zevon, M. A., & Tellegen, A. (1982). The structure of mood change: An idiographic/nomothetic analysis. *Journal of Personality and Social Psychology, 43,* 111–122.

5

Laboratory Research on Defense Mechanisms

DAVID S. HOLMES
KEVIN D. McCAUL

Defense mechanisms play an important role in our thinking about personality, the control of stress, and psychopathology. For example, we frequently hear comments such as, "His behavior is the result of *repressed* desires," "She is *projecting* her problems onto others," and "He is *denying* the implications of his illness." In view of the important role defense mechanisms play in our theorizing about personality, it is essential that their existence and function be tested experimentally. For the most part, this task has fallen to laboratory researchers.

A complete examination of the laboratory research on defenses is beyond the scope of this chapter. We elected to consider only the research on *repression, projection,* and *suppression* (avoidant thinking).[1] These defenses were selected because (1) they are very basic to much of the theorizing

---

[1] David Holmes took responsibility for the discussions of repression and projection, and Kevin McCaul developed the material on suppression.

about personality and psychopathology, (2) research on them has posed some intriguing methodological problems, (3) the results that have been generated are particularly interesting and sometimes controversial, and (4) they are defenses on which we have worked actively. In discussing these defenses, we will limit ourselves to asking two questions about each: *Does the defense in question actually exist,* and if it does, *does it actually reduce stress?* Even with these limitations, space considerations preclude an exhaustive coverage. With this material as background, the reader might go on to works by other authors in the area (e.g., Lazarus & Folkman, 1984).

REPRESSION

We will begin with a discussion of repression because from some theoretical standpoints it is the most important defense mechanism. Indeed, Freud (1914/1957a) called repression "the cornerstone on which the whole structure of psychoanalysis rests (p. 16)." Before discussing the research, four points concerning the concept of repression should be noted. These points are important because they have (or should have) guided the laboratory procedures that were used to test the concept. First, repression is *motivated selective forgetting.* More specifically, repression is used to eliminate from consciousness those memories or related associations that cause the individual "pain" (Freud, 1915/1957b). Second, unlike suppression with which it is sometimes confused, repression is *not under voluntary control.* Third, repressed material is not lost but instead is *stored in the unconscious* and can be returned to consciousness if the anxiety or pain that is associated with the memory is removed (Freud, 1911/1957c). Fourth and finally, there are *two kinds of repression.* On the one hand, there is what Freud (1915/1957c) called "repression proper" or "after expulsion." This type of repression occurs when a person consciously recognizes something as threatening and then represses the thought to avoid the stress. On the other hand, there is "primary repression" in which threatening material is relegated to the unconscious before it is consciously recognized as stressful. With those points clarified, we can go on to consider the ways in which repression has been studied in the laboratory.

Differential Recall of Pleasant and Unpleasant Experiences

In some of the earliest research on repression, investigators had subjects make lists of their pleasant and unpleasant experiences. Later the subjects were asked unexpectedly to recall the experiences that they had recorded. The investigators then compared the two lists to determine whether there had been a greater forgetting of pleasant or unpleasant experiences. In most studies, it was found that unpleasant experiences were more likely to be forgotten, and those findings were taken as evidence for repression (e.g., Jersild, 1931; Meltzer, 1931; Stagner, 1931).

In contrast to the data indicating that it is the *type* of affect (pleasantness vs. unpleasantness) that determines recall, there was another body of data suggesting that it was the *intensity* of affect that determined recall (e.g., Menzies, 1936; Waters & Leeper, 1936). In this research, it was found that emotionally intense experiences were more likely to be recalled than less intense experiences regardless of whether they were pleasant or unpleasant. These findings were used to challenge the concept of repression.

In an attempt to reconcile these two bodies of conflicting data and develop a more comprehensive explanation for the differential recall of different types of experiences, Holmes proposed that: (1) the recall of experiences is determined by the intensity of the affect associated with the experiences *at the time of recall*, (2) the *intensity of the affect associated with the experiences declines over time* (between the experience and the recall), and (3) the *affect associated with unpleasant experiences is more likely to decline or will decline faster than the affect associated with pleasant experiences* (Holmes, 1970). To test that possibility, college students were first asked to keep a diary of their pleasant and unpleasant experiences for seven days and to score each experience for pleasantness-unpleasantness on a nine-point scale. Each experience was recorded on a card, and the affect score for the experience was recorded on the back of the card. A week later the subjects were unexpectedly asked to write down all of the experiences they had recorded on their diary cards. When that was completed, the subjects were given their diary cards and asked to read each experience and to give the experience a score on a nine-point scale in terms of how pleasant-unpleasant it was *at that time*. (Note that the original scores for affect were on the backs of the cards and thus could not influence the subjects' second scoring.) With this procedure, it was possible to measure differential recall and to measure changes in affect for pleasant and unpleasant experiences that were and were not recalled. The results indicated that (1) more initially pleasant than unpleasant experiences were recalled, (2) more initially intense than less intense experiences were recalled, (3) experiences that declined in affective intensity were less likely to be recalled than experiences that remained constant in affective intensity, and most importantly, (4) *unpleasant experiences showed greater declines in affective intensity than pleasant experiences.* These results account for all of the previous findings and indicate that rather than being caused by repression, reduced recall of unpleasant experiences is due to a reduced affective intensity associated with the unpleasant experiences.

One caveat concerning these results must be noted. This investigation did not indicate *why* there were greater declines in the affective intensity associated with unpleasant than pleasant experiences. It could be argued that the declines were due to denial or repression of the unpleasant affect, thus returning the explanation for the forgetting to a dynamic level. There are, however, two alternative (and perhaps better) explanations for the decline in intensity of unpleasant experiences. First, given the lapse of time between the occurrence and the recall, the subject may discover that the experience did not result in the dire consequences that were expected (failing a test in French is not the end of the world!) or the subject may take some remediative action that alters the nature of the experience (studying harder may improve future performance in French.) The absence of dire consequences or remediative action could serve to reduce the original negativity of the experience and in turn reduce the likelihood of its recall. The second explanation is based on the findings that: (1) subjects think more about intense experiences than neutral experiences (D'Zurilla, 1965; Menzies, 1936; Waters & Leeper, 1935) and (2) repeated exposure results in more positive attitudes toward stimuli (Zajonc, 1968). It then may be that the attention given to unpleasant experiences results in their becoming less unpleasant (and thereby less intense).

It might also be noted that if the decline in affect or reduction in recall of unpleasant experiences was indeed due to repression, it would be expected that individual differences in personality would be associated with the changes in affect/recall (e.g., it would be expected that "hysterics" would be more likely to show the effect than "nonhysterics"). However, an extensive investigation of the influence of individual differences on the differential recall of pleasant and unpleasant experiences failed to reveal any of the effects that would be expected on the basis of repression (Holmes, 1973). It appears that the differential recall of pleasant and unpleasant experiences cannot be used to support the concept of repression.

Differential Recall of Completed and Incompleted Tasks

A second approach to studying repression involved having subjects work on a series of tasks that were constructed so that some could be completed whereas others could not. Later the subjects were tested for their recall of the completed and incompleted tasks. If incompletions are interpreted by subjects as failures (i.e., ego threats), it might be expected that incompletions would be more likely to be repressed and recalled less well than completions.

Paradoxically, this line of research originally was begun to test the Gestalt notion that incompletions create "tension systems" and thus will be *more* likely to be recalled (Butterfield, 1964; Lewin, 1940; Prentice, 1944). In the early tests of that prediction, it was generally found that subjects recalled more incompletions than completions, but there were notable exceptions. These exceptions were sometimes explained by suggesting that embarrassment over failure to complete a task led the subject to repress the recall of the task (Lewis & Franklin, 1944; Zeigarnik, 1927). Experimenters then seized on the completed/incompleted task procedure as a technique for manipulating ego threat and testing for repression, and there followed a long series of such experiments (Eriksen, 1952a, 1952b; Forest, 1959; Gilmore, 1954;

Glixman, 1948; Green, 1963; Rosenzweig, 1943; Rosenzweig & Mason, 1934; Sanford & Risser, 1948; Smock, 1957; Tudor & Holmes, 1973). In the six most methodologically refined experiments in this group, subjects participated under conditions of high stress (tasks were presented as an intelligence test) and low stress (no importance was attached to the tasks). It was predicted that under high stress fewer incompletions than completions would be recalled (i.e., incompletions would be repressed because they were threatening) whereas under low stress there would not be a difference in the recall of incompletions and completions. This was found to be the case in all six of the experiments (Eriksen, 1952a, 1952b; Gilmore, 1954; Glixman, 1948; Lewis & Franklin, 1944; Smock, 1957; Tudor & Holmes, 1973), thus apparently providing considerable evidence for the existence of repression.

Because individual differences in personality might influence the degree to which subjects used repression, a variety of other investigations were conducted to examine the interaction between the recall of completions versus incompletions and personality factors such as ego-strength, hysteria, hypnotizability, and need for success (Alper, 1946, 1948, 1957; Atkinson, 1953; Atkinson & Raphelson, 1956; Caron & Wallach, 1957, 1959; Coopersmith, 1960; Eriksen, 1954; Jourard, 1954; Petrie, 1948; Rosenzweig & Sarason, 1942; Tamkin, 1957; Tudor & Holmes, 1973; Weiner, 1965; Weiner, Johnson, & Mehrabian, 1968). The only consistent finding in this line of research was that subjects with high need for achievement recalled more incompletions under high stress than low stress. It appears that when subjects were confronted with unsolvable problems in ego-involving situations, the high need for success subjects persisted in working on or thinking about the problems rather than repressing them (Coopersmith, 1960; Weiner, 1965). These findings based on individual differences fail to provide support for the concept of repression.

Although the general research on the differential recall of completed and incompleted tasks provides some support for the concept of repression, there is a very serious problem with the paradigm that might drastically influence the conclusions to be drawn from the results. Specifically, the differences in the recall of completed and incompleted tasks may not be due to differences in the degree to which the tasks were forgotten (repressed), but instead the differences may be due to differences in the degree to which they were *originally learned*. In other words, in these experiments differential learning may have been misinterpreted as differential forgetting. Fortunately, there are some data on the question of differential learning versus forgetting.

In one experiment (Caron & Wallach, 1957), the subjects in a "continued stress" group were exposed to the completed and incompleted tasks under stress and then tested for recall under stress as had been done in most of the research. On the other hand, the subjects in a "relief" group were exposed to the tasks under stress, *then debriefed* (i.e., the hoax was revealed and therefore the stress was eliminated), and then the subjects were tested for recall. If recall was influenced by repression, the continued stress group should recall fewer incompletions than the relief group because the anxiety had been eliminated in the relief group and therefore the subjects in that group would not have a reason to repress. On the other hand, if recall was a function of original learning, no differences in the recall of incompletions would be expected between the groups because the conditions under which they had learned the materials were identical. The results supported the latter prediction, and the authors concluded that "recall tendencies in the present study are due to a *selective learning* rather than a selective remembering mechanism" (emphasis added; Caron & Wallach, 1957, p. 378). Similar results were produced in my laboratory (Holmes, 1973). It appears then that what originally looked like repression was in fact differential learning, and thus we must look elsewhere for evidence for repression.

Introduction and Recall of Ego Threat

A third approach to studying repression in the laboratory involves two experimental manipulations, one to induce ego threat and provoke repression, and a second to eliminate the ego threat and provide an opportunity for the repressed material to return to consciousness (the "return of the repressed"). These experiments are also an improvement over the previous ones in that procedures were used to insure that the material that was to be "repressed" was equally learned by both experimental and control subjects prior to the experimental manipulation of threat.

In these experiments, subjects in the experimental and control conditions were first tested for their ability to recall a set of neutral materials (nonsense syllables, words, etc.). This was done to make sure that the subjects actually knew the materials for which recall would be tested later. The subjects in the experimental condition were then exposed to an "ego threat" (failure, negative personality feedback, etc.). The threat was directly related to the materials to be recalled (e.g., the materials may have been part of a test that the subject was led to fail) or the threat occurred in the same situation in which the recall materials had been presented. The major point was that the anxiety generated by the ego threat became associated with the neutral materials causing the neutral materials to be painful or anxiety provoking. After the experimental manipulation of threat, the subjects were tested for recall. It was typically found that subjects in the ego-threat condition recalled fewer of the previously neutral materials than subjects in the control condition, a finding that was interpreted as evidence for repression.

The second experimental manipulation involved eliminating the stress. Specifically, subjects in the threat condition were exposed to success (good performance on a test, positive personality feedback) or they were simply debriefed about the deception that was used to induce the stress. All of the subjects were then tested again for their recall of the material. Typically, recall improved after the stress was eliminated ("return of the repressed") and there were then no longer differences in the recall between the groups. This patterning of findings has been reported in numerous experiments, and in many cases it was concluded that the findings provided evidence for repression and the return of the repressed (Aborn, 1953; D'Zurilla, 1965; Flavell, 1955; Holmes, 1972; Holmes & Schallow, 1969; Merrill, 1954; Penn, 1964; Truax, 1957; Zeller, 1950, Exp I & II; Zeller, 1951).

There is a serious interpretative problem with this research. Although the *performance* of the subjects in these experiments is consistent with what would be expected on the basis of repression, most of these experiments did not offer evidence concerning the *process* that was responsible for the performance. It was assumed that repression was the process, but this might not necessarily be the case. A major competing hypothesis is that the decrease in recall performance was due to the *interfering effects of stress* (Russell, 1952; Truax, 1957). As early as 1952, it was pointed out that, "it is possible also that failure situations may produce a drive state (frustration, anxiety, or insecurity) which affects behavior in this case through the elicitation of *competing* responses (emphasis added; Russell, 1952, p. 214)." Consistent with this possibility, postexperimental interviews revealed that subjects in the threat condition thought more about the threat to which they had been exposed than subjects in the no-threat condition thought about the neutral experience to which they had been exposed (D'Zurilla, 1965). This is certainly in sharp contrast to what would be expected on the basis of repression. It might be that thinking about the stress interfered with the recall performance.

To test the hypothesis that the decreases in recall following stress were due to interference rather than repression, two experiments were conducted in which subjects were exposed to ego-threatening, interfering, or neutral conditions (Holmes, 1972; Holmes & Schallow, 1969). In one experiment, the subjects first had their recall tested for a group of nouns. They then took a "multiple choice Rorschach test" in which the words from the recall list were the response alternatives. During the test, the subjects in an *ego-threat* condition received bogus feedback indicating that 6 of their 10 responses were signs of serious pathology. Subjects in an *interference* condition received bogus feedback that their responses indicated that they were very creative and showed signs of leadership (i.e., something to think about that was not threatening). Finally, subjects in a control condition received neutral personality feedback (Holmes, 1972). After taking the bogus test, the subjects were again tested for their recall of the words. Finally, the subjects were debriefed concerning the deception and then their recall for the words was tested again. The results indicated that after the threat/interference manipulation, the subjects in the threat and interference conditions showed comparable levels of recall that were poorer than that of the subjects in the control condition. After being debriefed concerning the deception, the subjects in all of the conditions showed comparable levels of recall. These results are presented in Figure 5.1. From

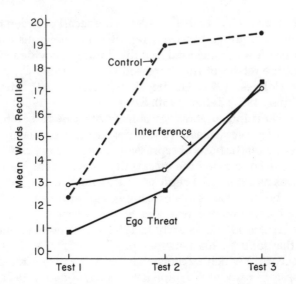

FIGURE 5.1.   Patterns of recall under three experimental conditions.

these results it was concluded that decreased recall following stress was due to interference rather than to repression.

It could be argued, of course, that the comparable patterns of recall that were found in the ego-threat and interference conditions were due to different processes. Specifically, it is possible that repression was operating in the ego-threat condition, whereas interference was operating in the interference condition. Although it is impossible to demonstrate conclusively that identical processes were operating in the two conditions, some suggestive data have been offered. Specifically, if repression were operating, it would be expected that the decrease in recall would be greater for those stimulus words that were directly associated with the threat (words used as responses that led to negative feedback) than for words that were not directly associated with the threat. That was not found to be the case; words not associated with the threat were just as likely to be forgotten as words that were associated with the threat. That effect could be accounted for better by interference than by repression (Holmes, 1972).

Individual Differences and the Search for Repression

In studying repression, some investigators have devised scales or other psychometric techniques for identifying "repressors," and then they studied the recall patterns of those persons. The most notable attempt in this area was the development of the *Repression-Sensitization Scale* (*R-S* scale; Byrne, Barry, & Nelson, 1963) that spawned hundreds of studies. The *R-S* scale is made up of items from the MMPI that ask about the presence of symptoms. Persons who acknowledge a high number of symptoms are said to be sensitizers, whereas persons who do not acknowledge many symptoms are said to be repressors. Unfortunately, there is a very serious logical problem with this approach in that there is no way to distinguish between persons who actually have symptoms and *do not* report them (repressors or, more likely, deniers) and persons who do not have any symptoms and therefore *cannot* report them (nonrepressors). In other words, *individuals without symptoms are falsely classified as repressors.* Obviously, this scale cannot be used to support the notion that some individuals are more likely to use repression than others, and its use by researchers who did not consider the logic of the test has served only to add irrelevant data and erroneous conclusions to this body of literature.

A more recent but equally erroneous approach to identifying repressors involved using measures of social desirability and anxiety (Davis & Schwartz, 1987; Weinberger, Schwartz, & Davidson, 1979). In these studies, subjects who had high scores on the Marlowe-Crowne Social Desirability scale and low scores on the Taylor Manifest Anxiety Scale were identified as "repressors." It was found that these subjects were less likely than other subjects to report threatening or unpleasant events. The problem here is that persons who are high on social desirability may be upset by and less willing to report undesirable events, but that does not mean *that they are not aware of them.* Indeed, the investigators reported that although "repressors" did not report undesirable events, they showed higher physiological arousal than other subjects. If they had actually repressed the material and were unaware of it, they would not have been aroused. Overall then, this research does not provide evidence for the existence of repression.

Perceptual Defense

Thus far, the discussion has been focused on "repression proper" or "after expulsion," but before concluding some brief attention should be given to "primary repression." Theoretically, with primary repression the threatening materials are relegated to the unconscious *before the person even becomes aware of their existence.* In studying primary repression, investigators have generally sought to determine whether subjects were less likely to *perceive* threatening than nonthreatening material ("perceptual defense;" see review by Eriksen & Pierce, 1968). For example, threatening and nonthreatening words were flashed on a screen for very short periods of time, and it was the subjects' task to read the words. In most of the early research, it was found that the threatening words had to be on the screen for longer periods of time than nonthreatening words before the subjects were able to read them, and it was therefore concluded that the subjects were defending against (repressing) the recognition of the threatening words by simply not seeing them. Unfortunately, subsequent research indicated that the differences in the time required for recognition of the two types of words was due to factors other than repression. For example, it turned out that the threatening words were less familiar than the nonthreatening words, and familiarity influences recognition. It was also found that subjects were less willing to say the threatening ("dirty") words until they were absolutely sure that it was those words that were being flashed, and that hesitancy rather than lack of recognition influenced their reporting of words. When familiarity was equated across the two types of words, and when social constraints were eliminated from the situation, the perceptual defense or repression effect disappeared.

About 10 years ago, interest in perceptual defense was revived (Erdelyi, 1974; Erdelyi & Goldberg, 1979). Specifically, a variety of interesting cognitive theories were developed to explain primary repression or perceptual defense. The problem, however, is that the investigators provided explanations for the phenomenon, but they did not provide controlled evidence that the phenomenon existed. Instead, they relied on anecdotal clinical evidence. Despite the lapse of over 10 years, that situation has not changed, and therefore we are still without firm evidence supporting the existence of primary repression.

Conclusions Concerning Repression Based on Laboratory Research

There is no consistent laboratory evidence to support the hypotheses derived from the theory of repression. The lack of evidence is especially striking in view of the large amount of research that has been conducted on the topic over the past 50 years. Given the amount of research, it is surprising that some evidence was not found simply on the basis of chance.

It is possible to dismiss all of the laboratory research as irrelevant for one reason or another; the procedures were "contrived," the stresses were not great enough, the stresses were not relevant, and so forth. In that regard, it is interesting to note that in 1934 when Rosenzweig wrote to Freud about his laboratory research supporting the concept of repression, Freud wrote back saying that he did not "put much value" on such demonstrations, but added that they could at least "do no harm" (MacKinnon & Dukes, 1964). However, if we define all of the situations that have been pursued in the laboratory as irrelevant, the remaining situations in which repression could occur are very limited, thus greatly diminishing the potential application of the concept.

With regard to the relevance of laboratory research, it is noteworthy that when a particular laboratory technique initially produced results that appeared to provide support for the concept of repression, the advocates of the psychodynamic position often embraced the technique as a relevant means of studying and confirming repression in the laboratory. It was only later, when the results were found to be due to some other process such as declines in affective intensity, differential learning or interference, that the advocates rejected the technique as irrelevant.

Does the absence of empirical evidence for repression lead to the conclusion that repression does not exist? Certainly not. *It is impossible to prove the null hypothesis that something does not exist.* Instead, all we can do is conclude that thus far there is no controlled evidence for the concept.

Although there is no laboratory evidence for repression, we must not dismiss the possibility of selectivity in memory, for certainly such selectivity does exist. Almost every one of the procedures we examined reflected some selectivity (pleasant experiences are more likely to be recalled than unpleasant experiences, completed tasks were more likely to be recalled than incomplete tasks, stress reduced recall). In every case, however, the selectivity could be accounted for better by processes other than repression (declines in affective intensity, differential learning or attention, cognitive interference).

PROJECTION

Projection plays an important role in psychology in two ways. First, projection is thought to be a defense mechanism that is effective for reducing stress. Second, it is thought that by examining a person's projections we can learn about that person's personality (i.e., projective testing). Although the focus of this chapter is on defense mechanisms, the research has implications for understanding the role that projection may play as a means of assessing personality.

In general, projection is said to occur when a person attributes traits or characteristics to other persons as a function of his or her own personality. Numerous types of projection have been suggested, and therefore our first task will be to organize the various types and determine which of them exist. With that done, we can go on to determine whether those types that do exist serve a defensive function.

Types of Projection

The numerous types of projection that have been suggested can be organized in terms of two dimensions (see Table 5.1; Holmes, 1968). The first dimension deals with *what* is projected. In some cases, persons project on to other persons the *same trait that they have* (a frightened person sees others as frightened), whereas in other cases persons project onto other persons a *trait that is different from their own* (a frightened person sees others as frightening). Note that when different traits are projected, they are not random traits but are the *complement* or *cause* of the trait that the projector possesses.

The second dimension of projection deals with the *awareness* or *insight* that persons have about their possession of the trait that underlies the projection. Theoretically, in some cases persons are not aware of their

TABLE 5.1.   TYPES OF PROJECTION

Person's Awareness	Same Trait Projected	Different Trait Projected
Person aware of trait in self	Attributive projection	Complementary projection
Person not aware of trait in self	Similarity projection	

possession of the trait that underlies their projection (e.g., the hostile person who projects hostility onto others may not be aware that he or she is hostile). On the other hand, in many cases persons may be very much aware of their possession of the trait they are projecting (e.g., frightened persons who see others as frightened are probably aware of the fact that they are frightened). With regard to the awareness dimension, it should be noted that we are referring to awareness about the *possession of the trait* and not to awareness of the *process of projection*. Persons may or may not be aware of their possession of a particular trait, but when they project that trait onto others, *they are not aware of the fact that they are attributing the trait to someone else because they themselves have the trait*.

The types of projection that result from these two dimensions of projection are presented diagramatically in Table 5.1. We can now go on to consider the evidence for the existence of each type. After examining the evidence concerning their existence, we will review the evidence concerning their hypothesized defensive function.

Evidence for the Existence of the Types of Projection and Their Defensive Function

Attributive Projection.[2]   Attributive projection occurs when a person possesses a characteristic, is aware of his or her possession of the characteristic, and then attributes that same characteristic to another person. There is a wide variety of evidence supporting the existence of attributive projection. For example, subjects' levels of happiness were correlated with the degree to which they saw others as happy (Goldings, 1954), children's generosity was correlated with their ratings of the generosity of others (Wright, 1942), students who were frightened or made anxious by impending electrical shocks or tests were more likely to see others as frightened or

---

[2] Attributive projection has also been referred to as *assimilative projection* (Cameron & Margaret, 1951), *supplementary appreceptive projection* (Murray, 1943), *naive projection* (Murstein, 1957), *similarity projection* (Burish & Houston, 1979), and *false consensus bias* (Ross, Green, & House, 1977). Actually, the term attributive projection may not be a good one because all projections involve attributions.

anxious (Feshbach & Singer, 1957; Singer, Feshbach & Singer, 1962), cheating students were more likely than noncheating students to believe that others cheated (Katz & Allport, 1931), children's ages were positively associated with their judged age of Peter Pan (Mintz, 1956), and persons who held specific political beliefs overestimated the number of others who held those beliefs (Calvin, Hanley, Hoffman, & Clifford, 1959; Hayes, 1936; Thomsen, 1941; Travers, 1941; Wallen, 1941).

Freud did not discuss the possible defensive function of attributive projection, but Bramel (1962) suggested a process by which attributive projection might reduce the anxiety associated with the possession of an undesirable trait. He suggested that,

> By attributing it to *respected* people, the projector may enable himself to re-evaluate the trait. If respected persons possess it, then perhaps it is not so bad a thing after all. . . . Another possibility is that the person may attribute the trait to members of his reference or *comparison* group. In this way he could convince himself that he does not deviate from the persons with whom he ordinarily compares himself (p. 122).

Three predictions can be derived from this conception of attributive projection. First, *persons who possess undesirable traits should project those traits onto desirable persons but not onto undesirable persons*. It would not help to see yourself as being like an undesirable person, but it might help to see yourself as being like a desirable or respected person. This predicted patterning of projection has been examined in four experiments, and those experiments have yielded very consistent results. In each experiment, it was found that when subjects were convinced that they possessed an undesirable trait, they projected that trait onto persons whom they saw as desirable (Bramel, 1962, 1963; Edlow & Kiesler, 1966; Secord, Backman, & Eachus, 1964). On the other hand, however, in three of the experiments it was found that the subjects also projected their undesirable traits onto undesirable persons (Bramel, 1962, 1963; Edlow & Kiesler, 1966). The results of the fourth experiment suggested that after subjects learned that they possessed undesirable traits they did not increase their projection of those traits onto undesirable persons (Secord et al., 1964), but it appears that the effects may have been limited by a "ceiling effect." That is, the subjects had already attributed a high degree of the negative traits to the undesirable persons and thus could not increase the level after they learned that they themselves had the trait.

Rather than being motivated by some defensive function, it may be that the projection onto the desirable persons may simply have been due to *assumed similarity* (Cronbach, 1955; Hanks, 1936). That is, the subjects saw the desirable persons as generally like themselves and, independent of any defensive strategy, they may have assumed that the other persons had the same traits they did. In that regard, it is noteworthy that in one experiment it was found that low self-esteem subjects did not project their traits onto desirable persons, probably because the low self-esteem subjects did not see themselves as generally similar to the desirable persons (Bramel, 1962). On the other hand, undesirable traits might be projected onto undesirable persons simply because the possession of those traits would be consistent with the general view of the persons. In other words, a negative "halo effect" might account for that projection (Guilford, 1954; Thorndike, 1920). It appears that the patterning of attributive projection that has been found is inconsistent with what would be expected if attributive projection served a defensive function. Furthermore, the patterning that has been found can be easily explained with reference to simpler processes.

The second prediction concerning the hypothesized defensive function of attributive projection is that *the projection of the undesirable traits onto desirable persons will result in a positive reevaluation of the trait.* That possibility has been examined in two experiments, but neither provided any evidence for the predicted reevaluation (Bramel, 1963; Secord et al., 1964). Persons may project their undesirable traits onto others, but doing so does not appear to change their evaluations of those traits.

The third and most basic hypothesis is that *persons who project their undesirable traits onto others will show a reduction in anxiety.* There are six published experiments in which the stress-reducing effect of attributive projection was tested. Two of those experiments provided some support for the stress-reducing effect of attributive projection (Bennett & Holmes, 1975; Burish & Houston, 1979). In both of these experiments, subjects who had experienced an anxiety-producing failure and were then given an opportunity to project anxiety onto others subsequently reported less anxiety than subjects who had experienced the anxiety-producing failure but were not given the opportunity to project. (It might be noted that Burish and Houston also examined the projection of depression and anger as a consequence of the failure but did not find that those projections reduced those states.)

The remaining four experiments did not indicate that attributive projection reduced stress (Heilbrun, 1978; Holmes & Houston, 1971; Stevens & Reitz, 1970; Zemore & Greenough, 1973; see reviews by Holmes, 1978, 1981). Overall then, it appears that there is a modicum of evidence suggesting that attributive projection of anxiety serves to reduce anxiety, but more research will be necessary before we can draw firm conclusions.

Complementary Projection. Complementary projection is said to occur when a person possesses a characteristic, is aware of his or her possession of that characteristic, and then attributes the cause of that characteristic onto others. Evidence for the existence of complementary projection is provided by research indicating that: (1) after being frightened, young girls saw men as more frightening (Murray, 1933; Feshbach & Feshbach, 1963; Feshbach & Singer, 1957); (2) college students who were strapped into an "electric chair" showed an increased tendency to rate others as "dangerous, frightening, and threatening" (Hornberger, 1960); and (3) male college students who were led to believe that they were aroused (they heard increases in what they thought were their heart rates), rated pictures of seminude women as more attractive (i.e., "If I'm aroused, they must be attractive;" Valins, 1966).

With regard to its potential defensive function, it has been suggested that complementary projection can be used to provide explanations or justifications for feelings and beliefs. For example, seeing others as frightening justifies one's own fear, and seeing others as attractive justifies one's own arousal. Insofar as it provides explanations or justifications for feelings and beliefs, complementary projection would be anxiety reducing because holding unexplained or unjustified beliefs would be anxiety provoking.

This theory was partially tested in an experiment in which one group of subjects was shown a frightening movie about the threat Russia poses for the United States (a movie that would justify fear), whereas another group of subjects was shown a series of neutral slides related to Russia (slides that would not justify fear; Bramel, Bell, & Margulis, 1965). While the subjects watched the movie or slides, they were given false physiological feedback indicating that they were afraid. Finally, after watching the movie or the slides and getting the false feedback, the subjects rated the level of threat they thought the Russians posed. It was predicted that when the subjects felt that they were aroused, those who saw the neutral sides (no justification for fear) would project more threat onto the Russians than the subjects who saw the threatening film (justification for fear). In other words, it was predicted that in the absence of justification for their feelings, they would project the cause of their feelings onto the Russians and see the Russians as frightening. That indeed is exactly what was found. It should be noted, however, that although the patterning of projection was consistent with what would be expected on the basis of the defensive theory of projection, changes in anxiety were not assessed and therefore from this experiment we cannot determine whether in fact the projection was effective in reducing stress.

Similarity Projection.   Similarity projection is said to occur when a person possesses a trait, is unaware of his/her possession of the trait, and then projects the trait onto others. This type of projection is very important because it provides the basis for the projective tests with which psychologists attempt to measure persons' unconscious characteristics and motivations. This type of projection is also important in terms of psychological defense because in theory it protects the individual from the knowledge that he or she possesses the undesirable trait. Not only is the possession of the trait repressed by the person (a questionable assumption to begin with), but greater distance between the person and the trait is achieved by projecting it out (Freud, 1957d).

A large amount of research has been conducted on similarity projection (Campbell, Miller, Lubetsky, & O'Connel, 1964; Lemann, 1952; Murstein, 1957; Murstein & Pryer, 1959; Norman & Ainsworth, 1954; Norman & Leiding, 1956; Page & Markowitz, 1955; Rokeach, 1945; Sears, 1936; Singer, 1963; Wells & Goldstein, 1964; Wylie, 1961; Zimmer, 1955; Zucker, 1952). Despite the numerous investigations and the theoretical importance of this type of projection, at the present time *there is no adequately controlled evidence supporting the existence of similarity projection.* A thorough review of this body of research is beyond the scope of this chapter. For a review of the methodological problems, conceptual confusions, and erroneous conclusions, the reader is referred to an earlier review (Holmes, 1968). However, because of the importance of the question of whether or not similarity projection occurs, some attention will be given to an investigation conducted by Campbell, Miller, Lubetsky, and O'Connel (1964) that is undoubtedly the best and most revealing study on the topic.

The subjects used by Campbell and his colleagues were persons who were in the lowest third of a distribution based on their self-description for a particular trait (e.g., hostility). Within that group, "insightful" subjects were then identified as those whose reputations indicated that they in fact did not possess the trait, and "noninsightful" subjects were those whose reputations indicated that they actually did possess the trait. The projections of the insightful and noninsightful subjects were then compared to determine, for example, whether hostile-noninsightful subjects would project more hostility than hostile-insightful subjects. Of the 112 comparisons that were made over a variety of traits, only one difference in the predicted direction reached statistical significance at the .05 level. Because that was well below what would be expected on the basis of chance alone, their research provided no evidence for the existence of similarity projection. Because there is no evidence that similarity projections exist, there is no point in considering the possibility that it reduces stress.

Conclusions Concerning Projection Based on Laboratory Research

There are two noteworthy conclusions that can be drawn from the laboratory research on projection. First, although there is abundant evidence that persons project traits that they know they possess, there is no evidence that persons project traits that they possess but which they are not aware of possessing. When originally published 20 years ago (Holmes, 1968), it was assumed that the conclusion would stimulate a flood of methodologically sound new research that would lead to a reversal of the conclusion. After all, that type of projection supposedly plays a crucial role in diagnostic testing, to say nothing of the role it plays for some theorists in their assumptions concerning personality functioning. Numerous persons indicated that research was planned or in progress, but to date no data have appeared that conflict with the original conclusion. In one case, another reviewer attempted to refute the original interpretations (Sherwood, 1981), but the numerous errors in interpreting the procedures used in experiments do not provide a basis for changing the conclusion (see Holmes, 1981).

Second, it can be concluded that the evidence for the stress-reducing effects of projection is too limited to draw firm conclusions. The stress-reducing effects of complementary projection have not been tested, and the evidence concerning the effects of attributive projection is weak and inconsistent at best (only 2 of 6 experiments offered any evidence). It is my *subjective impression* that attributive and complementary projection do reduce stress, but as a scientist I must also admit that I have no evidence to support my hunch.

CONCLUSIONS CONCERNING REPRESSION AND PROJECTION

In considering the research that has been reviewed, it is noteworthy that very little of that research has been published recently. Reviews were published in which methodological and interpretative problems with the existing research were pointed out, but unlike what often happens, those reviews did not stimulate new, different, and better research that might provide evidence where other investigations failed. It is possible that the reviews did stimulate new research, but that the research also failed to provide confirmatory evidence. It may be that because the new research did not produce new findings, it was not published.

Whether or not the reviews stimulated new research, it is clear that documenting the absence of evidence had little if any influence on the general understanding or evaluation of the concepts. Most contemporary textbooks still discuss the existence and effects of repression and projection as unquestionable truths. Ironically, the lack of recognition or acceptance of the absence of evidence for repression and projection may provide the best evidence for the existence of repression—or at least massive denial.

We now go on to consider the topic of avoidant thinking, a process for which there does seem to be some support.

AVOIDANT THINKING

When faced with a threatening event, it is possible to suppress thinking about it, to devote one's thoughts to a more pleasant topic, to avoid thinking about possible harm. *Avoidant thinking,* also termed suppression, attentional diversion, or distraction, involves an attempt to cope with stress-produced anxiety by thinking about something other than the threatening situation. Avoidant thinking can be distinguished from other defenses in a couple of ways. First, it is often—though not necessarily—a conscious process. If pondering an upcoming dental appointment is liable to provoke fear and anxiety, a person might say "It scares me, so I'm just not going to think about it." Note that, in this example, the person is conscious of both feelings of anxiety as well as the use of the coping strategy. Second, avoidant thinking should be explicitly distinguished from denial, since even though the defenses seem similar, it appears that they are differentially effective (McCaul & Malott, 1984; Suls & Fletcher, 1985). Denial involves the selective attention to and reinterpretation of the stressful situation (Holmes, 1985). Rather than avoiding thoughts about a menacing dental appointment, one might deny that it is stressful in the first place (e.g., "I'm not even worried about it") or one might attend to the positive aspects of a dental visit (e.g., "I'm actually looking forward to it—it's such a stimulating experience"). In either example, the focus of attention is directed to the event, unlike avoidant thinking in which attention is directed away from the stressor.

Similar to the treatment of repression and projection, we will address two general issues concerning avoidant thinking. First is the issue of whether persons ever use the coping strategy, a question that will be dismissed rather quickly with an affirmative answer. The more important point for this particular defense is whether avoidant thinking effectively reduces anxiety. We will consider that question by first discussing theoretical rationales for why avoidant thinking might work and then covering the empirical literature that tests those rationales. As in other sections, our review is not meant to be exhaustive. Rather we will highlight important examples of laboratory research in which the use of avoidant thinking was manipulated.

Using Avoidant Thinking

For some defenses, notably repression, the most crucial research question is whether the defense even exists. This question can be particularly difficult to answer when defenses are supposedly used unconsciously: How can an experimenter get persons to reveal what is supposed to be inaccessible material?

Fortunately, there is no such problem in determining whether persons use avoidant thinking, because the defense is often used purposely. Thus, we can simply ask persons who have confronted stress whether they attempted to use the defense. Good evidence that persons cope by using avoidant thinking comes primarily from control conditions in which subjects are not provided with a coping strategy but in which they are asked to describe their coping efforts during the stressful experience. For example, Monat, Averill, and Lazarus (1972) reported that subjects who were anticipating receiving electric shock preferred to think about "things not related to this experiment, such as exams, movies, songs, dates, sex, etc." (p. 239). The avoidance continued up until the moment when the shock was supposed to be delivered, when subjects finally reported thinking about (preparing for?) the stimulus. Monat et al. (1972) further reported that when there was a great deal of uncertainty about when the shock would occur, subjects consistently used avoidant thinking throughout the experimental period.

There is additional evidence from experiments focusing on pain as a stressor that people attempt to cope by using avoidant thinking. Control subjects frequently report retrospectively that they tried to avoid thinking about the pain (e.g., Avia & Kanfer, 1980; Barber & Cooper, 1972), and they believe that avoidant thinking is a very *effective* strategy for dealing with pain. For example, persons prefer avoidant thinking over alternative strategies, as demonstrated both in the laboratory (McCaul & Haugtvedt, 1982) and in the field (Leventhal, Schacham, Boothe, & Leventhal, 1981); these studies also show that a preference for avoidant thinking persists even when other strategies are actually more effective. Thus, it seems clear that persons use avoidant thinking and that they like the strategy. Perhaps they have learned that the defense is effective, the question to which we now turn.

Why Should Avoidant Thinking Work?

The proposition that avoidant thinking can reduce anxiety associated with a stressful event is implicitly based on two assumptions. First, we must assume that in order for stress to result in emotional distress, one has to think about the stressful stimulus. If anxiety occurs without thought, then there is no point in avoidant thinking. At one level, this assumption is certainly true—few of us fear events of which we are unaware (unless one allows for a general fear of the unknown and then one is probably "thinking about" the unknown). At another level, however, it could be argued that we can be anxious about an event even when thoughts about that event are not presently in consciousness. One might experience a nagging sense of upset, a low-level anxiety that cannot be directly attributed to a particular source (i.e., "free-floating anxiety").

Although it is probably the case that we *can* experience anxiety about an event even when it is not foremost in our thoughts, a more special case of the first assumption would still allow for the proposal that avoidant thinking can reduce anxiety. Specifically, it is only necessary to assume that *less* thinking about a stressor produces *less* anxiety about that event. Here we are on safer ground as there is sufficient evidence that persistent or obsessive thinking about a stressor can exacerbate anxiety. In any case, this more limited assumption can be addressed empirically—it is essentially the question of whether avoidant thinking (i.e., less stress-directed thinking) "works."

For avoidant thinking to be effective, an assumption involving limited attentional capacity must also be introduced. That is, for avoidant thinking to be effective, it must be difficult to process multiple events at once. If this were not the case, of course, then one could think about both the stressor and something more pleasant at the same time, and avoidant thinking would serve no beneficial purpose. For example, one could read a humorous story and simultaneously ponder impending electric shock. Fortunately, there is good evidence that it is very difficult to simultaneously process multiple events *well* (with the possible exception of some special instances in which processing of one task occurs without drawing on attentional capacity, a process termed automatic processing (cf. Kahneman, 1973; LaBerge, 1981). It is also likely, however, that a distracting or avoidant thinking task will not consume *all* of one's attentional resources. It would be fairly easy, for example, for persons to shift their attention, moving from a distraction task to the stressor and back again—perhaps many times even in a brief interval. The assumption of limited attentional capacity, while a reasonable one, forces a consideration of the nature of the avoidant thinking task and suggests that some tasks will be better than others.

Does Avoidant Thinking Work?

Any question as to whether a defense "works" is a comparative question: Does it work compared to what? In the laboratory, the simplest comparison is a "no-strategy" control, and it is this type of experiment (or conditions within an experiment) that is reviewed next. It is important to note at the outset, though, that uninstructed control subjects are not simply passive observers of the stressful stimulus, they use their own strategies (Houston & Holmes, 1974; Scott & Barber, 1977). Given that distraction is often a preferred coping technique, experimenters may sometimes be comparing an experimental manipulation of distraction to subjects' spontaneous use of the same strategy.

The "problem" of subjects using their own strategy led to some early evidence suggesting that avoidant thinking would be *ineffective* for coping with stress. Houston and Holmes (1974) instructed experimental subjects to read a humorous passage out loud during a two-minute period in which they expected to receive a painful electric shock (no shocks were actually delivered). Compared to control subjects who were simply asked to sit quietly, those who engaged in avoidant thinking exhibited higher pulse rates and skin resistance, though comparable self-reports of anxiety. However, subsequent examination of postexperimental questionnaires revealed that the control subjects failed to simply "sit quietly;" instead, many of them took the opportunity to reappraise the shocks (which they had never received) as painless. Thus, the avoidant-thinking strategy may have prevented subjects from using a denial strategy that, with an ambiguous stressor, happened to be more effective than the avoidant-thinking strategy.

Later research showed that avoidant thinking was clearly superior to a no-strategy condition when the stimulus was difficult to reappraise. In a paradigm very similar to that employed by Houston and Holmes (1974), Bloom, Houston, Holmes, and Burish (1977) first exposed all subjects to a sample, painful shock. Presumably this initial experience made it less difficult to deny that the shocks might be painful, because in a subsequent anticipatory period, subjects instructed to use avoidant thinking by reading an amusing children's book showed lower pulse rates and skin resistance compared to control subjects.

Although the above experiments dealt with the anticipation of a stressful event, most experiments addressing avoidant thinking have dealt with actual confrontation with the event, usually a painful stimulus. Table 5.2 shows 19 selected laboratory experiments in which an avoidant thinking strategy was compared to a "no instructions" control condition. In addition, the table shows the type of stimulus and the type of avoidant thinking task used in each experiment. The experiments portrayed in Table 5.2 were chosen to represent different stressors and strategies; in addition, they *all* showed that avoidant thinking successfully reduced anxiety on at least one measure (i.e., self-report, tolerance, and physiological). It would be too lengthy to describe and contrast each of the studies in Table 5.2, but it is worth illustrating the type of laboratory research summarized there with two examples: The experiments conducted by Stevens and Heide (1977) and Ribordy, Holmes, and Buschsbaum (1980).

Stevens and Heide (1977) conducted a laboratory experiment that examined components common to prepared childbirth techniques (e.g., Lamaze). Undergraduate women first were exposed to two cold pressor trials in which they reported pain until they reached the top of a scale (labeled "not endurable"); at that time, they were instructed to withdraw their hand from the ice water. Half of the subjects were subsequently instructed to focus upon a blank spot on the wall while "excluding all other

TABLE 5.2. SAMPLING OF SELECTED LABORATORY EXPERIMENTS THAT INCLUDED AVOIDANT THINKING AND NO-STRATEGY CONTROL CONDITIONS

Study	Avoidant Thinking Task	Stressful Stimulus
Worthington & Shumate, 1981	Pleasant imagery	Cold pressor
Grimm & Kanfer, 1976	Neutral imagery	Cold pressor
Stevens & Heide, 1977	Focus away	Cold pressor
Mefferd & Wieland, 1965	Word association	Cold pressor
McCaul & Haugtvedt, 1982	Watching slides	Cold pressor
Clum et al., 1982	Pleasant imagery	Pressure pain
Barber & Cooper, 1972	Mental arithmetic	Pressure pain
Lavine et al., 1976	Music	Electric shock
Bloom et al., 1977	Reading humorous passage	Threat of shock
Ribordy et al., 1980	Reading jokes	Ego-threat

images and thoughts" (p. 431).[3] The other half of the women were given no instructions for focusing their attention. All participants then participated in four additional cold pressor trials that ended when they could no longer tolerate the noxious stimulation.

The results were reported in terms of tolerance changes. Attention focusing was quite successful in increasing tolerance compared to no instructions; indeed, by the last trial, women engaged in avoidant thinking more than doubled the tolerance times of control women. Similar findings were obtained for the self-report ratings of pain.

The Stevens and Heide (1977) experiment is not too dissimilar from the basic paradigm used in much of the research shown in Table 5.1, particularly because of its focus on "pain" as a stressor. Although a very different paradigm was used by Ribordy et al. (1980), parallel results were obtained. Ribordy et al. first asked 126 male undergraduates to complete a supposed test of intelligence (the Critical Thinking Appraisal Test) in a group setting. In a subsequent session, conducted with each person individually, participants were given false feedback indicating that they had scored in either the 97th, 45th, or 6th percentiles, and they then were given a second bogus test that was used to reinforce the false feedback (e.g., successful subjects were given an easy task so that they would succeed again). The students then completed an anxiety inventory.

Following the manipulation of stress, participants were exposed to different levels and types of avoidant thinking. Specifically, 1/3 of the subjects read and rated jokes, 1/3 read and rated quotations that were similar in length and interest to the jokes, and the final group was simply asked to wait quietly. Scores on a subsequent anxiety inventory were compared to the anxiety experienced by participants immediately following receipt of their test scores and the data revealed that reading jokes significantly reduced anxiety compared to reading quotes and sitting quietly, whereas the latter groups did not differ. Interestingly, there was no anxiety by avoidant-thinking interaction, which might have been expected if the defense was only operating to protect those who had confronted a stressful event.

The Stevens and Heide (1977) and Ribordy et al. (1980) experiments illustrate a general point that can be drawn from the experiments shown in Table 5.1: Avoidant thinking appears to be a consistently superior coping strategy compared to no instructions. This is true across different types of stressors (e.g., cold pressor stimulation, "ego-threat"), different avoidant-thinking tasks (e.g., imagery, reading out loud), and different dependent measures (e.g., self-reported distress, physiological measures). Avoidant-thinking conditions don't *always* work compared to no-treatment control conditions (e.g., Holmes & Houston, 1974; Scott & Barber, 1977), but they usually do (McCaul & Malott, 1984; Suls & Fletcher, 1985).

---

[3] Stevens and Heide (1977) included additional conditions with variations in relaxation instructions that are not considered here.

Despite the appearance of the supportive research in Table 5.1, however, there are some clues that avoidant thinking may not be so successful, or at least the evidence may be less overwhelming than we have made it appear. There are three questions that can be raised: (1) Does the type of distraction strategy make a difference?; (2) Does the dependent measure make a difference?, and (3) Is there a difference in effectiveness over time? As we shall see from discussion of these questions, there is research left to do in order to decide whether avoidant thinking is indeed an effective strategy.

Strategy Type.   Are some types of avoidant-thinking tasks better than others? If the defense works *only* because it draws attention away from the stressful situation, then one would argue that the more attentionally demanding the task, the better it should work. But it is important to remember that the purpose of defenses is to reduce anxiety. Thus, it could also be suggested that avoidant thinking that involves positive affect would be more successful than affectively neutral thoughts.

Unfortunately, the literature does not provide consistent support for either of the above two suppositions. There are almost no experiments in which avoidant thinking-tasks that quantitatively differ in their demands on attentional resources are compared for their anxiety-reducing properties (cf. McCaul & Malott, 1984). The few experiments that do exist have produced mixed evidence. Barber and Cooper (1972) found that adding aloud (by 7s) produced lower pain reports than counting aloud (by 1s), presumably because the former strategy required more attention. But this finding was not obtained in a conceptually similar experiment conducted by Brucato (1978), who discovered that a difficult number classification task failed to improve cold pressor tolerance compared to a moderately difficult task. Finally, as far as we are aware, there is not a single study in which a stressor other than pain has been used and in which avoidant-thinking strategies that differ only in demands on attentional capacity have been tested.

Comparisons of strategies that differ in affective quality also fail to provide a clear answer as to whether emotionally positive strategies are best. The Ribordy et al. experiment (1980), discussed earlier, demonstrated that reading jokes—but not quotes—reduced anxiety following ego threat. More convincing evidence, however, could have been provided by asking subjects how they felt about their test score per se rather than assessing their general anxiety levels. As far as we know, the Ribordy et al. experiment is the only one in which affectively different avoidant-thinking strategies have been compared in response to a nonpainful stressor. There are a number of experiments, though, that compare strategy effectiveness in response to pain. Still, there is no clear answer to the question. Some experiments, for example, show that pleasant imagery (e.g., vividly imagining a pleasant scene) is no more effective for improving pain tolerance than affectively "neutral" strategies (e.g., counting; Akins, Hollandsworth, & Alcorn, 1983; Beers & Karoly, 1979; Worthington, 1978). Other, similar experiments, suggest that pleasant imagery is preferable (Horan & Dellinger, 1974; Stone, Demchik-Stone, & Horan, 1977). Finally, in one intriguing experiment (and one that is clearly worthy of replication and extension), Wescott & Horan (1977) demonstrated that affectively *negative* avoidant thinking may have potential for reducing pain. In that experiment, women who engaged in anger imagery tolerated cold pressor stimulation longer than uninstructed women.

Although it would be predicted theoretically that attentionally demanding and affectively pleasant avoidant thinking would be superior to other distraction thinking strategies, the evidence is unconvincing. Further, it may be difficult to construct strategies that vary *only* on one or the other of these dimensions. For example, extremely pleasant imagery may simultaneously be more demanding of attentional capacity; extremely difficult tasks may also be unpleasant. There is room here for creative experimentation to avoid such confounded manipulations.

Dependent Measures.   It is a cliche to note that in order to measure anxiety reduction, three types of anxiety measures should be obtained. But the need for self-report, behavioral, and physiological measures may be particularly important in research on avoidant thinking, because a reliance on self-report measures alone suffers from demand problems that are especially likely in this area. As we have already noted, people *believe* that avoidant thinking works. Thus, self-reported anxiety might simply reflect subject's expectancies about strategy effectiveness. The expectancy problem is further exacerbated because many avoidant-thinking tasks look as if they should be enjoyable (e.g., reading jokes; pleasant imagery). Because of these problems, experimenters should make an effort to include more than just self-report measures.

It should also be noted that the inclusion of physiological measures, though helpful, does not provide a substitute for self-reports. On the plus side, physiological measures are difficult to fake whereas self-reports can be manipulated easily (Houston & Holmes, 1975). On the other hand, physiological measures are strongly influenced not only by anxiety but by the avoidant-thinking task itself. This fact necessitates a set of no-stress control conditions that allow for the examination of strategy effects alone.

Effects over Time.   The American stereotype of appropriate ways to cope with difficulties emphasizes problem solving—"don't ignore your problems; *do* something about it." This ethic conflicts directly with the use of avoidant thinking as a defense and with our findings that avoidant thinking is an effective strategy for coping with stress. In short, we have argued that the defense works for reducing anxiety (although we may be unsure about precisely why it works).

It is likely, however, that avoidant thinking may be differentially effective during different time periods. Suls and Fletcher (1985), relying chiefly on a review of nonlaboratory work, concluded that avoidant thinking was effective in the short run but less so over a longer time. McCaul & Malott (1984) drew a similar conclusion in their review of research on avoidant thinking and pain, although they argued that avoidant thinking was less effective for strong pain stimuli (i.e., when it would be difficult, if not impossible, to exclude the noxious stimulation from attention). Since, in pain research, time and sensations are frequently confounded (sensations are more intense as the stressor continues to be applied), it could not be definitively stated which was more responsible for the different effects of avoidant thinking.

In laboratory research, it is not clear whether avoidant thinking is more or less effective over time. Of course, this is partly because of the upper limits that are placed on time effects in the lab. Still, it is certainly possible to study at least two conceptually different time periods: anticipation and confrontation. Nearly all pain research focuses only on the latter—distress responses to sensation impact. The few studies on nonpainful stressors that we have described tend to focus on anticipatory responses (e.g., responses while waiting for electric shock). Future research should include measurement across these two periods.

Conclusions on Avoidant Thinking

There is convincing evidence from the laboratories of a number of different researchers that people use avoidant thinking to cope with stress and that the defense is frequently effective for reducing anxiety. It is less clear whether different types of avoidant-thinking strategies are differentially effective, particularly whether strategies that consume larger amounts of attention or those that produce positive affect are best. Further, physiological measures have been neglected in much of the research that we reviewed, leaving open the possibility that some of the observed effectiveness of avoidant thinking is due to demand characteristics imbedded in the experiments. Finally, there is a need for further study of whether avoidant thinking is differentially effective upon stressor impact as compared to the anticipation of an unpleasant experience.

References

Aborn, M. (1953). The influence of experimentally induced failure on the retention of material acquired through set and incidental learning. *Journal of Experimental Psychology, 45,* 225–231.

Akins, T., Hollandsworth, J. G., Jr., & Alcorn, J. D. (1983). Visual and verbal modes of information processing and cognitively-based coping strategies: An extension and replication. *Behavior Research and Therapy, 21,* 69–73.

Alper, T. (1946). Memory for completed and incompleted tasks as a function of personality: An analysis of group data. *Journal of Abnormal and Social Psychology, 41,* 403–420.

Alper, T. (1948). Memory for completed and incompleted tasks as a function of personality: Correlation between experimental and personality data. *Journal of Personality, 17,* 104–137.

Alper, T. (1957). Predicting the direction of selective recall; its relation to ego strength and N achievement. *Journal of Abnormal and Social Psychology, 55,* 149–165.

Atkinson, J. (1953). The achievement motive and recall of interrupted and completed tasks. *Journal of Experimental Psychology, 46,* 381–390.

Atkinson, J., & Raphelson, A. (1956). Individual differences in motivation and behavior in particular situations. *Journal of Personality, 24,* 349–363.

Avia, M. D., & Kanfer, F. H. (1980). Coping with aversive stimulation: The effects of training in a self-management context. *Cognitive Therapy and Research, 4,* 73–81.

Barber, T. X., & Cooper, B. J. (1972). Effects on pain of experimentally induced and spontaneous distraction. *Psychological Reports, 31,* 647–651.

Beers, T. M., Jr., & Karoly, P. (1979). Cognitive strategies, expectancy, and coping style in the control of pain. *Journal of Consulting and Clinical Psychology, 47,* 179–180.

Bennett, D. H., & Holmes, D. S. (1975). Influence of denial (situation redefinition) and projection on anxiety associated with threat to self-esteem. *Journal of Personality and Social Psychology, 32,* 915–921.

Bloom, L., Houston, B. K., Holmes, D. S., & Burish, T. (1977). The effectiveness of attentional diversion and situation redefinition for reducing stress due to a non-ambiguous threat. *Journal of Research in Personality, 11,* 83–94.

Bramel, D. (1962). A dissonance theory approach to defensive projection. *Journal of Abnormal and Social Psychology, 64,* 121–129.

Bramel, D. (1963). Selection of a target for defensive projection. *Journal of Abnormal and Social Psychology, 66,* 318–324.

Bramel, D., Bell, J., & Margulis, S. (1965). Attributing danger as a means of explaining one's fear. *Journal of Experimental Social Psychology, 1,* 267–281.

Brucato, D. B. (1978). *The psychological control of pain: The role of attentional focusing and capacity on the experience of pain.* Unpublished doctoral dissertation, Kent State University.

Burish, T. G., & Houston, B. K. (1979). Causal projection, similarity projection, and coping with threat to self-esteem. *Journal of Personality, 47,* 57–70.

Butterfield, E. (1964). The interruption of tasks: Methodological, factual, and theoretical issues. *Psychological Bulletin, 62,* 309–322.

Byrne, D., Barry, J., & Nelson, D. (1963). The revised repression-sensitization scale and its relationship to measures of self-description. *Psychological Reports, 13,* 323–334.

Calvin, A., Hanley, C., Hoffman, F., & Clifford, L. (1959). An experimental investigation of the "pull" effect. *Journal of Social Psychology, 49,* 275–283.

Cameron, N., & Magaret, A. (1951). *Behavior pathology.* Boston: Houghton Mifflin.

Campbell, D., Miller, N., Lubetsky, J., & O'Connel, E. (1964). Varieties of projection in trait attribution. *Psychological Monographs, 78,* (15, Whole No. 592).

Caron, A., & Wallach, M. (1957). Recall of interrupted tasks under stress: A phenomena of memory or learning? *Journal of Abnormal and Social Psychology, 55,* 372–381.

Caron, A., & Wallach, M. (1959). Personality determinants of repressive and obsessive reactions to failure stress. *Journal of Abnormal and Social Psychology, 59,* 236–245.

Clum, G. A., Luscomb, R. L., & Scott, L. (1982). Relaxation training and cognitive redirection of strategies in the treatment of acute pain. *Pain, 12,* 175–183.

Coopersmith, S. (1960). Self-esteem and need achievement as determinants of selective recall and repetition. *Journal of Abnormal and Social Psychology, 60,* 310–317.

Cronbach, L. (1955). Processes affecting scores on "understanding of others" and "assumed similarity." *Psychological Bulletin, 52,* 177–193.

Davis, P. J., & Schwartz, G. E. (1987). Repression and the inaccessibility of affective memories. *Journal of Personality and Social Psychology, 52,* 155–163.

D'Zurilla, T. (1965). Recall efficiency and mediating cognitive events in "experimental repression." *Journal of Personality and Social Psychology, 3,* 253–256.

Edlow, D., & Kiesler, C. (1966). Ease of denial and defensive projection. *Journal of Experimental Social Psychology, 2,* 56–69.

Erdelyi, M. H. (1974). A new look at the new look: Perceptual defense and vigilance. *Psychological Review, 81,* 1–25.

Erdelyi, M. H., & Goldberg, B. (1979). Let's not sweep repression under the rug: Toward a cognitive psychology of repression. In J. F. Kihlstrom & F. J. Evans (Eds.), *Functional disorders of memory* (pp. 355–402). Hillsdale, NJ: Erlbaum.

Eriksen, C. (1952a). Defense against ego threat in memory and perception. *Journal of Abnormal and Social Psychology, 47,* 231–236.

Eriksen, C. (1952b). Individual differences in defensive forgetting. *Journal of Experimental Psychology, 44,* 442–443.

Eriksen, C. (1954). Psychological defenses and "ego strength" in recall of completed and incompleted tasks. *Journal of Abnormal and Social Psychology, 49,* 45–50.

Eriksen, C., & Pierce, J. (1968). Defense mechanisms. In E. Borgatta & W. Lambert (Eds.), *Handbook of personality theory and research.* Chicago: Rand McNally.

Feshbach, S., & Feshbach, N. (1963). Influence of the stimulus object upon the complementary and supplementary projection of fear. *Journal of Abnormal and Social Psychology, 66,* 498–502.

Feshbach, S., & Singer, R. (1957). The effects of fear arousal and suppression of fear upon social perception. *Journal of Abnormal and Social Psychology, 55,* 283–288.

Flavell, J. (1955). Repression and the "return of the repressed." *Journal of Consulting Psychology, 19,* 441–442.

Forest, D. (1959). The role of muscular tension in the recall of interrupted tasks. *Journal of Experimental Psychology, 58,* 181–184.

Freud, S. (1911/1957a). On the history of the psycho-analytic movement. *The complete psychological works of Sigmund Freud* (Vol. 14). London: Hogarth.

Freud, S. (1915/1957b). Repression. *The complete psychological works of Sigmund Freud* (Vol. 14). London: Hogarth.

Freud, S. (1911/1957c). Psychoanalytic notes upon an autobiographical account of a case of paranois (dementia paranoides). *The complete psychological works of Sigmund Freud* (Vol. 12). London: Hogarth.

Freud, S. (1957d). Instincts and their vicissitudes. *The complete psychological works of Sigmund Freud.* London: Hogarth.

Gilmore, J. (1954). Recall of success and failure as a function of subjects' threat interpretations. *Journal of Psychology, 38,* 359–365.

Glixman, A. (1948). An analysis of the use of the interruption technique in experimental studies of repression. *Psychological Bulletin, 45,* 491–506.

Goldings, H. J. (1954). On the avowal and projection of happiness. *Journal of Personality, 23,* 30–47.

Green, D. (1963). Volunteering and the recall of interrupted tasks. *Journal of Abnormal and Social Psychology, 66,* 392–401.

Grimm, L., & Kanfer, F. H. (1976). Tolerance of aversive stimulation. *Behavior Therapy, 7,* 593–601.

Guilford, J. P. (1954). *Psychometric methods.* New York: McGraw-Hill.

Hanks, L. M. (1936). Prediction from case material to personality test data: A methodological study of types. *Archives of Psychology, 29,* No. 207.

Hayes, S. P., Jr. (1936). The predictive ability of voters. *Journal of Social Psychology, 7,* 183–191.

Heilbrun, A. B. (1978). Projective and repressive styles of processing aversive information. *Journal of Consulting and Clinical Psychology, 46,* 156–164.

Holmes, D. S. (1968). Dimensions of projection. *Psychological Bulletin, 69,* 248–268.

Holmes, D. S. (1970). Differential change in affective intensity and the forgetting of unpleasant personal experiences. *Journal of Personality and Social Psychology, 15,* 234–239.

Holmes, D. S. (1972). Repression or interference: A further investigation. *Journal of Personality and Social Psychology, 22,* 163–170.

Holmes, D. S. (1973). *Differential recall of pleasant experiences and personality.* Unpublished manuscript.

Holmes, D. S. (1978). Projection as a defense mechanism. *Psychological Bulletin, 85,* 677–688.

Holmes, D. S. (1981). Existence of classical projection and the stress-reducing function of attributive projection: A reply to Sherwood. *Psychological Bulletin, 90,* 460–466.

Holmes, D. S. (1985). *The encyclopedia of psychology.* New York: Wiley. pp. 347–350.

Holmes, D. S., & Houston, B. K. (1971). The defensive function of projection. *Journal of Personality and Social Psychology, 20,* 208–213.

Holmes, D. S., & Schallow, J. R. (1969). Reduced recall after ego threat: Repression or response competition? *Journal of Personality and Social Psychology, 13,* 145–152.

Horan, J. J., & Dellinger, J. K. (1974). "In vivo" emotive imagery: A preliminary test. *Perceptual and Motor Skills, 39,* 359–362.

Hornberger, R. (1960). The projective effects of fear and sexual arousal on the rating of pictures. *Journal of Clinical Psychology, 16,* 328–331.

Houston, B. K., & Holmes, D. S. (1974). Effectiveness of avoidant thinking and reappraisal in coping with threat involving temporal uncertainty. *Journal of Personality and Social Psychology, 30,* 382–388.

Houston, B. K., & Holmes, D. S. (1975). Role playing versus deception: The ability of subjects to simulate self-report and physiological responses. *The Journal of Social Psychology, 96,* 91–98.

Jersild, A. (1931). Memory for the pleasant as compared with the unpleasant. *Journal of Experimental Psychology, 14,* 284–288.

Jourard, S. (1954). Ego strength and the recall of tasks. *Journal of Abnormal and Social Psychology, 49,* 51–58.

Kahneman, D. (1973). *Attention and effort.* Englewood Cliffs, NJ: Prentice Hall.

Katz, D., & Allport, F. (1931). *Students' attitudes.* Syracuse: Craftsman.

LaBerge, D. (1981). Automatic information processing: A review. In J. Long & A. Baddeley (Eds.), *Attention and performance* (Vol. 9, pp. 173–186). Hillsdale, NJ: Erlbaum.

Lavine, R., Buchsbaum, M. S., & Poncy, M. (1976). Auditory analgesia: Somatosensory evoked response and subjective pain rating. *Psychophysiology, 13,* 140–146.

Lazarus, & Folkman. (1984) *Stress, appraisal and coping.* New York: Springer.

Lemann, G. F. J. (1952). Group characteristics as revealed in sociometric patterns and personality ratings. *Sociometry, 15,* 7–90.

Leventhal, H., Shacham, S., Boothe, L. S., & Leventhal, E. (1981). *The role of attention in distress and control during childbirth.* Unpublished manuscript, University of Wisconsin–Madison.

Lewin, K. (1940). Formalization and progress in psychology. Studies in topological and vector psychology. *University of Iowa Studies, Studies in Child Welfare, 16,* 9–44.

Lewis, H., & Franklin, M. (1944). An experimental study of the role of the ego in work: II. The significance of task-orientation in work. *Journal of Experimental Psychology, 34,* 195–215.

McCaul, K. D., & Haugtvedt, C. (1982). Attention, distraction, and cold-pressor pain. *Journal of Personality and Social Psychology, 43,* 154–162.

McCaul, K. D., & Mallot, J. M. (1984). Distraction and coping with pain. *Psychological Bulletin, 95,* 516–533.

Mefferd, R. B., Jr., & Wieland, B. A. (1965). Modification in autonomically mediated physiological responses to cold pressor by word associations. *Psychophysiology, 2,* 1–9.

Meltzer, H. (1931). Sex differences in forgetting pleasant and unpleasant experiences. *Journal of Abnormal Psychology, 25,* 450–464.

Menzies, R. (1936). The comparative memory value of pleasant, unpleasant, and indifferent experiences. *Journal of Experimental Psychology, 18,* 267–279.

Merrill, R. (1954). The effect of pre-experimental and experimental anxiety on recall efficiency. *Journal of Experimental Psychology, 48,* 167–172.

Mintz, E. (1956). An example of assimilative projection. *Journal of Abnormal and Social Psychology, 52,* 270–280.

Monat, A., Averill, G. R., & Lazarus, R. S. (1972). Anticipatory stress and coping reactions under various conditions of uncertainty. *Journal of Personality and Social Psychology, 24,* 237–253.

Murray, H. A. (1933). The effect of fear upon estimates of the maliciousness of other personalities. *Journal of Social Psychology, 4,* 310–339.

Murray, H. A. (1943). *Thematic apperception test manual.* Cambridge, MA: Harvard University Press.

Murstein, B. I. (1957). Studies in projection: A critique. *Journal of Projective Techniques, 21,* 129–136.

Murstein, B. I., & Pryer, R. S. (1959). The concept of projection: A review. *Psychological Bulletin, 56,* 353–374.

Norman, R., & Ainsworth, P. (1954). The relationships among projection, empathy, reality, and adjustment, operationally defined. *Journal of Consulting Psychology, 18,* 53–58.

Norman, R., & Leiding, W. (1956). The relationship between measures of individual and mass empathy. *Journal of Consulting Psychology, 20,* 79–82.

Page, H. A., & Markowitz, G. (1955). The relationship of defensiveness to rating scale bias. *Journal of Psychology, 40,* 431–435.

Penn, N. (1964). Experimental improvements on an analogue of repression paradigm. *Psychological Record, 14,* 185–196.

Petrie, A. (1948). Repression and suggestability as related to temperament. *Journal of Personality, 16,* 445–458.

Prentice, W. (1944). The interruption of tasks. *Psychological Review, 51,* 329–340.

Ribordy, S. C., Holmes, D. S., & Buchsbaum, H. K. (1980). Effects of affective and cognitive distractions on anxiety reduction. *Journal of Social Psychology, 112,* 121–127.

Rokeach, M. (1945). Studies in beauty: II. Some determiners of the perception of beauty in women. *Journal of Social Psychology, 22,* 155–169.

Rosenzweig, S. (1943). An experimental study of "repression" with special reference to need-persistive and ego-defensive reactions to frustration. *Journal of Experimental Psychology, 32,* 64–74.

Rosenzweig, S., & Mason, G. (1934). An experimental study of memory in relation to the theory of repression. *British Journal of Psychology, 24,* 247–265.

Rosenzweig, S., & Sarason, S. (1942). An experimental study of the triadic hypothesis: Reactions to frustration, ego-defense, and hypnotizability. I. Correlational approach. *Character and Personality, 11,* 1–19.

Ross, L., Green, D., & House, P. (1977). The false consensus effect: An egocentric bias in social perception and attribution processes. *Journal of Experimental Social Psychology, 13,* 279–301.

Russell, W. (1952). Retention of verbal material as a function of motivating instructions and experimentally induced failure. *Journal of Experimental Psychology, 43,* 207–216.

Sanford, R., & Risser, J. (1948). What are the conditions of self-defensive forgetting? *Journal of Personality, 17,* 244–260.

Scott, D. S., & Barber, T. X. (1977). Cognitive control of pain: Effects of multiple cognitive strategies. *Psychological Record, 2,* 373–383.

Sears, R. (1936). Experimental studies of projection: I. Attribution of traits. *Journal of Social Psychology, 7,* 151–163.

Secord, P., Backman, C., & Eachus, H. (1964). Effects of imbalance in the self-concept on the perception of persons. *Journal of Abnormal and Social Psychology, 68,* 442–446.

Sherwood, G. G. (1981). Self-serving biases in person perception: A reexamination of projection as a mechanism of defense. *Psychological Bulletin, 90,* 445–459.

Singer, R. D. (1963). A cognitive view of rationalized projection. *Journal of Projective Techniques, 27,* 236–243.

Singer, R. D., & Feshbach, S. (1962). Effects of anxiety in psychotics and normals upon the perception of anxiety in others. *Journal of Personality, 30,* 574–587.

Smock, C. (1957). Recall of interrupted or non-interrupted tasks as a function of experimentally induced anxiety and motivational relevance of the task stimuli. *Journal of Personality, 25,* 589–599.

Stagner, R. (1931). The reintegration of pleasant and unpleasant experiences. *American Journal of Psychology, 43,* 463–468.

Stevens, H., & Reitz, W. (1970). An experimental investigation of projection as a defense mechanism. *Journal of Clinical Psychology, 26,* 152–154.

Stevens, R. J., & Heide, F. (1977). Analgesic characteristics of prepared childbirth techniques: Attention focusion and systematic relaxation. *Journal of Psychosomatic Research, 21,* 429–438.

Stone, C. I., Demchik-Stone, D. A., & Horan, J. J. (1977). Coping with pain: A component analysis of Lamaze and cognitive-behavioral procedures. *Journal of Psychosomatic Research, 21,* 451–456.

Suls, J., & Fletcher, B. (1985). The relative efficacy of avoidant and non-avoidant coping strategies: A meta-analysis. *Health Psychology, 4,* 249–288.

Tamkin, A. (1957). Selective recall in schizophrenia and its relation to ego strength. *Journal of Abnormal and Social Psychology, 55,* 345–349.

Thomsen, A. (1941). Psychological projection and the election: A simple class experiment. *Journal of Psychology, 11,* 115–117.

Thorndike, E. L. (1920). A constant error in psychological ratings. *Journal of Applied Psychology, 4,* 25–29.

Travers, R. M. W. (1941). A study in judging the opinions of groups. *Archives of Psychology,* No. 266.

Truax, C. B. (1957). The repression response to implied failure as a function of the hysteria-psychasthenia index. *Journal of Abnormal and Social Psychology, 55,* 188–193.

Tudor, T. G., & Holmes, D. S. (1973). Differential recall of successes and failures: Its relationship to defensiveness, achievement motivation, and anxiety. *Journal of Research in Personality, 7,* 208–224.

Valins, S. (1966). Cognitive effects of false heart-rate feedback. *Journal of Personality and Social Psychology, 4,* 400–408.

Wallen, R. (1941). Individual estimates of group attitudes. *Psychological Bulletin, 38,* 539–540.

Waters, R., & Leeper, R. (1936). The relation of affective tone to the retention of experiences in everyday life. *Journal of Experimental Psychology, 19,* 203–215.

Weinberger, D. A., Schwartz, G. E., & Davidson, R. J. (1979). Low-anxious, high-anxious, and repressive coping styles: Psychometric patterns and behavioral and physiological responses to stress. *Journal of Abnormal Psychology, 88,* 369–380.

Weiner, B. (1965). The effects of unsatisfied achievement motivation on persistence and subsequent performance. *Journal of Personality, 33,* 428–442.

Weiner, B., Johnson, P., & Mehrabian, A. (1968). Achievement motivation and the recall of incompleted and completed examination questions. *Journal of Educational Psychology, 59,* 181–185.

Wells, W., & Goldstein, R. (1964). Sears' study of projection: Replications and critique. *Journal of Social Psychology, 64,* 169–179.

Westcott, T. B., & Horan, J. J. (1977). The effects of anger and relaxation forms of an in vivo emotive imagery on pain tolerance. *Canadian Journal of Behavioral Science, 9,* 216–223.

Worthington, E. L., Jr. (1978). The effects of imagery content, choice of imagery content, and self-verbalization on the self-control of pain. *Cognitive Therapy and Research, 2,* 225–240.

Wright, B. (1942). Altruism in children and the perceived conduct of others. *Journal of Abnormal and Social Psychology, 37,* 218–223.

Wylie, R. (1961). *The self concept: A critical survey of pertinent research literature.* Lincoln, NE: University of Nebraska Press.

Zajonc, R. D. (1968). Attitudinal effects of mere exposure. *Journal of Personality and Social Psychology, 9,* Monograph Suppl. No. 2, Part 2.

Zeigarnik, B. (1927). Uber das behalten von erledigten und underledigten handlungen. *Psychologische, Rorschung, 9,* 1–85.

Zeller, A. (1950). An experimental analogue of repression: II. The effect of individual failure and success on memory measured by relearning. *Journal of Experimental Psychology, 40,* 411–422.

Zeller, A. (1951). An experimental analogue of repression: III. The effect of induced failure and success on memory measured by recall. *Journal of Experimental Psychology, 42,* 32–38.

Zemore, R. & Greenough, T. (1973). Reduction of ego threat following attributive projection. *Proceedings of the 81st Annual Convention of the American Psychological Association (Summary),* 343–344.

Zimmer, H. (1955). The roles of conflict and internalized demands in projection. *Journal of Abnormal and Social Psychology, 50,* 188–192.

Zucker, K. (1952). *Experimental investigation of correlates of projection.* Unpublished master's thesis, Case Western Reserve University, Cleveland, Ohio.

PART **III**

FIELD AND CLINICAL
INVESTIGATIONS

6

Techniques for Data Acquisition and Analysis in Field Investigations of Stress

ROD A. MARTIN

Field research on psychological stress has mushroomed over the past two decades. Rapid growth in the number of studies published has been accompanied by increasingly sophisticated theoretical conceptualizations and complex methodologies and statistical techniques. Early research with simple case-control designs and retrospective correlational methodologies has given way to prospective and longitudinal research examining moderator variables using multiple regression analyses and, more recently, complex causal modeling techniques. Numerous theoretical papers and review articles have discussed the relative merits of a variety of techniques for the measurement of stressful life events, social support, coping strategies, and so on.

The aim of this chapter is to survey the various techniques that are available for collecting and analyzing data in field research on stress and to point out where possible those approaches that appear to be most promising for future work. The emphasis is on methodology rather than on substantive research findings. In view of the plethora of methods and measures available, this discussion will of necessity be fairly selective. An attempt will be made to briefly discuss some of the controversial issues in the field and, where further discussion is needed, references to more in-depth review articles will be cited.

Although this chapter is limited to field research as opposed to laboratory analog studies, it is not the author's intention to imply that the former approach is the only, or even better, way to proceed in stress research. Coyne and Lazarus (1980) have argued strongly in favor of field research rather than laboratory studies of stress. They point out that laboratory research is subject to a number of limitations, including restricted ecological validity; an inability to examine stress processes over time; the limited duration, severity, and complexity of stressors that are ethically feasible in laboratory research; the artificial constraints placed on variables; and the lack of robustness of such research. Although their points are well taken, it can be argued that naturalistic field research is also subject to limitations, including a high vulnerability to threats to internal validity, poor control of extraneous variables, and limited ability to clarify causal relationships between variables. As stated by Laux and Vossel (1982), laboratory and field methodologies may be viewed as complementary, each approach making significant contributions to the furtherance of the other. (See also Wortman, Abbey, Holland, Silver, & Janoff-Bulman, 1980, for further discussion of this issue.)

This chapter is divided into two sections, first focusing on methods of collecting data on variables that are relevant to stress, and second, focusing on data analytic techniques.

DATA ACQUISITION TECHNIQUES

Much confusion in the early stress research literature existed concerning the definition of stress. Is stress to be viewed as a *response* of the organism (e.g., Selye's concept of the General Adaptation Syndrome, 1956) or as a characteristic of certain environmental events (*stimuli*) impinging on the organism (e.g., Holmes & Rahe's Social Readjustment Scale, 1967)? Recently there appears to be a growing consensus in agreement with the contention of Lazarus and colleagues that stress is best viewed as a *transaction* between the person and the environment in which the situation is appraised by the individual as in some way exceeding his or her resources and endangering his or her well-being (e.g., Lazarus & Folkman, 1984). This definition highlights three separate domains that need to be sampled in stress research: (1) characteristics of the environment (the independent variables); (2) characteristics, resources, and actions of the individual such as personality variables, appraisal, cognitive styles, social support, and coping strategies (the moderating variables); and (3) the effects of this stressful transaction on the individual, such as physiological and psychological illness outcomes (the dependent variables). Although researchers differ in their use of terminology (e.g., some use the term "stress" to refer to the independent variable while others use it for the dependent variable), most would agree that these three classes of variables may be conceptually distinguished. The present discussion of methods of data acquisition will therefore follow this general classification scheme.

Assessment of Independent Variables

A number of methods have been devised for investigating the sources of stress in naturalistic settings. The stressors measured generally fall into four categories: (1) major disruptive life events, (2) minor daily irritants, (3) chronic role strains, and (4) specific environmental stressors. Research using the first three (i.e., self-report data) usually involves the selection of representative subject samples from the general population and investigating relationships between scores on the particular stressor measure and a variety of stress outcomes, either retrospectively or prospectively (the *normal population survey*). An alternative strategy using such measures is to identify a sample of subjects displaying a particular symptom assumed to be caused by stress (e.g., myocardial infarction, depression) and retrospectively compare them with a suitable control group using a particular stressor measure (the *retrospective case-control method*). The fourth measurement method listed usually involves the identification of a group of individuals who have all experienced the same specific, objectively defined stressor (e.g., a natural disaster, spinal cord injury) and comparing them with a suitable control group on a variety of stress outcomes (the *prospective case-control method*). Alternatively, relationships between various individual difference variables and patterns of symptomatology may be examined within such a commonly stressed group (the *case-only design*). (See Kessler, 1983 for a more complete discussion of these methodologies.)

Measures of Major Life Events.   Approaches to stress research that examine the cumulative effects of major life disruptions originated in the work of Adolph Meyer (1951) who attempted to relate such events to the medical status of patients using his "life chart" method. This approach was given major impetus by the development of the Schedule of Recent Experience (SRE) by Holmes and Rahe (1967). Drawing on the equilibrium theory of Walter Cannon (1932), these researchers hypothesized that stress occurs as a result of an accumulation of major changes that require adaptation. Such changes may be either undesirable (e.g., death of a spouse) or desirable (e.g., outstanding personal achievement). The SRE comprised a list of 43 events generated by systematic study of life charts of over 5000 patients. Recognizing that these events varied in the degree of change and adaptation involved, Holmes and Rahe (1967) further refined their measure by assigning weights to each item based on standardized ratings obtained from a number of judges. For example, death of a spouse received a weight of 100 life change units (LCUs), marriage was weighted at 50, and vacation at 12. The revised measure was named the Social Readjustment Rating Scale (SRRS). A subject's total life stress score is computed by summing the weights of each of the events he or she reports having experienced during a recent interval of time, usually 6 to 24 months. A voluminous body of research literature has been published using this measure (cf. Holmes & Masuda, 1974; Rahe, 1972, 1974; Rahe & Arthur, 1978; Rahe & Lind, 1971), and it is still fairly widely used.

Although it has inspired a flurry of research activity, the Holmes and Rahe (1967) measure has also been criticized. One problem has to do with the assumption that change per se is stressful regardless of the desirability or undesirability of the events (e.g., Brown, 1974; Mechanic, 1975; Sarason, DeMonchaux, & Hunt, 1975). Numerous critics argued that undesirable events (e.g., death of a spouse) would have a more deleterious effect than desirable events (e.g., outstanding personal achievement). In support of the "change per se" hypothesis, Dohrenwend (1973) found that total change scores (weighted desirable + undesirable events) were more highly correlated with a measure of psychiatric functioning than were scores derived by subtracting weighted desirable from weighted undesirable events. However, several other studies (Gersten, Langner, Eisenberg, & Orzeck, 1974; Mueller, Edwards, & Yarvis, 1977; Myers, Lindenthal, & Pepper, 1971; Paykel, 1974; Ross & Mirowsky, 1979; Vinokur & Selzer, 1975) obtained higher correlations with stress outcomes using undesirable events alone. Desirable events have generally been found to be nonsignificantly related to a variety of dependent measures, and the general consensus at present is that life event measures should include only undesirable events.

A related issue has to do with whether the ratings of desirability should be obtained from the subjects themselves or from independent judges. The former method has been criticized on the grounds that subjects' own ratings are contaminated by their present psychological state, and therefore this method introduces a confound between the independent and dependent variables. This problem is particularly acute when both the life events and the outcome measures are obtained retrospectively at the same time. On the other hand, having the subjects rate the desirability of events has the advantage of allowing for individual differences in appraisals which are seen as important factors in the stress process (e.g., Lazarus & Folkman, 1984). One reasonable strategy might be to make use of subjects' ratings in prospective studies and objective judges' ratings in retrospective studies. However, this issue may not be as critical as it appears, in view of the fact that the data obtained by Mueller et al., (1977) and by Vinokur and Selzer

(1975) indicate that both methods yield comparable results even when data are collected retrospectively.

Another issue regarding the SRE has to do with the weighting of life changes. The original assumption that different life events will have varying degrees of impact on the individual seems reasonable. However, a number of researchers have found correlations in the order of .95 between weighted and unweighted (i.e., simple frequency counts of) life event scores and, in addition, have found that the two types of scores produce correlations of similar magnitude with various stress outcomes (e.g., Gersten et al., 1974; Lei & Skinner, 1980; Mueller et al., 1977; Ross & Mirowsky, 1979; Vinokur & Selzer, 1975; Zimmerman, 1983). Mueller et al., (1977, p. 316) conclude that "on the basis of this evidence, it seems safe to conclude that weighting techniques have little impact on results."

One further point concerning the weighting of events needs to be made, however. Weighted life events scores have the advantage of being more normally distributed and therefore more conforming to the assumptions of widely-used statistical procedures, whereas unweighted frequency counts of life events tend to be quite highly positively skewed. One solution to this problem when using unweighted scores is to compute a logarithmic transformation of the data and use these transformed scores in the subsequent analyses. The logarithmic transformation has the effect of spreading out scores at the lower end of the distribution and compressing the higher end. This procedure may mean the difference between significant and non-significant results, particularly when using such statistical methods as multiple regression analyses with interaction terms (i.e., cross-product of independent and moderator variables; this statistical technique will be discussed in more detail later).

A third criticism of the SRE relates to the particular items included in the scale. First, a number of the items are vague and ambiguous (e.g., major change in social activities). Such ambiguity precludes the possibility of determining a priori whether the event is likely to be viewed by the respondent as desirable or undesirable. In addition, such ambiguous items require a subjective interpretation and it is likely that subjects will vary in their tendency to endorse them as having occurred. As Schroeder and Costa (1984) point out, subjects who are physically ill or suffering from psychological distress may attribute their conditions to external events and may interpret and recall events in support of this attribution. More objective events with specifically defined criteria are required to ensure accurate recall of their occurrence on the part of respondents.

A related issue concerns the "symptom contamination" of a number of the events listed in the SRE. Hudgens (1974) pointed out that 29 of the 43 items on the scale might be viewed as symptoms rather than causes of physical illness (e.g., major personal injury or illness, change in eating habits, change in sleeping habits). Similarly, Schroeder and Costa (1984) noted that several of the SRE items may be either direct symptoms of psychopathology (e.g., sexual difficulties) or events that result from neurotic traits or tendencies (e.g., divorce, being fired from a job). Therefore, conclusions regarding the etiological significance of life events derived from correlations obtained between the SRE and either physical or psychological illness may be suspect. Tennant, Bebbington, and Hurry (1981) argued that the validity of all research using the SRE is undermined by the inclusion of such criterion contaminated events.

In a study relating life events to symptoms of illness, Schroeder and Costa (1984) found that "when health-related, neuroticism-related, and subjective items were included in the life event measure, the customary low-to-moderate correlation with reported illness was obtained. However, as suspected, when these contaminated items were excluded, the remaining items were not correlated with illness, which suggests that illness is essentially independent of the occurrence of life event changes per se" (pp. 859–860). These authors argue quite forcefully that evidence for etiological effects of stressful life events on illness is due to artifacts. They advocate that research using simple life events lists be abandoned. It should be noted, however, that Schroeder and Costa's study employed a retrospective design. Other authors (e.g., Zimmerman, O'Hara, & Corenthal, 1984) have suggested that the problem of symptom-related events may be circumvented by the use of prospective studies or, in retrospective studies, accurately dating the occurrence of events relative to the date of illness onset. However, Paykel (1983) has pointed out that it is difficult to date the onset of certain disorders such as schizophrenia, and has argued that life events lists should be limited to events that are unlikely to have been brought about by illness (cf. Brown, Sklair, Harris, & Birley, 1973).

In view of the above criticisms of Holmes and Rahe's (1967) measure, a number of investigators have constructed alternate scales that attempt to improve on the shortcomings of the SRE while retaining the general approach of assessing major life disruptions. Sarason, Johnson, and Siegel (1978), for example, developed the Life Experience Survey (LES), a 57-item self-report measure which allows respondents to rate both the desirability or undesirability and the severity of impact at the time of occurrence of each reported event. An attempt was also made to either eliminate ambiguous items or make them more specific. The LES has been widely used in recent research.

Other life events measures have been developed for specific populations such as children (Coddington, 1972), college students (Sandler & Lakey, 1982), adolescents (Newcomb, Huba, & Bentler, 1981), and athletes (Bramwell, Masuda, Wagner, & Holmes, 1975).

One issue which concerns the validity of all self-report measures of life events is the problem of "event fall-off." Jenkins, Hurst, and Rose (1979) found that when subjects were asked to report the life events that had occurred during the same 6-month period on two separate occasions nine months apart, their total scores on the second report were 34 to 46 percent lower than those from the first report. Similarly, Uhlenhuth, Haberman, Balter, and Lipman (1977) had subjects indicate the occurrence of life events over the preceding 18 months on a month-by-month basis. They found that the number of events reported decreased by approximately 5% per month, calling into question the validity of retrospective recall of life events due to forgetting of events with time. Funch and Marshall (1984a) obtained similar results, noting that major disruptive events (e.g., divorce, death of a spouse) are less likely to be underreported than more minor events, particularly those that primarily concerned another person (e.g., illness of a family member).

Several solutions to this problem have been suggested. One is to keep the recall period short (e.g., six months), although this method precludes the possibility of assessing the longer-term impact of life events. Another solution that is more costly and time-consuming is to use a diary technique, having subjects record the occurrence of life events as they occur over an extended period of time. Several authors (e.g., Brown & Harris, 1982; Paykel, 1983) have argued that the best approach for obtaining reliable life event data is to use a structured interview format. Interviewers can be trained to probe into details regarding the background and dating of events and the relation of events to one another. Brown and Harris (1982) report minimal fall-off rates using this procedure for a 12-month recall period. Paykel (1983) concludes that "self-report event questionnaires are inadequate for the 1980s; some form of interview method should be used, preferably one permitting enough probing to establish detail" (p. 350). Besides the measures developed by Brown and Harris (1982), interview-based scales have been developed by Tennant and Andrews (1976) and by Dohrenwend, Krasnoff, Askenasy, and Dohrenwend, (1978—the PERI life events scale).

Measures of Minor Daily Irritants. In view of the numerous conceptual, methodological, and empirical difficulties with scales assessing major life events, Richard Lazarus and his colleagues (e.g., Lazarus, 1984; Kanner, Coyne, Schaefer, & Lazarus, 1981; DeLongis, Coyne, Dakof, Folkman, & Lazarus, 1982) have proposed a major change in focus in research on life stress. Lazarus (1984, p. 376) notes "the overemphasis on change, the failure to consider the individual significance of events, the person's coping resources and liabilities, and the low explanatory power of life events with respect to health outcomes." These investigators have proposed that a more important source of stress than major life change events are "daily hassles," which are defined as "the irritating, frustrating, distressing demands that to some degree characterize everyday transactions with the environment" (Kanner et al., 1981, p. 3).

In order to measure such irritants, they developed the 117-item Daily Hassles Scale (Kanner et al., 1981), which includes such items as "misplacing or losing things," "trouble relaxing," "not enough time for family," and "too many things to do." Subjects are instructed to indicate the hassles that oc-curred during a specified period of time (usually 1 to 12 months) and then to rate the severity of each reported item on a scale from 0 to 3.

Research using this scale (Kanner et al., 1981; DeLongis et al., 1982; Hola-han, Holahan, & Belk, 1984; Zarski, 1984) has generally found that, although hassles are moderately correlated with major life events, hassles are signifi-cantly correlated with psychological symptomatology even when variance associated with major life events is partialled out. In contrast, major life events do not add to the prediction of symptoms once hassles have been partialled out. It should also be pointed out that, although Kanner et al. (1981) also presented a "Daily Uplifts Scale" comprising positive daily expe-riences, this measure has generally not been found to be related to symptom outcome.

Despite these promising findings, the Daily Hassles Scale is subject to the criticism of criterion contamination seen earlier with the SRE. Accord-ing to Burks and Martin (1985), as many as 34 of the 117 events listed in the scale (e.g., concerns about health; physical illness) may be seen as introduc-ing a confound between the independent and dependent measures when the Hassles Scale is used to predict health outcomes.

Similar criticism of the Daily Hassles Scale has been voiced by Dohrenwend, Dohrenwend, Dodson, and Shrout (1984). In a survey of 371 clinical psychologists, these authors found that 90 of the 117 Hassles Scale items were rated as "likely" or "about as likely as not" to be symptoms of psychological disorder, suggesting that the correlations between has-sles and psychological health outcomes may merely be due to a confound between the two measures. In a rebuttal to this article, Lazarus, DeLongis, Folkman, and Gruen (1985) demonstrated that correlations of almost equal magnitude were obtained between the Hopkins Symptom Checklist and items that were found by Dohrenwend et al., (1984) to be either confounded or unconfounded with psychological disorder. Lazarus and his colleagues further argued that an interactional view of stress pre-cludes the possibility of using a "clean" measure of environmental stres-sors (i.e., one that does not tap into individuals' appraisals of events), since "stress does not exist in the absence of the person-environment relationship and the processes that explain this relationship" (p. 778). Dohrenwend and Shrout (1985) subsequently argued that adequate inves-tigation of Lazarus's transactional model requires measures of the ob-jective characteristics of environmental events that are distinct from measures of individuals' perceptions of, and responses to, those events. Clearly, there is still much debate concerning the most appropriate meth-ods of measuring the independent variable in stress research in general, and the appropriateness of the Daily Hassles Scale in particular.

A potential alternative to the Daily Hassles Scale is the 34-item Everyday Problem Scale (Burks & Martin, 1985), which takes the same general ap-proach, but seeks to avoid the problem of confounding between hassles and their effects. These authors obtained results similar to those reported earlier with the Daily Hassles Scale, i.e., significant correlations between scores on the Everyday Problem Scale and psychological symptoms even after major life events are partialled out. Monroe (1983) has also developed a shortened "minor life events" scale (36 items) which attempts to avoid the contamination problem and which has yielded comparable results in a prospective study relating minor life events to psychological symptoms. Although these measures are new and have received only limited empirical attention, the initial promising results warrant further investigations with them.

Social Role Strains.   Another alternative to life events in the assessment of sources of stress is the concept of role strains, which derives from sociological theory (Pearlin & Lieberman, 1979). Pearlin and Schooler (1978) suggested that "from a sociological perspective many of the difficult problems with which people cope are not unusual problems impinging on exceptional people in rare situations, but are persistent hardships experienced by those engaged in mainstream activities within major institutions" (p. 3). Thus, these authors' approach is similar to the "daily hassles" approach in that it focuses on persistent problems in daily living. However, it differs from the latter approach in its emphasis on chronic "strains" or stressors that arise from the social roles that people adopt.

On the basis of data obtained from unstructured interviews with over 100 subjects, Pearlin and Schooler (1978) identified four role areas in which people commonly experience persistent strain: roles as marriage partners, economic managers, parents, and workers. They went on to develop a structured interview to assess role strain in each of these areas. Sample items assessing strains in the four role areas are: (1) "How strongly do you agree with the statement, 'I cannot completely be myself around my spouse'?" (marriage role); (2) "How often do you have to give attention to the correction of your child(ren) failing to get along with others the same age?" (parenting role); (3) "How much difficulty do you have in meeting the monthly payment on bills?" (economic manager role); and (4) "How much of the time do you have more work than you can handle?" (occupational role).

In a large-scale interview survey of 2300 people aged 18 to 65 in the Chicago area, Pearlin and Schooler (1978) investigated the relation between these role strains and self-reported emotional disturbance (which these authors refer to as "stress"), examining also the effectiveness of various coping strategies and resources. In an extensive follow-up study with the same sample, Pearlin, Menaghan, Lieberman, and Mullan (1981) further investigated causal models of the relationships between role strain, major life events, mediating factors, and depression. The role strain approach was also taken by Kandel, Davies, and Raveis (1985) in an investigation of the effects of marital, occupational and household role strains on psychiatric symptomatology in a sample of women. The particularly rich yield of data obtained in these studies indicates that the role strain approach to stress research is worthy of further investigation.

Specific Stressors. The methods of assessing sources of stress described thus far (major life events, minor daily problems, and chronic strains of social roles) all make use of summary scores of cumulative, nonspecific stressors. These methods also all employ self-report techniques and the data are usually obtained retrospectively. A fourth strategy for examining stress in naturalistic settings is to investigate samples of individuals who have all experienced a specific major stressful event. Individual differences may be investigated within such samples by examining relationships between various stress outcomes and such factors as personality variables, social support, coping style, and so on (case-only designs), or, alternatively, such samples may be compared with appropriate control groups of individuals who have not been subjected to the particular event in question (prospective case-control designs). These sorts of research strategies have been employed in investigations of the effects of a variety of specific stressors, including the Three Mile Island nuclear accident (Cleary & Houts, 1984; Collins, Baum, & Singer, 1983; Schaeffer & Baum, 1984); enrollment in medical school (Murphy, Nadelson, & Notman, 1984); university examinations (Folkman & Lazarus, 1985; Krantz, 1983; McClelland, Ross, & Patel, 1985); environmental noise (Heft, 1979; Stansfeld, Clark, Turpin, Jenkins, & Tarnopolsky, 1985); environmental crowding (Baum & Valins, 1977; Rodin, 1976); abortion (Cohen & Roth, 1984); assault (Sales, Baum, & Shore, 1984); parenting a handicapped child (Petersen, 1984); widowhood (Helsing, Szkio, & Comstock, 1981); combat duty in the Vietnam War (Borus, 1974; Faulkner & McGraw, 1977); a supper club fire (Green, Grace, & Gleser, 1985); and a flood disaster (Gleser, Green, & Winget, 1981).

The investigation of specific stressors provides some advantages over the previously described techniques in that it focuses on an objective, usually time-limited event and is not subject to the distortions and biases of self-report and recall of subjects. Thus, there is less problem of confounding between the independent, dependent, and moderator variables, a problem which, as we have seen, continues to be the subject of much debate in the literature. However, this method also has several limitations, including the large number of uncontrolled variables, the problem of obtaining personality and coping data after the occurrence of the event, and the limited generalizability to other sorts of stressor events. Some of these problems may be minimized by selecting subjects and obtaining antecedent data prior to the occurrence of an anticipated event such as academic examinations or surgical interventions and then obtaining outcome data in follow-up. However, this strategy is not always feasible, as only a small number of stressful events may be predicted in advance.

There is a wide variety of methods available for the assessment of the "independent variable" in field research on stress. Each of these techniques arises from different theoretical conceptualizations of the stress process and each has its particular advantages and disadvantages. The increasing recognition of the complexity of the stress process would indicate the need for a combination of methods within research projects. Models of stress that take into account the cumulative and interactional effects of both major life disruptions and chronic irritants and strains need to be developed and empirically tested. Hypotheses regarding stress processes and outcomes, coping and moderating variables may be profitably examined by means of research programs that include both studies employing self-report measures of nonspecific stressors, hassles, and strains, and investigations of specific stressful events as they occur. We turn now to a discussion of the sorts of dependent variables employed in naturalistic stress research.

Assessment of Dependent Variables

Although the original work of Selye (e.g., 1956) emphasized the physiological effects of stress particularly in the hypothalamic-pituitary-adrenocortical axis, subsequent investigations have examined stress outcomes in a wide range of domains. At the biochemical level, studies have examined the effects of stress-related arousal on psychophysiological, neuroendocrinological, and immunological functioning (cf, Frankenhauser, 1980; Jemmott & Locke, 1984; Riley, 1981; Sterling & Eyer, 1981). Stress has been implicated in the etiology of a variety of physical disorders including peptic ulcers, heart disease, hypertension, asthma, cancer, and arthritis (cf. Creed, 1985; Moss, 1973; Miller, 1980; Minter & Kimball, 1980; Sterling & Eyer, 1981; Weiner, 1977; Womack, Vitaliano, & Maiuro, 1983). At the psychological level, researchers have examined effects of stress on psychiatric symptoms such as schizophrenia (Rabkin, 1980) and depression, as well as on general mood levels (e.g., anxiety), and on behavioral functioning such as problem-solving abilities and social relationships (Cohen, 1980).

The researcher who is interested in studying stress is confronted with a bewildering array of possible dependent measures from which to choose, including numerous self-report scales as well as various psychophysiological and biochemical assay techniques. Researchers' reasons for selecting particular dependent measures are often not clear. Investigators who are primarily interested in examining the etiological role of stress in the development of a particular disorder (e.g., depression, heart disease) will select dependent measures relevant to that disorder. However, those who are focusing on particular stress measurement techniques (e.g., life events vs. daily hassles) or who wish to investigate the role of particular moderating variables (e.g., social support) frequently appear to choose their dependent measures rather arbitrarily on the basis of convenience and ease of administration. The assumption seems to be that one measure is as good as another and that equivalent results are to be expected regardless of the outcome assessed, and as a result the majority of studies utilize a single (usually self-report) dependent measure. Baum, Grunberg, and Singer (1982) have pointed out that "different measures of stress [i.e., stress outcome] are not necessarily correlated with each other" (p. 219) and have called for a multi-level approach to the measurement of stress effects. The present author would agree with their suggestion that "a combination of self-report, performance, and biologically based measures constitutes a measurement strategy that provides an optimal understanding of stress in any given situation" (p. 219).

We continue with a survey of the various techniques available for assessing stress outcomes. Given the large number of such techniques, this review is necessarily highly selective and limited in terms of the evaluative discussion provided. Baum et al. (1982) have categorized stress outcome measures into four basic groups: self-report, performance, psychophysiological, and biochemical. The following discussion is organized according to this framework.

Self-Report Measures.   The vast majority of published psychological studies in the stress field have relied on self-report techniques for assessing outcomes of stress, and numerous scales have been developed. These measures may be divided into four types: physical illness, psychiatric disturbance, mood, and perceived stress.

Physical Illness.   A number of self-report checklists have been developed for assessing the presence of a variety of physical symptoms. One of the most widely used is the Seriousness of Illness Survey (Wyler, Masuda, & Holmes, 1968), which comprises a list of 126 symptoms. In the development of this scale, a severity weight for each symptom was obtained by having the symptoms rated by a large sample of physicians and lay persons. These ratings were made on the basis of prognosis, duration, threat to life, degree of disability, and degree of discomfort. In research with this scale, subjects are typically asked to check off the symptoms which they have experienced during a given period of time (usually 1 month to 1 year) and an overall score is computed by summing the weights of all of the symptoms checked off. Similar measures were developed by Belloc, Breslow, and Hochstim (1971; Belloc & Breslow, 1972), and by Cline and Chosy (1972). Many researchers (e.g., Antoni, 1985; Billings & Moos, 1982; Cronkite & Moos, 1984; Miller & Ingham, 1979; Sarason, Sarason, Potter, & Antoni, 1985) construct their own symptom checklists by adapting published measures to their own purposes.

There is some question, however, regarding the validity of such self-report measures of health. Although Meltzer and Hockstim (1970) reported favorable comparisons between self-report checklists and objective medical records, recent work reported by Antoni (1985) was less positive. In a study of 73 men enrolled in a submarine school, Antoni found a correlation of only .37 ($p < .10$) between self-reported illnesses and illnesses recorded in medical files. Since these military subjects obtained scheduled, mandatory physical examinations and had access to free, on-call medical services, it was assumed that the data from the medical records were more accurate. Interestingly, this study found significant longitudinal relationships between life events and illness when medical records were used, but not using the self-reported illness data. It would appear that self-reports of symptoms of illness may be subject to many of the sorts of biases and recall "drop-off" problems that have been found with self-reports of life events. In order to ensure the accuracy of health outcome data, researchers might do well to supplement self-report illness measures with data from subjects' medical records, or else use a diary technique in which subjects record illness occurrence over a period of time.

Psychiatric Disturbance and Mood.   Several measures have been constructed for assessing levels of general psychiatric symptomatology in epidemiological research. Langner (1962) published a 22-item scale that was developed for the Midtown Study of mental disorder in Manhattan. It was not designed to identify individual cases of psychiatric illness, but rather to provide a "rough indication of where people lie on a continuum of impairment in life functioning due to very common types of psychiatric symptoms" (Langner, 1962, p. 269). The items, derived from the MMPI and other measures, reflect psychophysiological problems, depression, and social withdrawal, and a total score is computed by summing the number of symptoms endorsed by the respondent.

The General Health Questionnaire (Goldberg, 1972) is a similar measure that is composed of 60 items assessing symptoms of depression, anxiety, behavioral disturbances, and hypochondriasis. Another widely used measure is the Hopkins Symptom Checklist (HSCL—Derogatis, Lipman, Rickels, Uhlenhuth, & Covi, 1974), a 58-item scale with five factors: somatization, obsessive-compulsive symptoms, interpersonal sensitivity, depression, and anxiety. This checklist has been demonstrated to have good reliability and validity, and to be sensitive to low levels of symptoms in normal populations (Uhlenhuth, Lipman, Balter, & Stern, 1974). The SCL-90 (Derogatis, Lipman, & Covi, 1973) is an expanded 90-item version of the HSCL with four additional factors: hostility, phobic anxiety, paranoid ideation, and psychoticism. A 29-item Psychiatric Screening Inventory has also been developed using items from the HSCL (Ilfeld, 1976).

All of these scales have been widely used as dependent measures in stress research (e.g., Billings & Moos, 1982; Burks & Martin, 1985; Coyne, Aldwin, & Lazarus, 1981; Kanner et al., 1981; Monroe, 1983). As with the checklists of physical illness symptoms, various researchers have also developed checklists of psychiatric symptoms by borrowing from various published scales (e.g., Grant, Sweetwood, Yager, & Gerst, 1981; Lindenthal & Myers, 1979; Mueller et al., 1977). For a discussion of such measures see Dohrenwend, Shrout, Egri, and Mendelsohn (1980).

Self-report measures of mood are also frequently used as dependent measures in naturalistic stress research. The Beck Depression Inventory (BDI—Beck, Ward, Mendelson, Mock, & Erbaugh, 1961) and Centre for Epidemiological Studies Depression Scale (CES—D—Radloff, 1977) are widely employed for assessing levels of depression in normal populations. Anxiety may be assessed by means of the State-Trait Anxiety Inventory (Spielberger, Gorsuch, & Lushene, 1970). The Multiple Affect Adjective Check List (MAACL—Zuckerman & Lubin, 1965) and the Profile of Mood States (POMS—McNair, Lorr, & Droppleman, 1971) are mood adjective checklists that provide an overall "mood disturbance" score as well as sub-scale scores for specific moods such as anxiety, depression, hostility, fatigue, and confusion. Depending on whether they wish to assess day-to-day mood fluctuations or more enduring mood levels, researchers may vary the instructions given to respondents to complete these scales in terms of "how you are feeling at this moment" or "how you have generally been feeling over the past week (month)."

Perceived Stress.   Cohen, Kamarch, and Mermelstein (1983) have published the Perceived Stress Scale (PSS), a 14-item self-report measure of the degree to which situations in respondent's lives are perceived as stressful. These authors noted that "PSS items were designed to tap the degree to which respondents found their lives unpredictable, uncontrollable, and overloading. These three issues have been repeatedly found to be central components of the experience of stress. . . ." (p. 387). Sample items from the scale are "how often have you felt nervous and 'stressed'?" and "how often have you felt difficulties were piling up so high that you could not overcome them?" Subjects are instructed to respond to the items in terms of how they have been feeling over the past month using 4-point rating scales (never) to (very often). In their initial validational research, Cohen and associates (1983) found small to moderate correlations between the PSS and life events scales (.17 to .49) and fairly strong correlations between the PSS and measures of physical symptomatology (.52 to .70) and depression (.65 to .76).

One practical difficulty with the PSS is that it is not clear whether it should be viewed as an independent variable (e.g., as an alternative to life events or hassles scales), as a dependent measure, or as a moderator variable (e.g., mediating the relationship between life events and physical health). Cohen and associates (1983) seem to suggest all three possibilities. In a more recent article, however, Cohen (1986) suggests that the PSS should be used as an alternative to the Daily Hassles Scale as an independent variable predicting stress outcomes. He cites data from a two-month prospective study that demonstrated that the PSS predicted physical and psychological symptoms even after symptoms at time 1 were partialled out. In terms of the classification system used in the present chapter, however, the PSS might best be viewed as a "mediating" variable, assessing the outcome of the interaction between independent (i.e., objective events) and moderating (i.e., appraisal and coping) variables, and having a causal effect on other dependent variables such as physical and psychiatric symptoms. In any event, the emphasis on the subjective appraisal of stress is consonant with current conceptualizations of stress processes (e.g., Lazarus & Folkman, 1984), and the utility of this measure remains to be determined in future research.

Another recently developed tool for assessing global stress responses is the Strain Questionnaire, a self-report scale developed by Lefebvre and Sandford (1985). These authors conceptualized "strain" as "a syndrome of physical, behavioral, and cognitive symptoms that are elicited, to varying degrees, by environmental demands upon the individual" (p. 70). The Strain Questionnaire is composed of 48 items (e.g., "feeling out of control," "tense muscles," "racing heart"), and subjects are instructed to indicate how frequently they have experienced each symptom over the preceding week on a 5-point scale ranging from "never" to "constantly." Weighted scores are computed for total strain (all 48 items), and for physical (28 items), behavioral (12 items), and cognition (8 items) subscales. Initial research has indicated acceptable levels of reliability and moderate correlations with the Beck Depression Inventory. Again, further research is needed to determine the utility of this measure as a multi-modal measure of stress effects.

In summary, self-report scales are the most frequently used method of obtaining data regarding the outcomes of stress. Their popularity is no doubt due to the fact that they are relatively inexpensive and are easily administered to large samples of subjects. However, the problem remains that self-report methods are susceptible to both intentional and unintentional biases. Baum, Grunberg, and Singer (1982) have pointed out that increases in self-reported physical and psychiatric symptoms may be overestimated due to changes in subjects' awareness, attributions or concerns when they are experiencing stress, rather than being accurate estimates of actual changes in functioning. In addition, exaggerations in reported symptoms may be politically or socially motivated when subjects perceive that their responses may be instrumental in effecting changes in their environmental conditions.

On the other hand, subjects may also underestimate or minimize symptoms or mood disturbances. Weinberg, Schwarz, and Davidson (1979) found that subjects with high scores on a need for approval scale reported low levels of anxiety on a self-report measure but showed high levels of arousal as measured by heart rate, skin conductance, and muscle tension as well as poor performance on a phrase association task. In contrast, subjects with low need for approval scores revealed positive correlations between self-reported anxiety and the psychophysiological and behavioral measures. These authors interpreted the need for approval scores as reflecting repression, and suggested that researchers need to distinguish between repressors and truly low-anxious subjects in stress research using self-report methods. (However, see Chapter 5 by Holmes and McCaul in the present volume for an alternative interpretation.) In any event, the problems of bias indicate the need for supplementing self-report measures with other types of dependent measures, including behavioral, psychophysiological, and biochemical assessments.

Behavioral Measures.   Cohen (1980) has reviewed research on the effects of stress on performance and social behavior. These studies, which have largely been laboratory experiments, have generally shown that exposure to stress results in poorer performance on a variety of tasks, including solving line puzzles and anagrams, proofreading typewritten material for grammatical and typographic errors, and the Stroop color-word task. In addition, observed effects of stress on social behavior include increased aggressiveness, decreased group cohesiveness, decreased helping of others, and decreased recognition of social roles.

Only a few studies have examined such behavioral and performance effects in naturalistic field settings, although such research appears to have considerable potential. One example of the use of task performance measures in field research is provided by Collins, Baum, and Singer (1983) in a study of stress in subjects living in proximity to the Three Mile Island (TMI) nuclear plant. The subjects in this study were given two tasks that require concentration. In the first of these, subjects were asked to proofread seven pages of typewritten material for five minutes, looking for typographical errors, misspellings, and grammatical errors that had been inserted into the text. The second was an embedded figures task in which subjects were required to locate single target figures in a series of more complex geometric figures. The results obtained showed that the TMI area residents, as compared with a control group of subjects living in another area, found significantly fewer errors in the proofreading task and solved fewer of the embedded figures.

Besides task performance measures, a variety of other behavioral outcomes may be examined in naturalistic stress research, such as drug use (Bruns & Geist, 1984; Krueger, 1981), traffic accidents (Selzer & Vinokur, 1974), athletic injuries (Bramwell, Masuda, Wagner, & Holmes, 1975), academic performance (Lloyd, Alexander, Rice, & Greenfield, 1980), and suicide (Paykel, Prusoff, & Myers, 1975).

Psychophysiological Measures.   Psychophysiological measures have frequently been used in experimental laboratory research on stress. Increases in sympathetic nervous system arousal, as reflected in changes in heart rate, blood pressure, skin temperature, and skin conductance, as well as increases in muscle tension and changes in EEG patterns and respiration have long been associated with stress responses in the lab (e.g., Lazarus,

Speisman, Mordkoff, & Davison, 1962; Lazarus, 1966). Very little work has been done, however, in examining the generalizability of these findings to naturalistic field settings.

Part of the reason for the relative neglect of psychophysiological measurement in field research is that, until recently, the instruments required for obtaining such data (e.g., polygraphs) have been bulky and subject to decalibration with movement. One exception is the measurement of blood pressure, which may be done with a simple sphygmanometer. Field studies have examined relationships between blood pressure and job loss (Kasl & Cobb, 1970), chronic exposure to aircraft noise (Stansfeld et al., 1985; Cohen, Evans, Krantz, & Stokols, 1980), crowded living conditions in prison (Paulus, McCain, & Cox, 1978), and self-reported life events (Svensson & Theorell, 1983). It should be noted that factors such as height and weight should be controlled in analyses of blood pressure.

Recent technological advances have led to the development of small portable psychophysiological recording devices which can be used to record such responses as heart rate and skin conductance on standard audio cassette tapes. These tapes can later be replayed at high speed and either written out on a chart using a polygraph or analyzed directly using an analogue-to-digital converter and a computer (Turpin, 1985). Such techniques were employed by Stansfeld and associates (1985) in examining the effects of exposure to chronic aircraft noise on heart rate and skin conductance. These authors pointed out that the collection of data in the subjects' homes permitted measures of tonic physiological activity rather than the phasic responses obtained in artificial laboratory environments.

There are some difficulties with psychophysiological techniques, including the costs involved, the obtrusiveness of attaching electrodes to subjects, and the possible reactive effects of such procedures in inexperienced subjects. However, these are not insurmountable, and the wealth of data potentially available would seem to make such techniques a desirable adjunct to currently used methodologies.

Biochemical Measures.   The early work by Selye (1956) emphasized the importance of changes in endocrine functioning in the stress response. Subsequent laboratory research with both animal and human subjects has demonstrated stress-related increases in arousal in the sympathetic-adrenal medullary and pituitary-adrenal cortical systems (cf. Baum et al., 1982; Frankenhauser, 1975, 1980). The medulla of the adrenal glands is innervated by the sympathetic nervous system and secretes the catecholamines epinephrine and norepinephrine, so that measures of catecholamine levels (e.g., in the bloodstream or urine) provide assessments of general sympathetic arousal. The adrenal cortex, which is stimulated by adrenocorticotrophic hormone (ACTH) from the pituitary, secretes corticosteroids, primarily cortisol in humans. Baum, Grunberg, and Singer (1982) point out that "measurement of corticosteroids in the blood and urine can provide a sensitive and reliable index of psychological and emotional states associated with stress" (p. 227).

Baum et al. also point out that "many psychologists do not realize that the state of the art in biochemical assay techniques is such that endocrinological measurements can and should be added to the armamentarium of behavioral, psychological, and physiological techniques already being used. Gathering the required samples for bioassay (e.g., urine) is a minor procedural addition to psychological protocols and it provides important additional data" (p. 218). They state that measures obtained from urine samples are relatively inexpensive, are noninvasive and nonpainful and do not require medical supervision as do blood samples, and provide more stable estimates of long-term (e.g., 24 hours) catecholamine levels. They offer a number of useful suggestions regarding appropriate methods for obtaining samples and conducting bioassays.

The study by Collins, Baum, and Singer (1983) of residents living in the area of the Three Mile Island nuclear plant made use of urinary catecholamine measures in addition to the task performance measures noted earlier. They found higher levels of norepinephrine ($p < .001$) and epinephrine ($p < .07$) in urine obtained from TMI residents as compared to the control group (cf. Schaeffer & Baum, 1984). McClelland, Ross, and Patel (1985) have also described a method for obtaining catecholamine measures from human saliva samples, although they caution that the relationship between salivary and blood plasma catecholamine levels has not been fully examined.

Another area of biochemical functioning which is receiving increased attention in stress research is the immune system. Jemmott and Locke (1984) have reviewed studies on the relationship between psychosocial factors and immunological functioning. Two types of immunological reactions have been identified: humoral and cell-mediated. Humoral reactions occur more rapidly and involve the synthesis and release of immunoglobulins (antibodies) into the bloodstream and lymph in defense against a variety of viral and bacterial infections. Cell-mediated immunity is involved in delayed hypersensitivity reactions (e.g., tuberculin skin test), transplantation rejection, and defense against cancer cells and some viruses and bacteria. Considerable laboratory research has demonstrated stress-related depressions in immunocompetence, although enhancement of some aspects of immune functioning has also been observed. Although the exact mechanisms are not yet well understood, the research evidence obtained thus far suggests that decreases in immune functioning resulting from stress may play a role in increasing individuals' susceptibility to a variety of disorders, including cancer, autoimmune disorders, allergies, and respiratory illnesses (Fox, 1981; Jemmott & Locke, 1984; Solomon, 1981; Stein, 1981).

In a series of studies investigating the effects of stress and need for power on immune functioning, McClelland and his associates (e.g., McClelland, Alexander, & Marks, 1980; McClelland, Floor, Davidson, &

Saron, 1980; McClelland et al., 1985) have employed a relatively simple method for assessing concentrations of Immunoglobulin A (IgA) in saliva samples. IgA is believed to be involved in the defense against pathogens entering through the mouth and nose which produce upper respiratory infections (e.g., colds, flu, sinusitis). Prepared agar plates impregnated with antibodies to human IgA are available at reasonable cost from commercial suppliers and minimal additional equipment is required for assaying saliva for IgA levels. Since saliva samples are quite easily obtained from subjects, this type of procedure is another potentially useful addition to the dependent measures currently in use.

It should be noted that fluctuations in biochemical substances such as catecholamines, corticosteroids, and immunoglobulins occur as a function of a variety of factors such as diurnal cycles and food ingestion as well as stress. In addition, successful assays depend on proper collection, storage, and preparation of the samples. Researchers who are interested in employing such measures would be well advised to familiarize themselves with the relevant literature in order to ensure that their procedures are maximally reliable and valid. Finally, as Baum and associates (1982) point out, it should be noted that self-report, performance, psychophysiological, and biochemical measures of stress are not necessarily highly intercorrelated. Each approach provides unique kinds of information, and a combination of all of them is likely to offer an optimal understanding of stress outcomes.

Assessment of Moderator Variables

In an oft-cited review of earlier stress research, Rabkin and Struening (1976) pointed out that, although reliable correlations had been obtained both retrospectively and prospectively between life events and illness, these correlations were generally quite weak, ranging from .20 to .30. At best, stressful life events appeared to account for less than 10 percent of the variance in illness outcomes. These authors suggested that predictive accuracy might be improved by examining variables that moderate or mediate the relationship between life stress and illness. They defined such "mediating factors" as "those characteristics of the stressful event, of the individual, and of his social support system that influence his perception of or sensitivity to stressors" (p. 1014). In addition to increasing the proportion of explained variance in the dependent measures, it was suggested that research on moderator variables might allow for the identification of individuals who are at greater risk of illness following stress, and these individuals might be targeted for preventive intervention. Several other authors echoed these suggestions (e.g., Johnson & Sarason, 1979).

The introduction of moderator variables into life events research represented something of a "paradigm shift" in the field. Researchers began to examine a number of potential stress-moderating variables, including social support and a variety of personality variables including locus of control, sensation seeking, "hardiness," cognitive style, and the sense of humor. More recently, a second shift seems to have occurred as researchers emphasizing "process" rather than "static" models of stress (e.g., Coyne & Holroyd, 1982; Lazarus & Folkman, 1984; Pearlin & Schooler, 1978; Pearlin et al., 1981) have argued that what an individual *does* (i.e., coping responses) is potentially more important in mediating the impact of stress than what the person *is* (e.g., personality variables) or *has* (e.g., social support). These authors pointed out that the "moderator variable" approach, although an improvement over the simple stimulus-response model, is still a unidirectional, "static" model of stress, generally relying on cross-sectional research methods. In contrast, studies of the processes involved in coping with stress over time, based on a "transactional" model of stress, require longitudinal designs. Furthermore, they argued, the latter approach potentially offers a greater yield of information regarding useful intervention strategies, as it is easier for people to change what they *do* in responding to stress (i.e., cognitive and behavioral strategies) than to change their enduring personality traits or social environments. We now turn to a brief overview of methods for assessing social support, personality variables, and coping strategies in stress research. It should be noted that, for the purposes of the present discussion, we include all three types of variables as "moderator variables," as they all relate to the ways in which individual differences influence the outcomes of stressful events.

Social Support.   An environmental factor which may play an important role in mediating the impact of stressful life experiences is the degree of social support available to the individual. A number of investigators have hypothesized that individuals who have a network of friends and relatives to turn to for material and emotional aid in times of stress are less likely to suffer the deleterious consequences of stress than are those with fewer such resources available to them. A large body of research literature investigating this hypothesis has accumulated (for reviews see Dean & Lin, 1977; Haggerty, 1980; Liem & Liem, 1978; Thoits, 1982; Turner, 1983; Wallston, Alagna, DeVellis, & DeVellis, 1983).

Considerable confusion continues to abound in this literature regarding the exact meaning of social support and methods of operationalizing it. As Thoits (1982, p. 146) observed, "most investigators have not attempted to formulate a precise definition of social support, and few have attempted to develop valid or reliable indicators of the concept." The variety of definitions and descriptions that have been offered focus on a diversity of aspects of social support, including provision of information or material aid, availability of a confidant, gratification of basic emotional and social needs, and so on (Wallston et al., 1983). Thoits (1982) notes that social support is a multi-dimensional rather than a unitary construct, and that it can be broken down into such dimensions as (1) *amount* of support, (2) *types* of support (e.g., emotional versus instrumental), (3) *sources* of support (e.g., spouse, friends, relatives, co-workers), and (4) *structure* of support network (e.g., size, density, accessibility, stability). Not all sources or types of support may be equally effective in attenuating the impact of stress.

Similarly, Schaefer, Coyne, and Lazarus (1981) distinguished between *social network* (i.e., the number of individuals potentially available for support) and *perceived support* (i.e., the individual's perception of the supportive value of these relationships). These authors suggest that these two dimensions of support may be quite differently related to health and psychological functioning. They hypothesize that perceived support is positively related to morale and health, whereas social network may be unrelated or even negatively related to well-being because of the demands, constraints and disappointments often inherent in large social networks. They also distinguish between three types of social support: emotional, tangible and informational. These distinctions correspond to Wallston and associates' (1983) observations of two primary dimensions in social support: (1) a quantitative versus qualitative dimension (cf. social network vs. perceived support); and (2) an instrumental versus expressive dimension (cf. tangible and informational aid vs. emotional support).

As Thoits (1982) points out, much of the earlier work on social support relied on information from one or two items extracted from available data (e.g., presence or absence of a spouse or confidant, living alone or with others). Alternatively, measures were used which included items relating to a variety of factors in addition to social support (e.g., the measure of psychosocial assets used by Nuckolls, Cassel, & Kaplan, 1972). More recently, investigators have begun to develop more carefully designed scales which attempt to reflect theoretical developments in the field (e.g., Bruhn & Philips, 1984; Donald, Ware, Brook, & Davies-Avery, 1978; Lin, Dean, & Ensel, 1981). The Social Support Questionnaire by Schaefer, Coyne, and Lazarus (1981) was developed to assess both social network size and perceived support along the dimensions of tangible, informational and emotional support. These authors report acceptable levels of reliability and validity with this measure, and their initial data have tended to corroborate the conceptual distinction between social network and perceived support (cf. Sarason, Sarason, Potter, & Antoni, 1985).

Wallston and associates (1983) have offered guidelines for the selection of an appropriate social support measure. They suggest that in choosing a scale researchers should attend to (1) the degree to which the measure matches one's theoretical-conceptual preferences; (2) the comprehensiveness of the data it provides; (3) the potential confound between items on the scale and the particular dependent variable(s) of interest; and (4) the amount and quality of prior research using the scale.

Personality Variables.   Research examining moderator variables is predicated on the assumption that individuals differ in the degree to which they are adversely affected by stressful experiences. Investigations have been conducted on a wide variety of personality dimensions which have been hypothesized to exert such a stress-buffering effect. Examples of such personality variables include: locus of control and perceived control (Johnson & Sarason, 1978; Lefcourt, Miller, Ware, & Sherk, 1981); sensation seeking (Smith, Johnson, & Sarason, 1978); sense of humor (Martin & Lefcourt, 1983); metamotivational dominance (Martin, 1985); self-efficacy (Holahan et al., 1984); need for power (McClelland et al., 1985; McClelland & Jemmott, 1980); Type A personality (Blumenthal, Williams, Kong, Schanberg, & Thompson, 1978); and MMPI Scales (Lichtenberg, Skehan, & Swensen, 1984). Kobasa (1979; Kobasa, Maddi, & Courington, 1981; Kobasa, Maddi, & Kahn, 1982) has conceptualized a personality dimension which she terms "hardiness," comprising perceptions of control, challenge and commitment to goals, and which she has extensively examined as a stress-buffering factor. Individual differences in cognitive style have also been examined as moderating variables, such as monitoring versus blunting (Miller, 1980), screening versus nonscreening (Mehrabian & Ross, 1977), and being field dependent/ independent (Lazarus, Averill, & Opton, 1974). Several studies have examined interactions between various personality factors and social support in moderating stress effects (e.g., Funch & Marshall, 1984b; Kobasa & Puccetti, 1983; Lefcourt, Martin, & Saleh, 1984; Sandler & Lakey, 1982).

In view of the large number of individual difference variables that might be investigated for stress-buffering effects, no attempt will be made here to discuss measurement issues regarding specific variables. Several general observations may be made, however. First, it is important that researchers using this general strategy ensure that their investigations are based on sound theoretical rationale. A "shot-gun" approach using personality scales for which there is no theoretical basis for assuming stress-moderating effects is only likely to add to confusion in the field. Second, researchers should carefully select well-validated personality measures which are specific to their conceptual definitions and which are not confounded with the independent and dependent measures under investigation.

Finally, a comment is in order regarding the argument of some authors (e.g., Lazarus & Folkman, 1984) that research on personality measures as moderators should be abandoned because it fails to take into account the processes involved in person-environment stress transactions and it does not provide useful information regarding potential intervention strategies. Although the present author would agree with the need for process-oriented research, this does not mean that personality-oriented research is without merit. Increased understanding of both the stress process and the nature of particular personality traits would be obtained by combining these research strategies, examining how individuals with various personalities vary in the ways they appraise and cope with stressful experiences over time. For example, the finding of lower correlations between self-reported life events and mood disturbance among individuals with a stronger sense of humor (Martin & Lefcourt, 1983) might be followed by longitudinal investigations into the specific ways in which these people make use of humor in dealing with stress. In addition, although the clinical relevance and usefulness of stress research is an important consideration, this should not be the sole criterion for evaluating research. Of potentially equal value are the refinements in theoretical conceptualizations of particular personality constructs that may be obtained from such research (e.g., Martin, 1985). For further critical discussion of personality variables as moderators of stress, see Chapter 7 by Cohen and Edwards in this volume.

Coping Strategies.   Whereas social support concerns the environmental resources that a person *has,* and personality variables have to do with what the person *is,* coping is concerned with what the individual *does* in dealing with stress (Coyne & Lazarus, 1980; Lazarus & Folkman, 1984; Pearlin & Schooler, 1978). Lazarus and Launier (1978, p. 311) defined coping as "efforts, both action oriented and intrapsychic, to manage (that is, to master, tolerate, reduce, minimize) environmental and internal demands and conflicts among them which tax or exceed a person's resources." Thus coping is seen to include both behavioral and cognitive types of strategies. Coping strategies may also have several different functions, including (1) the modification of the stressor itself (problem-focused coping), (2) alteration of one's own evaluation or appraisal of the stressor in order to reduce perceptions of threat (appraisal-focused coping), and (3) management of one's somatic or emotional reactions to the stressor (emotion-focused coping) (Pearlin et al., 1981; Pearlin & Schooler, 1978).

Singer (1984) has noted that there are two general strategies that have been adopted for the study of coping with stress. The first strategy makes use of scales or other measuring instruments tapping various categories of coping strategies derived from a theoretical framework. Research is conducted to assess the relative effectiveness of each category of coping strategy in attenuating the relationship between stressors (e.g., life events, hassles) and various outcome measures (e.g., illness, mood disturbance). The second strategy is to examine a particular stressor (e.g., bereavement or a life-threatening illness such as myocardial infarction or breast cancer) and compare the coping strategies of individuals who cope successfully with this situation and those who do not, as indicated by mood and health outcomes. The first (theory-based) strategy has the advantage of potentially providing more generalizable results and improving theoretical understanding of the stress process, but it is limited in that it may fail to examine certain coping strategies which may be effective but which are not included in the theoretical framework. On the other hand, the second (stressor-based) strategy produces less generalizable data, but it allows for a more comprehensive catalogue of coping strategies that are effective in dealing with a specific stressor and may therefore be of greater clinical utility.

Several scales have been developed to assess individuals' coping strategies. The Ways of Coping Checklist (Lazarus & Folkman, 1984) comprises 67 items such as "I try to analyze the problem in order to understand it better" and "I talk to someone who can do something concrete about the problem." Respondents are instructed to rate on a four-point scale the degree to which they made use of each strategy in coping with a particular stressful situation. Factor analyses of this measure have yielded eight factors: problem-focused coping, wishful thinking, distancing, emphasizing the positive, self-blame, tension-reduction, self-isolation, and seeking social support (Folkman & Lazarus, 1985). Scores may be obtained on each of these factors by summing the respondent's ratings of relevant items.

Billings and Moos (1981) described a 19-item coping scale which assesses coping strategies along two dimensions: (1) focus of coping (problem-focused versus emotion-focused), and (2) method of coping (active cognitive versus active behavioral versus avoidance). They found moderate levels of internal consistency for each of these subscales and low intercorrelations among them (mean $r = .21$), indicating that they are relatively independent. An interview-based measure of coping strategies containing 17 factors was developed by Pearlin and Schooler (1978) for assessing strategies of coping with role strains in marriage, parenting, household economics, and occupation.

Stone and Neale (1984) have developed a measure of coping with daily problems for use in longitudinal studies with repeated assessments. Their initial attempts to develop a checklist of specific coping behaviors and cognitions were abandoned because of difficulties in obtaining adequate homogeneity in the subscales. Instead, they adopted an open-ended response format in a questionnaire that presents one-sentence descriptions of eight general coping strategies (e.g., distraction, situation redefinition, direct action). Subjects are asked to check whether or not they used each of these strategies in coping with a specific stressor and then briefly describe the particular thoughts or actions that they engaged in. Further work is needed to determine the validity and utility of this measure for examining coping processes.

Research on coping requires not only suitable measuring instruments, but also appropriate research designs. Advocates of coping research (e.g., Folkman & Lazarus, 1985) have emphasized the need for longitudinal rather than cross-sectional research methodologies if coping is to be conceptualized as a process which changes over time. Unfortunately, much of the research to date has been limited to single cross-sectional assessments of coping behavior. This practice leads to the inference of trait-like notions of "coping style" that conceptually resemble the personality variables that advocates of coping research have decried. Future research in this domain will require extensive longitudinal studies that make repeated assessments of coping strategies as well as stressful experiences and stress outcomes.

DATA ANALYSIS TECHNIQUES

We now turn our attention to methods of data analysis in field research on stress. As noted in the previous section, theoretical approaches to stress research have become increasingly sophisticated over the past two decades. These developments have been paralleled by improvements in statistical methodologies. Three major overlapping stages in the research may be delineated: (1) simple correlational models; (2) interactional models; and (3) transactional or process models.

Simple Correlational Models

Early field research on stress focused on the simple relationship between stressful life events and various physical and psychiatric health outcomes. Two general strategies have been adopted in such research. The first strategy is to obtain data from surveys of normal populations, correlating scores obtained on life events measures with indices of health impairment, either by obtaining both measures retrospectively (e.g., Holmes & Masuda, 1974; Rahe, 1972), or in a prospective design with health outcome data obtained some time after the collection of the life events data (e.g., Rubin, Gunderson, & Arthur, 1971). The second strategy is the retrospective case-control method which focuses on a specific target disorder such as myocardial in-farction (Theorell & Rahe, 1971) or multiple sclerosis (Antonovsky & Kats, 1967). In this approach t-tests are performed to compare retrospectively obtained life events scores between a sample of subjects who manifest the target disorder and a symptom-free control group matched on the basis of age, sex, socioeconomic status, and so on.

The simple correlational model represents an initial step in examining the assumed relationship between stressful experiences and health. Although it has been subjected to considerable criticism on both conceptual and method-ological grounds (e.g., Dohrenwend & Dohrenwend, 1974; Mechanic, 1974; Rabkin & Struening, 1976), this approach stimulated a good deal of interest and discussion, leading to more sophisticated methodologies.

Interactional Models

As noted earlier, a shift in theoretical models of stress occurred with the introduction of moderator variables into the research. This model assumes an interaction between the independent measure of stress and the moderator variable (e.g., social support, locus of control) in predicting stress outcomes. In other words, the magnitude of the correlation between the independent and dependent variables varies as a function of the moderator variable.

Early work with this model divided subjects via median splits on the independent and moderator variables and then conducted an analysis of variance in a 2 × 2 factorial design on the dependent measures (e.g., Smith, Johnson, & Sarason, 1978). Alternatively, subjects were divided into two groups via a median split on the moderator variable only and correlation coefficients were computed between the independent and dependent stress measures within each group. A significant difference in the two correlations (tested by means of a t-test using Fisher Z transformations of the correlations) was viewed as support for the hypothesized interaction effect (e.g., Johnson & Sarason, 1978). (See Cohen & Edwards, Chapter 7, for a critique of these methods.)

A more efficient and powerful technique, however, is to conduct a hierarchial multiple regression analysis using an interaction term (Cohen & Cohen, 1983, Chap. 8). This technique is comparable to analysis of variance but makes more efficient use of continuous independent variables. In this approach, a multiple regression equation is computed, using the outcome measure (e.g., illness symptoms) as the criterion or dependent variable, and entering first the independent stress measure (e.g., life events), then the moderator variable (e.g., social support), and finally the product of these latter two measures (i.e., the interaction term). A significant increase in R^2 for this product term indicates an interaction between the independent and moderator variables. In other words, the magnitude of the correlation between the independent and dependent measures varies as a function of the moderator variable. The computer printout of such an analysis provides a regression equation of the form:

$$Y' = c + b_1 X_1 + b_2 X_2 + b_3 X_1 X_2$$

where Y' is the predicted score for the dependent variable, X_1 is the independent measure of stress, X_2 is the moderator variable, c is a constant, and b_1, b_2, and b_3 are the unstandardized regression weights. The direction of the interaction may then be examined by plotting predicted scores on a graph showing the independent variable (X_1) on the abscissa and the dependent variable (Y') on the ordinate. Using the regression equation, two separate regression lines can be plotted, one for subjects with low scores on the moderator variable (using a score one standard deviation below the mean on X_2), and one for those with high scores (one standard deviation above the mean). Visual inspection of the slopes of these lines will then determine whether the interaction is in the predicted direction (see Martin & Lefcourt, 1983 for an example of this procedure).

This procedure may be used with data obtained either retrospectively or prospectively in a longitudinal study. More complex relationships may also be examined using the same general procedure. For example, three-way interactions may be computed when the moderating effect of one variable (e.g., social support) is hypothesized to vary as a function of a second moderator variable (e.g., locus of control; cf. Lefcourt et al., 1984). It should be noted that meaningful interpretation of interaction terms requires that all lower-level interactions and "main effects" be previously entered into the hierarchical analysis. Thus, when examining a three-way interaction, one must first enter the three main effects and the three two-way interactions (cf. Kessler, 1983).

Curvilinear relationships may also be investigated by means of quadratic components computed by squaring subjects' scores on one of the variables. For example, in an investigation of stress from the perspective of reversal theory, Martin (1985) predicted that the relation between life events and mood disturbance would be linear for subjects with high scores on a personality variable called telic dominance, but U-shaped for subjects with low scores on this moderator variable. To test this hypothesis, a hierarchial multiple regression equation of the following form was computed:

$$Y' = c + b_1 X_1 + b_2 X_2 + b_3 X_1 X_2 + b_4 X_2^2 + b_5 X_1 X_2^2$$

A significant increase in R^2 produced by the last component $(X_1 X_2^2)$ provided support for the hypothesized relationship, and a graph of predicted mood scores derived from the obtained regression weights indicated that the regression lines were shaped as hypothesized. Thus, multiple regression analysis represents a general analytic technique with a wide variety of potential applications in stress research (see Kessler, 1983, and Cohen & Edwards, Chapter 7, this volume, for more thorough discussions of methodological issues).

Transactional Models

The importance of conceptualizing stress and coping in terms of a process rather than a stable relationship has been most forcefully expressed by Lazarus and his colleagues (e.g., Lazarus & Folkman, 1984). Folkman and Lazarus (1985, p. 150) state that, "the essence of stress, coping, and adaptation is change. . . . Therefore, unless we focus on change we cannot learn how people come to manage stressful events and conditions." According to these authors, much of the current research on stress and coping emphasizes stable, structural properties of the person and the environment rather than examining the changes that occur over time as the process of stress and coping unfolds.

Research of the type advocated by Lazarus and his colleagues requires a longitudinal methodology. Measures of stressful environmental events, coping strategies, and emotional and physiological effects need to be obtained from the same groups of subjects on several different occasions. The difficulty with this research is that appropriate statistical procedures are not always available for adequate analysis of the data.

One statistical method which might be appropriate in some research of this sort is path analysis (cf. Cohen & Cohen, 1983, Chap. 9; Kenny, 1979; Pedhazur, 1982, Chap. 15). In this procedure the researcher first draws a path diagram indicating the hypothesized causal relationships amongst the variables under investigation. Multiple regression analyses are then conducted to obtain regression weights (path coefficients) indicating the strength of the relationships between the variables in the model. Statistical tests may be performed to determine whether these path coefficients are significantly different from zero. In addition, overidentified models (i.e., these in which certain paths are deleted on the basis of prior theoretical assumptions) may be tested for goodness of fit by comparing the obtained correlation matrix with a matrix that is reproduced according to certain rules. If these matrices do not differ significantly, then one can conclude that the hypothesized causal model is consistent with the data. It shall be noted, however, that this does not *prove* that the model is correct; any number of alternative models may "fit" the data equally well. A detailed explanation of these techniques is beyond the scope of the present paper; the interested reader should refer to any of the excellent presentations cited above. A study by Billings and Moos (1982) provides an example of such techniques applied to longitudinal research on stressful life events and psychiatric symptomatology.

However, path analysis is subject to several important restrictions which may render it unsuitable for many of the kinds of investigations conducted on stress. Path analysis requires that: (1) the variables are measured without error; (2) the residuals are not intercorrelated; and (3) causal relationships are unidirectional (i.e., recursive) (Pedhazur, 1982, p. 636). It is highly unlikely, in fact, that these assumptions are tenable in longitudinal research in which variables with only moderate reliability and validity are measured repeatedly and causal relationships are assumed to be reciprocal (e.g., emotional responses both affect and are affected by coping strategies). Kessler (1983) discusses the use of "instrumental variables" (i.e., variables that are theoretically related to one of the variables but not the other) in sorting out reciprocal causation effects between two variables. This method may also be useful in resolving problems of contamination in stress research, such as the reciprocal relations between chronic role strains or life events and distress.

Many of the difficulties may also be circumvented by employing more sophisticated and versatile techniques such as LISREL (Joreskog & Sorbom, 1977; 1979). This technique, essentially a combination of factor analysis and path analysis, subsumes path analysis as a special case, but also allows for reciprocal causation, measurement errors and correlated residuals. LISREL distinguishes between latent (unmeasured, hypothetical) constructs and observed (measured) variables. The goodness of fit of causal models may be tested by examining relations between the hypothesized latent variables, using several different measures as indicators of each of the latent variables. Once again, it is important to recognize that results indicating that a particular causal model "fits" the data do not *prove* that the model is correct. In addition, models must be developed a priori on the basis of theory rather than using LISREL procedures to engage in a "fishing expedition" to find a model that fits the data. It should be noted also that causal modeling techniques such as LISREL are still quite controversial and there is considerable discussion regarding appropriate statistical tests, robustness to assumption failures, and so on (cf. Bentler, 1980; see also Bynner & Romney, 1985; Cohen & Cohen, 1983, Chap. 9; Pedhazur, 1982, Chap 16). An example of longitudinal research on the stress process using LISREL may be found in a study published by Pearlin and associates (1981).

Other data analytic techniques may also be useful with certain types of data. For example, Kessler (1983) describes methods for estimating block models in which parameters are generated describing relationships among *groups* of variables rather than among *individual* variables (e.g., Marsden, 1982). These models are capable of including blocks of interaction terms as well as main effects. Thus, in research examining complex theories of stress comprising multiple independent stressor variables, moderator variables, and outcome variables, analytic models may be employed in which each of these sets of variables, as well as interactions, are combined into blocks. Parameters estimated from such analyses are more reliable than those obtained from analyses of partial effects of individual variables.

Finally, stochastic process analysis of Markov chains (cf. Neufeld, 1977, pp. 57–62) may be a useful technique for examining stress processes over time. This approach provides estimates of the probability of occurrence of categorical events following other categorical events in a sequential chain. As applied to stress research, it might be used to examine the likelihood of a particular symptom or problem behavior occurring within a specified period of time subsequent to the occurrence or nonoccurrence of a particular stressor event. The occurrence or nonoccurrence of a particular coping strategy might also be entered into the analysis to examine changes in outcome probabilities effected by such a strategy. Probability values may be submitted to an analysis of variance to examine such stochastic processes averaged across a group of subjects (see also Hertel, 1972; Kemeny & Snell, 1960).

As theoretical models and research designs in the field of stress become increasingly complex, researchers will need to keep abreast of the developments in statistical methodologies and will be required to make innovative use of such techniques.

CONCLUSION

A wide variety of data acquisition methods, research designs and data analysis techniques are available to the researcher who wishes to conduct field investigations of stress. In assessing the "independent variables" of stress, one may choose from a number of measures of major life events, minor daily irritants, and chronic role strains. Outcome measures for determining the impact of such stressors include self-report scales assessing physiological and psychological health and moods, behavioral assessments of problem-solving or social performance, psychophysiological recordings, and biochemical assays. Individual differences in stressor-outcome relations may be examined using various measures of social support, personality and cognitive styles, and cognitive and behavioral coping strategies.

Research designs appropriate to such investigations include surveys of normal populations, retrospective and prospective case-control designs, and case-only designs (Kessler, 1983). Data analysis techniques range from simple correlations and t-tests through multiple regression analyses to complex causal modeling programs that allow for reciprocal causation and multiple indicators of latent variables.

The choice among the various measurement instruments, research designs and analysis techniques will depend upon theoretical and practical considerations of the individual researcher. For example, the choice will be simplified by considering whether one is primarily concerned with examining the range of stress outcomes that may result from a particular stressor; the variety of stressors that may be associated with a particular illness or disorder; the effectiveness of a particular coping strategy in dealing with a heterogeneous group of stressors; the typical process of coping with a particular stressor over time; buffering effects of a particular personality variable in moderating the relation between a variety of stressors and health outcomes, or some other aspect of the stress process.

In conclusion, two general points raised in earlier discussion need to be reiterated. First, whenever possible researchers should make use of multiple independent and/or dependent measures in order to improve construct validity and to ascertain the generality of phenomena under investigation. In particular, past reliance on self-report measures needs to be augmented by other sources of data such as behavioral observations and psychophysiological and biochemical measurements.

Finally, theoretical models of stress are becoming increasingly complex as researchers recognize that earlier conceptualizations are inadequate for understanding the accumulating research findings. Such complex models require sophisticated research designs and multivariate statistical analysis techniques. In addition, inadequate success with existing measurement devices necessitates continued psychometric progress. Thus further advances in stress research will depend in large part upon concurrent refinement of reliable and valid measurement devices and advances in data analytic strategies. In view of the complexity of the phenomena under investigation, researchers in this area would do well to remain on the leading edge of advances in research methodologies.

References

Antoni, M. (1985). Temporal relationship between life events and two illness measures: A cross-lagged panel analysis. *Journal of Human Stress, 11,* 21–26.

Antonovsky, A., & Kats, R. (1967). The life crisis history as a tool in epidemiological research. *Journal of Health and Social Behavior, 8,* 15–21.

Baum, A., Grunberg, N. E., & Singer, J. E. (1982). The use of psychological and neuroendocrinological measurements in the study of stress. *Health Psychology, 3,* 217–236.

Baum, A., & Valins, S. (1977). *Architecture and social behavior.* Hillsdale, NJ: Erlbaum.

Beck, A., Ward, C., Mendelson, M., Mock, J., & Erbaugh, J. (1961). An inventory for measuring depression. *Archives of General Psychiatry, 4,* 53–63.

Belloc, N. B., & Breslow, L. (1972). Relationship of physical health status and health practices. *Preventive Medicine, 1,* 409–421.

Belloc, N. B., Breslow, L., & Hochstim, J. R. (1971). Measurement of physical health in a general population survey. *American Journal of Epidemiology, 93,* 328–336.

Bentler, P. M. (1980). Multivariate analysis with latent variables: Causal modeling. *Annual Review of Psychology, 31,* 419–456.

Billings, A. C., & Moos, R. H. (1981). The role of coping responses in attenuating the impact of stressful life events. *Journal of Behavioral Medicine, 4,* 139–157.

Billings, A. C., & Moos, R. H. (1982). Stressful life events and symptoms: A longitudinal model. *Health Psychology, 1,* 99–117.

Blumenthal, J. A., Williams, R. B., Kong, H., Schanberg, S. M., & Thompson, L. W. (1978). Type A behavior pattern and coronary artherosclerosis. *Circulation, 58,* 634–639.

Borus, J. F. (1974). Incidence of maladjustment in Vietnam returnees. *Archives of General Psychiatry, 30,* 554–557.

Bramwell, S. T., Masuda, M., Wagner, N. N., & Holmes, T. H. (1975). Psychosocial factors in athletic injuries. *Journal of Human Stress, 1,* 6–20.

Brown, G. W. (1974). Meaning, measurement, and stress of life events. In B. S. Dohrenwend, & B. P. Dohrenwend (Eds.), *Stressful life events: Their nature and effects.* New York: Wiley.

Brown, G. W., & Harris, T. (1982). Fall-off in the reporting of life events. *Social Psychiatry, 17,* 23.

Brown, G. W., Sklair, F., Harris, T. O., & Birley, T. L. T. (1973). Life-events and psychiatric disorders. Part I: Some methodological issues. *Psychological Medicine, 3,* 74.

Bruhn, J. G., & Philips, B. U. (1984). Measuring social support: A synthesis of current approaches. *Journal of Behavioral Medicine, 7,* 151–169.

Bruns, C., & Geist, C. (1984). Stressful life events and drug use among adolescents. *Journal of Human Stress, 10,* 135–139.

Burks, N., & Martin, B. (1985). Everyday problems and life change events: Ongoing versus acute sources of stress. *Journal of Human Stress, 11,* 27–35.

Bynner, J. M., & Romney, D. M. (1985). Lisrel for beginners. *Canadian Psychology, 26,* 43–49.

Cannon, W. B. (1932). *Bodily changes in pain, hunger, fear, and rage.* New York: Appleton.

Cleary, P. D., & Houts, P. S. (1984). The psychological impact of the Three Mile Island incident. *Journal of Human Stress, 10,* 28–34.

Cline, D. W., & Chosy, J. J. (1972). A prospective study of life changes and subsequent health changes. *Archives of General Psychiatry, 27,* 51–53.

Coddington, R. (1972). The significance of life events as etiologic factors in the disease of children. I: A survey of professional workers. *Journal of Psychosomatic Research, 16,* 7–18.

Cohen, J., & Cohen, P. (1983). *Applied multiple regression/correlation analysis for the behavioral sciences* (2nd Ed.). Hillsdale, NJ: Erlbaum.

Cohen, S., & Edwards, J. R. (1989). Personality characteristics as moderators of the relationship between stress and disorder. In R. W. J. Neufeld (Ed.), *Advances in the investigation of psychological stress* (pp. 235–283). New York: Wiley

Cohen, L., & Roth, S. (1984). Coping with abortion. *Journal of Human Stress, 10,* 140–145.

Cohen, S. (1980). Aftereffects of stress on human performance and social behavior: A review of research and theory. *Psychological Bulletin, 88,* 82–108.

Cohen, S. (1986). Contrasting the hassles scale and the perceived stress ccale: Who's really measuring appraised stress? *American Psychologist, 41,* 716–718.

Cohen, S., Evans, G. W., Krantz, D. S., & Stokols, D. (1980). Physiological, motivational, and cognitive effects of aircraft noise on children: Moving from the laboratory to the field. *American Psychologist, 35,* 231–243.

Cohen, S., Kamarch, T., & Mermelstein, R. (1983). A global measure of perceived stress. *Journal of Health and Social Behavior, 24,* 385–396.

Collins, D. L., Baum, A., & Singer, J. E. (1983). Coping with chronic stress at Three Mile Island: Psychological and biochemical evidence. *Health Psychology, 2,* 149–166.

Coyne, J. C., Aldwin, C., & Lazarus, R. S. (1981). Depression and coping in stressful episodes. *Journal of Abnormal Psychology, 90,* 439–447.

Coyne, J. C., & Holroyd, K. A. (1982). Stress, coping and illness. In T. Millon, C. J. Green, & R. B. Meagher (Eds.), *Handbook of clinical health psychology.* New York: Plenum.

Coyne, J. C., & Lazarus, R. S. (1980). Cognitive style, stress perception, and coping. In I. L. Kutash & L. B. Schlesinger (Eds.), *Handbook on stress and anxiety* (pp. 144–158). San Francisco: Jossey-Bass.

Creed, F. (1985). Life events and physical illness. *Journal of Psychosomatic Research, 29,* 113–123.

Cronkite, R. C., & Moos, R. H. (1984). The role of predisposing and moderating factors in the stress-illness relationship. *Journal of Health and Social Behavior, 25,* 372–393.

Dean, A., & Lin, N. (1977). The stress-buffering role of social support: Problems and prospects for systematic investigation. *Journal of Nervous and Mental Disease, 165,* 403–417.

DeLongis, A., Coyne, J. C., Dakof, G., Folkman, S., & Lazarus, R. S. (1982). Relationship of daily hassles, uplifts, and major life events to health status. *Health Psychology, 1,* 119–136.

Derogatis, L. R., Lipman, R. S., & Covi, L. (1973). The SCL-90: An outpatient psychiatric rating scale. *Psychopharmacological Bulletin, 9,* 13–28.

Derogatis, L. R., Lipman, R. S., Rickels, K., Uhlenhuth, E. H., & Covi, L. (1974). The Hopkins symptom checklist (HSCL): A self-report symptom inventory. *Behavioral Science, 19,* 1–15.

Dohrenwend, B. P., & Dohrenwend, B. S. (1974). Social and cultural influences on psychopathology. *Annual Review of Psychology, 25,* 417–452.

Dohrenwend, B. P., & Shrout, P. E. (1985). "Hassles" in the conceptualization and measurement of life stress variables. *American Psychologist, 40,* 780–785.

Dohrenwend, B. P., Shrout, P. E., Egri, G., & Mendelsohn, F. S. (1980). What psychiatric screening scales measure in the general population: II. The components of demoralization by contrast with other dimensions of psychopathology. *Archives of General Psychiatry, 37,* 1229–1236.

Dohrenwend, B. S. (1973). Life events as stressors: A methodological inquiry. *Journal of Health and Social Behavior, 14,* 167–175.

Dohrenwend, B. S., Dohrenwend, B. P., Dodson, M., & Shrout, P. E. (1984). Symptoms, hassles, social supports, and life events: Problem of confounded measures. *Journal of Abnormal Psychology, 93,* 222–230.

Dohrenwend, B. S., Krasnoff, L., Askenasy, A. R., & Dohrenwend, B. P. (1978). Exemplification of a method for scaling life events: The PERI life events scale. *Journal of Health and Social Behavior, 19,* 205–229.

Donald, C. A., Ware, J., Brook, R. H., & Davies-Avery, A. (1978). *Conceptualization and measurement of health for adults in the health insurance study: Vol. IV. Social health.* Santa Monica, CA: The Rand Corporation.

Faulkner, R. R., & McGraw, D. B. (1977). Uneasy homecoming: Stages in reentry transition of Vietnam veterans. *Urban Life, 6,* 303–328.

Folkman, S., & Lazarus, R. S. (1985). If it changes it must be a process: Study of emotion and coping during three stages of a college examination. *Journal of Personality and Social Psychology, 48,* 150–170.

Fox, B. H. (1981). Psychosocial factors in the immune system in human cancer. In R. Ader (Ed.), *Psychoneuroimmunology* (pp. 103–158). New York: Academic.

Frankenhaeuser, M. (1975). Sympathetic-adrenomedullary activity, behavior and the psychosocial environment. In P. H. Venables & M. J. Christie (Eds.), *Research in Psychophysiology.* London: Wiley.

Frankenhaeuser, M. (1980). Psychobiological aspects of life stress. In S. Levine & H. Ursin (Eds.), *Coping and health.* New York: Plenum.

Funch, D. P., & Marshall, J. R. (1984a). Measuring life stress: Factors affecting fall-off in the reporting of life events. *Journal of Health and Social Behavior, 25,* 453–464.

Funch, D. P., & Marshall, J. R. (1984b). Self-reliance as a modifier of the effects of life stress and social support. *Journal of Psychosomatic Research, 28,* 9–15.

Gersten, J. C., Langner, T. S., Eisenberg, J. G., & Orzeck, L. (1974). Child behavior and life events: Undesirable change or change per se? In B. S. Dohrenwend & B. P. Dohrenwend (Eds.), *Stressful life events: Their nature and effects* (pp. 159–170). New York: Wiley.

Gleser, G. C., Green, B. L., & Winget, C. (1981). *Prolonged psychosocial effects of disaster: A study of Buffalo Creek.* New York: Academic.

Goldberg, D. P. (1972). *The detection of psychiatric illness by questionnaire.* London: Oxford University Press.

Grant, I., Sweetwood, H. L., Yager, J., & Gerst, M. (1981). Quality of life events in relation to psychiatric symptoms. *Archives of General Psychiatry, 38,* 335–339.

Green, B. L., Grace, M. C., & Gleser, G. C. (1985). Identifying survivors at risk: Long-term impairment following the Beverly Hills Supper Club fire. *Journal of Consulting and Clinical Psychology, 53,* 672–678.

Haggerty, R. H. J. (1980). Life stress, illness and social support. *Developmental Medicine and Child Neurology, 22,* 391–400.

Heft, H. (1979). Background and focal environmental conditions of the home and attention in young children. *Journal of Applied Social Psychology, 9,* 47–69.

Helsing, K. J., Szkio, M., & Comstock, G. W. (1981). Factors associated with mortality after widowhood. *American Journal of Public Health, 71,* 802–809.

Hertel, R. K. (1972). Application of stochastic process analyses to the study of psychotherapeutic processes. *Psychological Bulletin, 77,* 421–430.

Holahan, C. K., Holahan, C. J., & Belk, S. S. (1984). Adjustment in aging: The roles of life stress, hassles, and self-efficacy. *Health Psychology, 3,* 315–328.

Holmes, T. H., & Masuda, M. (1974). Life change and illness susceptibility. In B. S. Dohrenwend & B. P. Dohrenwend (Eds.), *Stressful life events: Their nature and effects.* New York: Wiley.

Holmes, T. H., & Rahe, R. H. (1967). The social readjustment rating scale. *Journal of Psychosomatic Research, 11,* 213–218.

Hudgens, R. W. (1974). Personal catastrophe and depression: A consideration of the subject with respect to medically ill adolescents, and a requiem for retrospective life-event studies. In B. S. Dohrenwend & B. P. Dohrenwend (Eds.), *Stressful life events: Their nature and effects* (pp. 119–134). New York: Wiley.

Ilfeld, F. W. (1976). Further validation of a psychiatric symptom index in a normal population. *Psychological Reports, 39,* 1215–1228.

Jemmott, J. B., & Locke, S. E. (1984). Psychosocial factors, immunologic mediation, and human susceptibility to infectious diseases: How much do we know? *Psychological Bulletin, 95,* 78–108.

Jenkins, C. D., Hurst, M. W., & Rose, R. M. (1979). Life changes: Do people really remember? *Archives of General Psychiatry, 36,* 379–384.

Johnson, J. H., & Sarason, I. G. (1979). Moderator variables in life stress research. In I. G. Sarason & C. D. Spielberger (Eds.), *Stress and anxiety* (Vol. 6). Washington, DC: Hemisphere.

Johnson, J. H., & Sarason, I. G. (1978). Life stress, depression and anxiety: Internal-external control as a moderator variable. *Journal of Psychosomatic Research, 22,* 205–208.

Joreskog, K. G., & Sorbom, D. (1979). *Advances in factor analysis and structural equation models.* Boston: Abt Books.

Joreskog, K. G., & Sorbom, D. G. (1977). Statistical models and methods for analysis of longitudinal data. In D. J. Aigner & A. S. Goldberger (Eds.), *Latent variables in socioeconomic models.* Amsterdam: North Holland Publishing 285–325.

Kandel, D. B., Davies, M., & Raveis, V. H. (1985). The stressfulness of daily social roles for women: Marital, occupational and household roles. *Journal of Health and Social Behavior, 26,* 64–78.

Kanner, A. D., Coyne, J. C., Schaeffer, C., & Lazarus, R. S. (1981). Comparison of two modes of stress measurement: Daily hassles and uplifts versus major life events. *Journal of Behavioral Medicine, 4,* 1–39.

Kasl, S. V., & Cobb, S. (1970). Blood pressure changes in men undergoing job loss: A preliminary report. *Psychosomatic Medicine, 32,* 19–39.

Kemeny, J. G., & Snell, J. L. (1960). *Finite Markov chains.* New York: Van Nostrand.

Kenny, D. A. (1979). *Correlation and causality.* New York: Wiley.

Kessler, R. C. (1983). Methodological issues in the study of psychosocial stress. In H. B. Kaplan (Ed.), *Psychosocial stress: Trends in theory and research* (pp. 267–341). New York: Academic.

Kobasa, S. C. (1979). Stressful life events, personality and health: An inquiry into hardiness. *Journal of Personality and Social Psychology, 37,* 1–11.

Kobasa, S. C., Maddi, S. R., & Courington, S. (1981). Personality and constitution as mediators in the stress-illness relationship. *Journal of Health and Social Behavior, 22,* 368–378.

Kobasa, S. C., Maddi, S. R., & Kahn, S. (1982). Hardiness and health: A prospective study. *Journal of Personality and Social Psychology, 42,* 168–177.

Kobasa, S. C., & Puccetti, M. C. (1983). Personality and social resources in stress resistance. *Journal of Personality and Social Psychology, 45,* 839–850.

Krantz, S. E. (1983). Cognitive appraisals and problem-directed coping: A prospective study of stress. *Journal of Personality and Social Psychology, 44,* 638–643.

Krueger, D. W. (1981). Stressful life events and the return to heroin use. *Journal of Human Stress, 7,* 3–8.

Langner, T. S. (1962). A twenty-two item screening score of psychiatric symptoms indicating impairment. *Journal of Health and Social Behavior, 3,* 269–276.

Laux, L., & Vossel, G. (1982). Paradigms in stress research: Laboratory versus field and traits versus processes. In L. Goldberger & S. Breznitz (Eds.), *Handbook of stress: Theoretical and clinical aspects* (pp. 203–211). New York: Free Press.

Lazarus, R. S. (1966). *Psychological stress and the coping process.* New York: McGraw-Hill.

Lazarus, R. S. (1984). Puzzles in the study of daily hassles. *Journal of Behavioral Medicine, 7,* 375–389.

Lazarus, R. S., Averill, S. R., & Opton, E. M. (1974). The psychology of coping: Issues of research and assessment. In G. V. Coelho, D. A. Hamburg, & J. E. Adams (Eds.), *Coping and adaptation.* New York: Basic Books.

Lazarus, R. S., DeLongis, A., Folkman, S., & Gruen, R. (1985). Stress and adaptational outcomes: The problem of confounded measures. *American Psychologist, 40,* 770–779.

Lazarus, R. S., & Folkman, S. (1984). *Stress, appraisal and coping.* New York: Springer.

Lazarus, R. S., & Launier, R. (1978). Stress-related transactions between person and environment. In L. A. Pervin & M. Lewis (Eds.), *Perspectives in interactional psychology* (pp. 287–327). New York: Plenum.

Lazarus, R. S., Speisman, J., Mordkoff, A., & Davison, L. (1962). A laboratory study of psychological stress produced by a motion picture film. *Psychological Monographs, 76,* (Whole No. 553).

Lefcourt, H. M., Martin, R. A., & Saleh, W. E. (1984). Locus of control and social support: Interactive moderators of stress. *Journal of Personality and Social Psychology, 47,* 378–389.

Lefcourt, H. M., Miller, R. J., Ware, E. E., & Sherk, D. (1981). Locus of control as a modifier of the relationship between stressors and moods. *Journal of Personality and Social Psychology, 41,* 337–369.

Lefebvre, R. C., & Sandford, S. L. (1985). A multi-modal questionnaire for stress. *Journal of Human Stress, 11,* 69–75.

Lei, H., & Skinner, H. A. (1980). A psychosomatic study of life events and social readjustment. *Journal of Psychosomatic Research, 24,* 57–65.

Lichtenberg, P. A., Skehan, M. W., & Swensen, C. H. (1984). The role of personality, recent life stress and arthritic severity in predicting pain. *Journal of Psychosomatic Research, 28,* 231–236.

Liem, R., & Liem, J. (1978). Social class and mental illness reconsidered: The role of economic stress and social support. *Journal of Health and Social Behavior, 19,* 139–156.

Lin, N., Dean, A., & Ensel, W. M. (1981). Social support scales: A methodological note. *Schizophrenia Bulletin, 7,* 73–89.

Lindenthal, J. J., & Myers, J. K. (1979). The New Haven longitudinal survey. In I. G. Sarason & C. D. Spielberger (Eds.), *Stress and anxiety* (Vol. 6, pp. 269–288). Washington, DC: Hemisphere.

Lloyd, C., Alexander, A. A., Rice, D. G., & Greenfield, N. S. (1980). Life events as predictors of academic performance. *Journal of Human Stress, 6,* 15–25.

Marsden, P. V. (1982). A note on block variables in multiequation models. *Social Science Research, 11,* 127–140.

Martin, R. A. (1985). Telic dominance, stress and moods. In M. J. Apter, D. Fontana, & S. Murgatroyd (Eds.), *Reversal theory: Applications and developments* (pp. 59–71). Cardiff, Wales: University College Cardiff Press.

Martin, R. A., & Lefcourt, H. M. (1983). Sense of humor as a moderator of the relation between stressors and moods. *Journal of Personality and Social Psychology, 45,* 1313–1324.

McClelland, D. C., Alexander, C., & Marks, E. (1980). The need for power, stress, immune function, and illness among male prisoners. *Journal of Abnormal Psychology, 10,* 93–102.

McClelland, D. C., Floor, E., Davidson, R. J., & Saron, C. (1980). Stressed power motivation, sympathetic activation, immune function, and illness. *Journal of Human Stress, 6,* 11–19.

McClelland, D. C., & Jemmott, J. B. (1980). Power motivation, stress, and physical illness. *Journal of Human Stress, 6,* 6–15.

McClelland, D. C., Ross, G., & Patel, V. (1985). The effect of an academic examination on salivary norepinephrine and immunoglobulin levels. *Journal of Human Stress, 11,* 52–59.

McNair, D. M., Lorr, M., & Droppleman, L. F. (1971). *The profile of mood states.* San Diego, CA: EDITS.

Mechanic, D. (1974). Discussion of research programs on relations between stressful life events and episodes of physical illness. In B. S. Dohrenwend & B. P. Dohrenwend (Eds.), *Stressful life events: Their nature and effects* (pp. 87–97). New York: Wiley.

Mechanic, D. (1975). Some problems in the measurement of stress and social readjustment. *Journal of Human Stress, 1,* 43–48.

Mehrabian, A., & Ross, M. (1977). Quality of life change and individual differences in stimulus screening in relation to incidence of illness. *Psychological Reports, 41,* 267–278.

Meltzer, J., & Hockstim, J. (1970). Reliability and validity of survey data on physical health. *Public Health Reports, 85,* 1075–1086.

Meyer, A. (1951). The life chart and the obligation of specifying positive data in psychopathological diagnosis. In E. E. Winters (Ed.), *The collected papers of Meyer. Vol 3: Medical teaching.* Baltimore: Johns Hopkins Press.

Miller, P. M., & Ingham, J. C. (1979). Reflections on the life-events-to-illness link with some preliminary findings. In I. G. Sarason & C. D. Spielberger (Eds.), *Stress and anxiety* (Vol. 6, pp. 313–336). Washington, DC: Hemisphere.

Miller, S. M. (1980). When is a little information a dangerous thing? Coping with stressful events by monitoring versus blunting. In S. Levine & H. Ursin (Eds.), *Coping and health: Proceedings of a NATO conference* (pp. 145–169). New York: Plenum.

Minter, R. E., & Kimball, C. P. (1980). Life events, personality traits, and illness. In I. L. Kutash & L. B. Schlesinger (Eds.), *Handbook on stress and anxiety* (pp. 189–206). San Francisco: Jossey-Bass.

Monroe, S. M. (1983). Major and minor life events as predictors of psychological distress: Further issues and findings. *Journal of Behavioral Medicine, 6,* 189–205.

Moss, B. E. (1973). *Illness, immunity and social interaction.* New York: Wiley.

Mueller, D. P., Edwards, D. W., & Yarvis, R. M. (1977). Stressful life events and psychiatric symptomatology: Change or undesirability? *Journal of Health and Social Behavior, 18,* 307–317.

Murphy, J. M., Nadelson, C. C., & Notman, M. T. (1984). Factors influencing first-year medical students' perceptions of stress. *Journal of Human Stress, 10,* 165–173.

Myers, J., Lindenthal, J. J., & Pepper, M. P. (1971). Life events and psychiatric impairment. *Journal of Nervous and Mental Disease, 152,* 149–157.

Neufeld, R. W. J. (1977). *Clinical quantitative methods.* New York: Grune & Stratton.

Newcomb, M. D., Huba, G. J., & Bentler, P. M. (1981). A multidimensional assessment of stressful life events among adolescents: Derivation and correlates. *Journal of Health and Social Behavior, 22,* 400–415.

Nuckolls, C., Cassel, J., & Kaplan, B. H. (1972). Psycho-social assets, life crises, and the prognosis of pregnancy. *American Journal of Epidemiology, 95,* 431–441.

Paulus, P. B., McCain, G., & Cox, V. C. (1978). Death rates, psychiatric commitments, blood pressure, and perceived crowding as a function of institutional crowding. *Environmental Psychology and Nonverbal Behavior, 3,* 107–116.

Paykel, E. S. (1974). Life stress and psychiatric disorder: Applications of the clinical approach. In B. S. Dohrenwend & B. P. Dohrenwend (Eds.), *Stressful life events: Their nature and effects* (pp. 135–149). New York: Wiley.

Paykel, E. S. (1983). Methodological aspects of life events research. *Journal of Psychosomatic Research, 27,* 341–352.

Paykel, E. S., Prusoff, B. A., & Myers, J. K. (1975). Suicide attempts and recent life events: A controlled comparison. *Archives of General Psychiatry, 32,* 327–333.

Pearlin, L. I., & Lieberman, M. A. (1979). Social sources of emotional distress. In R. Simmons (Ed.), *Research in community and mental health* (Vol. 1, pp. 217–248). Greenwich, CT: JAI Press.

Pearlin, L. I., Menaghan, E. G., Lieberman, M. A., & Mullan, J. T. (1981). The stress process. *Journal of Health and Social Behavior, 22,* 337–356.

Pearlin, L. I., & Schooler, C. (1978). The structure of coping. *Journal of Health and Social Behavior, 19,* 2–21.

Pedhazur, E. J. (1982). *Multiple regression in behavioral research: Explanation and prediction* (2nd Ed.). New York: Holt, Rinehart & Winston.

Peterson, P. (1984). Effects of moderator variables in reducing stress outcome in mothers of children with handicaps. *Journal of Psychosomatic Research, 28,* 337–344.

Rabkin, J. G. (1980). Stressful life events and schizophrenia: A review of the research literature. *Psychological Bulletin, 87,* 408–425.

Rabkin, J. G., & Struening, E. L. (1976). Life events, stress, and illness. *Science, 194,* 1013–1020.

Radloff, L. S. (1977). The CES-D Scale: A self-report depression scale for research in the general population. *Applied Psychological Measurement, 1,* 385–401.

Rahe, R. H. (1972). Subjects' recent life changes and their near-future illness susceptibility. *Advances in Psychosomatic Medicine, 8,* 2–19.

Rahe, R. H. (1974). The pathway between subjects' recent life changes and their near future illness reports: Representative results and methodological issues. In B. S. Dohrenwend & B. P. Dohrenwend (Eds.), *Stressful life events: Their nature and effects.* New York: Wiley.

Rahe, R. H., & Arthur, R. J. (1978). Life change and illness studies: Past history and future directions. *Journal of Human Stress, 4,* 3–15.

Rahe, R. H., & Lind, E. (1971). Psychosocial factors and sudden cardiac death: A pilot study. *Journal of Psychosomatic Research, 15,* 19–24.

Riley, V. (1981). Psychoneuroendocrine influences on immunocompetence and neoplasia. *Science, 212,* 1100–1109.

Rodin, J. (1976). Crowding, perceived choice and response to controllable and uncontrollable outcomes. *Journal of Experimental Social Psychology, 12,* 564–578.

Ross, C. E., & Mirowsky, J. (1979). A comparison of life-event weighting schemes: Change, undesirability, and effort-proportional indices. *Journal of Health and Social Behavior, 20,* 166–177.

Rubin, R. T., Gunderson, E. K. E., & Arthur, R. J. (1971). Life stress and illness patterns in the U.S. Navy: V. Prior life change and illness onset in a battleship's crew. *Journal of Psychosomatic Research, 15,* 89–94.

Sales, E., Baum, M., & Shore, B. (1984). Victim readjustment following assault. *Journal of Social Issues, 40,* 117–136.

Sandler, I. N., & Lakey, B. (1982). Locus of control as a stress moderator: The role of control perceptions and social support. *American Journal of Community Psychology, 10,* 65–80.

Sarason, I. G., DeMonchaux, C., & Hunt, T. (1975). Methodological issues in the assessment of life stress. In L. Levi (Ed.), *Emotions: Their parameters and measurement.* New York: Rover.

Sarason, I. G., Johnson, J. H., & Siegel, J. M. (1978). Assessing the impact of life changes: Development of the life experiences survey. In I. G. Sarason & C. D. Spielberger (Eds.), *Stress and anxiety* (Vol. 6, pp. 131–149). Washington, DC: Hemisphere.

Sarason, I. G., Sarason, B. R., Potter, E. H., & Antoni, M. H. (1985). Life events, social support, and illness. *Psychosomatic Medicine, 47,* 156–163.

Schaefer, C., Coyne, J. C., & Lazarus, R. S. (1981). The health-related functions of social support. *Journal of Behavioral Medicine, 4,* 381–406.

Schaeffer, M. A., & Baum, A. (1984). Adrenal cortical response to stress at Three Mile Island. *Psychosomatic Medicine, 46,* 227–237.

Schroeder, D. H., & Costa, D. T. (1984). Influence of life event stress on physical illness: Substantive effects or methodological flaws? *Journal of Personality and Social Psychology, 46,* 853–863.

Selye, H. (1956). *The stress of life.* New York: McGraw-Hill.

Selzer, M. L., & Vinokur, A. (1974). Life events, subjective stress, and traffic accidents. *American Journal of Psychiatry, 131,* 903–906.

Singer, J. E. (1984). Some issues in the study of coping. *Cancer, 53,* 2303–2315.

Smith, R. E., Johnson, J. H., & Sarason, I. G. (1978). Life change, the sensation seeking motive, and psychological distress. *Journal of Consulting and Clinical Psychology, 46,* 348–349.

Solomon, G. F. (1981). Emotional and personality factors in the onset and course of autoimmune disease, particularly rheumatoid arthritis. In R. Ader (Ed.), *Psychoneuroimmunology,* pp. 259–280. New York: Academic.

Spielberger, C. D., Gorsuch, R. C., & Lushene, R. F. (1970). *Manual for the state-trait anxiety inventory.* Palo Alto, CA: Consulting Psychologists Press.

Stansfeld, S. A., Clark, C. R., Turpin, G., Jenkins, L. M., & Tarnopolsky, A. (1985). Sensitivity to noise in a community sample: II. Measurement of psychophysiological issues. *Psychosomatic Medicine, 15,* 255–263.

Stein, M. (1981). A biopsychosocial approach to immune function and medical disorder. *Pediatric Clinics of North America, 4,* 203–221.

Sterling, P., & Eyer, J. (1981). Biological basis of stress-related mortality. *Social Science and Medicine, 15E,* 3–42.

Stone, A. S., & Neale, T. M. (1984). New measure of daily coping: Development and preliminary results. *Journal of Personality and Social Psychology, 46,* 892–906.

Svensson, J., & Theorell, T. (1983). Life events and elevated blood pressure in young men. *Journal of Psychosomatic Research, 27,* 445–456.

Tennant, C., & Andrews, G. (1976). A scale to measure the stress of life events. *Social Psychiatry, 17,* 23–28.

Tennant, C., Bebbington, P., & Hurry, J. (1981). The role of life events in depressive illness: Is there a substantial causal relation? *Psychological Medicine, 11,* 379–389.

Theorell, T., & Rahe, R. H. (1971). Psychosocial factors and myocardial infarction: I. An inpatient study in Sweden. *Journal of Psychosomatic Research, 15,* 25–31.

Thoits, P. A. (1982). Conceptual, methodological, and theoretical problems in studying social support as a buffer against life stress. *Journal of Health and Social Behavior, 23,* 145–159.

Turner, J. (1983). Direct, indirect, and moderating effects of social support on psychological distress and associated conditions. In H. B. Kaplan (Ed.), *Psychosocial stress: Trends in theory and research* (pp. 105–155). New York: Academic.

Turpin, G. (1985). Ambulatory psychophysiological monitoring: Techniques and applications. In D. Papakostopoulos, S. Butler & I. Martin (Eds.), *Experimental and clinical neuropsychophysiology.* Beckenham: Croom Helm.

Uhlenhuth, E. H., Haberman, S. J., Balter, M. D., & Lipman, R. S. (1977). Remembering life events. In J. S. Strauss, H. M. Babigan, & M. Ruff (Eds.), *The origins and course of psychopathology.* New York: Plenum.

Uhlenhuth, F. H., Lipman, R. S., Balter, M. B., & Stern, M. (1974). Symptom intensity and life stress in the city. *Archives of General Psychiatry, 31,* 759–764.

Vinokur, A., & Selzer, M. L. (1975). Desirable versus undesirable life events: Their relationship to stress and mental distress. *Journal of Personality and Social Psychology, 32,* 329–337.

Wallston, B., Alagna, S. W., DeVellis, B. M., & DeVellis, R. F. (1983). Social support and physical health. *Health Psychology, 2,* 367–391.

Weinberg, D. A., Schwarz, G. E., & Davidson, R. J. (1979). Low-anxious, high-anxious and repressive coping styles: Psychometric patterns and behavioral and physiological responses to stress. *Journal of Abnormal Psychology, 88,* 369–380.

Weiner, H. (1977). *Psychobiology and human disease.* New York: Elsevier.

Womack, W. M., Vitaliano, P. P., & Maiuro, R. D. (1983). The relation of stress to health and illness. In J. E. Carr & H. A. Dengerink (Eds.), *Behavioral science in the practice of medicine.* New York: Elsevier.

Wortman, C. B., Abbey, A., Holland, A. E., Silver, R. L., & Janoff-Bulman, R. (1980). Transitions from the laboratory to the field: Problems and progress. In L. Bickman (Ed.), *Applied social psychology annual.* Beverly Hills, CA: Sage Publications.

Wyler, A. R., Masuda, M., & Holmes, T. H. (1968). Seriousness of illness rating scale. *Journal of Psychosomatic Research, 11,* 363–375.

Zarski, J. (1984). Hassles and health: A replication. *Health Psychology, 3,* 243–251.

Zimmerman, M. (1983). Using personal scalings on life event inventories to predict dysphoria. *Journal of Human Stress, 9,* 32–38.

Zimmerman, M., O'Hara, M. W., & Corenthal, C. P. (1984). Symptom contamination of life event scales. *Health Psychology, 3,* 77–81.

Zuckerman, M., & Lubin, B. (1965). Normative data for the multiple affect adjective checklist. *Psychological Reports, 16,* 438.

7

Personality Characteristics as Moderators of the Relationship between Stress and Disorder

SHELDON COHEN
JEFFREY R. EDWARDS

Evidence of an association between recent stressful life events and a variety of psychological and physical disorders has steadily accumulated over the last 20 years. Life events have been linked to depression, neurotic impairment, coronary heart disease, cancer, infectious diseases, and a host of other physical and psychological disorders (cf. Dohrenwend & Dohrenwend, 1978, 1981; Thoits, 1983). However, correlations between life event scores and measures of health and well-being have rarely risen above .30 suggesting

Preparation of this chapter was supported in part by NIMH Research Scientist Development Award (K02 MH00721) to the first author. The authors wish to thank Robyn Dawes, Scott Monroe, Shelley Taylor, Jerry Suls, and Peggy Thoits for their helpful comments on an earlier draft.

that life events may account at best for 9% of the variance in illness. Upon initial consideration, this suggests that even if a causal link exists between life stress and physical and psychological outcomes, it is small and the etiological significance of stress may be exaggerated.

In response to this attack on the significance of stress in the etiology of mental and physical disorder, a number of investigators have proposed that the relationship between stress and illness varies with both personal and social characteristics (e.g., see reviews by Cohen et al., 1982; Cohen & Wills, 1985; Gentry & Kobasa, 1985; Johnson & Sarason, 1979; Rabkin & Struening, 1976). That is, differences in social support systems, skills, attitudes, beliefs, and personality characteristics render some persons relatively immune to stress-induced illness and others relatively susceptible. These moderating variables are commonly referred to as stress-buffering resources because they are presumed to protect or buffer people from the pathogenic effects of stress.

The vast majority of existing research on stress buffering has focused on the possible moderating role of social resources. This literature suggests that perceptions of the availability of stress-responsive social support provide relative protection from stress-induced symptomatology, while social network membership per se does not (see recent reviews by Cohen & Wills, 1985; Kessler & McLeod, 1985). This chapter explores the roles of *personal* resources (relatively stable individual differences) in the buffering of stress-induced disorder. Examples of personal resources studied include hardiness, locus of control, self-esteem, private self-consciousness, and type A behavior pattern.[1] We propose a model suggesting how personal characteristics might influence the process by which stress results in disorder, discuss methodological and conceptual issues involved in testing the moderating role of personal resources, and critically review the existing literature. Because most of the studies reviewed in this chapter index symptoms of psychological or physical distress rather than extreme disorder such as clinical depression or chronic physical illness, we use the term *symptomatology* to refer to criterion variables.

In general, we find little convincing evidence for personality factors operating as stress buffers. Although there is suggestive evidence in regard to a number of specific person resources that may influence stress appraisal and/or coping, statistical and conceptual problems, a lack of consistency of results across existing studies, and inadequate numbers of independent replications make much of the evidence difficult to interpret. Only in the case of generalized internal locus of control do we feel there is sufficient evidence to make even a tentative conclusion consistent with stress buffering.

---

[1] It can be argued that perceived availability of social support is a person rather than social resource since these perceptions may be partly or totally attributable to stable personality factors (Cohen, Sherrod, & Clark, 1986; Gore, 1985). Because this literature is adequately reviewed elsewhere (Cohen & Wills, 1985; Kessler & McLeod, 1985), we will not address it in this chapter.

STRESS BUFFERS

For our purposes, we posit that stress arises when one appraises a situation as threatening or otherwise demanding and does not have an appropriate coping response (cf. Lazarus, 1966; Lazarus & Launier, 1978). As noted by Sells (1970), these situations are ones in which the person perceives that it is important to respond but an appropriate response is not immediately available. Characteristic effects of stress appraisal include negative affect, elevation of physiological response, and behavioral adaptations (cf. Baum, Singer, & Baum, 1981). The specific mechanisms through which psychosocial stress is linked to mental health and physical illness, however, remain to be clarified. At a general level, it is assumed that stress leads to negative psychological states such as anxiety or depression. In turn, these psychological states may ultimately influence physical health, either through a direct effect on biological processes that influence susceptibility to disease, or through behavioral patterns that increase risk for disease and mortality.

In earlier work (Cohen & McKay, 1984; Cohen & Wills, 1985), we proposed that there are two major points at which social or personal resources may influence the effects of psychosocial stress on health (also see Gore, 1981; House, 1981).[2] These stress-buffering mechanisms are depicted in Figure 7.1.

First, resources may intervene between stressful events (or event expectations) and a stress reaction by attenuating or preventing a stress appraisal. For example, the perception that necessary resources are available may redefine the threat posed by a situation and/or bolster perceived coping efficacy, thereby preventing a particular situation from being appraised as highly stressful. Second, resources may intervene between the experience of stress and the onset of the pathological outcome by influencing coping ability or effort in a way that facilitates successful coping with either the stressor itself (problem focused) or with the stress reaction (emotion focused), or by facilitating healthful behaviors that counteract the effects of stress reactions.

Thus far, we have indicated that personal characteristics may short-circuit threat appraisal or facilitate coping. In some cases, however, stress-buffering effects may be attributable to the *absence* of a personal characteristic (or the presence of an opposite characteristic) resulting in increased susceptibility to stress-induced pathology rather than the presence of a characteristic resulting in resistance (buffering). Let us consider type A behavior pattern as an example. Presumably, individuals with type B behavior pattern (the lack of the type A pattern) are buffered from the pathogenic effects of stressful events. This implies that there is something about being a type B that either short-circuits stress appraisal or facilitates coping with events appraised as

---

[2] A social or personal resource may also prevent the occurrence of objective stressful events. We view this as independent of the hypothesis that a resource protects [buffers] people from the potentially pathogenic effect of experiencing stressful events.

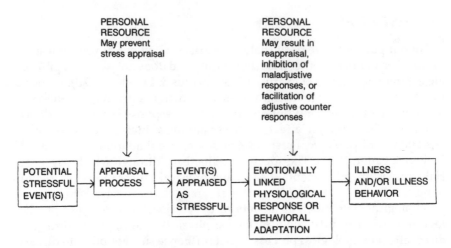

FIGURE 7.1. Two points at which personal resources may intervene with the hypothesized causal link between stressful events and illness (Adapted from Figure 1, Cohen & Wills, 1985). Stress social support and the buffering hypothesis (*Psychological Bulletin, 98,* 310–357. Copyright 1985 by the American Psychological Association).

stressful. Alternatively, it is possible that persons with the type A behavior pattern are more likely to appraise a situation as stressful and to cope inappropriately once a stress appraisal is made. Hence type B individuals may be better off, not because they possess some beneficial personal characteristic, but merely because they are not type A.

Dynamics of Model.   Although it is convenient to think of transactions with stressors as static, cross-sectional occurrences, many common stressful events are chronic or repetitious. It is likely that the stress-buffering effectiveness of some resources may vary over the course of a stressful event or series of events. For example, as we continue to draw on a resource, the appropriateness and/or availability of that resource may change; some resources may be depletable and others increase with practice or use (Gore, 1985). Of particular concern when discussing personal resources is that continued transactions with a stressor may alter the resource itself. For example, self-esteem and feelings of personal control may increase when coping is successful and decrease when it is unsuccessful. Wheaton's (1982; also see Gore, 1985) distinction between resources that influence ability and those that influence effort may be especially useful in this context since resources that affect effort may be more susceptible to success-failure induced change than those that affect ability. In addition, different coping resources may be appropriate at different phases of a stressful event (Lazarus & Folkman, 1984). For example, avoidant strategies may be more effective in the initial stages of encounter and nonavoidant strategies in later stages (see review by Suls & Fletcher, 1985b).

Matching Stressors and Resources.   In our earlier work, we proposed that buffering effects occur when there is a reasonable match between the needs elicited by stressful events and available resources (Cohen & McKay, 1984; Cohen & Wills, 1985; also see Hobfoll, 1985). We have also argued that a common effect of stressors is to threaten feelings of self-esteem and personal control. Therefore, resources that enhance these feelings are likely to match up with a broad range of stressful events. The adequacy of the match between stressor and resource may also be influenced by the specificity of the resource. For example, elevated self-esteem or control in a specific domain (e.g., academics) is more likely to operate as a buffer in that domain than global measures of esteem or control. In theory, global feelings are only useful to the extent that they generate stressor-specific cognitions (cf. Folkman, 1984).

METHODOLOGICAL ISSUES

A minimum condition for testing the buffering hypotheses is a factorial design including at least two levels of stress and two levels of the personal resource under examination. (Studies reviewed in this article will be limited to those that meet the above criterion.) A buffering effect is indicated when the resource reduces (Figure 7.2a) or eliminates (Figure 7.2b) the effects of stress on symptomatology. In either case, if the sample is large enough (allowing for sufficient statistical power), there would be a significant stress × resource interaction.

Statistical Analyses

Common statistical procedures used in stress-buffering studies include two-way analysis of variance with stress and the personal resource as factors, or equivalently, multiple regression analysis with the cross-product term (stress × resource) forced into the equation after the main effect terms for stress and the resource. When appropriate data are available, the regression analysis is preferred because it treats the predictor variables as continuous. Using this procedure, the stress × resource interaction term represents an index of the difference between the slope of the stress-symptom relationship for persons low on the resource and the slope of the stress-symptom relationship for persons high on the resource (cf. Arnold, 1984; Cohen & Cohen, 1975). Also, given certain assumptions are met, both regression and analysis of covariance models provide a means of control for initial symptom level in prospective data analyses.[3]

---

[3] For a discussion of use of covariance in prospective models see Byrk and Weisberg (1977) and Weisberg (1979).

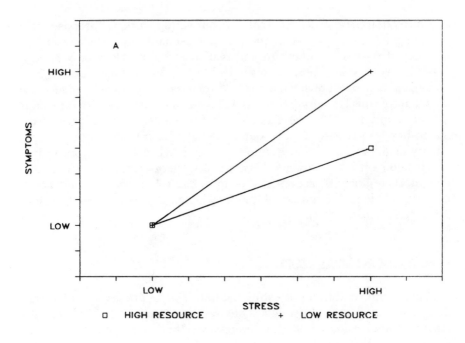

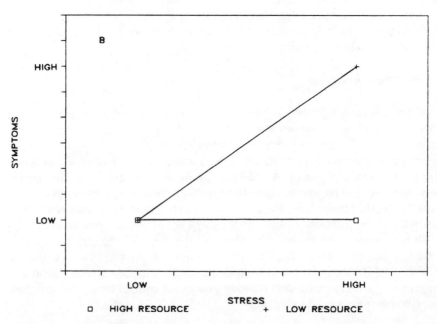

FIGURE 7.2. Depiction of the two forms of the stress × resource buffering interaction supportive of stress-buffering.

Another common statistical procedure used in this literature is subgrouping analysis of correlations. In this analysis, correlations between stress and symptoms are examined separately for persons high (above the median) and low (below the median) on the personality moderator under consideration. (For the purpose of this discussion, we assume that the variable is scored so that the higher the resource level, the greater the stress-buffering.) In general, results have been deemed supportive of stress buffering if (1) there is a significant positive relationship between stress and symptoms for persons with low scores on the coping resource; (2) the relationship between stress and symptoms for persons with high scores on the coping resource is positive or zero; and (3) the correlation between stress and symptoms for persons with low scores on the coping resource is significantly greater than the same correlation for persons with high scores on the resource.

Unfortunately, inappropriate use of the subgrouping of correlations procedure and the inadequate provision of information regarding the form of observed relationships render many of the stress-buffering studies using this procedure uninterpretable. Because the subgrouping of correlations procedure tests differences in the amount of variance explained rather than differences between slopes, it does not provide a test of stress buffering. Moreover, because of a common and mistaken belief that just the presentation of the correlations (or slopes) is sufficient evidence for interpreting the form of the stress × resource interaction, most of the studies in this literature using subgrouping analyses are technically uninterpretable.

Why is it that subgrouping of correlations does not provide an appropriate test of stress buffering? As discussed earlier, a test of stress buffering depends on a significant difference between the slope of the stress-symptom relationship for persons low on the resource and the slope of the stress-symptom relationship for persons high on the resource (see Figure 7.2). Subgrouping analysis of correlations does *not* test the difference between slopes (regression coefficients), but rather the difference in amount of variance explained (correlation coefficients). Slopes and correlations are only identical if the ratio of standard deviations of both variables (stress and symptoms) are the same in both subgroups (high and low resource groups) (see e.g., Arnold, 1982; Tukey, 1969). However, equality of ratios will seldom hold when the pattern of data is supportive of stress buffering. For example, given the standard deviation for stress is equal across subgroups, a steeper slope for one subgroup implies (assuming a normal distribution of scores) a greater standard deviation for symptom scores in that group (see Arnold, 1984, p. 147). Assume, for example, that all points in Figure 7.2b lie very close to the plotted lines. In this case, the standard deviation of symptoms for the high resource group would be close to 0, while the standard deviation for symptoms of the low resource group would be some positive value. In short, if we hold the variance of stress constant across groups, a flatter regression line is generally associated with a smaller variance in symptoms than a steeper regression line. Because of this inequality of standard deviations, subgrouping of correlations is an inappropriate statistical test of stress buffering or of any theory predicting differences in absolute values of slopes across subgroups. A cursory examination of Figure 7.2a suggests the fallacy in the subgrouping of correlation approach. Although the slopes of the two subgroups are different, the correlations could be identical, larger for the steeper slope, or smaller for the steeper slope. A subgrouping comparison of the *slopes* of high and low resource groups, instead of the correlations, avoids this problem (e.g., studies by Krause & Stryker, 1984; Suls & Fletcher, 1985a).

Why are the data patterns from most of these studies uninterpretable? In all but one of the subgrouping (of both correlations and slopes) studies, information is not provided (means, description of mean patterns, or regression slopes *and* intercepts) to allow discrimination between stress-buffering patterns (Figure 7.2a & 7.2b) and forms of the stress × resource interaction in which persons high on the personal coping resource have higher symptom scores than some or all of those who are low (e.g., Figure 7.3a & 7.3b). Although all of the patterns depicted in Figures 7.2 and 7.3 are consistent with the differences in slopes as tested by subgrouping of slopes analysis, only those depicted in Figure 7.2 are supportive of the stress-buffering hypothesis.[4]

It would be justifiable to exclude most of the subgrouping studies as totally uninformative. However, because of the common usage of this technique, and the controversy this critique is sure to raise, we take a middle ground. We present the authors' interpretation of the analysis as well as our own, and interpret the reported conclusions as speculative guesses as to the nature of the data.

Sample Size

The interaction depicted in Figure 7.2b, a *monotone* interaction, is difficult to demonstrate statistically, because the buffering effect (a discrepant mean in only one cell of a 2 × 2 matrix) is divided between main effect terms and the interaction term in the analysis of variance or regression (Dawes, 1969; Reis, 1984). As a result, reasonably reliable measurement and a large number of subjects are required to detect a significant monotone interaction. Thus in studies where measurement procedures or sample size are suboptimal, it is common to find a significant main effect and a pattern of means consistent with a buffering effect without a significant interaction (cf. Kessler & McLeod, 1985).

---

[4] All of these patterns are also consistent with a stress × resource interaction in analysis of variance or regression. However, investigators using these techniques have typically reported the information required to determine the form of the interaction, that is, group means or slopes and intercepts.

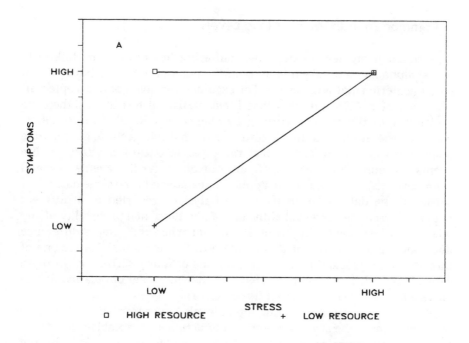

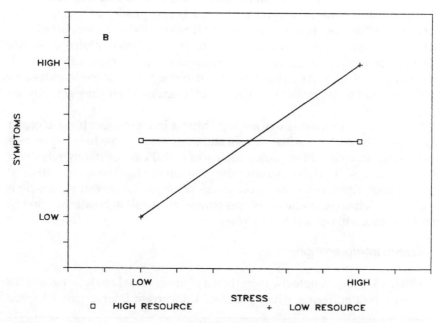

FIGURE 7.3. Depiction of stress × resource interactions consistent with a significant difference between slopes as indicated by subgrouping analysis but not supportive of stress-buffering.

Common Errors in Setting Alpha Levels

A common problem in the stress-buffering literature is the failure to adjust alpha levels to take into account the number of tests conducted in a study (experimental wide error). For example, the commonly accepted alpha level of $p < .05$ indicates that *if one* statistical test is run, then the probability of the result occurring by chance is 1 in 20. Unfortunately, many of the studies in the literature run multiple tests (e.g., separate interactions are conducted to test the possible buffering effects of life events × resource for several different outcomes, for life events × several resources, etc.). (The same issue applies to reanalysis of the same data set or subset of the data set even if that reanalysis is reported in a different paper.) Using an uncorrected alpha of $p < .05$, the actual probability of any one of *two* tests appearing to be significant when the sample difference does not actually represent a population difference is $p < .10$, for one of three tests the probability is $p < .14$, for one of four $p < .18$, etc.[5] In these cases, sample differences are treated as if they represent population differences when they actually do not (type I error).

There are also cases of setting alpha levels too conservatively. Because only one form of the stress × resource interaction is acceptable as evidence for stress buffering (negative signed beta; see Figures 7.2a & 7.2b), the stress × resource interaction can be tested with a one-tailed test. That is, for a single test, a two-tailed level of $p < .10$ is acceptable. In short, we are arguing that because fewer than half of all possible stress × resource interactions support stress buffering, the usual two-tailed alpha does not provide an accurate estimate of the probability of a confirmatory result occurring by chance. As a result, sample differences are sometimes treated as if they do not represent population differences when they actually do (type II error).

The two issues raised above are not entirely independent. If we accept a two-tailed alpha of $p < .10$ as significant, then it is possible to interpret two tests using unadjusted two-tailed alphas of $p < .05$ as accurately reflecting a one-tailed $p < .05$ alpha. Because the problem of more than one statistical test without alpha adjustment occurs so often in the literature, we limit specific criticisms of studies to places where the violation is extreme, that is, *multiple* tests without adjusted alphas.

Causal Interpretation

Finally, we should note the importance of using causal analytic models for data on stress buffering when possible. Concurrent interactions between

---

[5] $1-(1-\text{alpha})^k$ where k = number of uncorrelated tests. See Miller (1966) for discussion of this problem and alternative solutions for both correlated and uncorrelated tests.

stress and a buffering resource in the prediction of well-being are amenable to three alternative causal interpretations. They may reflect the predicted stress buffering of the resource, or illness causing changes in stress and resource levels (reverse causation), or a third factor, for example, social class, causing changes in stress and resource levels and in illness (spuriousness). Clearly, work employing methodological and statistical models that aid in distinguishing between these alternative interpretations is imperative. A discussion of the methodological and statistical techniques available to aid in causal inference from stress-buffering data exceeds the scope of this chapter. The reader is referred to an overview of available statistical techniques and their limitations provided by Dooley (1985) and discussions of prospective data analysis and its limitations by Kasl (1983) and Kessler (1985).

REVIEW

As noted earlier, the following review is limited to studies including both stress and a personal resource presumed to act as a stress buffer. We include studies published through January 1986 as well as several in-press articles available to us at that time.[6] The review is organized into three sections: Composite indices of stress-protective resources; interpersonal predispositions; and intrapersonal predispositions. For the sake of brevity, we often refer to a main effect for stress or a main effect for a personal resource without indicating direction of the effect. Unless otherwise noted, a main effect for stress refers to higher stress associated with *increased* symptomatology, and a main effect for personal coping resource refers to greater resource levels associated with *decreased* symptomatology.

Composite Indices of Stress-Protective Resources

In this section, we discuss studies that use measures that combine various personal and social resources into composite indices. These studies can be divided into those using what have traditionally been termed "psychosocial asset" measures and those using "hardiness" measures. Psychosocial asset measures usually include personal characteristics, health, and social support. Hardiness measures include scales assessing personal control, commitment, and challenge. In both cases, these combined resources are presumed to aid persons in the face of stressful events by providing increased ability or motivation to cope with events or their consequences.

---

[6] Recent published studies that are relevant to past work have been inserted or footnoted in appropriate sections. Other work published since January 1986 reports stress-buffering properties for self-complexity (Linville, 1987), sex-role orientation (Roos & Cohen, in press), and the joint operation of a number of personality and social factors (Holahan & Moos, 1986).

Psychosocial Assets. In a study reported by De Araujo, van Arsdel, Holmes, and Dudley (1973), 36 asthma patients completed a life events checklist (the SRE), and the Berle Psychosocial Assets Index, which provides a score based on three subscales. The first subscale included age, social status, and past medical history; the second subscale tapped the patient's perceptions of family and interpersonal relationships; and the third was based on a physician's rating of the patient's personality structure and attitudes toward illness. The total score was based on a weight of 20 for the first subscale, 28 for males and 20 for females on the second, and 40 points for the third. Hence the overall score is heavily weighted for the physician ratings of patient personality and beliefs. One year after administration of the scales, patients' medical records were reviewed and the mean daily dosage of adrenocortiscosteriods (medication used to control asthma) was calculated.

The results of this study suggested a buffering effect. The mean dosage for patients with low life events scores was relatively low irrespective of the psychosocial assets score. Patients with high life events scores had a relatively high dosage of medication if their psychosocial assets score was low, but had a level equivalent to the low life events groups if their assets score was high. T-tests of all possible pairs of cells indicated that the high stress, low psychosocial asset group had higher steroid intake than any of the other three groups, while these three groups were not different from one another. (These analyses use inappropriate error terms, but they are at least suggestive.) Although a prospective design was employed, there was no control for initial steroid dosage. One problem in interpreting these results is that physician ratings of patient personality make up most of the psychosocial asset scale and the outcome is physician-prescribed drug dosage. Hence the physician's behavior may have been influenced by his or her interpretation of patients' personal abilities to cope.

An oft-cited study by Nuckolls, Cassel, and Kaplan (1972) examined the role of a psychosocial assets score as a moderator of the relationship between life change and medical complications during pregnancy in a sample of 170 women. Measures of stressful life events (the SRE) and of psychosocial assets were obtained during the twenty-fourth and thirty-sixth week of pregnancy; a measure of medical complications was obtained from medical records after delivery, and cases were scored as either complicated or uncomplicated. The psychosocial assets scale was a composite measure including equally weighted scores for self-esteem, marital adjustment, family relationships, friendship patterns, and feelings about pregnancy.

Subjects were cross-classified on the basis of (1) stressful life events (normatively weighted score) in the two years before pregnancy, (2) stressful life events during pregnancy, and (3) psychosocial assets. Although no statistical test of the stress × psychosocial assets interactions were reported, there was a substantial elevation in medical complications for subjects with high stress both before and during pregnancy and low psychosocial assets in comparison with all other groups. However, because of the multiple cross-classifications, this result was based on very few subjects ($n = 11$ in the high stress before pregnancy/high stress during pregnancy/low assets cell). The lack of appropriate statistical analysis, lack of a buffering-like effect for persons who had low stress scores before pregnancy and high stress during pregnancy, and small sample size render the support for stress buffering reported in this study suggestive at best.

In a study reported by Norris and Murrell (1984), a community sample of 1402 older (55 and over) adults were tested five times separated by six-month intervals. Only data from the first two waves are reported in this article. A measure of depressive symptoms (CES-D) and a psychosocial assets scale were administered at the first interview session. Depressive symptoms were measured again during the second interview along with undesirable life events (56 items designed for older adults) and a global (perceived) stress question about how stressful life had been during the last six months. The psychosocial asset scale was the equally weighted sum of the standardized scores from scales measuring social support, functional health, self-esteem, education, and urbanicity (life in urban or rural area). Regression analysis examined the role of time 2 life events and time 1 assets in predicting time 2 depressive symptoms (traditional buffering interaction) and also in predicting time 2 perceived stress. A similar analysis examined the roles of perceived stress and assets in predicting depressive symptoms. Hence, this study provided separate tests of whether personal coping resource influences appraisal of stressful events (life events and assets predicting perceived stress) and/or influences the relationship between appraised stress and symptomatology (perceived stress and assets predicting depression). In regressions that provided additional controls for sex, age, and depression at the first panel, these authors found support for psychosocial assets buffering the relationship between perceived stress and depression but not for either the traditional buffering test or for buffering of the relationship between life events and perceived stress. In short, the study provides support for assets operating as buffers only *after* stress appraisal.

In another article, Murrell and Norris (1984) examined the relationship between undesirable life events (as measured at time 1 and 2) and changes in depression from the first to third interview waves of the *same* study. Multivariate analyses of variance indicated a significant interaction between resources and undesirable events on depression. As predicted by a stress-buffering hypothesis, increases in depression over time were limited to the combined condition of weak resources and high levels of undesirable events. However, weak resource persons with low or moderate undesirable events showed modest (and unpredicted) improvements in depression. In a regression analysis of the same data (resources and events treated as continuous variables), the undesirable event × resources interaction did not reach significance.

In sum, all of these studies provide some evidence suggesting a buffering role of psychosocial assets. However, scale differences and problems in the statistical analysis and interpretation of the two earlier studies make it diffi-cult to interpret the significance of these results. In all of these cases, sepa-rate analyses with each subscale would have helped determine whether the entire complex of assets is necessary for buffering to occur or a specific aspect or aspects of these composite measures were responsible.

Hardiness.   Hardiness is defined as a personality construct composed of three characteristics: (1) *control,* which refers to believing in one's ability to influence the course of events; (2) *commitment,* which refers to approaching life with curiosity and sense of meaningfulness; and (3) *challenge,* which refers to the expectation that change is normal and stimulates development (Kobasa, Maddi, & Courington, 1981).

In a prospective study, Kobasa, Maddi, and Courington (1981) col-lected three sets of data separated by one-year intervals from a sample of 259 executives. Stress was measured using the Schedule of Recent Life Events (SRE; Holmes & Rahe, 1967), and self-reports of recent illness by the Seriousness of Illness Survey (SIS; Wyler, Masuda, & Holmes, 1968). At time 1, hardiness was measured by six scales, with commitment meas-ured with the alienation from self and work scales of the Alienation Test (Maddi, Kobasa, & Hoover, 1979), control measured with Rotter's locus of control scale (Rotter, Seeman, & Liverant, 1962) and the control scale of the Alienation Test (Maddi et al., 1979), and challenge measured with the security scale of the California Life Goals Evaluation Schedule (Hahn, 1966) and the cognitive structure scale of the Personality Research Form (Jackson, 1974). Factor analysis revealed that five of the six subscales (all but cognitive structure) loaded on a single factor. These five scales were combined (sum of equally weighted standard scores) into a composite hardiness score. Because only these five scales are included in the com-posite score, this hardiness measure (used in all reviewed studies employ-ing a composite measure) assigns weights of 2 to both control and commitment, and 1 to challenge. Using reported illness summed over time 2 and 3 as the dependent variable and time 1 stressful life events, hardi-ness, and constitutional predisposition (a measure of parents' illness) as predictors, analysis of variance indicated significant main effects for stressful life events, hardiness, and constitutional predisposition. After controlling for time 1 illness, only the main effects for hardiness and constitutional predisposition remained significant. Although no interac-tions were significant in either analysis, the pattern of group means were consistent with a buffering effect for hardiness.

Kobasa, Maddi, and Kahn (1982) report further prospective analyses of the *same data* just described, again using reported illness summed over time 2 and 3 as the dependent variable. After dropping constitutional predisposition from the model and controlling for time 1 illness, the main effect for time 1 stressful life events was not significant, but the interaction of stress and time 1 hardiness reached significance. Similar results were obtained in a cross-sectional analysis of these *same* data using concurrent stressful life events (summed over time 2 and time 3) rather than stressful life events from time 1. Significant main effects were found for both stress and hardiness, as well as an interaction consistent with the operation of hardiness as a stress-buffer.

In three subsequent articles, Kobasa and her colleagues report the impact of hardiness and several other factors (exercise, social assets, type A behavior pattern) on the relationship between life events stress and reported illness. (Only the results pertaining to hardiness are discussed here.) In each of these cross-sectional studies, stress, illness, and hardiness (5 scales) were measured with the same instruments used in the Kobasa, Maddi, and Courington (1981) study. Two articles report analyses from the *same* sample of 204 managers of a large utility company, differing by the inclusion of either exercise (Kobasa, Maddi, & Puccetti, 1982) or social assets (Kobasa & Puccetti, 1983) as an additional moderator and by final sample sizes due to incomplete protocols. In both cases, results indicated main effects for both stressful life events and hardiness and a buffering effect for hardiness. The third report (Kobasa, Maddi, & Zola, 1983) involved a sample of 140 managers and included type A behavior as an additional moderator. Again, main effects were found for both stressful life events and hardiness. Though an interaction was not found between hardiness and total life events stress, a marginally significant buffering effect was found when only work-related life events were considered.

Rhodewalt and Agustdottir (1984) used the same hardiness scales used by Kobasa and her colleagues. Six-hundred undergraduates completed the hardiness scales, the JAS (see section on type A), the 22-item Langner Psychiatric Impairment Scale, and the College Schedule of Recent Life Events. For each life event, subjects indicated the degree to which the event was desirable (yes, no), controllable (high, moderate, low), and expected (yes, no). Only data from subjects scoring in the upper or lower third of *both* the hardiness and type A scales were used for analysis, yielding a final sample of 339. Subgrouping analyses of correlations indicated that, for low hardiness subjects, life events which were either undesirable or not totally controllable were significantly related to psychological distress. For high hardiness subjects, only life events which were moderately controllable were related to psychological distress. Differences between correlations were not tested. The authors interpret these results as consistent with the buffering hypothesis. As discussed earlier, the subgrouping analysis does not provide an appropriate test of stress buffering. Moreover, neither group means nor slopes and intercepts were reported to clarify the form of the observed interaction.

A final study, reported by Ganellen and Blaney (1984), used a hardiness measure that differs from the five scales described above. In this study, a revised version of the locus of control scale (Levenson, 1974)[7] and five of the original 18 hardiness scales were used to measure hardiness. The five scales were drawn from the Alienation Test (Maddi et al., 1979) and included dimensions of control (powerlessness, nihilism), commitment (alienation from self), and challenge (vigorousness and adventurousness). Instead of combining these scales into a single measure, however, each was used separately in a series of ANOVA's (along with stress and social support) to test their individual contribution to the prediction of depression. Main effects were found for stressful life events, social support, two of the hardiness scales, alienation from self (commitment) and vigorousness (challenge). A buffering effect was found for alienation from self, but not for any of the other five scales.

If unique samples rather than number of articles are counted, five independent studies of hardiness as a moderator of stress and symptoms have been conducted. Of the four studies which used a composite measure of hardiness, one found a significant buffering effect, one found a buffering effect in one analysis of the data but not another, one found no buffering effect for total life events and a marginal (unpredicted) effect for work related events, and one was uninterpretable. (Also see recent failures to find buffering effect of hardiness by Funk & Houston, 1987; Schmied & Lawler, 1986; and Wiebe & McCallum, 1986; and failure with similar construct by Zika & Chamberlain, 1986.) In short, the evidence that the hardiness construct operates as a stress buffer is weak at best. This may be partly attributable to the poor internal consistency of the hardiness measure. Indeed, Kobasa, Maddi, and Courington (1981) report surprisingly low correlations between pairs of scales used to measure each of the three components of hardiness (ranging from .15 to .53), and a factor analysis of the five scales reveals a single dimension accounting for only 46.5% of the variance. When separate dimensions of hardiness were tested, only lack of alienation from self was found to buffer the effects of stress (Ganellen & Blaney, 1984). Because Kobasa and her colleagues did not analyze these dimensions separately, we do not know whether the composite is a more effective buffer than any of the components. Thus, though some components of hardiness may ameliorate the negative effects of stressful life events, it is unclear what these components are and whether they should be considered separately or grouped together as a single meaningful construct (cf. Funk & Houston, 1987; Ganellen & Blaney, 1984; Hull, Van Treuren, & Virnelli, 1987; Scheier & Carver, 1985).

---

[7] Recall that Kobasa and her colleagues used the Rotter scale and the control scale from the Alienation Test. The effectiveness of different locus of control scales is discussed later in this chapter.

Interpersonal Factors

The studies reviewed in this section all focus on personal differences in abilities, attitudes, and feelings about others. They include social skills, social interests, and alienation.

Social Skills.   Social skills refer to stable individual differences that contribute to abilities to form and maintain interpersonal relationships, and to obtain desired rewards from the social environment. These skills are presumed to operate as stress buffers because socially skilled persons would be more capable of coping with stressful events (especially interpersonal events) and more able to mobilize and maintain available social resources when actively coping with stressful events.

The buffering effectiveness of three social skills—social anxiety, self-disclosure, and social competence—were studied in 483 college freshmen by Cohen, Sherrod and Clark (1986). Instruments assessing these skills included the social anxiety subscale of the Self-Consciousness Scale (Fenigstein, Scheier, & Buss, 1975). Jourard's (1971, appendix 12) self-disclosure questionnaire, and a modified version of Levenson and Gottman's (1978) social competence scale. The perception of cumulative stress was measured by the Perceived Stress Scale (Cohen, 1986; Cohen, Kamarck, & Mermelstein, 1983) and depressive symptoms by the CES-D. Three separate hierarchical regressions indicated a stress-buffering effect only in the case of social anxiety; accounting for a mere .57% increment in variance. A relatively smaller sample size for the social competence analysis ($n = 130$; because of missing data on that variable) led the authors to suggest that their failure to find a stress × social competence interaction could be attributable to insufficient power.

Social Interests.   Social interest refers to interest in developing and maintaining interpersonal relationships. Two rather different measures of this concept were used in the only published work examining social interest as a stress moderator (Crandall, 1984): the Social Interest Scale (SocIS; Crandall, 1975) and the Social Interest Index (SII; Greever, Tseng, & Friedland, 1973). The SocIS measures the desire for traits that reflect an interest in and concern for others, such as helpfulness, sympathy, generosity, and so on. The SII measures the desire to contribute, cooperate, and develop in four life areas, including work, friendship, love, and self-significance. Thus, while the SocIS measures concern for others in an altruistic sense, the SII measures involvement in and integration with society. Social integration (traditionally considered a structural [latent] measure of social support rather than a personality factor) could buffer stress because it implies the availability of others to aid. Sensitivity and concern for others may act as a buffer because such feelings may imply social skills that allow persons to draw from their social networks.

Crandall (1984) administered both of these scales, along with the 43-item stressful life events scale (SRRS) and an affect measure (MAACL), to 87 undergraduates. Subgrouping of correlations analyses were performed, with separate correlations between life events and anxiety, depression, and hostility computed for high and low social interest subjects. Results indicated positive correlations between life events and both anxiety and depression only for subjects low in social interest. However, the difference between correlations for high versus low social interest subjects was significant only for subjects classified according to the SocIS. As discussed earlier, this analysis does not provide an appropriate test of the stress-buffering interaction. Moreover, neither means nor slopes and intercepts were reported making it unclear whether the form of the results are consistent with stress buffering.

Anomie.   In a prospective study, Jenkins (1979) examined the moderating effects of anomie in the relationship between stressful life events and psychiatric symptoms among air traffic controllers. A lack of anomie or alienation from society could operate as a buffer because the nonalienated have stronger support networks or are more capable of maintaining and drawing on these networks. Anomie could also result in persons caring less about their own welfare and hence putting less effort into coping with stressful events. At time 1, the Psychiatric Status Schedule was used to identify subjects who were free from clinically significant psychological problems. The 348 subjects who met this criteria were administered a 100-item life event scale and an anomie scale designed to measure alienation from society. Approximately 27 months later, psychiatric symptoms were again assessed. Chi-square analyses were calculated with incidence of impulse control problems at time 2 as the dependent variable. The pattern of results were not supportive of stress-buffering.

Summary.   In short, the evidence for differences in abilities, attitudes, and feelings about others acting as buffers of life stress is, at best, mixed. Evidence for buffering is reported in only two cases: for persons relatively low on social anxiety and for those relatively high in social interests (when defined as concerns about others). There are no replications of this work at this time and the size of the effects appear small. Stress-buffering effects were not found for social competence, self-disclosure, social interests (when defined as social integration), or lack of anomie (not being alienated). Finally, the inappropriate use of subgrouping analysis in the social interest study renders both the confirming and nonconfirming results reported in this study questionable.

Intrapersonal Factors

This section reviews a range of individual differences that are nonsocial in nature. We have categorized these variables into sections on personal control, type A behavior, coping styles, coping flexibility, self-esteem, and private self-consciousness.

Generalized Expectancies of Control.   If persons believe that their outcomes are within their own control, it follows that they should be active (effortful) copers. Because effortful coping increases the likelihood of successful coping, feelings of control are presumed to operate as a stress buffer (Lefcourt, 1985; Wheaton, 1982).

Generalized expectancies regarding control are variously referred to as locus of control, fatalism, mastery, and personal competence. These terms seem to be similar descriptions of the same concept deriving from different traditions or disciplines. Locus of control is the term used most often in the stress-buffering literature. Rotter (1966) defines locus of control as a generalized belief concerning personal control over important outcomes. An *internal* locus of control refers to a generalized belief that events are contingent upon one's own behavior, whereas an *external* locus of control refers to a generalized belief that events are contingent upon external factors, such as fate, luck, chance, or powerful others.

A number of different measures of locus of control have been used in studies of generalized control as a stress buffer. The most popular is the Rotter scale (Rotter, 1966) which was designed to measure a unidimensional, generalized expectancy of control over a wide variety of life domains. Subsequent factor analyses, however, support a multidimensional interpretation of the scale. For example, Mirels (1970) uncovered two meaningful dimensions, one concerning control over personal goals, achievements, and outcomes, and the other concerning control over social-political systems. Reid and Ware (1973) describe the former factor as fatalism and the latter as social systems control (SSC). Reid and Ware (1974) elaborated these dimensions in the development of a three-factor locus of control scale, which, in addition to subscales concerning fatalism and SSC, contains a self-control (SC) subscale that reflects beliefs concerning the ability to regulate one's own responses. The fatalism and SSC dimensions of this scale are highly related to the corresponding dimensions in the Rotter scale, while the SC dimension appears to be fairly distinct from the dimensions identified in the Rotter scale.

Lefcourt, von Baeyer, Ware, and Cox (1979) also expanded upon the multidimensional nature of locus of control in their development of the Multidimensional-Multiattributional Causality Scale (MMCS). This measure contains two subscales, one pertaining to locus of control concerning personal achievement and one pertaining to locus of control concerning affiliations with others. Both MMCS subscales are positively correlated with the Rotter (1966) scale, with correlations ranging from .23

to .62 for the achievement scale and .37 to .55 for the affiliation scale (Lefcourt et al., 1979).

Several studies have examined the moderating effects of locus of control as measured by each of the instruments just described. The majority of this work used the Rotter scale, and evidence for internal control operating as a stress buffer derives primarily from studies using this scale. In the earliest published study, Johnson and Sarason (1978) collected concurrent data on stressful life event (LES), locus of control (Rotter Scale), and symptoms of anxiety (STAI) and depression (BDI) from 124 college students. Subgrouping of correlations analyses indicated that only negative life events experienced by externals were significantly (and positively) related to both depression and trait anxiety. The authors interpret these findings as supportive of the hypothesis that internal control acts as a stress buffer. However, the appropriateness of the subgrouping analysis is in question. Moreover, neither group means nor slopes and intercepts were reported to clarify the form of the observed relationship.

Wheaton (1982) used a six-item version of the Rotter scale in a study in which locus of control is referred to as fatalism—accepting personal outcomes as inevitable, predetermined, and unalterable. Wheaton tested a random sample of 132 Anglo Americans and 108 Mexican Americans living in El Paso, Texas. Two measures of stress were used, including a life event inventory designed to measure acute stressors and a nine-item measure tapping the number of chronic sources of stress, such as separation or divorce, excessive marital problems, and feelings of being a failure in one's work. Depressive symptoms were measured using a self-report scale concerning the frequency of occurrence of 40 symptoms. Regression analyses indicated that, after controlling for sex, church attendance, education, physical problems, and social desirability, low fatalism (internal locus of control) buffered acute (life events) but not chronic stress. In an analysis of a subsample (132 Anglos) from the *same* data set, Wheaton (1983) examined two additional outcomes, symptoms of schizophrenia and anxiety, as well as reanalyzing the data on depressive symptoms. As in the larger version of the data set, low fatalism (internal control) buffered acute stress in the prediction of depressive symptoms. In the new analyses, low fatalism buffered both acute and chronic stress in the prediction of schizophrenic symptoms but neither acute nor chronic stress in the prediction of symptoms of anxiety.

Lefcourt, Miller, Ware, and Sherk (1981) reported three cross-sectional studies examining the impact of various measures of locus of control on the relationship between life events and psychological strain. Only the first used the Rotter scale. In this study, 59 undergraduates completed a life events scale focusing on high school years, both the Rotter and MMCS locus of control scales, and an affect measure (POMS). Separate hierarchical regression analyses, each using total mood disturbance as the dependent variable, were performed for each measure of locus of control. Main effects were found for negative life events and Rotter's locus of control (favoring internals). The interaction between these two variables was also significant and consistent with the hypothesis that internal locus of control operates as a stress buffer. The interaction accounted for 7% of the variance in mood disturbance. A similar stress buffering effect was found for the MMCS affiliation scale, though it reached only marginal significance (4% variance accounted for).

Krause and Stryker (1984) examined the moderating effects of locus of control in a longitudinal study of 2090 middleaged men. A shortened version of the Rotter scale and two items measuring global health status were administered at time 1. Two years later (time 2), the shortened version of the Rotter scale was again administered, along with a six-item index of recent job and economic events and a seven-item measure of psychological and physical distress. Cases were divided at the mean of the locus of control scale, and only men with the same locus of control orientation at both panels were retained for analysis ($n = 1763$). Subgrouping analysis of slopes indicated that, after controlling for time 1 distress and demographic information, the slope representing the relationship between time 2 stress and time 2 distress was significantly greater for externals, though significant for both groups. Further analysis involved four groups formed by dividing the two earlier groups at plus and minus one standard deviation from the mean (extreme externals, moderate externals, moderate internals, extreme internals). Multiple comparisons indicated that the slope representing the relationship between stress and time 2 distress was steepest for moderate externals and flattest for moderate internals (differences significant at the $p < .05$ level), though the slopes were significant for all four groups. Unfortunately, neither intercepts nor group means were reported to clarify the form of these relationships. Nonetheless, this study suggests the possibility of a curvilinear moderating effect of locus of control.

In a later article, Krause (1985) noted that persons high in need for social approval may under report socially undesirable experiences such as negative life events (e.g., divorce, financial, and legal problems) and depressive symptomatology. To control for this, a measure of social desirability (Crowne & Marlowe, 1964) was included in a study of life events (12-item scale), locus of control (Rotter scale), and depression (CES-D) among 300 married women. Before controlling for social desirability, main effects for negative life events and locus of control were significant, while their interaction was not. After controlling for social desirability, however, the main effect for negative life events remained significant and the stress × control interaction attained significance, accounting for 1.2% of depressive symptom variance. The interaction was consistent with the hypothesis that internal locus of control acts as a stress buffer. These results indicate that controlling for social desirability response bias may aid the detection of control as a stress buffer.

In a study by Sandler and Lakey (1982), undergraduates were classified as internals (52 subjects) or externals (41 subjects) according to their scores on the fatalism dimension of the Rotter scale (Mirels, 1970). Those whose scores range from 0–3 were classified as internals and those with scores of 5–9 as externals. These subjects were administered a 111-item life event scale in which they were asked to rate each event for personal control over occurrence and consequences, an anxiety measure (STAI), and a depressive symptom scale (BDI). Subgrouping of correlations analyses indicated positive relationships between negative life events and both depression and anxiety for all subjects, with stronger relationships for subjects with an external locus of control. These data were interpreted by the authors as supportive of stress buffering. Unfortunately, the analyses provided an inappropriate test of the buffering hypothesis. Moreover, because group means were not reported, it is not possible to determine whether the pattern of data were supportive of stress buffering. In the case of personal control over life event occurrence and consequences, the patterns and magnitudes of correlations were clearly not consistent with stress buffering. Furthermore, locus of control and personal control over life events were not correlated, which is contrary to the assumption that an internal locus of control leads to more effective coping due to greater personal control over life events.

Turner and Noh (1983) also examined the stress buffering effects of locus of control as measured by the fatalism dimension of the Rotter scale. A sample of 312 women completed a 22-item life events scale, a 9-item version of the fatalism dimension of the Rotter scale, and a psychological distress measure focusing on anxiety (7 items), depression (6 items), and anger/aggression (6 items). Regression analysis using the summary psychological distress measure as the dependent variable indicated significant main effects for life events and locus of control. The interaction between life events and locus of control was not significant for the overall sample. However, separate analyses for lower, middle, and upperclass women suggested a buffering effect for locus of control specifically among middleclass women (neither statistical test nor significance level of this effect was not reported).

Two studies using the Rotter scale failed to find any stress-buffering effects. In a prospective study, McFarlane, Norman, Streiner, and Roy (1983) interviewed 428 subjects at three points in time separated by six-month intervals. At each interview, subjects completed a psychological distress scale (Langner, 1962) and a 42-item life events scale (SRE) with each event assessed for desirability, expectedness, and personal control over occurrence. During the first and third interviews, subjects also completed the Rotter scale and a measure of social support. Other health measures included a health diary in which symptoms were recorded for consecutive three-day intervals every two weeks and a diagnosis and treatment form completed by family physicians after each visit. Prospective analyses indicated that uncontrollable events evaluated as either undesirable or neutral were most strongly related to all symptoms, and further analyses involved only these life events. Moderating effects were tested cross-sectionally, using time 2 psychological distress scores and time 2 number of symptoms reported in the health diaries as dependent variables in separate regression analyses. After controlling for time 1 symptom scores, stressful life events as assessed at time 2 were significantly related to psychological distress, but neither the main effect for locus of control nor its interaction with stressful life events reached significance. Similarly, stressful life events were significantly related to reported physical symptoms after controlling for previously reported symptoms, while locus of control exhibited neither main nor moderating effects.

Nelson and Cohen (1983) collected longitudinal data from 110 undergraduates at two times separated by an eight-week interval. Measures collected at both time 1 and time 2 included a 57-item life events scale (LES) with each event rated for personal control over the outcome of the event, an anxiety scale (STAI), a psychological discomfort scale, and Rotter's locus of control scale. Depressive symptoms (BDI) was measured only at time 2. Cross-sectional analyses at both times 1 and 2 indicated the expected main effects on anxiety and discomfort for both negative life events and locus of control (externals have more symptoms). There were no stress × locus of control or stress × personal control interaction in either analysis. A similar lack of buffering interactions was found in a reanalysis of time 2 data controlling for time 1 anxiety and discomfort. As in the Sandler and Lakey (1982) study, ratings of personal control over life events were independent of locus of control orientation.

Unlike studies using the Rotter scale, those using the MMCS and Reid and Ware scales have not generally found internal control acting as a stress buffer. Two studies reported in Lefcourt el al. (1981) measured locus of control with the Reid and Ware scale and the MMCS. In the first, 102 undergraduates completed a life events scale (LES), an affect measure (POMS), and the Reid and Ware (1974) SC subscale. Results indicated no main effect for life events but a significant main effect for self-control (favoring internals). A significant interaction between negative life events and self-control was also found. However, rather than representing a buffering effect, plotted means indicated a positive relationship between negative life events and mood disturbance only for internals, while externals experienced high levels of mood disturbance regardless of life event scores (Figure 7.3a).

In the second study, 55 undergraduates were administered the LES, the POMS, the MMCS, and all three subscales of the Reid and Ware three-factor locus of control scale. Main effects were found for negative life events and control over affiliations with others (marginal), as well as interactions between negative life events and both control over affiliations with others and control over achievements. The form of the interaction between life events and control over affiliation with others was not consistent with a locus of control buffering hypothesis. Control over achievements demonstrated a buffering effect favoring internals (accounting for 7% of the variance), though strong positive relationships between negative life events and mood disturbance were found for both internals and externals.

Generalized feelings of control were also studied under the rubric of "personal competence" in a study reported by Husaini, Neff, Newbrough, and Moore (1982). White married adults ($n = 965$) from rural areas in Tennessee, Oklahoma, and Ohio were randomly sampled. Personal competence was measured with a seven-item scale developed by Campbell, Converse, Miller, & Stokes (1960) designed to measure an individual's sense of competence or instrumental efficacy. Stressful life events were measured with a 52-item modified version of the Holmes and Rahe scale, and depressive symptoms were measured with the CES-D. Respondents also completed an eight-item scale tapping eight dimensions of social support. Eight separate hierarchical regression analyses were performed, each controlling for demographics and including a different measure of social support. All eight analyses indicated a significant main effect for life events and, in seven of eight analyses, a significant interaction between life events and personal competence. Results were consistent with the hypothesis that internal locus of control operates as a stress buffer. When these analyses were recalculated separately for males ($n = 335$) and females ($n = 624$), the control buffering effect was not found in any of the analyses of male data and occurred only in two of eight analyses of female data. These results may indicate that locus of control is more important for females, or alternatively may reflect the lower statistical power in the smaller sample of males.

Finally, a study of the stress-buffering properties of "mastery" is reported by Hobfoll and Walfisch (1984). In this study, 68 Israeli women were interviewed immediately prior to undergoing biopsy for suspected cancer ("acute" stress) and again three months later ("everyday" stress). Mastery was measured (prebiopsy) with the sense of mastery scale used by Pearlin and Schooler (1978). Measures of psychological distress collected both pre- and postbiopsy included state anxiety (STAT) and depressive symptoms (CES-D). Data from women diagnosed as having cancer at prebiopsy were omitted, and the remaining group was assumed to be under high stress at time 1 (prior to biopsy) and low stress at time 2 (3 months postbiopsy). An inappropriate subgrouping of correlations analyses did not support stress buffering for mastery. Enough information was available to determine that data for anxiety was probably not supportive of buffering. The reported data were insufficient to make any estimate in the case of depression.

Overall, the detection of internal locus of control as a stress buffer appears to depend upon the instrument used to measure locus of control and the dependent variable under consideration. In particular, most studies reporting a moderating effect measured locus of control with the Rotter scale (or a subset of its items) and used psychological symptomatology as the dependent variable (Johnson & Sarason, 1978; Krause, 1985; Krause & Stryker, 1984; Lefcourt et al., 1981, study 1; Turner & Noh, 1983; Wheaton, 1982, 1983).

However, inappropriate statistical analysis (Johnson & Sarason, 1978), and failure to provide sufficient data to determine the form of the interaction (Johnson & Sarason, 1978; Krause & Stryker, 1984) raise questions regarding the results of two of these studies.[8] With the exception of Husaini et al. (1982), the few studies using locus of control measures other than the Rotter scale produced inconsistent and inconclusive results (Ganellen & Blaney, 1984 [discussed in composite index section]; Hobfoll & Walfisch, 1984; Lefcourt el al., 1981, studies 1, 2, & 3). It is not clear that the facets of locus of control measured by these scales (particularly the affiliation, achievement, and social-systems control scales) are relevant for the attenuation of stress-related outcomes.

The relative success of the Rotter scale may be attributable to its generality and its emphasis on control of external events (as opposed to self-control). Because stressful life events scales assess the occurrence of a range of different stressors, eliciting needs in different domains, a global control scale like the Rotter instrument may provide a good match of stressors and resources. Moreover, life events are generally conceptualized as external occurrences requiring personal control of the environment. In sum, the studies reviewed offer tentative support for locus of control (as measured by the Rotter scale) as a buffer of the relationship between life events stress and psychological strain.

Type A Behavior Pattern.   Type A behavior pattern is characterized by excessive competitive drive, impatience, hostility, and accelerated speech and motor movements, while the type B pattern is defined as the relative absence of these characteristics (Friedman & Rosenman, 1959; Glass, 1977; Matthews, 1982). Epidemiologic studies have established that type A individuals are more likely than type B individuals to develop coronary heart disease. According to Glass (1977), challenging, competitive, or uncontrollable environmental conditions tend to trigger the type A pattern in susceptible individuals, which in turn intensifies their psychophysiological reactions to these conditions. Hence, one might predict that the type B pattern would act as a stress buffer, either because type B behavior helps protect people from stress-induced pathology or because the type A behavior enhances stress-induced pathology (Krantz & Manuck, 1984; Manuck & Krantz, 1984).

The two measures of type A behavior pattern used most often in this literature are the Structured Interview (SI; Rosenman et al., 1975) and the Jenkins Activity Survey (JAS; Jenkins, Rosenman, & Zyzanski, 1974). While both of these measures exhibit acceptable reliability, the overlap between measures is only moderate. Several studies have indicated that the JAS produces the same type A/B classification made by the Structured Interview in

---

[8] A recently published study by Caldwell, Pearson, and Chin (1987) failed to find a stress-buffering effect of a version of the Rotter scale.

only about 60 to 70% of the cases examined (see review by Matthews, 1982). Thus, while each of these measures may reliably tap some dimension of the type A pattern, it is doubtful that the same dimensions are addressed by each.

Though laboratory research has demonstrated the heightened reactivity to stressful conditions of type A individuals (Houston, 1983), most field research has examined type A behavior pattern as a main effect in the prediction of pathology (Haynes, Feinleib, & Kannel, 1980; Rosenman et al., 1975). We located seven published field studies that examined the differential reactivity of type A and type B individuals in reaction to stressful conditions. At best, these studies provide only suggestive evidence that type B individuals are relatively protected from stress-induced pathology.

In the earliest study, Caplan and Jones (1975) examined the impact of type A behavior pattern on the relationship between stress associated with a campus computer shutdown and symptomatology in college students. During the three days before the announced shutdown, 122 male computer users were administered a questionnaire including measures of subjective stress (workload and role ambiguity); a self-report type A behavior questionnaire (Vickers, 1973), and scales measuring anxiety, depression, and resentment. Heart rate was measured after completion of the questionnaire. Five months later, all measures were again collected from 73 (60%) of the original respondents. All data were converted to change scores by partialing out the time 1 value of each variable. Path analyses involving the entire sample indicated a positive relationship between change in workload and change in anxiety, positive relationships between change in role ambiguity and changes in both depression and resentment, and positive relationships between changes in both anxiety and resentment and change in heart rate. Subgrouping of correlations analyses were used to test differences between type A and type B students in the relationship between stressors and symptoms. Of the nine analyses performed (2 stressors × 3 psychological outcomes as well as 3 psychological outcomes as predictors of heart rate), the only difference between type A and type B students was interpreted as consistent with stress buffering and involved the association between change in workload and change in anxiety. The correlation was significant only in the case of type A individuals, and the magnitude of the correlations were significantly different. A similar but nonsignificant difference was found for the relationship between change in anxiety and change in heart rate. Unfortunately, the alpha level (set at $p < .10$) was not appropriately adjusted to account for the number of analyses performed. Moreover, although slopes were presented (greater slope for type A individuals as predicted by buffering), failure to report intercepts or group means results in uncertainty regarding the exact nature of the stress × type A interaction.

Suls, Gastorf, and Witenberg (1979) examined the relationship between life events and psychological distress in a sample of 125 undergraduates classified as extreme type A or type B according to a version of the JAS adapted for college students (Glass, 1977). Life events were measured using a version of the SRE modified for college students with each event assessed in terms of desirability, personal controllability, and expectedness (yes, no, unable to determine). Psychological distress was measured using Langner's anxiety scale. Subgrouping analyses were performed, with data divided according to the 3 (desirability, controllability, expectedness) × 3 (yes, no, unable to determine) categorization of life events just described and the type A/type B classification. These matrices result in 9 possible subgrouping of correlations comparisons. If type A behavior is only triggered by unpredictable and uncontrollable events, buffering effects would only be expected for comparisons involving undesirable, uncontrollable, and unexpected life events. Data interpreted by the authors as consistent with the buffering hypothesis were found for two of these comparisons: undesirable and unexpected events, and also for events for which degree of personal control was indeterminable. Unfortunately, the subgrouping of correlations analysis used in this study is inappropriate for testing stress buffering. Moreover, neither group means nor slopes and intercepts were reported, making any interpretation of the form of the observed relationship speculative at best.

Controllability, desirability, and predictability of life events were also assessed in two studies of the stress-buffering role of the type A behavior pattern reported by Rhodewalt and his colleagues. In the first study (Rhodewalt & Agustdottir, 1984), 600 undergraduates completed the hardiness scale, the JAS, the Langner psychological distress scale, and a college student life events scale. The details of this study are discussed in the section on hardiness. Subgrouping analyses of correlations indicated that, for type A subjects, life events which were either undesirable or not totally controllable were significantly related to psychological distress. For type B subjects, only life events which were undesirable were related to psychological distress. As indicated earlier, an inappropriate analysis as well as a failure to report group means or slopes and intercepts renders this study uninterpretable.

Rhodewalt, Hays, Chemers, and Wysocki (1984) report a study in which 49 university administrators completed the JAS, a 24-item job stress scale, a life events scale (SRE), a 26-item physical symptom and illness checklist, and the Langner 22-item psychiatric impairment scale. Each applicable item in the life events scale was rated by the respondent for desirability, predictability, and controllability. Six multivariate analyses of variance were conducted. Analyses involving job stress scores indicated significant main effects for both job stress and type A scores and a stress-buffering effect (favoring type B subjects). Further univariate analyses of variance indicated that the buffering effect corresponded to scores on the Langner scale but was not significant for overall physical symptoms. However, when only symptoms pertaining to cardiovascular health were included, a significant buffering effect (favoring type B subjects) was found. Findings for life events rated as both undesirable and moderately controllable were consistent with those for job stress, indicating a buffering effect (favoring type B subjects) in the prediction of psychological distress and cardiovascular symptoms.

In two cross-sectional studies, Ivancevich, Matteson, and Preston (1982) assessed the relationship between job stress and various psychological and physiological outcomes for type A and type B managers and nurses. In the first study, 339 managers completed the job stress measures (quantitative and qualitative workload, lack of career progression, family situation, supervisor relations, and role conflict), a type A scale similar to the JAS, and a job satisfaction measure. Physiological measures included serum cholesterol and triglycerides, systolic and diastolic blood pressure, and percent body fat. Subgrouping of correlations analyses looked only at persons in the extremes; classifying persons as type A if they were in the top third of scale scores and as type B if they were in the bottom third. Of the 30 subgrouping analyses performed (6 stress measures × 5 outcomes), three were interpreted by the authors as consistent with a type B stress-buffering hypothesis; indicating insignificant correlations for type B managers and significantly greater relationships for type A managers. These included the relationship between quantitative workload and both systolic and diastolic blood pressure and the relationship between role conflict and systolic blood pressure. Unfortunately, this subgrouping analysis was inappropriate and group means or slopes and intercepts clarifying the nature of the observed relationships were not reported. In a follow-up study involving 57 female registered nurses, job stress (same as above except that family situation and lack of job progression were replaced with physician relations and time pressure) and the psychological and physiological criterion variables were measured as before, but the type A behavior pattern was assessed using the structured interview. Of the 30 subgrouping of correlations analyses performed, four were interpreted by the authors as consistent with type B stress buffering; indicating nonsignificant relationships for type B subjects and significantly greater relationships for type A nurses. These included the relationships between time pressures, role conflict, and quantitative workload and serum cholesterol, and the relationship between quantitative work overload and systolic blood pressure. Group means suggest that the form of these interactions were consistent with the stress-buffering hypothesis. Overall, even if the authors' interpretation of statistical significance were accepted, these data are suggestive at best with only 7 of 60 analyses supporting type B buffering.

Two studies failed to find even suggestive evidence that type B subjects are less effected by stress than type A subjects. In the first, Somes, Garrity, and Marx (1981) examined differences in the relationship between life events and physical and psychological symptomatology among 145 type A and type B undergraduates. The life events instrument was a 47-item scale, and measures of symptomatology included four physical health scales and

Langner's index of mental health. Structured interviews categorized 41 students as extreme type A (type A_1) and the remaining 104 students as either type A_2 or type B. Due to difficulty in making a reliable distinction between type A_2 and type B students, the latter two groups were combined for analysis. Analyses involving the entire sample indicated positive relationships between life events and both physical and psychological symptoms. Results of subgrouping of correlations analyses were not supportive of type B buffering in either the entire sample or in separate analyses for males and females.

Finally, Kobasa, Maddi, and Zola (1983) examined the moderating effects of type A behavior and hardiness on the relationship between stress and illness. Managers ($n = 140$) completed the 58-item life events list (SRE), a self-reported illness scale (SIS), and the JAS. Analysis of variance revealed a main effect for stressful life events (more events resulting in more illness), but neither a main effect nor an interaction were found for type A behavior.

Overall, the evidence for persons with type B patterns being relatively protected from stress-induced pathology is at best suggestive. Although some supportive effects are reported by Caplan and Jones (1975), Ivancevich et al. (1982), Suls et al. (1979), and Rhodewalt et al. (1984), there is a distinct possibility of type I error, with only 13 of 83 analyses (16%) reaching significance; 13 of 89 of the remaining two studies are also included.[9] Moreover, the majority of these studies may be uninterpretable in terms of their implications for stress buffering because of statistical shortcomings. Only Kobasa, Maddi, and Zola (1983) and Rhodewalt et al. (1984) used appropriate analytic techniques. Moreover, among the studies using subgrouping of correlations, only Ivancevich et al. (1982) reported sufficient information to allow determination of whether the difference in reactivity between type A and type B individuals is indicative of a buffering effect.

This is clearly an area where better conceptualization of the process would help clarify the possible role of type B behavior pattern in stress buffering (or type A in stress enhancing). Recall that type A individuals are expected to exhibit greater reactivity to stressors characterized by challenge, competitiveness, or uncontrollability (Glass, 1977). Unfortunately, only Suls et al. (1979), Rhodewalt and Agustdottir (1984), and Rhodewalt et al. (1984) assessed any of these characteristics. The results of the Rhodewalt et al. study are statistically flawed and uninterpretable, while the remaining two studies offer partial support for Glass' proposition. Further research is needed to determine whether type B behavior actually buffers the effects of stress and whether the characteristics of the stressor are important in eliciting type A behavior.

---

[9] A study of a large sample of working men reported by French, Caplan, and Van Harrison (1982) similarly found support for type A as a buffer in only one of 128 tests.

Coping Styles. The following section reviews the roles of stable (as opposed to situation specific) coping styles in stress buffering. Although there is substantial literature on the effectiveness of coping styles in response to stress (e.g., review by Suls & Fletcher, 1985), few of these studies include the low or no stress controls required for a test of the stress-buffering hypothesis. Hence it is unclear whether the effects of these personal coping styles occur only under stress. Of the studies we review, one examines the roles of avoidant (emotional focused) and approach (problem focused) coping, and the other of an index of two styles said to influence stressor appraisal, positive comparison, and stressor devaluation. Coping measures in both studies appear to assess stable person variables rather than situational specific coping.

Cronkite and Moos (1984) suggest that approach coping—dealing directly with a problem, may be more effective than avoidance coping—avoiding the problem or dealing with the emotional reactions it elicits. However, it seems likely that approach coping styles would be more effective when persons are faced with controllable stressful events, while avoidant styles would be more effective if the events are uncontrollable (Cohen, Evans, Stokols, & Krantz, 1986; Lazarus & Folkman, 1984).

We found only one published study examining the stress-buffering roles of active and avoidant coping styles. Cronkite and Moos (1984) conducted a longitudinal study of the relationship between life stress and indices of depression, physical symptoms, and alcohol consumption among 247 married couples. Time 1 measures included depression and physical symptoms (Health and Daily Living Form [HDL]), and alcohol consumption—the amount of beer, wine, and liquor consumed on a typical drinking day. Time 2 measures included depressive and physical symptoms, alcohol consumption, and two stress scales (respondent's undesirable life events, and a scale combining spouse's depression, physical symptoms, and alcohol consumption), and indices of self-esteem, family support, and approach and avoidance coping responses. To assess coping style, respondents were asked to recall a recent stressful life event and indicate the frequency with which they used each of 17 different coping responses. These responses were then classified according to which referred to approach and which to avoidance coping.

Hierarchical regression analysis was used to examine buffering effects, with separate analyses conducted for husbands and wives (2), for each stressor (4), each coping style (2), and each dependent variable (3). When including additional variables examined in this study (family support and self-esteem), 96 possible interactions were tested and only one (involving approach coping) reached significance ($p < .01$). Since one interaction should have reached significance by chance alone, these results cannot be interpreted as offering support for the role of any of the assessed coping strategies in stress buffering. Because coping strategies used in response to a single arbitrarily chosen stressor may not be representative of the range of coping responses available for coping with other stressors, this study may not have provided a fair test of the stress-buffering role of these coping styles.

Positive comparison refers to comparing one's own situation to that of persons who are worse off, and stressor devaluation refers to devaluating the importance of a stressor. Both of these coping strategies are presumed to lessen the impact of stressors by influencing the appraisal process; that is, by attributing benign meaning to them. In a longitudinal study of job disruption in a large community sample, Pearlin, Lieberman, Menaghan, and Mullan (1981) combined measures of positive comparison and devaluation of monetary success into one index. Respondents were interviewed twice with a four-year interval. Interview questions included four-event measure of job disruption (being fired, laid off, downgraded, or leaving work because of illness), economic role strains such as difficulties in acquiring life necessities and extras, the coping index, self-esteem, mastery, and depressive symptoms. Job disruption at the initial interview was treated as a stressor and coping as measured at the second interview as a potential stress buffer in the prediction of second interview measures of economic strain, self-esteem, mastery and depression. Economic strain as measured at the first interview was treated as a stressor and coping as measured at the second interview a stress buffer in the prediction of second interview measures of self-esteem, mastery, and depression. Regression coefficients indicated interactions consistent with coping operating as a stress buffer of job disruption in the prediction of economic strain, self-esteem, and depression. None of the interactions between economic strain and coping were significant. Because positive comparison and devaluation are presumed to influence appraisal, it is not surprising that they operated to reduce the influence of objective events, but were not operative after the events were appraised as stressful.

In sum, the limited work on the stress-buffering role of coping strategies fails to find any evidence for a stress-buffering role of approach or avoidant coping and finds some evidence for a stress-buffering role of coping strategies that influence the interpretation of an event (positive comparison and devaluation). However, given the number of interactions tested, even these results must be viewed as merely suggestive.

Coping Flexibility and Complexity.   Coping flexibility refers to a predisposition to use a wide range of coping situations in dealing with stressful events. An inflexible person would be less likely to use different coping strategies even if these strategies were within their repertoire. Complexity refers to the number of different coping resources in a person's repertoire, that is, the number that could theoretically be brought to bear in a stressful situation (Lazarus & Folkman, 1984). Both flexibility and complexity presumably operate through their effects on ability. That is, persons with a greater range of usable coping behaviors have a higher likelihood of effectively coping with any event or events.

The measure of inflexibility used in this work (Wheaton, 1982) is a seven-item scale in which subjects rated their similarity to persons with designated characteristics such as "initial mistrust of others, believing that people are honest only because they are afraid of being caught if they are not . . . , being 'on guard' with friendly people, a particular emphasis on neatness or cleanliness in the workplace or home, and believing in sticking rigidly to standards" (Wheaton, 1982, p. 301). The instrument assessed the personality trait of flexibility-rigidity (as well as aspects of interpersonal mistrust and susceptibility to conformity) and does not provide a specific assessment of coping flexibility.

Wheaton (1982) studied 132 Anglo Americans and 108 Mexican Americans from a randomly chosen sample of persons living in El Paso, Texas. Two measures of stress were used in an interview procedure: a life event inventory (acute stressors), and a nine-item measure tapping the number of relatively stable sources of stress (chronic stressors), for example, separation or divorce, excessive marital problems, feelings of being a failure in one's work. The outcome measure was the frequency of occurrence of 40 depressive symptoms. A series of regression equations controlling for sex, education, church attendance, physical problems, and social desirability, found that flexibility operated as a buffer of both acute and chronic stress.

In an analysis of a subsample (132 Anglos) of the *same* data set described above, Wheaton (1983) examined the roles of stress and flexibility in the prediction of symptoms of schizophrenia and anxiety as well as depression. As in the analysis of the larger form of this data set, flexibility was found to buffer both acute and chronic stress in the case of depressive disorder. A similar effect was found in the prediction of schizophrenia but not in the prediction of anxiety.

Billings and Moos (1984) examined the possible stress-buffering role of coping complexity (the number of coping responses typically used) in a sample of 424 patients entering treatment for depression. Coping responses were assessed by asking respondents to recall a recent stressful life event and to indicate on a four-point scale the frequency with which they used each of 32 different coping responses (Billings & Moos, 1981). The responses represented appraisal-focused, problem-focused, and emotion-focused coping strategies. These responses were combined into a summary index (number of strategies) for analysis. A stress index averaged the standardized scores of stress indices assessing negative life events, personal illness, children's illness, spouse symptoms, negative home environment, family strains, and work stress. Social resources and severity of depression were also assessed. Hierarchical regression was used to examine the buffering effects of social resources and coping responses, with separate analyses conducted for men and women and for each moderator variable. After controlling for sociodemographic factors, significant main effects were found for stress, social resources, and coping responses. No interactions were significant in any of the four analyses conducted. The assumption that the range of coping responses used in response to one stressful event are representative of those available for other events may be flawed and result in an insensitive if not invalid measure of complexity.

In summary, the few existing studies on coping complexity and flexibility provide evidence for flexibility as a buffer in the case of both chronic and acute stressors and no evidence for either complexity, approach or avoidant coping styles as stress buffers. The dearth of studies in this area make any conclusions based on this work suggestive at best.

Arousal and Sensation Seeking.   Sensation or arousal seeking can be thought of as preference for high or low stimulation. For example, sensation seeking has been described as the need for varied and novel complex sensations and experiences and the willingness to take risks for the sake of such experiences (Zuckerman, 1974). Persons relatively high on sensation or arousal seeking may be better able to cope with the increased arousal brought about by the stress experience and hence arousal or sensation seekers may be less affected by stressful events.

A study of the buffering potential of sensation seeking was reported by Smith, Johnson, and Sarason (1978). College students ($n = 75$) were administered a 60-item life event scale (LES), the Zuckerman et al. (1964) Sensation-Seeking Scale (SSS), and a neuroticism scale. There were no significant main effects or interaction effects in analyses of variance involving either positive or total life change scores. However, there was a significant main effect for negative life change and a marginal (p unspecified) stress-buffering interaction of negative life events and sensation seeking; those high in sensation seeking were relatively protected from the increased neuroticism associated with increased stress.

A failure to replicate the Smith et al. (1978) results is reported by Cohen (1982). College students ($n = 211$) completed the same scales (more recent revision of the SSS) as in the previously described study. Three separate analyses of variance using positive, negative, and total life change respectively all failed to indicate significant or near significant life stress by sensation seeking interactions.

In a study of 76 college students, Johnson, Sarason, and Siegel (1978; described in Johnson & Sarason, 1979) examined the potential buffering influence of arousal seeking on anxiety, depression, and hostility. Arousal seeking was assessed with the Mehrabian and Russell (1973) Arousal-Seeking Scale. This scale (like the Sensation-Seeking Scale) assesses the tendency of individuals to engage in or avoid activities and situations which might increase arousal. The LES was used to measure stressful life events, and subscales of the MAACL were used to assess anxiety, depression, and hostility. The positive life change score of the LES was not related to any of the outcomes. In the case of negative life change, correlations between stress and anxiety, depression and hostility ranged from −.04 to .05 when arousal seeking scores were high, and .23 to .46 when arousal seeking scores were low. The anxiety and hostility correlations were significant, but the depression correlation was not. Unfortunately, the use of correlational subgrouping analysis is an inappropriate test of stress buffering. Moreover, the authors fail to provide information regarding the exact form of the stress × arousal-seeking interaction.

Self-Esteem.   A measure of self-esteem was included in the Cronkite and Moos (1984) study described earlier in the coping section and in the Hobfoll and Walfisch (1984) study described in the control section. In the former study, respondents indicated how well each of six adjectives (aggressive, ambitious, confident, successful, outgoing, energetic) described them on a five-point scale ranging from "not at all like me" to "very much like me" (Gough & Heilbrun, 1965). Recall that this longitudinal study examined the relationship between life stress and indices of depression, physical symptoms, and alcohol consumption among 247 married couples. Separate regression analyses tested the role of life events and self-esteem in each outcome. None of the life event × self-esteem interactions were significant.

In the later study, women were tested both prebiopsy (high stress) and postbiopsy (low stress) (Hobfoll & Walfisch, 1984). Self-esteem was measured (prebiopsy) with the six-item Pearlin and Schooler (1978) adaptation of the Rosenberg (1965) self-esteem scale. Recall that measures of psychological distress collected both pre- and postbiopsy included state anxiety (STAT) and depressive symptoms (CES-D). Inappropriate subgrouping of correlations analyses did not provide support for stress buffering for self-esteem for either distress measure. Because the authors failed to provide either group means or slopes and intercepts, we view these data as uninterpretable.

In a later study (Hobfoll & Leiberman, 1987), 99 Israeli women, each experiencing various degrees of birth complications, were interviewed immediately after giving birth and again three months later. Self-esteem, anxiety, and depression were measured as in the previous study. Similar to the earlier study, women were assumed to be under high stress immediately after giving birth and low stress three months later. A repeated-measures ANOVA indicated main effects for both time (stress) and self-esteem, and group means suggested an interaction consistent with the buffering hypothesis. Unfortunately, the time × self-esteem interaction was not reported.

Overall, the data from studies examining the possible moderating role of self-esteem is inconclusive. There is a suggestion in the study by Hobfoll and Leiberman (in press) that self-esteem operates as a buffer, disconfirming results in the Cronkite and Moos (1984) study, and uninterpretable results in the Hobfoll and Walfisch (1984) study.

Private Self-Consciousness.   Suls and his colleagues have focused on private self-consciousness as a moderator of the relationship between life events stress and physical illness (Mullen & Suls, 1982; Suls & Fletcher, 1985a). Private self-consciousness (PrSC) is defined as a focus on internal aspects of the self, for example, one's feelings, beliefs, and privately held attitudes. Suls argues that PrSC should ameliorate the effects of stress because persons high in self-consciousness are: (a) more aware of internal bodily states and hence more sensitive to stressful experiences; and (b) more likely to recognize discrepancies between desired and current states and as a result engage in coping attempts to reduce these discrepancies. He further argues that if people low in private self-consciousness fail to take action to reduce stress-induced physiological activity, continued activation could eventually result in lowered body resistance and increased suscepti- bility to illness.

Two studies examined PrSC as a moderator of the relationship between life events stress and physical symptomatology. In both studies, PrSC was measured using a 10-item scale which assesses the degree to which the respondent focuses on his or her own thoughts, moods, bodily states, etc. (Fenigstein et al., 1975). The first was a prospective study of 88 under- graduates (Mullen & Suls, 1982). At time 1, subjects filled out a 45-item life events scale adapted for college students, including assessments of event controllability and desirability, an open-ended illness scale refer- ring to any illnesses in the preceding three weeks, and the PrSC scale just described. Three weeks later, the life events and illness scales were ad- ministered again. Analyses included subgrouped cross-lagged correla- tions and regression analyses controlling for time 1 illness. Data interpreted by the authors as consistent with private self-consciousness acting as a stress buffer was found in only one of the five subgrouping comparisons. When life events were perceived as both undesirable and uncontrollable, a larger correlation was found for the association between time 1 life events and time 2 illness for persons low in PrSC (.43) than for those high in PrSC (−.01). Similar results (same one of five interactions) were found in the regression analyses. Unfortunately, neither group means nor intercepts were presented, making exact interpretation of the reported interaction impossible.

In a two-month longitudinal study, Suls and Fletcher (1985a) adminis- tered a 65-item life events scale and the PrSC instruments described above to a sample of 120 undergraduates, substituting a physical symptom check- list for the open-ended illness measure. Separate path analyses examined the relationship between stress and symptoms for persons high and low on private self-consciousness, with a comparison of betas (slopes) used in subgrouping comparisons. Data interpreted as consistent with private self- consciousness acting as a stress-buffer was found in two of the five sub- grouping comparisons. When life events were perceived as uncontrollable and undesirable, the beta for low PrSC was positive and significant and for high PrSC was nonsignificant. Similar results were found for uncontrol- lable, desirable events. Statistical comparison of betas were not reported, and a failure to report intercepts or group means make interpretation of the form of this interaction speculative at best.

Taken together, these studies offer consistent evidence for a stronger relationship between uncontrollable life events and illness for subjects low in PrSC. However, due to a failure to report either means or slopes *and* intercepts, and to test the differences between slopes, the studies are un-interpretable in regard to stress buffering.[10]

Summary of Intrapersonal Section.   As a whole, only the work on locus of control provides even tentative evidence for stress buffering, and even these effects are not entirely consistent and are primarily limited to control as conceptualized by the Rotter scale. There are hints of stress-buffering effects for persons high in arousal and sensation seeking, for those using coping strategies aimed at reappraising the stressfulness of an event, and for those high in private self-consciousness. There is also a possibility that a tightly conceptualized approach to type B behavior pattern as a buffer might be fruitful. At this point, there is just not enough research in any of the remaining areas to make even tentative conclusions.

DISCUSSION

What Person Variables Operate as Stress Buffers?

Only in the case of locus of control is there a large enough data base and consistent enough results to even tentatively suggest a stable effect in the prediction of psychological symptoms. In particular, when defined as a generalized concept applying only to control of things outside oneself, the data are consistent with the operation of internal control as a stress buffer. (As discussed earlier, this may also be attributable to external control as a stress enhancer). The weakness in this literature is that none of the studies use a prospective design or causal analytic techniques that allow for elimination of alternative causal explanations.

Arousal and sensation seeking, private self-consciousness, hardiness, and psychosocial assets each have at least two studies that provide some evidence for their operation as stress buffers. However, these literatures suffer from inconsistencies in results and statistical and methodological problems that make more definitive statements impossible. Moreover, in the case of both of the indices (psychosocial assets and hardiness), it is as yet unclear whether these measures represent unidimensional resources or merely operate because of one or more "active" components. For example, the hardiness scales used by Kobasa and her colleagues include the Rotter

---

[10] In a personal communication, the studies' author suggested that appropriate re-analysis of these data provided support for stress buffering.

locus of control scale and the psychosocial asset scales include subscales measuring social support.

In several cases, evidence that is either consistent or inconsistent with stress buffering was derived from a single study. Consistent evidence was reported in the cases of alienation from self, social interests defined as concern for others, and social anxiety, while inconsistent evidence was found in the cases of social competence, self-disclosure, social interests when defined as social integration, lack of anomie, and components of the alienation scale (powerlessness, nihilism, vigorousness, and adventurousness). The lack of a sufficient data base, as well as the serious statistical problems in one of these studies, precludes any conclusions in these areas.

Evidence for the stress-buffering properties of self-esteem derive from three studies; two reporting disconfirming results and one suggestive confirming evidence. However, the data analysis in one of the disconfirming studies was inappropriate and the confirming study's evidence was based on group means without analysis.

Finally, the studies on type A behavior provide an unconvincing view of the behavior pattern (type B) as a stress buffer. However, much of this work is uninterpretable because of inappropriate statistical analyses. Moreover, it is generally poorly conceptualized; lacking a sensitivity to the types of stressors that elicit behavioral reactions from type A individuals. Hence further work examining type A and B reactions to stressors characterized by challenge, competitiveness, and uncontrollability could help provide a clearer picture in this case.

Do Stress Buffers Allow Us to Account for More Variance?

At the beginning of this chapter we suggested that it might be possible to improve the predictive validity of psychosocial stress by separately looking at those who are more or less susceptible to stress-induced illness. One approach to addressing this issue is to look at the percent of variance accounted for by stress × resource buffering interactions. Although variance accounted for (or even enough information to calculate it) is provided in few studies, the results are interesting. In the case of internal locus of control as a stress buffer, Krause (1985) reported accounting for an additional 1.2% in depressive symptoms, and Lefcourt et al. (1981) between 4 and 7% in total mood disturbance. Cohen, Sherrod, and Clark (1986) found the stress × social-anxiety buffering interaction accounted for a mere .57% of the variance in depressive symptoms. The small increment in variance accounted for by these buffering effects is consistent with what has been found in the social support literature (discussions in Cohen, Sherrod, & Clark, 1986; Kessler & McLeod, 1985) and may underestimate the role of this interaction because the variance in this monotone interaction is shared between main effects of stress and the buffering resource, and the interaction term (Dawes, 1969; Reis, 1984).

A more liberal estimate of the contribution of person moderators to understanding symptomatology can be obtained by examining the correlation between stress and outcome for persons low in the buffering resource under consideration. This provides an upper end estimate; that is, the most variance we are likely to account for in the stress-symptomatology relationship. These data are also disappointing. The correlations (as reported in studies using subgrouping analyses interpreted by the authors as supportive of stress buffering) range from .25 to .45. Hence, it appears that at best, the addition of these buffering resources allow us to account for a *total* of 20% of symptom variance.

In fairness, percent of variance accounted for may not provide an adequate test of the etiological importance of personality stress buffers. Arnold (1984) has argued that percent of variance accounted for is not an accurate measure of the importance of an interaction term, and Brown (1981) has pointed out that even small percentages of variance may account for substantial increases or decreases in risk of disorder.

How Do Person Variables Influence Stress Coping?

Earlier, we proposed a model in which person variables may influence either the initial appraisal of potentially stressful events or the coping activity that occurs after they have been appraised as stressful (see Figure 7.1). Two studies provide evidence in regard to the point in this process at which a resource operates. In a direct test of the role of psychosocial assets both during and after appraisal, Norris and Murrell (1984) provided support for psychosocial assets operating as buffers only *after* stress appraisal. On the other hand, Pearlin et al. (1981) found that an index of coping strategies assumed to influence appraisal (positive comparison and devaluation) operated to reduce the influence of objective events, but were not operative in reducing stress-induced strain (after the events were appraised as stressful). It is also possible to view other studies that used perceived stress measures in their analyses as addressing at least the second stage of this model. For example, Cohen, Sherrod, and Clark (1986) found that social anxiety moderated the relationship between perceived stress and depressive symptoms, although there were no stress-buffering effects of social competence, or social anxiety. Although inconclusive at this point, the existing work focusing on the stage of the stress process in which a resource operates suggests that this distinction is worthwhile. Clearly, additional studies distinguishing between buffering effects as appraisal versus post appraisal processes would help clarify the processes by which different coping resources operate.

Influence on Coping Processes. In arguing for various personal factors as stress buffers, most authors based their hypotheses on the premise that persons with a particular characteristic (e.g., internal control, private self-consciousness) would be more successful in dealing with stressful events because they would be more likely to engage in coping or more likely to cope appropriately. Others have argued that some of these factors influence ability to cope, while others influence effort. Unfortunately, *not one* of the reviewed studies directly examined coping activities of their subjects leaving these hypotheses untested.

Matching Resources with Stressors

The necessity of a match between stressor and resource is especially difficult to address given the nature of the reviewed studies. The work reviewed in this chapter is almost totally based on cumulative (global) measures of stress. The research on generalized and specific expectancies of control may, however, provide some insight into this issue. Recall that we argued that a common effect of stressors is to threaten feelings of *self-esteem* and *personal control*. Hence resources that increase these feelings are likely to match up well with a broad range of stressful events. Contrary to our hypothesis, control specific to the stressors under consideration did not operate as buffers (Nelson & Cohen, 1983; Sandler & Lakey, 1982). These data are subject to criticism, however, because of the questionable validity of the specific control measures (summed ratings of individual events). Moreover, generalized (global) feelings of control may in fact provide a better match with global stress than the specific measures used in these studies. As discussed earlier, there is some evidence that a generalized expectancy of control operates as a stress buffer.

Unfortunately, there is little interpretable data on self-esteem as a stress buffer. In the three published studies we reviewed, the results were mixed and analyses in two of the studies were lacking or inappropriate. Other work, however, using a social support measure that assessed "self-esteem" support in terms of feelings that the respondent is better than others and that others think highly of him or her does provide suggestive evidence that self-esteem may operate as a stress buffer (Cohen, Mermelstein, Kamarck, & Hoberman, 1985). Further work with different samples, stress measures, and self-esteem measures is necessary to determine what forms of self-esteem operate as stress buffers and under what conditions this occurs.

Wheaton (1982, 1983) argued that stress-resource matching is based on the dimensions of effort and ability. He derived a stability matching hypothesis that predicts that buffering of chronic stress occurs when a resource increases ability (stable stressor and stable resource) and that buffering of acute stress occurs when a resource increases effort (instable stressor and instable resource). Because control influences effort, he hypothesized that internal control buffering would only occur in the case of acute (life events) but not chronic stress. Moreover, because flexibility assesses coping ability, he predicted that persons with greater flexibility would be protected from chronic but not acute stressors. Wheaton's own data is not generally supportive of his hypotheses. For example, when acting as a stress buffer, flexibility seems to work in the case of both acute and chronic stress. None of the remaining studies provide a fair test of Wheaton's theory since none use both acute and chronic stress measures. Moreover, because most life event scales include chronic as well as acute events, existing research cannot even be viewed as a test of whether acute stressors are buffered by personal resources influencing effort. A more reasonable use of effort and ability in a matching scheme would suggest that ability should increase effective coping for *all stressors*, while effort may be most effective in the case of acute stressors. Because effort is influenced by experience with a particular stressor, it seems reasonable that resources influencing effort may be more important early on in the coping process or when the stressor is short-lived. It is unclear, however, why resources influencing "stable" ability wouldn't be important for both acute (instable) and chronic (stable) stressors. Wheaton's data, in fact, are relatively consistent with this revised approach.

Superordinate Moderators

It is possible that the scattered stress-buffering effects found in this literature occur because of a common influence on one or more superordinate mechanisms that reduce the impact of stress on illness. That is, some overriding mechanism that is common to a variety of measures. In light of the reviewed studies, the most likely possibility is feelings of personal control (Brown & Harris, 1978; Cohen & Wills, 1985; Pearlin & Schooler, 1978; Wheaton, 1982). Other possibilities include self-efficacy or self-esteem (Cohen & Wills, 1985; Husaini et al., 1982; Pearlin & Schooler, 1978); effort or ability (Wheaton, 1982, 1983), and optimism (Scheier & Carver, 1985).

Studies that measure both mechanisms that may operate at a superordinate level as well as other potential stress buffers would provide evidence to evaluate superordinate hypotheses. Appropriate analyses would first separately evaluate the moderating role of each resource and then examine the contribution of the stress × resource interaction with the role of other moderators under study partialled out.

Combined Resistance Resources

Should we expect resistance to stressors to increase with increased number of resources? In general, it is likely that whether or not additional resources increase stress resistance depends on the effectiveness of available resources, overlap with other resources, and whether additional resources are more closely matched to the stressful event or events.

Effectiveness could be supplemented if additional resources provided a wide coping repertoire, that is, provide a greater range of choices and hence a greater likelihood (and perceived likelihood) of having an appropriate response. Effectiveness could also be increased if additional resources additively increased the impact of existing resources on a specific process or influenced a second relevant process unaffected by other resources. On the other hand, there might be a maximum possible impact of resistant resources on the stress appraisal process with increased resources having little or no additional impact. In that case, if a resource is very effective, additional resources may make little difference. We would also expect additional resources to be relatively ineffective to the extent that they redundantly influenced the same process, for example, operate as proxies for superordinate moderator such as control, self-esteem, or optimism or increase ability or effort. Finally, it is likely that the effectiveness of a resource depends on its match with the needs elicited by a stressful event or events. Hence additional resources would only increase resistance if they provide a similar or better match.

There are few studies in this literature that examine two or more personal resources (exceptions include Wheaton, 1982, 1983; Ganellen & Blaney, 1984; Cohen, Sherrod, & Clark, 1986). Only Wheaton (1983) examines the simultaneous (independent) contributions of the resources under study. Again, adequate understanding of such overlap requires examining both individual and simultaneous contributions to variance of the stress by resource interaction.

CONCLUSION

From a practical perspective, research on personality factors as buffers of stress-induced pathology has not been very successful. As noted earlier, a liberal estimate of the impact of such moderators on total variance accounted for in the relationship between stress and symptomatology is rather small. From a theoretical perspective, the contribution of this literature is somewhat mixed. On the one hand, it has provided suggestive evidence in regard to a number of specific person resources that may influence the appraisal and/or coping process. On the other hand, statistical and conceptual problems, a lack of consistency of results across existing studies, and inadequate numbers of replications make much of the evidence difficult to interpret.

Clearly, the most impressive literature reviewed in this chapter is the work on generalized expectancies of control. A tentative finding that internal control operates as a stress buffer fits well with theoretical conceptions of the stress and coping process that view perceptions of control as essential components of stress appraisal.

Another interpretation of this literature is that there is just not enough methodologically competent, conceptually sophisticated research on personality factors as buffers of stress-induced pathology to make even tentative conclusions. We are not entirely in disagreement with this argument. This interpretation suggests that less emphasis be placed on the results of existing work, and more on learning from the mistakes of the past.

Where to go from here? In order for our understanding of personal resources as stress buffers to increase, future work needs to be designed to test theoretically based questions. What are the superordinate stress-buffering mechanisms? What overlap is there between established moderators? Do these moderators influence stress appraisal and/or coping activity, style or effort? Hopefully, by addressing issues central to process, results of studies will speak to the operation of a range of personal and social resources rather than to just the efficacy of the stress moderator under consideration.

References

Arnold, H. J. (1984). Testing moderator variable hypothesis: A reply to Stone and Hollenbeck. *Organizational Behavior and Human Performance, 34,* 214–224.

Baum, A., Singer, J. E., & Baum, C. S. (1981). Stress and the environment. *Journal of Social Issues, 37,* 4–35.

Beck, A. T. (1967). *Depression: Clinical, experimental and theoretical aspects.* New York: Harper & Row.

Billings, A. G., & Moos, R. H. (1981). The role of coping responses and social resources in attenuating the stress of life events. *Journal of Behavioral Medicine, 4,* 2, 139–157.

Billings, A. G., & Moos, R. H. (1984). Coping, stress, and social resources among adults with unipolar depression. *Journal of Personality and Social Psychology, 46,* 877–891.

Brown, G. W. (1981). Life events, psychiatric disorder and physical illness. *Journal of Psychosomatic Research, 25,* 461–473.

Brown, G. W., & Harris, T. (1978). *Social origins of depression: A study of psychiatric disorders in women.* London: Tavistock.

Byrk, A. S., & Weisberg, H. I. (1977). Use of the nonequivalent control group design when subjects are growing. *Psychological Bulletin, 84,* 950–962.

Caldwell, R. A., Pearson, J. L., & Chin, R. J. (1987). Stress-moderating effects: Social support in the context of gender and locus of control. *Personality and Social Psychology Bulletin, 13,* 5–17.

Campbell, A., Converse, P. E., Miller, W. E., & Stokes, D. E. (1960). *The American voter.* New York: Wiley.

Caplan, R. D., & Jones, K. W. (1975). Effects of work load, role ambiguity, and type A personality on anxiety, depression, and heart rate. *Journal of Applied Psychology, 60,* 6, 713–719.

Cohen, F., Horowitz, M. J., Lazarus, R. S., Moos, R. H., Robins, L. N., Rose, R. M., & Rutter, M. (1982). Panel report on psychosocial assets and modifiers of stress. In G. R. Elliot & C. Eisdorfer (Eds.), *Stress and human health analysis and implications of research* (Springer Series on Psychiatry 1). New York: Springer.

Cohen, J., & Cohen, P. (1975). *Applied multiple regression/correlation analysis for the behavioral Sciences.* Hillsdale, NJ: Erlbaum.

Cohen, L. (1982). Life change and the sensation-seeking motive. *Personality and Individual Differences, 3,* 221–222.

Cohen, S. (1986). Contrasting the hassles scale and the perceived stress scale: Who's really measuring appraised stress? *American Psychologist, 41,* 716–719.

Cohen, S., Evans, G. W., Stokols, D., & Krantz, D. S. (1986). *Behavior, health, and environmental stress.* New York: Plenum.

Cohen, S., Kamarck, T., & Mermelstein, R. (1983). A global measure of perceived stress. *Journal of Health and Social Behavior, 24,* 385–396.

Cohen, S., & McKay, G. (1984). Social support, stress and the buffering hypothesis: A theoretical analysis. In A. Baum, S. E. Taylor, & J. E. Singer (Eds.), *Handbook of psychology and health.* Hillsdale, NJ: Erlbaum.

Cohen, S., Mermelstein, R., Kamarck, T., & Hoberman, H. (1985). Measuring the functional components of social support. In I. G. Sarason & B. R. Sarason (Eds.), *Social support: Theory, research and application.* The Hague, Holland: Martinus Nijhoff.

Cohen, S., Sherrod, D. R., & Clark, M. S. (1986). Social skills and the stress-protective role of social support. *Journal of Personality and Social Psychology, 50,* 963–973.

Cohen, S., & Wills, T. A. (1985). Stress, social support, and the buffering hypothesis. *Pschological Bulletin, 98,* 2, 310–357.

Crandall, J. E. (1975). A scale for social interest. *Journal of Individual Psychology, 31,* 187–195.

Crandall, J. E. (1984). Social interest as a moderator of life stress. *Journal of Personality and Social Psychology, 47,* 164–174.

Cronkite, R. C., & Moos, R. H. (1984). The role of predisposing and moderating factors in the stress-illness relationship. *Journal of Health and Social Behavior, 25,* 372–393.

Crowne, D., & Marlowe, D. (1964). *The approval motive.* New York: Wiley.

Dawes, R. M. (1969). Interaction effects in the presence of asymmetrical transfer. *Psychological Bulletin, 71,* 55–57.

De Araujo, G., van Arsdel, P. P., Holmes, T. H., & Dudley, D. L. (1973). Life change, coping ability and chronic asthma. *Journal of Psychosomatic Research, 17,* 359–363.

Dohrenwend, B. S., & Dohrenwend, B. P. (1978). Some issues in research on stressful life events. *Journal of Nervous and Mental Disease, 166,* 7–15.

Dohrenwend, B. S., & Dohrenwend, B. P. (1981). *Stressful life events and their contexts.* New York: Neale Watson.

Dooley, D. (1985). Casual inference in the study of social support. In S. Cohen & S. L. Syme (Eds.), *Social support and health.* New York: Academic.

Fenigstein, A., Scheier, M., & Buss, A. H. (1975). Public and private self-consciousness: Assessment and theory. *Journal of Consulting and Clinical Psychology, 43,* 522–527.

Folkman, S. (1984). Personal control and stress and coping processes: A theoretical analysis. *Journal of Personality and Social Psychology, 46,* 839–852.

French, J. R. P., Caplan, R. D., & Van Harrison, R. (1982). *The mechanisms of job stress and strain.* New York: Wiley.

Friedman, M., & Rosenman, R. H. (1959). Association of specific overt behavior pattern with increases in blood cholesterol, blood clotting time, incidence of arcus senilis and clinical coronary artery disease. *Journal of the American Medical Association, 169,* 1286–1296.

Funk, S. C., & Houston, B. K. (1987). A critical analysis of the hardiness scale's validity and utility. *Journal of Personality and Social Psychology, 53,* 572–578.

Ganellen, R. J., & Blaney, P. H. (1984). Hardiness and social support as moderators of the effects of life stress. *Journal of Personality and Social Psychology, 47,* 145–155.

Gentry, W. D., & Kobasa, S. C. (1985). Social and psychological resources mediating stress-illness relationships in humans. In W. D. Gentry (Ed.), *Handbook of behavioral medicine* (pp. 87–116). New York: Guilford.

Glass, D. C. (1977). *Behavior patterns, stress, and coronary disease.* Hillsdale, NJ: Erlbaum.

Gore, S. (1981). Stress-buffering functions of social supports: An appraisal and clarification of research models. In B. S. Dohrenwend & B. P. Dohrenwend (Eds.), *Stressful life events and their contexts* (pp. 202–222). New York: Prodist.

Gore, S. (1985). Social support and styles of coping with stress. In S. Cohen & S. L. Syme (Eds.), *Social support and health* (pp. 263–280). New York: Academic.

Gough, H. G., & Heilbrun, A. B., Jr. (1965). *The adjective check list manual.* Palo Alto: Consulting Psychologists Press.

Greever, K. B., Tseng, M. S., & Friedland, B. U. (1973). Development of the social interest index. *Journal of Consulting and Clinical Psychology, 41,* 454–458.

Hahn, M. E. (1966). *California life goals evaluation schedule.* Palo Alto: Western Psychological Services.

Haynes, S. G., Feinleib, M., & Kannel, W. B. (1980). The relationship of psychosocial factors to coronary heart disease in the Framingham study: III. Eight-year incidence of coronary heart disease. *American Journal of Epidemiology, 111,* 37–58.

Hobfoll, S. E. (1985). Limitations of social support in the stress process. In I. G. Sarason & B. R. Sarason (Eds.), *Social support: Theory, research, and applications* (pp. 319–414). The Hague, the Netherlands: Marinus Nijhoff.

Hobfoll, S. E., & Leiberman, J. R. (1987). Personality and social resources in immediate and continued stress-resistance among women. *Journal of Personality and Social Psychology, 52,* 18–26.

Hobfoll, S. E., & Walfisch, S. (1984). Coping with a threat to life: A longitudinal study of self-concept, social support, and psychological distress. *American Journal of Community Psychology, 12,* 87–100.

Holahan, C. J., & Moos, R. H. (1986). Personality, coping, and family resources in stress resistance: A longitudinal analysis. *Journal of Personality and Social Psychology, 51,* 389–395.

Holmes, T. H., & Rahe, R. H. (1967). The social readjustment rating scale. *Journal of Psychosomatic Research, 11,* 213–218.

House, J. (1981). *Work stress and social support.* Reading, MA: Addison-Wesley.

Houston, B. K. (1983). Psychophysiological responsivity and the type A behavior pattern. *Journal of Research in Personality, 17,* 22–39.

Hull, J. G., Van Treuren, R. R., & Virnelli, S. (1987). Hardiness and health: A critique and alternative approach. *Journal of Personality and Social Psychology, 53,* 518–530.

Husaini, B., Neff, J., Newbrough, J. R., & Moore, M. C. (1982). The stress-buffering role of social support and personal competence among the rural married. *Journal of Community Psychology, 10,* 409–426.

Ivancevich, J. M., Matteson, M. T., & Preston, C. (1982). Occupational stress, type A behavior, and physical well being. *Academy of Management Journal, 25,* 373–391.

Jackson, D. N. (1974). *Personality research form manual.* Goshen, NY: Research Psychologists' Press.

Jenkins, C. D. (1979). Psychosocial modifiers of response to stress. In J. E. Barrett, R. M. Rose, G. L. Klerman (Eds.), *Stress and mental disorder* (pp. 265–278). New York: Raven.

Jenkins, C. D., Rosenman, R. H., & Zyzanski, S. J. (1974). Prediction of clinical coronary heart disease by a test for the coronary-prone behavior pattern. *New England Journal of Medicine, 23,* 1271–1275.

Johnson, J. H., & Sarason, I. G. (1978). Life stress, depression, and anxiety: Internal-external control as a moderator variable. *Journal of Psychosomatic Research, 22,* 205–208.

Johnson, J. H., & Sarason, I. G. (1979). Moderator variables in life stress research. In I. G. Sarason & C. D. Speilberger (Eds.), *Stress and anxiety* (Vol. 6, pp. 151–167). New York: Wiley.

Jourard, S. M. (1971). *Self-disclosure: An experimental analysis of the transparent self.* New York: Wiley.

Kasl, S. V. (1983). Pursuing the link between stressful life experiences and disease: A time for reappraisal. In C. L. Cooper (Ed.), *Stress research.* New York: Wiley.

Kessler, R. C. (1985). Methodological issues in the study of psychosocial stress. In H. B. Kaplan (Ed.), *Psychosocial stress* (pp. 267–341). New York: Academic.

Kessler, R. C., & McLeod, J. D. (1985). Social support and mental health in community samples. In S. Cohen & S. L. Syme (Eds.), *Social support and health* (pp. 219–240). New York: Academic.

Kobasa, S. C., Maddi, S. R., & Courington, S. (1981). Personality and constitution as mediators in the stress-illness relationship. *Journal of Health and Social Behavior, 22,* 368–378.

Kobasa, S. C., Maddi, S. R., & Kahn, S. (1982). Hardiness and health: A prospective study. *Journal of Personality and Social Psychology, 42,* 168–177.

Kobasa, S. C., Maddi, S. R., & Puccetti, M. C. (1982). Personality and exercise as buffers in the stress-illness relationship. *Journal of Behavioral Medicine, 5,* 391–404.

Kobasa, S. C., Maddi, S. R., & Zola, M. A. (1983). Type A and hardiness. *Journal of Behavioral Medicine, 6,* 41–51.

Kobasa, S. C., & Puccetti, M. C. (1983). Personality and social resources in stress resistance. *Journal of Personality and Social Psychology, 45,* 4, 839–850.

Krantz, D. S., & Manuck, S. B. (1984). Acute psychophysiologic reactivity and risk of cardiovascular disease: A review and methodologic critique. *Psychological Bulletin, 96,* 435–464.

Krause, N. (1985). Stress, control beliefs, and psychological distress: The problem of response bias. *Journal of Human Stress, 11*–19.

Krause, N., & Stryker, S. (1984). Stress and well-being: The buffering role of locus of control beliefs. *Social Science and Medicine, 18,* 783–790.

Langner, T. S. (1962). A twenty-two item screening score of psychiatric symptoms indicating impairment. *Journal of Health and Human Behavior, 3,* 269–276.

Lazarus, R. S. (1966). *Psychological stress and the coping process.* New York: McGraw-Hill.

Lazarus, R. S., & Folkman, S. (1984). *Stress, coping, and adaptation.* New York: Springer.

Lazarus, R. S., & Launier, R. (1978). Stress-related transactions between person and environment. In L. A. Pervin and M. Lewis (Eds.), *Perspective in interactional psychology* (pp. 287–327). New York: Plenum.

Lefcourt, H. M. (1985). Intimacy, social support, and locus of control as moderators of stress. In I. G. Sarason & B. R. Sarason (Eds.), *Social support: Theory, research, and applications* (pp. 155–172). Dordrecht: Martinus Nijhoff.

Lefcourt, H. M., von Baeyer, C. L., Ware, E. E., & Cox, D. J. (1979). The multidimensional-multiattributional causality scale: The development of a goal specific locus of control scale. *Canadian Journal of Behavioral Science, 11,* 286–304.

Lefcourt, H. M., Miller, R. S., Ware, E. E., & Sherk, D. (1981). Locus of control as a modifier of the relationship between stressors and moods. *Journal of Personality and Social Psychology, 41,* 357–369.

Levenson, H. (1974). Activism and powerful others: Distinctions within the concept of internal-external control. *Journal of Personality Assessment, 38,* 377–383.

Levenson, H., & Gottman, J. M. (1978). Toward the assessment of social competence. *Journal of Consulting and Clinical Psychology, 46,* 453–462.

Linville, P. W. (1987). Self-complexity as a cognitive buffer against stress-related illness and depression. *Journal of Personality and Social Psychology, 52,* 663–676.

Maddi, S. R., Kobasa, S. C., & Hoover, M. (1979). An alienation test. *Journal of Humanistic Psychology, 19,* 73–76.

Manuck, S., & Krantz, D. S. (1984). Psychophysiologic reactivity in coronary heart disease. *Behavioral Medicine Update, 6,* 11–15.

Matthews, K. A. (1982). Psychological perspectives on the type-A behavior pattern. *Psychological Bulletin, 91,* 293–333.

McFarlane, A., Norman, G., Streiner, D., & Roy, R. (1983). The process of social stress: Stable, reciprocal, and mediating relationships. *Journal of Health and Social Behavior, 24,* 160–173.

Mehrabian, A., & Russell, J. D. (1973). A measure of arousal seeking tendency. *Environment and Behavior, 5,* 315–333.

Miller, R. G., Jr. (1966). *Simultaneous statistical inference.* New York: McGraw-Hill.

Mirels, H. L. (1970). Dimensions of internal versus external control. *Journal of Consulting and Clinical Psychology, 34,* 226–228.

Moos, R. H., Cronkite, R. C., Billings, A. G., & Finney, J. W. (1982). *Health and daily living form manual.* Social Ecology Laboratory, Department of Psychiatry and Behavioral Sciences, Stanford University School of Medicine, Stanford, CA.

Mullen, B., & Suls, J. (1982). "Know thyself": Stressful life changes and the ameliorative effect of private self-consciousness. *Journal of Experimental Social Psychology, 18,* 43–55.

Murrell, S. A., & Norris, F. H. (1984). Resources, life events, and changes in positive affect and depression in older adults. *American Journal of Community Psychology, 12,* 445–464.

Nelson, D. W., & Cohen, L. H. (1983). Locus of control and control perceptions and the relationship between life stress and psychological disorder. *American Journal of Community Psychology, 11,* 705–722.

Norris, F. H., & Murrell, S. A. (1984). Protective function of resources related to life events, global stress, and depression in older adults. *Journal of Health and Social Behavior, 25,* 424–437.

Nuckolls, K. B., Cassel, J., & Kaplan, B. H. (1972). Psychological assets, life crisis and the prognosis of pregnancy. *American Journal of Epidemiology, 95,* 431–441.

Pearlin, L. I., Leiberman, M. A., Menaghan, E. G., & Mullen, J. T. (1981). The stress process. *Journal of Health and Social Behavior, 22,* 337–356.

Pearlin, L. I., & Schooler, C. (1978). The structure of coping. *Journal of Health and Social Behavior, 19,* 2–21.

Rabkin, J., & Struening, E. (1976). Life events, stress, and illness. *Science, 194,* 1013–1020.

Radloff, L. (1977). The CES-D scale: A self-report depression scale for research in the general population. *Applied Psychosocial Measurement, 1,* 385–401.

Reid, D., & Ware, E. E. (1973). Multidimensionality of internal-external control: Implications for past and future research. *Canadian Journal of Behavioral Science, 5,* 264–271.

Reid, D., & Ware, E. E. (1974). Multidimensionality of internal versus external locus of control: Addition of a third dimension and non-distinction of self versus others. *Canadian Journal of Behavioral Science, 6,* 131–142.

Reis, H. T. (1984). Social interaction and well-being. In S. Duck (Ed.), *Personality relationships: Vol. 5. Repairing personal relationships* (pp. 21–45). London: Academic Press.

Rhodewalt, F., & Agustdottir, S. (1984). On the relationship of hardiness to the type A behavior pattern: Perception of life events versus coping with life events. *Journal of Research in Personality, 18,* 212–223.

Rhodewalt, F., Hays, R. B., Chemers, M. M., & Wysocki, J. (1984). Type A behavior, perceived stress, and illness: A person-situation analysis. *Personality and Social Psychology Bulletin, 10,* 149–159.

Rosenberg, M. (1965). *Society and adolescent self-image.* Princeton: Princeton University Press.

Rosenman, R. H., Brand, R. J., Jenkins, C. D., Friedman, M., Straus, R., & Wurm, M. (1975). Coronary heart disease in the western collaborative group study: Final follow-up experience of 8 1/2 years. *Journal of the American Medical Association, 233,* 872–877.

Roos, P. E., & Cohen, L. H. (in press). Sex roles and social support as moderators of life stress adjustment. *Journal of Personality and Social Psychology.*

Rotter, J. B. (1966). Generalized expectancies for internal versus external control of reinforcement. *Psychological Monographs: General and Applied, 80,* 1 (Whole No. 609).

Rotter, J. B., Seeman, M., & Liverant, S. (1962). Internal vs. external locus of control of reinforcement: A major variable in behavior theory. In N. F. Washburne (Ed.), *Decisions, values, and groups* (pp. 473–516). London: Pergamon.

Sandler, I. N., & Lakey, B. (1982). Locus of control as a stress moderator: The role of control perceptions and social support. *American Journal of Community Psychology, 10,* 65–80.

Scheier, M. F., & Carver, C. S. (1985). Optimism, coping, and health: Assessment and implications of generalized outcome expectancies. *Health Psychology, 4,* 219–247.

Schmied, L. A., & Lawler, K. A. (1986). Hardiness, type A behavior, and the stress-illness relation in working women. *Journal of Personality and Social Psychology, 51,* 1218–1223.

Sells, S. B. (1970). On the nature of stress. In J. E. McGrath (Ed.), *Social and psychological factors in stress* (pp. 134–139). New York: Holt.

Smith, R. E., Johnson, J. G., & Sarason, I. G. (1978). Life change, the sensation seeking motive, and psychological distress. *Journal of Consulting and Clinical Psychology, 46,* 348–349.

Somes, G. W., Garrity, T. F., & Marx, M. B. (1981). The relationship of coronary-prone behavior pattern to the health of college students at varying levels of recent life change. *Journal of Psychosomatic Research, 25,* 565–572.

Spielberger, C. D., Gorsuch, R. L., & Lushene, R. E. (1969). *The state-trait anxiety inventory.* Palo Alto: Consulting Psychologists Press.

Suls, J., & Fletcher, B. (1985a). Self-attention, life stress and illness: A prospective study. *Psychosomatic Medicine, 47,* 469–481.

Suls, J., & Fletcher, B. (1985b). The relative efficacy of avoidant and nonavoidant coping strategies: A meta-analysis. *Health Psychology, 4,* 249–288.

Suls, J., Gastorf, J. W., & Witenberg, S. H. (1979). Life events, psychological distress and the type A coronary-prone behavior pattern. *Journal of Psychosomatic Research, 23,* 315–319.

Thoits, P. A. (1983). Dimensions of life events that influence psychological distress: An evaluation and synthesis of the literature. In H. B. Kaplan (Ed.), *Psychosocial stress: Trends in theory and research* (pp. 33–104). New York: Academic.

Tukey, J. W. (1969). Analyzing data: Sanctification or detective work? *American Psychologist, 24,* 89.

Turner, R. J., & Noh, S. (1983). Class and psychological vulnerability among women: The significance of social support and personal control. *Journal of Health and Social Behavior, 24,* 2–15.

Vickers, R. (1973). *A short measure of the type-A personality.* Ann Arbor: University of Michigan, Institute for Social Research.

Weisberg, H. I. (1979). Statistical adjustments and uncontrolled studies. *Psychological Bulletin, 86,* 1149–1164.

Wheaton, B. (1982). A comparison of the moderating effects of personal coping resources in the impact of exposure to stress in two groups. *Journal of Community Psychology, 10,* 293–311.

Wheaton, B. (1983). Stress, personal coping resources, and psychiatric symptoms: An investigation of interactive model. *Journal of Health and Social Behavior, 24,* 208–229.

Wiebe, D. J., & McCallum, D. M. (1986). Health practices and hardiness as mediators in the stress-illness relationship. *Health Psychology, 5,* 425–438.

Wyler, A. R., Masuda, M., and Holmes, T. H. (1968). Seriousness of illness rating scale. *Journal of Psychosomatic Research, 11,* 363–375.

Zika, S., & Chamberlain, K. (1986). Relations of hassles and personality to subjective well-being. *Journal of Personality and Social Psychology, 53,* 155–162.

Zuckerman, M. (1974). The sensation-seeking motive. In B. Haher (Ed.), *Progress in experimental personality research* (Vol. 7). New York: Academic.

Zuckerman, M., Kolin, E. A., Price, L., & Zoob, I. (1964). Development of a sensation-seeking scale. *Journal of Consulting Psychology, 26,* 250–260.

8

Treatment of Psychological Stress Responses in Healthy Type A Men

ETHEL ROSKIES
PETER SERAGANIAN
ROBERT OSEASOHN
CHRISTINE SMILGA
NORMAND MARTIN
JAMES A. HANLEY

INTRODUCTION

Three short-term intervention programs (aerobic exercise, cognitive-behavioral stress management, and weight training) have been used to modify the behavioral and physiological stress responses of individuals classified

The research reported here was financed by grant no. 6605-1883-46 from Health and Welfare, Ottawa to Roskies, Seraganian, Oseasohn, and Hanley.

Ms. Pierrette Koppel was responsible for the aerobic exercise intervention, Drs. Ethel Roskies and Lorraine Poitras served as cotherapists for the stress management program, and Mr. Tom Brown led the weight training program.

as type A. Although currently healthy, these individuals were considered at risk for coronary heart disease (CHD) because of their exaggerated manner of responding to everyday stress situations. The treatment programs were used to reduce the quality, intensity, and/or duration of stress responses by changing stress appraisals, coping strategies, and/or coping resources (Lazarus & Folkman, 1984).

The interventions presented were employed in the Montreal Type A Intervention Project (MTAIP), a clinical trial conducted between October 1982 and June 1984. This trial compared the ability of the three treatments to modify putative mechanisms for CHD in a selected sample of healthy type A men. Male managers were enrolled in the program after being screened for absence of heart disease, presence of type A, and presence of exaggerated cardiovascular and endocrine reactivity to psychosocial stress. The 118 managers selected were randomly assigned to the three interventions and evaluated on behavioral, physiological, and psychological response to stress before and after the treatment period. Changes in behavioral reactivity were assessed by comparing pre- and post-treatment Structured Interview scores using the protocol developed by Dembroski and his associates (Dembroski & MacDougall, 1983). Changes in physiological reactivity were assessed by comparing pre- and post-treatment values of heart rate, blood pressure, plasma cathecholamines, and cortisol in response to laboratory psychosocial stressors (i.e., the Stroop test, mental arithmetic). A detailed description of the study design and rationale has been presented elsewhere (Roskies et al., 1986), here, we present content and delivery details.

The individual treatment techniques used in our intervention programs (e.g., cognitive restructuring, jogging, progressive muscular relaxation) were not unique to this program; on the contrary, all are frequently employed in general stress management and health promotion packages and most have been applied to type A individuals (Blumenthal, Williams, Williams, & Wallace, 1980; Jenni & Wollersheim, 1979; Levenkron, Cohen, Mueller, & Fisher, 1983; Roskies, Spevack, Surkis, Cohen, & Gilman, 1978; Roskies, 1979; Roskies, 1983; Suinn, 1975; Suinn & Bloom, 1978). Our treatment of type A individuals differs from previous efforts in its utilization of stress theory to achieve greater specificity in diagnosis and treatment. Rather than applying a broadside blast of treatment techniques with the hope of a general, nonspecific improvement in functioning, we have used a theoretical stress model (Lazarus & Folkman, 1984), first to pinpoint the deficiencies in stress management exhibited by the target population, then to delineate the changes considered desirable and possible, and finally to examine the various intervention techniques available in terms of their specific ability to produce these changes. In short, stress theory served as our guide both to understanding the coronary risk of type A individuals, and to selecting treatments likely to modify this risk.

A second major characteristic of our intervention approach was the attention devoted to marketing. No true test of a specific treatment approach could occur unless the program representing it was appealing enough to attract and keep a sufficient number of suitable volunteers. The nature of our target audience made the process of recruitment and retention far from assured: Healthy, busy, time-pressured, impatient type A individuals were unlikely to come to or remain in treatment unless the benefits of intervention could be clearly understood, quickly felt, and soon outweighed the costs. The challenge, therefore, was not only to develop treatment programs incorporating the best available knowledge, but also to present them successfully to a highly critical consumer group.

TYPE A: A STRESS DISORDER

Individuals manifesting the type A behavior pattern (TABP) have been shown to be twice as likely to develop coronary heart disease as the more relaxed, easygoing type B counterparts (Rosenman et al., 1975). A review panel, charged with reviewing the evidence linking type A to heart disease, concluded that for employed middle-aged persons in the United States, at least, type A was a risk factor of the same magnitude as age, hypertension, elevated cholesterol, or smoking (Review Panel on Coronary-Prone Behavior and Coronary Heart Disease, 1981). Moreover, the type A behavior pattern is extremely widespread with a prevalence rate of 50 to 75% in selected North American samples of employed persons (Howard, Cunningham, & Rechnitzer, 1977; Rosenman et al., 1975). Finally, the TABP poses a challenge to current social values: TABP appears to be the occupational disease of high achievers. In contrast to the other risk factors for heart disease that are associated with blue collar status, TABP is most prevalent among upwardly mobile, achievement-oriented managers and professionals (Matthews, Helmreich, Beane, & Lucker, 1980; Mettlin, 1976).

The classic definition of the TABP is of "a characteristic action-emotion complex which is exhibited by those individuals who are engaged in a relatively *chronic struggle* to obtain an *unlimited* number of *poorly defined* things from their environment in *the shortest period of time* and, if necessary, against the opposing efforts of other things or persons" (Friedman, 1969, p. 84). There are a number of methods for assessing the presence of the pattern, including a Structured Interview (Rosenman, 1978), and two questionnaires—the Jenkins Activity Survey (Jenkins, Zyzanski, & Rosenman, 1971), and the Framingham Scale (Haynes, Levine, Scotch, Feinleib, & Kannel, 1978). All are valid in terms of their ability to predict heart disease, but unfortunately each appears to be measuring a different aspect of the pattern, since the intercorrelation between them is low (Matthews, Krantz, Dembroski, & MacDougall, 1982).

The most valid assessment device in terms of its predictive capacity is the Structured Interview. This is a 15–20 minute interview in which the interviewer poses a set series of questions relating to daily activities. A typical question is "What irritates you most about your work or the people with whom you work?" In contrast to the usual clinical interview, the interviewer tends to be challenging, rather than sympathetic. He or she may deliberately interrupt or challenge the respondent's statement, or alternately ask an obvious question in a deliberately slow manner. The scoring of the interview is based mainly on style of response (e.g., speech stylistics, manifestations of hostility), rather than on content. On the basis of the interview, respondents are classified either as fully developed type A individuals (A_1), somewhat A (A_2), midway between A and B (X), or definitely non-A (B).

The presence of the type A behavior pattern can signal a serious threat to health, but it is far from obvious why it should be classified as a stress disorder. As a group, type A individuals have not been exposed to the type of severe stress situation capable of producing recognized clinical syndromes, such as the post-traumatic stress disorder of Vietnam veterans or the reactive depression of bereaved spouses. Even in terms of the less traumatic but more persistent occupational stress, the managerial and professional jobs in which type A individuals are most commonly found are not rated highest. In fact, physical and mental problems directly linked to occupation are far more likely to be found in blue collar workers (Kasl, 1978). Managerial type A individuals may describe their lives as busy and pressured, but there is no basis for explaining their increased coronary risk as a result of exposure to unusually stressful life circumstances.

Type A individuals do not fall into the category of persons suffering from stress disorders because of obvious deficiencies in coping resources and strategies. On the contrary, type A managers with whom we worked are so full of energy and activity that they give the impression of being super healthy. Even a short interview reveals their mental alertness, emotional expressiveness, and rapid pace of thought and speech. Their ability to fulfill valued social roles is also noteworthy. All hold responsible managerial positions, and most add to their job demands a host of family obligations and community activities. In spite of these multiple pressures, there are remarkably few complaints of anxiety and depression. Some of the type A men state that they thrive on challenge and tight deadlines—the more the better. Even when a man does experience malaise, be it in the form of tight shoulder muscles or difficulty in falling asleep, the usual tendency is to minimize the degree of discomfort and to accept it as a necessary part of the stress of modern life.

In short, type A individuals as a group do not appear to live in unusually stressful life circumstances, nor do they manifest obvious deficiencies in coping resources for managing the stresses they do encounter. Nevertheless, the TABP is considered a stress disorder because of the type A individuals' psychological vulnerability to the demands of daily life, the disposition to perceive threat and/or challenge where the type B individual does not (Pittner & Houston, 1980; Van Egeren, Abelson, & Sniderman, 1983; Vickers, Hervig, Rahe, & Rosenman, 1981). Various explanations have been offered for the type A individual's tendency to appraise daily happenings as stress encounters: Some authors postulate a need to exert control over the environment (Glass, 1977), while others claim that type A individuals manifest an intense ego involvement leading to increased emotionality (Scherwitz, Berton, & Leventhal, 1978; Scherwitz, Leachman, et al., 1978, 1983). A third view attributes the type A individual's perceptual hypersensitivity to an uncertain sense of self-worth, leading to the necessity to continuously prove oneself (Prince, 1982). Regardless of the specific beliefs and commitments underlying this perceptual hypersensitivity, however, the consequence is the same: The type A individual is more often at war than at peace, repeatedly mobilizing his or her resources to confront perceived threats and challenges. A game of tennis, a difference of opinion with a colleague at work, and a too-slow elevator, all produce a stress reaction in the hypersensitive type A person.

The resulting stress is expressed both behaviorally and physiologically. Behaviorally, the type A individual is characterized by pressured drive (e.g., time hurry, impatience, push for achievement, explosive speech) and potential for hostility (i.e., interactions with others marked by anger, suspiciousness, and hostility) (cf. Thoresen & Ohman, 1985). The relationship of these behavioral manifestations to heart disease has been established empirically. Increased coronary risk was successfully predicted by classifying the individual according to behavioral style on the Structured Interview (Rosenman et al., 1975), while Friedman and his colleagues have recently reported that in a sample of post-infarct patients treatment which successfully reduced behavioral indices of the TABP, as measured by a variant of the Structured Interview, also successfully reduced recurrence of heart attacks and mortality (Friedman et al., 1984).

On the physiological level, the type A individual's vulnerability to the demands of daily life is manifested by frequent, excessive innervations of the sympathetic-adrenomedullary system. Type A and B individuals do not differ physiologically when at rest, but in response to typical laboratory stress tasks or simply the pressures of the working day, type A individuals are more likely than type B individuals to show greater elevations in blood pressure, heart rate, and circulating cortisol, epinephrine, and norepinephrine (Dembroski, MacDougall, Shields, Petito, & Lushene, 1978; Friedman et al., 1960; Glass et al., 1980; Manuck, Craft, & Gold, 1978; Williams et al., 1982). Moreover, type A individuals appear to lack a necessary feedback loop alerting them to fatigue and illness (Carver, Coleman, & Glass, 1976; Matthews & Carra, 1982; Schlegel, Wellwood, Copps, Gruchow, & Sharratt, 1980); not only do they become more aroused, but there is a deficiency in the signaling process that would lead them to seek rest and relaxation. The link between exaggerated physiological reactivity in type A individuals and their increased risk of heart disease still awaits empirical confirmation, but these innervations of the sympathetic-adrenomedullary system could conceivably serve as a biological pathway between behavior and disease by potentiating arteriosclerosis and, eventually, CHD (Herd, 1981; Krantz & Manuck, 1984).

The relationship between the behavioral and physiological manifestations of the pattern is still unclear. It is usually assumed that the behavioral manifestations give rise to the physiological reactions, though Krantz and Durel (1983) suggest that the sequence may be reversed, with the type A individual suffering from a constitutional physiological hyperreactivity. In this latter view, it is the effort to give meaning to a pounding heart or rising blood pressure that leads the type A individual to "feel" anger or impatience. A third possibility is that the behavioral and sympathetic stress responses are independent, with behavior linked to disease by another, as yet unknown, biological mechanism.

Regardless of where the cycle begins and through what mechanisms it operates, however, most observers agree on one basic point: The type A individual does not necessarily handle any single stress episode badly, but it is the cumulative impact of perceiving too many situations as stressful and reacting too intensely and for too long, that defines his or her increased vulnerability to CHD. There are two empirical lines of evidence that lend credibility to this model of type A individual as a problem in tolerating and coping with the minor irritants of daily life. The first, based on the work of Lazarus and his colleagues (Kanner, Coyne, Schaefer, & Lazarus 1981; DeLongis, Coyne, Dakof, Folkman, & Lazarus, 1982; Lazarus, 1984), indicates that daily hassles—the minor irritants of everyday living—can be as, or even more, harmful to health than the more dramatic major life changes. The second line of evidence arises from attempts to improve the diagnostic specificity of the Structured Interview by analyzing what it is really measuring. These analyses indicate physiological reactions similar to those observed in reaction to other laboratory psychosocial stress tasks (Dembroski, MacDougall, & Lushene 1979; Krantz et al., 1981). The basis for classifying an individual as A or not-A is coping style (e.g., loud voice, manifestation of hostility), rather than interview content (Schuker & Jacobs, 1977). Essentially, the Structured Interview is a measure of behavioral reactivity to the laboratory analog of a daily hassle.

CHOICE OF TREATMENT GOALS AND METHODS

Based on our view that type A managers as a group did not suffer from an unusually stressful environment, we did not seek to radically restructure work or home environments. Similarly, because we did not consider type A individuals as a group to be generally psychologically vulnerable, we rejected broad-band psychological interventions that would seek major personality reconstruction. Instead, because we believed that the type A individuals' stress difficulties were a problem of too frequent, too intense, and too long-lasting daily hassles, the focus of our interventions was on modifying the nature and consequences of these minor stress episodes.

Three broad lines of approach were available: pharmaceutical, cognitive-behavioral, and physical. Medications such as beta blockers show promise in reducing the physical signs of arousal in stressful situations, but any medication powerful enough to affect the sympathetic-adrenomedullary system could also be expected to have multiple side-effects. Some undesirable secondary effects have been identified; others remain to be discovered (cf. Durel, Krantz, Eisold, & Lazar, in press). Moreover, experience with hypertensives has highlighted the serious difficulties involved in convincing symptomless individuals to embark on a lifelong program of daily medication. For these reasons, we considered the pharmaceutical approach to be a line of last defense, to be tried only when other approaches had been proved wanting.

In contrast to the pharmaceutical approach, stress management and physical exercise do not carry the connotation of illness and, hence, are likely to prove more acceptable within the context of a preventive program. Moreover, in appropriately selected samples, stress management has no apparent negative effects, while those resulting from exercise are less prevalent and usually less serious than the negative side-effects of medication. Accordingly, in seeking to modify the type A individual's daily stress encounters, we selected cognitive-behavioral stress management and physical exercise as the basic treatment approaches. The specific techniques selected, and the reasons for choosing them, are detailed in the descriptions of the individual treatment programs.

In seeking to compare treatments within a given study, there are inevitable conflicts between the experimental need for standardization of treatment delivery procedures and the varying clinical needs of individual treatments; for instance, while it would be desirable for experimental purposes to have the same number of sessions for all treatments, aerobic exercise programs are most effective using three to four sessions per week, in contrast to the one or two weekly sessions considered optimal for the stress management program. Similarly, the cognitive-behavioral treatment is based on homework assignments, while physical exercise interventions have no homework requirement. Our decision was to standardize treatment delivery only to the degree that it did not affect clinical validity; thus, 10 weeks was considered to be the minimum time necessary to achieve significant aerobic effects and, in the absence of conflicting needs of the other treatments, this length of treatment was adopted as the standard. For frequency of sessions and homework assignments, in contrast, treatments were permitted to vary according to their individual needs.

PROGRAM MARKETING

The Montreal offices of two large Canadian corporations, conveniently located close to testing and treatment facilities, provided a pool of thousands of managers, many of whom were presumably hyperreactive and type A. Program marketing was based both on mass mailings to selected levels of these managers and articles in their company newspapers. Previous experience with healthy type A individuals (Roskies, 1983; Roskies et al., 1978, 1979) led us to believe that these men were less concerned with future disease than with current productivity. Accordingly, rather than dwelling on the type A individual's risk of developing heart disease sometime in the future, we emphasized, instead, the wasted energy and unnecessary tension these men were currently experiencing. Our interventions promised to make them more efficient by teaching them to accomplish as much, if not more, with a lower expenditure of energy and less discomfort.

The multi-stage screening process provided numerous opportunities to reinforce the sales message. For instance, while informing prospective candidates of their classification as type A and physiologically hyperreactive, we could point out that some co-workers, occupying positions of similar responsibility in the same company, did not react in the same intense way they did. Interpersonal relations marked by hostility and competitiveness were not a necessary condition of successful job performance. In fact, previous studies with the same laboratory stress tasks had repeatedly confirmed that type A individuals, in spite of their higher heart rate, blood pressure, and levels of catecholamine and cortisol excretion, do not perform better than type B individuals (Dembroski et al., 1978; Lundberg & Forsman, 1979; Manuck et al., 1978). The obvious conclusion here was that hyperreactive type A individuals are inefficient in expending more effort to get the same job done.

The need to follow a complex experimental protocol (careful screening of subjects, counterbalancing time of day of testing, random assignment to treatment groups, etc.) is not entirely compatible with good clinical practice. Careful screening of subjects may require us to exclude the man who most needs and wants treatment, and random assignment to treatment groups may violate individual preferences. We did not find a completely satisfactory answer to this problem, but within the limits of our research protocol, the individual welfare of volunteers was our primary consideration. The best way of showing this concern, of course, was by the quality of the treatments offered, but the people who screened potential participants and delivered the interventions were also important. Project personnel having direct contact with participants were selected for their clinical abilities, and each of the selection, testing, and treating activities was under the direct supervision of a specific principal investigator, charged with maintaining a high standard of professional conduct.

To further help volunteers feel like collaborators rather than experimental subjects, we attempted to provide as much information as possible: A full description of the project was provided at the initial selection appointment, staff members provided additional explanations as the selection proceeded, and the principal investigators were available to answer further questions or concerns. Just before the beginning of treatment, all participants were invited to a general information meeting with the staff. Each participant was promised that, at the end of the project, he would receive both his own individual records and a report of the general outcome. Individuals declared ineligible were furnished the reasons for their elimination (e.g., not type A), and referred to other stress management or exercise programs if they requested it.

We were particularly sensitive to the possible negative psychological effects on an individual who was declared medically ineligible, possibly discovering a hitherto unsuspected medical problem. To minimize anxiety, we emphasized from the outset that we were looking for a sample with specific characteristics, leading us to reject the majority of volunteers. Letters concerning medical exclusions were signed by a physician, who explained the nature of the problem, and invited the individual to contact him for further information or discussion. At the request of the participant, his medical record would be sent to the physician of his choice, or we would refer him to a suitable medical facility.

Before enrolling eligible participants in the program, we required a deposit of $200, as a sign of good faith. This money was refundable at the end of the program, with interest, if the participant attended the required number of treatment sessions. The sum of money involved was probably not sufficiently high to keep a person in a program he truly disliked, but the necessity for a monetary deposit did help to distinguish those who were seriously interested from the merely curious. The deposit is particularly helpful during the first few weeks of the interventions when the costs of treatment may appear to outweigh the gains.

Once a participant was enrolled, we tried to keep him in the program by making the interventions as attractive and convenient as possible. Interventions were limited to the minimum period considered necessary to produce significant aerobic effects (10 weeks) and the groups were scheduled to avoid the Christmas break or the summer holiday period. Sessions were held at the beginning of the working day (7:30 and 8 A.M.) in locations at or near the workplace. Each of the programs had provisions for allowing a participant to keep up with his group even if he had to miss a few sessions because of illness or business travel. Program leaders were all highly trained and experienced in working with a managerial population. Finally, the group structure itself was used to provide social support for change.

AEROBIC TRAINING PROGRAM

The rationale for subjecting hyperreactive type A individuals to physical fitness training derives from the finding that a regular program of isorhythmic/aerobic exercise (15–30 minutes/3 times/week) leads to short-term improvement in cardiovascular efficiency. Indices of improved functioning are increased oxygen utilization and stroke volume; decreased resting, active, and recovery heart rate; decreased blood pressure, and decreased catecholamines. Significant for our purposes, is the possibility that this enhancement in cardiovascular efficiency not only leads to faster recovery from physiological stressors such as exercise, but also modifies the response to psychosocial stress.

A number of authors have reported more rapid physiological recovery from psychosocial stress of physically fit individuals compared to unfit ones (Cox, Evans, & Jamieson, 1979; Keller & Seraganian, 1984; Light, Obrist, & James, 1984; Sinyor, Schwartz, Perronet, Brisson, & Seraganian, 1983). In addition, there is one treatment study of the effects of physical fitness on type A individuals (Blumenthal et al., 1980). No direct test of reactivity was made, but the authors do report generally improved physiological and psychological functioning. These data suggest that improved physical fitness might reduce the negative consequences of a stressful encounter, because the fit individual would be aroused for a shorter time period. A program that improved aerobic fitness would, by increasing resiliance, literally put the person in better shape to withstand stress. Given the current popularity of physical fitness, such an intervention would have the added advantage of credibility.

Jogging was chosen as the most practical aerobic exercise for the climate, time, and resources available. Length of training was established at 10 weeks on the basis that the most significant changes in aerobic fitness occur during this period, with further training yielding progressively smaller increments in fitness. A frequency of 3 to 4 times a week was chosen as the best balance between maximizing fitness gains while minimizing risk of muscular and skeletal injuries (ACSM Position Statement, 1978; Pollack et al., 1977). Classes were held four times a week (Mondays, Wednesdays, Thursdays, and Fridays from 8 to 9 A.M.) under the leadership of a physical education specialist experienced in working with sedentary middleaged men. The locale of treatment was a private exercise club, located close to the worksite, with a padded jogging track reserved for the exclusive use of participants during class periods, as well as excellent locker facilities, sauna, and whirlpool.

Three classes per week were required, a fourth was optional, and participants were expected to attend a minimum of 27 of the 40 classes offered. At the beginning of treatment, each participant received a manual that described the rationale of treatment, furnished directions for minimizing chances of injury, and provided an exercise program that an individual could follow on his own if he were absent from a session. By following these directions, a participant could miss up to one week of classes without apparent disruption of progress.

Each class was designed to last for approximately 45 minutes. The first and last 10 to 15 minutes of each class served as warm-up and cool-down periods, consisting of calisthetics and stretching exercises. The principal cardiovascular component, an individually tailored jogging program, was sandwiched into the middle 20 to 25 minutes of each class. Although it is this cardiovascular component that is largely responsible for changes in aerobic fitness, failure to provide adequate warm-up and cool-down periods increases risk of injury, and, consequently, diminishes program compliance.

Considerable attention was given to the intensity parameter. The safest and most effective method for specifying aerobic exercise intensity is in terms of the heart rate (HR) achieved. If the jogging activity in the middle 20 to 25 minutes of each class is not sufficiently intense to elevate HR above a certain (individually determined) threshold, then little gain in aerobic fitness can be expected over the 10 weeks. Conversely, if an individual works too intensely and elevates his heart rate above a ceiling value, he will fatigue prematurely, suffer undue discomfort, and greatly increase risk of injury.

Recent literature suggests that the best way to calculate target heart rate is as a percentage of total heart rate range. Using a bicycle ergometer with a modified version of the Astrand-Rhyming protocol (Siconalfi, Cullinane, Carleton, & Thompson, 1982), a maximal heart rate was estimated for each subject. Heart rate range was then obtained by subtracting basal HR from maximal HR. Once this heart rate range was determined, the participant was given a range of target exercise heart rates, based on his age and physical condition. For instance, for a 35-year-old person with a basal HR of 80 and an estimated maximal HR of 190, the total heart rate range was calculated as 110 (190 − 80). This subject was instructed to aim for an increase of 65% of his heart rate range during exercise, that is an increase of 73 (65% of 110) beats per minute. In practical terms, this meant that the minimal desirable heart rate during exercise was 135 bpm (80 + 50% of 110) and the maximal rate was 163 bpm (80 + 75% of 110).

A major concern in working with type A men is to ensure that participants keep to the designated heart rate, and do not incur injury by seeking to compete with other group members who are younger, or in better physical condition. For some participants this was likely to be especially difficult, since their exercise prescription called for alternate walking and jogging, while others were allowed to jog for the entire 20-minute period. To counteract this competitiveness, the group leader emphasized the importance of monitoring heart rate at frequent intervals, and participants were taught how to take their pulse. Pulse taking was made more attractive by distributing a number of wristwatch electronic pulse monitors among participants. During the critical first weeks, when risk of injury is highest, a graduate student served as an additional supervisor monitoring heart rate and jogging style.

A number of additional techniques were used to minimize dropout resulting from injury. To ensure that all participants had appropriate, well-fitting jogging shoes, we had them fitted with new jogging shoes at our expense. At each session, the men were asked to report any pain experienced, and, if necessary, were referred to a sports medicine clinic which had agreed to see them quickly. If pain or injury made jogging undesirable, participants were switched to an exercise bicycle until they had recovered.

COGNITIVE-BEHAVIORAL PROGRAM

Numerous studies have shown that individuals can be provided with cognitive and behavioral skills that will significantly alter how they perceive and respond to a wide range of potential stressors (cf. Foryet & Rathjen, 1978; Kendall & Hollon, 1979; Meichenbaum & Jaremko, 1983; Motofsky, 1976). Our goal in devising a stress management program for these hyperreactive type A managers was first to define as operationally as possible what was most harmful in their response to stress, and then to select cognitive and behavioral techniques for modifying these coping deficiencies. Next, and most important, the teaching of these skills had to be organized into a 10-week program that divided the learning process into a series of graded steps. Each session had the double objective of providing a useful learning experience by itself and, at the same time, fitting into a hierarchial sequence of skill acquisition and application.

The first step was to delineate as clearly as possible our understanding of what was harmful about participants' present style of coping and the changes we hoped to achieve by treatment. We defined the hyperreactivity of type A individuals as, essentially, a tendency to expend energy unnecessarily and/or ineffectively in coping with the inevitable hassles of daily life. Compared to less reactive individuals, program participants were more likely to evaluate even minor challenges or annoyances as stressful, more likely to react in a stereotyped, undifferentiated fashion to a wide variety of stress situations, and more likely to proceed directly from one stressful situation to the next without allowing for rest and recuperation. Instead of carefully evaluating the nature of a potential stressor and the resources available to deal with it, the type A person repeatedly reacts in an automatic all-or-none fashion.

Most of our participants had some awareness of their hyperreactivity, but felt that this was the inevitable cost of an active, productive lifestyle. We agreed that stress—particularly in the form of daily hassles—is an inevitable part of their lifestyle and, indeed, all lives. The competent coper is no more able than the deficient one to completely avoid potentially stressful situations. Where he differs, however, is in his mental preparedness for the possibility of stress, his differentiated evaluation of external events and internal states, and his broad repertoire of coping techniques. This ability to be aware of and exert effective control over thoughts, behavior, and physical reactions allows the competent coper to respond to challenge or threat in a manner that maximizes impact and minimizes strain.

Hyperreactive type A individuals, in contrast, were not incompetent copers, but simply inefficient ones. They had adopted a coping style that permitted considerable achievement and brought many rewards, but which was both unnecessarily wasteful of their own energy and unnecessarily disruptive of their relationships with others. Admittedly, it was not easy to change deeply engrained habits that had seemed to serve them well. But learning to cope more efficiently is hardly the first difficult situation that these men had successfully faced. Fortunately, the same qualities of intelligence and persistence could be brought to bear on this new challenge.

The exaggerated stress responses of type A individuals occur on many levels—physiological, behavioral, emotional, and cognitive—and responses occurring on different levels interact synergistically to intensify and prolong the reaction. For instance, a raging headache may lead us to shout at a meeting, but the act of shouting may in itself increase the level of physical tension. To maximize the possibilities for effective self-control, therefore, we could not rely on a single all-purpose technique, but would have to provide participants with multiple skills for controlling the multiple facets of tension. Moreover, because the pattern of hyperreactive coping is not limited to a few situations but occurs in response to a multitude of stimuli, significant change in hyperreactivity would depend on the ability to generalize new skills beyond the initial learning situation. The objectives of the program, therefore, became:

1. increased awareness of the many levels of and the many situations in which dysfunctional responses were occurring
2. acquisition of multiple new coping strategies for evaluating and responding to potential stressors
3. repeated practice of new coping patterns in an ever-widening variety of situations until these new patterns themselves became habitual

The first two thirds of the 10-week (20-session) program were devoted to acquisition of basic coping skills; Focusing on physiological, behavioral, and cognitive stress responses in sequence, participants were helped to discriminate "bad" stress responses from "good" ones and then to acquire and practice coping strategies for transforming the former into the latter. All sessions in this part of the program followed a similar pattern. Beginning with physical tension, participants first learned to become aware of variations in physical tension by keeping a stress diary, and then to become proficient in progressive muscular relaxation as a means of controlling such tension. For behavioral tension, a similar stress diary was used to increase awareness, but the techniques used for control were more varied: pause, engaging in behavior incompatible with the action to be avoided (e.g., when tempted to interrupt, focus on what the other person is saying), and learning to discuss difficult issues in a constructive fashion. Learning to control unproductive thinking, involved a stress diary of what is termed "self-talk," distinguishing between helpful and unhelpful self-talk, and conscious efforts to substitute the former for the latter.

Once the basic techniques of managing stress were acquired, the emphasis shifted to application. Stress situations were divided into two categories, predictable and unpredictable, and participants were encouraged to identify as many as possible of the former (e.g., the daily commute to work, a weekly project meeting) and to take preventive action against dysfunctional stress responses by seeking to change the situation, their reaction to it, or a combination of both. For unpredictable stress situations (e.g., an unexpected car breakdown), the emphasis was on short-circuiting the initial loss of emotional control or regaining control as quickly as possible, so that appropriate action could be taken. The final sections of the course dealt with increasing stress resistance by planning (1) to incorporate small pleasures into the daily routine and (2) how to maintain the changes effected once the course ended.

Given the nature of the course material, the bulk of the learning would take place in filling the homework assignments, outside the twice weekly group meetings. A number of strategies were used to increase compliance with the homework assignments. At the beginning of each section of the course (e.g., productive thinking), participants were furnished a small booklet detailing the purpose of this form of stress management, the skills required, and the possible applications. Homework assignments were completed in prepared booklets, each of which contained a cover page detailing the purpose of the homework assignment, and what specifically the respondent was being asked to do. A second introductory page provided an example of a completed homework assignment. The aim was to increase clarity of purpose and to minimize response cost.

To further increase compliance, most of the group meetings were devoted to a discussion of the most recent homework assignment, and participants were encouraged to read directly from their homework assignments. The group leaders attempted to establish an atmosphere of tolerance and humor, so that participants could learn to share some of their difficulties in confronting minor domestic and work crises. Because participants worked in the same companies and would necessarily meet in other contexts, the degree of exposure was controlled; the emphasis was on irritants of daily life that anybody could confront. Some of the problems raised could be humorous (e.g., planning Christmas with two sets of competing in-laws), and an effort was made to encourage laughter and mutual support. At the end of each session, homework assignments were collected, permitting group leaders to better follow individual progress, and further encouraging participants to complete them.

Group sessions were held in a meeting room in one of the participating companies, Monday and Thursday mornings from 8 to 9 A.M. A third makeup session at Friday noon was directed primarily towards individuals who had missed a session or who expected to be away during the following week. The usual attendance at a makeup session was 2 to 3 people, in contrast to the 10 to 12 at a regular session. Therefore, individuals who wished to discuss something more privately with a group leader would occasionally use this third weekly session as a supplementary one. The program was based on 20 sessions (there were 19 homework assignments), and participants were required to attend a minimum of 18.

WEIGHT TRAINING PROGRAM

In contrast to aerobic exercise and cognitive-behavioral stress management, we were unaware of any data that directly linked weight training to a reduction of behavioral or physiological response to stress. Instead, weight training was included in this clinical trial as a nonspecific treatment, to control for attention-placebo and expectancy effects on outcome. It was important that the treatment be as credible as the others and treatment conditions be as similar as possible.

The program was designed to mimic the aerobic fitness training, while avoiding techniques that would generate improvements in cardiovascular fitness itself. Classes were held between 7:30 to 8:30 A.M. in the health spa of a large downtown Montreal hotel, located close to the workplace of program participants. During classes, participants had exclusive use of the spa's facilities, including the Nautilus training stations.

The training period was 10 weeks, the same as the other programs. Three classes per week were offered, two were recommended, and participants were expected to attend a minimum of 18 sessions. All participants received a detailed manual which outlined the rationale behind the weight training program and summarized the principles involved. This manual helped participants to maintain training, even if they had to miss one or two classes.

The warm-up and cool-down periods mimicked those used in the aerobic exercise program. Where the two programs differed, was in the type of exercise employed in the middle 20 to 25 minutes of each class. Instead of jogging, participants in the weight training program exercised on Nautilus equipment at individually tailored intensities that generally exceeded the aerobic range, but for durations far shorter than those required to produce aerobic adaptations. To increase the credibility of this program, "before" and "after" measures of strength were included in the testing protocols (Wilmore, 1974, Clarke & Clarke, 1967).

EVALUATION OF TREATMENTS

The primary evaluation of these treatments was in terms of their ability to produce the desired behavioral and physiological changes, but a necessary first step in this process was the verification of treatment delivery. Failure to verify that the treatments were delivered as intended, a common omission in assessments of behavioral treatments, makes it impossible to interpret the subsequent findings. For instance, lack of observed change can be the result of ineffective treatments or simply of inadequately delivered ones.

Fortunately for our purposes, the four process measures used all indicated that the three treatments had been delivered as intended. The criterion of minimum attendance at 90 percent of sessions for inclusion in evaluation of treatment effects meant that all participants received adequate exposure to the treatments. Participants' equally high ratings of their respective programs indicated that all three treatments were acceptable and credible; on a 7-point scale of "worthwhileness," 82 percent of the sample (82 percent in the aerobic exercise group, 81 percent in the stress management group, and 83 percent in the weight training group) rated their treatment as 6 or 7, that is, very worthwhile. For the two physical fitness programs, it was also possible to verify changes in aerobic fitness and muscle strength. As expected, the joggers increased estimated maximal oxygen uptake and decreased basal heart rate significantly, but the other two groups did not; conversely, and also as expected, the weight training group showed substantial increases on six of the seven strength determinations, the aerobic group improved on three determinations, and the stress management group remained virtually unchanged. The positive results of these process measures effectively ruled out inadequacies in treatment delivery as a possible cause of the inability of one or more of these treatments to achieve the desired results.

The next step in the evaluation process was to focus on the treatment effects themselves; these have been reported in detail elsewhere (Roskies et al., 1986) and we shall simply summarize the highlights here. Essentially, changes in behavioral reactivity were assessed by comparing pre- to post-treatment verbal stylistics on the Structured Interview. For changes in physiological reactivity, participants' pretreatment responses to a series of laboratory tests were compared to their post-treatment ones; the parameters measured were plasma epinephrine and norepinephrine, cortisol, heart rate, systolic and diastolic blood pressure.

When the various treatments were then compared in terms of their ability to modify behavioral reactivity, one treatment—cognitive-behavioral stress management—was clearly and consistently superior to the rest. The Dembroski protocol (Dembroski & MacDougall, 1983) provides for a global type A rating, as well as ratings on six component scores (loud speech, explosive speech, rapid and accelerated speech, quick response latency, potential for hostility and verbal competitiveness). The cognitive-behavioral treatment was significantly superior to the other two treatments on global score and five of the six components, showing reductions of 13 to 23 percent below pretreatment values. In sharp contrast, the aerobic exercise group generally showed no change, while the weight training group was intermediate between the two others, with smaller and less consistent reductions of 0 to 12 percent; the differences between the two physical exercise groups, however, were not statistically significant. The credibility of these findings is enhanced by the fact that there were three groups per treatment, and the results were virtually identical in the different groups within each treatment.

For physiological stress responses, in contrast, none of the treatments achieved meaningful reductions. Three of the six measures had to be discarded because of measurement problems (epinephrine, norepinephrine, and cortisol) and of the three that remained (heart rate, systolic, and diastolic blood pressure) the pre- to post-treatment differences observed, while statistically significant, did not differentiate between groups and, in any case, were no greater than those attributable to habituation alone. These results may reflect the inability of behavioral treatments in general to modify physiological hyperreactivity, but they may also be the result of the inability of existing measures to accurately capture physiological changes that do occur because of "noise" in the measuring instruments and/or situations.

CONCLUSION

The material presented here reflects but a single chapter in the continuing efforts to understand the TABP better and to develop treatments that will alleviate its harmful effects. Both the positive and negative findings of our particular research effort suggest avenues of further exploration. The positive behavioral effects apparently produced by the stress management treatment need to be tested for replicability, durability, and ability to reduce incidence of heart disease itself. The negative physiological results highlights the need both for improved measures and for clarification of the relationship between exaggerated physiological reactivity, the TABP, and coronary heart disease. Our aim was to illustrate the use of stress theory to achieve greater precision in the diagnosis and treatment of stress disorders. Based on the positive process measures for all interventions, and the promising outcome for one, we believe that stress and coping theory has much to contribute to the clinical practice of teaching coping skills.

References

ACSM Position Statement. (1978). The recommended quantity and quality of exercise for developing and maintaining fitness in healthy adults. *Medicine and Science in Sports, 10,* 7–10.

Blumenthal, J. A., Williams, R. S., Williams Jr., R. B., & Wallace A. G. (1980). Effects of exercise on the type A (coronary-prone) behavior pattern. *Psychosomatic Medicine, 4,* 289–296.

Carver, C. S., Coleman, A. E., & Glass, D. C. (1976). The coronary-prone behavior pattern and the suppression of fatigue on a treadmill test. *Journal of Personality and Social Psychology, 33,* 460–466.

Clarke, H. H., & Clarke D. H. (1967). *Developmental and adapted physical education.* Englewood Cliffs, N.J.: Prentice-Hall.

Cox, J. P., Evans, J. F., & Jamieson, J. L. (1979). Aerobic power and tonic heart rate responses to psychosocial stressors. *Personality and Social Psychology Bulletin, 5,* 160–163.

DeLongis, A., Coyne, J. C., Dakof, G., Folkman, S., & Lazarus, R. S. (1982). Relationship of daily hassles, uplifts, and major life events to health status. *Health Psychology, 1,* 119–136.

Dembroski, T. M., & MacDougall, J. M. (1983). Behavioral and psychophysiological perspectives on coronary-prone behavior. In T. M. Dembroski, T. H. Schmidt, and G. Blumchen (Eds.), *Biobehavioral bases of coronary heart diseases,* 106–129. Basel: Karger.

Dembroski, T. M., MacDougall, J. M., & Lushene, R. (1979). Interpersonal interaction and cardiovascular response in type A subjects and coronary patients. *Journal of Human Stress, 5:* no. 4, 28–36.

Dembroski, T. M., MacDougall, J. M., Shields, J. L., Petito, J., & Lushene, R. (1978). Components of the type A coronary-prone behavior pattern and cardiovascular response to psychomotor challenge. *Journal of Behavioral Medicine, 1,* 159–176.

Durel, L. A., Krantz, D. S., Eisold, J. F., & Lazar, J. D. (in press). Behavioral effects of beta-blockers, with emphasis on the reduction of anxiety, acute stress and type A behavior. *Journal of Cardiac Rehabilitation.*

Foreyt, J. P., & Rathjen, D. P. (Eds.) (1978). *Cognitive-behavior therapy: research and application.* New York: Plenum.

Friedman, M. (1969). *Pathogenesis of coronary artery disease.* New York: McGraw-Hill.

Friedman, M., St. George, S., Byers, S. O., & Rosenman, R. H. (1960). Excretion of catecholamines, 17 kerosteroids, 17 hydroxy-corticoids and 5 hydroxyindole in men exhibiting a particular behavior pattern (A) associated with high incidence of clinical coronary artery disease. *J Clinical Investigation, 39:* 758–764.

Friedman, M., Thoresen, C. E., Gill, J. J., Powell, L., Ulmer, D., Thompson, L., Price, V., Rabin, D. D., Breall, W. S., Dixon, T., Levy, R. A., & Bourg, E. (1984). Alteration of type A behavior and reduction in cardiac recurrences in post-myocardial infarction patients. *American Heart Journal, 108,* 237–248.

Glass, D. C. (1977). *Behavior patterns, stress and coronary disease.* Hillsdale, NJ: Erlbaum.

Glass, D. C., Krakoff, L. R., Contrada, R., Hilton, W. F., Kehoe, K., Mannucci, E. G., Collins, C., Snow, B., and Elting, E. (1980). Effect of harassment and competition upon cardiovascular and catecholamine responses in type A and B individuals. *Psychophysiology, 17,* 453–463.

Haynes, S. G., Levine, S., Scotch, N., Feinleib, M., & Kannel, W. (1978). The relationship of psychosocial factors to coronary heart disease in the Framingham study. *American Journal of Epidemiology, 107,* 362–383.

Herd, J. A., (1981). Behavioral factors in the physiological mechanisms of cardiovascular disease. In S. M. Weiss, J. A. Herd, & B. H. Fox (Eds.), *Perspectives on behavioral medicine,* 55–66. New York: Academic.

Howard, J. H., Cunningham, D. A., & Rechnitzer, P. A. (1977). Work patterns associated with type A behavior: A managerial population. *Human Relations, 30,* 825–836.

Jenkins, C. D., Zyzanski, S. J., & Rosenman, R. H. (1971). Progress toward validation of a computer-scored test for the type A coronary-prone behavior pattern. *Psychosomatic Medicine. 33,* 193–202.

Jenni, M. A., & Wollersheim, J. P. (1979). Cognitive therapy, stress management training and the type A behavior pattern. *Cognitive Therapy and Research, 3,* 61–73.

Kanner, A. D., Coyne, J. C., Schaefer, C., & Lazarus, R. S. (1981). Comparison of two modes of stress measurement: Daily hassles and uplifts versus major life events. *Journal of Behavioral Medicine, 4,* 1–40.

Kasl, S. (1978). Epidemiological contributions to the study of work stress. In C. L. Cooper & R. Payne (Eds.), *Stress at work,* 3–50. New York: Wiley.

Keller, S. M., & Seraganian, P. (1984). Physical fitness level and autonomic reactivity to psychological stress. *Journal of Psychosomatic Research, 28,* 279–287.

Kendall, P. C., & Hollon, S. D. (Eds.). (1979). *Cognitive-behavioral interventions: theory, research and procedures.* New York: Academic.

Krantz, D. S., & Durel, L. A. (1983). Psychobiological substrates of the type A behavior pattern. *Health Psychology, 2,* 393–411.

Krantz, D. S., & Manuck, S. B. (1984). Acute psychophysiological reactivity and risk of cardiovascular disease. *Psychological Bulletin, 96,* 435–464.

Krantz, D. S., Schaeffer, M. A., Davia, J. E., Dembroski, T. M., MacDougall, J. M., & Shaffer, R. T. (1981). Extent of coronary atherosclerosis, type A behavior and cardiovascular response to social interaction. *Psychophysiology, 18,* 654–664.

Lazarus, R. S. (1984). Puzzles in the study of daily hassles. *Journal of Behavioral Medicine, 7,* 375–389.

Lazarus, R. S., & Folkman, S. (1984). *Stress, appraisal and coping.* New York: Springer.

Levenkron, J. C., Cohen, J. D., Mueller, H. S., & Fisher Jr., E. B. (1983). Modifying the type A coronary-prone behavior pattern. *Journal of Consulting and Clinical Psychology, 51,* 192–204.

Light, K. C., Obrist, P. A., James, S. A. (1984). Self-reported exercise levels and cardiovascular responses during rest and stress. *SPR Abstracts, 21,* 586.

Lundberg, U., & Forsman, L. (1979). Adrenal-medullary and adrenal-cortical responses to understimulation and overstimulation: Comparison between type A and type B persons. *Biological Psychology, 9,* 79–89.

Manuck, S. B., Craft, S. A., & Gold, K. J. (1978). Coronary-prone behavior pattern and cardiovascular response. *Psychophysiology, 15,* 403–411.

Matthews, K. A., & Carra, J. (1982). Suppression of menstrual distress symptoms: A study of type A behavior. *Personality and Social Psychology Bulletin, 8,* 146–151.

Matthews, K. A., Helmreich, R. L., Beane, W. E., & Lucker, G. W. (1980). Pattern A, achievement striving and scientific merit: Does pattern A help or hinder? *Journal of Personality and Social Psychology, 39,* 962–967.

Matthews, K. A., Krantz, D. S., Dembroski, T. M., & MacDougall, J. M. (1982). Unique and common variance in structured interview and Jenkins activity survey measures of the type A behavior pattern. *Journal of Personality and Social Psychology, 42,* 303–313.

Meichenbaum, D., & Jaremko, M. E. (Eds.). (1983). *Stress reduction and prevention.* New York: Plenum.

Mettlin, C. (1976). Occupational careers and the prevention of coronary-prone behavior. *Social Science and Medicine, 10,* 367–373.

Motofsky, D. I. (Ed.). (1976). *Behavior control and modification of physiological activity.* Englewood Cliffs NJ: Prentice-Hall.

Pollack, M. L., Gutman, L. R., Milesis, C. A., Bah, M. D., Durstine, L., & Johnson, R. B. (1977). *Medicine and Science in Sports, 9,* 31–36.

Pittner, M. S., & Houston, B. K. (1980). Response to stress, cognitive coping strategies and the type A behavior pattern. *Journal of Personality and Social Psychology, 39,* 147–157.

Prince, V. (1982). *Type A behavior pattern.* New York: Academic.

Review Panel on Coronary-Prone Behavior and Coronary Heart Disease. (1981). Coronary-prone behavior and coronary heart disease: A critical review. *Circulation, 63,* 1199–1215.

Rosenman, R. H. (1978). The interview method of assessment of the coronary-prone behavior pattern. In T. M. Dembroski, S. M. Weiss, J. Shields, S. G. Haynes, & M. Feinleib (Eds.), *Coronary-prone behavior,* 55–70. New York: Springer-Verlag.

Rosenman, R. H., Brand, R. J., Jenkins, D., Friedman, M., Straus, R., & Wurm, M. (1975). Coronary heart disease in the western collaborative group study: Final follow-up experience of 8 1/2 years. *Journal of the American Medical Association, 233,* 872–877.

Roskies, E. (1983). Stress management for type A individuals. In D. Meichenbaum & M. Jaremko (Eds.), *Stress reduction and prevention.* New York: Plenum.

Roskies, E., Kearney, H., Spevack, M., Surkis, A., Cohen, C., & Gilman, S. (1979). Generalizability and durability of treatment effects in an intervention program for coronary-prone type A managers. *Journal of Behavioral Medicine, 2,* 195–207.

Roskies, E., Seraganian, P., Oseasohn, R., Hanley, J. A., Collu, R., Martin, N., & Smilga, C. (1986). The Montreal type A intervention project: Major findings. *Health Psychology, 5,* 45–69.

Roskies, E., Spevack, M., Surkis, A., Cohen, C., & Gilman, S. (1978). Changing the coronary-prone type A behavior pattern in a non-clinical population. *Journal of Behavioral Medicine, 1,* 201–216.

Scherwitz, L., Berton, K., & Leventhal, H. (1978). Type A behavior, self-involvement and cardiovascular response. *Psychosomatic Medicine, 40,* 593–609.

Scherwitz, L., McKelvain, R., Laman, C., Patterson, J., Dutton, L., Yusim, S., Lester, J., Kraft, I., Rochelle, D., & Leachman, R. (1983). Type A behavior, self-involvement, and coronary atherosclerosis. *Psychosomatic Medicine, 45,* 47–57.

Schlegel, R. P., Wellwood, J. K., Copps, B. E., Gruchow, W. H., & Sharratt, M. T. (1980). The relationship between perceived challenge and daily symptom reporting in type A vs. B postinfarct subjects. *Journal of Behavioral Medicine, 3,* 191–204.

Schuker, B., & Jacobs Jr., D. R. (1977). Assessment of behavioral risk for coronary disease by voice characteristics. *Psychosomatic Medicine, 39,* 219–228.

Siconalfi, S. F., Cullinane, E. M., Carleton, R. A., & Thompson, P. D. (1982). Assessing Vo_2 max in epidemiological studies: Modification of the Astrand-Rhyming test. *Medicine and Science in Sports and Exercise, 14,* 335–338.

Sinyor, D., Schwartz, S. G., Perronet, F., Brisson, G., & Seraganian, P. (1983). Aerobic fitness level and reactivity to psychosocial stress: Physiological, biochemical and subjective measures. *Psychosomatic Medicine, 45,* 205–218.

Suinn, R. M. (1975). The cardiac stress management program for type A patients. *Cardiac Rehabilitation, 5,* 13–15.

Suinn, R. M., & Bloom, L. J. (1978). Anxiety management training for pattern A behavior. *Journal of Behavioral Medicine, 1,* 25–35.

Thoresen, C. A., & Ohman, A. (1985). The type A behavior pattern: A person-environment interaction perspective. In D. Magnusson & A. Ohman (Eds.), *Psychopathology: An interaction perspective.* New York: Academic.

Van Egeren, L. F., Abelson, J. L., & Sniderman, L. D. (1983). Interpersonal and electrocardiographic responses of type A and type B individuals in competitive socioeconomic games. *Journal of Psychosomatic Research, 27,* 53–61.

Vickers, R. R., Hervig, L. K., Rahe, R. H., & Rosenman, R. H. (1981). Type A behavior pattern and coping and defense. *Psychosomatic Medicine, 43,* 381–403.

Williams, R. B., Lane, J. D., Kuhn, C. M., Melosh, W., White, A. D., & Schanberg, S. M. (1982). Type A behavior and elevated physiological and neuroendocrine responses to cognitive tasks. *Science, 218,* 483–485.

Wilmore, J. H. (1974). Alterations in strength, body composition and anthropometric measurement consequent to a 10-week training program. *Medicine and Science in Sports, 6,* 133–138.

9

Psychological Stress and Coping in End-Stage Renal Disease

YITZCHAK M. BINIK
GERALD M. DEVINS
CAROLEE M. ORME

INTRODUCTION

Until the early 1960s, end-stage renal disease (ESRD; i.e., irreversible kidney failure) was essentially a fatal condition. With the development of maintenance hemodialysis and renal transplantation, however, normal kidney functioning could be sufficiently replaced to prolong life. This transition from an experimental medical procedure to a standard clinical application was accompanied by a concern about the quality of life it provided. In order to provide a context for the psychosocial issues involved in the

The writing of this chapter was supported in part by a grant from the National Health Research and Development Program of Health and Welfare Canada to Y. M. Binik and G. M. Devins and through a National Health Research Scholar Award to Gerald M. Devins.

treatment of ESRD in adults, we will provide a brief overview of the medical background.

Medical Background

The onset of ESRD is usually defined by a 95% reduction in kidney function. Renal failure may be caused by a variety of conditions (cf. Friedman, 1979) that may develop insidiously over prolonged periods or may occur instantaneously (e.g., in a motorcycle accident). Failure to treat ESRD will result in death within a matter of weeks. Epidemiological information concerning ESRD is available through the annual report of the European Dialysis and Transplant Association (London, EDTA) and the Canadian Renal Failure Register. Although ESRD may occur at any age, the highest reported rates are generally for ages 45 to 74. In Canada, incidence has been estimated to be 52.8 new patients/million/year (Posen, 1982).

Before 1960, treatment for ESRD was essentially palliative. Since then two major forms of treatment, dialysis and transplantation, have been developed. The most common form of dialysis is called hemodialysis in which a person's blood is circulated outside of the body through an artificial kidney for sessions of 3 to 5 hours, three times a week. In this type of treatment, patients must also take a variety of medications and adhere to stringent dietary and fluid restrictions. For instance, most hemodialysis patients are asked to drink no more than 500 ml/day. Patient participation and the location of treatment may vary depending on local facilities, patient interest, and physical status. In home hemodialysis, for example, the patient and a helper, usually a spouse, are responsible for carrying out the dialysis procedure.

In peritoneal dialysis, the peritoneum is used as an artificial kidney by filling the abdominal cavity with a dialysate fluid so that waste products and excess fluid can be extracted from the blood vessels of the peritoneal membrane into the dialysate by a process of diffusion. This type of treatment may be delivered either intermittently (intermittent peritoneal dialysis) or continuously (continuous ambulatory peritoneal dialysis, CAPD).

Renal transplantation is the second major form of treatment for ESRD. Successful transplantation probably most closely approximates a return to pre-ESRD physical functioning and usually only requires the use of immunosuppressive medication. However, the availability of a suitable kidney for transplantation is limited primarily by the availability of an immunologically matched donor. It is also important to note that even in the case of successful transplantation, the recipient's body may immediately or ultimately reject the transplanted kidney, forcing the recipient to return to dialysis or die. Recently, a new immunosuppressive drug, cyclosporin, appears to have dramatically increased the number of successful transplants. Its long term effects, however, are still being evaluated. There is much controversy among nephrologists and transplant surgeons concerning the best form of treatment.

There is little disagreement that ESRD and its treatment involve major stressors and stresses. Among the most commonly identified stresses are: uncertainty about survival, dependencies on medical technology, economic burdens, limited reproductive capacity, severe diet and fluid restrictions, reduced mobility, general feelings of malaise, and a variety of medication side-effects. What is striking, however, is the great variation in how well individuals are able to cope with ESRD.

Until recently, research and clinical intervention in ESRD have been based on the consultation liaison psychiatry model (Levy, 1981, 1984). Researchers working within the model have been responsible for stimulating and maintaining the interest of mental health professionals in this area through major conferences, books, and the coining of the term "Psychonephrology" (Levy, 1981b, 1983). Unfortunately, the research conducted within this model has focused on evaluating immediately practical problems of interest to health care practitioners working with dialysis and transplant patients (e.g., the psychosocial advantages or disadvantages associated with different forms of treatment). This research is important and sometimes provides crucial information concerning choice of treatment or outcome; however, it does little to further our understanding of how patients cope with this life threatening illness.

From our point of view, the consultation psychiatry model has also tended to overemphasize the prevalence of psychopathology, particularly depression. In addition, it has almost exclusively focused on the individual and has attempted to explain behavior on the basis of intrapsychic mechanisms. The importance of the larger context, e.g., the dialysis unit, the family, and other social networks, generally has been downplayed while great emphasis has been placed on the management of "the difficult patient." Finally, psychosocial aspects of transplantation have received relatively little emphasis compared to those of dialysis with the implication that ESRD related problems disappear with successful transplantation. From a methodological perspective, this research is characterized by a number of problems including: over-reliance on nonobjective and idiosyncratic measures, inadequate quantification procedures, lack of specification of patient populations or comparison groups, and failure to control for psychosocial influences attributable to relevant demographic, medical or response style variables.

While we believe that it is appropriate to continue carrying out evaluative research in this area, our major purpose in this chapter will be to suggest that future research in this area should attempt to apply general theoretical models from other areas of psychology. To exemplify this approach, we will focus on three psychosocial areas of concern in ESRD, mood-depression, compliance, and marital functioning. In each area, we will briefly review and critique the available literature in adults while relying on research that we or others have carried out to illustrate the utility of applying theory. Before doing this, however, we will briefly examine several important methodological issues.

METHODOLOGICAL ISSUES

Since much of the psychosocial research concerning ESRD is by necessity quasi-experimental all of the usual methodological guidelines concerning this type of research are relevant here as well. These have been reviewed in detail elsewhere (Cook & Campbell, 1979), therefore, we will only deal with methodological issues specific to ESRD patients.

Population Factors

The demographics of ESRD differ from that of the general population in at least two respects. First, renal failure appears to be more common among men by a ratio of approximately 3:2 (Friedman, 1979). Second, the average age of new adult patients receiving their first treatment is approximately 50 years old (Posen, 1982). The second factor, in particular, must be carefully evaluated in trying to compare renal patient data with that of other groups.

In addition, a variety of factors may make it difficult to compare ESRD samples between studies. In any given study, it is crucial to know how patients were sampled and to determine the percentage of patients unable or unwilling to participate in the research because of language difficulties, defensiveness, or other factors. Intercurrent nonrenal illnesses (e.g., diabetes, hypertension), in particular, pose a serious threat insofar as they often accompany ESRD and may add independently to variability in individual psychosocial adaptation.

It is also our experience that particular ESRD facilities favor some forms of treatment over others and this may result in deviations even from the ESRD demographic norms. Moreover, characteristics such as age and general nonrenal health vary systematically across individuals receiving different forms of treatment. Transplant recipients, for example, are typically younger and healthier than dialysis patients. In addition, home hemodialysis patients are typically younger and healthier than their hospital counterparts. Some centers reserve CAPD for older and sicker patients who cannot tolerate hemodialysis while others favor it for a wider range of patients.

Socioeconomic status and the availability of social support may also vary across treatment modalities. Home hemodialysis, for example, usually requires the owning of a home or of an apartment that can be partially renovated to permit the installation of special equipment. The availability of a significant other (e.g., a spouse) as a home helper is also required. If the effects of such background factors on dependent measures are not controlled, they may seriously compromise the validity of experimental findings.

Dependent Measures

Confusion of Medical and Psychosocial Symptoms.   Some of the symptoms that comprise the uremic syndrome in ESRD are also common components of the psychosocial distress response. These include apathy, inability to concentrate, fatigue, anorexia and weight loss, decreased libido, and disturbed sleep patterns. Indeed, depression is probably among the nonrenal disturbances most frequently confused with the uremic syndrome due to the substantial overlap of symptoms (Schreiner, 1959). This overlap introduces at least three potential problems that must be ruled out before one can conclude that an hypothesized (psychosocial) stressor contributes to increased distress among ESRD patients. Perhaps most obvious is the possibility that uremic symptoms may simply be misidentified as components of a distress response. It is important, therefore, that criterion measures of distress not be contaminated by overlapping uremic symptoms (Devins et al., 1985).

A second potential problem is that the symptoms of irreversible renal failure may actually be stressors, themselves, insofar as they introduce physical discomforts, uncertainties, and threats with which the patient must cope. Thus failure to control for confounded variability in general nonrenal health levels across patient groups may also lead to erroneous conclusions regarding stress in ESRD (Binik, 1983). Finally, given that similar symptoms may entail both stressors and distress responses, it is likely that an element of overlap in instrument content may be present in many investigations. Extreme caution must be exercised to develop operational definitions of "independent" and "dependent" variables that do not derive from a common underlying dimension (cf. Dohrenwend & Shrout, 1985, for an excellent discussion of this problem in the most general context of stressful life events and psychosocial distress).

Medication Effects. Dialysis patients are typically taking numerous medications. Little is known about the effects of these medications on typical psychosocial measures and there appears to be great variation among units in physicians' prescription practices as well as in patient adherence. It has been suggested, for example, that the large doses of immunosuppressive medications, prescribed shortly following renal transplantation, can have a significant although variable influence on mood levels. Antihypertensive medications may seriously affect erectile abilities in males. While it may not be possible to directly control for medication effects, strategies for evaluating and minimizing them may include: (1) using the dosage of relevant drugs as a covariate; (2) comparing groups taking specific medication(s) with those not taking them; (3) comparing patients before, during, and after they take certain drugs.

Data Collection Procedures

There are numerous issues concerning data collection procedures that have not been investigated in ESRD patients. Dialysis patients, in particular, are highly dependent on their physicians and nurses and it appears likely to us that their self-reports may be influenced by the nature of this relationship. Staff must usually be convinced that the study is important lest they give patients the message directly or indirectly that participation in the research is unimportant. Whether data is better collected via interview or anonymous questionnaire has not been investigated. In some settings, great care must be taken to preserve the anonymity of the participant.

One potentially important issue is whether one should standardize the time for testing of hemodialysis patients with respect to their dialysis treatments (e.g., might indices of psychosocial adjustment be affected by differential concentrations of metabolic waste products between dialysis treatments?). Only one study has investigated the effect of this physiological variation (McCauley & Brenner, 1984), and it has indicated that mood and quality of life indices appear not to be affected by variations in the timing of administration (e.g., testing patients while they are "on" vs. "off" hemodialysis, or at the beginning vs. the end of a dialysis run).

Design Considerations

Priority of Causal Influences. Much of the literature concerning psychological stress in ESRD has focused on its psychosocial *impact* upon patients—i.e., adjustment problems that are produced by the stressors entailed in the illness and its treatment. The working hypothesis underlying the majority of studies has been that ESRD and its treatment can be highly stressful for patients and that, as a result, psychosocial adjustment difficulties are inevitable for many (Kemph, 1970; Levy, 1981a). Such symptoms cannot be attributed to ESRD or to its treatment, however, before ruling out the competing hypothesis that their onset actually antedated the development of renal failure. This is a difficult point to establish. One approach might be to conduct cross-sectional comparisons between groups of patients at different stages of renal failure (e.g., before vs. after reaching the endstage). Such comparisons are likely to be confounded by increasing mortality rates associated with more advanced stages of the condition. A longitudinal approach in which relevant data are collected both before and after the onset of uremic symptoms and their treatment by dialysis and transplantation is, therefore, more desirable. Unlike many chronic illnesses, ESRD patients are typically identified and followed medically long before they reach the end stage of progressive renal failure (i.e., before the onset of significant uremic symptoms). Despite the feasibility of conducting longitudinal comparisons of individuals before and after the onset of symptoms, there appears to be only one published study in which such a design has been implemented (Procci & Martin, 1985).

DEPRESSION

The traditional perspective has been that depression is highly prevalent among ESRD patients with as many as 45 to 53% reported to experience depressions of clinical severity (De-Nour & Czaczkes, 1976; Hughson, Collier, Johnston, & Tiller, 1974). One study has even reported a prevalence rate of 100% (Reichsman & Levy, 1972)! However, the data have been mixed; a number of investigations have reported substantially lower estimates (Farmer, Bewick, Parsons, & Snowden, 1979; Livesley, 1979; Lowry & Atcherson, 1979; Maher et al., 1983). Consistent with these latter studies, our own work has actually indicated that the prevalence of depression in ESRD does not appear to differ from the rates observed among the general (i.e., non-ESRD) population (Devins et al., 1985; Devins, Binik, Hollomby, Barre, & Guttmann, 1981; Devins et al., 1984). These striking differences among results may be attributable to a number of conceptual and methodological differences across studies such as (1) sample size; (2) measures of and criteria for depression; (3) the inclusion of appropriate control groups or selection criteria; and (4) other controls against potential biases due to confounded demographic and medical background variables and/or response styles. Table 9.1 summarizes the major studies that have examined depression in ESRD and illustrates the variation in the above mentioned factors. Particularly striking are the absence of controls for confounded demographic, medical, or response-style variables, and the emphasis on in-center hemodialysis, the variable sample sizes, the variance in measures of depression, and their psychiatric emphasis.

Tests of Theoretical Models of Depression in ESRD

In examining depression and its determinants in ESRD, our work has focused on learned helplessness, self-efficacy, and defensive denial.

Learned Helplessness. The reformulated learned helplessness theory of depression (Abramson, Seligman, & Teasdale, 1978) postulates that depression is the result of an expectation that one cannot control important outcomes. Individuals exposed to objective noncontingency between their actions and the outcomes that affect them are hypothesized to perceive this lack of control and to formulate a causal attribution to account for it. Attributions have been hypothesized to involve at least three dimensions: (1) *internality*, the degree to which the lack of control is attributable to personal characteristics of the individual; (2) *stability*, the degree to which the cause is likely to be present and in effect in the future; and (3) *globality*, the degree to which the cause is likely to be operative in situations beyond the original one in which uncontrollability occurred. The theory has posited that an expectation of uncontrollability over important outcomes in the future is established subsequent to the formulation of a causal attribution and that helplessness and depression are produced to the extent that this expectation involves the belief that one will be unable to affect important outcomes in future.

TABLE 9.1. STUDIES OF DEPRESSION IN ESRD

Reference	N	Sample Composition	Control Groups or Selection Criteria	Assessment Methods and Instruments	Controls for Confounded Demographic, Medical, or Response Style Variables	Estimated Prevalence of Depression
Burke (1979)	77	In center hemodialysis	Pre-dialysis chronic renal failure patients ($n = 77$) served as controls. Also compared MMPI profiles of study sample with previously published data. Participation rate not specified; selection criteria not specified	MMPI	None	No prevalence estimate provided. Average T-score elevations on D scale was 73. No differences were detected across the profiles of the various groups. Concluded that pre-dialysis, dialysis and general medical patient profiles were characterized by "remarkable . . . psychological similarity."
Cassileth et al. (1984)	60	In center hemodialysis, CAPD	All consecutive new arthritis, depression, diabetes, cancer & dermatologic disorders patients in 1 year; participation rate = 96%	Beck depression inventory, Spielberger state trait anxiety inventory, general well-being schedule	None	Depression in ESRD equivalent to that in other medical groups. All medical groups were significantly less depressed than the depressed psychiatric group. No prevalence estimates.
Crammond et al. (1967)	21	Chronic renal failure but not yet on dialysis; hemodialysis; peritoneal dialysis; posttransplant	No control groups; all available patients included; participation rate = 100%	Unstandardized clinical observations	None	24%

Study	N	Sample/Treatment	Design	Measures	Controls	Prevalence/Results
De-Nour & Czaczkes (1970)	100	In center hemodialysis	No control group. All new patients over 2-year period; participation rate = 74%	Clinical evaluation based on semi-structured interview by a psychiatrist.	None	53% were moderately or severely depressed.
Devins et al. (1981)	70	Hemodialysis (in center & home); posttransplant	No control group. Complex selection criteria based on a) nonrenal pathology b) length of treatment c) eligibility for other forms of treatment. Participation rate = 82%	Beck Depression Inventory, Coopersmith Self-Esteem Inventory, Rotter I-E Locus of Control Scale, Health Locus of Control Scale; Laboratory Concept Formation Test; ratings by hospital staff and significant other	Covariance controls for age, SES, IQ, general nonrenal health, number of previous transplant failures	4%
Devins et al. (1984)	70	Hemodialysis (staff-care, self-care), home hemodialysis; CAPD; posttransplant	No control groups. Selection criteria based on age, sex, general nonrenal health, and number of previous transplant failures; participation rate = 89%	Beck Depression Inventory-SF; Rosenberg Self-Esteem Inventory, Profile of Mood States, Affect Balance Scale, Life Happiness Rating Scale, Hamilton Rating Scale for depression	Convariance controls for age, SES, general nonrenal health and defensive response style	5%
Farmer, Snowden & Parsens (1979)	32	Home hemodialysis	No control group; all available patients included; participation rate = 100%	Standardized psychiatric interview	None	13%
Foster et al. (1973)	21	Hemodialysis	No control group; all available patients included; participation rate = 100%	Structured interview generating a (global) rating of psychopathology; I-E Locus of Control Scale, Cornell Medical Index, Mood Adjective Check List, Karnofsky Performance Scale	None	No estimate provided. Patients who had died subsequent to assessment displayed significantly higher levels of depression than did patients who survived.

TABLE 9.1. (Continued)

Reference	N	Sample Composition	Control Groups or Selection Criteria	Assessment Methods and Instruments	Controls for Confounded Demographic, Medical, or Response Style Variables	Estimated Prevalence of Depression
Glassman & Siegel (1970)	7	Hemodialysis	No control group or selection criteria. Participation rate not specified	California Personality Inventory, Shipman Anxiety Scale, Shipman Depression Scale.	None	0%
Hughson et al. (1974)	56	Posttransplant	No control group; all available patients included; participation rate = 89%	Semi-structured interview by social worker generated a global assessment.	None	45% showed moderate to marked increases in neurotic symptoms, including depression.
Isiadinso et al. (1975)	84	In center hemodialysis	No control group; 2 exclusion criteria-senility and language problems; Participation rate = 82%	WAIS, MMPI, Rorschach, TAT, Taylor Manifest Anxiety Scale, Draw-A-Person test, Rotter Sentence Completion Test	None	No estimate provided. Depression was described as prominent among patients who could not pursue their instinctual drives or achieve their goals because of the limitation imposed by their illnesses.
Kemph (1970)	37	Posttransplant (also examined as many donors as were willing to participate—N not specified	No control group or selection criteria. Participation rate not specified	Psychiatric evaluation; projective tests (no specific instruments were identified)	None	No estimate provided. Depression was reported to occur frequently among both transplant recipients and donors.
Kutner et al. (1985)	128	In center hemodialysis; home hemodialysis	No control group. Selection criterion: participants must have	Zung Self-Rating Scale, Zung Self-Rating Anxiety Scale,	None	Psychiatric scales (Zung Depression and Anxiety) indicated a

Study	N	Setting	Sampling / Design	Measures	Treatment	Results
			been on hemodialysis for 3 months. Participation rate unspecified	Differential Emotions Scale, Test of Emotional Styles, Social Dysfunction Rating Scale.		prevalence of 26.6% for clinically elevated depression. Other scales indicated that patients did not perceive themselves to be unhappy or depressed.
Livesley (1979)	85	In center hemodialysis	No control group; or 2 exclusion criteria = medical or comprehension problems, participation rate = 93%	General Health Questionnaire	None	22%
Lowry & Atcherson (1980)	83	Hemodialysis patients entering training for home hemodialysis	No control group; all available patients included; participation rate not specified	Structured interview by social worker; data obtained & applied to Research Diagnostic Criteria for major depressive disorders by a psychiatrist.	None	18%
Maher et al. (1983)	262	In center hemodialysis	No control group; numerous selection criteria; participation rate = 84%	MMPI, MAACL, I-E Locus of Control, WAIS Vocabulary, Life Events Checklist, Social Adjustment Scale, Self-Report Structured and Scaled Interview to Assess Maladjustment (SSIAM)	None	No formal estimate. Patients who withdrew their participation from the study before its completion were significantly more depressed than were those who completed the entire experiment. No evidence of clinically elevated depression among those patients who completed the entire experiment.

TABLE 9.1. (Continued)

Reference	N	Sample Composition	Control Groups or Selection Criteria	Assessment Methods and Instruments	Controls for Confounded Demographic, Medical, or Response Style Variables	Estimated Prevalence of Depression
Numan et al. (1981)	74	In center hemodialysis	All available patients included; participation rate = 95%	Depression Adjective Check List	Statistical controls for number of recent hospitalizations	No prevalence rate estimated. Increased rates of hospitalization and death were significantly associated with increased depression levels over a period of 12 months.
Reichsman & Levy (1972)	25	In center hemodialysis	No control groups; all available patients included; participation rate = 100%	Multiple clinical interviews by a psychiatrist	None	100% were diagnosed as depressed prior to treatment by hemodialysis; 64% became nondepressed following initiation of treatment by dialysis.
Shea et al. (1965)	9	In center hemodialysis	No control group or selection criteria Participation rate not specified	Clinical observations; psychological testing (no specific instruments identified)	None	67%
Smith et al. (1985)	60	In center hemodialysis; posttransplant	No control groups; selection criteria = on dialysis for 1 year, participation rate not specified	Beck Depression Inventory, Multiple Affect Adjective Check List; Schedule for Affective Disorders and Schizophrenia, using DSM-III criteria	None	Different rates were estimated on the basis of each instrument: the BDI identified 47% as depressed; the MAACL identified 10%; and the SADS/DSM-III identified 5%.

Study	N	Population	Design notes	Measures	Control group	Estimate
Treischmann & Sand (1971)	83	Pre-dialysis chronic renal failure	No control group; participation rate = 84%; selection criteria based on age, psychological status and anticipation of renal failure	WAIS, MMPI	None	12%
Wright et al. (1966)	12	In center hemodialysis	Corresponding test scores from nonequivalent control groups of college student normals and tubercular patients. Selection criteria participation rate not specified	MMPI, TAT, Rorschach; Clinical Interview by psychiatrist	None	0%
Ziarnik et al. (1977)	47	In center hemodialysis	No control group; Selection criteria based on survival; participation rate not specified.	MMPI	None	No estimate provided. All of the patients who had died within one year of initiating dialysis ($n = 14$) displayed significantly higher levels of depression than did patients who survived.

A number of authors have commented on the helplessness implicit in ESRD, noting that personal control over a broad range of important life areas appears to be reduced (e.g., Blagg, 1978). Such observations, together with reports that depression and distress were widespread among individuals with ESRD, led us to test the reformulated learned helplessness theory in ESRD (Devins et al., 1981). Two groups of hypotheses were developed. The first related to control over treatment, given that hemodialysis can be delivered in at least three different ways that vary in patient participation (control). We hypothesized that *staff-hospital* hemodialysis, performed in a hospital unit and in which the entire procedure is conducted by unit staff, would offer the lowest degree of control over the treatment whereas *home* hemodialysis, which is conducted in the individual's home and requires the patient to perform the procedure, would offer the highest degree of control. *Self-hospital* hemodialysis, in which the patient performs his/her own treatment in a hospital or satellite center, was hypothesized to provide a moderate amount of control. In keeping with the reformulated learned helplessness model, we also hypothesized that hemodialysis patients who perceived themselves as lacking control over their treatment and who attributed this to internal, stable, and global causes would evidence higher levels of helplessness and depression than would individuals who reported increased levels of control and/or who attributed their lack of control to external, unstable, and specific causes.

Our second group of hypotheses related to control over nonillness aspects of life. While patients on dialysis may differ in perceived control over their treatments, they may all perceive their treatment as imposing severe limitations on the amounts of control that they are able to exercise over nonillness life dimensions (e.g., marital and family relationships, work, leisure activities). Recipients of a successful kidney transplant, on the other hand, ought not to be subject to such limitations. Thus we hypothesized that relative to patients on any form of maintenance hemodialysis, kidney transplant recipients would experience higher levels of control over a variety of nonillness aspects of life and that, as a result, they would display lower levels of helplessness and depression. Once again, the hypotheses regarding perceived lack of control and attributional style were applied to nonillness aspects of life.

A sample of 45 ESRD patients on hemodialysis including each of the three modalities, and 25 post-transplant patients from four local hospitals participated. A series of three hypothesis-specific inclusion criteria were employed. For dialysis patients these were: (1) absence of serious nonrenal pathology; (2) equal capability of receiving treatment by any of the three modes of delivery; and (3) initiation of treatment and/or related training had been completed no less than three months prior to participation in the study. For post-transplant patients, the criteria were: (1) absence of serious nonrenal pathology; (2) no current rejection crisis; and (3) a minimum of one year since transplantation.

A standardized interview procedure was employed, including self-report measures, an experimental task, and ratings by significant others. The self-report instruments included measures of depression, self-esteem, internal-external locus of control, health locus of control, and a self-rating of helplessness. A concept formation task provided five separate measures that had been used widely in previous human helplessness research. Significant others (e.g., spouses) and hospital staff members who were familiar with the participant provided collateral ratings of each individual. These measures were then factor analyzed via a principal-components analysis that extracted six factor scores that were submitted individually to hierarchical multiple regression/correlation (MRC) analyses in which the two groups of hypotheses were examined. In addition to the treatment modality variable, patients' perceived control over their treatment and over a variety of nonillness life dimensions (e.g., work, family relations, leisure) was assessed via a series of rating scales. Causal attributions were assessed via the Attributional Style Questionnaire (ASQ; Peterson et al., 1982); attributions for control over dialysis were measured by adapting the ASQ questions to relate to the specific issue of control over the dialysis procedure.

Preliminary correlational analyses identified five demographic and medical variables that were significantly associated with helplessness and depression—age, socioeconomic status, intelligence, general nonrenal health, and number of previous transplant failures—therefore, these were entered into the regression equation in an initial step to control for their effects statistically. Surprisingly, the results indicated that helplessness and depression were much less prevalent among ESRD patients than might have been anticipated on the basis of the literature (less than 5% of participants evidenced depressive symptoms of clinical severity; i.e., Beck Depression Inventory scores greater than 20). The results also failed to yield any support for the reformulated learned helplessness theory. While patients receiving the various forms of hemodialysis did perceive themselves as exerting significantly different amounts of control over the treatment as anticipated, perceived control over dialysis did not correlate significantly with symptoms of helplessness and depression. Similarly, causal attributions for control (or lack of control) over dialysis were unrelated to these symptoms. Contrary to current medical opinion, there were no significant differences in helplessness and depression among patients receiving any of the dialysis treatments or between post-transplant and dialysis patients, collectively, in their overall levels of depression. All of these patient groups displayed equally low symptom levels. Similarly, attributional style was unrelated to these mood states. Perceived control over nonillness aspects of life, however, was significantly related to helplessness and depression— low levels of perceived control were associated with increased levels of distress. Perceived control over nonillness aspects of life was also significantly related to generalized and health locus of control. Consistent with findings in nonmedical groups, low levels of perceived control were associated with external generalized and health locus of control.

Self-Efficacy. The finding that low levels of perceived control, external locus of control, and increased depression intercorrelated significantly seemed to suggest that the expectancy of response-outcome independence may account, in part, for the relationship between depression and perceived control. However, the magnitude of these correlations was relatively low (in the range of .3 to .5), indicating that a more complete explanation was required. In a reanalysis of the above data, therefore, Bandura's (1977) distinction between efficacy and outcome cognitions was explored as a potential source of additional explanatory power (Devins et al., 1982). Bandura defined an *outcome* belief as one's estimate of the extent to which a given behavior is capable of producing certain outcomes. This seems to correspond closely to helplessness theory's expectancy of response-outcome contingency (Seligman, 1975) as well as Rotter's (1966) construct of internal-external locus of control. Bandura defined an *efficacy* cognition, on the other hand, as the conviction that one is capable of successfully executing the behavior required to produce a given outcome. Bandura (1978) hypothesized that the combination of strong outcome and weak self-efficacy expectancies would produce increased levels of depression via a self-critical social comparison process in which a negative self-evaluation is produced when one realizes that he or she is incapable of producing the outcomes that others are able to accomplish (i.e., an Outcome × Efficacy interaction).

Outcome beliefs regarding health and nonhealth life domains were operationally defined in terms of participants' scores on the health and I–E locus of control scales, respectively. Corresponding perceived control scores were constructed to reflect perceived self-efficacy regarding health and nonhealth aspects of life. Dependent variables included the self-report measures of helplessness, depression, and self-esteem. Once again, hierarchical MRC analyses—controlling for age, general nonrenal health, and number of previous transplant failures—were conducted. While the results failed to evidence the hypothesized interaction between efficacy and outcome expectations, they did indicate that each of these two cognitive variables was an important and independent contributor to distress levels. Weak efficacy and weak outcome beliefs, each, correlated significantly and uniquely with increased feelings of helplessness, depression, and low self-esteem. Bandura's distinction, thus, added useful explanatory power regarding the relationship between depression and perceived control.

Defensive Denial. One surprising observation has been that the prevalence of clinical depression in ESRD does not appear to be elevated. While it may be true that ESRD patients are simply no more depressed than are individuals among the general population, it might also be argued that our observations are the product of *defensive denial.* This defense mechanism has traditionally been invoked to account for unexpected findings of limited depression in ESRD. It has been suggested, for example, that the psychological situation faced by ESRD patients—especially those on maintenance hemodialysis—may simply be too threatening to maintain in conscious awareness (Czaczkes & De-Nour, 1978; Short & Wilson, 1969; Yanagida, Streltzer, & Siemsen, 1981). While this is an interesting possibility, it has proved very difficult to assess due to conceptual problems related to the nature of the defense mechanism and also due to the absence of a psychometrically adequate instrument with which it can be measured.

Such limitations notwithstanding, the overall pattern of findings that we observed in the helplessness and depression study seemed to be consistent with this explanation. First, the overall prevalence of clinical depression was low. Second, reduced perceived control over nonillness life dimensions correlated significantly with increased helplessness and depression and with external generalized and health locus of control, and yet perceived control over dialysis did not. Finally, perceived control over dialysis was unrelated to perceived control over nonillness life dimensions. Collectively, these findings are interpretable as consistent with the defensive denial hypothesis: ESRD patients may cope with the stresses imposed by their life-threatening illness by isolating and excluding illness-related events from their overall experiences of life, minimizing their impact, and maintaining a nondepressed emotional status as a result.

A study (Devins et al., 1984) provided a further opportunity to examine this hypothesis. Once again, a total of 70 patients participated, including hemodialysis ($n = 35$), CAPD ($n = 10$), and post-transplant patients ($n = 25$). This sample was stratified, however, to represent the widest possible ranges of age, general nonrenal health, and number of previous transplant failures, variables that our earlier study had identified as importantly related to depression in ESRD. Data were again collected via standardized self-report measures. Given the relatively low levels of depression observed in our earlier study, however, the focus was expanded to include relatively normal positive and negative mood states, overall life happiness, and somatic symptoms of distress in addition to pathological depression symptoms. Participants also rated their perceived control over and the degree to which they perceived ESRD and/or its treatment to interfere (intrusiveness) with several aspects of life.

As anticipated and consistent with earlier findings, patients' perceptions of intrusiveness and control, each were associated significantly and uniquely with mood states as indicated by analyses of partial variance (Cohen & Cohen, 1983) in which the potential effects of confounded background variables were controlled statistically. Decreased perceived control and increased perceived intrusiveness were both related to increased negative and decreased positive moods, and so on. Also consistent with earlier findings was the observation of a low prevalence of depression of clinical severity.

Data were also collected that permitted a test of the hypothesis that ESRD patients may defensively minimize illness-related experiences. A card-sort task obtained patients' perceptions of the degrees of similarity among the life dimensions for which perceived intrusiveness and control had been rated. These data were then submitted to a multidimensional scaling analysis to examine the underlying "structure" of patients' perceptions of their life space (e.g., Do they perceive illness-related and nonillness dimensions as separate aspects of life?). The results of this analysis were then applied in an analysis of partial variance in which the consistency of relationships between perceptions of intrusiveness and control for each cluster, on the one hand, and positive and negative moods, on the other, was examined. One specific set of inconsistencies was hypothesized to correspond to the operation of denial. The defensive minimization of illness-related experiences was hypothesized to be evidenced by: (1) illness-related aspects of life emerging as a separate cluster of life dimensions from nonillness ones in the multidimensional scaling analysis and (2) a differential pattern of relationships between patients' moods and their perceptions of intrusiveness and control across illness-related as compared to nonillness aspects of life. More specifically, our hypothesis was that a minimization of illness-related experiences would be evidenced by a pattern of correlations in which perceived control over nonillness aspects of life would be importantly related to positive and negative moods (as we had observed in our earlier studies) but also in which perceived control over illness-related ones would not. Perceived intrusiveness, on the other hand, was hypothesized to exhibit precisely the opposite pattern—i.e., perceived intrusiveness of ESRD into illness-related life domains should be related to mood levels but perceived intrusiveness into nonillness aspects should not because of a minimization of the impact of illness-related events upon one's overall experience of life.

With regard to the first of these hypotheses, the multidimensional scaling analysis yielded three clearly separate clusters of life domains corresponding to "health," "personal life," and "social life," suggesting that ESRD patients do, in fact, discriminate among illness-related and nonillness aspects of life. An analysis of partial variance controlling for age and general nonrenal health, failed to generate support for the second hypothesis, however. For each of the three clusters of life domains, patients' perceptions of intrusiveness and control correlated significantly with mood levels (with only one exception), suggesting that no such selective or defensive minimization was operating. Under relatively stable circumstances, therefore, the majority of ESRD patients appear to adapt effectively to the psychosocial stresses to which they are routinely exposed without the need for defensive minimization of illness-related experiences.

MARITAL ADJUSTMENT AND ESRD

Review and Critique of the Literature

Virtually all investigators in this area have assumed that the onset of ESRD must have stressful effects on the spouse. The empirical evidence, collected to date, has indicated that the severity and generality of these effects can range widely. Some reports have reported almost no measurable stress while others have indicated that stress observed in the spouse may equal that in the patient. In reviewing the available studies concerning marital adjustment in ESRD (cf. Table 9.2), several points become apparent. The majority of these studies concern home dialysis patients and are descriptive, relying on comparisons of individual personality or adjustment measures obtained separately from the patient and spouse.

A variety of methodological flaws characterize many of the studies. None of them, for example, have employed non-ESRD control groups and many have used idiosyncratic measures and very small sample sizes. In addition, studies have typically failed to evaluate the influence of confounded background factors, such as sex, age, types and duration of treatment, physical status, health status, position in family life cycle, or degree of successful adjustment. Attempts to measure interactions between the members of the dyad are neglected despite the recognition that the partner's individual ability to cope with the disease may be more dependent on the nature and flexibility of the marital interaction than on the nature of their individual psyches. This omission is especially surprising in view of the now extensive systems theory literature in which couple functioning has been conceptualized in terms of a complex interactional phenomenon rather than as the algebraic sum of individual coping styles (see Table 9.2).

Marital Role Theory as Applied to ESRD

A study by Chowanec (1983) was designed to remedy many of the methodological shortcomings in this area and to test several aspects of marital role theory. Briefly, marital role theory (Quick & Jacob, 1973) posits that individuals develop specific role expectations for themselves and their partners in marriage. Marital happiness and individual well-being are hypothesized to occur to the extent that these role expectations are met. However, to the extent that expectations are not satisfied, role strain will occur, resulting in a continuing decline in role reciprocations and increased psychological morbidity. The onset of a major chronic life-threatening illness, such as ESRD, presents an unfortunate but useful situation in which to test marital role theory insofar as virtually all aspects of marital life may be affected and successful psychosocial adaptation may force substantial role changes within a couple. For example, the "male provider" may find himself unable to continue working, forcing his formerly dependent wife to assume that role. These role changes

Study	N							Findings
Fishman & Schneider (1972)	12*	X		X			X	For both patients and the assistant relatives, the greater the expression of emotional problems early in the home training program, the worse the first year emotional adjustment.
Holcomb & MacDonald (1973)	23	X		X			X	Both patients and their spouses report feelings of depression and frustration; effects seem to moderate with time.
Lowry & Atcherson (1984)	29	X		X			X	At 6 months after home hemo-dialysis training, psycho-pathology levels and marital disease were low for patients and spouses.
Mlott (1976)	35	Unspecified		X			X	Patients were prone toward guilt fantasies; sex differences in adjustment.
Brown et al. (1978)	40	X		X		X		Home dialysis places consider-able strain upon the dialysis partner.
Speidel et al. (1979)	186*	XO		X			X	Unit dialysis seems to influence patients and partners towards social incompetence
4. Marital Dyad								
Pentecost (1970)	11	X		X	X	X	X	Family study appears to be a useful service for home dialysis centers.
De-Nour & Czackes (1970)	8	X	X	X		X		Five factors which influence patients' resistance to home dialysis are objective aspects of dialysis, attitude of the medical team, patient's person-ality, attitude of spouse, and financial situation.
Bailey et al. (1972)	125	X	X	X		X		Four basic patterns of reactions in spouse pairs are sharing, obsessive-compulsive, parent-child, master-slave.

TABLE 9.2. SUMMARY OF STUDIES INVESTIGATING PATIENTS' AND THEIR SPOUSES' ADJUSTMENT TO DIALYSIS

	Subjects		Methodology					Results		Findings
				Standardized Procedures		Dyadic Observations[†]				
Focus	N Couples	Type of Dialysis Home = X Unit = 0	Clinical Case Reports	Individual*	Dyadic**			Descriptive	Statistically Analyzed	
1. Patient, Secondarily on Spouse										
Malmquist & Hagberg (1974)	13	X		X				X		Dialysis affects patients and spouses as co-workers on the same team.
Pentecost et al. (1976)	40	X		X		X			X	Success in home dialysis is associated with the patients' expression of their own identity and their families' acceptance of such expression.
Bergstein et al. (1977)	47*	X0		X				X		Spouses experienced strain, yet many felt their relationship had become closer.
Farmer et al. (1979)	32	X		X					X	Patient survival was associated with a coping spouse.
2. Patient's Family or Spouse										
Shambaugh & Kanter (1969)	14*	0		X				X		Spouses exhibited extreme emotional closeness to their ill partners.
Friedman et al. (1970)	20	0		X				X		Good long-term adjustment was achieved by a majority of families.
Goldman et al. (1980)	8	X		X				X		Family members underwent role changes to adjust to alterations imposed by dialysis.
3. Patient and Spouse, Individually										
Heale et al. (1970)	24*	Unspecified	X					X		ESRD can have a considerable impact on the patient's family and financial situation.

TABLE 9.2. (Continued)

Focus	N Couples	Type of Dialysis Home = X Unit = 0	Clinical Case Reports	Individual*	Dyadic**	Dyadic Observations†	Descriptive	Statistically Analyzed	Findings
Marshall et al. (1975)	22	X		X				X	Failure on home dialysis training correlated with use of denial by both partners.
Mass & De-Nour (1975)	13	0	X				X		Couples displaced their hostility onto the outside environment.
Streltzer et al. (1976)	16	X	X				X		Success in home dialysis is at risk when the spouse is dependent on the patient.
Maurin & Schenkel (1976)	20*	X0			X	X	X		Withdrawal from social life into a very family-centered existence.
Finkelstein et al. (1976)	17	X0		X	X			X	The stress imposed by dialysis frequently results in marital discord, as rated by the investigators, though patients and spouses view their marriage as being nearly problem free.
Steele et al. (1976)	17	X0		X	X			X	A strong relationship between severity of depression and severity of sexual dysfunction existed for patients but not for the mates.
Brackney (1979)	12	X		X	X			X	Attention should shift from the patient alone to include the spouse and the marital relationship.

The columns are grouped under: **Subjects** (N Couples; Type of Dialysis), **Methodology** (Clinical Case Reports; Standardized Procedures: Individual*, Dyadic**, Dyadic Observations†), and **Results** (Descriptive; Statistically Analyzed).

*Focus of measurements either intra (*) inter (**)-personal or observations of couple interactions (†). Not all patients had spouses: in some cases a significant other was used.

have become increasingly more significant as life expectancy in ESRD has been strikingly increased over the past 25 years due to technological and medical advances.

Chowanec divided the progression of renal failure into four conceptual stages based on illness severity and intrusiveness. In increasing order, these stages were (1) minimal renal disease not leading to ESRD; (2) ESRD currently treated by transplantation; (3) renal disease leading to ESRD and requiring treatment within one year; and (4) ESRD currently requiring treatment by dialysis. A sample of 89 patients and their spouses were recruited from four hospitals in Montreal and one in Ottawa. Equal numbers of male and female patients were selected for each category. The dialysis group ($n = 35$) was divided between hospital and home hemodialysis since it was believed that this dimension might have an effect on marital adjustment. The home dialysis group included individuals receiving either CAPD or home hemodialysis. Patients and their spouses were tested on a variety of measures of marital relations, role strain, and happiness. In addition, measures of individual psychosocial well-being were administered, including overall life happiness, positive and negative moods, self-esteem, and an index of psychopathology. A number of demographic, medical, and response style variables were also assessed in anticipation of their potential appropriateness for statistical controls.

Results confirmed the hypothesized ESRD intrusiveness continuum; however, no significant differences were observed across the groups for any of the measures of marital or individual well-being. Scores for all measures were in the normal ranges. This finding was observed regardless of whether the data were analyzed separately for patients and their spouses as individuals or combined into couple scores. This failure to find differences in psychological well-being and marital relations suggests that previous clinical studies may have overemphasized the degree of psychopathology among ESRD patients as opposed to non-ESRD patients. A second important result concerned sex differences. Although women tended to report more psychopathology than did men, there was no interaction between sex and ESRD. This contradicts the assumption that it is easier for women than for men to adapt to role changes that may be induced by a chronic illness (Levy, 1984). Moreover, there was no indication that ESRD or its associated treatments differentially affected the psychological well-being of patients or their spouses. Perhaps the most important result in this study was that marital role strain significantly correlated with psychological well-being for individuals and their spouses after several demographic, medical, and response style variables were controlled statistically. Interestingly, the magnitude of this correlation increased significantly as the intrusiveness of the illness increased. The two dialysis groups, in particular, exhibited the strongest correlations between marital role strain and psychological well-being. One interpretation of this finding is consistent with the observation of Maurin and Schenkel (1976) that "dialysis couples" may be especially dependent upon each other for the fulfillment of their psychosocial needs, that their social sphere becomes more circumscribed, and that this may produce a much more family-centered life, as a result.

Androgyny and Sex Roles

Another facet of the study entailed an alternative examination of the role of potential sex differences by recategorizing subjects according to sex role (Bem Sex Role Inventory) rather than using biological sex as the determining factors. This categorization, if valid, has intuitive appeal within a systems theory approach because it is the role associated with biological sex that has been hypothesized to contribute to marital strain rather than biological sex, per se. Androgyny scores have, in fact, been interpreted by Bem (1974, 1979) as a trait measure of behavioral role flexibility. In the context of our study, therefore, such role flexibility might be anticipated to facilitate effective adaptation to the stresses imposed by chronic illness. Also of secondary interest was Bem's prediction that androgynous, as opposed to sex-typed, individuals are more psychologically healthy. Thus we predicted that androgynous as opposed to sex-typed individuals would evidence lower levels of marital role strain. This hypothesis was not supported by our data, however. Our analysis of the relationship between androgyny and psychological well-being indicated that the sex-type of masculinity—and not androgyny—was the most important correlate of well-being, especially when the latter is conceptualized as self-esteem (e.g., Taylor & Hall, 1982).

ADHERENCE

The most complex medical regimen associated with the treatment of ESRD is that which accompanies maintenance hemodialysis and, in fact, adherence to this regimen has received the majority of the research attention. The hemodialysis diet restricts the intake of protein, sodium, potassium, and fluids. Failure to follow these restrictions can lead to an accumulation of toxic fluids and metabolic end products in the blood that may result in weakness, nausea, cardiovascular difficulties, and even death. In addition, phosphate-binding medications are usually prescribed to prevent dangerous increases in serum phosphorous, decreases in serum calcium, secondary hyperparathyroidism, and metabolic bone disease. Dietary and fluid restrictions are much less severe for CAPD than for hemodialysis patients; however, CAPD entails four daily dialysate exchanges, each requiring 30 to 60 minutes to complete and meticulous attention to aseptic technique. Post-transplant patients have minimal dietary restrictions; however, they must adhere closely to a regimen of immunosuppressive medications. These regimen demands and restrictions, and the possible sequelae of nonadherence with them, represent an important source of stress for ESRD patients. The bulk of the evidence suggests, however, that many patients do not cope well with these demands, that many, even those post-transplant (e.g., Armstrong & Weiner, 1981–82), do not adhere to one or more aspects of their regimen.

Extent of the Problem

A number of studies have focused on the actual extent of nonadherence in ESRD, particularly among hemodialysis patients (Table 9.3). Variability across these studies in sampling and in the conceptualization and measurement of adherence, however, has rendered them difficult to integrate or compare. The confusion generated by this inconsistency is further compounded by the tendency to classify and report patients as belonging in either an "adherent" or "nonadherent" group, thus eliminating potentially important individual variation within these categories.

These problems are compounded when the validity of the methods used to assess adherence is considered. Interdialysis weight gain, for example, may be affected by residual kidney function, activity level, caloric intake, and even the amount of perspiration. Serum potassium and serum phosphorous levels may be affected by the presence of co-existing catabolic processes and the adequacy of the previous dialysis.

Self-report concerning adherence to regimens (e.g., Hilbert, 1985; Hume, 1982; O'Brien, 1980) has generally been considered an inferior source of information due to the operation of social desirability biases. Studies in a variety of populations have reported that the levels of adherence obtained using physiological techniques are reliably lower than are those indicated by self-report (e.g., Norell, 1981). When correlations between the two methods have been calculated, however, these have consistently been significant and positive (Fletcher, Pappius, & Harper, 1979; Norell, 1981; Roth & Caron, 1978), suggesting that self-report may still represent a valuable source of information. No comparable data are available for ESRD patients, however.

In general, staff ratings have also been found to underestimate the level of nonadherence in comparison with more objective indices (Preston & Miller, 1964; Caron & Roth, 1968; Moulding, Onstad, & Sbarbaro, 1970; Hadden et al., 1975; Blackburn, 1977; Mushlin & Appel, 1977; Roth & Caron, 1978; Norell, 1981; Witenberg, Blanchard, McCoy, Suls, & McGoldrick, 1983). In the ESRD context, Witenberg et al. (1983) compared staff subjective ratings of hemodialysis patients' dietary adherence with ratings based on laboratory values and found that the levels of adherence assigned by the staff were significantly higher than those determined from the physiological data. Blackburn (1977), however, concluded that staff estimates of who was and who was not adherent were accurate in relation to a classification based on physiological measures.

TABLE 9.3. RATES OF NONCOMPLIANCE WITH DIALYSIS REGIMENS

Authors	Sample	Type of Measure	Target Behaviors	Findings	Comments
Agashua et al. 1981	35 in center and 35 home hemodialysis patients	Interdialysis weight gain	Fluid and dietary adherence	Depending on criterion for weight gain and time of measurement adherence rates ranged from 31.4–85.7%	Failed to control for residual kidney function No stated selection criteria
Blackburn, 1977	53 in center hemodialysis patients—entire unit	All interdialysis, weight gains, serum potassium levels, serum phosphorous levels over varying time periods (3–14 months) If within specified acceptable range 50% of the time, considered adherent	Various aspects of dietary, medication, and fluid compliance	79% were potassium adherent 62% were phosphorous adherent 49% were weight adherent	Controlled for residual kidney function
Bollin & Hart, 1982	Convenient sample of 30 of 52 in center hemodialysis patients dialyzed for at least 10 months	Mean interdialysis weight gain over 12 sessions, monthly potassium levels measured against explicit criteria; patient knowledge of prescribed diet and recall of food intake	Fluid and potassium adherence, dietary recall	53.3% fluid adherent 93.3% potassium adherent 50% dietary recall	Controlled for residual kidney function
Borkman (1976)	661 patients out of total of 852 from 93 out of a total 120 hemodialysis centers in U.S.	Staff classification as excellent, adequate or poor	Water, salt, and protein restriction; shunt care	13–16% rated as poor compliers with each of 3 dietary restrictions; 8% poor at shunt care; 30% poor in one or more	Data collected in 1967 population probably not representative of today's patients No stated criteria for staff classification

Study	Sample	Adherence	Measure	Results	Comments
Hartman & Becker, 1978	40 chronic in center hemodialysis patients	Dietary, fluid and phosphate binding medication adherence	Interdialysis weight gain; serum phosphorous levels; serum potassium levels collected on 6 occasions used to classify subjects into high, medium, and low adherence categories	1. 78% were adherent re: weight gain more often than not 2. 39% were adherent re: phosphate-binding meds more often than not 3. 74% were adherent re: potassium more often than not	Mean time on dialysis only 1.5 years; effects of residual kidney function on weight gain not controlled; acceptable compliance range determined by staff judgments. Selection criteria—all of the unhospitalized stable patients receiving dialysis at one hospital plus convenient samples from other centers.
De-Nour & Czaczkes, 1972	43 in center hemodialysis patients from 6 units had to be on dialysis 6 months	Fluid and dietary adherence	Interdialysis weight gain, predialysis potassium levels and post-dialysis blood pressure over last 3 months used to construct five-point scale (excellent to great abuse) according to explicit criteria.	46.5% classified as abusers of diet	Failed to control for residual kidney function
De-Nour & Czaczkes, 1976	32 patients seen predialysis and at 6 months, 1, 2, and 3 years after starting dialysis from a total initial sample of 120 from 6 units	Fluid and dietary adherence	Interdialysis weight gain, potassium and BUN levels used by nephrologist to classify adherence as good, fair and bad by a detailed set of criteria	At last followup, 50% were rated as good, 25% as fair, and 25% as bad	No explicit selection criteria; high attrition rate (120 to 32); failure to control for effects of residual kidney function

TABLE 9.3. (Continued)

Authors	Sample	Type of Measure	Target Behaviors	Findings	Comments
Procci, 1981	31 in center hemodialysis patients	Interdialysis weight gain and mean serum potassium levels over 6-month period were examined in relation to pre-established criteria	Severe dietary abuse	22.6% classified as severe abusers based on weight gain; 3.2% based on potassium levels	Failed to control for residual kidney function No stated selection criterion
Schlebush & Levin, 1982	25 hemodialysis patients. All who did not wish to volunteer were excluded.	Unspecified staff ratings	Overall adherence	55% were classified as adherent	Validity of compliance classification unknown; failed to control for residual kidney function
Yanagida et al., 1981	46 out of 70 self- and limited-care hemodialysis patients in one hospital	Interdialysis weight gain averaging (1) 2.5 kgs. or more 50% of time across 75 observations (nonadherent); or (2) 2 kgs. or less more than 75% of time (adherent)	Adherence to fluid restrictions	34.8% were classified as nonadherent 33.3% were classified as adherent	Failed to control for residual kidney functions; no stated selection criterion
Hume (1982)	25 intermittent peritoneal dialysis patients; convenient sample from 5 units	Serum potassium, blood urea nitrogen and interdialysis weight gains classified as good, adequate, poor; self-report of adherence as very good, fairly good, poor. No explicit criteria	Fluid and dietary adherence	80% were rated as good based on serum potassium and BUN; 1/3 rated as good, adequate and poor based on weight gains	How classification determined not reported; no control for residual kidney function

Study	Sample	Measures	Concept	Results	Limitations
Yanitski (1982)	29 out of 31 in center hemodialysis patients (21 at final data point)	Interdialysis weight gains and monthly serum phosphorous and potassium levels for 3–6 month time periods. If stated criteria were met more than 50% of the time, patient was classified as compliant on that measure for that 6-month period	Fluid and sodium restrictions; diet and medication adherence	28% rated selves as very good, 48% as fairly good, and 24% as poor. 19–38% were compliant with fluid and sodium restrictions; 90% were compliant with diet; 56–59% were compliant with phosphate binding medication	Failed to control for residual kidney function
Hilbert (1985)	26 out of 45 in center hemodialysis patients	All interdialysis weight gains and monthly serum phosphorous and potassium levels for 3 months. Self-reported compliance with diet, medication, and fluid intake. (Likert Scale, 0–4)	Fluid, diet and medication adherence	Based on self-report, 69% were compliant with fluid restrictions; 66% were compliant with diet restrictions; and 97% were compliant with phosphate binding medication.	Reliance on self-report, even when significantly negatively correlated with physiological data; failed to control for residual kidney function; high non-participation rate; did not report levels of compliance based on laboratory measures.

Determinants of ESRD Patients' Nonadherence

Most of the research concerning determinants of nonadherence in ESRD has lacked a specific theoretical focus. Despite this, a number of potential determinants have been investigated, including demographic characteristics, personality factors, psychopathology, suicide, social support, and health beliefs. With respect to demographic characteristics, there is little evidence in ESRD that factors, such as age, sex, race, socioeconomic status, religion, or marital status are systematically related to adherence (Blackburn, 1977; O'Brien, 1980). This finding parallels data from other illness populations (Haynes, 1976, 1979; Kirscht & Rosenstock, 1979).

Personality Factors

To the best of our knowledge, there is no rigorous evidence in any illness population of a defaulting, or nonadherent, personality type. There is some evidence, however, of an association between specific stable intrapersonal characteristics and adherence, although many of the findings are not consistent. This appears to be equally true in ESRD. Investigators have examined a number of personality variables, including I-E and health locus of control (Bollin & Hart, 1982), (Poll & De-Nour, 1980; Blackburn, 1977), self-concept and self-esteem (Basta, 1981), defensive denial (Yanagida, Streltzer, & Siemsen, 1981), as well as general personality profiles (Schlebush & Levin, 1982). No consistent pattern has emerged, however.

Psychopathology

A number of studies have used psychiatric interviews to identify and assess psychopathology as a determinant of nonadherence. Among the problems that have been reported to be associated with nonadherence are depression (De-Nour & Czaczkes, 1976; Procci, 1981), frustration tolerance and gains from the sick role (De-Nour & Czaczkes, 1972); anxiety and "psychotic complications" (De-Nour & Czaczkes, 1976) and dependency/independency conflicts (Procci, 1981). However, no significant associations were found between nonadherence and acting out, homicidal behavior (directed against the patient), superstition, prejudices, or body image problems (De-Nour & Czaczkes, 1972). Unfortunately almost all of these studies have been methodologically flawed (cf. above).

Suicide

When treatment of ESRD by dialysis first became available, it was regarded as such a major life stress as to engender a heightened risk of suicide. Reasoning that nonadherence might actually represent suicidal behavior,

Abram, Moore and Westervelt (1971) surveyed 201 U.S. hemodialysis centers concerning patient suicides, attempted suicides, withdrawals from treatment, accidental deaths, and deaths from not following the regimen. Abram et al. estimated that the suicide rate in the dialysis population was 100–400 times greater than that in the general population. Included in these calculations were 117 (out of 2706) patients whose deaths were attributed to nonadherence, 22 patients who withdrew from dialysis programs, and 20 whose deaths were considered suicide by the respondents. The classification of nonadherent patients as suicides has been criticized (De-Nour & Czaczkes, 1972), however, because no evidence was presented of intentionality. Further, Levy (1978) has suggested that Abram et al. underestimated the suicide rate in the general population. Even so, a more recent study of suicide in Swiss dialysis patients (Haenel, Brunner, & Battegay, 1980) has estimated that suicide may occur 4 to 5 times more frequently in this group than in the general population. Neither of these studies, however, included controls for a variety of background factors that are known to affect suicide rates nor have they made the appropriate comparisons with other chronically ill groups.

Social Support

One basic assumption has been that adherence to the therapeutic regimen may be facilitated by a supportive social network. Similarly, illness-related disruptions to family life are believed to exert a deleterious effect on adherence. Research directed at each of these issues has failed to provide clearcut support, however (Pentecost, Zwerenz, & Manuel, 1976; Steidl et al., 1980; O'Brien, 1980; Hilbert, 1985; Cummings, Becker, Kirscht, & Levin, 1982; Sherwood, 1983; Armstrong & Woods, 1983). The fundamental problem with much of this work, however, is the absence of an adequate conceptualization and operational definition of social support. As a result, the two basic assumptions concerning social support and adherence appear not yet to have received a fair test.

Health Belief Model (HBM)

The underlying premise of the HBM is that behavior is a function of the value placed by an individual on a particular health outcome and of the individual's perception of the probability that a given behavior will result in that outcome (Maiman & Becker, 1974). Four health-related perceptions have been identified relating to: (1) severity of the disease if it were to occur; (2) personal susceptibility to the disease; (3) benefits of a specific action in reducing the risk; and (4) barriers to taking the action. "Cues to action," stimuli that trigger the perception of threat and a general health motivation (concern) are also hypothesized determinants of health-related behavior.

A number of investigators have examined various aspects of this model in relation to ESRD. Generally, there has been little support and results have been highly inconsistent (Hartman & Becker, 1978; Bollin & Hart, 1982; Yanitski, 1982; Cummings et al., 1982; Armstrong & Woods, 1983). There does not appear to be strong support for this model in other chronic illnesses such as diabetes (e.g., Orme, 1983). A major ongoing problem for the HBM has been the lack of standardized measures for its central constructs. Thus each investigator has created new measures whose relationship to previous instruments is unclear. Inconsistent results are likely to continue as long as this persists.

CONCLUSION

For reasons that are not entirely clear to us, ESRD has been virtually ignored in the health psychology literature (e.g., Millon, Green, & Meagher, 1982; Special Issue on Behavioral Medicine, *Journal of Consulting & Clinical Psychology,* 1982; Stone, Cohen, & Adler, 1980). Considering some of the unique medical aspects of ESRD and the resulting psychosocial effects, this lack of attention appears unwarranted. We believe that theoretical models can be usefully tested in this population in order to provide clinically relevant illness specific information as well as to further enrich and develop psychological theory. It also appears to us important to begin to embark on comparative psychosocial studies of other chronic illness. While we have stressed the unique medical situations of ESRD patients, it is not at all clear to us that this situation translates into unique coping processes or psychological effects. An important next step will be to apply existing theories of stress and coping to a variety of illness populations in order to identify the common underlying processes and mechanisms.

References

Abram, M. S., Moore, G. L., & Westervelt, F. B. (1971). Suicidal behavior in chronic dialysis patients. *American Journal of Psychiatry, 127,* 1199–1204.

Abramson, L. Y., Seligman, M. E. P., & Teasdale, R. (1978). Learned helplessness in humans: Critique and reformulation. *Journal of Abnormal Psychology, 87,* 49–74.

Agashua, P. A., Lyle, R. C., Livesley, W. J., Slade, P. D., Winney, R. J., & Irwin, M. (1981). Predicting dietary non-compliance of patients on intermittent hemodialysis. *Journal of Psychosomatic Research, 4,* 289–301.

Armstrong, S., & Weiner, M. (1981–82). Noncompliance with posttransplant immunosuppression. *International Journal of Psychiatry in Medicine, 11,* 89–95.

Armstrong, S., & Woods, A. (1983). Patient self-reported adjustment and health beliefs in compliant versus noncompliant hemodialysis patients. In N. B. Levy (Ed.), *Psychonephrology 2: Psychological problems in kidney failure and their management* (pp. 53–69). New York: Plenum.

Bailey, G. L., Mocelin, A. J., Hampers, C. L., & Merrill, J. P. (1972). Home dialysis: 30,000 treatments later. *Postgraduate Medicine, 32,* 190–193.

Bandura, A. (1977). Self-efficacy: Toward a unifying theory of behavioral change. *Psychological Review, 84,* 191–215.

Bandura, A. (1978). Reflections on self-efficacy. *Advances in Behavioral Research and Therapy, 1,* 237–269.

Basta, P. J. (1981). Compliant and noncompliant hemodialysis patients: A comparison of self-concept components. *Military Medicine, 146,* 863–867.

Bem, S. L. (1974). The measurement of psychological androgyny. *Journal of Consulting and Clinical Psychology, 42,* 155–162.

Bem, S. L. (1979). Theory and measurement of androgyny: A reply to the Pedhazur-Tetenbaum and Locksley-Colten critiques. *Journal of Personality and Social Psychology, 37,* 1047–1054.

Bergstein, E., Asaba, H., & Bergstrom, J. (1977). A study of patients on chronic hemodialysis. *Scandinavian Journal of Social Medicine, 11,* 3–31 (supplement).

Binik, Y. M. (1983). Coping with chronic life-threatening illness: Psychosocial perspectives on end-stage renal disease. *Canadian Journal of Behavioral Science, 15,* 373–391.

Blackburn, S. L. (1977). Dietary compliance of chronic hemodialysis patients. *Journal of the American Diabetic Association, 70,* 31–37.

Blagg, C. R. (1978). Objective quantification of rehabilitation in dialysis and transplantation. In E. A. Friedman (Ed.), *Strategy in renal failure* (pp. 415–433). New York: Wiley.

Bollin, B. W., & Hart, L. K. (1982). The relationship of health belief motivations, health locus of control and health valuing to dietary compliance of hemodialysis patients. *AANNT Journal,* 41–47.

Borkman, T. S. (1976). Hemodialysis compliance: The relationship of staff estimates of patients' intelligence and understanding to compliance. *Social Science and Medicine, 10,* 385–392.

Brackney, B. (1979). The impact of home hemodialysis on the marital dyad. *Journal of Marital Family Therapy, 5,* 60.

Brown, D. J., Craick, C. C., Davies, S. E., Johnson, M. L., Dawborn, J. K., & Heale, W. F. (1978). Physical, emotional and social adjustments to home dialysis, *Medical Journal of Australia, 1,* 246.

Burke, H. R. (1979). Renal patients and their MMPI profiles. *Journal of Psychology, 101,* 229–236.

Caron, H. S., & Roth, H. P. (1968). Patients' cooperation with a medical regimen. *Journal of the American Medical Association, 203,* 922–926.

Cassileth, B. R., Lusk, E. J., Strouse, T. B., Miller, D. S., Brown, L. L., Cross, P. A., & Tenaglia, A. N. (1984). Psychosocial status in chronic illness: A comparative analysis of six diagnostic groups. *The New England Journal of Medicine, 311,* 506–511.

Chowanec, G. D. (1983). *End stage renal disease and (ESRD) and the marital dyad.* Doctoral dissertation, McGill University.

Chowanec, G. D., & Binik, Y. M. (1982). End stage renal disease and the marital dyad: A literature review and critique, *Social Science and Medicine, 16,* 1551, 1558.

Cohen, J., & Cohen, P. (1983). *Applied multiple regression/correlation analysis for the behavioral sciences* (2nd ed.), Hillsdale, NJ: Erlbaum.

Cook, T. D., & Campbell, D. T. (1979). *Quasi experimentation: Design and analysis issues for field settings.* Chicago: Rand McNally.

Crammond, W. A., Knight, P. R., & Lawrence, J. R. (1967). The psychiatric contribution to a renal unit undertaking chronic haemodialysis and renal homotransplantation. *International Journal of Psychiatry, 113*, 1201–1212.

Cummings, K. M., Becker, M. H., Kirscht, J. P., & Levin, N. W. (1982). Psychological factors affecting adherence to medical regimens in a group of hemodialysis patients. *Medical Care, 20*, 567–580.

Czaczkes, J. W., & De-Nour, A. K. (1978). *Chronic hemodialysis as a way of life.* New York: Brunner/Mazel.

De-Nour, A. K., & Czaczkes, J. W. (1970). Resistance to home dialysis. *Psychiatric Medicine, 1*, 207–221.

De-Nour, A. K., & Czaczkes, J. W. (1972). Personality factors in chronic hemodialysis patients causing noncompliance with medical regimen. *Psychosomatic Medicine, 34*, 333–334.

De-Nour, A. K., & Czaczkes, J. W. (1976). The influence of patient's personality on adjustment to chronic dialysis: A predictive study. *The Journal of Nervous and Mental Disease, 162*, 323–333.

Devins, G. M., Binik, Y. M., Gorman, P., Dattel, M., McCloskey, B., Oscar, G., & Briggs, J. (1982). Perceived self-efficacy, outcome expectancies, and negative mood states in end-stage renal disease. *Journal of Abnormal Psychology, 91*, 241–244.

Devins, G. M., Binik, Y. M., Hollomby, D. J., Barre, P. E., & Guttmann, R. D. (1981). Helplessness and depression in end-stage renal disease. *Journal of Abnormal Psychology, 90*, 531–545.

Devins, G. M., Binik, Y. M., Hutchinson, T. A., Hollomby, D. J., Barre, P. E., & Guttmann, R. D. (1984). The emotional impact of end-stage renal disease: Importance of patients' perceptions of intrusiveness and control. *International Journal of Psychiatry in Medicine, 13*, 327–343.

Devins, G. M., Binik, Y. M., Mandin, H., Burgess, E. D., Taub, K., Slaughter, D., Letourneau, P. K., Buckle, S., & Low, G. L. (1985). Denial as a defense against depression in end-stage renal disease. Manuscript submitted for publication.

Dohrenwend, B. P., & Shrout, P. E. (1985). Hassles in the conceptualization and measurement of life stress variables. *American Psychologist, 40*, 780–785.

European Dialysis and Transplant Association. *EDTA Registry*, London, Annual.

Farmer, C. J., Bewick, M., Parsons, V., & Snowden, S. A. (1979). Survival on home hemodialysis: Its relationship with physical symptomatology, psychosocial background and psychiatric morbidity. *Psychological Medicine, 9*, 515–523.

Farmer, C. J., Snowden, A., & Parsons, V. (1979). The prevalence of psychiatric illness among patients on home haemodialysis. *Psychological Medicine, 9*, 509–514.

Finkelstein, F. O., Finkelstein, S. H., & Steele, T. E. (1976). Assessment of marital relationships of hemodialysis patients. *American Journal of Medical Science, 271*, 24–25.

Fishman, D. B., & Schneider, C. J. (1972). Predicting emotional adjustment in home dialysis patients and their relatives. *Journal of Chronic Disease, 25*, 99–105.

Fletcher, S., Pappius, E., & Harper, S. (1979). Measurement of medication compliance in a clinical setting. *Archives of Internal Medicine, 139,* 635–638.

Foster, F. G., Cohn, G. L., & McKegney, F. P. (1973). Psychobiologic factors and individual survival on chronic renal hemodialysis—A two year follow-up: Part 1. *Psychosomatic Medicine, 35,* 64–82.

Friedman, E. A. (1979). Etiology of chronic renal failure. In S. B. Cheyatte (Ed.) *Rehabilitation on chronic renal failure,* Baltimore: Williams & Williams.

Friedman, E. A., Goodwin, N. J., & Chaudhury, L. (1970). Psychosocial adjustment of family to maintenance hemodialysis. *New York State Journal of Medicine, 70 (1),* 767–774.

Glassman, B. M., & Siegel, A. (1970). Personality correlates of survival in a long-term hemodialysis program. *Archives of General Psychiatry, 22,* 566–574.

Goldman, R. H., Cohn, G. L., & Longnecker, R. E. (1980–81). The family and home hemodialysis: Adolescents' reactions to a father on home dialysis. *International Journal of Psychiatry in Medicine, 10,* 235–241.

Hadden, D., Montgomery, D., Skelly, R., Trimble, E., Weaver, J., Wilson, E., & Buchanan, K. (1975). Maturity onset diabetes mellitus: Response to intensive dietary management. *British Medical Journal, 3,* 276–278.

Haenel, T., Brunner, F., & Battegay, R. (1980). Renal dialysis and suicide: Occurrence in Switzerland and in Europe. *Comprehensive Psychiatry, 21,* 140–145.

Hartman, P., & Becker, M. (1978). Noncompliance with prescribed regimen among chronic hemodialysis patients: A method of prediction and educational diagnosis. *Dialysis and Transplantation, 9,* 978–987.

Haynes, R. B. (1976). A critical review of the determinants of compliance with therapeutic regimens. In D. L. Sackett & R. B. Haynes (Eds.), *Compliance with therapeutic regimens* (pp. 26–39). Baltimore: John Hopkins University Press.

Haynes, R. B. (1979). Determinants of compliance: The disease mechanics of treatment. In R. Haynes, D. Taylor, & D. Sackett (Eds.), *Compliance in health care* (pp. 49–62). Baltimore: John Hopkins University Press.

Heale, W. F., Liesgang, J., & Nhan, J. F. (1970). Chronic renal disease: A socioeconomic study. *Medical Journal of Australia, 2,* 623–625.

Hilbert, G. A. (1985). An investigation of the relationship between social support and compliance of hemodialysis patients. *ANNA Journal, 12,* 133–136.

Holcomb, J., & MacDonald, R. (1973). Social functioning of artificial kidney patients. *Social Science and Medicine, 7,* 109–119.

Hughson, B. J., Collier, E. A., Johnston, J., & Tiller, D. J. (1974). Rehabilitation after renal transplantation. *The Medical Journal of Australia, 2,* 732–735.

Hume, M. R. (1982). Factors influencing dietary adherence as perceived by patients on long-term intermittent peritoneal dialysis. *Nursing Papers, 16,* 38–54.

Isiadinso, D. A., Sullivan, J. F., & Baxter, J. E. (1975). Psychological adaptation to long-term hemodialysis: A study of 84 patients. *Bulletin of the New York Academy of Medicine, 51,* 797–804.

Journal of Consulting and Clinical Psychology (1982), *50,* 795–1053 (special issue in Behavioral Medicine).

Kemph, J. P. (1970). Observations of the effects of kidney transplantation on donors and recipients. *Diseases of the Nervous System, 31,* 323–325.

Kirscht, J. P., & Rosenstock, I. M. (1979). Patients' problems in following health recommendations of experts. In G. C. Stone, F. Cohen & E. Adler (Eds.), *Health psychology—A handbook*. San Francisco: Jossey-Bass.

Kutner, N. G., Fair, P. L., & Kutner, M. H. (1985). Assessing depression and anxiety in chronic dialysis patients. *Journal of Psychosomatic Research, 29*, 23–31.

Levy, N. (1978). Psychological sequelae to hemodialysis. *Psychosomatics, 19*, 329–331.

Levy, N. B. (1981a). Psychological reactions to machine dependency: Hemodialysis. *Psychiatric Clinics of North America, 4*, 351–363.

Levy. N. B. (1981b). *Psychonephrology 1*. New York, Plenum.

Levy, N. B. (Ed.)(1983). *Psychonephrology 2*. New York, Plenum.

Levy, N. B. (1984). Psychological complications of dialysis. *Bulletin of the Menninger Clinic, 48(3)*, 237–250.

Livesley, W. J. (1979). Psychiatric disturbance and chronic haemodialysis. *British Medical Journal, 2*, 306–308.

Lowry, M. R., & Atcherson, E. (1979). Characteristics of patients with depressive disorder on entry into home hemodialysis. *The Journal of Nervous and Mental Disease, 167*, 748–751.

Lowry, M. R., & Atcherson, E. (1980). A short-term followup of patients with depressive disorders on entry into home dialysis training. *Journal of Affective Disorders, 2*, 219–227.

Lowry, M. R., & Atcherson, E. (1984). Spouse assistant's adjustment to home hemodialysis, *Journal of Chronic Diseases, 37*, 253–300.

Maher, B. A., Lamping, D. L., Dickenson, C. A., Murawski, B. J., Olivier, D. C., & Santiago, G. C. (1983). Psychosocial aspects of chronic hemodialysis: The national cooperative dialysis study. *Kidney International, 23*, (Suppl. 13), 550–557.

Maiman, L. A., & Becker, M. H. (1974). The health belief model: Origins and correlates in psychological theory. *Health Education Monographs, 2*, 336–353.

Malmquist, H., & Hagberg, B. (1974). A prospective study of patients in chronic hemodialysis–V. *Journal of Psychosomatic Research, 18*, 323.

Marshall, J. R., Rice, D. G., O'Mera, M., & Shelp, W. D. (1975). Characteristics of couples with poor outcome in dialysis home training. *Journal of Chronic Disease, 28*, 375–381.

Mass, M., & De-Nour, A. K. (1975). Reactions of families to chronic hemodialysis. *Psychotherapy and Psychosomatics, 26*, 30.

Maurin, J., & Schenkel, J. (1976). A study of the family unit's response to hemodialysis. *Journal of Psychosomatic Research, 20*, 165–166.

McCauley, C. R., & Brenner, B. A. (1984, May 31). Temporal and situational stability of quality of life measures in an ESRD patient population. Paper presented at CPA, Ottawa.

Millon, T., Green, C., & Meagher, R. (Eds.)(1982). *Handbook of clinical health psychology*. New York: Plenum.

Mlott, S. R. (1976). Fantasy and self-esteem of renal dialysis patients and their spouses. *Southern Medical Journal, 69*, 1323.

Moulding, T., Onstad, G., & Sbarbaro, J. (1970). Supervision of outpatient therapy with the medication monitor. *Annals of Internal Medicine, 73,* 559–564.

Mushlin, A. I., & Appel, F. A. (1977). Diagnosing patient noncompliance. *Annals of Internal Medicine, 137,* 318–321.

Norell, S. E. (1981). Accuracy of patient interviews and estimates by clinic staff in determining medication compliance. *Social Science and Medicine, 15E,* 57–61.

Numan, I., Barklind, K. S., & Lubin, B. (1981). Correlates of depression in chronic dialysis patients: Morbidity and mortality. *Research in Nursing and Health, 4,* 295–297.

O'Brien, M. E. (1980). Hemodialysis regimen compliance and social environment: A panel analysis. *Nursing Research, 29,* 250–255.

Orme, C. M. (1983). *Measuring and predicting diabetic patients' compliance.* Unpublished doctoral dissertation, Montreal, McGill University.

Pentecost, R. L. (1970). Family study in home dialysis. *Archives of General Psychiatry, 22,* 532–546.

Pentecost, R. L., Zwerenz, B., & Manuel, J. W. (1976). Intrafamily identity and home dialysis success. *Nephron, 17,* 88–103.

Peterson, C., Semmel, A., von Baeyer, C., Abramson, L. Y., Metalsky, G. I., & Seligman, M. E. P. (1982). The attributional style questionnaire. *Cognitive Therapy and Research, 6,* 287–299.

Poll, I. B., & De-Nour, A. K. (1980). Locus of control and adjustment to chronic haemodialysis. *Psychological Medicine, 10,* 153–157.

Posen, G. A. (1982). *Canadian Renal Failure Register: 1981 report.* Kidney Foundation of Canada.

Preston, D. F., & Miller, F. T. (1964). The tuberculosis outpatients' defection from therapy. *American Journal of the Medical Sciences, 247,* 21–24.

Procci, W. R. (1981). Psychological factors associated with severe abuse of the hemodialysis diet. *General Hospital Psychiatry, 3,* 111–118.

Procci, W. R., & Martin, D. J. (1985). Effect of maintenance hemodialysis on male sexual performance. *Journal of Nervous and Mental Disease, 173,* 366–372.

Quick, E., & Jacobs, T. (1973). Marital disturbance in relation to role theory and relationship theory. *Journal of Abnormal Psychology, 82,* 309–316.

Reichsman, F., & Levy, N. B. (1972). Problems in adaptation to maintenance hemodialysis: A four-year study of 25 patients. *Archives of Internal Medicine, 130,* 859–865.

Roth, H. P., & Caron, H. S. (1978). Accuracy of doctors' estimates and patients' statements on adherence to a drug regimen. *Clinical Pharmacology and Therapeutics, 23,* 361–370.

Rotter, J. B. (1966). Generalized expectancies for internal versus external locus of control of reinforcement. *Psychological Monographs, 80,* (1, Whole No. 609).

Schlebusch, L., & Levin, A. (1982). Psychotherapeutic management of good and poor compliance in patients on haemodialysis. *South African Medical Journal, 16,* 92–94.

Schreiner, G. (1959). Mental and personality changes in the uremic syndrome. *The Medical Annals of the District of Columbia, 28,* 316–324.

Seligman, M. E. P. (1975). *Helplessness: On depression, development, and death.* San Francisco: Freeman.

Shambaugh, P. W., & Kanter, S. S. (1969). Spouses under stress: Group meetings with spouses of patients on hemodialysis. *American Journal of Psychiatry, 125,* 928–936.

Shea, E. J., Bogdan, D. F., Freeman, R. B., & Schreiner, G. E. (1965). Hemodialysis for chronic renal failure IV. Psychological Considerations. *Annals of Internal Medicine, 62,* 558–563.

Sherwood, R. J. (1983). The impact of renal failure and dialysis treatments on patients' lives and on their compliance behavior. In N. B. Levy (Ed.), *Psychonephrology 2: Psychological problems in kidney failure and their management* (pp. 53–69). New York: Plenum.

Short, M. J., & Wilson, W. P. (1969). Roles of denial in chronic hemodialysis. *Southern Medical Journal, 20,* 433–437.

Smith, M. D., Hong, B. A., & Robson, A. M. (1985). Diagnosis of depression in patients with end-stage renal disease. *The American Journal of Medicine, 79,* 160–166.

Speidel, H., Koch, U., Balck, F., & Kniess, J. (1979). Problems in interaction between patients undergoing long-term hemodialysis and their partners. *Psychotherapy and Psychosomatics, 31,* 240.

Steele, T. E., Finkelstein, S. H., & Finkelstein, F. G. (1976). Hemodialysis patients and spouses. *Journal of Nervous and Mental Disorders, 162,* 225.

Steidl, J. H., Finkelstein, F. O., Wexler, J. P., Feigenbaum, H., Kitsen, J., Kliger, A. S., & Quinlan, D. M. (1980). Medical condition, adherence to treatment regimens, and family functioning. *Archives of General Psychiatry, 37,* 1025–1027.

Stone, G. C., Cohen, F., & Adler, N. E. (Eds.)(1980). *Health psychology—A handbook.* San Francisco: Jossey–Bass.

Streltzer, J., Finkelstein, F., Feigenbaum, H., Kitsen, J., & Cohn, G. L. (1976). The spouse's role in home hemodialysis. *Archives of General Psychiatry, 33,* 57–58.

Taylor, M. C., & Hall, J. A. (1982). Psychological androgyny: Theories, methods, and conclusions. *Psychological Bulletin, 92,* 347–366.

Treischmann, R. B., & Sand, P. L. (1971). WAIS and MMPI correlates of increasing renal failure in adult medical patients. *Psychological Reports, 29,* 1251–1262.

Witenberg, S., Blanchard, E., McCoy, B., Suls, J., & McGoldrick, M. (1983). Evaluation of compliance in home and center hemodialysis patients. *Health Psychology, 2,* 227–237.

Wright, R. G., Sand, P., & Livingston, G. (1966). Psychological stress during hemodialysis for chronic renal failure. *Annals of Internal Medicine, 64,* 611–621.

Yanagida, E. H., Streltzer, J., & Siemsen, A. (1981). Denial in dialysis patients: Relationship to compliance and other variables. *Psychosomatic Medicine, 43,* 271–280.

Yanitski, A. E. (1982). *Primary nursing and compliance of the hemodialysis patient.* Kidney Foundation of Canada.

Ziarnik, J. P., Freeman, C. W., Sherrard, D. J., & Calsyn, D. A. (1977). Brief communication: Psychological correlates of survival on renal dialysis. *The Journal of Nervous and Mental Disease, 164,* 210–213.

10

The Relevance of Stress to Rheumatoid Arthritis

MYLES GENEST

Stress has long been assumed to play a crucial role in rheumatoid arthritis (RA). As far back as 1909, a text on arthritis was unequivocal in claiming, "That mental shocks, continuous anxiety, and worry may determine the onset or provoke an exacerbation of rheumatoid arthritis is, I think, beyond question" (Jones, 1909, quoted by Moos, 1964, p. 41). Views of both stress and RA have matured since the first decade of the century. This chapter examines the current status of the role of stress in the disease. Both research and clinical works will be referenced, and comments will at times reflect informal observations from a current study of RA at the University of Saskatchewan.

CHARACTERISTICS OF THE DISEASE

Rheumatoid arthritis is a chronic disorder affecting from 0.5 to 1% of the population between the ages of 20 and 80, and about 4.5% of those

Work on this chapter was supported in part by a grant from Health and Welfare Canada. The author appreciates the editorial and research assistance of Sharon Genest, and work by Harry van Eyck and Colleen Wilkie.

between 55 and 75 (McDuffie, 1985). The personal costs of the disease comprise a litany of pain and loss—loss of physical function, of positive body image, and of earnings, social activities, and independence. Societal costs include $777 million in out-of-pocket medical expenses in the United States in 1983 and indirect costs of $215 million in lost productivity.

Rheumatoid arthritis involves inflammation of the joint tissues, frequently with additional systemic changes. Its course is capricious and unpredictable, spontaneously remitting and flaring. Repeated relapses or continued inflammation lead to a thickening of the synovium, a membrane surrounding the joint, which secretes a transparent viscid fluid into the joint cavity. Granular tissue may form, extend over the surface of the cartilage and burrow into the bone (Rodnan, McEwen, & Wallace, 1973). Structural damage occurs primarily through destruction of cartilage. Large areas of bone may be denuded of cartilage; this can lead to adhesions between joint surfaces and resulting inflexibility. This firm union of previously jointed bones, called ankylosis, renders the joints partially or completely immobile. Even without ankylosis, loss of cartilage and bone, and weakened tendons and ligaments may lead to instability of joints, or partial dislocation (subluxation).

Systemic involvement may lead to nonarticular manifestations that can constitute more serious health threats than the joint disability. These can involve organs such as the heart, lung, or eye, or may be complications such as anemia, skin lesions, including rashes and gangrene, or chronic leg ulcers. Some of these are common—anemia, for example, occurs to some extent in most cases—whereas others, such as heart problems, are rarer.

The diagnosis of RA is difficult, especially in the early stages, and presents a major methodological stumbling block for interpreting much of the research in the area (Genest, 1983). Because the etiology is not well understood, definitive diagnostic criteria have remained elusive. None of the numerous manifestations of the disease is universal (Kellgren, 1968), and many may be symptoms and signs of other rheumatic or nonrheumatic diseases (Rodnan et al., 1973). Especially problematic for research is the common practice of making diagnosis on the basis of ill-defined clinical judgments. If heterogeneous groups result from insufficiently rigorous diagnostic procedures, significant effects may be obscured, or spurious effects obtained. Several systems for collecting data and making classification decisions from these data are available (see Genest, 1983, for summary). In particular, the American Rheumatism Association criteria have attained general recognition and fortunately are becoming more visible in the literature (Mitchell & Fries, 1982).

THE IMPACT OF STRESS ON RA

In recent years, an interactional view of stress has become predominant among stress researchers (e.g., Cameron & Meichenbaum, 1982; Lazarus &

Folkman, 1984; Leventhal & Nerenz, 1983). Much of the research concerning stress and RA predates this theoretical development, and was undertaken with simpler, often unidirectional models of stress is mind. In the sections that follow, the variety of models that have guided this research is represented: Stress in RA has been treated as a function of person-based variables, of situational characteristics or of an interaction of the two.

Stress-Related Personality Variables

Since the 1930s, a substantial literature has been concerned with the relationship of psychological stress to RA. By far the largest portion of these writings has assumed that the most appropriate locus of attention is the personality of those afflicted. Similar to stress research that focuses attention on the traits of the individual (e.g., Kobasa, 1979), this research on RA has hypothesized that there is a group of individuals who have personality characteristics that lead them to react to stressful events in ways that are self-defeating—in this instance, destructive to their joints (Prick & van de Loo, 1964). This view of stress in RA is limited: It emphasizes psychodynamics at the expense of a full consideration of interactions among intrapsychic and external events and the impact of the disease on the individual. Though it also suffers considerable methodological problems, the research raises several important issues concerning psychological distress and RA.

Psychosomatic Studies.   Psychoanalytic conceptions of the etiology of disease fueled the development of the psychosomatic approach to medicine (Alexander, 1950; Alexander, French, & Pollock, 1968). RA, according to this view, originates from a combination of unexpressed rage, often attributed to early lengthy separation from one or both parents and a weak ego, which together lead external stressors to be transformed into particular physiological stresses predisposing individuals to the disease.

> Previous to the onset of the rheumatoid arthritis, such patients divert their hostile impulses into a variety of competitive sports (men) and domestic work (women), but at the onset of the disease, this anger is turned inward, sublimation into physical activity ceases, and the combination of the rheumatoid factor and weak ego somehow directs the whole process to the pathology of rheumatoid arthritis. (Geist, 1966, p. 79)

Until the 1960s, most of the claims for a relationship between personality variables and arthritis were based on scientifically inadmissable evidence. Reports of uncontrolled, single case studies or of small, heterogeneous groups of arthritics without comparison or control groups reiterated such views as Geist's (1966), but provided little acceptable empirical basis for their claims. In a scorching review of the evidence, Scotch and Geiger (1962) concluded, "In short, the studies are without scientific merit" (p. 1053).

Other investigators proposed a link between body image and response to stress in RA (e.g., Moos & Engel, 1962; Moos & Solomon, 1964, 1965). Arthritics, it was contended, tended to have body images that are shell-like, well-defined, and hard:

> The arthritic . . . has found it necessary to convert his body into a containing vessel whose walls would prevent the outbreaks of these impulses . . . selectively utilizing a particular layer of his body (striate musculature) to achieve a protective wall about himself. His muscle stiffness seemed to be equated with inhibition and making his body exterior tough and resistant. (Fisher & Cleveland, quoted in Nalven & O'Brien, 1964, p. 18)

This body image would tend to lead to individual specific physiological responses to stress (Lacey, Bateman, & Van Lehn, 1953) linked to the development of the disease. In experimental conditioning trials, Moos and Engel (1962) found that arthritics showed higher heart rate and skin conductance levels and greater reactivity in skin conductance than did a comparison group of hypertensives. This pattern, different from the hypertensives' proclivity to adapt in muscle tension but sustain elevations in blood pressure, was taken as evidence for response specificity. The investigators did not assess body image, however, so the hypothesized basis for the relationships was not examined.

An elaboration of the psychophysiological link was proposed by Anderson, Stoyva, and Vaughn (1982), who looked for evidence bearing on Sternbach's (1966) model of psychosomatic disease. The model proposes that if there exist (1) individual response stereotypy, (2) inadequate homeostatic response, and (3) exposure to the activating stressors, then psychosomatic episodes will result. Different psychosomatic diseases would result from different response stereotypies. Anderson et al. (1982) found evidence that arthritics were stereotypical muscle responders, rather than vascular responders (compared to migraine and tension headache subjects and hypertensives). In addition, arthritics did display slow homeostatic recovery after stress, although it was unclear whether this delay was significantly different from that of subjects in the other groups. Unfortunately, small numbers of subjects, and many potentially confounding variables (age, heterogeneity within groups, medications, longevity of symptoms, etc.) render the findings tentative.

Other investigations of specificity of stress responses among arthritics have also failed to obtain clear and consistent results (e.g., Fisher & Cleveland, 1960; Gottschalk, Serota, & Shapiro, 1950; Taylor, Gatchel, & Korman, 1982; Walker & Sandman, 1977). In a recent review, Anderson, Bradley, Young, McDaniel, and Wise (1985) found sufficient evidence only for these differences: Compared to normals and other chronic disease groups, RA patients have higher EMG levels near affected joints, show greater EMG increases and slower return to usual levels upon stress, and show greater increases in electrodermal activity with stress. These conclusions, however, must be qualified by the inconsistencies that have been found, the small Ns in those studies that do detect differences (e.g., Anderson et al., 1982), and the variations in methodology that make it difficult to make comparisons among studies.

Other Trait Studies.   There are numerous atheoretical studies of rheumatoid arthritics, although they derive from psychosomatic theory. Examples abound of administrations of personality scales, and comparisons of arthritics to norms or to other groups. Bourestrom and Howard's (1965) study is typical. These authors gave the MMPI to 90 RA patients, 74 patients with Multiple Sclerosis (MS), and 100 spinal-cord-injured patients. As in many of these studies, the criteria used to classify patients were unspecified in the report—a severe limitation in a study of two diseases (RA and MS) that are notoriously difficult to diagnose. Nevertheless, the investigators reported that all three groups had significant elevations above norms on the neurotic triad (hypochondriasis, hysteria, and depression scales), with MS patients scoring the highest and RA patients scoring between the other two groups.

Polley, Swenson, and Steinhilber's (1970) study had the most impressive number of subjects to date, although the methodology is essentially the same. Seven hundred, twenty-six RA patients were compared to 50,000 general medical patients, and 1576 "normal healthy" individuals on MMPI scale scores and individual items. Once again, the RA group was found significantly higher than the others (about 1.5 s.d. above the mean) on the hypochondriasis, depression, and hysteria scales. The RA group and general medical patients also scored lower than normals on the hypomania scale. Similar results, indicating higher neurotic profiles have been obtained by other investigators with the MMPI (e.g., Liang, Rogers et al., 1984; Nalven & O'Brien, 1964; Wilson, Olson, Gascon, & Brumback, 1982), and with the Eysenck Personality Inventory (Gardiner, 1980). Using the Maudsley Personality Inventory, Ward (1971) obtained the opposite results, lower neuroticism among arthritics, although the samples were very small in this study (10 per group).

The fairly consistent findings of a higher incidence of depression, hysteria, and other neurotic features among rheumatoid arthritics does not, however, support an etiological argument. This line of investigation was originally undertaken to demonstrate the particular scenario of a physically stress-inducing, maladaptive constellation of traits that predisposes individuals to arthritis. At least equally plausible, however, is the contention that these measured psychological characteristics are *reactions* to RA, or perhaps to any chronic disease at all, rather than causes of it. Concerning their extensive data, Polley et al. (1970) concluded,

> In this and other reported studies to date, however, the predominant or statistically significant differences in responses to the MMPI test in patients with

rheumatoid arthritis are most readily explained on the basis of symptoms and effects of a disease that is chronic, painful, and potentially disabling. (p. 48)

This interpretation of the neurotic and other personality characteristics found among rheumatoid arthritics has received support from numerous investigators and reviewers (e.g., Anderson et al., 1985; Spergel, Ehrlich, & Glass, 1978; Wilson et al., 1982).

Comparisons within RA. Studies that have compared different groups of RA patients provide data relevant to this hypothesis. Robinson, Kirk, and Frye (1971) compared RA patients diagnosed within the last six months (the "new RA" group) to those diagnosed at least three years previously ("old RA" group), as well as to diabetics, TB patients, and hypertensives, using the 16PF personality inventory. The new RA patients were found not to differ statistically from the new disease control groups. They did differ from the published test norms in being less emotionally stable. The old RA group differed somewhat more from the controls: They were more unstable, guilt prone, and depressive and evidenced greater needs for self-sufficiency and less control than diabetic patients. They were more sophisticated, guilt prone, and depressive than hypertensives.

These results do not unequivocally disconfirm the predisposing trait hypothesis for RA etiology, but they are consistent with the idea that the pain and disability of the disease tend to lead to particular emotional responses that become more pronounced as the disease progresses. The initial emotional instability of the new RA group could be seen as a reaction to the sudden changes resulting from a recent diagnosis of this significance, and the differences of the old RA group from the other chronic disease patients may have resulted from the particular demands for adjustment placed on the arthritics. A limitation of the study is that it involved small numbers and included a large number of significance tests without controlling for experiment-wise error rates.

In a similar study, Robinson, Kirk, Frye, and Robertson (1972) found that there was a tendency for old and new RA groups and a group of pain patients (primarily with ruptured lumbar discs or neck problems following car accidents) to have similar scores on neurotic scales of the 16PF, such as anxiety and depression. The authors suggested that the observed personality traits of the RA patients, "represent attempts on their part to adjust to and cope with stresses encountered in their environment" (Robinson et al., 1972, p. 56), rather than constituting part of the stress constellation that leads to RA. They continued, "A person who reacts to the stresses of a chronic, painful disease with anxiety and depression may not be making a desirable adjustment, but it is one which common sense would predict" (p. 56).

Supporting evidence for this view is provided by several studies. Jacob, Robinson, and Masi (1972) provided data suggesting that "need deficiencies" arose soon after the onset of RA, but did not exist prodromally. Crown and Crown (1973) compared personality traits assessed by the Middlesex Hospital Questionnaire in patients with RA of recent onset to a normal and a neurotic sample. They found that the new RA sample did not differ from the normal group and was markedly different from the neurotic group. In a longitudinal study of 28 RA patients who were assessed every two months for a year, severe depressive symptoms appeared only in those who had very severe, active, painful, and disabling disease with changes occurring in disease pathology over the year (Mindham, Bagshaw, James, & Swannell, 1981).

Psychological or Somatic?   But perhaps the apparent personality characteristics or psychological symptoms that develop in RA patients are, in fact, illusory. The items that typically comprise the self-report scales used to assess neurotic traits are often somatic in content and would be answered in a pathological direction by patients experiencing many disabling diseases (Nalven & O'Brien, 1964; Smythe, 1984). As examples, Smythe (1984) pointed out these (paraphrased) items, all of which appear on the hypochondriasis, depression, and hysteria scales of the MMPI:

My sleep is fitful and disturbed.
I feel weak all over much of the time.
I have few or no pains.
I do not tire quickly.
During the past few years I have been well most of the time.
I am in just as good physical health as most of my friends.
I am about as able to work as I ever was.

Smythe counted 32 such somatic-content questions on the hypochondriasis scale, 26 of which he judged were predictably associated with painful conditions. Similarly, he found 22 somatic questions (12 pain-related) in the 60-item depression scale, and 29 somatic questions (22 pain-related) in the 60-item hysteria scale. Calculating on the basis of nonindependent scales with repeated questions, he reasoned that there was a built-in bias towards a neurotic score of up to 38% for pain patients. "This bias arises inescapably from the symptoms and even from the formal definitions of these syndromes, since the questions are essentially paraphrases of commonly used diagnostic criteria" (Smythe, 1984, p. 417).

Stress, Personality, and RA: Conclusions.   Smythe's critique presents serious difficulties for attempts to untangle personality-stress processes in the disease from the extant literature. Personality characteristics found among RA patients may be explained as neither physically stress-inducing traits nor changes that result from stresses of the disease, but as invalid measurements, the product of confounding physical and psychological assessment. It will require careful attention to the measures used, with more reliance on behavioral and less on self-report data, preferably in longitudinal studies, to answer this challenge.

Nevertheless, our view of the area is changing. Most previous reviews were able to conclude only that no valid data support the contention that an arthritic personality, contributing to disease onset, exists (King, 1955; Moos, 1964; Scotch & Geiger, 1962; Weiner, 1977). Evidence seems to be converging on a few points: (1) It is clearer that arthritics do not differ from the general population in prodromal personality measures; (2) RA does lead to changes in emotional measures over time; and (3) RA patients may have characteristic patterns of physiological responding to stress, in particular, higher EMG levels near affected joints and greater EMG increases and slower homeostatic response upon stress, although whether these exist before or only after the development of RA has not been determined.

Stressful Life Events

The life-events approach to the study of stress in RA contrasts with personality-based conceptions. Deriving from stress research that has emphasized the role of life change in producing negative outcomes (Dohrenwend & Dohrenwend, 1979; Holmes & Rahe, 1967), this approach assumes that stress can best be defined in terms of situations.

A rationale for the role of life events in the etiology of RA was provided by Moos and Solomon (1964). They suggested that stressful events could alter immunological reactivity, thus predisposing one to auto-immune disorders. The role of stress in the immune system has recently been emphasized by investigators working in other areas (Jemmott & Locke, 1984; Locke et al., 1984), but the specific mechanisms linking stress, immune responses, and RA remain to be explored.

An early attempt to support the role of life events in RA reported that for an entire sample of 12 RA patients, onset or exacerbation of symptoms was temporally related to a major life crisis involving separation (Shochet et al., 1969). The study suffered from several fatal flaws, however, and its conclusions cannot be trusted. Data were collected primarily by interviews with three different professionals (the study's investigators), who through unreported means, arrived at composite descriptions of patients. There were no controls for the investigators' expectancies concerning the findings, and data were primarily qualitative in nature. Further, data reduction procedures were not described, no control sample was used, and no hypothesis tests carried out.

More recently, Baker (1982), using somewhat better defined methodology, reached similar conclusions. He compared 22 RA patients to 22 age- and sex-matched controls, apparently nonrheumatic-disease patients of a general practitioner. Fifteen of the RA group, compared to 8 controls, reported significant life events in the year preceding onset of symptoms. Despite its use of a control sample, this study suffered from major limitations. The samples were inadequately specified, especially the comparison group. More importantly, data-collection procedures appear to have been insufficiently rigorous: The rheumatologist carried out interviews concerning life events without adhering to a strict protocol. The possibility for expectancy effects to have influenced the results cannot be discounted.

More objective data are available from a study by Hendrie, Paraskevas, Baragar, and Adamson (1971). Twenty-one arthritics were compared with hospital staff controls matched for age, sex, and socioeconomic class and with 74 patients with primary depression, of similar age and sex distribution but from a lower socioeconomic class. Participants completed the Rahe social readjustment scale (Holmes & Rahe, 1967), which provides an index of life events that are typically considered stressful. The arthritics and the staff control sample were not found to differ in life-change scores for the year preceding the onset of arthritis. In contrast, the depressed sample had a significantly higher score. Interestingly, this more rigorous investigation failed to support prior reports that stressful life events play a role in the onset of RA.

Other data from the Hendrie et al. (1971) study were intriguing in light of the proposal that stress and immune-system responses may be relevant in RA. It was found that when the 8 arthritics with elevated immunoglobulin levels were compared with the 13 without elevations, there were significant differences in life-change scores. The mean raw score for the elevated group was 290 (s.d. = 151), whereas it was 100 (s.d. = 87) for the nonelevated group ($p < .01$). Elevated levels of immunoglobulins have been noted in RA, although their significance is not clear. Further study is needed to clarify the import of the Hendrie et al. findings.

A recent 15-year follow-up study of 74 female patients with RA suggested that stressful experiences may play a different role for different subgroups of rheumatoid arthritics. Rimón and Laakso (1985) examined the course of the disease for two groups that had been originally classified in a major conflict group (MCG) or nonconflict group (NCG), depending upon onset of the disease: For the MCG, and not the NCG patients, an emotionally traumatic life event was judged to have provoked a psychic or psychophysiological reaction in the year before the onset of the illness. In addition, the pattern of onset differed between the two groups:

> In the MCG, the onset of RA was sudden, and the symptoms were clinically unequivocal and even severe . . . a hereditary predisposition to the disease was low or lacking. In the NCG, on the other hand, the rheumatoid symptoms came on insidiously, the disease progressed slowly and there was a hereditary predisposition, in that about half these patients had relatives with RA. (Rimón & Laakso, 1985, p. 38)

An initial one-year study had found that exacerbations of the illness continued to be associated with emotionally traumatic life events for the MCG, but not generally for the NCG (Rimón, 1969).

Upon reexamination 15 years later, 20 of the 41 MCG patients had continued to experience episodic exacerbations of the disease, compared to 9 of the 33 NCG patients. By comparison, 13 of the NCG patients evidenced a continuous, insidious disease progression without major exacerbations, compared to 8 of the MCG.

Unfortunately, the Rimón data are subject to some of the same qualifications that have been discussed with reference to other studies. Since a "relatively non-directive" (Rimón & Laakso, 1985, p. 39) interview was the primary method of psychosocial data collection, a variety of competing explanations for the findings cannot be ruled out. For example, it may have been that the MCG and NCG patients were distinguished not by differential rates of major life stresses, but by differential attention to such events, willingness to report them, or styles of presentation in an interview. If the two groups were reliably different in life events, it remains possible that the experience of repeated flares in the MCG may have played a role in causing more significant disruptions in their lives, rather than vice versa.

But other studies have also provided grounds for distinguishing two groups of RA patients. Crown, Crown, and Fleming (1975) found that the presence or absence of rheumatoid factor (RF) differentiated RA patients into two distinct psychological groups. The seropositive (SP) group had lower overall psychopathology scores on the Middlesex Hospital Questionnaire. Female SP patients also had lower free-floating anxiety scores. In a follow-up, higher psychopathology scores tended to be associated with milder joint disease, whereas lower psychopathology was associated with more severe disease. Similarly, Gardiner (1980) found that SP patients were less susceptible to psychiatric disturbance (assessed by the Eysenck Personality Inventory, Zung Depression Scale, and Semantic Differential) than were SN patients, although in his samples, psychological variables were not related to disease activity.

Vollhardt, Ackerman, Grayzel, and Barland (1982) also obtained congruent results. Using the Profile of Mood States and the psychopathology scales of the SCL-90, these investigators attempted to find psychological factors that would distinguish SP from SN RA patients, and from a mixed, non-RA group of arthritics. They identified a factor that enabled correct classification of 100% of the SP group solely on the basis of psychological test results. The other two groups were less uniformly classifiable, with accuracy of about 65%. The factor differentiating the SP group from the other two was comprised of measures of tension/anxiety, depression/dejection, anger/hostility, fatigue/inertia, confusion/bewilderment, obsessive-compulsiveness, depression, anxiety, and psychoticism. The SP group was lower (i.e., better adjusted) on all these. These results need replication before they can be treated as reliable, since the classification factor was tested with the same sample as was used to develop it.

What do these differences among arthritic groups mean? Rimón and Laakso (1985) suggested that there are two separate types of RA: one, a disease form less connected with genetic factors and more influenced by major psychodynamic conflict, and a second form more associated with hereditary predisposition and less influenced by environmental psychosocial changes. A more parsimonious interpretation of the Rimón data is that the disease will tend to follow a natural course of insidious progression, unless the patient experiences major life stressors, and that some individuals may, by virtue of either their dispositions or life circumstances, be more likely to experience repeated stresses. But this explanation breaks down in attempting to account for the seropositive-seronegative differences obtained by other investigators. With the limited, sometimes conflicting data available from studies with numerous methodological problems, no clear conclusions can be drawn. But the possibility that two classes of the disease may be related to psychological differences, and that stresses may play more of a role in the development of one class, deserves further attention. New investigations, however, need to take into account the critiques of psychological RA studies (e.g., Achterberg-Lawlis, 1982; Anderson et al., 1985; Genest, 1983; Moos, 1964; Weiner, 1977); otherwise, new data will be no more enlightening.

THE STRESSFUL IMPACT OF RA

To this point, we have examined research concerned with the ways in which the experience of stress may contribute to the development or progression of RA. But for the individual with RA, it is probably less significant that stresses may have played a role in the origin of his or her disease than it is that having the disease now leads to a dramatically increased burden. Recently, more research attention has been paid to this causal direction, the contribution of RA to the experience of stress in patients' lives.

From an interactional perspective, stress is a function of a dynamic interaction of the demands being made on the individual, the individual's assessment of both the demands and his or her ability to meet them, and the coping attempts he or she employs. Stress is, therefore, neither an event nor a physical nor psychological characteristic of an individual, but a state that exists dependent upon interacting, internal and external variables. A chronic, debilitating disease obviously leads to increased demands for adaptation at the same time as it diminishes the individual's capacity to act. The potential for higher levels of stress among such individuals is therefore heightened at both ends of the process. RA, with its unpredictable, often painful and vicious course, is among the most stress-inducing of diseases.

In looking at the RA-stress relationship from this end, we must first briefly consider the increased demands RA entails, the additional limitations it causes, and then the evidence concerning levels of stress experienced among arthritics.

Problems Resulting from RA

Physical problems are paramount in RA, but they in turn can cause difficulties in almost all other areas of patients' lives. Pain, fatigue, limitations to movement, and other physical effects were noted earlier. The fact that swelling and tenderness in joints, pain, especially upon movement, fatigue, stiffness, restricted range of joint motion, weakness, and disabling and disfiguring deformities are all characteristics that contribute to diagnosis of this disease clearly indicates the extent of physical problems that can result. Difficulties with everyday mechanical movements, such as grasping, pulling, and lifting, even combing hair, can result from deformities, and, more commonly, from active disease, which diminishes strength and causes instability of joints (Morisawa, 1984).

Pain.   An investigation by Kazis, Meenan, and Anderson (1983) highlighted the importance of pain for patients with various arthritic ailments (59% of their sample of 729 had RA). Using the Arthritis Impact Measurement Scales (AIMS, Meenan, Gertman, & Mason, 1980), the authors found that pain was more important than either psychological (depression and anxiety) or physical (dexterity, physical activity, mobility, household activities, and activities of daily living) disability in explaining medication usage, accounting for 16% of the variance. The findings were similar for the RA group alone, but with a lower proportion of the variance explained (9%). Pain also was the factor most responsible for the patients' judgments about their overall health status, and the status of their arthritis specifically. Current pain level was the best predictor of pain six months later, and was significantly predictive of subsequent levels of physical disability. Lambert (1981) also found the pain level among RA women to bear significantly on psychological well-being.

Sexual Function.   One would expect that the difficulty and pain in movement among arthritics would also lead to inhibition of sexual expression, with resulting personal frustration and increased tension between partners. The clinical literature has generally assumed such difficulties commonly exist (e.g., Buckwalter, Wernimont, & Buckwalter, 1982; Chesson, 1984), but there have been no adequate systematic investigations (Richards, 1980), largely because of the type of reluctance expressed by Helewa, Goldsmith, and Smythe (1982) in their discussion of development of a new scale for functional disability:

> Sexual function . . . was purposely omitted as we felt it was too sensitive a subject for RA subjects with active disease and if pressed, it might have resulted in a substantial number of refusals. (p. 794)

A high rate of sexual dysfunction among arthritics is suggested by reports of improvement in sexual function among those experiencing surgical reconstructions or replacement for severe hip problems (Baldursson & Brattström, 1979), and in a comparison of RA patients to those with another debilitating disease, ankylosing spondylitis, and to healthy individuals (Elst et al., 1984). In addition, Yoshino and Uchida (1981) found that 50% of women with RA reported a diminished desire for sex since the onset of the illness. Although no control group was assessed, it was reported that fear of a worsening condition on the day following intercourse was a factor for many among the majority who reported usually or always refusing sexual advances. Only 4%, however, reported that the anticipated exacerbation generally occurred, and 18% said it happened sometimes.

Clearly more data are required before any general conclusions can be drawn about the extent of sexual problems among RA patients. Some of the sexual changes that occur may be viewed by many patients as a normal part of the aging process. As Follick, Smith, and Turk (1984) showed with ostomy patients, just because health professionals expect sexual adjustment difficulties to be severe among a disease group, does not mean that they actually are. Elst et al. (1984) found more similarities than differences between control and arthritic groups in sexual preferences and behavior, though increasing disability seemed to be more associated with increasing sexual problems. It appears that further data might not be as difficult to collect as Helewa et al. (1982) expected: Yoshino and Uchida (1981) achieved an 81% return rate among their sample of 112 women, and Elst et al. (1984) found no difference in response rate between the arthritic sample (71%) and the control sample (73%).

Mobility.   The Sickness Impact Profile (SIP, Gilson, Gilson, Bergner, Bobbitt, Kressel, Pollard, & Vesselago, 1975) is an excellent health status questionnaire, designed to assess a broad range of functions that may be affected by illness. Seventy-nine consecutive RA clinic patients who completed the SIP evidenced considerable disability in movement (Deyo, Inui, Leininger, & Overman, 1982). Ambulation, body care and movement, and mobility scales were strongly affected on average. The proportion of patients endorsing a sample of items illustrates the impact of the disease:

SIP Item, Paraphrased	Checking Item (%)
Walk more slowly	73
Walk shorter distances or frequent rests	63
Walk with difficulty, e.g., limp, wobble	56
Move hand or fingers with limitation or difficulty	62
Stand for only short periods	43

A longitudinal study of carefully documented rheumatoid arthritics found severe declines in physical capacity over nine years (Pincus et al., 1984). Unfortunately, this study lacked a control group, making it difficult to assess to what extent these changes were a result of factors such as aging. Nevertheless, the extent and degree of changes documented paint a disturbing picture of the potential physical impact of RA. And as Lambert (1981) found, limitations on physical activities are viewed by patients as one of the most frustrating aspects of the illness.

Economic and Occupational Disability.   At the same time as limited physical abilities reduce arthritic patients' means of coping with extra demands, these physical limits increase the sources of pressure on them and their families. Financial concerns are one of the most serious sources of self-identified stress among rheumatoid arthritics (Crosby, 1984). But in our work with some older arthritics, we have found the disease to have less financial impact, since many of these patients adjust to retirement and lower incomes before suffering severe limitations from RA.

There has recently been substantial documentation of major financial and work losses among rheumatoid arthritics. Direct costs are experienced by many, though not all patients with RA (Liang, Larson, et al., 1984). Liang, Larson et al. reported that 80% incurred costs for arthritis-related purchases, 78% paid for outpatient visits, and 7% had inpatient costs. For some patients, total yearly costs exceeded $5,000, with $1,000 of that paid out-of-pocket (1979 U.S. dollar amounts). Average costs for their sample were $682 per year, with about $150 paid out-of-pocket. Spitz (1984) reported that the average medical costs alone for one year amounted to $2,329 in 1981. These are only direct costs.

Losses because of work disability have been estimated to amount to an average of over 30% of family income per year by nine years after disease onset (Meenan, Yelin, Nevitt, & Epstein, 1981). A cross-section (although not necessarily representative) of 245 RA patients from 25 rheumtologists in the United States was found to be earning on average only 50% of the income predicted for them had they not had arthritis (Meenan et al., 1981). Fifty-nine percent of those who had been working at the time their disease began (an average of nine years earlier) were no longer working, and 82% of these individuals attributed the change directly to RA. In the Pincus et al. (1984) study, work disability was found in 85% of the patients under 65 who had been working full-time at disease onset. A one-year prospective, diary study of 99 RA patients randomly sampled from a rheumatology clinic found that an average of 6.8 days of activity were restricted each month because of arthritis symptoms (Liang, Larson, et al., 1984). In Czechoslovakia, a stratified, apparently representative sample of 545 RA patients was found to have only 45% able to retain their pre-morbid employment and 40% of those experienced difficulty continuing in their work (Urbánek, Sitajová, & Hudáková, 1984). By comparison, among a similar sample of 170 patients with ankylosing spondylitis, 61% were able to continue their work. Similar proportions were obtained by Allander (1970), in a Scandinavian study. He reported that from "slight" to "severe" disease (based on a combination of clinical criteria), the average proportion of persons employed is halved, from 67 to 37% for females, and 95 to 50% for males.

As with the studies of physical limitations, these reports of occupational changes generally suffer from having no control or comparison samples, rendering interpretation of the descriptive data difficult. It is clear from preliminary data on our own work, for example, that there are large groups of arthritic women for whom no significant financial disability is experienced. Many older women in particular, never worked outside the home or had their own source of income, so that even severe physical changes do not affect their financial status. Once again, however, descriptive data from several studies are sufficient to indicate severe stresses on the ability of many patients to work effectively and maintain financial independence.

Social Stressors.   Along with decreased physical ability, many RA patients report substantial social changes resulting from the disease. The U.S. divorce rate among patients with rheumatoid arthritis was estimated at 18% at a time when the national average was 11%, amounting to a 70% increase (Meenan et al., 1981). Recreation and pastimes, and social interaction are reported to be substantially disrupted for between 50 and 85% of RA patients (Deyo et al., 1982; Meenan et al., 1981; Spitz, 1984). Yet, as Matzilevich (1982) showed, higher social activity among rheumatoid arthritics is associated with more positive self-esteem.

Families also often have to make adjustments, even to the point of changing places of residence and employment status to compensate for difficulties imposed by the illness (Meenan et al., 1981). In a report by Sawyer (1983), disease activity was found to be correlated with severity of daily hassels, though it is not clear whether the disease influenced the daily stressors or stressors influenced the disease.

Emotional Impact of RA-Related Problems

There are no simple ways to measure the degree to which RA patients actually are stressed, and the extent to which that stress is a function of their disease. In fact, assessing stress is difficult in general, since it is no longer viewed as a unidimensional construct. One of the means by which investigators have attempted to assess the stressful impact of RA is by targeting emotional adjustment, which one would expect to be affected by severe stress.

As noted earlier, the findings of elevated levels of depression, and other psychological problems among arthritics have been interpreted by some as resulting from the stress of the disease. Smythe (1984), it may be recalled, expressed grave misgivings about the confounding of disease-relevant and psychological dysfunction items in the MMPI. A study by Zaphiropoulos and Burry (1974) avoided this pitfall in assessing depression by using only the nonphysical-symptom items from the Beck Depression Inventory. Fifty unselected ARA-criteria RA patients and 32 patients suffering a variety of painful, chronic, noninflammatory locomotor disorders were examined. Forty-six percent of the RA group were found mildly to severely depressed, compared to 19% of the control group ($p < .05$).

These results support the view that RA does involve increased levels of depression for many patients. It would be consistent with an interactional view of stress to see this depression as both a possible contributor to and consequence of the disease. The fact that the RA patients were found more depressed than another group of chronic pain patients (comprised primarily of sufferers from osteoarthrosis, chronic backache, or sciatica) points toward unique aspects of RA as important:

> the systemic nature of rheumatoid disease, the greater persistence of pain and disability, or constant uncertainty about what the future might hold. All these factors constitute a pattern of constantly changing adjustment, a demand specific to rheumatoid disease. (Zaphiropoulos & Burry, 1974, p. 134)

The disfigurement from RA also sets this disease apart. It is quite common for patients to complain of having to wear clunky shoes because of changes in the shape of their feet, or to hide their hands, or wear gloves.

Results from studies such as this must still be weighed against investigations that have found no elevations of psychological dysfunction among RA patients compared to other patients and the general public (e.g., Cassileth, et al., 1984; Earle et al., 1979).

Yet, perhaps the issue of whether arthritics are *on average* emotionally debilitated by the effects of their disease is less important than considering what factors moderate the impact of the disease. There is no disagreement that RA can have a negative impact on many functions. From the interactional view of stress, one might ask what moderating variables ameliorate the potentially destructive impact of the disease. The psychologically destructive potential is not realized consistently or to such a degree that it appears regardless of the circumstances and methods of the research. This lack of robustness in finding disturbed functioning argues that there is considerable variation across individuals with RA—depression, apathy, and so forth, cannot be considered inevitable consequences, even of severe disease.

In posing the question about moderating variables, one may learn more not only about what the effects of the disease are, but about how it produces changes in individuals' lives, and how individuals can best manage the increased demands. In addition, it may be helpful to distinguish among areas of function, since emotional, financial, physical, and social well-being, may not be congruent, and the factors influencing one may be irrelevant for the other. Two projects that examine coping among rheumatoid arthritics, currently in progress, may provide some of these data (DeVellis & Hochbaum, 1985; Genest, Mitchell, & Laverty, 1987).

Moderators of the Impact of RA. There has been a recent accumulation of evidence supporting long-standing clinical claims that there is no monotonic relationship between severity of RA and patient function; in fact, the correlation between function and biological markers of disease is weak at best (Shoor & Holman, 1984). Pincus and his colleagues, for example, found that physical difficulties did not always involve low levels of patient satisfaction with functional ability (Pincus, Summey, Soraci, Wallston, & Hummon, 1983). Burckhardt (1982) also found that an arthritic sample reported a range of satisfaction, with the quality of their lives comparable to that found in the general population. A few reports are now available that indicate factors that may moderate the impact of RA.

As in many areas of health research, there is evidence that having better social supports and using them are associated with better adjustment among arthritics (Burckhardt, 1982; Cohen & Wills, 1985; Johnson, 1983). Unfortunately, it has also been found that the disease tends to lead to a depletion of social support resources (Johnson, 1983).

Concerning work-related disability, although occupational category in itself has no impact upon ability to continue employment, workplace factors do play an important role (Meenan et al., 1981). Among a broad cross section of RA patients ($N = 245$), the probability of restricted employment was significantly decreased in those who were self-employed or who enjoyed substantial workplace autonomy, that is, who could exercise control over the pace and content of their work. In fact, workplace factors were found to be as important as disease factors in a discriminant analysis of disability. Sociodemographic factors, by contrast, had no important effect on work disability (see Cohen, Chapter 7 in this volume, on "Main effects for resources").

Shoor and Holman (1984) were interested in the contribution of the patient's sense that he or she can successfully have an impact upon the disease or function related to the disease. They developed a scale to assess this dimension of self-efficacy (Bandura, 1977) and related it to pain (assessed by a visual analog scale) and disability (measured by the Stanford Health Assessment Questionnaire), on two occasions, four weeks apart, with 250 arthritics, 25% of whom had RA. It was found that perceived self-efficacy was a powerful predictor of future pain and future disability. This predictive value of perceived self-efficacy was independent of treatment with steroids or remittive agents, functional status, type of arthritis, sex, age, and education level. These results are consistent with those from other studies in which self-efficacy has been shown to modulate the impact of various stressors, from experimentally induced pain (Reese, 1983) to childbirth (Cogan, Henneborn, & Klopfer, 1976).

Along similar lines, a recent investigation developed a scale to assess arthritics' perceptions of loss of control with arthritis (Nicassio, Wallston,

Callahan, Herbert, & Pincus, 1985). Among 219 RA patients, higher scores on this Arthritis Helplessness Index (AHI) were related to generally poorer function, including depression, anxiety, and impairment in performing activities of daily living. Changes in helplessness over a year were correlated with changes in the difficulty of carrying out daily activities. Greater helplessness was also evident among older patients and those with less education.

Cognitive coping strategies, including information seeking and cognitive restructuring, were reported to be related to positive emotional affect among a group of 170 patients with one of four chronic illnesses (hypertension, diabetes mellitus, cancer, and RA) (Felton, Revenson, & Hinrichsen, 1984). Emotional strategies, such as avoidance, blame, and emotional ventilation, were reported to be related to negative affect, lowered self-esteem, and poorer adjustment to illness. There are substantial problems with this study, however, resulting from the combination of the small number of subjects in each group, the large number of variables examined, and the complexity of interaction effects that were being tested. Nevertheless, the study provides some support for the contention that psychological adjustment among chronic disease patients is moderated by individual efforts to cope with the effects of the disease.

Lambert's (1981) dissertation also provided data concerning emotion-focused coping. Among the RA women in this study, the use of emotion-focused coping was associated with less education. Together with pain, emotion-focused coping was one of the best predictors of psychological dysfunction.

Earlier work by Moos and Solomon (1964, 1965) examined the relationship between severe emotional reactions and the progress of the disease. On the basis of MMPI scores, Moos and Solomon (1965) differentiated patients with less functional capacity than would be expected given the stage of their illness from those whose functional capacity matched or exceeded the progression of their illness. The more handicapped group was found to have higher scores reflecting depression, general neurotic, psychotic, and impulse problems. The authors speculated that the stress experienced by the more pathological group might predispose them to more auto-immune problems by altering immunological reactivity. In a similar study, Moos and Solomon (1964) identified MMPI scales differentiating patients whose arthritis progressed relatively rapidly from those whose disease progressed relatively slowly. Rapid progression was associated with greater general maladjustment, anxiety, hostility, and imperturbability, whereas slow progression was associated with higher compliance-subservience, perfectionism, denial of hostility, capacity for status, social responsibility, and social status.

This work brings us the full circle, as would be expected from current views of stress. From wondering whether such variables as general maladjustment might form part of a stress scenario that causes arthritis, we have returned to the point of suggesting that when greater psychological disability is present in the disease, it may exacerbate destructive physical processes. The evidence for all of the links is not available. But a cycle of destruction is possible: RA leads to increased stresses, which in turn worsen the disease, causing greater stress, and so forth. Attempts to break the cycle by ameliorating the impact of the disease need not stand or fall on the validity of the model. For even if it should be shown conclusively that stress can in no manner have an impact on RA, interventions would nevertheless have had a beneficial direct effect for patients.

SUMMARY

This chapter began by considering the stress variables that have been claimed to influence the disease process, from personality dispositions to stressful life events. Although early personality-based conceptions of arthritic etiology were judged to have been long on rhetoric and short on data, it was found that recent links among personality and psychophysiological processes suggest new and promising areas for investigation. The differences in personality variables obtained in some studies were, when not simply a methodological artifact, more likely a result of the disease than a cause. Another recent research direction has suggested different subtypes of RA, based on congruent psychological and physiological evidence. Early data are intriguing, but remain to be confirmed.

Though it was not clear that stress factors played a role in causing RA, there was more evidence presented that RA increases demands made upon individuals, and alters their ability to respond to those demands—in other words, leads to more stress. Physical, economic, and social stressors are reported, and have their impact in measurably increased emotional distress. Early attempts to examine moderators of the stress in RA have barely scratched the surface of what may be the most practically useful direction for future research. In any case, interventions that attempt to moderate the impact of RA are certainly appropriate, given the potential distress resulting from the disease. There is no need to wait for more data to undertake experimental programs attempting to alleviate the problems caused by arthritis. Data collection in conjunction with such programs may, however, lead to a better understanding of the disease and ways to lessen its impact.

References

Achterberg-Lawlis, J. (1982). The psychological dimensions of arthritis. *Journal of Consulting and Clinical Psychology, 50,* 984–992.

Alexander, F. (1950). *Psychosomatic medicine.* New York: Norton.

Alexander, F., French, T. M., & Pollock, G. H. (1968). *Psychosomatic specificity: Experimental study and results.* Chicago: University of Chicago Press.

Allander, E. (1970). A population survey of rheumatoid arthritis: Epidemiological aspects of the syndrome, its pattern and effect on gainful employment. *Scandinavian Journal of Rheumatology* (Suppl.), *15*, 86–100.

Anderson, K. O., Bradley, L. A., Young, L. D., McDaniel, L. K., & Wise, C. M. (1985). Rheumatoid arthritis: Review of psychological factors related to etiology, effects, and treatment. *Psychological Bulletin, 98*, 358–387.

Anderson, C. D., Stoyva, J. M., & Vaughn, L. J. (1982). A test of delayed recovery following stressful stimulation in four psychosomatic disorders. *Journal of Psychosomatic Research, 26*, 571–580.

Baker, G. H. B. (1982). Life events before the onset of rheumatoid arthritis. *Psychotherapy and Psychosomatics, 38*, 173–177.

Baldursson, H., & Brattström, H. (1979). Sexual difficulties and total hip replacement in rheumatoid arthritis. *Scandinavian Journal of Rheumatology, 8*, 214–216.

Bandura, A. (1977). Self-efficacy: Toward a unifying theory of behavioral change. *Psychological Review, 84*, 191–215.

Bourestom, N. C., & Howard, M. T. (1965). Personality characteristics of three disability groups. *Archives of Physical Medicine and Rehabilitation, 46*, 626–632.

Buckwalter, K. C., Wernimont, T., & Buckwalter, J. A. (1982). Musculo-skeletal conditions and sexuality (Part II), *Sexuality and Disability, 5*, 195–207.

Burckhardt, C. A. S. (1982). The impact of arthritis on quality of life. *Dissertation Abstracts International, 43*, 1041-B. (University Microfilms No. DA8221060)

Cameron, R., & Meichenbaum, D. (1982). The nature of effective coping and the treatment of stress related problems: A cognitive-behavioral perspective. In C. Goldberger & A. Breznitz (Eds.), *Handbook of stress*. New York: Free Press.

Cassileth, B. R., Lusk, E. J., Strouse, T. B., Miller, D. S., Brown, L. L., Cross, P. A., & Teneglia, A. N. (1984). Psychosocial status in chronic illness: A comparative analysis of six diagnostic groups. *The New England Journal of Medicine, 311*, 506–510.

Chesson, S. (1984). Social and emotional aspects of rheumatoid arthritis. *Medical Education (International) Ltd.*, 914–915.

Cogan, R., Henneborn, W., & Klopfer, F. (1976). Predictors of pain during prepared childbirth. *Journal of Psychosomatic Research, 20*, 523–533.

Cohen, S., & Wills, T. A. (1985). Stress, social support, and the buffering hypothesis. *Psychological Bulletin, 98*, 310–357.

Crosby, L. J. (1984). Stress factors, emotional stress, and rheumatoid arthritis disease activity. *Dissertation Abstracts International, 45*, 1428-B.

Crown, S., & Crown, J. M. (1973). Personality in early rheumatoid disease. *Journal of Psychosomatic Research, 17*, 189–196.

Crown, S., Crown, J. M., & Fleming, A. (1975). Aspects of the psychology and epidemiology of rheumatoid disease. *Psychological Medicine, 5*, 291–299.

DeVellis, B., & Hochbaum, G. M. (1985). Arthritis patient education model: Further explorations of coping and compliance. Research in progress. University of North Carolina at Chapel Hill.

Deyo, R. A., Inui, T. S., Leininger, J., & Overman, S. (1982). Physical and psychosocial function in rheumatoid arthritis. *Archives of Internal Medicine, 142*, 879–882.

Dohrenwend, B. P., & Dohrenwend, B. S. (1979). The conceptualization and measurement of stressful life events: An overview of the issues. In R. Depue (Ed.), *The psychobiology of the depressive disorders; Implications for the effects of stress* (pp. 105–124). New York: Academic.

Earle, J. R., Perricone, P. J., Maultsby, D. M., Perricone, N., Turner, R. A., & Davis, J. (1979). Psycho-social adjustment of rheumatoid arthritis patients from two alternative treatment settings. *The Journal of Rheumatology, 6,* 80–87.

Elst, P., Sybesma, T., van der Stadt, R. J., Prins, A. P. A., Muller, H. W., & den Butter, A. (1984). Sexual problems in rheumatoid arthritis and ankylosing spondylitis. *Arthritis and Rheumatism, 27,* 217–220.

Felton, B. J., Revenson, T. A., & Hinrichsen, G. A. (1984). Stress and coping in the explanation of psychological adjustment among chronically ill adults. *Social Science and Medicine, 18,* 889–898.

Fisher, S., & Cleveland, S. (1960). A comparison of psychological characteristics and physiological reactivity in ulcer and rheumatoid arthritis groups. *Psychosomatic Medicine, 22,* 290–293.

Follick, M. J., Smith, T. W., & Turk, D. C. (1984). Psychosocial adjustment following ostomy. *Health Psychology, 3,* 505–517.

Gardiner, B. M. (1980). Psychological aspects of rheumatoid arthritis. *Psychological Medicine, 10,* 150–163.

Geist, H. (1966). *The psychological aspects of rheumatoid arthritis.* Springfield, IL: Thomas.

Genest, M. (1983). Coping with rheumatoid arthritis. *Canadian Journal of Behavioural Science, 15,* 392–408.

Genest, M., Mitchell, D., & Laverty, W. (1987). *Coping with chronic disease: Rheumatoid arthritis.* Research in progress. University of Saskatchewan, Saskatoon, Saskatchewan.

Gilson, B. S., Gilson, J., Bergner, M., Bobbitt, R. A., Kressel, S., Pollard, W. E., & Vesselago, M. (1975). The sickness impact profile: Development of an outcome measure of health care. *American Journal of Public Health, 65,* 1304–1310.

Gottschalk, L. A., Serota, H. M., & Shapiro, L. B. (1950). Psychologic conflict and neuromuscular tension: I. Preliminary report on a method, as applied to rheumatoid arthritis. *Psychosomatic Medicine, 12,* 315–319.

Helewa, A., Goldsmith, C. H., & Smythe, H. A. (1982). Independent measurement of functional capacity in rheumatoid arthritis. *The Journal of Rheumatology, 9,* 794–797.

Hendrie, H. C., Paraskevas, F., Baragar, F. D., & Adamson, J. D., (1971). Stress, immunoglobulin levels and early polyarthritis. *Journal of Psychosomatic Research, 15,* 337–342.

Holmes, T. H., & Rahe, R. H. (1967). The social readjustment rating scale. *Journal of Psychosomatic Research, 11,* 213–218.

Jacob, D. L., Robinson, H., & Masi, A. T. (1972). A controlled home interview study of factors associated with early rheumatoid arthritis. *American Journal of Public Health, 62,* 1532–1537.

Jemmott, J. B., & Locke, S. E. (1984). Psychological factors, immunologic mediation, and human susceptibility to infectious diseases: How much do we know? *Psychological Bulletin, 95,* 78–108.

Johnson, R. J. (1983). The impact of chronic illness on social supports. *Dissertation Abstracts International, 44,* 3499-A. (University Microfilms No. DA8404875)

Kazis, L. E., Meenan, R. G., & Anderson, J. J. (1983). Pain in the rheumatic diseases: Investigation of a key health status component. *Arthritis and Rheumatism, 26,* 1022–1027.

Kellgren, J. H. (1968). Epidemiology of rheumatoid arthritis. In J. J. R. Duthie & W. R. M. Alexander (Eds.), *Rheumatic disease.* Edinburgh University Press, Pfizer Medical Monographs, No. 3.

King, S. H. (1955). Psychosocial factors associated with rheumatoid arthritis. *Journal of Chronic Rheumatology, 2,* 287–302.

Kobasa, S. C. (1979). Stressful life events, personality and health: An inquiry into hardiness. *Journal of Personality and Social Psychology, 37,* 1–11.

Lacey, J. I., Bateman, E. E., & Van Lehn, R. (1953). Autonomic response specificity: An experimental study. *Psychosomatic Medicine, 15,* 8–21.

Lambert, V. A. (1981). Factors affecting psychological well-being in rheumatoid arthritic women. *Dissertation Abstracts International, 42,* 4017-B. (University Microfilms No. DA8207626)

Lazarus, R. S., & Folkman, S. (1984). *Stress, appraisal, and coping.* New York: Springer.

Leventhal, H., & Nerenz, D. R. (1983). A model for stress research with some implications for the control of stress disorders. In D. Meichenbaum & M. E. Jaremko (Eds.), *Stress reduction and prevention* (pp. 5–38). New York: Plenum.

Liang, M. H., Larson, M., Thompson, M., Eaton, H., McNamara, E., Katz, R., & Taylor, J. (1984). Costs and outcomes in rheumatoid arthritis and osteoarthritis. *Arthritis and Rheumatism, 27,* 522–529.

Liang, M. H., Rogers, M., Larson, M., Eaton, H. M., Murawski, B. J., Taylor, J. E., Swafford, J., & Schur, P. H. (1984). The psychosocial impact of systemic lupis erythematosus and rheumatoid arthritis. *Arthritis and Rheumatism, 27,* 13–19.

Locke, S. E., Kraus, L., Leserman, J., Hurst, M. W., Heisel, S., & Williams, R. M. (1984). Life change stress, psychiatric symptoms, and natural killer cell activity. *Psychosomatic Medicine, 46,* 441–453.

Matzilevich, J. J. (1982). Psychosocial correlates of successful achievement in individuals with rheumatoid arthritis. *Dissertation Abstracts International, 43,* 2319-B. (University Microfilms No. DA8227361)

McDuffie, F. C. (1985). Morbidity impact of rheumatoid arthritis on society. *The American Journal of Medicine, 78,* 1–5.

Meenan, R. F., Gertman, P. M., & Mason, J. H. (1980). Measuring health status in arthritis: The arthritis impact measurement scales. *Arthritis and Rheumatism, 23,* 146–152.

Meenan, R. F., Yelin, E. H., Nevitt, M., & Epstein, R. V. (1981). The impact of chronic disease: A sociomedical profile of rheumatoid arthritis. *Arthritis and Rheumatism, 245,* 544–549.

Mindham, R. H. S., Bagshaw, A., James, S. A., & Swannell, A. J. (1981). Factors associated with the appearance of psychiatric symptoms in rheumatoid arthritis. *Journal of Psychosomatic Research, 25,* 429–435.

Mitchell, D. M., & Fries, J. F. (1982). An analysis of the American Rheumatism Association criteria for rheumatoid arthritis. *Arthritis and Rheumatism, 25,* 481–487.

Moos, R. H., (1964). Personality factors associated with rheumatoid arthritis: A review. *Journal of Chronic Diseases, 17,* 41–55.

Moos, R. H., & Engel, B. T. (1962). Psychophysiological reactions in hypertensive and arthritic patients. *Journal of Psychosomatic Research, 6,* 227–241.

Moos, R. H., & Solomon, G. F. (1964). Personality correlates of the rapidity of progression of rheumatoid arthritis. *Annals of Rheumatic Diseases, 23,* 145–151.

Moos, R. H., & Solomon, G. F. (1965). Personality correlates of the degree of functional incapacity of patients with physical disease. *Journal of Chronic Diseases, 18,* 1019–1038.

Morisawa, S. (1984). Functional disability and hand deformity in rheumatoid arthritis. *The Ryumachi, 24,* 18–24.

Nalven, F. B., & O'Brien, J. F. (1964). Personality patterns of rheumatoid arthritic patients. *Arthritis and Rheumatism, 7,* 18–28.

Nicassio, P. M., Wallston, K. A., Callahan, L. F., Herbert, M., & Pincus, T. (1985). The measurement of helplessness in rheumatoid arthritis. The development of the arthritis helplessness index. *Journal of Rheumatology, 12,* 462–467.

Pincus, T., Callahan, L. F., Sale, W. G., Brooks, A. L., Payne, L. E., & Vaughn, W. K. (1984). Severe functional declines, work disability, and increased mortality in seventy-five rheumatoid arthritis patients studied over nine years. *Arthritis and Rheumatism, 27,* 864–972.

Pincus, T., Summey, J. A., Soraci, S. A., Jr., Wallston, K. A., & Hummon, N. P. (1983). Assessment of patient satisfaction in activities of daily living using a modified Stanford health assessment questionnaire. *Arthritis and Rheumatism, 26,* 1346–1353.

Polley, H. F., Swenson, W., & Steinhilber, R. M. (1970). Personality characteristics of patients with rheumatoid arthritis. *Psychosomatics, 11,* 45–49.

Prick, J. J. G., & van de Loo, K. J. M. (1964). *The psychosomatic approach to primary chronic rheumatoid arthritis.* Philadelphia: Davis.

Richards, J. S. (1980). Sex and arthritis. *Sexuality and Disability, 3,* 97–104.

Rimón, R. A. (1969). A psychosomatic approach to rheumatoid arthritis. *Acta Rheumatologica Scandinavica,* Supplement No. 3.

Rimón, R. A., & Laakso, R. (1985). Life stress and rheumatoid arthritis: A 15-year follow-up study. *Psychotherapy and Psychosomatics, 43,* 38–43.

Robinson, H., Kirk, R. F., Jr., & Frye, R. L. (1971). A psychological study of rheumatoid arthritis and selected controls. *Journal of Chronic Diseases, 23,* 791–801.

Robinson, H., Kirk, R. F., Jr., Frye, R. F., & Robertson, J. T. (1972). A psychological study of patients with rheumatoid arthritis and other painful diseases. *Journal of Psychosomatic Research, 16,* 53–56.

Rodnan, G. P., McEwen, C., & Wallace, S. L. (Eds.). (1973). *Primer on the rheumatoid diseases.* (7th ed.). Atlanta, GA: Arthritis Foundation.

Sawyer, T. E. (1983). Cognitive mediators of health status in rheumatoid arthritis. *Dissertation Abstracts International, 44,* 747-B. (University Microfilms No. DA8315825)

Scotch, N. A., & Geiger, H. J. (1962). The epidemiology of rheumatoid arthritis: A review with special attention to social factors. *Journal of Chronic Diseases, 15,* 1037–1067.

Shochet, B. R., Lisansky, E. T., Schubart, A. F., Fiocco, V., Kurland, S., & Pope, M. (1969). A medical-psychiatric study of patients with rheumatoid arthritis. *Psychosomatics, 10,* 271–279.

Shoor, S. M., & Holman, H. R. (1984). Development of an instrument to explore psychological mediators of outcome in chronic arthritis. *Clinical Research, 32,* 325–331.

Smythe, H. A. (1984). Problems with the MMPI. *Journal of Rheumatology, 11,* 417–418.

Spitz, P. W. (1984). The medical, personal, and social costs of rheumatoid arthritis. *Nursing Clinics of North America, 19,* 575–582.

Spergel, P., Ehrlich, G. E., & Glass, D. (1978). The rheumatoid arthritic personality: A psycho-diagnostic myth. *Psychosomatics, 19,* 79–86.

Sternback, R. A. (1966). *Principles of psychophysiology,* New York: Academic.

Taylor, J. A., Gatchel, R. J., & Korman, M. (1982). Psychophysiological and cognitive characteristics of ulcer and rheumatoid arthritis patients. *Journal of Behavioral Medicine, 5,* 173–188.

Urbánek, T., Sitajová, H., & Hudáková, G. (1984). Problems of rheumatoid arthritis and ankylosing spondylitis patients in their labor and life environments. *Czechoslovak Medicine, 7,* 78–89.

Vollhardt, B. R., Ackerman, S. H., Grayzel, A. I., & Barland, P. (1982). Psychologically distinguishable groups of rheumatoid arthritis patients: A controlled, single blind study. *Psychosomatic Medicine, 44,* 353–361.

Walker, B. B., & Sandman, C. A. (1977). Physiological response patterns in ulcer patients: Phasic and tonic components of the electrogastrogram. *Psychophysiology, 14,* 393–400.

Ward, D. J. (1971, May 8). Rheumatoid arthritis and personality: A controlled study. *British Medical Journal, 2,* 297–299.

Weiner, H. (1977). *Psychobiology and human disease.* New York: Elsevier.

Wilson, H., Olson, W. H., Gascon, G. G., & Brumback, R. A. (1982). Personality characteristics and multiple sclerosis. *Psychological Reports, 51,* 791–806.

Yoshino, S., & Uchida, S. (1981). Sexual problems of women with rheumatoid arthritis. *Archives of Physical Medicine and Rehabilitation, 62,* 122–123.

Zaphiropoulos, G., & Burry, H. C. (1974). Depression in rheumatoid disease. *Annals of the Rheumatic Diseases, 33,* 132–135.

11

Stress and Cognitive Vulnerability for Depression: A Self-Worth Contingency Model

NICHOLAS A. KUIPER
L. JOAN OLINGER

This chapter provides an overview of our research program focusing on stress and cognitive vulnerability for depression. The theoretical model underlying this work is a self-worth contingency model of depression. In this model, we propose that perceptions and evaluations of self-worth play a fundamental role in the etiology, maintenance, and remission of depressive symptomatology. Furthermore, this model suggests that certain individuals display a cognitive vulnerability for depression, centering around their rigid and inappropriate contingencies for evaluating self-worth. This self-worth model is presented next, followed by a discussion of the possible role of the self in the etiology and maintenance of depression. Here, we have also developed a self-schema model of depression. This model relates the severity of depressive symptomatology to the type of content (positive/negative) represented in an individual's self-schema. This model also highlights the importance of the degree of organization or consolidation of that information. The key elements of this self-schema model, especially as they relate to stress and cognitive vulnerability for depression, are presented in detail. Additional research focusing on further characteristics of vulnerable individuals, including coping styles, stress appraisals, and heightened levels of arousal and anxiety, is also presented. Finally, the chapter concludes by examining the empirical and theoretical relationships between certain life stresses, cognitive vulnerability for depression, and the expression of depressive symptomatology.

AN OVERVIEW OF THE SELF-WORTH CONTINGENCY MODEL OF DEPRESSION

Basic to the self-worth model are dysfunctional attitudes, or excessively rigid and inappropriate rules for guiding one's life (Beck, Rush, Shaw, & Emery, 1979). One instrument typically used for measuring these attitudes is the Dysfunctional Attitudes Scale (DAS; Dobson & Shaw, 1986; Oliver & Baumgart, 1985). Example items on this scale include, "If I do not do well all of the time, people will not respect me," or "If I do not perform as well as others, it means that I am an inferior human being." In our model, individuals endorsing a large number of dysfunctional attitudes are considered to be cognitively vulnerable to depression. For these individuals, dysfunctional attitudes establish unrealistic contingencies for evaluating self-worth (Kuiper & Olinger, 1986). In particular, these contingencies relate to a heightened concern over performance evaluation and an excessive need for approval by others (Cane, Olinger, Gotlib, & Kuiper, 1986). To illustrate, for the dysfunctional attitude, "My value as a person depends upon what others think of me," the implicit condition for self-worth is approval from others. Thus, as long as a vulnerable individual perceived that significant others were approving, her evaluations of self-worth would generally remain positive, limiting the expression of depressive symptomatology. In other words, the perception that dysfunctional contingencies for evaluating self-worth were being met would preclude the development of depression. If, however, this individual perceived that she was not well thought of, then her evaluations of self-worth would likely diminish, contributing to the further development of depressive symptomatology.

In the self-worth model, it is proposed that an individual's use of dysfunctional attitudes may relate to a parenting style that fosters dependency and self-criticism (Kuiper & Olinger, 1986; Kuiper, Olinger, & MacDonald, 1988). In preliminary support of this proposal, work in our own laboratory has indicated a significant correlation between mothers and daughters scores on the DAS ($r = .53$). Furthermore, research with former depressives has shown that these individuals maintain high levels of narcissistic vulnerability, even when in a nondepressed state (Cofer & Wittenborn, 1980). This exaggerated concern with evaluation and the approval of others is a central feature of dysfunctional self-worth contingencies.

The self-worth model also provides details concerning the changes that occur when vulnerable individuals move from a nondepressed to depressed state (Kuiper & Olinger, 1986; Kuiper, Olinger, & MacDonald, 1988). In particular, these changes relate to failed attempts to fulfill self-worth contingencies (e.g., "My value as a person depends greatly on what others think of me."). When circumstances hamper the opportunity to fulfill approval-based contingencies, the vulnerable individual responds by attempting to modify, reduce, or eliminate these stressful conditions. Mild threats to self-worth occur frequently for the vulnerable individual, who is highly dependent upon social and environmental feedback for self-esteem maintenance. Depression might thus be provoked by the occurrence of culminating minor stressors (continuing interpersonal conflicts as one example) or highly undesirable major stressors (loss of employment or loss of a significant other as examples) (see also Cohen & Edwards, Chapter 7, this volume, for a description of stress by resource interactions). In any case, these events all have their impact through an actual or expected lack of fulfillment of self-worth contingencies. With each failed attempt to meet self-worth contingencies, an increase in depressive types of responding is expected within the domains of cognition, affect, behavior, and physiology. Ultimately, these responses may reach a sufficient magnitude to constitute a depressive episode.

While attempting to modify their stressful situations, important changes are expected in the way vulnerable individuals attempt to cope with the stress, interact with others, and view themselves (Kuiper & Olinger, 1986). Specifically, vulnerable individuals are expected to rely increasingly on emotional regulation of their responses to stress (rather than persist in direct problem-solving attempts). Vulnerable individuals are also expected to begin to interact with others in a manner that elicits the rejection they expect. Finally, vulnerable individuals are expected to increase their self-focused attention, and shift from a positive view of self to a negative one.

A SELF-SCHEMA MODEL OF DEPRESSION

Over the past several years, we have also explored the nature of negative self-referent information processing in depression (Kuiper & Olinger, 1986; Kuiper, Olinger, & MacDonald, 1988). This research, which is based upon a social cognition approach, defines the self as a cognitive structure or schema. In particular, the self is viewed as an organized memory structure containing representational self-referent material. This schema is postulated to play a central role in the interpretation, organization, and memory for personal information.

In this research, we have developed a self-schema model of depression. This model considers both content and consolidation components and relates these to severity of depression. Content refers to the type of material represented in the self-schema. This material may be either depressed (e.g., hopeless, inferior) or nondepressed (e.g., orderly, helpful). Consolidation refers to the degree of integration of self-schema content. Kuiper and Olinger (1986) have proposed that a well-integrated or consolidated self-schema processes relevant personal material in a highly efficient and consistent manner. They also suggest that a poorly consolidated self-schema displays the opposite effect, leading to the inefficient and inconsistent processing of personal information.

Self-Schema Content.   Several of our studies have provided empirical evidence relating to the content of the depressive self-schema. Derry and Kuiper (1981) found that personal adjectives congruent with the content represented in an individual's self-schema were better recalled than adjectives which were incongruent. In particular, clinically depressed individuals in this study displayed enhanced self-referent recall only for depressed content adjectives. Nondepressed controls, on the other hand, showed enhanced self-referent recall only for nondepressed content adjectives.

Further research established the effects of milder levels of depression on self-schema content (see Kuiper & Olinger, 1986 for a detailed review of this work). In these studies, normal controls and mildly depressed individuals provided self-referent personality judgments for the depressed and nondepressed content adjectives. Following this, normal controls recalled far more nondepressed than depressed adjectives, suggesting a positive content base for their self-schema. Mild depressives, however, displayed equivalent self-referent recall for both types of content. This latter finding is consistent with the proposal that both positive and negative content is represented in the self-schema of mild depressives.

Self-Schema Consolidation.   When investigating the self-schema consolidation component, we have used a rating time measure to focus on processing efficiency. Kuiper and MacDonald (1982), for instance, used rating times (RTs) for self-referent personality decisions as an index of schematic processing efficiency. For normals it was found that schema congruent positive information was processed more efficiently (with quicker RTs) than schema incongruent negative information. Similar RT findings have been reported for the normal controls in other self-reference studies (Dance & Kuiper, 1988; Derry & Kuiper, 1981; MacDonald & Kuiper, 1985). Mild depressives, however, do not appear to display efficient processing for either type of personal content. As one illustration, Kuiper and MacDonald (1982) found that mild depressives displayed extremely long RTs for self-referent judgments concerning either positive or negative content. Finally, clinical depressives appear to display efficient processing, but only for self-referent negative material. MacDonald and Kuiper (1985), for example, found that clinical depressives processed self-schema congruent material (e.g., negative content) more quickly than incongruent material (e.g., positive content). In general, these findings suggest that both clinical depressives and normals employ a well-consolidated self-schema to assist in self-referent judgments, albeit for negative and positive content, respectively.

Summary.   When combined, these studies provide empirical support for a self-schema model of depression. A major tenent of this model is that severity of depression is a primary factor in determining both the content and consolidation components of the self-schema. Both normals and clinical depressives are characterized by a well-consolidated self-schema. For normals, this results in the efficient and consistent processing of positive self-referent material. Conversely, for clinical depressives, this results in the efficient and consistent processing of negative personal information. Mild depressives incorporate both types of content, but with a lower degree of consolidation. At milder levels of depression, an individual may begin to recognize and incorporate negative experiences into their self-schema. At the same time, they may begin to increasingly question the validity of positive self-referent attributes. As such, these processes reduce the overall degree of consolidation of the mild depressive's self-schema.

Cognitive Vulnerability for Depression and the Self-Schema Model

Self-Schema Content.   The self-worth model predicts that cognitively vulnerable individuals, when not depressed, should exhibit primarily positive content in their self-schema (Kuiper & Olinger, 1986; Kuiper, Olinger, & MacDonald, 1988). This prediction is based on the assumption that these individuals perceive they are currently fulfilling the self-worth contingencies of their dysfunctional attitudes. As such, these individuals would have a positive view of self, which, in turn, limits the expression of depressive symptomatology. If a vulnerable individual perceived repeated failures in attempts to meet dysfunctional self-worth contingencies, however, it is expected that negative aspects of self would become increasingly salient. As outlined earlier, this negative focus would contribute to the further expression of depressive symptomatology. Overall, then, it is proposed that the emergence of negative self-schema content is a concomitant of depression and not a vulnerability factor.

Several of our studies have offered empirical support for the proposal that negative self-schema content is an episodic or concomitant feature of depression. In one study, Kuiper, Olinger, MacDonald, and Shaw (1985) used the self-reference incidental recall paradigm employed in previous research. Consistent with the self-schema model of depression, normals recalled positive self-schema content, whereas mild depressives recalled equal amounts of positive and negative content. Of special interest was the type of content recalled by vulnerable, but currently nondepressed, individuals [i.e., those scoring high on the DAS, but low on the Beck Depression Inventory (BDI)]. As predicted by the self-worth model, it was found that these individuals did not display any evidence of negative self-schema content. Consistent with the normal controls, these vulnerable but currently nondepressed individuals recalled far more nondepressed than depressed content adjectives.

These findings have been replicated in two further studies using slightly different procedures and data analyses. In the first of these, Dance and Kuiper (1988) again used the self-reference incidental recall paradigm with vulnerable individuals, mild depressives, and normal controls. This research employed an overall proportion positive recall measure to determine self-schema content. Scores on this measure could range from 0 to 1, with higher numbers indicating a greater proportion of positive content recall. As expected, a hierarchical multiple-regression analysis revealed a significant main effect of depression, with proportion positive recall scores decreasing as BDI scores increased (low BDI recall score = .98; high BDI recall score = .74). Interestingly, the regression analysis also revealed that vulnerability to depression (as measured by the DAS) did not add significantly to the prediction of proportion positive recall scores. In other words, vulnerable individuals, when nondepressed, did not show lower positive recall scores than normals. This pattern is again consistent with the proposal that negative self-schema content is an episodic feature of depression, and not a vulnerability factor.

A further study (Kuiper, Olinger, & Swallow, 1987) used a different procedure to assess self-schema content. Rather than relying on a recall measure, participants in this study were simply asked to circle, in a set of presented adjectives, those they felt were self-descriptive. As in previous research, half of the adjectives were depressed in content, whereas half were nondepressed. An overall positivity score ranging from 0 to 1 was again employed, with higher numbers indicating a more positive orientation. In this study, both normal and vulnerable subjects exhibited a highly positive view of self (means of .95 and .94, respectively). In contrast, mildly depressed subjects were significantly less positive (mean = .60) than both of these groups. This pattern is again consistent with the self-worth model, in that an increasingly negative view of self is considered to be a concomitant or episodic feature of depression, and not a vulnerability factor.

Self-Schema Consolidation.   Although the self-worth model proposes that vulnerable individuals have a positive view of self when nondepressed, it also suggests that this self-schema is poorly consolidated (Kuiper &

Olinger, 1986; Kuiper, Olinger, & MacDonald, 1988). In particular, it is proposed that vulnerable individuals often engaged in assessments of their self-worth, as determined by the contingencies outlined in their dysfunctional attitudes (e.g., "Do significant others really approve of me?"). As such, their positive view of self is subject to frequent re-evaluation and interpretation. In these re-evaluations, the vulnerable individual may be extremely concerned about whether their positive view of self is justified or warranted. These processes result in a poorly consolidated self-schema, in contrast to the well-integrated self-schema exhibited by normals.

Empirical evidence relating to self-schema consolidation comes from two sources. One type of study has revealed that vulnerable individuals display a lower degree of decision consistency across independent sets of self-referent judgments than normal controls (MacDonald, Kuiper, & Olinger, 1985). Poorer consistency is congruent with the notion that vulnerable individuals are generally less certain about the self-referent status of personal adjectives than normals. In turn, this uncertainty is reflected in the vulnerable individual's poorer consolidation of self-referent material.

A second source of evidence concerning consolidation comes from research employing RTs as a measure of processing efficiency. One study, employing this measure with vulnerable individuals, was briefly described earlier. In this study, Dance and Kuiper (1988) obtained a rating time measure for each self-referent judgment made by participants. As expected, a regression analysis revealed that efficiency decreased significantly as depression level increased (low BDI RT = 1,278 msec; high BDI RT = 1,323 msec). This result is consistent with the self-schema model, as it suggests that normals have a well-consolidated view of self, whereas mild depressives do not. Of special interest was the finding that increasing levels of vulnerability also resulted in a decrease in self-schema processing efficiency, over and above that accounted for by current depression level (low DAS RT = 1,204 msec; high DAS RT = 1,404 msec). Thus, as predicted by the self-worth model, individuals scoring high on the DAS displayed a lower degree of self-schema consolidation than individuals scoring low on this measure.

Summary.   The above studies offer convergent evidence for both components of the self-schema model of depression when applied to vulnerable individuals. In accord with the self-worth contingency model, vulnerable individuals who are not currently depressed do not exhibit negative content in their self-schema. Instead, these individuals, as well as normal controls, display a primarily positive content self-schema. The critical distinction between these two groups is that only normals exhibit a strong degree of self-schema consolidation. Vulnerable individuals exhibit poor self-schema consolidation, due to the frequent reassessments of self, based on dysfunctional self-evaluative contingencies.

A central aspect of our model is that vulnerable individuals are only expected to maintain their positive view of self if they continue to perceive that their dysfunctional self-worth contingencies are being met. If a vulnerable individual is unable, over a period of time, to fulfill dysfunctional self-worth contingencies, then positive aspects of the self-schema become pre-empted by negative self-referent material. Using this self-schema, personal and social information of relevance to the vulnerable individual is processed in a negative fashion. The emergence of this negative content self-schema, along with the coping stress associated with failures to meet self-worth contingencies, contributes to the development of further depressive symptoms. As one illustration, the individual's negative view of self, and the perceived failure to meet self-worth contingencies, may contribute to increased feelings of self-rejection. This negativistic, self-critical presentation style may then enhance the possibility that others will reject the vulnerable individual, making it extremely difficult for this person to fulfill dysfunctional self-esteem contingencies.

FURTHER CHARACTERISTICS OF VULNERABLE INDIVIDUALS

Cognitive Vulnerability as an Enduring Personality Characteristic

One of the major assumptions of the self-worth model is that cognitive vulnerability for depression is a relatively enduring characteristic. In other words, it is expected that vulnerable individuals will generally endorse a large number of dysfunctional attitudes, regardless of their current level of depression. In preliminary empirical support of this proposal, investigators have found higher test-retest reliabilities for the DAS than for the BDI. Oliver and Baumgart (1985), for example, found a 6-week test reliability of .73 for the DAS and .54 for the BDI. Findings such as these suggest that level of vulnerability is a more stable characteristic than level of depression. This view has been corroborated by longitudinal research using different techniques. Eaves and Rush (1984), for example, obtained DAS scores from clinical depressives and community controls at two points in time. Of special interest was the finding that remitted depressives at time 2 still exhibited DAS scores that were significantly higher than those obtained by normal community controls. Again, this pattern supports the proposal that cognitive vulnerability for depression is a relatively enduring characteristic, and one that is not solely contingent upon current level of depression.

A longitudinal study in our own laboratory examined the stability issue, but from a slightly different perspective. In this study, we administered the BDI, the DAS, and the Ways of Coping Scale to a sample of 88 undergraduate females at two points in time, three months apart (Kuiper, Olinger, & Air, in press). The Ways of Coping Scale was developed by Lazarus and his colleagues (Folkman & Lazarus, 1985) and consists of a two-part questionnaire. Part one asks subjects to describe, in detail, one event or situation that was most stressful to them during the previous month. Part two is a 66-item self-report measure of coping strategies used by an individual to deal with this stressful event (e.g., "I try to analyze the problem in order to understand it better," or "I avoid being with people in general").

In our study, BDI and DAS scores were used simultaneously to categorize subjects into one of three groups—depressed, vulnerable, or normal controls. As a first step, those subjects scoring above a median split of 120 on the DAS were considered vulnerable, whereas those scoring below were considered nonvulnerable. Similarly, those scoring in the range of 0–9 on the BDI were considered nondepressed, whereas those scoring above 9 were considered depressed. Thus, the depressed group in our research consisted of those scoring above 9 on the BDI (and above 120 on the DAS). In contrast, the vulnerable group consisted of those individuals scoring above 120 on the DAS, but also currently nondepressed (BDI score of 0–9). Finally, the normal control group consisted of individuals below the median on the DAS, and also in the nondepressed range of the BDI (0–9).

Using this procedure, we classified participants into one of three groups at time 1. The relationship between this initial classification and a subsequent group classification three months later at time 2, gave an indication of the general stability of group membership across time. The self-worth model suggests that cognitive vulnerability for depression is a relatively stable and enduring attribute. As such, it was expected that the vulnerable individuals identified at time 1 (be they depressed or nondepressed at this time) would generally remain in one of the vulnerable categories at time 2 (be it depressed or nondepressed).

The data relating to these predictions is presented in Table 11.1a. A chi-squared analysis revealed a significant relationship between group membership at times 1 and 2, $p < .001$. An inspection of the main diagonal of Table 11.1a indicates a relatively high degree of stability, with the majority of individuals retaining the same group membership across the three-month time period (60% or greater for each category). Of special importance to the self-worth model, however, was the finding that vulnerable individuals who did not remain in the same group generally shifted to the expected alternate group. Thus, over 90% of the vulnerable (and nondepressed) individuals at time 1 were either in the same group at time 2 (64% vulnerable and still nondepressed), or were now in the depressed group (27% vulnerable and now depressed). Similarily, 90% of the depressed (and vulnerable) individuals at time 1 remained in one of the two vulnerable groups at time 2 (60% depressed and still vulnerable; 30% vulnerable and now nondepressed). Consistent with the self-worth model, this pattern suggests that whereas depression level may shift, vulnerability to depression is a relatively enduring and stable characteristic.

TABLE 11.1.   LONGITUDINAL FINDINGS

a. General Stability of Group Membership Across 3 Months

	Group Membership at Time 2		
Group Membership at Time 1	Depressed (& Vulnerable)	Vulnerable (& Nondepressed)	Normal Controls
Depressed (& Vulnerable)	60%	30%	10%
Vulnerable (& Nondepressed)	27%	64%	9%
Normal Controls	5%	29%	66%

b. Predicting Time 2 Group Membership from Time 1 Stressful Event

		Group Membership at Time 2	
Group at Time 1	Time 1 Event	Depressed (& Vulnerable)	Vulnerable (& Nondepressed)
Depressed (& Vulnerable)	Resolved	20%	60%
	Unresolved	74%	20%

c. Predicting Time 2 Group Membership from Time 2 Stressful Event

		Group Membership at Time 2	
Group at Time 1	Time 2 Event	Depressed (& Vulnerable)	Vulnerable (& Nondepressed)
Vulnerable (& Nondepressed)	Resolved	16%	75%
	Unresolved	40%	50%

Source: Kuiper, Olinger, & Air, in press

Predicting Changes in Depression Level for Vulnerable Individuals

The self-worth model also provides a theoretical framework to account for changes in depression level exhibited by vulnerable individuals. As detailed previously, vulnerable individuals are expected to become depressed if they perceive that their self-worth contingencies are not being met. Once depressed, however, these individuals are expected to become nondepressed if they perceive that the conditions necessary to fulfil their self-worth contingencies have been re-established (Kuiper & Olinger, 1986; Kuiper, Olinger, & MacDonald, 1988).

Based on this theoretical premise, we reasoned that one possible method of determining whether self-worth contingencies were being met was to examine more closely the nature of the stressful events described by each participant in our longitudinal study. An initial examination of these descriptions, as provided in part one of the Ways of Coping Scale, revealed that the majority of these stressors involved interpersonal difficulties (i.e., conflicts with friends, family members, etc.); with further categories including adjustment concerns (i.e., leaving home, financial pressures), and academic problems (i.e., doing poorly in required courses, time pressures related to course assignments and studying for exams, career decisions).

It was also possible to categorize each stressful event as being unresolved or resolved. An event was considered unresolved if the description was written in the present tense and/or clearly indicated that the stressor was an ongoing aspect of the participant's current life situation. In contrast, an event was rated as resolved if the description employed the past tense, and/or described the event as having occurred during a specified time period (e.g., during a particular weekend), or otherwise clearly indicated that it was no longer a problem. Thus, resolved events were discrete, time-limited stressors, such as preparing for an exam that was now past, or an argument with a significant other that was now concluded. Unresolved events, in contrast, included ongoing problems in various domains, such as interpersonal difficulties and academic concerns. Using these criteria, two independent raters obtained an agreement rate of over 80%, with the remaining descriptions being conferenced to arrive at a final event classification.

Given the continuing intrapsychic/interpersonal conflicts associated with unresolved events, it was proposed that these particular stressors would especially hamper the vulnerable individual's ability to meet dysfunctional self-worth contingencies. Resolved events, in contrast, were not expected to have this adverse impact. Thus, it was generally predicted that vulnerable individuals reporting unresolved stressful events would have a higher likelihood of being depressed than those reporting resolved events.

Several analyses were conducted in order to test these hypotheses. Of particular relevance are those analyses performed to determine if stressful event categorization would add further to the predictability of time 2 group membership. One illustration is presented in Table 11.1b. Here, the stressful events described by depressed (and vulnerable) individuals at time 1 were used to predict time 2 group membership, three months later. In accord with the self-worth model, the majority of these depressed (and vulnerable) individuals with resolved events at time 1 were no longer depressed at time 2 (only 20% remained depressed whereas 60% were now nondepressed but still vulnerable). Conversely, but again in accord with the self-worth model, the majority of these depressed (and vulnerable) individuals with unresolved events at time 1 were still depressed (and vulnerable) at time 2 (i.e., 74%). This rather dramatic effect obtained for depressed (and vulnerable) individuals at time 1; but was not as evident for vulnerable individuals who were not depressed during the initial assessment. Instead, it was necessary to consider the nature of the stressful event at time 2 for these individuals. As shown in Table 11.1c, the vast majority of vulnerable individuals with a resolved stressful event at time 2 remained nondepressed (75%). In contrast, and compared to vulnerable individuals with a resolved event, a much higher percentage of vulnerable individuals with an unresolved event at time 2 became depressed (16% vs. 40%, respectively). Overall, these findings provide further empirical support for the self-worth model. In addition, they suggest that the type of stressful event categorization employed in this research carries with it a powerful degree of predictive validity.

Cognitive Vulnerability and Coping with Stressful Events

A further component of the self-worth model pertains to the coping strategies employed by vulnerable individuals when they encounter stressful events. Past research indicates that depressed persons often rely on less effective coping strategies than nondepressed persons. Depressed individuals appear to focus on the emotional regulation of responses to stressful events, but often at the expense of more direct problem-solving techniques (Billings & Moos, 1983). Such emotion-focused coping strategies may take several forms, with Folkman and Lazarus (1985) delineating several possible categories. These include wishful thinking (e.g., "Wish that I can change what is happening or how I feel"), distancing ("Try to forget the whole thing"), self-blame ("Criticize or lecture myself"), and self-isolation ("Avoid being with people in general"). In contrast, problem-focused coping typically involves strategies that deal more directly with the stressful event ("I'm making a plan of action and following it"). All of these strategies are tapped in part 2 of the Ways of Coping Scale, as described earlier.

Of special interest are the potential links between these coping strategies and cognitive vulnerability for depression. In general, we have proposed that vulnerable individuals may, under certain circumstances, display coping strategies that are less than optimal, and perhaps even similar to those displayed by currently depressed individuals. Based upon the self-worth model, we have further proposed that when circumstances hamper the opportunity to fulfill dysfunctional contingencies, vulnerable individuals will respond with an overall increase in coping responses (Kuiper & Olinger, 1986). Some of these responses may involve problem-focused attempts at modifying, reducing, or even eliminating the stressful conditions that prohibit the fulfillment of self-worth contingencies. Given the irrational and extreme nature of these contingencies, however, these attempts may often prove unsuccessful. Furthermore, the interpersonal and assertion difficulties displayed by vulnerable individuals (Kuiper, Olinger, & Swallow, 1987; Olinger, Shaw, & Kuiper, 1987), combined with a reticence in letting others know that self-worth contingencies are not being met, may lead the vulnerable individual to an increasing reliance on emotion-focused coping responses. Here, self-isolation may be viewed as a particularly viable coping strategy by vulnerable individuals, since it may reduce the perceived negative social interaction consequences of failing to meet self-worth contingencies (i.e., "I am a worthless person unless others think highly of me"). In other words, once vulnerable individuals have rejected themselves (by failing to meet self-worth contingencies), they would also expect others to reject them, making the thought of social interactions aversive.

We have provided a preliminary empirical test of these proposals in a longitudinal research study employing the Ways of Coping Scale (Kuiper, Olinger, & Air, in press). As outlined earlier, participants in this study also completed the BDI and DAS (with three groups of subjects then being formed, based on these scores). Table 11.2 presents the means for the eight Ways of Coping subscales, for each of these three groups, at both times 1 and 2.

Congruent with past research findings, depressed individuals reported the use of significantly more emotion-focused coping strategies than normal controls. Thus, in response to stressful events at time 1, depressed individuals displayed significantly more wishful thinking, distancing, self-blame, and self-isolation, when compared to normal controls (all

TABLE 11.2. MEANS FOR WAYS OF COPING SUBSCALES

Ways of Coping Subscale		Group Membership at Time 1		
		Depressed (& Vulnerable)	Vulnerable (& Nondepressed)	Normal Controls
Emotion-Focused				
Wishful thinking	T1	1.97	1.44	1.19
	T2	2.13	1.28	1.03
Distancing	T1	1.22	.88	.82
	T2	1.04	.72	.62
Emphasizing the positive	T1	1.27	1.23	1.33
	T2	1.46	1.46	1.25
Self-blame	T1	1.57	1.14	.88
	T2	1.85	1.39	1.01
Tension reduction	T1	1.08	1.07	.91
	T2	.83	.77	.67
Self-isolation	T1	1.19	.86	.50
	T2	1.18	.98	.52
Problem-Focused				
Problem-focused	T1	1.34	1.34	1.25
	T2	1.56	1.59	1.37
Seeking social support	T1	1.63	1.58	1.37
	T2	1.73	1.74	1.41

Note: Scores on each subscale can range from 0 to 3, with higher numbers indicating more frequent use. T1 = Time 1, T2 = Time 2. Seeking social support is both problem- and emotion-focused.

Source: Kuiper, Olinger, & Air, in press

ps < .01). Vulnerable individuals, in contrast, were not significantly different from normal controls on these coping subscales. It was only in the case of self-isolation that vulnerable individuals were equivalent to currently depressed individuals, with both of these groups reporting significantly more self-isolation than normal controls (p < .001).

The overall pattern of coping responses at time 2 was virtually identical to that found for time 1. Thus, when faced with a further stressful event at time 2, those individuals depressed at time 1 still engaged in significantly more wishful thinking, distancing, self-blame, and self-isolation, relative to normal controls (all ps < .05). In contrast, those initially classified as vulnerable (and nondepressed) were only differentiated from normal controls on the basis of coping through self-isolation (p < .05). This coping difference for self-isolation was also found using group classification based on time 2 BDI and DAS scores; and was further replicated in an additional study reported by Kuiper et al. (in press).

These coping findings support the proposal that vulnerable individuals, regardless of their current level of depression, may be reticent to seek out others for discussion of their problems and concerns. From the vulnerable individual's point of view, such discussions may lead to disapproval and rejection by others. Thus such a coping style would be viewed as unacceptable. The increased use of self-isolation is also consistent with previous research indicating assertion problems among vulnerable individuals, and higher levels of subjective discomfort when interacting with others (Olinger, Shaw, & Kuiper, 1987). Ironically, increases in self-isolation may produce a state of affairs in which those persons who need the approval of others most intently (i.e., vulnerable individuals) may actually have the greatest difficulty in obtaining it.

Vulnerable individuals may view self-isolation as a reasonable strategy for dealing with stressful events. Unfortunately, this may not always be the case. In particular, an increase in self-isolation may also lead to an overall increase in the vulnerable individual's level of self-focused attention (Kuiper, Olinger, & Swallow, 1987). This latter increase is undesirable, as self-focused attention may serve to heighten negative affect, increase social interaction problems, and increase levels of self-criticism and self-blame (Kuiper & Olinger, 1986). In turn, these adverse effects might enhance the general level of stress experienced by the vulnerable individual, and could thus contribute to the further development and expression of depressive symptomatology.

Complementing this research on coping strategies is additional work exploring the social support systems of vulnerable and nonvulnerable individuals. Preliminary research suggests that vulnerable individuals may have inadequate social support networks, even when they are nondepressed. Kuiper, Olinger, & Swallow (1987), for example, found that vulnerable individuals, even when nondepressed, rated their social relationships as being significantly less satisfying than normal controls. This finding suggests that inadequate social networks may play a role in the etiology, as well as maintenance of depression. In other words, vulnerable individuals may not enjoy the same degree of support as nonvulnerable individuals, contributing further to their sense of social isolation and making it increasingly difficult to satisfy their dysfunctional self-worth contingencies.

Cognitive Vulnerability, Stress Appraisals, and Anxiety

A further implication of the self-worth model is that vulnerable individuals will exhibit heightened levels of personal stress and anxiety, even when in a nondepressed state. This prediction stems from the proposal that vulnerable individuals often engage in assessments of their self-worth, as determined by their dysfunctional contingencies. Given the generally unrealistic and rigid nature of these self-imposed contingencies, this high level of evaluative concern becomes taxing for the vulnerable individual and results in chronically enhanced levels of arousal, stress, anxiety.

These stress-related predictions were tested empirically in a series of studies. In the first of these, Olinger, Kuiper, and Shaw (1987) found that individuals with high DAS scores, regardless of their current level of depression (as measured by the BDI), reported feeling overwhelmed and out of control of major aspects of their lives (as evidenced by increased scores on the Perceived Stress Scale: Cohen, Kamarck, & Mermelstein, 1983).

This enhanced stress level may derive from several sources. As one possibility, vulnerable individuals may ruminate unduly on the various negative aspects of situations or events that have special relevance to their self-worth contingencies. As another possibility, and one that is not unrelated, vulnerable individuals may be particularly concerned about how other people perceive or evaluate them. These ruminations and evaluative concerns may then contribute to the increased stress levels exhibited by vulnerable individuals. In support of this proposal, Olinger, Kuiper, and Shaw (1987) have also found significant relationships between DAS scores and stress appraisals of events relevant to dysfunctional attitudes. Specifically, individuals scoring high on the DAS thought about these events more often and rated them as having greater importance and emotional impact than individuals scoring low on the DAS. Thus vulnerable individuals seem to monitor closely events that are relevant to their dysfunctional attitudes, and this monitoring, along with ruminative self-evaluations, may be one source of self-generated stress for these individuals.

An additional source of internally generated stress for vulnerable individuals may relate to self-presentational concerns. In vulnerable individuals, a need for approval by others, coupled with an increased fear of rejection, may foster an exaggerated concern with the adequacy of social performance. Accordingly, these social evaluative concerns were assessed in a study by Kuiper, Olinger, and Swallow (1987). Among other measures, this study employed the BDI, the DAS, and the self-consciousness scale (Buss, 1980). This latter scale provides measures of both public self-consciousness (e.g., "I usually worry about making a good impression") and social anxiety (e.g., "I have trouble when someone is watching me"). Consistent with proposals from the self-worth model, findings from this research indicated that vulnerable individuals, regardless of their current depression level, did indeed evidence higher levels of social anxiety and public self-consciousness than nonvulnerable individuals.

Additional research employing both self-report and psychophysiological measures has further documented the increased levels of anxiety and arousal evident in vulnerable individuals (Kuiper, Olinger, & Martin, in press). In this study, subjects participated in a computerized videogame task. One condition of this task was designed to minimize evaluative concerns, with participants being instructed to simply perform the task for fun. A second condition was designed to elicit moderate social evaluative concerns. Here participants were instructed to try to do the best they could, while their performance was monitored continuously by the experimenter. In this condition, the participant's own score was prominently displayed on the screen, along with the highest previous score obtained in this task.

Anxiety and arousal levels were assessed in this research with various self-report and psychophysiological measures, including heart rate and skin conductance. In support of the proposal that dysfunctional attitudes enhance stress appraisals and negative affect, it was found that vulnerable individuals displayed increased self-reported anxiety, self-consciousness, and greater physiological arousal throughout the entire experimental procedure.

When considering physiological responses more specifically, this study found that those individuals scoring high on the DAS evidenced a significantly higher degree of autonomic emotional arousal than did low DAS scorers. In terms of spontaneous skin response (SSR), vulnerable individuals showed significantly higher rates of SSRs than nonvulnerable subjects. This pattern obtained in both videogame conditions, but was especially evident in the moderately stressful condition. Similarly, the heart rate data also pointed to a higher level of autonomic arousal in individuals with a large number of dysfunctional attitudes. These individuals maintained a consistently high heart rate in both conditions, whereas individuals scoring low on the DAS showed significant heart rate deceleration in the low stress condition. Finally, self-reports of feeling states differed significantly between vulnerable and nonvulnerable individuals. Those scoring high on the DAS rated their arousal in the moderately stressful condition as being unpleasant and anxiety provoking. In contrast, nonvulnerable individuals viewed their physiological arousal in this condition as being pleasant and exhilarating.

Summary. The studies reviewed here suggest that anxiety may be a further negative emotion which relates to dysfunctional attitudes. As indicated earlier, these attitudes are assumed to be pervasive and general, and individuals who exhibit them are therefore likely to be frequently engaged in assessing their self-worth. Since these contingencies are extreme and rigid, it is difficult for individuals to meet them consistently. Thus individuals with dysfunctional attitudes are likely to find themselves often in situations where the perceived probability of meeting all of their self-worth contingencies is low. Under these conditions, such individuals are likely to experience heightened arousal, anxiety, and stress regarding the possibility of negative self-evaluation and loss of self-worth.

In considering the self-worth model more generally, the studies reviewed here may help elucidate more clearly the possible relationships between various negative emotions, such as anxiety and depression, and dysfunctional self-evaluative contingencies. It has often been suggested in the literature that anxiety is a precursor to depression (Beck, Brown, Steer, Eidelson, & Riskind, 1987; Rholes, Riskind, & Nevill, 1985). Anxiety is proposed to be more prevalent as long as the individual continues to actively cope with a threat and maintains some hope of avoiding the threatened outcome. In contrast, depression is likely to ensue when the individual begins to despair of the effectiveness of coping attempts, and therefore loses hope of avoiding threat. Therefore, for individuals with a large number of dysfunctional attitudes, perceived difficulties in meeting self-worth contingencies may, in the first instance, lead to increased anxiety. If the vulnerable individual begins to lose hope of being able to cope successfully and perceives that contingencies for self-worth have not been met, then that individual is likely to also experience feelings of depression. At mild to moderate levels of depression, there may still be a significant level of anxiety, as the vulnerable individual fluctuates between perceptions of loss and threat.

Cognitive Vulnerability Interacting with Negative Life Events

A consistent finding in the stress literature concerns the relationship between negative life events and depression. Across a variety of subject populations, assessment instruments, and research methodologies, it has been found that depressed persons experience a greater number of negative life events than nondepressed persons. Furthermore, a focus on microstressors and their relationship to depression level has yielded similar results (Kanner, Coyne, Schaefer, & Lazarus, 1981). Depressed persons report significantly more daily hassles and minor frustrating events than do nondepressed persons.

Negative life events by themselves, however, cannot fully account for the occurrence of depressive symptomatology. Only a minority of individuals who experience the loss of a significant other, for example, become depressed (Costello, 1985). Similar findings have been reported for other negative events and have led to the general conclusion that the percent of variance accounted for by life events alone is relatively modest.

In light of this modest relationship, we have conducted research exploring the possible links between stressful life events, cognitive vulnerability for depression, and the expression of depressive symptomatology. Based on the self-worth model, we have proposed that cognitive vulnerability for depression serves as a moderator variable. Individuals scoring high on the DAS are postulated to be particularly susceptible to the adverse impact of certain life events, whereas individuals scoring low on this measure are proposed to be significantly less affected. To illustrate, a vulnerable individual with the attitude that her worth was dependent upon the approval of significant others may begin to experience depressive symptomatology if she encountered a situation or life event that lead to the belief that significant others were disapproving. Conversely, an individual with few dysfunctional attitudes is not expected to display as negative an emotional reaction to this event.

Vulnerability and the Number of Stressful Life Events.   Several studies support the proposal that dysfunctional attitudes may serve as a moderator variable between stressful life events and negative emotions. Wise and Barnes (1986), using a sample of college students, found a significant interaction between DAS scores and the number of major negative life events, when predicting depression. Among subjects with low DAS scores, there was no relationship between negative life stressors and depression, whereas subjects with high DAS scores revealed a significant positive relationship between these two variables. In other words, it was only those individuals with a large number of dysfunctional attitudes and a large number of negative life events that showed significant depressive symptomatology.

Similar interactive findings have been reported for research in our own laboratory. Olinger, Kuiper, and Shaw (1987) conducted two studies using different measures of stressful life events. Again, there was a significant moderating effect of the DAS on the relationship between life events and BDI scores. In particular, it was only for subjects high on dysfunctional attitudes that an increase in the number of negative life events had a substantial negative impact on depression scores. This pattern obtained for life events specifically related to dysfunctional attitudes (Study 1), as well as a broader range of negative life events relating to social, occupational, financial, interpersonal, family, health, and academic concerns (Study 2).

Finally, a third study by Kuiper, Olinger, and Martin (in press) focused on the role of microstressors and their possible relationship to cognitive vulnerability and depression. In this study, subjects completed the BDI, the DAS, and the Hassles Scale (Kanner et al., 1981). The Hassles Scale covers a broad range of potential daily irritants, including such topics as unexpected company, auto maintenance, troublesome neighbors, social obligations, and not enough time for the family. Respondents circle each hassle that has occurred in the past month, and also indicate how severe that particular hassle was. A series of regression analyses offered further support for the proposal that dysfunctional attitudes act as a moderator variable. For low levels of vulnerability, an increase in the number of microstressors has a negligible impact on depression level. For high levels of vulnerability, however, the effect was significant. Here, an increase in the number of hassles produced more than a two-fold increase in depression level (see also Martin, Chapter 6, for a discussion of central issues surrounding stress moderator research in field settings).

Vulnerability and Characteristics of the Most Stressful Event. In addition to the research just discussed, we have also examined more closely the characteristics of the most stressful event reported by an individual. As one example, Kuiper, Olinger, and Air (in press) proposed that for vulnerable individuals, stressful events that impinged most directly on their dysfunctional self-worth contingencies would have the greatest impact on depression level. To test this proposal, subjects in this study completed the BDI, the DAS, and the Ways of Coping Scale. As outlined earlier in this chapter, part one of the Ways of Coping Scale asks subjects to describe, in detail, their most stressful event during the past month.

Based on the self-worth model, we reasoned that an impinging event for a vulnerable individual would display two major characteristics. First, such an event would contain strong elements of disapproval from a significant other. Second, such an event would still be unresolved or ongoing in the individual's life. Using these criteria, two independent raters classified each described stressful event as impinging or nonimpinging (with 89% agreement). In addition, vulnerability level was determined using a median split of 122 on the DAS. Those individuals scoring below this median split were classified as low on vulnerability, those above were classified as high.

With respect to depressive symptomatology, the self-worth model predicted a significant interaction between vulnerability level and stressful event classification. In other words, vulnerable individuals with an impinging stressful event were expected to display the highest levels of depressive symptomatology. As shown in Table 11.3a, this pattern was found. An analysis of variance of the BDI scores revealed a significant interaction between vulnerability level and stressful event categorization ($p < .01$). Consistent with the model, those vulnerable individuals with a stressful event impinging on their dysfunctional self-worth contingencies displayed the highest BDI scores (mean of 15.18). In contrast, event categorization was of much less concern to individuals low on vulnerability. Here, the type of event (impinging versus nonimpinging) did not have a significant impact on depression level (BDI means of 8.15 versus 5.26, respectively). This finding is also consistent with the self-worth model, as impinging events should generally have little relevance for individuals with few dysfunctional evaluative contingencies.

A further study by Kuiper, Olinger, and Air (in press) also examined the interaction of event characteristics and vulnerability to depression. Although this study used a simpler event categorization technique, it revealed essentially the same pattern of results as just described. As indicated

TABLE 11.3.   THE INTERACTION OF VULNERABILITY AND STRESSFUL EVENT
CHARACTERISTICS

(a) Kuiper, Olinger, & Air (in press: Study 1)

	Low Vulnerability		High Vulnerability	
	Nonimpinging Event	Impinging Event	Nonimpinging Event	Impinging Event
BDI Means	5.26	8.15	7.51	15.18

(b) Kuiper, Olinger, & Air (in press: Study 2): Time 1 Only

	Low Vulnerability		High Vulnerability	
	Resolved Event	Unresolved Event	Resolved Event	Unresolved Event
BDI Means at Time 1	3.64	4.30	7.55	14.05

(c) Kuiper, Olinger, & Air (in press: Study 2): Predicting Time 2 BDI scores

	Low Vulnerability		High Vulnerability	
	Resolved Event	Unresolved Event	Resolved Event	Unresolved Event
BDI Means at Time 2	4.20	4.00	8.50	15.78

earlier, this longitudinal study classified events described on the Ways of
Coping Scale as being either resolved or unresolved in nature. Using this
technique, and a median split on the DAS to determine vulnerability level,
an analysis of variance of depression scores revealed a significant interaction at time 1 ($p < .025$). As shown in Table 11.3b, vulnerability to depression moderated the relationship between stressful event categorization and
depression. Consistent with the self-worth model, only those individuals
with unresolved events and high DAS scores exhibited significant depressive symptomatology (BDI mean of 14.05).

Given the longitudinal nature of this second study, we also attempted
to predict depression level at time 2 (three months later), using time 1
vulnerability level and stressful event categorization. When all stressful
events at time 1 were included, an analysis of variance of BDI scores at
time 2 revealed only a marginal interaction ($p = .13$). However, a separate
analysis for interpersonal stressful events (the largest category of events
at time 1), revealed a significant interaction ($p < .05$). This interaction is
shown in Table 11.3c. Again, vulnerability level served to moderate the
relationship between stressful event characteristics and depression level.
In particular, it was only those vulnerable individuals with an unresolved
interpersonal stressful event at time 1 that showed significant depressive

symptomatology at time 2 (BDI mean of 15.78). In light of the three-month time period covered by this analysis, the obtained interaction suggests that unresolved interpersonal stressful events are especially problematic for vulnerable individuals. In particular, such unresolved events seem to contribute to chronically enhanced depression levels.

Summary.   The findings from the studies reviewed here offer empirical support for the proposal that depressive symptomatology is related to the interaction of negative life events and cognitive vulnerability for depression. As predicted by the self-worth model, vulnerability for depression moderates the relationship between (1) the number of negative life events and depression, and (2) characteristics of the most stressful event and depression. For those low on cognitive vulnerability, these particular life-event attributes have only a modest impact on depression level. For those high on vulnerability, however, the relationship is more pronounced, and can be predicted across time.

CONCLUSIONS AND FUTURE DIRECTIONS

This chapter has provided a brief overview of our current research program focusing on the complex relationships between stress, cognitive vulnerability for depression, and negative emotions, such as anxiety and depression. As shown in Table 11.4, this program has been guided by a theoretical model which proposes that certain individuals display dysfunctional contingencies for evaluating self-worth. In this model, it is further proposed that these aberrant evaluative standards have a pervasive and negative impact on the vulnerable individual's overall quality for life and sense of well-being.

In our research, we have documented a number of major characteristics associated with individuals cognitively vulnerable for depression, including their self-perceptions and reactions to stressful situations. Even when in a nondepressed state, vulnerable individuals display an increased concern about evaluations of others and how these evaluations may relate to perceptions of self-worth. Thus vulnerable individuals, regardless of their current level of depression, exhibit increased levels of anxiety and autonomic arousal. Furthermore, the coping strategies employed by vulnerable individuals, such as self-isolation, may actually serve to enhance the intrapsychic and interpersonal difficulties encountered by these individuals. Therefore, when coping attempts are perceived as failing to meet self-worth contingencies, the vulnerable individual may increasingly emphasize negative content aspects of self. As a result of these self-schema changes, the vulnerable individual experiences increasing depressive symptomatology in the cognitive, affective, motivational, and physiological realms. Only when the individual again perceives that dysfunctional self-worth contingencies are being

TABLE 11.4. SELF-WORTH CONTINGENCY MODEL OF DEPRESSION: MAJOR CHARACTERISTICS OF INDIVIDUALS COGNITIVELY VULNERABLE FOR DEPRESSION

Vulnerability Characteristics	Representative Studies
Endorse dysfunctional self-worth contingencies, as measured by the DAS. Contingencies relate to an excessive need for approval from significant others. These contingencies are rated as important and show a reasonable degree of stability across time.	Kuiper & Olinger (1986) Olinger, Kuiper, & Shaw (1987) Kuiper, Olinger, & Air (in press) Cane, Olinger, Gotlib, & Kuiper (1986)
Display a positive content self-schema when nondepressed, but incorporate negative content as depression level increases. This self-schema is poorly consolidated, however, even when in a nondepressed state.	Kuiper et al. (1985) Dance & Kuiper (1988) Kuiper, Olinger, & Swallow (1987) MacDonald, Kuiper, & Olinger (1985) MacDonald & Kuiper (1984)
Display heightened levels of internally generated stress, even when nondepressed. Relates to increased social anxiety, high public self-consciousness, ruminations over self-worth contingencies, and a generalized perception that life stresses are overwhelming. Also includes greater anxiety and increased physiological arousal, even when nondepressed. Finally, when coping with stressful events, show increased self-isolation.	Olinger, Kuiper, & Shaw (1987) Kuiper, Olinger & Swallow (1987) Kuiper, Olinger, & Air (in press) Kuiper, Olinger, & Martin (in press)
Display depressive responses to life events which, in contrast, have a minimal impact on individuals with few dysfunctional self-worth contingencies. Both the number and nature of these events influence subsequent depression levels. Interpersonal situations appear to be particularly problematic for vulnerable individuals to resolve, as they display poor assertion and social skills.	Olinger, Kuiper, & Shaw (1987) Kuiper, Olinger, & Martin (in press) Kuiper, Olinger, & Air (in press) Olinger, Shaw, & Kuiper (1987)

met is there a reduction in overt depressive symptomatology, and a return to a positive content view of self (albeit it is poorly consolidated).

Finally, it should be noted that although our research program has been informative, many fundamental issues and questions still remain. As one illustration, we have just begun to explore the possible theoretical and empirical links between major social roles, self-schemata, and the self-worth model of depression (Dance & Kuiper, 1987). In the depression domain, a number of investigators have implicated role loss or role strain as an important factor in the etiology of this disorder (Oatley & Bolton, 1985). Accordingly, we are currently focusing on the perception of roles as an integral aspect of self, and are examining how multiple roles and role complexity may interact with dysfunctional self-evaluative standards to produce negative affect. As a second illustration of future research directions, we have recently begun to develop a more explicit model of the social comparison processes and individual difference factors which may enhance negative self-evaluations and depression (Swallow & Kuiper, 1987). In this model, a number of aspects of self are identified (e.g., complexity, accessibility, and consolidation) and related to social comparison processes (e.g., choice of comparison others, choice of comparison dimensions), individual difference variables (e.g., dysfunctional attitudes), and negative affect. Overall, these two illustrations provide examples of further theoretical and research directions which may help clarify the role of vulnerability and stress factors in the expression of negative emotions.

References

Beck, A. T., Brown, G., Steer, R. A., Eidelson, J. I., & Riskind, J. H. (1987). Differentiating anxiety and depression: A test of the cognitive content-specificity hypothesis. *Journal of Abnormal Psychology, 96,* 179–183.

Beck, A. T., Rush, A. J., Shaw, B. F., & Emery, G. (1979). *Cognitive therapy of depression.* New York: Guilford.

Billings, A. G., & Moos, R. H. (1983). Psychosocial theory and research on depression: An integrative framework and review. *Clinical Psychology Review, 2,* 213–237.

Buss, A. H. (1980). *Self-consciousness and social anxiety.* San Francisco: Freeman.

Cane, D. B., Olinger, L. J., Gotlib, I. H., & Kuiper, N. A. (1986). Factor structure of the dysfunctional attitude scale in a student population. *Journal of Clinical Psychology, 42,* 307–309.

Cofer, D. H., & Wittenborn, J. R. (1980). Personality characteristics of formerly depressed women. *Journal of Abnormal Psychology, 84,* 693–700.

Cohen, S., & Edwards, J. R. (1989). Personality characteristics as moderators of the relationship between stress and disorder. In R. W. J. Neufeld (Ed.), *Advances in the investigation of psychological stress* (pp. 235–283). New York: Wiley.

Cohen, S., Kamarck, T., & Mermelstein, R. (1983). A global measure of perceived stress. *Journal of Health and Social Behavior, 24,* 385–396.

Costello, C. G. (1985). Major depression: A comparison of the routes to prevention. *Canadian Psychology, 26,* 187–194.

Dance, K. A., & Kuiper, N. A. (1987). Self-schemata, social roles, and a self-worth contingency model of depression. *Motivation & Emotion, 11,* 251–268.

Dance, K. A., & Kuiper, N. A. (1988). *Self-schema content and consolidation: The impact of depression level and cognitive vulnerability for depression.* Unpublished Manuscript. University of Western Ontario, London, Ontario, Canada.

Derry, P. A., & Kuiper, N. A. (1981). Schematic processing and self-reference in clinical depression. *Journal of Abnormal Psychology, 90,* 286–297.

Dobson, K. S., & Shaw, B. F. (1986). Cognitive assessment with major depressive disorders. *Cognitive Therapy & Research, 10,* 13–30.

Eaves, G., & Rush, A. J. (1984). Cognitive patterns in symptomatic and remitted unipolar major depression. *Journal of Abnormal Psychology, 93,* 31–40.

Folkman, S., & Lazarus, R. S. (1985). If it changes it must be a process: Study of emotion and coping during three stages of a college examination. *Journal of Personality and Social Psychology, 48,* 150–170.

Kanner, A. D., Coyne, J. C., Schaefer, C., & Lazarus, R. S. (1981). Comparison of two modes of stress measurement: Daily hassles and uplifts versus major life events. *Journal of Behavioral Medicine, 4,* 1–39.

Kuiper, N. A., & MacDonald, M. R. (1982). Self and other perception in mild depressives. *Social Cognition, 1,* 223–239.

Kuiper, N. A., & Olinger, L. J. (1986). Dysfunctional attitudes and a self-worth contingency model of depression. In P. C. Kendall (Ed.), *Advances in cognitive-behavioral research and therapy* (Vol. 5, pp. 115–142). New York: Academic.

Kuiper, N. A., Olinger, L. J., & Air, P. A. (in press). Stressful events, dysfunctional attitudes, coping styles, and depression. *Personality & Individual Differences.*

Kuiper, N. A., Olinger, L. J., & MacDonald, M. R. (1988). Vulnerability and episodic cognitions in a self-worth contingency model of depression. In L. B. Alloy (Ed.), *Cognitive processes in depression* (pp. 289–309). New York: Guilford.

Kuiper, N. A., Olinger, L. J., MacDonald, M. R., & Shaw, B. F. (1985). Self-schema processing of depressed and nondepressed content: The effects of vulnerability to depression. *Social Cognition, 3,* 77–93.

Kuiper, N. A., Olinger, L. J., & Martin, R. A. (in press). Dysfunctional attitudes, stress appraisals, and negative emotions. *Cognitive Therapy & Research.*

Kuiper, N. A., Olinger, L. J., & Swallow, S. R. (1987). Dysfunctional attitudes, mild depression, views of self, self-consciousness, and social perceptions. *Motivation & Emotion,* 379–401.

MacDonald, M. R., & Kuiper, N. A. (1985). Efficiency and automaticity of self-schema processing in clinical depressives. *Motivation & Emotion, 9,* 171–184.

MacDonald, M. R., Kuiper, N. A., & Olinger, L. J. (1985). Vulnerability to depression, mild depression, and self-schema consistency. *Motivation & Emotion, 9,* 369–379.

Martin, R. A. (in press). Techniques for data acquisition and analysis in field investigations of stress. In R. W. J. Neufeld (Ed.), *Advances in the investigation of psychological stress.* New York: Wiley.

Oatley, K., & Bolton, W. (1985). A social-cognitive theory of depression in reaction to life events. *Psychological Review, 92,* 372–388.

Olinger, L. J., Kuiper, N. A., & Shaw, B. F. (1987). Dysfunctional attitudes and stressful life events: An interactive model of depression. *Cognitive Therapy & Research, 11,* 25–40.

Olinger, L. J., Shaw, B. F., & Kuiper, N. A. (1987). Nonassertiveness, dysfunctional attitudes, and mild levels of depression. *Canadian Journal of Behavioural Science, 19,* 40–49.

Oliver, J. M., & Baumgart, E. P. (1985). The dysfunctional attitude scale: Psychometric properties and relation to depression in an unselected adult population. *Cognitive Therapy & Research, 9,* 161–167.

Rholes, W., Riskind, J. H., & Neville, B. (1985). The relationship of cognitions and hopelessness to depression and anxiety. *Social Cognition, 3,* 36–50.

Swallow, S. R., & Kuiper, N. A. (1987). Social comparison and negative self-evaluations: An application to depression. *Clinical Psychology Review, 8,* 1–22.

Wise, E. H., & Barnes, D. R. (1986). The relationship among life events, dysfunctional attitudes, and depression. *Cognitive Therapy & Research, 10,* 257–266.

12

Forms and Mechanisms of Susceptibility to Stress in Schizophrenia

IAN R. NICHOLSON
RICHARD W. J. NEUFELD

INTRODUCTION AND OVERVIEW

The psychiatric disorder that is presently termed schizophrenia has been known for thousands of years. Sanskrit writings from as early as the fourteenth century B.C. contain references to such a disorder (Doran, Brier, & Roy, 1986). Psychiatric texts throughout the nineteenth century include references to variants of the subtypes of schizophrenia (Cancro, 1985). Yet it was not until the diagnostic system developed by Emil Kraepelin during the 1890s that these various disorders were grouped under the major category of "dementia praecox." This diagnostic category stood apart from previous descriptions of the disorder because it included three previously separate forms of mental disorder—catatonic, hebephrenic, and paranoid. Kraepelin believed that several symptoms were common to these three forms, including progressive mental deterioration (i.e., dementia) and onset during puberty or adolescence (i.e., praecox).

He revised his diagnostic categories several times in the years before his death in 1927, the last complete version appearing in 1913. In this version, he described dementia praecox as "a *series of states*, the common characteristic of which is a peculiar destruction of the internal connections of the psychic personality. The effects of this injury predominate in the emotional and volitional spheres of mental life." (1913/1919, p. 3, italics added). Kraepelin never hypothesized that there was only one single clinical entity responsible for all of these groups. Instead, he grouped together a series of poorly understood psychotic syndromes. This use of a common overarching diagnostic category allowed for general predictions as to the cause and outcome of the three syndromes but also allowed for variations that did not exactly fit into his schema.

During the time in which Kraepelin was revising his text, Eugen Bleuler's (1911/1950) text on schizophrenia appeared. It made a major impact for several important reasons. First, Bleuler introduced the term "schizophrenia" to overcome difficulties inherent in the use of the term "dementia praecox." Such inherent difficulties included the use of the term praecox, since there was a considerable number of cases in which the disorder presented itself in adulthood, not during puberty or adolescence. Second, he reinforced the three categories that were united originally by Kraepelin and added a fourth—"simple" schizophrenia. Third, he posited that schizophrenia should be viewed as a single clinical entity since there were several primary characteristics common to all subtypes (e.g., inappropriate emotional responses). Bleuler's view has since dominated the majority of theory and research on schizophrenia (Cromwell, 1975).

Since the time of Emil Kraepelin and Eugen Bleuler, several different diagnostic manuals have appeared. Organizations such as the New York Academy of Medicine, the World Health Organization (WHO), and the American Psychiatric Association (formerly the American Medico-Psychological Association) have all published diagnostic systems, each system with its own set of criteria and terminology. Furthermore, several researchers and theorists have similarly published their own sets of criteria, each emphasizing different aspects of schizophrenia (e.g., Astrachan et al., 1972; Carpenter, Strauss, & Bartko, 1973; Feighner et al., 1972). At the present time, the most commonly applied diagnostic system is the revised third edition of one published by the American Psychiatric Association (1987)—*Diagnostic and Statistical Manual of Mental Disorders* (DSM-III-R).

The diagnostic criteria for active adult schizophrenia in the DSM-III-R are modifications of criteria from other systems (Spitzer, Andreasen, & Endicott, 1978), primarily focusing on those employed by the Research Diagnostic Criteria (RDC, Spitzer, Endicott, & Robins, 1978). The diagnosis of schizophrenia now centers around the persistence of characteristic psychotic symptoms (e.g., bizarre delusions, prominent auditory hallucinations, catatonic rigidity, grossly inappropriate emotional responses), a marked decline in functioning in social areas (e.g., work, self-care), and a duration of disturbance of at least six months. Furthermore, other disorders (e.g., psychotic depression, organic disturbance) are ruled out. As a diagnostic system for schizophrenia, the DSM-III-R is viewed by many researchers as the best in that, although it is narrowly defined, it has a high degree of predictive specificity (Helzer, Brockington, & Kendell, 1981; Stephens, Astrup, Carpenter, Shaffer, & Goldberg, 1982).

The general aim of this chapter will be to examine the role of stress in schizophrenia. The importance of the role of stress in psychopathology generally can be seen by its inclusion in the DSM-III-R. The DSM-III included a new multiaxial evaluation system when it was introduced by the American Psychiatric Association in 1980. With this multiaxial system, patients are rated on a variety of different axes (i.e., classes of information). The five axes are: (I) clinical syndromes, (II) developmental disorders and personality disorders, (III) physical disorders and conditions, (IV) severity of psychosocial stressors, and (V) global assessment of functioning. Axis II, Axis IV, and Axis V were new and important additions to the diagnostic system. Although these additions have been both praised and criticized for a variety of reasons, Axis IV has been primarily questioned due to its low reliability. This problem resulted from the difficulty many clinicians experienced in assessing the severity of a psychosocial stressor (Polyson, Miller, & Shank, 1987; Rey, Stewart, Plapp, Bashir, & Richards, 1987). Nevertheless, its inclusion in the DSM-III was supported by many of its critics (Spitzer & Forman, 1979). Though many improvements have been made to Axis IV in the revised third edition of the manual, some difficulties remain.

The addition of Axis IV in the DSM-III allowed for greater comprehensiveness than could previously be achieved in the evaluation on an individual's condition. Such increased comprehensiveness then allows for a greater understanding of likely etiological factors when planning treatment and charting prognosis. As such, the American Psychiatric Association's inclusion of Axis IV signifies that the association officially recognizes that psychosocial factors play a role in onset, continuance, and exacerbation of disorders (Millon, 1986).

Although the emphasis of the present discussion will be on schizophrenia, many of the issues discussed will be applicable to other forms of psychopathological disorder. In the first part of this chapter, stress will be discussed in terms of the early research of stress as an antecedent to schizophrenia. This discussion will center on vulnerability-stress hypotheses of schizophrenia, particularly Zubin and Spring's (1977) model. Although it is recognized that such models have an important role in the development of theory and research, the present review will be evaluative. Controversies and questions regarding these models will be reviewed, with attention paid to three areas: stress, schizophrenia, and the unique relation between stress and schizophrenia. In the second portion of this chapter, selected mechanisms that may be responsible for the adverse effects of stress on schizophrenics will be considered. One possibility is that schizophrenics may display a proclivity toward an increased level of stress arousal which, among other consequences, may impair cognitive processes. A second possibility is that schizophrenics may suffer from a reduced attentional capacity that undermines their ability to cope with their environment.

STRESS AS AN ANTECEDENT TO SCHIZOPHRENIA

Almost since schizophrenia was first recognized as a diagnostic entity, clinicians and researchers have speculated as to its cause. For example, Bleuler viewed the origins of schizophrenia to have an organic basis. Jung (1939) believed that such conclusions were hasty. Instead, he saw that "the usual aetiology consists in a competition between various conditions" (p. 1008). The conditions that he believed were primary, in the majority of cases, had a psychological basis—"an emotional shock, a disappointment, a difficult situation, a reversal of fortune, etc." (p. 1008). Such organic-psychological or genetic-environmental arguments continued for decades.

One area where these disputes led theorists and researchers was the relation between stress and schizophrenia. Little research was published on this relation before the late 1960s (e.g., Schofield & Balian, 1959). At that time, however, a considerable amount of research began on stressors (i.e., stressful life events) as the etiological agent for schizophrenia (e.g., Brown & Birley, 1968). Stressful life events, as referred to in the context of this research, included primarily dramatic occurrences (e.g., death of a spouse, witnessing a serious road accident, development of a life-threatening illness). Unfortunately, the research was disappointing with regard to the early hypothesis that stressful life events were necessary factors for the development of schizophrenia. Often, researchers failed to discover any instances of precipating stress in schizophrenic etiology (e.g., Beck & Worthen, 1972). In other instances, when possible precipitating stress was discovered, its level was less for schizophrenia than that level discovered for other psychiatric disorders (e.g., depression; Jacobs, Prusoff, & Paykel, 1974). Likewise, when precipitating life events were related to psychotic symptomatology, stronger relations were found between events and nonpsychotic symptomatology (e.g., anxiety, somatic concerns; Schwartz & Myers, 1977). In reviewing over 10 years of research on the subject, Rabkin (1980) concluded that "the events reported are not in themselves sufficient, either quantitatively or qualitatively, to account for illness onset . . . nor are they a necessary precursor of illness" (p. 424). Nevertheless, in reviewing much of the same literature Dohrenwend and Egri (1981) concluded that "the consensus that recent life events have only a trivial impact on the onset and course of schizophrenia is premature" (p. 22). Dohrenwend and Egri finish their review with a call for more research to be undertaken to better understand the "enigmatic" role played by stressful life events in the development of schizophrenia.

Furthermore, research and theory in the 1970s suggested numerous other factors that may play important roles in the development of schizophrenia. Such factors include genetics (Gottesman & Shields, 1972), aberrant family interactions (Jacob, 1975), environmental and social influences (Hammer, Makiesky-Barrow, & Gutwirth, 1978), neurological dysfunctions such as an impairment of the left hemisphere of the brain (Gur, 1978) or excessive cortical atrophy (Weinberger, Torrey, Neophytides, & Wyatt, 1979), biochemical dysfunctions such as a dysfunctional endorphin-dopamine linkage (Volavka, Davis, & Ehrlich, 1979) or dopaminergic hyperactivity (Matthysse, 1974), etc. With these various perspectives all claiming special status as the necessary factor in the development of schizophrenia, research interests increased in diversity. Nevertheless, researchers tended to reach a theoretical standstill in terms of what could be explained.

VULNERABILITY MODELS

In an attempt to explain, to a greater degree, the etiology and course of schizophrenia, Zubin and Spring (1977) reviewed six major scientific models (ecological, developmental, learning theory, genetic, internal environment, and neurophysiological models). In a logical factor analysis (described by the authors as a method in which they "squeeze the juice out of all these models into a goblet and see what the elixer consists of," p. 109), Zubin and Spring suggested that a common denominator could be a higher level theory termed the "vulnerability model." This model proposed "that each of us is endowed with a degree of vulnerability that under suitable circumstances will express itself in an episode of schizophrenic illness" (p. 109). Vulnerability was viewed as a persistent trait that resulted from a genetic endowment. This trait can be influenced early in the life cycle through both life events and biological events.

This vulnerability results in a "tolerance threshold" for each individual. If his or her level of stressful life events (i.e., "suitable circumstances") is below the tolerance threshold, the individual can absorb the stress homeostatically. If the level of events exceeds this threshold, it will then result in an episode of schizophrenia. Once this stress abates and falls below the level of the vulnerability threshold, the episode will terminate and the individual will return to the level of adjustment that existed prior to the episode. If such stressor events, either endogenous or exogenous, are to be defined as suitable circumstances for the underlying vulnerability to express itself, they must occur within the two years prior to the beginning of the schizophrenic episode (i.e., the beginning of a period of florid symptomatology).

Independent of an individual's vulnerability is his or her "adaptation." This characteristic "describes the extent to which an organism responds adequately and appropriately to life's exigencies" (Zubin & Spring, 1977; p. 110). As such, adaptation is comprised of three separate factors: coping effort, competence, and coping ability. The term "coping effort" refers to the energy exerted when simple reflexive action is not enough to deal with a situation. The individual's "competence" consists of the skills and abilities that are employed to deal with the situation that he or she encounters. Finally, "coping ability" is the "result of the coping effort, or initiative, and the competence, or skill, that an organism brings to bear on formulating strategies to master life situations" (pp. 116–117). A person with a high level of vulnerability will be more at risk for psychopathology when he or she has low coping ability than if the individual possessed a high coping ability. The two constructs of coping ability and vulnerability, however, do not directly affect one another in Zubin and Spring's model.

Furthermore, later versions of the vulnerability model for schizophrenia recognized the role played by moderating variables. These new variables (e.g., personality characteristics; cf. Cohen & Edwards, Chapter 7, this volume) may cushion the impact of the stressful life event. Such cushioning could then prevent the occurrence of the initial or of possible recurrent episodes of schizophrenia (Zubin, Steinhauer, Day, & van Kammen, 1985). As in the case of coping ability, these moderating variables are assumed to be independent of both the level of vulnerability and of the triggering events.

It should be noted that the concept of a vulnerability model is not unique to Zubin and Spring (1977). For example, such vulnerability models have since been hypothesized for the development of other adult psychopathology (e.g., depression, Kuiper & Olinger, Chapter 11, this volume) and for the development of child psychopathology (e.g., Felner, 1984), including schizophrenia during adolescence (e.g., Asarnow & Goldstein, 1986). Furthermore, similar vulnerability models of the etiology and course of schizophrenia have appeared prior to 1977. For example, such a vulnerability model for schizophrenia was originally proposed by Meehl (1962). In his model, individuals born with a specific neural integrative defect were termed *schizotaxic*. Through his or her history of social learning, the individual then developed a personality organization termed *schizotypic*. These schizotypic men and women were viewed as vulnerable to decompensating (i.e., losing their "normal ability") into clinical schizophrenia. Meehl further hypothesized that nonschizotaxic individuals could never become schizotypic and, therefore, never decompensate into schizophrenia. The worst they could develop is a character disorder or a psychoneurosis. Only a minority of schizotypic individuals, however, actually developed schizophrenia. The remainder of these schizotypes would never decompensate. What caused this differential tendency for decompensation was unclear to Meehl. He believed, however, that the important factor might be the schizotypic's mother's child-rearing practices that were believed to be destructive to a child's normal development. A future version of this model viewed stress as the decompensating factor (the "diathesis-stress" model, Rosenthal, 1970). Thus Zubin and Spring's version of the vulnerability model, to a degree, can be viewed as an extension of these previous accounts.

This model of schizophrenia has numerous strengths in its description of both the etiology and course of schizophrenia. First, the vulnerability hypotheses draw on research from a variety of disparate domains (e.g., behavioral genetics, stress). Second, Zubin and Spring allowed for the investigation of potential "markers" that could characterize the individuals who are prone to episodes of schizophrenia. This type of investigation has been the center of research by Zubin and his colleagues for several years (e.g., Zubin & Steinhauer, 1981; Zubin et al., 1985). Zubin reviewed the major scientific models for schizophrenia and proposed lists of likely markers. These hypothesized markers are wide and varied, including an absence of intimacy in adolescence, postnatal cerebral damage, etc. Third, such models allow for a distinction between the *state* of schizophrenia (a distinct episode of psychotic behavior such as hallucinations and delusions) and the *trait* (the vulnerability or predisposition toward the development of this psychotic behavior). Finally, this model attempts to explain the course of schizophrenia such that chronic schizophrenia is "an artifact and perhaps a temporary aberration which may eventually disappear if proper preventive methods are applied" (Zubin, 1986, p. 478). Zubin views chronicity as possibly due to the adverse effects of institutionalization, medication, understimulation, highly critical families, labeling, continuing stressful life events or a combination of any or all of these factors. If the proper therapeutic intervention is discovered, then the chronic symptomatology should disappear. Zubin concludes that "chronicity is not a natural, inevitable outcome of schizophrenia anymore than that poverty is a natural outcome of physical disorders" (Zubin, 1986, p. 481). All things considered, these vulnerability models have been useful for organizing research findings and supporting certain avenues of investigation (e.g., markers of proneness to schizophrenic episodes). Meanwhile, certain extensions and alterations of these models have been necessary to explain more fully schizophrenic etiology and the course of the disorder.

Accordingly, numerous additions and modifications of the vulnerability-stress hypothesis for schizophrenia have continued to appear since Zubin and Spring's (1977) version was published. As modifications of the vulnerability model have appeared in recent years, each has centered on different constructs. Some of these models and the changes involved will be briefly discussed in order to provide an overview of where some vulnerability researchers have focused their attention during the past decade.

For example, Spring and Coons (1982) developed a schematic model of the vulnerability hypothesis that better explained the temporal aspect of schizophrenia as well as containing additional factors. One such factor was the plasticity of an individual's vulnerability, a dimension previously considered by Zubin and Spring (1977) to be "a relatively permanent, enduring trait" (p. 109).

The vulnerability model proposed by Gottesman and Shields (1982) incorporated schizophrenic spectrum disorders. These spectrum disorders approximate schizophrenia but are not diagnosed as such because some symptoms are missing or not at a diagnostic level. Examples of such spectrum disorders are the Cluster A Personality Disorders (Paranoid, Schizoid, and Schizotypal) in the DSM-III-R (APA, 1987). Individuals with the diagnosis of one of these personality disorders "often appear odd or eccentric" (p. 337).

Hartmann et al. (1984) proposed that, by reviewing childhood behavior patterns, one could determine who would be vulnerable to develop schizophrenia in later years. Such behaviors included an excessive amount of daydreaming, a failure to enter familiar situations with decreased apprehension, etc. Research supported the view that such behaviors were different in those children who later developed schizophrenia when compared to matched controls who remained free of the disorder.

Mirsky and Duncan's (1986) vulnerability model hypothesized that a specific biological vulnerability was necessary for the development of schizophrenia. This vulnerability was termed "schizophrenigenic brain abnormalities" (SBA). These abnormalities could result from, or be exacerbated by, intrauterine events or birth events.

In reviewing the literature on the detrimental effects of stress on the course of schizophrenia, Falloon (1986) concluded that such stress could result from a variety of sources apart from stressful life events. Work activities, social relationships, high emotional expression in the home, and urban stresses have all been implicated as sources of chronic ambient stress. High emotional expression is a term that was developed to describe the excessive emotional distress often displayed by families (or other caregivers) in response to the patient's schizophrenic behavior patterns. Such high emotional expression is poorly understood but has been repeatedly linked to the onset and recurrence of schizophrenic episodes (Goldstein, 1987).

A dual-deficit model for vulnerability was tentatively proposed by Asarnow and Goldstein (1986). Either a neurointegrative deficit (i.e., central nervous system damage) or a social skills deficit is necessary for a vulnerability to schizophrenia. These deficits can then be sources of stress in the individual's life, as can high emotional expression in the family or deviant parental communication patterns. Such stressors are viewed as resulting in increased dysfunction which, in turn, results in increased stress. Therefore "when these vulnerable children are confronted with the normative stress of adolescence, one would expect an elevated risk of breakdown" (p. 230). Asarnow and Goldstein conclude that this model is intended as a heuristic device and should be used to guide future research.

As can be seen even in such a brief overview, vulnerability models for the development of schizophrenia are at a stage of rapid growth. The models have shifted from the straight-forward model put forth by Zubin and Spring to complex multifactorial models (e.g., Nuechterlein & Liberman, 1985, cited

by Goldstein, 1987). Even with such changes, however, the present vulnerability-stress hypotheses are limited in their ability to offer a comprehensive
explanation of the complex relation between stress and the precipitation of
psychopathology (pre-episodic phase), the increase in its severity (episodic
phase), or the tendency for relapse (post-episodic phase).

LIMITATIONS OF THE VULNERABILITY FOR PSYCHOPATHOLOGY

Numerous questions surrounding vulnerability models have been discussed in the literature (Lukoff, Snyder, Ventura, & Nuechterlein, 1984;
Spring, 1981; Spring & Coons, 1982). These questions, as well as others,
can be divided into three general areas of concern: stress, schizophrenia,
and stress-schizophrenia relations. The "stress" questions include: How
does one define and measure a "stressful life event"? At what point does an
event become remote, thus contributing to vulnerability, and not recent,
contributing to the onset of an episode of psychopathology? The schizophrenia questions include: How do vulnerability theories explain the variety of characteristic symptoms often present in schizophrenia? How does
one define the actual time of onset of schizophrenia? Does a vulnerability-
stress hypothesis adequately describe the actual course of a disorder? The
stress-schizophrenia relations questions would include: Why would stress
result in schizophrenia, as opposed to any other disorder that has been
related to stress, such as coronary heart disease or depression? Doesn't
the peculiar behavior of the patient, before the onset of his or her psychotic
symptoms, result in stressful life events? Doesn't the often gross overreaction (or underreaction) to a stressful event by an individual with schizophrenia affect the impact of that event?

This section will attempt to explain why these questions are important,
especially in light of developments in research and theory on both stress
and schizophrenia. These questions will be discussed with regard to Zubin
and Spring's (1977) version of the model since it is the most frequently
employed and revised of the recent vulnerability models. Although this
section will center on reviewing questions surrounding the vulnerability-
stress hypothesis of schizophrenia, a number of the general problems in
research on stress and schizophrenia will be examined. Furthermore, it
should be remembered that, even though the emphasis in this chapter will
be on data surrounding schizophrenia, many of the arguments put forth are
applicable to stress research with other forms of psychopathology.

Questions Concerning Stress

How does one define and measure a stressful life event?

This question is central to any discussion on stressful events. A considerable number of problems are potentially inherent in the present measures of

stressful life events (cf. Martin, Chapter 6, this volume). For example, is it necessary to measure all life changes or might it be sufficient to measure only the undesirable events? By employing a specified list of possible major events, would the researcher neglect possible important events in the life of the respondent? How does a researcher control for "event fall-off," in which the number of minor stressful events that are remembered (and thus recorded) declines in proportion to the length of time since the events occurred? These and other concerns must be addressed before the measurement of stressful life events in psychopathology can proceed.

A number of other associated concerns relate more specifically to a vulnerability model. One such concern is that the level of stressful items reported at any one point in time is not independent of the level that is later reported (Eaton, 1978). One important reason for this relation is that items at any single point in time are not necessarily independent. Instead, these items cluster together, forming one larger stressful life event from several smaller ones (Hurst, 1979; Tausig, 1982). This clustering can be seen in an example from Brown and Birley (1968) who reported supposedly "independent" events in their schizophrenic patients' lives. These events can quite easily be viewed as interdependent. One of their patients left her job due to her pregnancy (event 1). Shortly thereafter she was admitted to hospital (event 2). She then had a baby (event 3). Even though nonorthogonality of life events such as these has been demonstrated, its implications have not been sufficiently related to the majority of present stress research and theory (Monroe, 1982), including the present vulnerability-stress hypotheses.

At what point does an event become remote, thus contributing to vulnerability, and not recent, contributing to the onset of an episode of psychopathology?

This question is important since the recent events are seen as the triggering episodes for the onset of schizophrenia. Conversely, the remote events are a part of the formative shaping of an individual's vulnerability to the disorder (Zubin & Spring, 1977). In a subsequent version of this model of vulnerability, "recent" was defined as being within the previous two years (Spring & Coons, 1982). If a stressful event has an effect that lasts longer than two years, is it then considered to be a remote life event? Since this change occurs, it is unclear if the converse is true. That is, are the events that are generally considered to be remote stressful life events (e.g., a highly emotional and distressing pattern of family interactions) ever considered to be recent? For example, at what age can a researcher indicate that the death of a parent is a recent life event and not a remote event?

Related to these concerns is the difficulty with stressful events gradually losing their impact over time (Brown, Harris, & Peto, 1973). For example, the death of a parent is more stressful the day after it occurs than it is two weeks later. The effect of this event at two weeks is greater than it would be 18 months later. Furthermore, the early death of a parent in an individual's life could have consequences far beyond the event. For example, the lack of parental support during adolescence could result in greater stress. It might be even more difficult to state in a vulnerability model any particular point in time when life events will suddenly become weaker and lose their effect as a trigger. Nevertheless, such issues arise when a strict definitional division is imposed between recent and remote stressful life events.

Questions Concerning Schizophrenia

How do vulnerability theories explain the variety of characteristic symptoms often present in schizophrenia?

Although the debate continues as to whether or not schizophrenia is one or several clinical entities (cf. Ciompi, 1984; Hays, 1984), it is generally recognized that it can express itself through a variety of symptoms (e.g., prominent auditory hallucinations, catatonic rigidity, bizarre systematized delusions). This heterogeneity of symptoms has long been viewed as responsible for the wide variance in schizophrenic responses to objective measures (Bannister, 1968; Shakow, 1963). Even so, research and theory often ignore this considerable heterogeneity among schizophrenics. Zubin (1986) argues that "the taxonomy depends upon the state of the art, and until we are forced to do otherwise by the weight of the evidence, we can hold on to a unitary concept of schizophrenia, despite its heterogeneity" (p. 485).

Later vulnerability models have attempted to explain this heterogeneity. For example, Spring and Coons (1982) hypothesize that heterogeneity in schizophrenia might be the result of different: (1) premorbid levels, (2) etiologies, or (3) manifestations of vulnerability (e.g., personality vs. abnormality of brain function). Research indicates, however, that there are definite distinctions between the schizophrenic subtypes and these distinctions are not addressed fully by this explanation.

A variety of mutually exclusive types are defined in the DSM-III-R (APA, 1987) diagnostic category of schizophrenia. These five types closely parallel the subtypes proposed by Kraepelin and Bleuler at the turn of the century. The "Catatonic Type" has the essential feature of marked psychomotor disturbance. The "Disorganized Type" is diagnosed by incoherence, marked loosening of associations, or grossly disorganized behavior combined with grossly inappropriate or flat affect. This type is sometimes referred to as "Hebephrenic" in other diagnostic systems (e.g., the Ninth Revision of the International Classification of Diseases (ICD-9), World Health Organization, 1977). Inclusion in the "Paranoid Type" is defined either by a preoccupation with systematized delusions or by frequent auditory hallucinations centering around a single theme. The "Undifferentiated Type" is for patients who display prominent psychotic symptoms but who are not classifiable into any one specific category. Finally, the "Residual Type" is diagnosed when an individual has had at least one episode of schizophrenia and has signs of the illness but does not display prominent psychotic symptoms at the time the diagnosis is being made.

There are several likely distinctions for subtyping schizophrenic subjects apart from those types proposed by the DSM-III-R. Some researchers use multivariate statistical techniques such as cluster analysis to determine what classification schemas can be identified by investigating the naturally occurring symptom groups (e.g., Carpenter, Bartko, Carpenter, & Strauss, 1976; Farmer, McGuffin, & Spitznagel, 1983). These methods, however, have inherent limitations that preclude their widespread usage in psychopathology research (Fleiss & Zubin, 1969; Skinner & Blashfield, 1982). As a result of such problems, the impact of this research has been limited (Meehl, 1979).

Crow (1980a, 1980b) hypothesized that there are two distinguishable forms of schizophrenia: Type I and Type II (see also Crow, 1985). The Type I schizophrenics were characterized by: (1) displaying more "positive symptoms," (2) being most commonly seen in acute schizophrenia, (3) indicating a good response to neuroleptic medication, (4) not displaying any indications of intellectual impairment, (5) having a disorder course which could be reversed, and (6) having an increased number of dopamine receptors. The positive symptoms are those symptomatic behaviors that are additional to an individual's normal behavior patterns (e.g., hallucinations). Crow hypothesized that these symptoms resulted from the accompanying increase in dopamine receptors.

Those symptoms that represent a deficit in normal functioning (e.g., the absence of appropriate emotional response) are termed "negative symptoms" and are displayed by Crow's Type II schizophrenics. These schizophrenics are also characterized by: (1) their higher degree of chronicity, (2) responding poorly to neuroleptics, (3) sometimes displaying signs of intellectual impairment, (4) often not having a reversible course to the disorder, and (5) symptoms that are thought to result from cell loss and structural changes in the brain. Although this classification scheme continues to inspire considerable research, it is also recognized as having several problems (cf. Andreasen, 1985; Sommers, 1985). For example, Zubin (1986) proposed that there is no clear evidence that the negative symptoms are the result of anything more than the adverse effects of long-term hospitalization and institutionalization and are present in a wide variety of individuals who exist in monotonous and stimulus-deprived environments.

The most investigated schizophrenic subtyping might be the division into a paranoid subtype and a nonparanoid subtype (e.g., Chapman & Chapman, 1973; Magaro, 1981). Although there are limitations in the use of this distinction (Berkowitz, 1981), it still inspires considerable research and theory (Magaro, 1984; Neufeld, in press). Research has indicated that appraisal, coping, and response strategies (see Chapters 1 and 2) may differ between paranoid and nonparanoid patients both quantitatively and qualitatively (Broga

& Neufeld, 1981; Dobson & Neufeld, 1982, 1988; Shean, 1982). Despite considerable heterogeneity, as outlined here, present vulnerability models do not adequately offer an explanation that encompasses subtype research. Nor does the present model hypothesize why differences in displayed symptom behaviors should exist among schizophrenic patients.

How does one define the actual time of onset of schizophrenia?

The timing of the onset of schizophrenia during its insidious course has remained one of the "thorniest issues" for the present vulnerability model (Spring, 1981). Does it arise at the time of the development of a preschizophrenic spectrum disorder such as a schizotypal personality disorder? Could it arise at the time of the arrival of prodromal (i.e., warning) symptoms such as an increased alienation from friends or family? Or does schizophrenia begin at the time of the onset of specific psychotic symptoms (Spring & Coons, 1982)? Some researchers have used the date of admission to hospital as the point of onset of psychiatric illness (Schless, Teichman, Mendels, & DiGiacomo, 1977). Research has found the need for exact timing of the onset of schizophrenia to be important because it allows for the distinction to be made between those life events that are causing the disorder and those events that result from it (e.g., Jacobs & Myers, 1976). Zubin and Spring recognize the necessity for exact timing in their version of the vulnerability model, not only for understanding previous research, but also for the proper investigation of many of the model's hypotheses.

Recommendations have been made in an attempt to overcome this limitation. Zubin and Spring (1977) suggested that evidence of a sharp plummeting of coping effectiveness could be employed as the indicator of onset. Yet, there is no method as to how this "sharp plummeting" can be objectively measured. Nor is the research evidence strongly supportive of such plummeting defining the onset of the disorder. As a result, this definition has not been employed widely.

It has also been suggested that measurements should be made at each stage in the development of schizophrenia to determine how each possible time of onset relates to stressful life events (Spring & Coons, 1982). Bebbington (1987) reports employing such a methodology because the correct time of onset was a major concern for the recent World Health Organization (WHO) international study of life events in schizophrenia. To investigate the differential impact of life events at the different stages in the development of the disorder, the WHO collaborative study investigated three separate stages of change: (1) from a state without symptoms, (2) from a state with only minor neurotic symptoms, and (3) from a state with mild psychotic symptoms. The results of this study will soon be reported and it is hoped that they will facilitate the explanation concerning the most important stage in which stressful life events affect onset.

Does a vulnerability-stress hypothesis adequately describe the actual course of a disorder?

Zubin and Spring's version of the vulnerability model proposes that the individual will return to his or her prior level of adjustment when the level of stressful events falls below the threshold. This view of schizophrenia, in terms of being either present or absent, does not allow for many aspects of the disorder to be investigated. For example, few schizophrenics return to their previous levels of functioning after the reduction of their initial psychotic symptoms. More often, their symptoms will first lessen in severity (or go into temporary remission) and then later increase (Carpenter, 1981). Furthermore, some patients will experience no relief of their symptoms. This chronic nature of the disorder could be explained by a schizophrenic perceiving the stressful events in his or her environment as being chronic. Some of the individual's symptoms may increase stress (e.g., persecutory auditory hallucinations). Likewise, research indicates that some difficulties are present throughout the life cycle of the schizophrenic (e.g., trouble with authority, Serban & Woloshin, 1974). Nonetheless, vulnerability models often view the course of a disorder in terms of a shifting between a dichotomy of "premorbid functioning" and "psychopathology." By such a proposition, however, the present vulnerability models seem limited in their ability to address specifically the fluctuating, sometimes chronic, levels of symptomatology.

Questions Concerning Stress-Schizophrenia Relations

Why would stress result in schizophrenia, as opposed to any other disorder that has been related to stress, such as coronary heart disease or depression?

It has been pointed out elsewhere that this vulnerability model does not contain any elements or make any statements concerning schizophrenia that could be considered unique to that disorder (Lukoff, Snyder, Ventura, & Nuechterlein, 1984). An increase in stressful life events has been linked to a considerable number of disorders, both medical and psychiatric (Rahe & Arthur, 1978). Furthermore, there appears to be no quantitative or qualitative difference in the stressful events that affect the various disorders (Rabkin, 1980). Thus Zubin and Spring's model does not appear to account for the development of schizophrenia, specifically, as opposed to the development of some other disorder. Those stressful aspects that can be considered unique to schizophrenia, such as distorted thought process and behavioral deviance within a patient's family (e.g., Lewis, Rodnick, & Goldstein, 1981) are not considered necessary in Zubin and Spring's vulnerability model.

Doesn't the often gross overreaction (or underreaction) to a stressful event by an individual with schizophrenia affect the impact of that event?

Related to this question is the difficulty regarding the present definition of stress incorporated by a vulnerability model. In the present model, stressors are defined as "objectively specifiable life events" (Spring & Coons, 1982, p. 36). This definition is used primarily because it allows the criterion and the predictor variables to be conceptually separate and distinct. Such an argument has been put forth by the DSM-III-R (APA, 1987). In a cautionary note on the rating of psychosocial stressors on the Axis IV, the DSM-III-R warns that the rating should be based on the severity of a stressor itself. The rating should not be based on the patient's idiosyncratic response to a particular stressor. Such responses are thought to reflect individual vulnerability. As a result of this type of separation, the stress that results from a life event would be viewed as equal both across different individuals in the same point in time and across different points in time in the same individual.

On the other hand, Lazarus and Folkman's (1984) prominent definition of stress could be every bit as applicable as the preceding definition to the present context. They hypothesize that "the judgment that a particular person-environment relationship is stressful *hinges on cognitive appraisal*" (p. 21; italics added). The inclusion of such idiosyncratic meanings for each patient, however, would make any large-scale research more difficult (Strauss, 1981). While less methodologically tidy than the approach associated with Axis IV of the DSM-III-R, the approach to stress of Lazarus and Folkman may provide considerable insight into otherwise enigmatic observations (cf. Dohrenwend & Shrout, 1985; Lazarus, DeLongis, Folkman, & Gruen, 1985).

Research has not generally found strong support for weighting life events in terms of how much of an impact the individual believes the event had on him or her (Ross & Mirowsky, 1979; Zimmerman, 1983). Some research on the prediction of severity of psychiatric symptoms, however, has indicated that subjective appraisals of life events are more accurate than the average weightings of life-event severity (Marziali & Pilkonis, 1986). It would seem reasonable to expect that certain everyday acts, such as watching a television program, could be very stressful for an individual who believed that a voice from the television was giving instructions to carry out evil behaviors. Rabkin (1980), in her review of stressful life events and schizophrenia, noted this problem: "Those who become schizophrenic are believed to be exceptionally sensitive to perceived or actual threats to self-esteem, and psychotic episodes may follow situations not ordinarily regarded as hazardous" (p. 411). In other words, when one compares schizophrenic appraisals of life events to the appraisals of nonschizophrenics, "a mountain in one life may be a molehill in another" (Spring & Coons, 1982, p. 34).

Such differences in the appraisal of stressful life events have been theorized previously. Unfortunately, little research has been done in the area of cognitive appraisal in psychopathology (Neufeld & Mothersill, 1980). The research that does exist indicates that the appraisals are both quantitatively and qualitatively different between nonpatient controls and schizophrenic patients (Dobson & Neufeld, in press; Shean, Faia, & Schmaltz, 1974). Although specific subjective appraisals are recognized as important by Zubin and Spring (1977), they did not expressly include such appraisals in their vulnerability model.

Doesn't the peculiar behavior of the patient, before the onset of psychotic symptoms, result in stressful life events?

Linked to the questions regarding the idiosyncratic appraisal of stress by schizophrenics and the actual timing of onset is the question of which came first: the stressful life event or the psychopathology. This issue is inherent in all research on the relation between illness and stressful life events (e.g., Billings & Moos, 1982). Nevertheless, it is in the area of psychiatric illness research where it perhaps causes the greatest amount of difficulty (Rabkin & Struening, 1976). Research indicates that the frequently employed measures of stress, such as the Schedule of Recent Events (SRE, Holmes & Rahe, 1967), are confounded with the symptoms of psychological disorder (Dohrenwend, Dohrenwend, Dodson, & Shrout, 1984). Even though Zubin and Spring (1977) state that such stressful life events, which occur as the patient "slides" toward schizophrenia, may not be independent of the disorder, they do not integrate this dependence in their version of the vulnerability model. Instead, they suggest that researchers try their best to separate the two constructs (i.e., schizophrenia and the initiation of stress) since it is the only way that they believe research can go ahead (Spring & Coons, 1982). Not all researchers, however, agree with this type of separation, viewing it as a loss of validity that is given for the sake of making an investigation more manageable (Kasl, 1983).

Zubin and Spring's (1977) vulnerability model of schizophrenia represented a much-needed effort to draw together previous research on the etiology of schizophrenia from a variety of disparate sources. The model has been extended and modified to incorporate additional features of stress-schizophrenia relations, and to accommodate more recent research and theory on these relations. Throughout, a premium has been placed on simplicity and clarity, to facilitate empirical research. More elaborate models have since been developed in response to apparent requirements for increased complexity stemming from existing evidence (e.g., Asarnow & Goldstein, 1986). These models, however, have not inspired as much research and debate as has that of Zubin and Spring.

MECHANISMS OF SUSCEPTIBILITY TO STRESS IN SCHIZOPHRENIA

The first part of this chapter dealt with some prominent accounts of the avenues that stress might take in contributing to schizophrenic psychopathology, and, to a lesser extent, those whereby pathological behavior might contribute to stress. In this section, we consider possible reasons as to why stress might present special problems to those experiencing episodes of schizophrenia and to those who may be vulnerable to experiencing such episodes. Our concern, then, is with the *mechanisms* of susceptibility to the adverse effects of stress among these individuals. Adverse effects may take the form of precipitating the disorder, increasing its severity, or fostering relapse, as discussed previously.

The present emphasis then, is on what had been referred to by Zubin and Spring as "coping ability," a component of "adaptation" to stress. Reduced coping ability was considered to raise susceptibility to stress and episodes of florid symptomatology. Our concern now primarily centers on certain factors that might compromise ability to cope. Note that stress, as referred to here, should not be viewed as stemming necessarily from relatively traumatic life events. It may be associated simply with moderate or mild environmental demands and everyday activities. This orientation is in keeping with the observations on the objective severity of life events and schizophrenia, as discussed in the first part of the chapter.

It was pointed out earlier that the avenues whereby stress might relate to schizophrenia were potentially complex and difficult to isolate. Stress might be (1) an antecedent of symptomatology, (2) a consequent, or (3) at different times an antecedent, and then a consequence of symptom increase. Pinpointing the sources of particular difficulty for schizophrenic patients is equally challenging when it comes to stress. How does stress impinge on those in pre-episodic, episodic, or post-episodic phases of schizophrenia in ways that it might not impinge on others? Related to the preceding question, how might schizophrenia reduce one's ability to cope? How might such problems manifest themselves in terms of symptomatology? Furthermore, the issues that are associated with these questions are in all likelihood interrelated. Perhaps reduced coping ability ushers in greater stress impact of certain events; greater stress impact, in turn, may disrupt any residual coping ability. Similarly, the disturbing effects of symptomatology on others and possibly on the patient him- or herself may exacerbate stress, leading to even further increases in symptomatology, and so on.

Clearly, the present topic could occupy an entire volume. The presentation of approaches to managing these problems could occupy an additional volume. The most that can be hoped for in the present discussion is to suggest tentative directions where some resolution of current enigmas may be lurking. The following strategy is used to tender such example directions. Accounts of psychological stress and coping are scrutinized for factors that may present special problems to those suffering from schizophrenia (or who might be prone to do so). At the same time, we examine some of the cognitive-behavioral abnormalities in schizophrenia with the accounts of stress and coping in mind. Of special interest are those abnormalities likely to compromise the individual's stress negotiation. This general tactic is intended to uncover potentially promising points of intersection between the domains of stress and coping, and that of schizophrenic disorders.

Stress Arousal and Its Possible Consequences in Schizophrenia

One source of susceptibility to stress in schizophrenia may comprise a tendency to experience elevated levels of stress arousal. In a certain sense, susceptibility to stress arousal may be an intrinsic feature of the disorder. Common measures of stress arousal were described in Chapter 3. The measures most relevant to the present discussion are psychophysiological measures, since they, more than the other measures discussed in Chapter 3, have been used in studies of schizophrenia.

An increased level of arousal, troublesome in and of itself, may have several untoward byproducts. A number of day-to-day activities required for self-maintenance may suffer. Such activities may involve hygiene, nutrition, and communication with others. An individual with elevated reactivity to activating stimulation generally may find it unsettling to engage in such daily self-maintenance activities. Withdrawal from such activities often is sufficient to occasion referral to mental health agencies, and perhaps hospitalization (Foulds, 1965; Sarbin, 1969). Taken to an extreme, such withdrawal may result in behaviors related to catatonia, such as stereotyped behavior or stuporous states. Thus elevated stress arousal to activating stimulation may undermine (negatively reinforce) transactions leading to a "normal life style" (see also Beuhring, Cudek, Mednick, Walker, & Schulsinger, 1982; Mednick & Schulsinger, 1974).

Note that such transactions often depend on cognitive operations—operations involving information processing and memory. The occupational setting, for example, may be one where the performance of cognitive tasks is routine. As observed in Chapter 2 of this volume, stress arousal can adversely affect memory and information processing. Consequently, the individual who has not withdrawn, but who continues to engage in daily self-maintenance and occupational duties, may not have escaped the repercussions of elevated stress arousal. This individual may find that such activities are impaired to the degree that they entail memory and information processing.

Based on these observations, it may be tempting to identify a proclivity toward elevated arousal as the principle mechanism of susceptibility to stress in schizophrenia. Although such proclivity may be undesirable in its own right, it may also have far-reaching consequences for the activities of daily functioning. Before embracing the above position, however, the following two notes of caution should be considered. First, a tendency toward elevated stress arousal is far from universal among schizophrenics. Indeed, a significant subset of schizophrenic samples have been characterized as "under-responsive" to activating stimulation. Descriptions of this heterogeneity in responsivity among schizophrenics have been amply provided elsewhere (e.g., Spohn & Patterson, 1979; Venables, 1983).

Second, consider the overlap between the adverse effects of stress on memory and information processing, on the one hand, and schizophrenic deficits in these functions, on the other. Some of the adverse effects of stress on information processing are paralleled by information-processing deficits in schizophrenia. One such instance involves the organization of presented items in memory so as to facilitate later recall (i.e., mnemonic organization). As noted in Chapter 2, mnemonic organization has been found to decrease somewhat with stress arousal. In like fashion, mnemonic organization has been observed to decline in schizophrenia (e.g., Koh, Kayton, & Berry, 1973).

Some of the adverse effects of stress, however, appear to be notably absent in schizophrenia. For example, the manipulation of information in "short-term" or "working memory" (e.g., manipulations that might be involved in solving simple numerical puzzles or unscrambling anagrams) seems to deteriorate with increased stress arousal (e.g., Hamilton, 1980; Millar, 1980; see also Eysenck, Chapter 4, this volume). Among schizophrenic samples, however, such short-term memory functions generally have been found *not* to be impaired (e.g., Broga & Neufeld, 1981).

This type of caution by no means disqualifies a tendency toward elevated stress arousal as a potentially important source of schizophrenic stress susceptibility. A number of difficulties encountered by many schizophrenics may be related to such a tendency. Note also that elevated arousal during incipient stages of the disorder subsequently may be enhanced by the development of certain symptoms. The DSM-III-R, for example, lists anger and argumentativeness as associated features of paranoid schizophrenia, along with unfounded anxiety.

Attentional Capacity, Information Processing, and Coping

Another possible mechanism of susceptibility to stress in schizophrenia may be that of reduced attentional capacity (e.g., Gjerde, 1983; Knight & Russell, 1978; Nuechterlein & Dawson, 1984). Reduced attentional capacity may undermine coping efficiency as will be seen momentarily.

Attentional capacity for the present purposes can be thought of as the pool of resources available to the individual for carrying out cognitive tasks (see Hasher & Zacks, 1979; Kahneman, 1973). The section on Stress and Information Processing of Chapter 2 contains a brief description of attentional capacity as it relates to stress.

It was noted in Chapter 2 that stress arousal may deplete the amount of attentional capacity available for the transaction of cognitive operations. As discussed in the preceding subsection, some schizophrenics may be prone toward heightened arousal. Heightened arousal, then, may reduce attentional capacity for such individuals.

However, reduction in attentional capacity may occur in schizophrenia for reasons other than elevation in stress arousal. Earlier theories of reduced attentional capacity among schizophrenics, for instance, did not necessarily rest on the construct of proneness toward elevated arousal (e.g., Knight & Russell, 1978). Thus a reduction in attentional capacity in schizophrenia may be a function of pathological processes other than those linked theoretically to heightened arousal.

How is diminished attentional capacity expressed empirically? Empirical consequences are thought to include slower rates of carrying out cognitive operations, and/or less accuracy in performing such operations (see, e.g., Townsend & Ashby, 1983). Furthermore, capacity reduction may express itself differently on different components of cognitive tasks. Some tasks or task components may withstand capacity reduction more than others. Task components that require less attentional capacity to maintain a given speed of execution and their level of accuracy may not deteriorate noticeably when available capacity is reduced. One example comprises certain manipulations of information in short-term memory, as was described earlier.

Other components of cognitive tasks, however, may be more sensitive to diminished capacity. One such component may be the initial assimilation or encoding of stimulus information. Stimulus encoding can be viewed approximately as the translation of stimulation in its raw form into a "cognitive format" that facilitates subsequent cognitive operations. Often, encoding involves the extraction of certain properties from the presenting stimulation that are particularly relevant to the task at hand. For instance, the raw stimulation might be a simple sentence referring to an adjacent object—"It is true that the block is red." The task at hand simply may be that of verifying the accuracy of this sentence. The verification process may be aided by condensing the sentence into a smaller set of linguistic components. The above sentence, for example, might be condensed into two components, one component representing the affirmative status of the sentence, and the other representing the object being referred to. This encoded version of the sentence schematically is portrayed as: "AFFIRMATIVE, RED BLOCK" (Carpenter & Just, 1975).

The encoding of raw stimulation into a format facilitating subsequent cognitive operations has been found quite consistently to be slower among schizophrenic samples, particularly those individuals classified as paranoid schizophrenic. Reduced speed of stimulus encoding among these subjects has been found to occur on a variety of both linguistic and nonlinguistic tasks (Neufeld, 1988).

A toll of such reduced attentional capacity, then, may take the form of slower encoding of presenting stimulation as discussed above. Many routine activities may be hampered by slower encoding. Catching the meaning of normally rapid speech may be difficult; if so, it could be discouraging to engage in conversation. If such individuals did engage in conversation, their speech would appear incoherent. They could also find it difficult to properly encode internal stimulation, resulting in hallucinations (Hoffman, 1986), and possibly inappropriate emotional response and disorganized thought processes (cf. George & Neufeld, 1985). Excessive concreteness and strong delusional systems could be viewed as attempts to force order on incoming stimuli that are unable to be properly encoded. More generally, the significance of any stimulation that changes quickly may be lost. A number of activities involved in daily self-maintenance behaviors may be undermined to the degree that such activities require intact speed of stimulus encoding.

Other activities that may be disrupted by slower stimulus encoding include those of coping with environmental threat, or with surges in environmental demands. Efficiency of coping as related to information processing is discussed in Chapter 2.

The possible mechanisms of susceptibility to stress in schizophrenia discussed here are but two examples of a variety of mechanisms that may be involved. An exhaustive treatment of this topic is not feasible here. However, the examples presented should serve to illustrate the identification of tentative sources of susceptibility to stress in schizophrenia by focusing on the intersection between the research domains of psychological stress and coping, and psychological functioning in schizophrenia. Note that several accounts of schizophrenic symptomatology (primarily thought disorder) have implemented stress as an integral construct. Such accounts have been reviewed previously (e.g., Neufeld & Mothersill, 1980).

It should be emphasized that many, if not most, of the observations on psychological functioning in schizophrenia have been drawn from data obtained from episodic, hospitalized patients. Extraneous variables associated with hospitalization (e.g., institutionalization; medication), can complicate the interpretation of such data (see, e.g., Neale & Oltmanns, 1980). These difficulties are not necessarily circumvented by studying patients whose symptoms have remitted (e.g., Asarnow & MacCrimmon, 1978; Dobson & Neufeld, in press). One advantage of studying episodic patients is that false positives—those incorrectly designated as "episode prone"—tend to be minimized in the research sample. In any event, generalization of inferences derived from data produced during periods of hospitalization to other phases of disturbance, clearly must be done with utmost caution, pending additional research.

SUMMARY

The first part of the chapter introduced the question of what is the role of stress in schizophrenia. The increasing recognition that stress can be related to psychopathology is noted by its inclusion as Axis IV in the DSM-III-R. The early research with respect to stress as an etiological agent for schizophrenia was briefly reviewed. While later research questioned the notion that high uncover potentially promising points of intersection between the domains of stress and coping, and that of schizophrenic disorders.

The vulnerability-stress hypotheses for the etiology of schizophrenia were then reviewed, with emphasis on Zubin and Spring's (1977) model. These models hypothesize that individuals differ with respect to their susceptibility to the development of schizophrenia, in part as a function of their susceptibility to stress. While these models have numerous strengths, general concerns and questions regarding their apparent limitations were discussed.

These questions centered around three areas. First, with respect to stress, difficulties in the measurement of stressful life events were discussed. Also discussed was how the time that passed since a stressful event affects its impact. Second, with respect to schizophrenia, questions were raised as to how the model explains the variety in symptomatology and how it explains the course of the disorder. Difficulties in the timing of onset of schizophrenia were also discussed. Third, with respect to the relation between stress and schizophrenia, the question was raised as to why stress would result in schizophrenia as opposed to any other medical or psychiatric disorder. Furthermore, the often unique appraisal by schizophrenics of stressful life events was discussed as was the possibility that a schizophrenic's unusual behavior before an episode of the disorder could, in and of itself, result in greater stress.

In the second part of this chapter, some possible sources of susceptibility to stress among those individuals undergoing, or prone to undergo, episodes of florid symptomatology were examined. It was suggested that cognitive deficits in schizophrenia and degrees of experienced stress may interact: Cognitive deficits in schizophrenia may undermine coping activity that normally would stem incremental stress; the rise in stress arousal, in turn, may exacerbate cognitive deficit.

The possibility of a tendency among schizophrenics to display evidence of increased stress arousal was raised. Implications of such a tendency for engaging in those day-to-day activities required for basic self maintenance were drawn out. Some limitations of a disposition toward heightened stress arousal and its consequences, as primary sources of stress-related difficulties in schizophrenia, were presented briefly.

Attentional capacity, the pool of resources devoted to cognitive operations, was then examined with respect to stress transactions in schizophrenia. It has been suggested that schizophrenic deficits in cognitive operations may result from *diminished* attentional capacity. Diminished attentional capacity may take its toll on some cognitive operations more than others. An example of the former case is the encoding of raw stimulus material into a format facilitating subsequent cognitive processing. Stimulus encoding was observed to be slower among schizophrenic samples, especially those designated as paranoid. Consequences of a reduced rate of encoding for transacting routine activities and for coping with threat were considered.

References

American Psychiatric Association. (1980). *Diagnostic and statistical manual of mental disorders* (3rd ed.). Washington, DC.

American Psychiatric Association. (1987). *Diagnostic and statistical manual of mental disorders* (3rd ed., rev. ed.). Washington, DC.

Andreasen, N. C. (1985). Positive vs. negative schizophrenia: A critical evaluation. *Schizophrenia Bulletin, 11,* 380–389.

Asarnow, J. R., & Goldstein, M. J. (1986). Schizophrenia during adolescence and early childhood: A developmental perspective on risk research. *Clinical Psychology Review, 6,* 211–235.

Asarnow, R. F., & MacCrimmon, D. J. (1978). Residual performance deficit in clinically remitted schizophrenics: A marker of schizophrenia? *Journal of Abnormal Psychology, 87,* 597–608.

Astrachan, R. M., Harrow, M., Brauer, A. I., Schwartz, A., Schwartz, C., & Tucker, G. (1972). A checklist for the diagnosis of schizophrenia. *British Journal of Psychiatry, 121,* 529–539.

Bannister, D. (1968). The logical requirements of research into schizophrenia. *British Journal of Psychiatry, 114,* 181–188.

Bebbington, P. E. (1987). Life events in schizophrenia: The WHO collaborative study. *Social Psychiatry, 22,* 179–180.

Beck, J. C., & Worthen, K. (1972). Precipitating stress, crisis theory, and hospitalization in schizophrenia and depression. *Archives of General Psychiatry, 26,* 123–129.

Berkowitz, R. (1981). The distinction between paranoid and nonparanoid forms of schizophrenia. *British Journal of Clinical Psychology, 20,* 15–23.

Beuhring, T., Cudek, R., Mednick, S. A., Walker, E. F., & Schulsinger, F. (1982). Vulnerability to environmental stress: High-risk research on the development of schizophrenia. In R. W. J. Neufeld (Ed.), *Psychological stress and psychopathology* (pp. 67–90). New York: McGraw-Hill.

Billings, A. C., & Moos, R. H. (1982). Stressful life events and symptoms: A longitudinal model. *Health Psychology, 1,* 99–117.

Bleuler, E. (1950). *Dementia praecox or the group of schizophrenias* (J. Zinkin, Trans.). New York: International Universities Press. (Original work published in 1911).

Broga, M. I., & Neufeld, R. W. J. (1981). Evaluation of information-sequential aspects of schizophrenic performance: Framework and current findings. *Journal of Nervous and Mental Disease, 169,* 559–568.

Brown, G. W., & Birley, J. L. T. (1968). Crises and life changes and the onset of schizophrenia. *Journal of Health and Social Behavior, 9,* 203–214.

Brown, G. W., Harris, T. O., & Peto, J. (1973). Life events and psychiatric disorders. Part 2: Nature of the causal link. *Psychological Medicine, 3,* 159–176.

Cancro, R. (1985). History and overview of schizophrenia. In H. I. Kaplan & B. J. Sadock (Eds.), *Comprehensive textbook of psychiatry* (4th ed., pp. 631–643). Baltimore, MD: Williams & Wilkins.

Carpenter, P. A., & Just, M. A. (1975). Sentence comprehension: A psycholinguistic processing model of verification. *Psychological Review, 82,* 45–73.

Carpenter, W. T., Jr. (1981). Commentary on "How to break the logjam in schizophrenia: A look beyond genetics" by Joseph Zubin and Stuart Steinhauer. *Journal of Nervous and Mental Disease, 169,* 495–496.

Carpenter, W. T., Jr., Bartko, J. J., Carpenter, C. L., & Strauss, J. S. (1976). Another view of schizophrenia subtypes: A report from the International Pilot Study of Schizophrenia. *Archives of General Psychiatry, 33,* 508–516.

Carpenter, W. T., Jr., Strauss, J. S., & Bartko, J. J. (1973). Flexible system for the diagnosis of schizophrenia: Report from the WHO international pilot study of schizophrenia. *Science, 182,* 1275–1278.

Chapman, L. J., & Chapman, J. P. (1973). *Disordered thought in schizophrenia.* New York: Appleton-Century-Crofts.

Ciompi, L. (1984). Is there really a schizophrenia? The long-term course of psychotic phenomena. *British Journal of Psychiatry, 145,* 636–640.

Cohen, S., & Edwards, J. R. (1989). Personality characteristics as moderators of the relationship between stress and disorder. In R. W. J. Neufeld (Ed.), *Advances in the investigation of psychological stress* (pp. 235–283). New York: Wiley.

Cromwell, R. L. (1975). Assessment of schizophrenia. In M. R. Rosenzweig & L. W. Porter (Eds.), *Annual review of psychology: Vol. 26* (pp. 593–619). Palo Alto, CA: Annual Reviews.

Crow, T. J. (1980a). Molecular pathway of schizophrenia: More than one disease process? *British Medical Journal, 280,* 66–68.

Crow, T. J. (1980b). Positive and negative schizophrenic symptoms and the role of dopamine: 2. *British Journal of Psychiatry, 137,* 379–386.

Crow, T. J. (1985). The two syndrome concept: Origins and current status. *Schizophrenia Bulletin, 11,* 471–486.

Dobson, D. J. G., & Neufeld, R. W. J. (1982). Paranoid-nonparanoid schizophrenic distinctions in implementing external conceptual constraints. *Journal of Nervous and Mental Disease, 170,* 614–621.

Dobson, D., & Neufeld, R. W. J. (1987). Span of apprehension among remitted schizophrenics using small visual angles. *Journal of Nervous and Mental Disease, 175,* 362–366.

Dobson, D., & Neufeld, R. W. J. (in press) Stress responses and coping propensity among paranoid and nonparanoid, episodic and remitted schizophrenics. *Canadian Journal of Behavioural Science.*

Dohrenwend, B. P., & Egri, G. (1981). Recent stressful life events and episodes of schizophrenia. *Schizophrenia Bulletin, 7,* 12–23.

Dohrenwend, B. P., & Shrout, P. E. (1985). "Hassles" in the conceptualization and measurement of life stress variables. *American Psychologist, 40,* 780–785.

Dohrenwend, B. S., Dohrenwend, B. P., Dodson, M., & Shrout, P. E. (1984). Symptoms, hassles, social supports, and life events: Problem of confounded measures. *Journal of Abnormal Psychology, 93,* 222–230.

Doran, A. R., Brier, A., & Roy, A. (1986). Differential diagnosis and diagnostic systems in schizophrenia. *Psychiatric Clinics of North America, 9(1),* 17–33.

Eaton, W. W. (1978). Life events, social supports, and psychiatric symptoms: A re-analysis of the New Haven data. *Journal of Health and Social Behavior, 19,* 230–234.

Eysenck, M. W. (1989). Personality, stress arousal, and cognitive processes in stress transactions. In R. W. J. Neufeld (Ed.), *Advances in the investigation of psychological stress* (pp. 133–160). New York: Wiley.

Falloon, I. R. H. (1986). Family stress and schizophrenia: Theory and practice. *Psychiatric Clinics of North America, 9(1),* 165–182.

Farmer, A. E., McGuffin, P., & Spitznagel, E. L. (1983). Heterogeneity in schizophrenia: A cluster-analytic approach. *Psychiatry Research, 8,* 1–12.

Feighner, J. P., Robins, E., Guze, S. B., Woodruff, R. A., Jr., Winouker, G., & Munoz, R. (1972). Diagnostic criteria for use in psychiatric research. *Archives of General Psychiatry, 26,* 57–63.

Felner, R. D. (1984). Vulnerability in childhood: A preventive framework for understanding children's efforts to cope with life stress and transitions. In M. Roberts & L. Peterson (Eds.), *Prevention of problems in childhood: Psychological research and applications* (pp. 133–169). New York: Wiley.

Fleiss, J. L., & Zubin, J. (1969). On the methods and theory of clustering. *Multivariate Behavioral Research, 4,* 235–250.

Foulds, C. A. (1965). *Personality and mental illness.* London: Tavistock.

George, L., & Neufeld, R. W. J. (1985). Cognition and symptomatology in schizophrenia. *Schizophrenia Bulletin, 11,* 264–285.

Gjerde, P. F. (1983). Attentional capacity dysfunction and arousal in schizophrenia. *Psychological Bulletin, 93,* 57–72.

Goldstein, M. J. (1987). Psychosocial issues. *Schizophrenia Bulletin, 13,* 157–171.

Gottesman, I. I., & Shields, J. (1972). *Schizophrenia and genetics: A twin study vantage point.* New York: Academic.

Gottesman, I. I., & Shields, J. (1982). *Schizophrenia: The epigenetic puzzle.* New York: Cambridge University Press.

Gur, R. E. (1978). Left hemisphere dysfunction and left hemisphere overactivation in schizophrenia. *Journal of Abnormal Psychology, 87,* 226–228.

Hamilton, V. (1980). An information processing analysis of environmental stress and life crises. In I. G. Sarason & C. D. Spielberger (Eds.), *Stress and anxiety: Vol. 7* (pp. 13–30). New York: Hamilton.

Hammer, M., Makiesky-Barrow, S., & Gutwirth, L. (1978). Social networks and schizophrenia. *Schizophrenia Bulletin, 4,* 522–545.

Hartmann, E., Milofsky, E., Vaillant, G., Oldfield, M., Falke, R., & Ducey, C. (1984). Vulnerability to schizophrenia: Prediction of adult schizophrenia using childhood information. *Archives of General Psychiatry, 41,* 1050–1056.

Hasher, L., & Zacks, R. T. (1979). Automatic and effortful processes in memory. *Journal of Experimental Psychology: General, 108,* 356–388.

Hays, P. (1984). The nosological status of schizophrenia. *Lancet, 1,* 1342–1345.

Helzer, J. E., Brockington, I. F., & Kendell, R. E. (1981). Predictive validity of DSM-III and Feighner definitions of schizophrenia: A comparison with research diagnostic criteria and CATEGO. *Archives of General Psychiatry, 38,* 791–797.

Hoffman, R. E. (1986). Verbal hallucination and language production processes in schizophrenia. *Behavioral and Brain Sciences, 9,* 503–548.

Hurst, M. W. (1979). Life changes and psychiatric symptom development: Issues of content, scoring, and clustering. In J. E. Barrett, R. M. Rose, & G. L. Klerman (Eds.), *Stress and mental disorder* (pp. 17–36). New York: Raven.

Jacob, T. (1975). Family interaction in disturbed and normal families: A methodological and substantive view. *Psychological Bulletin, 82,* 33–65.

Jacobs, S., & Myers, J. (1976). Recent life events and acute schizophrenic psychosis: A controlled study. *Journal of Nervous and Mental Disease, 162,* 75–87.

Jacobs, S. C., Prusoff, B. A., & Paykel, E. S. (1974). Recent life events in schizophrenia and depression. *Psychological Medicine, 4,* 444–453.

Jung, C. G. (1939). On the psychogenesis of schizophrenia. *Journal of Mental Science, 85,* 999–1011.

Kahneman, D. (1973). *Attention and effort.* Englewood Cliffs, NJ: Prentice-Hall.

Kasl, S. V. (1983). Pursuing the link between stressful life experiences and disease: A time for reappraisal. In C. L. Cooper (Ed.), *Stress research* (pp. 79–102). New York: Wiley.

Knight, R. A., & Russel, P. N. (1978). Global capacity reduction and schizophrenia. *British Journal of Social and Clinical Psychology, 17,* 275–280.

Koh, S. D., Kayton, L., & Berry, R. (1973). Mnemonic organization in young nonpsychotic schizophrenics. *Journal of Abnormal Psychology, 81,* 299–310.

Kraepelin, E. (1919). *Dementia praecox and paraphenia* (R. M. Barclay, Trans.). Huntington, NY: Krieger. (Original work published in 1913).

Kuiper, N. A., & Olinger, L. J. (1989). Stress and vulnerability to depression: A self-worth model. In R. W. J. Neufeld (Ed.), *Advances in the investigation of psychological stress* (pp. 367–391). New York: Wiley.

Lazarus, R. S., DeLongis, A., Folkman, S., & Gruen, R. (1985). Stress and adaptational outcomes: The problem of confounded measures. *American Psychologist, 40,* 770–779.

Lazarus, R. S., & Folkman, S. (1984). *Stress, appraisal, and coping.* New York: Springer.

Lewis, J. M., Rodnick, E. H., & Goldstein, M. J. (1981). Intrafamilial interactive behavior, parental communication deviance, and risk for schizophrenia. *Journal of Abnormal Psychology, 90,* 448–457.

Lukoff, D., Snyder, K., Ventura, J., & Nuechterlein, K. H. (1984). Life events, familial stress, and coping in the developmental course of schizophrenia. *Schizophrenia Bulletin, 10,* 258–292.

Magaro, P. A. (Ed.). (1981). Paranoia [Special Issue]. *Schizophrenia Bulletin, 7(4).*

Magaro, P. A. (1984). Psychosis and neurosis. In W. D. Spaulding & J. K. Cole (Eds.), *Nebraska symposium on motivation: Vol. 31. Theories of schizophrenia and psychosis* (pp. 157–230). Lincoln, NE: University of Nebraska Press.

Martin, R. A. (1989). Techniques for data acquisition and analysis in field settings. In R. W. J. Neufeld (Ed.), *Advances in the investigation of psychological stress* (pp. 195–233). New York: Wiley.

Marziali, E. A., & Pilkonis, P. A. (1986). The measurement of subjective response to stressful life events. *Journal of Human Stress, 12,* 5–12.

Matthysse, S. (1974). Dopamine and the pharmacology of schizophrenia: The state of the evidence. *Journal of Psychiatric Research, 11,* 107–113.

Meehl, P. E. (1962). Schizotaxia, schizotypy, schizophrenia. *American Psychologist, 17,* 827–838.

Meehl, P. E. (1979). A funny thing happened on the way to the latent entities. *Journal of Personality Assessment, 43,* 563–581.

Mednick, S. A., & Schulsinger, F. (1974). Studies of children at high risk for schizophrenia. In S. A. Mednick, F. Schulsinger, B. Bell, P. H. Venables, & K. O. Christiansen (Eds.), *Genetics, environment, and psychopathology* (pp. 103–116). New York: Elsevier.

Millar, K. (1980). *Loud noise and the retrieval of information.* Doctoral dissertation, University of Dundee.

Millon, T. (1986). The past and the future of the DSM-III: Personal recollections and projections. In T. Millon & G. L. Klerman (Eds.), *Contemporary directions in psychopathology: Toward the DSM-IV* (pp. 29–70). New York: Guilford.

Mirsky, A. F., & Duncan, C. C. (1986). Etiology and expression of schizophrenia: Neurobiological and psychosocial factors. In M. R. Rosenzweig & L. W. Porter (Eds.), *Annual Review of Psychology: Vol. 37* (pp. 291–319). Palo Alto, CA: Annual Reviews Inc.

Monroe, S. M. (1982). Life events assessment: Current practices, emerging trends. *Clinical Psychology Review, 2,* 435–453.

Neale, J. M., & Oltmanns, T. F. (1980). *Schizophrenia.* New York: Wiley.

Neufeld, R. W. J. (in press). Memory in paranoid schizophrenia. In P. A. Magaro & M. Johnston (Eds.), *Annual review of psychopathology,* (Vol. 1). Greenwich, CT: JAI Press.

Neufeld, R. W. J., & Mothersill, K. J. (1980). Stress as an irritant of psychopathology. In I. Sarason & C. D. Spielberger (Eds.), *Stress and anxiety* (Vol. 3). New York: Hemisphere.

Nuechterlein, K., & Dawson, M. (1984). A heuristic vulnerability/stress model of schizophrenic episodes. *Schizophrenia Bulletin, 10,* 300–312.

Polyson, J. A., Miller, H. L., & Shank, S. R. (1987). Axis IV: Experiment in progress. *Professional Psychology: Research and Practice, 18,* 447–451.

Rabkin, J. G. (1980). Stressful life events and schizophrenia: A review of the research literature. *Psychological Bulletin, 87,* 408–425.

Rabkin, J. G., & Struening, E. L. (1976). Life events, stress, and illness. *Science, 194,* 1013–1020.

Rahe, R. H., & Arthur, R. J. (1978). Life change and illness studies: Past history and future directions. *Journal of Human Stress, 4,* 3–15.

Rey, J. M., Stewart, G. W., Plapp, J. M., Bashir, M. R., & Richards, I. N. (1987). Sources of unreliability of DSM-III Axis IV. *Australian and New Zealand Journal of Psychiatry, 21,* 75–80.

Rosenthal, D. (1970). *Genetic theory and abnormal behavior.* New York: McGraw-Hill.

Ross, C. E., & Mirowsky, J. (1979). A comparison of life-event weighting schemes: Change, undesirability, and effort-proportional indices. *Journal of Health and Social Behavior, 20,* 166–177.

Sarbin, T. R. (1969). Schizophrenic thinking: A role-theoretical analysis. *Journal of Personality, 37,* 190–206.

Schless, A. P., Teichman, A., Mendels, J., & DiGiacomo, J. N. (1977). The role of stress as a precipitating factor of psychiatric illness. *British Journal of Psychiatry, 130,* 19–22.

Schofield, W., & Balian, L. (1959). A comparative study of the personal histories of the schizophrenic and nonpsychiatric patients. *Journal of Abnormal and Social Psychology, 59,* 216–225.

Schwartz, C. C., & Myers, J. K. (1977). Life events and schizophrenia. II. Impact of life events on symptom configuration. *Archives of General Psychiatry, 34,* 1242–1245.

Serban, G., & Woloshin, G. W. (1974). Relationship between pre- and postmorbid psychological stress in schizophrenics. *Psychological Reports, 35,* 507–517.

Shakow, D. (1963). Psychological deficit in schizophrenia. *Behavioral Science, 8,* 275–305.

Shean, G. (1982). Cognition, emotion, and schizophrenia. In R. W. J. Neufeld (Ed.), *Psychological stress and psychopathology* (pp. 55–66). New York: McGraw-Hill.

Shean, G., Faia, C., & Schmaltz, E. (1974). Cognitive appraisal of stress and schizophrenic subtype. *Journal of Abnormal Psychology, 83,* 523–528.

Skinner, H. A., & Blashfield, R. K. (1982). Increasing the impact of cluster analysis research: The case of psychiatric research. *Journal of Consulting and Clinical Psychology, 50,* 727–735.

Sommers, A. A. (1985). "Negative symptoms": Conceptual and methodological problems. *Schizophrenia Bulletin, 11,* 364–379.

Spitzer, R. L., Andreasen, N. C., & Endicott, J. (1978). Schizophrenia and other psychotic disorders in DSM-III. *Schizophrenia Bulletin, 4,* 489–509.

Spitzer, R. L., Endicott, J., & Robins, E. (1978). Research diagnostic criteria: Rationale and reliability. *Archives of General Psychiatry, 35,* 773–782.

Spitzer, R. L., & Forman, J. B. W. (1979). DSM-III Field Trials: II. Initial experience with the multiaxial system. *American Journal of Psychiatry, 136,* 818–820.

Spohn, H. E., & Patterson, T. (1979). Recent studies of psychophysiology in schizophrenia. *Schizophrenia Bulletin, 5,* 581–611.

Spring, B. (1981). Stress and schizophrenia: Some definitional issues. *Schizophrenia Bulletin, 7,* 24–33.

Spring, B., & Coons, H. (1982). Stress as a precursor of schizophrenia. In R. W. J. Neufeld (Ed.), *Psychological stress and psychopathology* (pp. 13–54). New York: McGraw-Hill.

Stephens, J. H., Astrup, C., Carpenter, W. T., Jr., Shaffer, J. W., & Goldberg, J. (1982). A comparison of nine systems to diagnose schizophrenia. *Psychiatry Research, 6,* 127–143.

Strauss, J. S. (1981). Comment on "How to break the logjam in schizophrenia." *Journal of Nervous and Mental Disease, 169,* 493–494.

Tausig, M. (1982). Measuring life events. *Journal of Health and Social Behavior, 23,* 52–64.

Townsend, J. T., & Ashby, F. G. (1983). *Stochastic modelling of elementary psychological processes.* London: Cambridge University Press.

Venables, P. H. (1983). Cerebral mechanisms, autonomic responsiveness, and attention in schizophrenia. In W. D. Spaulding & J. K. Cole (Eds.), *Nebraska symposium on motivation: Vol. 31. Theories of schizophrenia and psychosis* (pp. 47–91). Lincoln, NE: University of Nebraska Press.

Volvaka, J., Davis, L. G., & Ehrlich, Y. G. (1979). Endorphins, dopamine, and schizophrenia. *Schizophrenia Bulletin, 5,* 225–239.

Weinberger, D. R., Torrey, E. F., Neophytides, A. N., & Wyatt, R. J. (1979). Structural abnormalities in the cerebral cortex of chronic schizophrenia patients. *Archives of General Psychiatry, 36,* 935–939.

World Health Organization (1977). *Manual of the International Statistical Classification of Diseases, Injuries, and Causes of Death* (9th ed.). Geneva.

Zimmerman, M. (1983). Methodological issues in the assessment of life events: A review of issues and research. *Clinical Psychology Review, 3,* 339–370.

Zubin, J. (1986). Implications of the vulnerability model for DSM-IV with special reference to schizophrenia. In T. Millon & G. L. Klerman (Eds.), *Contemporary directions in psychopathology: Toward the DSM-IV* (pp. 473–494). New York: Guilford.

Zubin, J., & Spring, B. (1977). Vulnerability—A new view of schizophrenia. *Journal of Abnormal Psychology, 86,* 103–126.

Zubin, J., & Steinhauer, S. (1981). How to break the logjam in schizophrenia: A look beyond genetics. *Journal of Nervous and Mental Disease, 169,* 477–492.

Zubin, J., Steinhauer, S. R., Day, R., & van Kammen, D. P. (1985). Schizophrenia at the crossroads: A blueprint for the 80's. *Comprehensive Psychiatry, 26,* 217–240.

Author Index

Kazarian, S. S., 94, 127
Kazis, L. E., 354, 364
Kearney, H., 291, 303
Kehoe, K., 288, 301
Keinan, G., 95, 127
Keller, S. M., 293, 302
Kellett, D. S., 34, 42
Kellgren, J. H., 344, 364
Kemeny, J. G., 118, 127, 223, 228
Kemph, J. P., 310, 315, 339
Kendall, P. C., 140, 159
Kendell, R. E., 394, 416
Kendrick, M. J., 94, 127
Kenny, D. A., 115, 127, 221, 229
Kern, R. P., 93, 94, 102, 123
Kessler, R. C., 197, 221, 222, 223, 224, 229,
    236, 242, 245, 271, 279
Kiesler, C., 173, 187
Kilpatrick, D., 97, 127
Kimball, C. P., 205, 231
King, P. R., 27, 39, 82, 125
King, S. H., 350, 364
Kingma, J., 89, 127
Kirk, R. E., 113, 127
Kirk, R. F., Jr., 348, 365
Kirscht, J. P., 334, 335, 338, 340
Kitsen, J., 326, 335, 342
Kliger, A. S., 335, 342
Klopfer, F., 359, 362
Kneiss, J., 325, 342
Kniffin, C. W., 145, 157
Knight, P. R., 313, 338
Knight, R. A., 410, 411, 417
Kobasa, S. C., 216, 229, 236, 248, 249, 250,
    263, 278, 279, 280, 345, 364
Koch, U., 325, 342
Koh, S. D., 410, 417
Kolin, E. A., 267, 283
Kollar, E., 94, 129
Kong, H., 216, 225
Korman, M., 346, 366
Krakoff, L. R., 288, 301
Krantz, D., 49, 65
Krantz, D. S., 211, 226, 259, 264, 277, 279,
    280, 286, 289, 290, 301, 302, 303
Krantz, S. E., 204, 229
Krasnoff, L., 201, 227
Kraus, L., 350, 364
Krause, N., 242, 255, 258, 259, 271, 279,
    280
Kressel, S., 355, 363
Krueger, D. W., 210, 229
Kuczynski, M., 27, 39
Kuhn, C. M., 288, 304

Kuiper, N. A., 368, 369, 370, 371, 372, 373,
    374, 376, 378, 379, 380, 381, 382, 384, 385,
    386, 388, 389, 390
Kukde, M. P., 58, 66, 101, 127
Kurland, S., 350, 366
Kutner, M. H., 315, 340
Kutner, N. G., 315, 340
Kuzcynski, M., 82, 125

Laakso, R., 351, 352, 365
LaBerge, D., 180, 189
Lacey, B. C., 58, 66
Lacey, J. I., 10, 40, 58, 66, 346, 364
Lakatos, I., 89, 127
Lakey, B., 200, 216, 232, 255, 257, 273, 282
Lambert, F., 20, 41
Lambert, V. A., 354, 356, 360, 364
Lamping, D. L., 311, 315, 340
Lane, J. D., 288, 304
Lang, P., 140, 159
Langner, T. S., 198, 199, 207, 227, 229,
    256, 280
Lansman, M., 78, 87, 126
Lanzetta, J. T., 33, 40
Larson, M., 347, 356, 364
Laudenslager, M. L., 14, 40
Launier, R., 217, 229, 237, 280
Laux, L., 196, 229
Laverty, W., 358, 363
Lawler, K. A., 250, 282
Lawrence, J. R., 313, 338
Lawson, D. M., 94, 127
Lazar, J. D., 290, 301
Lazarus, R. S., 10, 11, 14, 15, 25, 27, 29, 30,
    40, 41, 42, 53, 55, 57, 65, 66, 73, 78, 79, 92,
    93, 100, 101, 118, 125, 127, 128, 134, 159,
    178, 179, 190, 196, 198, 201, 202, 204, 207,
    209, 210, 211, 214, 215, 216, 217, 218, 221,
    226, 227, 228, 229, 233, 236, 237, 264, 265,
    280, 285, 289, 301, 302, 344, 364, 374, 378,
    383, 384, 390, 406, 417
Lee, I., 17, 42
Leeper, R., 163, 164, 192
Lefave, M. K., 97, 99, 127
Lefcourt, H. M., 216, 220, 229, 230, 253, 254,
    257, 258, 259, 271, 280
Lefebvre, L. A., 58, 67, 101, 128
Lefebvre, R. C., 209, 230
Lei, H., 199, 230
Leiding, W., 176, 190
Leininger, J., 355, 357, 362
Lemann, G. F. J., 176, 189
Leonard, H. S., 49, 65
Leserman, J., 350, 364

Subject Index

Control/Controllability *(Continued)*
  implementation issues, 43–67
  instrumental, 56, 57, 58
  internality hypothesis, 51
  minimax hypothesis, 51
  minimax regret strategy, 60
  model, 44–46
  non-illness life dimensions, 321
  options, 58–62, 101
  perceptions, 50, 64, 318
  personal competence, 258
  of physiological reactions, 14
  potential control, 49
  predictability and, 48–49
  progression of alternate types (figure), 57
  research studies, 25
  secondary appraisal, 46
  stimulus-directed, 46, 47–48
  as stress buffer, 254
  stress-reducing effects, 35, 50, 64
  superordinate moderators, 274
  taxonomy, 54–56
  types of, 46–62
  utility considerations (figure), 59
  volitional, 58
Coping:
  ambiguity and, 37
  anxiety; vicious circle, 157
  appraisal-directed, 19, 20–21, 22, 25, 46, 54, 237
  approach/avoidance, 264
  arthritics, 360
  assessment of resources, 47
  avoidant thinking, 182
  buffering role, 253–259, 264, 265, 266
  cognitive factor, 134
  complexity, 265
  covert information processing, 101
  definition, 217
  effective strategy, 21
  emotion-focused, 360
  event probability and, 30
  flexibility, 265–267
  internally/externally-directed, 55
  laboratory studies, 47, 78, 100–101
  longitudinal studies, 218
  matching resources, 273–274
  options, 21, 44–46
  personal resources, 238
  person variables and, 272–273
  positive comparison, 265
  as process, 221
  reinforcement, by success, 21

renal disease, 305–342
research designs, 218
response-directed, 19, 20, 21, 25, 46, 54
schizophrenics, 408, 410–412, 413
single option (figure), 45
stimulus-directed, 19, 20, 22, 25
strategies, 23(figure), 217–218, 296
  assessment, 218
targets for, 18–19
type A behavior pattern, 289, 296, 300
types of behavior, 19, 22
vulnerability for depression, 369, 378, 379, 387
ways of coping subscale (table), 379
Coronary heart disease, 259
  See also Type A behavior pattern
Correlations, analysis of, 241–242, 319
Cortisol levels, 98
Counter-stress activity:
  ambiguity, 75, 82–83
  conveyed effectiveness (figure), 85
  effectiveness, 84, 121–122
  equations, 85, 86
  relative incidence (figure), 86
Covariance:
  adjustment; initial values, 110
  analysis of, 110–112, 113
  difference scores, 113
  individual differences, 117
Cross-lagged panel correlation, 109
Cyclosporin, 306

Daily Hassles Scale, 201–203, 208
Daily Uplifts Scale, 202
Danger:
  sports, 53–54
  threat, 10, 18
Data:
  acquisition techniques; field studies, 196–218
  analysis, 2, 219–224
    interactional models, 219–221
    simple correlational models, 219
    transactional models, 221–223
  collection, 77, 78
  curvilinear relationships, 221
  pre-analysis aggregation, 114–115
  renal disease research, 309–310
Decision-making, 13
  decisional control, 55, 56, 57, 58, 101
  decisional stress, 46
  maximizing strategy, 22
  personality and, 22
  satisficing strategy, 22